Student Teacher to Master Teacher

A Practical Guide for Educating  cial Needs

THIRD EDITION

Michael S. Rosenberg
Johns Hopkins University

Lawrence O'Shea
*Director of Special Education
Intermediate Unit One
Coal Center, Pennsylvania*

Dorothy J. O'Shea
Slippery Rock University of Pennsylvania

Merrill
Prentice Hall

Upper Saddle River, New Jersey
Columbus, Ohio

Library of Congress Cataloging in Publication Data

Rosenberg, Michael S.
    Student teacher to master teacher: a practical guide for educating students with special needs/Michael S. Rosenberg, Lawrence O'Shea, Dorothy J. O'Shea.--3rd ed.
      p. cm.
    Includes bibliographical references and index.
    ISBN 0-13-041372-0
    1. Handicapped children--Education--United States--Handbooks, manuals, etc. 2. Special education--United States--Handbooks, manuals, etc. 3. Teachers of handicapped children--Training of--United States--Handbooks, manuals, etc. I. O'Shea, Lawrence J. II. O'Shea, Dorothy J. III. Title.

LC4031 .R68 2002
371.9'0973--dc21

2001030386

Vice President and Publisher: Jeffrey W. Johnston
Executive Editor: Ann Castel Davis
Editorial Assistant: Keli Gemrich
Production Editor: Sheryl Glicker Langner
Production Coordination: Cliff Kallemeyn, Clarinda Production Services
Design Coordinator: Diane C. Lorenzo
Photo Coordinator: Valerie Schultz
Cover Designer: Thomas Borah
Cover art: SuperStock
Production Manager: Laura Messerly
Director of Marketing: Kevin Flanagan
Marketing Manager: Amy June
Marketing Coordinator: Barbara Koontz

This book was set in Palatino by The Clarinda Company. It was printed and bound by Courier, Kendallville, IN. The cover was printed by Lehigh Press.

Photo Credits: Scott Cunningham/Merrill, pp. 1, 57, 85, 155, 205; Anthony Magnacca/Merrill, pp. 29, 119, 251; Brad Feinknopf/Merrill, p. 283, Larry Hamill/Merrill, p. 315; Mary Hagler/Merrill, p. 339.

Prentice-Hall International (UK) Limited, *London*
Prentice-Hall of Australia Pty. Limited, *Sydney*
Prentice-Hall Canada, Inc., *Toronto*
Prentice-Hall Hispanoamericana, S.A., *Mexico*
Prentice-Hall of India Private Limited, *New Dehli*
Prentice-Hall of Japan, Inc., *Tokyo*
Prentice-Hall Singapore Pte. Ltd
Editora Prentice-Hall do Brasil, Ltda., *Rio de Janeiro*

Merrill
Prentice Hall

10 9 8 7 6 5 4 3 2 1
ISBN: 0-13-041372-0

Preface

Our basic purpose in preparing the third edition of *Student Teacher to Master Teacher* was to provide a reflective guide for use during supervised special education student teaching experiences or graduate field experience. We believe that field experiences are often the single most important component of a preservice level teacher development program.

The approach used in our guide is based on two interrelated assumptions. First, we believe that student teaching and initial field experiences should be rigorous and as realistic as possible. They should be developed to ensure that the preservice-level teacher enters the professional job market with the skills needed for both immediate survival and continued success. Few teacher educators would question this view, and many may regard it as an obvious, somewhat pious, statement of fact. Interpretation and actual implementation of this view appear to vary considerably, however, affecting the validity of the basic assumption in reference to specific teacher-training programs. In the absence of structured and purposeful activities or requirements, there may be no valid criteria for assessing easily delineated teaching skills across varied settings. In fact, the apparent discrepancy between theory and successful application may significantly reduce program credibility.

Second, special education field experiences should incorporate a variety of structured requirements and activities that collectively "bridge the gap" between methods and/or laboratory courses and actual independent, professional teaching. We recognize the need for more structured, reality-based, and relevant preservice experiences. When observing, supervising, managing, and evaluating preservice and beginning teachers, we found a critical need to link preservice training and field experience requirements to real teaching skills and actual on-the-job requirements. Topics and activities in this guide were chosen because we believe they represent many of the most pertinent issues that new teachers will face when they begin their field experiences or when they manage their first classrooms on their own.

Through our own experiences as classroom teachers and supervisors of developing teachers, we also realized the needs of college supervisors. We believe that individuals involved with the supervision of student teachers and field-experience students often are the forgotten souls, desperately trying to promote best practices in the face of problems of logistics, timing, and realities of modern schools. Often, these are individuals who must face experienced teachers' claims to novice teachers that "it can't be done like that" or "theory is only relevant in textbooks and it will never work here." To the university instructors' calls for "increased best practices" in the classrooms, we believe that college supervisors will welcome a commercially prepared resource to aid them in their roles. This guide was developed to reduce the amount of time needed by supervisory faculty and staff in the review and possible remediation of key concepts associated with successful teaching. We hope the use of this guide will allow more time for the important job of observing and providing feedback to preservice teachers and for supervisors' liaisons to classroom teachers and administrators, university faculty, and preservice teachers.

In summary, throughout this guide we provide tips and insights to preservice and beginning teachers to help them grow professionally with their chosen career over time, starting during their initial field experiences and continuing through their beginning years in teaching. We recognize the enormous amount of information that teachers new to special education must obtain and be able to demonstrate during their initial work with students with mild to moderate disabilities. This guide is meant to help new teachers make the transition from the role of student at the preservice level to the role of professional at the in-service level. Each topic in the guide has been judged a pertinent topic for new teachers and, we believe, will remain relevant to them as their experience grows.

ORGANIZATION OF THE TEXT

Chapter 1 provides an introduction to the student teaching experience and an overview of the field of working with students with mild to moderate disabilities. The chapter discusses the typical fears and concerns of student teachers and beginning special education teachers and reviews the characteristics of students with mild to moderate disabilities and the ways educational services are delivered (e.g., inclusion, continuum of service, and so on). The chapter also introduces ethical and professional standards of practice for teachers that will be highlighted throughout the subsequent chapters. Tips on using diplomacy in the workplace and an emphasis on maximizing people skills underscore our call for both effective interpersonal communication and teaching skills necessary to become "master teachers."

Chapter 2 gives the novice teacher an understanding of the legal bases for assessment and programming for students with disabilities. Pertinent legislation and litigation of the past three decades, most notably IDEA, are presented as the foundation of legal challenges that teachers today will face. Major components of federal mandates for school-age students and infants and toddlers are summarized, as are tips for working within the system to solve potential legal problems faced by teachers. Assumptions underlying successful mediation attempts with students, family members, and professionals are discussed as means to avoid unnecessary litigation.

Chapter 3 deals with the "nuts and bolts" of actual instructional themes of the classroom. Tips on organizing and managing instructional time, with an emphasis on effectiveness and consistency, are presented. Ways of setting up and maintaining effective scheduling procedures are discussed, and a system for the development of classroom rules and procedures, as well as other management strategies (e.g., planning for group size, arranging the physical environment) are provided. Available resources at the new teacher's disposal and tips for beginning the school year are included.

The major focus of Chapter 4 is on how the preservice and beginning teacher can link classroom-based assessment procedures to instruction. Initially, several basic assessment concepts are reviewed. These are followed by a concise delineation of step-by-step procedures for implementing curriculum-based assessments in special education and inclusive education environments.

Chapter 5 discusses the need for effective planning as a catalyst to appropriate instruction. Successfully planned lessons are illustrated to include the relationship of instructional objectives to students' individualized education programs (IEPs), the teacher's preparation for the demonstration of understanding of prerequisite skills for students, task analyses and learning sequences, the need for concise descriptions of instructional activities and materials linked to predetermined objectives, systematic methods to evaluate lessons, and anticipation of problems that might occur anywhere along the implementation phase of the instructional delivery to students. A section on lesson plan follow-up with tips on remediating and preventing actual problems observed during lessons, a review of instructional techniques used in varied lesson formats, and tips for lesson appraisal so that new teachers can practice self-evaluation are embedded within the chapter.

Chapter 6 stresses the importance of delivery of instruction. The concept of effective teacher behaviors is discussed along the dimensions of a structured academic focus, specific teaching of academic concepts, and a planned instructional sequence based on environmental variables and needs of students. Dimensions of direct instruction, the guided discovery approach, and strategic instruction are identified with numerous examples of teaching approaches throughout the chapter.

Chapter 7 provides developing and beginning teachers with a summary of the paperwork involved in special education and the documentation necessary in the referral process for special education. The chapter begins with the prereferral steps of helping students with problem behaviors or learning difficulties remain in the least restrictive environment (LRE) before calling for changes in students' educational placements. New teachers are provided with the steps of working with other professionals and parents to document precisely the need for all changes in educational decisions. Tips for working with parents, administrators, general educators, and others involved in educational planning teams are pinpointed. Additionally, IEPs and IEP meetings are discussed, stressing the IEP as a legal plan that parents and professionals develop together. The chapter concludes with suggestions to help developing and beginning teachers write reports of students' progress and to promote continuous methods of communication with parents and other significant professionals.

Chapter 8 is provided to encourage classroom management by the new teacher from the beginning of his or her involvement with students. The chapter was updated to underscore the importance of having a comprehensive school and classroom management program, as well as a series of strategies for the development of functional behavioral assessments of troubling behavior. A brief review of behavioral principles and rules governing classroom behavior is provided to highlight teachers' use of strategies to increase and/or maintain appropriate student behaviors and to decrease or eliminate inappropriate student behaviors. Tips for identifying, observing, recording, and illustrating problem behaviors are explained. Logistical concerns in developing large-group management and means of designing individual behavior change programs and reports are discussed. Finally, the chapter provides some practical strategies to teachers to facilitate and promote self-control strategies of their students.

Chapter 9, "Student and Family Transitions," provides an overview of transition issues related to very young children with disabilities and their families. Highlighted are the evaluation and assessment needs of young children and the various medical and physical issues encountered by families. Step-by-step procedures are provided for the construction of individualized family service plans (IFSPs). Also provided is a discussion of the transition services offered to school-age children and youth with disabilities. A common theme throughout the chapter is the need for interagency coordination and planning.

Chapter 10 provides insights into methods of collaborative consultation that new teachers will use when working with professionals and parents in school-based activities and educational meetings. The role of teaming is stressed throughout this guide as an important strategy to encourage effective educational decision making for all students. Chapter 10 is also intended to build a case for the necessity of strong interpersonal communication skills of teachers, including colleague relationships, stressing positive regard, empathy, and warmth toward peers.

Chapter 11 provides tips for the important search for employment. Typical job interview procedures are provided, and strategies for preparing attractive and relevant portfolios and résumés are described. Teacher burnout issues that may impede the master teacher process and means of recognizing and managing stress are also highlighted. Finally, the chapter concludes with suggestions for planning continued employment and advancement within the field. Specifically, readers are challenged to analyze their personal philosophy of special education as they maintain involvement in professional organizations, recertification and in-service programs, and advocacy groups.

By designing this guide as an easy-to-use, interactive resource, we hope the use of the text will not end once the field experience, student teaching, or first year of teaching ends. We believe that the chapters of the book reflect concerns typically faced by many teachers as they continue to grow as special educators. This guide was written with the hope of assisting beginning special education teachers to become master teachers and to maintain their status as such throughout their teaching careers.

FEATURES OF THE TEXT

Brief "Pause and Reflect" boxes are positioned frequently throughout each chapter to encourage the reader to think about what he or she has just read and relate the information to his or her own experiences and teaching situation.

Numbered boxes also frequently appear in each chapter to highlight issues and legislation, clarify definitions, and provide resources.

Following chapter summaries, Activities to Extend Your Knowledge are exercises provided to challenge the reader to learn more about special education by completing the activities.

We have added Point and Click sections to each of the chapters. These sections contain websites that provide useful materials and resources for both developing and beginning teachers.

ACKNOWLEDGMENTS

We wish to express our gratitude to the following individuals who devoted a great deal of personal and professional time to the task of helping us complete this book. The faculty and staff in the Department of Special Education at Johns Hopkins University, colleagues and staff at Intermediate Unit I in western Pennsylvania, and the faculty at Slippery Rock University provided much support and encouragement throughout all phases of this project. In particular, we acknowledge the artistic contributions of Sharon Lampkin and the overall assistance of Lori Jackman and Danielle Rollison. We are especially appreciative of the efforts of our colleagues Janeen Taylor, Stephanie Carpenter, and Peggy King-Sears, who took the time to contribute important new content to our text. We also gratefully acknowledge the many contributions of the experienced teachers we have worked with who continually remind us that there is a vast number of master special education teachers. In addition, we appreciate the efforts of the numerous developing teachers we have supervised over the past twenty years. They have inspired us to focus on their needs for survival and success. We appreciate the efforts of significant individuals who served as role models to us, including Bob Algozzine, Bill Reid, Paul Sindelar, and James Van Tassel. We also wish to express our appreciation to Ann Davis at Merrill/Prentice Hall, as well as the reviewers of this edition: Kevin J. Callahan, University of North Texas; Pam Gent, Clarion University (OH); Susan Gurganus, College of Charleston (SC); Kathryn Haring, University of Oklahoma; and Diane T. Woodrum, West Virginia University.

Finally, we wish to express our love and appreciation to our families in providing us with the support, encouragement, and patience to finish our task.

Discover the Companion Website Accompanying This Book

THE PRENTICE HALL COMPANION WEBSITE: A VIRTUAL LEARNING ENVIRONMENT

Technology is a constantly growing and changing aspect of our field that is creating a need for content and resources. To address this emerging need, Prentice Hall has developed an online learning environment for students and professors alike—Companion Websites—to support our textbook.

In creating a Companion Website, our goal is to build on and enhance what the textbook already offers. For this reason, the content for each user-friendly website is organized by topic and provides the professor and student with a variety of meaningful resources. Common features of a Companion Website include:

FOR THE PROFESSOR—

Every Companion Website integrates **Syllabus Manager**™, an online syllabus creation and management utility.

- **Syllabus Manager**™ provides you, the instructor, with an easy, step-by-step process to create and revise syllabi, with direct links into Companion Website and other online content without having to learn HTML.
- Students may log on to your syllabus during any study session. All they need to know is the web address for the Companion Website and the password you've assigned to your syllabus.
- After you have created a syllabus using **Syllabus Manager**™, students may enter the syllabus for their course section from any point in the Companion Website.
- Clicking on a date, the student is shown the list of activities for the assignment. The activities for each assignment are linked directly to actual content, saving time for students.
- Adding assignments consists of clicking on the desired due date, then filing in the details of the assignment—name of the assignment, instructions, and whether or not it is a one-time or repeating assignment.
- In addition, links to other activities can be created easily. If the activity is online, a URL can be entered in the space provided, and it will be linked automatically in the final syllabus.
- Your completed syllabus is hosted on our servers, allowing convenient updates from any computer on the Internet. Changes you make to your syllabus are immediately available to your students at their next logon.

FOR THE STUDENT—

Topic Overviews—outline key concepts in topic areas

Characteristics—general information about each topic/disability covered on this website

Read About It—a list of links to pertinent articles found on the Internet that cover each topic

Teaching Ideas—links to articles that offer suggestions, ideas, and strategies for teaching students with disabilities

Web Links—a wide range of websites that provide useful and current information related to each topic area

Resources—a wide array of different resources for many of the pertinent topics and issues surrounding special education

Electronic Bluebook—send homework or essays directly to your instructor's email with this paperless form

Message Board—serves as a virtual bulletin board to post—or respond to—questions or comments to/from a national audience

Chat—real-time chat with anyone who is using the text anywhere in the country—ideal for discussion and study groups, class projects, etc.

To take advantage of these and other resources, please visit the *Student Teacher to Master Teacher: A Practical Guide for Educating Students with Special Needs,* Third Edition, Companion Website at

www.prenhall.com/rosenberg

Contents

Chapter 7   The Paperwork   205

Chapter 8   Classroom Management   251

Chapter 9 Student and Family Transitions 283

(Coauthored by Janeen M. Taylor, Johns Hopkins University)

Chaper 10 Collaborative Programming and Consultation 315

Chapter 11   The Master Teacher   339

NOTE: Every effort has been made to provide accurate and current Internet information in this book. However, the Internet and information posted on it are constantly changing, so it is inevitable that some of the Internet addresses listed in this textbook will change.

Field Experiences with Students with Mild to Moderate Disabilities

In this chapter, we will

✔ review the categories of mild to moderate disabilities, with an emphasis on current definitions and typical characteristics

✔ discuss how special education services are typically delivered to students with disabilities

✔ define the attributes of inclusive educational programming and describe how such programs are designed and implemented

✔ describe the roles and responsibilities of key individuals involved in field experiences

✔ enumerate some commonsense tips that enable practicum students to realize the greatest benefits from their field experiences

*F*ield experiences are among the most important components in the professional development of quality teachers. As is the case with a variety of other human service professions (e.g., medicine, social work, counseling), supervised field experiences provide appropriately trained candidates with opportunities to apply freshly acquired skills within nurturing and supportive environments. In most teacher-training programs, field experiences are viewed as critical transition activities. Experiences are designed to link the knowledge base presented in the college classroom to the independent activities expected of beginning teachers. In sharp comparison with the unidirectional and vicarious nature of textbooks, journal articles, university lectures, and classroom simulations, field experiences bring emotion and immediacy to the teacher-education process. With a built-in network of support, developing teachers are (1) placed in real-world situations that allow for the constructive discovery of strengths and weaknesses, (2) given ample opportunities to improve on their assessed deficiencies, and (3) encouraged to enhance creatively their areas of strength. Working with students, parents, and colleagues, developing teachers experience the daily rewards and, at times, many of the challenges and frustrations inherent in their chosen profession.

In comparison with those of the past, today's teacher-training programs are allocating increased resources and amounts of time to field experiences, as well as exploring ways to deliver such experiences to nontraditional preservice populations (Rosenberg, Jackson, & Yeh, 1996). Developing teachers and their university supervisors are spending more of their time in direct contact with students and school personnel. Local education agencies (LEAs) and institutions of higher education are forming partnerships to ensure that developing and beginning teachers are provided with opportunities to become effective in today's schools. Recognizing the importance of field experiences, state lawmakers and varied professional organizations involved in the education of teachers (e.g., American Association of Colleges for Teacher Education) are advocating that field experiences be expanded and improved even more. For example, it has been recommended that clinical experiences include greater opportunities for analytic problem-solving activities and fewer tasks that merely require imitation (Case, Lanier, & Miskel, 1986). Such activities would produce reflective professionals who could apply their knowledge and skills to a range of challenges and, more important, use the results of their experiences to form new approaches to the education of the children in their charge.

In this introductory chapter, we address a wide range of issues faced by developing teachers who are placed in field-based practicum experiences with students identified as having mild to moderate disabilities. First, we describe the characteristics of students with mild to moderate disabilities. We give special attention to issues surrounding the categorical and noncategorical descriptions of this heterogeneous population of students. Second, we explore the variety of systems for delivering special education services and discuss how these systems have changed in recent years. Specifically, we provide an overview of inclusive education and describe what developing and beginning teachers can expect in education settings that have adopted inclusionary service delivery procedures. In a similar fashion, in a subsequent section we explore issues related to diversity; specific suggestions are provided for planning for academic diversity. Third, we explore the roles of the key people involved in field-based practicum activities, including the university supervisor, the cooperating teacher, and the practicum student. We conclude this chapter with a series of strategies that can help practicum students understand the social reality of schools, as well as become aware of their legal rights, responsibilities, and liabilities. We believe that these "sensible tips" can assist developing teachers in becoming effective participants in their field experiences.

ℙause and Reflect 1.1

For even the most prepared preservice special educator, the start of a new field experience can be a time of heightened anticipation. Clearly, this is a time of excitement, energy, enthusiasm, and yes, even some stress. Finally, all the things learned in university classes will be put into action. At times like these, it is often useful to write down some of the expectations and feelings you are experiencing. It is also useful to view how your teacher-development program has prepared you to meet your expectations and to deal with your emotions. In the space below, note some expectations you have for your field experience and some feelings you have regarding the start of this applied experience. Next, think back to how your courses and previous experiences have prepared you to succeed with this important activity. Use another sheet of paper if necessary.

Expectations/Feelings	How Prepared?
_____	_____
_____	_____
_____	_____
_____	_____

STUDENTS WITH MILD TO MODERATE DISABILITIES: DEFINITIONS AND CHARACTERISTICS

When developing teachers first enter the setting for students with mild to moderate disabilities, they realize that the children look like most other children. The children's outward appearance has no strange or alien quality; the layperson's conceptualization of what it means to have a disability doesn't seem to apply. From initial contacts, it seems nearly impossible to distinguish students with disabilities from students considered "normal." As the developing teacher spends more and more time in the classroom, however, learning and behavioral problems do become apparent, and students identified as having mild to moderate disabilities function with lower levels of success on academic tasks and have more difficulty in social situations than their nondisabled peers.

In most cases, children with mild to moderate disabilities are not identified until they enter school. There are two major reasons for the lack of success in the early detection of mild to moderate disabilities. First, many children display slight developmental difficulties that are virtually unnoticeable to the untrained eye. Even in cases where these difficulties are noted during the preschool years, there is no guarantee that these problems will persist into later developmental periods. Second, for many behaviors, there are no clear delineations as to what constitutes normal and abnormal functioning. In regard to hyperactivity or attention problems, for example, objective behavioral criteria that could assist in differentiating normal and problem preschoolers are virtually nonexistent. Thus, it is extremely difficult to differentiate a vigorous, unrestrained, and capricious 3-year-old child whose behavior is considered age-appropriate from another 3-year-old child whose behavior is overactive, inattentive, and impulsive to a clinically significant degree (Campbell, 1985). The beginning of school, however, is a time when professional educators first evaluate children's abilities in meeting age- and grade-appropriate expectations. Children who violate the norms of their school or grade level in terms of behavior, academic performance, acquisition of spoken and written language, motivation, and aspirations for achievement are those most often identified as having mild or moderate disabilities.

The definitions and descriptions of students' educational problems tend to vary according to the specific philosophies and policies of individual state education agencies (SEAs) and local education agencies (LEAs). As a result of this interstate and intrastate variation, developing and beginning teachers will experience a variety of nomenclatural and administrative arrangements used to describe students with mild to moderate disabilities. In fact, the Individuals with Disabilities Education Act (IDEA 97) now allows states and localities to use the generic term of developmental delay for children ages 3 through 9, an option previously used for those under the age of 5. Nonetheless, the variety of arrangements can be reduced to two broad approaches: the use of categorical referents and category-free clusters of characteristics. In the sections that follow, we (1) define the categories associated with mild to moderate disabilities and (2) describe the category-free cluster approach to problem identification.

Categories of Mild to Moderate Disabilities

The categories of exceptionality used most frequently to define students experiencing mild to moderate learning and behavioral problems are learning disabilities, emotional disturbance or behavioral disorders, mild/moderate mental retardation, and other health impairments (e.g., attention deficit disorders). Students identified as belonging to any one of these categories are presumed to share a specific behavior or pattern of behaviors. In recent years, the validity of this presumption has been the topic of considerable controversy.

Learning Disabilities. The vast majority of children having mild to moderate disabilities are considered to have a learning disability. Central to the diagnosis of learning disabilities, the newest major category in the field of special education, are problems in academic achievement. Specific learning disability is defined by IDEA 97 as:

> a disorder in one or more of the basic psychological processes involved in understanding or in using language, spoken or written, that may manifest itself in an imperfect ability to listen, think, speak, read, write, spell, or do mathematical calculations, including conditions such as perceptual disabilities, brain injury, minimal brain dysfunction, dyslexia, and developmental aphasia. The term does not include children who have learning problems that are primarily the result of visual, hearing, or motor disabilities, mental retardation, or emotional disturbance, or of environmental, cultural, or economic disadvantage.(U.S. Department of Education, 1997)

The National Joint Committee on Learning Disabilities (NJCLD), a national group of representatives of 10 major organizations (e.g., Council for Learning Disabilities [CLD], American Speech-Language-Hearing Association [ASHA], Learning Disabilities Association of America [LDAA]) committed to the education and welfare of individuals with learning disabilities, has defined learning disabilities as:

> a general term that refers to a heterogeneous group of disorders manifested by significant difficulties in the acquisition and use of listening, speaking, reading, writing, reasoning, or mathematical abilities. These disorders are intrinsic to the individual, presumed to be due to central nervous system dysfunction, and may occur across the life span. Problems in self-regulatory behaviors, social perception, and social interaction may exist with learning disabilities but do not by themselves constitute a learning disability. Although learning disabilities may occur concomitantly with other handicapping conditions (for example, sensory impairment, mental retardation, emotional disturbance) or with extrinsic influences (such as cultural differences, insufficient or inappropriate instruction), they are not the result of those conditions or influences. (NJCLD, 1988, p. 4)

As observed by Smith (1998), the major difference between the two definitions centers on the orientation about the causes of the disability. The federal definition, originally part of PL 94–142, the Education for All Handicapped Children's Act (EHA), is older and reflects a biophysical or medical orientation. The more recent NJCLD definition states that an individual's learning disability *may* have a biophysical cause (e.g., central nervous system dysfunction), but it allows for the inclusion of individuals who may not have such a dysfunction.

Not surprisingly, the federal definition of learning disabilities has been criticized widely and continues to spark emotional debates among professionals in the field. Some critics (e.g., Hallahan & Kauffman, 1982) have argued that the definition of learning disabilities needs to be broadened so that any child not achieving up to potential can receive special education services. Such a definition would not rely on causal explanations or exclude children who may have other disability conditions along with their learning disability. Other critics (e.g., Council for Learning Disabilities, 1986; Kirk & Gallagher, 1986) have tried to narrow the definition of learning disabilities and have remained steadfast in their view that not all underachieving students have a learning disability. In fact, these professionals view the excessive incidence of students with learning disabilities as a direct result of the inclusion of students whose low achievement or underachievement is a reflection of factors other than specific learning disabilities (e.g., depressed intellectual functioning, motivational problems, inadequate instruction). These professionals see learning disabilities as just one possible cause of underachievement and believe that specific interventions geared to specific learning disabilities can enhance remedial efforts. Underachievement stemming from extrinsic sources, such as poor environmental conditions, would be better served if society could change the living and learning environments.

Regardless of definitional controversies, most students identified as having a learning disability have average to above average intellectual ability as measured by intelligence tests. On measures of achievement, however, these students do not perform to levels commensurate with their assessed intellectual abilities. These differences between a student's intelligence test scores and achievement test scores are typically referred to as **discrepancies** between intellectual ability and educational performance. If a severe discrepancy is found between the intellectual ability and actual achievement of a student, he or she may be considered to have a learning disability. Unfortunately, there is no clear consensus as to what level of discrepancy between ability and achievement constitutes a severe discrepancy.

Emotional Disturbance or Behavioral Disorders. As with learning disabilities, it is difficult to identify and define formally the emotional and behavioral problems of school-age children. A major source of the difficulty is that a variety of terms are used to refer to problem behaviors. For example, professionals involved in the education and treatment of students with problem behaviors do not even agree on what generic name most appropriately captures the category. Under the provisions of IDEA 97, children who are disabled by their behavior have been referred to as having an *emotional disturbance*. Although this term is commonly used, many professionals (e.g., Council

Pause and Reflect 1.2

What type of identification procedure or formula does your state and/or school district use to operationalize the definition of learning disabilities? Do such procedures account for all children who require services for their learning disability? Do the procedures *overidentify* or *underidentify* students for special education services? Can you think of better ways to define and identify learning disabilities?

for Children with Behavior Disorders [CCBD]) believe that it is neither accurate nor beneficial to the educational process. The official position statement of the CCBD (Huntze, 1985) lists seven reasons for supporting the use of the term **behavioral disorder** over the traditional referent *emotional disturbance*. These seven reasons are highlighted in Box 1.1.

In IDEA 97, the Bower (1969) definition of emotional disturbance continues to be used for identifying students who may need special education services. Briefly, a student with emotional disturbance exhibits one or more of the following characteristics to a marked extent and over a long period of time:

- An inability to learn that cannot be explained by intellectual, sensory, or health factors
- An inability to build or maintain satisfactory relationships with peers and teachers
- Inappropriate types of behavior or feelings under normal circumstances
- A general pervasive mood of unhappiness or depression
- A tendency to develop physical symptoms or fears associated with personal or school problems

The federal categorical definition of emotional disturbance does embrace children who may be schizophrenic but does not include those who are socially maladjusted unless it is determined that they possess a serious emotional disturbance. One advantage to this definition is that it is descriptive. It does not attempt to explain the causes of emotional disturbance, but rather describes likely manifestations of whatever the problem might be.

Nonetheless, as with the definition of learning disabilities, the IDEA 97 definition of emotional disturbance has been the subject of widespread criticism, and it is quite possible that a new definition will be included in a future reauthorization of special education law. The major problem with the definition is that it contains many vague and neb-

---

Box 1.1   ## Seriously Emotionally Disturbed or Behaviorally Disordered? Is the Label Important?

In a controversial position paper, the Council for Children with Behavior Disorders (CCBD) advocated replacing the term *seriously emotionally disturbed* with the term *behaviorally disordered* as a descriptor for children and youth who are disabled by their behavior. Listed below are seven reasons for its support of this change. Detailed explanations for each component of the rationale are available in Huntze (1985). Do you agree or disagree with each of the stated reasons? Why or why not?

1. The term *behaviorally disordered* has far greater utility for education than the term *seriously emotionally disturbed*.
2. The term *behaviorally disordered* is not associated exclusively with any particular theory of causation and therefore with any particular set of intervention techniques.
3. The term *behaviorally disordered* affords a more comprehensive assessment of the population.
4. The term *behaviorally disordered* is less stigmatizing than the term *seriously emotionally disturbed*.
5. The term *behaviorally disordered* is more representative of students who are disabled by their behavior and currently served under IDEA.
6. The professional judgment of the field, generally, appears to be moving in the direction of the term *behaviorally disordered*.
7. The change in terminology is representative of a focus on the educational responsibility delineated in the statute and is descriptive of the population currently served.

ulous terms. Key terms and phrases are not defined, quantified, or operationalized. For example, the initial qualifying terms "to a marked extent" or "over a long period of time" are not quantified easily and are open to subjective interpretation. Similarly, the phrase "satisfactory interpersonal relationships" is much too general for precise decision making. Other problems with the definition include (1) its failure to consider problem behaviors as existing within a social context (Rosenberg, Wilson, Maheady, & Sindelar, 1997) and (2) the seemingly incongruous inclusionary and exclusionary caveats regarding schizophrenia and social maladjustment. Clearly, five criteria within the definition indicate that children with schizophrenia must be included and children with social maladjustment cannot be excluded from any conceptualization of emotional disturbance or behavioral disorder.

Unfortunately, there are no clear answers to the problems related to the identification of students with emotional disturbance. Many of us as educators believe that we know problem behaviors or indicators of emotional disturbance when we see them. The quantification of emotional disturbance under the present definition, however, is severely limited by a lack of quantitative measures for determining eligibility of services. This state of affairs has not limited the number of students referred as emotionally disturbed. In most school districts, **emotional disturbance** is defined socially by the relatively imprecise tolerance levels of teachers, administrators, and parents. Consequently, students identified as having emotional disturbance are a heterogeneous population that varies in behavioral characteristics both within and between individual classrooms, school buildings, and LEAs. At one extreme, these students may engage in high rates of acting out, aggressive behaviors; at the other extreme, students may be extremely withdrawn, with low rates of social interaction. In characterizing the range of behaviors associated with emotional disturbance, Rosenberg et al. (1997) have used the terms *high-incidence behavioral disorders* and *low-incidence behavioral disorders* to differentiate the types of behaviors that general and special educators tend to deal with on a regular basis. High-incidence behavioral disorders can include hyperactive behavior (overactivity, distractibility, impulsivity), aggression, rule-breaking/delinquency, and social withdrawal. Low-incidence behavioral disorders tend not to be observed by most educators and include a variety of psychotic behaviors exhibited by a relatively few children and youth in the general population. These behaviors can include self-stimulatory behavior, self-injurious behavior, social withdrawal, and delusional thinking.

Mild Mental Retardation. According to IDEA 97, **mental retardation (MR)** is formally defined as significantly subaverage general intellectual functioning existing concurrently with deficits in adaptive behavior and manifested during the developmental period that adversely affects a child's educational performance. Until recently, for a student to be identified as having MR, he or she must have had two specific deficits: (1) below-average intellectual functioning as measured by standardized tests of intelligence and (2) deficits in adaptive behavior—those everyday behaviors believed to be necessary for survival in our society (Grossman, 1977). Those students meeting the definitional criteria were diagnosed as having a level or degree of MR based on level of intelligence (as measured by IQ scores). Typically, students with scores between 55 and 69 on standardized intelligence tests were considered to have mild retardation; students with scores between 40 and 54 were considered to have moderate mental retardation; scores between 25 and 39 indicated severe retardation; and scores below 24 indicated profound retardation. Under this classification system, the large majority of individuals with MR (approximately 85%) fell into the mild retardation range and were believed able to master academic skills up to about the sixth grade and to learn job skills well enough to support themselves independently or semi-independently (Heward, 2000). Students with moderate retardation comprised approximately 7 to 10% of those identified as having MR and were believed to benefit from highly individualized instruction in those skills necessary for successful community integration (e.g., daily living skills, self-care skills, basic work skills, a functional vocabulary). Students with severe and profound mental retardation made up approximately 3 to 6% of those identified as having MR and were believed typically to require intensive instruction in self-care and basic communication skills.

In 1992, the American Association on Mental Retardation developed a new system for classifying mental retardation. Rather than levels of measured intelligence, this new system is based on an individual's unique strengths, weaknesses, and needs for special supports. As noted by Kozma and Stock (1993), the intent of this new classification system is to describe more accurately the variability in the way different people with similar IQ scores can function. The new system classifies individuals with MR by the amount of support or help that is needed across four dimensions (intellectual and adaptive skills; psychological and emotional considerations; physical/health/etiology consideration; and environmental considerations) related to success in their environment. For each of these dimensions, the four intensities of support are as follows:

1. **Intermittent:** Not requiring consistent support, yet needing support on a short-term basis (e.g., job loss, an acute medical crisis).
2. **Limited:** Requiring time-limited (yet not intermittent) support consistently over time (e.g., time-limited job training, transitional supports for school to work period).
3. **Extensive:** Requiring regular involvement (e.g., daily) in some environments and not time-limited (e.g., long-term job support, long-term home living support).
4. **Pervasive:** Requiring support characterized by constancy and high intensity across environments. Supports typically involve more staff members and intrusiveness than do extensive or time-limited supports and may be of a potential life-sustaining nature.

Students with mild mental retardation typically require supports at the intermittent or limited intensities and most often have problems in communication (e.g., delayed speech), attending to tasks, maintaining motivation, and generalizing from one task or setting to another, as well as with incidental learning.

Still, it bears mentioning that the use of mild mental retardation as a categorical referent is not without criticism. It has been argued that mild retardation is related more closely to such variables as socioeconomic status, family education level, and literacy than to IQ scores. In fact, some data support the view that children from poor families and minority groups tend to be overrepresented among the rosters of students identified with mild mental retardation. Although critics have noted that such students are questionable candidates for inclusion in the category of mild mental retardation, these children are undoubtedly in need of some type of special intervention if they are to succeed in school. The question, as posed by Edgar and Hayden (1985), remains: How can these students best be served?

Other Health Impairment (OHI). According to IDEA 97, OHI refers to students who have limited strength, vitality, or alertness, including a heightened alertness to environmental stimuli, that results in limited alertness to the educational environment. This may be due to chronic or acute health problems such as asthma, attention deficit disorder (ADD) or attention deficit hyperactivity disorder (ADHD), diabetes, epilepsy, a heart condition, hemophilia, lead poisoning, leukemia, nephritis, rheumatic fever, and sickle cell anemia. For the health impairment to be considered a disability it must adversely affect a child's educational performance.

A significant change in IDEA 97 has been the addition of ADD/ADHD to the list of eligible conditions under OHI. Under previous iterations of IDEA it had been specified that children with attention disabilities could receive special services if (1) their characteristics met one of the disability categories listed in the statute and (2) special education was needed because of that disability. Unfortunately, it was determined that many students with attention difficulties were not receiving services and it was necessary to formally codify ADD and ADHD as potential conditions under the law.

According to *DSM-IV* (APA, 1994), the essential feature of ADHD is a persistent pattern of inattention and/or hyperactivity-impulsivity that is more frequent and severe than what is found in individuals of comparable levels of development. Symptoms must be present in at least two settings (e.g., school, home), and there must be clear evidence of interference with developmentally appropriate social, academic, or occupational functioning. As noted by Rosenberg et al. (1997), the primary characteristics are overactivity and fidgetiness, distractibilty or inattention, impulsivity or judgment deficits, and excitability or negative affect. Among the secondary characteristics are learning problems or deficiencies in academic achievement, aggressive and antisocial behaviors, and poor self-concept or lack of self-esteem.

Category-Free Descriptions

Although the use of categorical referents is the traditional approach to the description of students with mild to moderate disabilities, many educators have found that it is more beneficial to adopt an alternative conceptualization—a category-free classification system. This category-free approach, often referred to as a **noncategorical or cross-categorical perspective**, puts greater emphasis on variables related to students' behavioral functioning than on the specific factors used to either include or exclude a student from a particular category. Operationally defined, **behavioral functioning** refers to the overt behaviors of students and their relationship to the environment. These are learned, often situation-specific behaviors that occur in response to the demands of different environmental settings (Gloecker & Simpson, 1988). Most important, students' levels of behavioral functioning are viewed as being, in part, modifiable through classroom intervention.

In general, the problem behaviors most typical of students with mild to moderate disabilities fall into several generic domains: academic underachievement, sensory and perceptual processing problems, perceptual-motor difficulties, attention deficit problems, long- and short-term memory deficits, receptive and expressive language disorders, hyperactivity, impulsivity, poor peer relationships, and deficient social-emotional skills. It should be remembered, however, that although students with mild to moderate disabilities as a group exhibit problem behaviors across all of these domains, no one student actually experiences difficulties in all domains.

Proponents of the noncategorical perspective cite three major reasons for advocating their position. First, the categorical approach to the description of students with mild to moderate disabilities implies a homogeneity within each of the categories. This is not the case. In fact, there is such heterogeneity of characteristics among students within each of the categories that the result is a blurring of categorical boundaries. The overlap between the traditional categories is most often noted in a sharing of common behavioral features including (but not limited to) deficient academic functioning, poor social skills, memory problems, impulsivity, and problems in the generalization and maintenance of newly acquired skills.

The second argument forwarded by proponents of the noncategorical orientation involves instructional procedures typical of most special education settings. In short, traditional methods of labeling or defining students with learning and behavioral problems are basically administrative procedures that have little impact on how to best teach students. In contrast, the precise definition of assessed problems constitutes the first step in providing appropriate instructional interventions. Because many of the criteria used to determine categorical eligibility include generic references to traits and etiological considerations, there is often little instructional relevance to a categorical label. Instruction based on strict categorical consideration has not been very successful (Hallahan, Kauffman, & Lloyd, 1985; Smith, Price, & Marsh, 1986).

The third reason forwarded by advocates for noncategorical programming is that the use of traditional categories promotes the faulty assumption that learning and behavioral difficulties can be attributed exclusively to the labeled student. Clearly, learning and behavioral problems are not solely student-based, but are often the result of a myriad of interacting ecological factors, including classroom setting, teacher behavior, community characteristics, and the entry-level behavior of a student (Blankenship & Lilly, 1981).

HOW SPECIAL EDUCATION SERVICES ARE DELIVERED

By far, one of the most contentious issues in special education is how to best deliver special education services while ensuring access to the general education curriculum. Most of the controversy has centered on how to best meet the educational needs of individuals with disabilities while in the least restrictive environment (LRE). For many years, the **cascade** or **continuum of services** was the primary benchmark for determining educational placement; recently, however, the principle of **inclusion** has been operationalized as an alternative means of delivery.

Continuum of Services

One of the first concepts presented to college students interested in pursuing a career in special education is the **cascade of educational services**. This cascade system, originally outlined by Reynolds (1962) and expanded by Deno (1970), suggests that the delivery of educational services to all students is best viewed as a continuum. As illustrated in Figure 1.1 and Box 1.2, the continuum ranges in both degree and type of special services required for an individual learner. Several assumptions are inherent in the cascade conceptualization of available educational services. First, the model assumes that a variety of service delivery options should be available to meet the specific educational needs of individual students. Rather than focus on classifications or labels, the ultimate goal is to tailor instructional programs and settings to meet the needs of students. Second, the triangular shape of the model indicates that the majority of students, those with disabilities and without disabilities, are appropriately placed in least restrictive settings. Third, the cascade assumes that placement within a particular setting is not permanent. Students should be able to move between levels of services on the basis of their educational performance. The greatest emphasis should be on returning students to less restrictive environments; movement to more restrictive settings should occur only when necessary.

Regardless of their categorical designation, most students with mild to moderate disabilities typically receive educational services within the general school environment. Therefore, many developing and beginning teachers find that they will be teaching in the traditional special education settings of full-time special classrooms, part-time special settings, or resource rooms. With the movement toward the increased integration of students with mild to moderate disabilities into general classroom settings, however, it is also possible that developing and beginning teachers will find themselves working in nontraditional service delivery roles—as consulting teachers, itinerant learning specialists, or cooperative partners in integrated classroom settings.

Although many practicum students will be in typical school environments, it is possible that some will sense an unusual estrangement from their general education colleagues. This feeling of separation is typically the result of a host of factors but is caused to a great degree by the lack of coordination between the special education and general education systems of educating students with problems. The significant growth and progress of the special education delivery system have resulted in one major deleterious by-product: a barrier between general and special educators as to who is responsible for the education of students identified as having disabilities. The growth of special education has resulted in a dual system of education—one for nondisabled

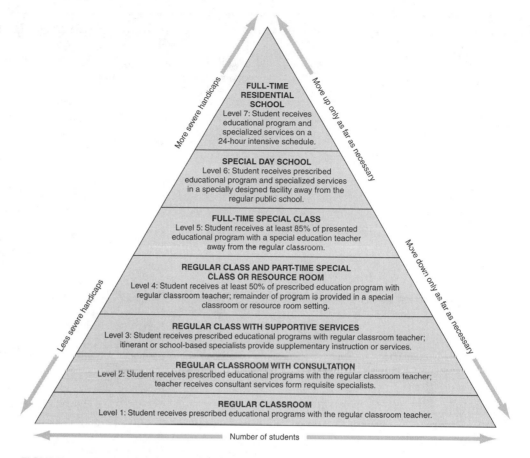

FIGURE 1.1 Cascade of Educational Services

Adapted from Deno, E. (1970) Special education as developmental capital. *Exceptional Children, 37*, 235; and Reynolds, M. C. (1962). A framework for considering some issues in special education. *Exceptional Children, 28*, 368.

youngsters and another for those with learning and behavioral difficulties. In settings where a dual system of education is institutionalized, many administrators and general classroom teachers believe they are no longer involved in the education of students with disabilities. Many general classroom teachers also believe they lack the specialized training that could enable them to teach the other 25 to 30 students in their classrooms along with students with disabilities. By virtue of identifying students as having a disability, the education of these problem students is viewed as the exclusive professional responsibility of a specialist—the special educator. Unfortunately, these attitudes do little to promote the reintegration and mainstreaming of students with disabilities and often put barriers between special and general educators.

By the time they enter the school environment, developing and beginning teachers are keenly aware that the success of students with mild to moderate disabilities depends on the collaborative efforts of general and special educators. This need to bring together general and special educators has been approached in a number of ways and with varying degrees of intensity. Several special educators have advocated a complete merging of special and general education efforts into a single, unified, *inclusive* system. Such restructuring would radically change how students with disabilities would be identified and served in their local communities. As observed by Stainback and Stainback (1984), the adoption of a unified system of education for all students would affect many facets of special education. Possible affected areas are summarized in Table 1.1.

Box 1.2   **Levels of the Cascade: Examples of Students Receiving Services**

1. *Full-time residential school:* Educational services are provided directly to the student in his or her place of residence on hospital or institutional grounds.

   Example: John has been diagnosed as having severe developmental disability, is deaf-blind, and requires full-time medical assistance. The LRE for John may be the Maryhurst Residential School and Treatment Center.

2. *Special day school:* Students with disabilities are educated in a special school with similar students.

   Example: Mary has been found to be functioning at a profound level of cognitive functioning. She requires the assistance of a wheelchair and feeding tubes during lunch. The LRE for Mary may be the Fanley Special Day Care Center.

3. *Full-time special class:* Students with disabilities are educated in a special class located on the grounds of a regular school.

   Example: Tara functions at a profound level of functioning although she displays no major problems with self-help skills or motor skills. She displays no medical difficulties. The LRE for Tara may be a full-time special class at Flanigan Middle School.

4. *Part-time general class and part-time special class:* Students with disabilities spend some part of the instructional week with regular peers.

   Example: Tommy displays problem behaviors—specifically, inattention to a task during academic instruction. He displays excellent motor skills, however, and is especially proficient in rhythm activities during music class. The LRE for Tommy may be a part-time special class in which he divides his time between instruction with regular students and instruction with students with disabilities at Santa Rosa High School.

5. *General class with supportive instructional services:* The majority of the student's classwork is provided during general class scheduling, but for a portion of the time, education is provided in a resource room setting.

   Example: Yusuf displays excellent reading and spelling skills but requires assistance by the teacher in the resource room for mathematics. Yusuf functions effectively in all aspects of the school curriculum. The LRE for Yusuf may be the resource room model at Tandy Elementary. His special education teacher may work on a consulting basis with the general class teacher to monitor Yusuf's progress in the mainstream.

6. *General class with consulting services for general class teacher:* Resource room teachers and itinerant teachers consult with general class teachers about modifications in the general curriculum. Prereferral strategies may be implemented for students who can profit by instruction with general class peers.

   Example: Ellen demonstrates adequate comprehension skills but has trouble reading the text. Teachers at Taylor School have consulted about the use of a tape-recorded text for her general class reading program. When she is allowed to hear stories read from the tape, Ellen demonstrates no difficulty following the written discourse. The LRE for Ellen may be the general class with consulting services. Use of the tape recorder may be monitored by her teachers through prereferral conferences.

7. *General classroom:* The LRE for education of all students is the general class.

   Example: Sara requires speech therapy for a diagnosed articulation problem although she displays no educational difficulties other than an articulation problem. Sara is 5 years old, and her LRE is the general class at Public School #16.

TABLE 1.1   Comparative Effects of Dual Versus Unified Systems of Education on Selected Areas of Concern

Concern	Dual System	Unified System
1. Student characteristics	Dichotomizes student into special and regular	Recognizes continuum among all students of intellectual, physical, and psychological characteristics
2. Individualization	Stresses individualization for student labeled special	Stresses individualization for all students
3. Instructional strategies	Seeks to use special strategies for special students	Selects from range of available strategies according to each student's learning needs
4. Type of educational services	Eligibility generally based on category affiliation	Eligibility based on each student's individual learning needs
5. Diagnostics	Large expenditures on identification of categorical affiliation	Emphasis on identifying the specific instructional needs of all students
6. Professional relationships	Establishes artificial barriers among educators that promote competition and alienation	Promotes cooperation through sharing resources, expertise, and advocacy responsibilities
7. Curriculum	Options available to each student are limited by categorical affiliation	All options available to every student as needed
8. Focus	Student must fit regular education program or be referred to special education	Regular education program is adjusted to meet all students' needs

From Stainback, W., & Stainback, S. (1984). A rationale for the merger of regular and special education. *Exceptional Children, 51*, 107. Copyright 1984 by The Council for Exceptional Children. Reprinted by permission.

Inclusive Education

Inclusive education is an effort to reconstruct general education classes so that all children representing the range of diversity present in a local community are welcome and provided with an appropriate, meaningful education (Giangreco, Baumgart, & Doyle, 1995). Therefore, *inclusion* means that students attend their home school with their age- and grade-appropriate peers, participate in extracurricular activities, and receive *special education and support services*, to the maximum extent possible, in the general education classroom. Inclusion does *not* mean that students must spend every moment of the school day in general education classes, or that students never receive small-group or individualized instruction (see Box 1.3) (York, Doyle, & Kronberg, 1992). However, the focus for inclusion is on where things are happening and the types of practices that are being used (King-Sears, 1997). Proponents of inclusion are quick to point out that inclusion is not synonymous with the term *mainstreaming*; mainstreaming occurs when a student with an identified disability leaves a special education class to participate in a general education class for part of the day to complete the same instructional goals set for other students. Within an inclusionary delivery system, special education and support services are delivered so that the student with a disability can benefit from being in the general education setting.

The rationale for inclusive education is quite compelling, particularly on philosophical and social grounds. Clearly, it is difficult to argue against the position that all children should reap the potential benefits of inclusive programming (e.g., attending one's neighborhood school in classrooms where there is a climate of acceptance, ending the segregation of large numbers of students, all students participating in shared

---

Box 1.3 Inclusion: What It Is and What It Is Not

Inclusion IS:	Inclusion is NOT:
• teaching students with disabilities in their home schools in general education settings regardless of the degree or severity of their disabilities	• serving students with disabilities only in separate schools or classes based on their disability label
• having a school and district mission that sets high expectations for all students, including those with disabilities	• setting low expectations for students with disabilities
• making sure that all students are placed in schools and classrooms appropriate to their age	• teaching students with disabilities in schools and classrooms that are not age-appropriate
• providing the planning, support, and services necessary for successful participation of students with disabilities in general education programs	• placing students with disabilities into general education classes without the planning, supports, and services needed for successful participation
• adapting teaching styles to meet the many different learning needs of all students	• failing to adapt instruction to meet the different learning needs of students
• providing professional development, training, and support for all staff regarding effective methods for the successful inclusion of students with disabilities	• providing separate staff development for regular teachers and special education teachers, thus reinforcing notions of separate systems
• encouraging activities that promote the development of friendships and relationships between students with and without disabilities	• maintaining separate daily activities for students with and without disabilities
• scheduling classes for all school activities in a way that maximizes opportunities for participation by students with disabilities	• scheduling students with disabilities for lunch and other activities at different times than other students are scheduled
• using "person first" language ("students with disabilities" instead of "disabled students") and teaching all students to understand and value human differences	• referring to students in stigmatizing terms such as "handicapped class" or the "retarded kids"

Source: Adapted from Maryland Coalition for Inclusive Education. (1993). *Inclusion: What it is and what it is not.* Laurel, MD: Author.

---

educational experiences with individualized outcomes). Most discussions on inclusion, however, have (1) ignored the barriers and conditions within the schools that preclude *successful* inclusive efforts and (2) minimized the real-life, day-to-day demands on teachers who are expected to teach an ever-increasing diversity of students with and without disabilities (Joint Committee on Teacher Planning for Students with Disabilities, 1995). From the results of four large-scale studies, the Joint Committee on Teacher Planning for Students with Disabilities found that, for students with disabilities to be successfully included in the general education classroom, educators need to think in terms of "supported inclusion," not simply inclusion (see Box 1.4).

Supported inclusion was defined as a set of instructional conditions in which classroom teachers

- are philosophically committed to meeting the needs of all students in the general education classroom, including those with mild disabilities
- have sufficient time to think about and plan for the diverse needs of students in their class(es)

ox 1.4   **Inclusion Checklist for Your Placement**

Rodgers (1993) prepared a checklist designed to assist school personnel in evaluating whether their current practices were consistent with the best intentions of the inclusive programming movement. Use this modified checklist to assess how your field placement measures up to some of the ideals proposed by inclusion advocates. Rate your placement with a + for each item in which the main statement best describes your placement and an 0 for each item in which the parenthetical statement best describes your school. As you consider the items, keep in mind that each 0 rating can serve as the basis for school improvement efforts.

_____ 1. Do the teachers, administrators, and staff at your school believe that each child belongs in the classroom that he or she would otherwise attend if not disabled (or do they believe that children with disabilities should be clustered into special groups, classrooms, or schools)?

_____ 2. Do the educators in your school individualize the instructional programs for all children whether or not they are disabled and provide the resources that each child needs to explore individual interests in the school environment (or do they tend to provide the same sorts of services for most children who share the same label or classification)?

_____ 3. Are the educators in your school fully committed to maintenance of a caring community that fosters mutual respect and support among staff, parents, and students and in which the educators honestly believe that disabled children can benefit from friendships with nondisabled children (or do the educators' practices tacitly tolerate children teasing or isolating some as outcasts)?

_____ 4. Have the general educators and special educators in your school integrated their efforts and their resources so that they work together as integral parts of a unified team (or are they isolated in separate rooms or departments with separate supervisors and budgets)?

_____ 5. Do the administrators at your school create a work climate in which staff are supported as they provide assistance to each other (or are teachers afraid of being presumed to be incompetent if they seek peer collaboration in working with students)?

_____ 6. Do the educators in your school actively encourage the full participation of children with disabilities in the life of the school, including extracurricular activities (or do they participate only in the academic portion of the school day)?

_____ 7. Are the educators in your school prepared to alter support systems for students as their needs change through the school year so that they can achieve, experience successes, and feel that they genuinely belong in their school and classes (or do they sometimes provide such limited services to them that the children are set up to fail)?

_____ 8. Do the educators in your school make parents of children with disabilities fully a part of your school community so they also can experience a sense of belonging (or do they give the parents a separate PTA and different newsletters)?

_____ 9. Do the educators give children with disabilities just as much of the full school curriculum as they can master and modify it as necessary so that they can share elements of these experiences with their classmates (or do the educators have a separate curriculum for children with disabilities)?

_____ 10. Have the educators in your school included children with disabilities supportively in as many as possible of the same testing and evaluation experiences as their nondisabled classmates (or have they excluded them from these opportunities while assuming that they cannot benefit from the experiences)

- incorporate teaching practices that enable them to better meet the needs of all students in their class(es)
- collaboratively work with special education teachers to assess, teach, and monitor student progress
- have the option for their students to receive *short-term*, intensive instructional support from a special education teacher
- have the option for their students to receive *sustained instruction* in basic skills or learning strategies that cannot be provided in the general education classroom (Joint Committee on Teacher Planning for Students with Disabilities, 1995, pp. 3–4)

These service delivery issues remain controversial within all levels of the teaching profession. Whether referred to as the regular education initiative, general education initiative, inclusion, or simply a merger between regular and special education systems, it is heartening to see that educators are continuing to seek more effective ways of delivering special education services to those who need them. There is little doubt that these efforts will provide better strategies for coordinating the efforts of all educators in delivering specialized educational services to those students in need.

However individual LEAs decide to restructure their systems of identifying and educating students with disabilities, cooperation between general and special educators still comes down to individuals and their interactions. Cooperation and collaboration involve people skills and mutual respect. Developing and beginning teachers of students with mild to moderate disabilities should avoid the "us versus them" mind-set when working with their general education colleagues and should instead actively seek to develop collaborative relationships. As with the many obstacles that people face in their personal lives, diplomacy is the key to achieving good working relationships and positive outcomes.

ROLES AND RESPONSIBILITIES

We have limited our discussions to definitions and characteristics of students with mild to moderate disabilities and descriptions of the various educational settings in which they are served. In the next section, we focus on the developing teacher and describe the roles and responsibilities of the individuals who are influential in determining the success of field-based practicum experiences. For developing teachers of students with mild to moderate disabilities to derive the maximum benefit from field-based practicum experiences, a well-planned team effort must be initiated and maintained. The primary members of this team are the university supervisor, the cooperating classroom teacher, and most important, the practicum student.

University Supervisor

The university supervisor assumes primary responsibility for the success of practicum students' field experiences. The supervisor is the direct representative of the university and serves as the liaison between the best interests of the practicum students and the requirements of the school or LEA. The university supervisor should foster professional development, provide honest performance feedback, and constructively smooth over possible rough spots during the teaching experience.

In addition to liaison responsibilities, the university supervisor typically assumes three responsibilities in the development of preservice special educators. First, the university supervisor arranges for the most appropriate placement for the practicum student. This entails the careful analysis of the practicum student's entry-level skills and the type of setting in which the student anticipates teaching (e.g., level of service, age or grade level, severity of disability). Factors also considered include the availability of both quality instructional settings and cooperating teachers within reasonable commuting distance of the practicum student and university supervisor.

Second, the university supervisor monitors the progress of the practicum student throughout the field experience. This typically involves periodic direct observation of lessons, meetings with the cooperating teacher and principal, and critiquing of lesson plans, unit projects, and behavioral change efforts. A critical component of this monitoring process is the delivery of feedback. The university supervisor accentuates the strengths of the developing teacher and identifies weaknesses for the purpose of improving performance. Feedback, in many cases, will be specific to the lessons observed, and suggestions for improving student achievement should be offered.

Third, the supervisor is the link between the practicum student's university-inspired idealism and the real-world pressures of the school. The supervisor can serve as the buffer between the way-things-ought-to-be approach typical of college classrooms and the complex, less-than-ideal realities of school settings. Some practicum students observe that some of their cooperating teachers' behaviors are not consistent with many of the principles of effective teaching covered in methods classes. The supervisor should clarify such inconsistencies and mediate diplomatically any disagreements between the practicum student and the cooperating teacher.

Cooperating Teacher

The cooperating teacher will have the greatest amount of direct contact with the practicum student. In the best of situations, a mentor relationship is forged between the cooperating teacher and the practicum student. Cooperating teachers are to (1) be models of effective instructional procedures and paragons of tempered professional practice, (2) be well schooled in the ability to share their instincts of teaching, (3) prepare their environment to maximize opportunities for novice teachers to succeed and learn from their errors, (4) observe and evaluate practicum student performance while ensuring that little damage is occurring to the often fragile self-concept of the novice teacher, and (5) set the pace for the integration of the practicum student into classroom activities, allowing gradually increased levels of responsibility. Box 1.5 lists the more commonly cited competencies desired of cooperating teachers. Although much is expected of cooperating teachers, it must be remembered that their first responsibility is to their students, ensuring that instruction of an appropriate quantity and quality is delivered consistently.

Practicum Student

For most practicum students, the transition from the role of university student to the role of professional teacher is completed with little difficulty. Nonetheless, the rigors and responsibilities of practicum experiences are considerable and should never be underestimated. How these responsibilities are met by the practicum student will dramatically affect the success of the experience itself, as well as the individual's future career in teaching. It is best to conceptualize the many responsibilities of the practicum student as falling into six specific domains of responsibilities:

1. Students and their parents
2. The cooperating teacher
3. The university
4. Awareness of legal rights, responsibilities, and liabilities
5. Personal professional growth
6. The profession

Responsibilities to Students and Their Parents. Practicum students must realize that the instruction they deliver is of vital importance to students in their classes. Every

---

B ox 1.5   **Commonly Cited Competencies Desired of Cooperating Teachers**

Competencies Related Primarily to the Working Relationship Between the Cooperating Teacher and the Practicum Student

The cooperating teacher

- remains available for consultation and moral support when needed
- analyzes with the practicum student the value of experiences: helps him or her discover which ones are most worthwhile
- helps the practicum student set his or her goals and formulate a personal educational philosophy
- shares in planning
- plans and teaches with another adult; originates and suggests new ideas without dominating the practicum student's thoughts and actions
- establishes a feeling of security for the practicum student by clarifying his or her responsibilities throughout the field experience
- offers criticism—continual, specific, and constructive—in an empathic manner
- invites the practicum student to participate in the professional and social activities of the staff
- helps the practicum student develop an understanding of his or her own strengths and weaknesses and build a healthy self-concept
- shows willingness to consider new and different techniques in an open-minded manner

Competencies Related to the Transition from the Observer Status of the Practicum Student to Active Teaching Status Later in the Field Experience

The cooperating teacher

- gradually allows the practicum student to accept increasing responsibility until full teaching responsibility is assumed
- helps the practicum student understand his or her job in relation to the entire school program
- helps the practicum student build teaching skills through observation of his or her own teaching
- helps the practicum student link theories to practice

Competencies Related Primarily to Instruction, Classroom Procedures, and Techniques

The cooperating teacher

- gives suggestions in matters of discipline
- acquaints the practicum student with routine matters
- displays accuracy in keeping records
- creates a democratic setting for learning—one in which students share in some decision-making experiences
- assists the practicum student in setting reasonable standards of performance for his or her instructional group
- encourages creative thinking and planning by the practicum student
- models effective instructional procedures during his or her own teaching

Competencies Related Primarily to Personal Characteristics or Traits of the Supervising Teacher That Might Be Emulated by the Practicum Student

The cooperating teacher

- sets a good example for the practicum student in personal appearance, grooming, speech, and appropriate mannerisms
- makes rational judgments, takes appropriate actions, and accepts responsibility for the consequences
- reflects a positive professional attitude and real liking and respect for teaching
- exhibits interest in continual self-improvement and educational advancement
- reflects a mature personality with enthusiasm and broad interests

Competencies Related Primarily to Developing Broad Professional and School Responsibilities

The cooperating teacher

- is an active participant in local and state teachers' organizations
- perceives the opportunity to work with future teachers as a professional responsibility
- actively participates with his or her colleagues in developing and enforcing standards fundamental to continual improvement of the profession and abides by those standards in practice
- exhibits willingness to accept out-of-class responsibilities
- participates effectively in faculty meetings and the work of professional committees
- is acquainted with sources of current thinking—journals, conferences, yearbook, workshops
- exhibits a cooperative attitude in relationships with other members of the staff

Source: Adapted from Ball State University (1981). *Competencies of the supervising teacher*. Muncie, IN: Author.

moment of available instructional time is of extreme value, particularly for students with mild to moderate disabilities. With this in mind, it is important that practicum students come prepared to teach effectively. This preparation should include thorough lesson planning and the necessary consultations with the cooperating teacher and university supervisor. Students' individualized education plans (IEPs) and diagnostic test information should also be reviewed (see Chapters 3 and 4 for greater detail).

In general, students enjoy working with developing teachers. The teachers' youth, vitality, and creativity are often seen as welcome changes of pace. Practicum students should be aware, however, that students in their classes will depend on them to follow through with planned activities. Therefore, practicum students should avoid unnecessary absences, be prompt in following through on promised events, and avoid promising things that will not be delivered. Practicum students should be models of appropriate decorum and controlled in their responses to negative or frustrating events. Initial

P*ause and Reflect 1.3*

You have just read what the expected roles and responsibilities typically are for university supervisors and cooperating teachers. On the basis of your unique needs and expectations, what types of supports would you like to receive from your university supervisor and cooperating teacher? What would be the most effective method for you to convey your expectations to these people? If problems with your placement were to arise, how would you like these individuals to approach you?

student enthusiasm toward working with the practicum student can be returned by becoming acquainted with students and by interacting with them in a lively, interested fashion. Practicum students should be careful not to become overly friendly, however, and should always conduct themselves in a firm, controlled, and impartial manner.

Practicum students may have the opportunity to interact with their students' parents. This may be a regularly scheduled IEP conference or the result of some critical incident requiring parental input. The practicum student must recognize parents as partners in the education process and, in concert with the cooperating teacher, must discuss constructively the behaviors of the student as they relate to the solution of the presenting problem.

Responsibilities to the Cooperating Teacher. Perhaps the most critical responsibility toward the cooperating teacher is the maintenance of clear communication. It is best to discuss situations in a direct, diplomatic manner without letting minor obstacles fester into major stumbling blocks. With the assistance of the university supervisor, the cooperating teacher should be made aware of the personal goals and aspirations of the practicum student, and a plan to achieve those goals within the context of the overall practicum experience should be developed and monitored. If questions about the methods used to pursue these goals arise, it is the responsibility of the practicum student to initiate requests for assistance. Finally, because the education of students in the class is the ultimate responsibility of the cooperating teacher, the practicum student should share activity or lesson plans well in advance of their implementation. This will allow the cooperating teacher to provide constructive feedback prior to the delivery of the activity or lesson.

Responsibilities to the University. As a practicum student in the local schools, the developing teaching is a representative of the sponsoring university. By placing a practicum student within a particular setting, the university is stating that the developing teacher is ready to assume the multifaceted responsibilities associated with teaching students with mild to moderate disabilities. Consequently, the behavior of each practicum student reflects on the institution that has provided training for that person.

The best ways for practicum students to represent their institutions are (1) putting forth the maximum effort possible in all facets of the field experience, (2) being open to suggestions from various school-based personnel, (3) becoming involved in team-based solutions to problems, (4) doing a fair share of the noninstructional and extracurricular duties required of teachers, (5) being enthusiastic and positive during instructional and noninstructional tasks, (6) facilitating the cooperative relationship between the visiting university supervisor and the school-based teachers and administrators, and (7) maintaining a professional and ethical demeanor when dealing with students' problem behaviors and confidential records. Practicum students should avoid falling into the trap of lounge gossip and must be careful whenever references to students, by name, are made during social situations away from the classroom.

Awareness of Legal Rights, Responsibilities, and Liabilities. For better or for worse, we are living in an increasingly litigious society. In all of the human service professions, especially those that involve children, it is critical that the service provider be aware of his or her legal status. Because laws and procedural safeguards regarding the status of those preparing to enter teaching vary from state to state, it is essential that each practicum student become aware of the specific requirements of his or her locality. Roe and Ross (1994) have recommended that practicum students be particularly aware of their district's policy on (1) reporting possible child abuse, (2) reporting accidents or injuries that occur among students, (3) using specific techniques (e.g., time-out, aversives) for discipline and behavioral management, (4) searching students' personnel belongings, (5) dealing with physically and verbally abusive advances of students, (6) administering first-aid, (7) making copies of instructional materials for students (so as to not violate copyright laws), (8) presenting seemingly controversial topics, and (9) needing liability insurance. Also, in this age of electronic information gathering and transmission, practicum students should be aware of policies regarding the acceptable use of computer technologies such as networks, video, and the Internet. Such information can be obtained from the office that administers field-based placements in your school or district.

Although it is extremely rare that developing teachers will face problems that require massive legal involvement, it is important that full documentation and disclosure of sticky situations be recorded and shared with the appropriate personnel (e.g., cooperating teacher, university supervisor).

Responsibilities to Personal Professional Growth. Although many practicum situations represent the culmination of a set of experiences within a special education training program, they are actually the cornerstones for future professional development activities. Instructing and managing challenging students in busy classrooms tend to illuminate specific content or skill areas that require additional growth or refinement. This feeling will recur throughout one's professional development. As a rule, professionals seldom let their acquired skills stagnate. In special education, instructional technology is advancing much too quickly for any teacher to neglect personal professional development.

Mechanisms exist for developing teachers to fulfill their own need for professional growth. The most convenient methods are to consult recent publications in the field and to scan the many web sites dedicated to special education and individuals with disabilities. A variety of professional textbooks, curriculum resource guides, and journals are available in regional resource centers, teacher development centers, and university libraries. Box 1.6 lists the professional journals that would be of greatest interest to developing teachers of students with mild to moderate disabilities. Also, at the end of each chapter we provided a short list of web sites that provide both informative content and links to other sites of interest (see Point and Click sections).

A second method for developing teachers to augment their skills is attendance at local, regional, or state conferences sponsored by professional organizations and advocacy groups involved in the education and treatment of students with disabilities. Schedules of such events can be obtained directly from the professional organizations or from listings in professional journals and newsletters.

A third means of professional development are in-service and staff development workshops provided by local school districts. These activities are usually open to all personnel within the district, and practicum students are typically urged to attend.

Finally, professional development can include taking additional courses in university settings. To begin considering the type of coursework or graduate programs that would most appropriately match professional development needs, practicum students can consult college catalogs. Most university libraries contain these catalogs in either hard copy or microfiche formats. In many cases, information can be obtained from university Web sites on the Internet.

Responsibilities to the Profession. The most critical responsibility toward the profession of special education is to behave in both an ethical and professional manner throughout field experiences. The trademark of any quality profession is its willingness to establish and abide by (1) a code of ethics and (2) corresponding standards that can provide a basis for evaluating professional practice related directly to a code of ethics (Heller, 1983). Whether or not special educators have reached the stage of true professionalism in the eyes of most members of society is arguable. What cannot be denied, however, is that all involved in the education and treatment of students with disabilities must continue to operate in a professional fashion if they are to expect those outside the profession to treat them as such.

B ox 1.6   Professional Journals of Interest to Developing and Beginning Teachers of Students with Mild to Moderate Disabilities

Listed below are the titles of the more prominent journals that would be of interest to those involved in the education of students with mild to moderate disabilities. Most of these publications are available at major university libraries. To contact the journals directly, use the business addresses provided.

American Journal of Mental Deficiency
American Association on Mental Deficiency
5101 Wisconsin Avenue, N.W.
Washington, DC 20016

Behavioral Disorders
Division for Children with Behavior Disorders
Council for Exceptional Children
1920 Association Drive
Reston, VA 22091

Beyond Behavior
Division for Children with Behavior Disorders
Council for Exceptional Children
1920 Association Drive
Reston, VA 22091

Career Development of Exceptional Individuals
Division of Career Development
Council for Exceptional Children
1920 Association Drive
Reston, VA 22091

Diagnostique
Council for Education Diagnostic Services
Council for Exceptional Children
1920 Association Drive
Reston, VA 22091

Education and Training in Mental Retardation
Mental Retardation Division
Council for Exceptional Children
1920 Association Drive
Reston, VA 22091

Exceptional Children
Council for Exceptional Children
1920 Association Drive
Reston, VA 22091

Education and Treatment of Children
Clinical Psychology Publishing Company
4 Conant Square
Brandon, VT 05733

Exceptional Parent 20
Providence Street
Boston, MA 03116

Focus on Exceptional Children
Love Publishing Company
1777 S. Bellaire Street
Denver, CO 80222

Intervention in School and Clinic
PRO-ED
8700 Shoal Creek Boulevard
Austin, TX 78735

Journal of Applied Behavior Analysis
Department of Human Development
University of Kansas
Lawrence, KS 66045

Journal of Emotional and Behavioral Disorders
PRO-ED
8700 Shoal Creek Boulevard
Austin, TX 78735

Journal of the Division of Early Childhood
Division of Early Childhood
Council for Exceptional Children
1920 Association Drive
Reston, VA 22091

Journal of Learning Disabilities
PRO-ED
8700 Shoal Creek
Boulevard Austin, TX 78735

Journal of Special Education
PRO-ED
8700 Shoal Creek Boulevard
Austin, TX 78735

Journal of Special Education Technology
Technology and Media Division
Council for Exceptional Children
1920 Association Drive
Reston, Va 22091

Learning Disabilities Research and Practice
Division for Children with Learning Disabilities
Council for Exceptional Children
1920 Association Drive
Reston, VA 22091

Learning Disabilities Quarterly
Council for Learning Disabilities
P.O. Box 40303
Overland Park, KS 66204

Mental Retardation
American Association on Mental Deficiency
5101 Wisconsin Avenue, N.W.
Washington, DC 20016

Remedial and Special Education
PRO-ED
8700 Shoal Creek Boulevard
Austin, TX 78735

Teaching Exceptional Children
Council for Exceptional Children
1920 Association Drive
Reston, VA 22091

Topics in Early Childhood Special Education
PRO-ED
8700 Shoal Creek Boulevard
Austin, TX 78735

In a major move toward the professionalization of special education, the Delegate Assembly of the Council for Exceptional Children (CEC) in 1983 adopted a code of ethics for educators of persons with exceptionalities. Responsibilities believed to form the basis of professional conduct in relation to three major areas—the exceptional student, the employer, and the profession—were formulated into a code of eight ethical principles. Correspondingly, this code of ethics was translated into a set of minimum standards of conduct called the Standards for Professional Practice. Together, both the code of ethics and the Standards for Professional Practice were viewed as providing guidelines for (1) professional etiquette, (2) effective interpersonal behavior, (3) resolution of ethical issues, and (4) making professional judgments concerning what constitutes competent practice. This CEC code of ethics is presented in Box 1.7. The complete set of standards is contained in the appendix.

Box 1.7   **Council for Exceptional Children's Code of Ethics**

We declare the following principles to be the Code of Ethics for educators of persons with exceptionalities. Members of the special education profession are responsible for upholding and advancing these principles. Members of the Council for Exceptional Children agree to judge and be judged by them in accordance with the spirit and provisions of this Code.

    I. Special education professionals are committed to developing the highest educational and quality-of-life potential of individuals with exceptionalities.

    II. Special education professionals promote and maintain a high level of competence and integrity in practicing their profession.

    III. Special education professionals engage in professional activities that benefit individuals with exceptionalities, their families, other colleagues, students, or research subjects.

    IV. Special education professionals exercise objective professional judgment in the practice of their profession.

    V. Special education professionals strive to advance their knowledge and skills regarding the education of individuals with exceptionalities.

    VI. Special education professionals work within the standards and policies of their profession.

    VII. Special education professionals seek to uphold and improve where necessary the laws, regulations, and policies governing the delivery of special education and related services and the practice of their profession.

    VIII. Special education professionals do not condone or participate in unethical or illegal acts, nor violate professional standards adopted by the Delegate Assembly of CEC.

SOURCE: Council for Exceptional Children. (2000). *What every educator must know: The international standards for the preparation and certification of special education teachers.* Reston, VA: Author.

PREPARING FOR A SUCCESSFUL PRACTICUM EXPERIENCE

In the previous sections, we discussed the behavioral characteristics of students with mild to moderate disabilities, as well as the many responsibilities required of practicum students during their field-based experiences. In this final section, we offer a listing of sensible tips that, if addressed, can enable practicum students to cope with their increased responsibilities and maximize the benefits of their field experiences:

1. **Have the opportunity to succeed.** The demands placed on practicum students during their field experiences are considerable. The time and effort required of most practicum experiences equal or even exceed those typical of full-time teaching positions. Wherever possible, limit the amount of time devoted to extracurricular activities, additional courses, and part-time jobs and allow for the maximum opportunity of success. Plan to get some well-deserved rest; teaching students with mild to moderate disabilities is a challenging and demanding job!

2. **Visit the assigned field-based setting prior to beginning the practicum.** Much of the anxiety related to a practicum student's impending experiences is the result of nonspecific fears of the unknown. It is wise, therefore, to get an "advance organizer" or mind-set of what will be experienced when the practicum officially begins. In addition to relieving some of the jitters, this visit will (1) convey to the cooperating teacher a genuine interest in the practicum process, (2) allow for a brief introduction to students, (3) provide important first impressions regarding the standards of protocol and comportment within the school, and (4) allow for the learning of school and classroom-specific policies.

3. **Present yourself appropriately.** Whether it is correct or not, people sometimes judge others rather superficially—on the basis of their appearance, comportment, and surface behaviors. To heighten the chances of making a favorable first impression, it is important that the practicum student be dressed and groomed appropriately. Moreover, the general tenor of how you express opinions and share personal lifestyles needs to be checked. Although many facets of a person's individuality are important components in the motivation of students, some forms of personal expression conflict with local community standards (however they tend to be defined) and are best saved for environments other than the school (Behling, 1978).

4. **Monitor all written work.** Practicum students are judged on the quality of the written documents (e.g., applications, personal statements) that are required for the field experience. Unfortunately, some developing teachers are identified as sloppy and careless merely because they do not make the extra effort of good written expression or do not proofread their written products prior to submission. Written products reflect directly on the author. Developing teachers should ensure that their written work contains correct punctuation and spelling, is grammatically correct, and possesses a logical sequence of ideas.

5. **Remain patient.** The assumption of instructional responsibilities by the practicum student is a gradual process. Although you may feel "all fired up and ready to take charge," a gradual integration into the flow of activities allows for observations of the cooperating teacher in action and for a general orientation to the operating procedures of the school. These observation periods also allow students in the class to become accustomed to the new teacher in the environment. Also, be sure to get the approval of the cooperating teacher prior to making any changes in instructional procedures or behavioral management programs. No matter how enthusiastic you may feel about implementing a change for a student, you must remember that the cooperating teacher is responsible for all programming within the classroom.

6. **Remain diplomatic.** Being the new person in the school means that many veteran teachers will give you advice on any number of topics related to education

(and life in general). Although some of this real-world advice may be in sharp contrast with what you believe or have learned about education, it is best to treat these interactions with colleagues as valuable learning experiences, as opportunities to get others' perceptions of certain issues. During these interactions, avoid arrogantly flaunting your knowledge of the innovative instructional procedures you have heard about in your methods classes. Keep interaction on a professional level, with efforts of mutual respect being initiated by the developing teacher.

7. Maintain enthusiasm in the face of others' disillusionment. As observed by Behling (1978), it is not unusual for practicum students to meet teachers and administrators who appear worn out, disillusioned, and apathetic. Although we anticipate that contacts with these people will be kept to a minimum, it is critical that developing teachers avoid falling into these highly contagious feelings of hopelessness and frustration. Even with the most challenging of students with disabilities, there is enough potential job satisfaction to merit enthusiasm.

8. Think "team," rather than individual. Practicum students face an overwhelming number of challenges related to the education and treatment of their students. An effort should be made to avoid trying to save the world singlehandedly. The problems faced by students in special education settings require collaboration and assistance from a variety of sectors within the school system. As is fully described in Chapters 8 and 9, successful efforts in meeting the challenges found in comprehensive special education programs typically require the enthusiasm and cooperation of a multidisciplinary team of professionals.

9. Get to know the other professionals and paraprofessionals. Each school has people who contribute to the effective schooling of children and youth. It is wise to use the practicum experience to learn the various roles and responsibilities of the individuals who populate the school. Certainly, visits with the school psychologist and social worker would allow for alternative perspectives on the student with mild to moderate disabilities. Also, getting to know the administrators of the school building and system could help when seeking a first teaching position.

SUMMARY

In this chapter, we addressed prerequisite issues associated with the initial field experiences of developing special education teachers. We opened with a brief description of the characteristics of students with mild to moderate disabilities. Specific emphases were given to both categorical and noncategorical conceptualizations of these disabilities. This was followed by a discussion of the range of service delivery options that are typical of most LEA placements. Issues related to (1) the LRE and (2) possible changes in how educators deliver educational service to students with disabilities were highlighted. The bulk of the chapter was devoted to the many roles and responsibilities of the key individuals involved in field-based teaching experiences. Concerns related to communication maintenance, professionalism, and preparation were emphasized. We concluded with a list of nine "sensible tips" related directly to the practical aspects of field-based experiences.

ACTIVITIES TO EXTEND YOUR KNOWLEDGE

1. Learning disabilities, emotional disturbance, and mild mental retardation are typically regarded as separate diagnostic categories by many special educators. Recently, however, a vocal and prolific group of researchers, theorists, and practitioners has

asserted that it is inappropriate and deleterious to continue using these nebulous and often overlapping categorical labels. Many of these dissenting special educators have advocated that service to students with mild to moderate handicaps be delivered through noncategorical (or multi- or cross-categorical) mechanisms. Can you clarify this categorical/noncategorical issue? Specifically,

- Can you demonstrate via differential definitions that you understand why learning disabilities, behavioral disorders, and mild mental retardation are traditionally treated as separate diagnostic entities?
- Can you outline the major issues in the categorical/noncategorical controversy, including both data-based assertions and theoretical positions?
- Can you explore the implications of adopting each of the service delivery alternatives in your LEA? How would the adoption of a noncategorical service delivery alternative affect instructional activities in your placement?
- Can you provide your own view of this most complex issue? Given the choice, would you advocate a categorical or noncategorical approach to the identification and education of students with mild to moderate disabilities?

2. Characterize the recent research on service delivery alternatives (inclusion, full continuum of services). What types of student outcomes have the researchers been considering? Is there any best way to deliver special education services to students with mild to moderate disabilities? Be sure you can defend your response.

3. How do the CEC code of ethics and the Standards for Professional Practice (see the appendix) compare with the codes and standards found in other professions (e.g., law, medicine, psychology)? In making such comparisons, critically evaluate the inclusiveness and comprehensiveness of the CEC code and standards. On the basis of your review, do you believe that the CEC code and standards are too rigorous or loose? What feedback would you provide to the CEC regarding the code of ethics and the Standards for Professional Practice?

POINT AND CLICK

These Web sites have information and links to additional information related to field experiences and students with mild to moderate disabilities.

Federal Resources for Educational Excellence (FREE)
http://www.ed.gov/free/

IDEA Practices
http://www.ideapractices.org/

K-12 Practitioners Home Page
http://nces.ed.gov/practitioners/

Selected Abstracts on Current Educational Issues
http://www.ascd.org/services/eric/facts.html

National Information Center for Children and Youth with Disabilities
http://www.nichcy.org/

What to Expect Your First Year of Teaching
http://www.ed.gov/pubs/FirstYear/

McREL: Mid-continent Research and for Education and Learning
http://www.mcrel.org

Council for Exceptional Children (CEC)
http://www.cec.sped.org

REFERENCES

American Psychiatric Association (APA). (1994). *Diagnostic and statistical manual of mental disorders (DSM-IV)*. Washington, DC: APA.

Ball State University. (1981). *Competencies of the supervising teacher*. Muncie, IN: Author.

Behling, H. (1978). *Some coping suggestions for student teachers* (Monograph No. 6). Annapolis: Maryland Association of Teacher Educators.

Blankenship, C., & Lilly, M. S. (1981). *Mainstreaming students with learning and behavior problems*. New York: Holt, Rinehart & Winston.

Bower, E. M. (1969). *Early identification of emotionally handicapped children in school*. Springfield, IL: Charles C. Thomas.

Campbell, S. B. (1985). Hyperactivity in preschoolers: Correlates and prognostic implications. *Clinical Psychology Review, 51,* 401-408.

Case, C. W., Lanier, J. E., & Miskel, C. G. (1986). The Holmes Group report: Impetus for gaining professional status for teachers. *Journal of Teacher Education, 37* (4), 36–43.

Council for Exceptional Children. (2000). *What every educator must know: The international standards for the preparation and certification of special education teachers*. Reston, VA: Author.

Council for Learning Disabilities. (1986). Inclusion of nonhandicapped low achievers and underachievers in learning disabilities programs: A position statement by the Board of Trustees of the Council for Learning Disabilities. *Learning Disability Quarterly, 9* (3), 246.

Deno, E. N. (1970). Special education as developmental capital. *Exceptional Children, 37,* 229–237.

Edgar, E., & Hayden, A. H. (1985). Who are the children special education should serve, and how many children are there? *Journal of Special Education, 18,* 523–539.

Giangreco, M. F., Baumgart, D. M. J., & Doyle, M. B. (1995). How inclusion can facilitate teaching and learning. *Intervention in School and Clinic, 30,* 273–278.

Gloecker, T., & Simpson, C. (1988). *Exceptional students in regular classrooms: Challenges, services, and methods*. Mountain View, CA: Mayfield.

Grossman, H. J. (1977). *Manual on terminology and classification in mental retardation* (7th ed.). Washington, DC: American Association on Mental Deficiency.

Hallahan, D. P., & Kauffman, J. M. (1982). *Exceptional children: Introduction to special education* (2nd ed.). Upper Saddle River, NJ: Prentice Hall.

Hallahan, D. P., Kauffman, J. M., & Lloyd, J. W. (1985). *Introduction to learning disabilities* (2nd ed.). Upper Saddle River, NJ: Prentice Hall.

Heller, H. W. (1983). Special education professional standards: Need, value, and use. *Exceptional Children, 50* (3), 199–204.

Heward, W. L. (2000). *Exceptional children* (6th ed.). Upper Saddle River, NJ: Merrill.

Huntze, S. L. (1985). A position paper of the Council for Children with Behavior Disorders. *Behavioral Disorders, 10,* 167–174.

Joint Committee on Teacher Planning for Students with Disabilities. (1995). *Planning for academic diversity in America's classrooms: Windows on reality, research, change, and practice*. Lawrence: University of Kansas.

King-Sears, M. E. (1997). Best academic practices for inclusive classrooms. *Focus on Exceptional Children, 29*(7), 1–22.

Kirk, S. A., & Gallagher, J. J. (1986). *Educating exceptional children* (5th ed.). Boston: Houghton Mifflin.

Kozma, C., & Stock, J. S. (1993). What is mental retardation? In R. Smith (Ed.), *Children with mental retardation: A parent's guide* (pp. 3–16). Rockville, MD: Woodbine House.

Maryland Coalition for Inclusive Education. (1993). *Inclusion: What it is and what it is not*. Laurel, MD: Author.

National Joint Committee on Learning Disabilities (NJCLD). (1988). *Learning disabilities: Issues on definition.* Austin, TX: Author.

Reynolds, M. C. (1962). A framework for considering issues in special education. *Exceptional Children, 28,* 367–370.

Rodgers, J. (1993). The inclusion revolution. *Research Bulletin of Phi Delta Kappa, 11,* 1–6.

Roe, B. D., & Ross, E. P. (1994). *Student teaching and field experiences handbook.* New York: Merrill/Macmillian.

Rosenberg, M.S., Jackson, L., & Yeh, C. (1996). Designing effective field experiences for nontraditional preservice special educators. *Teacher Education and Special Education, 19*(4) 331–341.

Rosenberg, M. S., Wilson, R., Maheady, L., & Sindelar, P. T. (1997). *Educating students with behavior disorders* (2nd ed.). Needham Heights, MA: Allyn & Bacon.

Smith, D. D. (1998). *Introduction to special education: Teaching in an age of challenge* (3rd ed.). Needham Heights, MA: Allyn & Bacon.

Smith, T. E. C., Price, B. J., & Marsh, G. E. (1986). *Mildly handicapped children and adults.* New York: West.

Stainback, W., & Stainback, S. (1984). A rationale for the merger of special and regular education. *Exceptional Children, 51,* 102–111.

U.S. Department of Education. (1997). IDEA: An Act To amend the Individuals with Disabilities Education Act, to reauthorize and make improvements to that Act, and for other purposes. (http://www.ed.gov/offices/OSERS/IDEA).

York, J., Doyle, M. B., & Kronberg, R. (1992). A curriculum development process for inclusive classrooms. *Focus on Exceptional Children, 25,* 1–16.

## CHAPTER 2

Legal Aspects of Special Education

A Brief Review

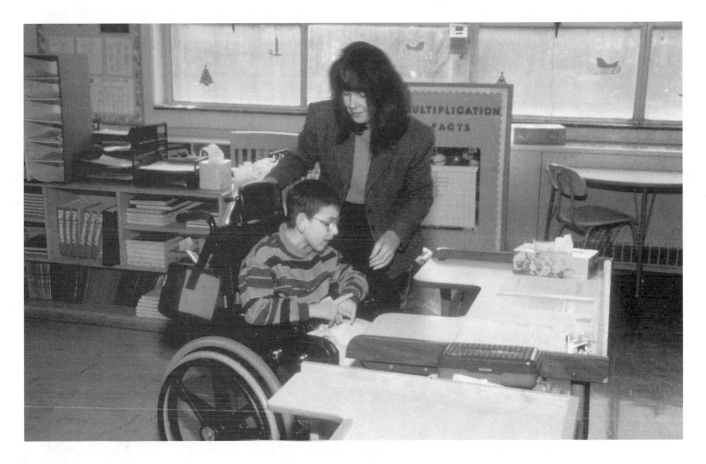

In this chapter, we will

- ✔ discuss the legal basis of educational rights for students with disabilities

- ✔ identify specific laws, rules, regulations, and procedural safeguards regarding students' planning and programming

- ✔ review recent court cases affecting special education and related services

- ✔ discuss recurring legal themes, including "rights and responsibilities" of parents, students, teachers, and schools

*L*egislation (laws and their accompanying regulations) and litigation (court cases) have influenced many changes in special education and the interpretation of rights and responsibilities of participants in the educational process. Recent changes in public policy have posed intense challenges to all professionals working with 21st-century students.

Preservice and beginning teachers who understand important laws may deal more effectively with the complex issues involved in providing a free and appropriate public education (FAPE) to students with disabilities. Awareness of legal issues may help developing teachers (1) provide a sound rationale for current administrative procedures and practices affecting their classrooms, (2) avoid past policy mistakes, and (3) ensure quality educational programming provided to the special-needs students they serve.

*P*ause and Reflect 2.1

Effective teachers require knowledge of and skills in legal issues affecting students with disabilities and their families. These issues can be very perplexing to new teachers, however. It may be useful to self-rate (5 highest, 1 lowest) your knowledge and skills of the following legal topics.

Legal Issue	Self-Rating Scale
Definition of individuals with exceptional learning needs	
Identification procedures for individuals with exceptional learning needs	
Applicable laws, rules, and regulations regarding the students' educational placement and program	
Procedural safeguards regarding students' educational placements and programs	
Typical procedures used for screening, prereferral, referral, and classification	
Legal provisions, regulations, and guidelines in student assessment	
"Rights and responsibilities" of parents, students, teachers, and schools as they relate to individuals with diverse learning needs and strengths	
Assurances and due process rights related to assessment, eligibility, and placement	
The attributes of local legal procedures	
Links between education placements and specially designed instruction	

LEGAL BASIS OF EDUCATIONAL RIGHTS FOR STUDENTS WITH DISABILITIES

Germane to all students with disabilities is federal legislation encouraging comprehensive services; that includes multidisciplinary evaluations and intervention services. The Individuals with Disabilities Education Act of 1997 (IDEA 97, hereafter IDEA) amended the original federal legislation (Education for All Handicapped Children's Act of 1975, EHA) to:

- strengthen the role of parents
- ensure access to general education curricula and reforms
- focus on teaching and learning while decreasing unnecessary paperwork
- respond to the growing needs of an increasingly diverse society
- assist educational agencies in addressing the costs of improving special education
- ensure schools are safe and conducive to learning
- encourage parents and educators to work out differences using nonadversarial means (IDEA).

These elements extend the fundamental underpinnings of previous federal legislation that ensured students with disabilities must be provided a free and appropriate public education (FAPE) in the least restrictive environment (LRE). Additionally, IDEA attempted to balance schools' needs to maintain safe and orderly environments while ensuring the rights of students with disabilities to receive FAPE (Yell, Katsiyannis, Bradley, & Kozalski, 2000).

Many educational practices have not always been in students' best interests. For example, in the past, students not meeting teacher or school expectations either were excluded from school altogether or were provided inappropriate services that did not match student needs. Such practices were to be eliminated through the enactment of federal and state laws, rules, regulations, and procedural safeguards upholding student and family rights in educational assessments and placements.

Unless teachers are informed consumers and users of legal knowledge, however, educational placement and programming decisions may revert to being misused or misdirected. Therefore, it is the responsibility of those who teach to have current knowledge and skills on legal issues affecting their students. All teachers can identify the limitations and benefits of pertinent laws and court cases by realizing that much progress and most educational innovations resulted from efforts of dedicated individuals who sought to change public policy, reform educational services, and uphold educational rights through legal means.

Importantly, every teacher in a public school setting will come in contact with the principles of IDEA. The original legislation and the subsequent amendments have changed the course of education of infants, children, and youth with special needs. During the mid-20th century, the social and political coalition of parents, concerned professionals, and advocates brought about the passage of landmark legislation at a time when children were being excluded from schools, misclassified through biased testing procedures, and/or served inadequately across the country. Without a strong commitment from a variety of people challenging existing school policies and legal procedures, progress would have remained very slow for students with disabilities. Educational services and programs would have continued to be inadequate and inconsistent from locality to locality.

Specific Legislation

Legislation entails the political processes by which elected members of the local, state, or federal government effect policy changes by proposing, debating, and passing laws. New laws and regulations evolve continually as policies are challenged and redefined, affecting the ever-changing field of special education. For the new teacher, this means that educational responsibilities are not static but rather continuously evolve as parents, professionals, and advocates effect changes in legal mandates and educational practices. This phenomenon is euphemistically referred to as the "shifting sands of special education."

Prior to the passage of EHA, some local and state statutes had guaranteed some degree of service to students in need of special help. Although these statutes were minimal and provided limited monies for the education of students with disabilities, they provided some direction (e.g., the commitment of procedural safeguards, assurances in state plans, education to school-age students residing in institutions, expansions or initiations of local programs). These laws, passed between 1950 and 1975, eventually provided the initial basis for federal mandates to provide services to all students in need of special education and related services. Box 2.1 presents pertinent laws directly bearing on special education. Today's professionals, familiar with these legal actions, may prevent educational injustices similar to those that occurred before these laws were passed.

Box 2.1   ## Laws Influencing Special Education

- **PL 83-531, Cooperative Research Act (1954),** was implemented to assist cooperative research in education. Of the $1 million appropriations, $675,000 was earmarked for research with students having mental retardation.
- **PL 85-926, Training of Professional Personnel (1958),** expanded teaching of students with mental retardation and facilitated grants to state agencies and to tertiary institutions, establishing a model for support to teacher trainees in special education.
- **PL 88-164, Mental Retardation Facilities and Community Mental Health Center's Construction Act (1963),** was a cornerstone legislative act for students with special needs. It brought together into one unit the "captioned film" program of PL 84-905 (1958), an expanded teacher-training program from PL 85-926, and a new research program for the education of students with disabilities.
- **PL 88-164, 302, Research and Demonstration Projects in Education of Handicapped Children,** authorized the commissioner of education to make grants to various state and local agencies in order to educate students with handicaps. PL 89-105 later supplemented PL 88-164, 302, by allowing funds to be used for construction, equipment, and operation of facilities for research and training of research personnel.
- **PL 89-10, Assistance to Children in Disadvantaged Areas (Elementary and Secondary Education Act, Title VI [1965]),** provided federal monies to initiate programs for schooling of children who were educationally deprived, especially children with handicaps in low-income families.
- **PL 89-313 (1965)** encouraged programs to educate children with disabilities who were residing in institutions and other similar state-operated or state-supported residential facilities.
- **PL 89-105, Community Mental Health Centers Act Amendments (1965),** provided additional traineeships and fellowships from original legislation developed by Congress and provided additional funds for research and demonstration projects in the education of students with special needs. It authorized construction of at least one research facility.
- **PL 89-750, Title VI, Education for Handicapped Children (1966),** allowed grants to states through the Elementary and Secondary Education Act (ESEA) for special needs students. PL 89-750 was particularly important because the Division of Handicapped Children and Youth had been disbanded in 1965.
- **PL 90-538, Handicapped Children's Early Education Assistance Act (1968),** was developed exclusively for children with disabilities and authorized the commissioner of

education, acting through the Bureau of Education for the Handicapped, to negotiate grants and contracts with both private and public agencies to establish experimental preschool and early education programs for special needs students.

- **PL 91-61, National Center of Educational Media and Materials for the Handicapped (1969),** provided the authority to the secretary of health, education, and welfare to contract a university to develop, construct, and operate a national center of educational media and materials for persons with disabilities.
- **PL 91-230, Elementary, Secondary, and Other Educational Amendments (1969),** consolidated a number of previous provisions on serving children with disabilities and divided into seven basic sections—Parts A through G—all of the categories of programs and services for educating children with special needs who receive federal assistance. Part B was intended to authorize grants for the initiation, expansion, and improvement of state and local educational programs for children requiring specialized help and was meant to specify the kind and amount of federal dollars to be provided to public agencies for special education.
- **PL 92-424, Economic Opportunity Amendments (1972),** mandated a minimum of 10% of the enrollment slots in Head Start programs be made available to students with disabilities.
- **PL 93-112, 504, 29 U.S.C. 794, Rehabilitation Act (1973),** specified that no handicapped individual in the United States shall, solely by reason of his or her handicap, be excluded from the participation in, be denied the benefits of, or be subjected to discrimination under any program or activity receiving federal financial assistance.
- **PL 93-380, Education Amendments (1974),** modified Part B to increase monies available to public agencies for the education of students with special needs and to expand the assurances in state plans for students' and parents' rights. Emanating from this law was the **Family Educational Rights and Privacy Act of 1974, also referred to as the Buckley Act,** which protected the confidentiality of school records and provided procedures to challenge questionable information contained in the records. Title VI extended and revised the Adult Education Act, the Education of the Handicapped Act, the Indian Education Act, and the Emergency School Aid Act. It required states to locate and serve all children with handicaps. The state must protect the rights of children with handicaps and their parents in making educational changes; it assured an education with one's peers, as possible; and it asked that evaluation materials be racially and culturally fair.
- **PL 94-142, Education for All Handicapped Children's Act (1975),** often referred to as the Bill of Rights for children with handicaps, guaranteed the availability of a "free appropriate education," including special education and related services programming to all students with disabilities. It assured "due process" rights of students with disabilities and their parents or guardians and monitored effectiveness of special education at all government levels. It mandated that an Individualized Education Program (IEP) or an individualized family services plan (IFSP) will be drawn up for every child or youth found eligible for special education or early intervention, pinpointing what kinds of special education and related services or the types of early intervention services each preschooler, child, or youth will receive. It called for annual planning and the assessment of students' strengths, needs, and interests.
- **PL 98-199, Parent Training and Information Centers (1983),** entailed the training and provision of information to parents and volunteers.
- **PL 99-457, Education of the Handicapped Student Act Amendments (1986),** extended the mandate from PL 94-142 to include special education and related services beginning at age 3 and created a discretionary early intervention program to serve children from birth through age 2. It provided monies to train early intervention teachers in clinical settings and preschools.
- **PL 101-476, Individuals with Disabilities Education Act (1990),** further amended the provisions of PL 94-142 and PL 99-487 and renamed the act. IDEA promoted the linkage of school and community experiences, development of postschool adult living objectives, and

development of daily living skills and functional vocational evaluations. It mandated that the IEP must include a statement of transition services, including, if appropriate, a statement of each public agency's and each participating agency's responsibilities or linkages or both before the student leaves the school setting.

- **PL 101-336, Americans with Disabilities Act (1990),** prohibited discrimination based on disabilities in the areas of employment, public services, transportation, public accommodations, and telecommunications. It provided that all affected entities must ensure "reasonable accommodation" to persons with disabilities. The law highlighted fair employment practices pertaining to private employers, state and local governments, employment agencies, and labor unions. It prohibited the use of employment tests that screen out individuals with disabilities, unless they are shown to be job-related, required of all applicants, and consistent with business necessity. It banned the use of preemployment medical examinations or inquires to determine whether an applicant has a disability. It prohibited discrimination based on a relationship or association with a person with a disability (e.g., protects people with spouses who are disabled from being denied employment because of an unfounded assumption that they would use excessive leave).

- **PL 101-392, Carl D. Perkins Vocational and Technology Education Act, (1990),** encouraged the competitiveness of the United States in the world economy by more fully developing the academic and occupational skills of all students. It provided resources on improving educational programs needed to work in a technologically advanced society. It guaranteed full vocational educational opportunities for all special populations.

- **PL 103-239, School to Work Opportunities Act (1994),** promoted collaboration and problem solving by the Departments of Education and Labor. It encouraged partnership models between school-based and employment-based sites at the local level by encouraging schools and employment site personnel to plan, implement, and evaluate integrated school-based and work-based learning. This law matched students and employers stating a need for career education, career development programs, and work-based linkages. It encouraged interagency agreements, technical assistance, and services to employers, educators, case managers, and others. It promoted postschool planning and assistance. The law linked youth development activities, academic and vocation learning, and employer strategies for upgrading worker skills.

- **PL 105-17, Reauthorized Individuals with Disabilities Education Act Amendments (1997),** established a number of new provisions designed to improve outcomes for students with disabilities. Provisions inherent in the reauthorized law, IDEA 97, include requirements that students with disabilities be included in statewide and district-wide assessments, that students' IEPs address the issue of students' access to general education curricula, and that states establish performance goals and indicators for students with disabilities.

Specific Litigation

Litigation entails court cases in which a judge and/or members of a jury examine evidence regarding the facts of an event or series of events. A decision is rendered about a particular case based on an application of the evidence (i.e., findings of fact) to the constructs of pertinent laws. Through the litigation process, laws have been challenged and redefined, thus creating new laws and regulations (Katsiyannis & Conderman, 1994; Turnbull, 1993; Weintraub, Abeson, Ballard, & LaVor, 1977). This process has resulted in significant changes not only for children and teachers but also for parents and guardians. For example, family members and professionals spearheaded a number of national goals, resulting in litigation emerging from their combined, collaborative struggles. In addition to the importance of the right to education for all students, litigation themes centered on family involvement in educational decision-making, the suspension and expulsion of students with disabilities, payment of attorneys' fees, extended school year programs, programs for children and youth with severe disabilities, and programs for children and youth with serious emotional disturbance.

Most legislative acts evolved because parents, educators, and advocates questioned, through litigation, practices occurring within the educational system that, from their standpoint, violated the rights of their children or others unable to defend themselves within the school setting. Again, new teachers familiar with recurring legal themes affecting their students and their students' classrooms and homes can help ensure quality services.

Recurring Legal Themes

The Fourteenth Amendment to the United States Constitution, illustrated in Figure 2.1, forbids states from depriving anyone of life, liberty, or property without due process and equal protection of law. The equal protection clause and the due process clause of the Fourteenth Amendment should be foremost in the developing teacher's mind. These components formed the basis of litigation resulting in the enactment of IDEA.

The Fourteenth Amendment to the Constitution applies to the states (not the federal government, which is bound by the first 10 amendments) and guarantees the rights of due process and equal protection to the citizens of each state. Turnbull (1993) described legal themes that hold today's professionals accountable for the way educational treatment of students is carried out under the constitutional tenets. Recognition of and respect for the legal themes form the basis of teachers' responsibilities to the students they serve. Box 2.2 presents recent legal themes having a direct bearing on special services.

Many participants in court decisions have relied on the constitutional basis to attack legal injustices occurring in public school settings (Turnbull, 1993). Accordingly, the benefits of an education are considered by the courts to be a **property interest,** and the reputation of an individual is considered to be a **liberty interest.** When students

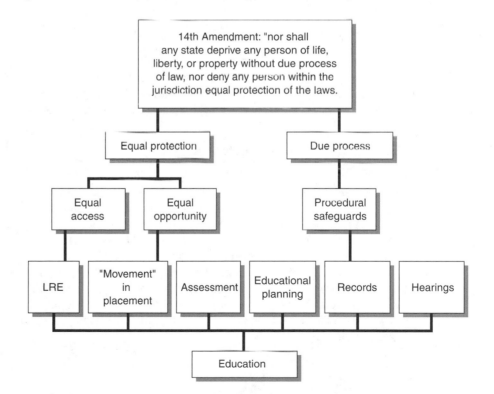

FIGURE 2.1   The Conceptual Structure of the Fourteenth Amendment to the United States Constitution as It Relates to Provisions for the Education of Students with Disabilities

Box 2.2

Legal Themes Influencing Special Education Laws

Procedural Due Process

Fair procedures must be followed before citizens can be denied certain interests. Due process entails procedural due process in which a person has the right to be heard and to protest if a government agency is about to take action affecting that person. Due process also entails substantive due process such that certain rights are inviolate and cannot be taken away by any state agency.

An example of a violation of procedural due process by a first-year teacher or other school official is a change in educational placement of a student without prior notice and without consulting the parents. The arbitrary institutionalization of a student by school officials is an illustration of a substantive due process claim. In other words, a teacher must notify parents and students of his or her intent to change an existing special education placement or service before changes can be made in students' education plans.

Equal Protection

The state must provide the same rights and benefits to individuals with disabilities as to persons without disabilities. They are guaranteed equal opportunity or access to participate in programs. Any variance must be justified.

An example of equal protection entails the opportunity for students with disabilities to participate in sports programs if such programs are available for students without disabilities. Another example is the provision of funds for band uniforms for special needs students if all other students are provided with band uniforms. School officials would be asked to justify why some students warrant school-related uniforms, whereas other students with disabilities do not.

Zero Reject

Individuals with disabilities must have the opportunity to be educated. No student can be denied educational services because of unalterable characteristics (including gender, cultural background, race, or disability). **Zero reject** means that any child or youth between ages 3 and 21 with disabilities must receive a free and appropriate education.

Assessment and Labeling

Traditionally, assessment and labeling procedures have been (and remain) powerful political tools capable of helping and harming diverse individuals. Assessment and labeling assist in identifying educational strengths and needs to serve the student better. Students are harmed by assessment that misplaces or wrongfully categorizes them to deprive them of educational opportunities and advancements. Some traditional assessment procedures are racially and culturally biased, often based on a single criterion rather than being multifactored. Many are administered inappropriately by untrained personnel. Federal law, now requiring a multidisciplinary assessment on an individual student done by many professionals, must include parent or guardian input. Multidisciplinary assessment uses multiple data sources to indicate what the individual student requires. All assessment and labeling must follow fair and appropriate testing procedures.

FAPE

Educational services are free and must be appropriate to the individual student. This means that education and related services must be provided at no cost to students, parents, or guardians. Additionally, students must have available a full range of educational services based on what the individual student requires. Federal law also gives preference to placement in the school the student would have attended if nondisabled unless participants in the educational process agree to some other arrangement. If a school district does not have a particular option, it may contract for the needed services.

Least Restrictive Environment

A continuum of special education service options must be available to meet the needs of special students in the setting closest to the "normal" general classroom setting. Special education, however, entails the services, not the setting per se. However, whereas the LRE for most students will be the education they receive with their peers without disabilities in the general education classroom, for some students the LRE may be a special class or a special school.

Parent Participation and Shared Decision-Making

Federal and state laws reaffirm parents' and guardians' legal right to participate in every decision related to the identification, evaluation, and placement of their child suspected of having or identified as having a disability. Accordingly, school district professionals must attempt to notify and contact the student's family when any changes are proposed, being considered, or made on behalf of the student. Additionally, for initial educational or related service changes, written parental or guardian consent is necessary.

---

with disabilities are provided with inadequate services, the denial of access to appropriate public education constitutes a deprivation of property. The negative effects of exclusion and labeling on their reputations are considered to be a deprivation of liberty. Furthermore, when groups of individuals are treated differently by agencies of the state, they are denied "equal protection" against infringement of their property and liberty interests. To address concerns by individuals or groups of individuals, there must be a set of procedures (i.e., due process) available to contest their treatment by agencies of the state. Under the IDEA, parents or school districts can redress their differences through mediation services, prehearing conferences, due process hearings, or civil courts at the state or federal levels. Consequently, new teachers should be aware of constitutional guarantees, especially due process rights, protecting all students from unilateral decisions by school personnel to deny students access to FAPE in the LRE.

Central Themes

Central themes occurring within school litigation have affected the practices of school personnel during past years. These issues are considered to be unconstitutional and should be actively avoided by new teachers.

Individuals have challenged unilateral decision-making by school professionals by initiating due process proceedings and taking school districts to a due process hearing or to state or federal civil court. Among relevant issues in past litigation are separate but not equal standards; disproportionate number of minority children assigned to special education; fairness practices in referral, assessment, or placement; and exclusion of students from programs (Ballard, Ramirez, & Weintraub, 1982).

After the passage of EHA, court litigation followed a slightly different course. Litigation of the 1980s entailed the interpretation of federal laws and regulations at the state and local levels, including delivery of special education programs and services; definition of related services; denial and/or unavailability of special education programming and services; financial issues in providing FAPE; and expulsion/suspension of students with disabilities (*Education for Students with Disabilities Law Report*, 1977–1988; Turnbull, 1993).

During the 1990s, issues centered on addressing instruction for diverse students and where best to provide services. Funding issues, including attorney fees and mediation prior to due process, became central. Discipline of students with disabilities highlighted FAPE discussions as parents won the right to raise discipline strategies at students' IEP meetings (Zirkel, 1995). In the 21st century, students' preschool needs, discipline practices, suspensions or expulsions, and transition from school to adult years are core to many due process proceedings (Yell et al., 2000).

Further, many citizen groups voiced a need for more effective instruction that will prepare all students for life in the 21st century. Many questioned whether services addressed students' needs in technology (Hanley, 1995), transitions across programs and services (Hodapp, 1993; McDonnell, 1993), and opportunities affecting students' quality of life, such as the appropriateness of services that facilitate students' acceptance into their schools and communities (Yell et al., 2000).

In current efforts, teachers are addressing how to prepare all students to exercise rights and responsibilities of citizenship. Foremost is productive employment in a modern economy. Recent reform agenda will have legal implications and an impact on developing teachers as they center their specially designed instruction on preparation for the lives of students with disabilities in the 21st century (i.e., transition services). Relevant are activities that will do the following:

- Define through the general education curriculum academic knowledge and skills that students are expected to have by the time they graduate from public schools
- Encourage local school districts to design curricula allowing students to achieve learning outcomes leading to completion of high school graduation requirements
- Include students with disabilities in statewide and districtwide assessment systems that measure student progress toward learning outcomes
- Encourage local school districts to implement educational reform according to a strategic plan developed at the local level
- Encourage active involvement in the educational process of parents, businesses and other community representatives, teachers, students, and school personnel (Pennsylvania Department of Education, 1995).

Additionally, major philosophical and logistical changes resulting from the reauthorized IDEA established new provisions designed to improve outcomes for students with disabilities. These include requirements that students with disabilities be included in statewide and districtwide assessments, that students' IEPs address issues of students' access to general education curricula, and that states establish performance goals and indicators for students with disabilities (Hehir, 1999; McLaughlin, 1999; Ysseldyke & Olsen, 1999).

As many legal interpretations to school reform emerge along with new perspectives on accepting and supporting students with disabilities, teachers continue to play a vital role: Teachers make appropriate services happen. Educational challenges in the form of technological advances, changing and community diversity, economic realities, and calls for school reform continue to set parameters for students with disabilities.

Standards-based teaching, in which teachers provide repetitive high-quality instruction for students to attain high-level goals, is also influencing the quality of teaching and learning in the 21st century. The standards movement applies to students with disabilities in that differentiated instruction geared toward their needs reflects the knowledge, skills, and dispositions valued by society (Tomlinson, 2000). These and other challenges require concerted efforts by new teachers to work with other professionals and students' families, using sharing processes and joint problem-solving skills to avoid legal injustices.

Box 2.3 presents pertinent litigation issues. New teachers should be familiar with components of litigation that have evolved to ensure fair, appropriate educational practices to students.

Box 2.3   **Pertinent Litigation Issues in Special Education**

Early 1950s–Mid 1970s	Mid 1970s–Early 1990s	Early 1990s–Present
• Separate but not equal standards • Disproportionate number of minority student in special education • Fairness in referral, assessment, and placements • Exclusion of students from schools and programs	• Delivery of special education programs and services • Definitions of related services • Denial/unavailability of special education programs and related services • Financial issues in transportation services and tuition • Expulsion/suspension of students with disabilities	• Serving diverse students • Instructional effectiveness • Technological advances • Transitions across programs • Graduation/learning outcomes • Attorney fees • Mediation processes • Funding appropriations

MAJOR COMPONENTS OF THE FEDERAL LAW

The reauthorized IDEA is the most important legislation supporting the education of children and youth with disabilities. It contains the framework from which students with special needs are educated today. Preservice and beginning teachers will be involved actively in implementing its mandates no matter what type of class placement teachers direct or where services are provided. Mandated components of the law form the basis of what teachers know and should be able to do and when or how teachers operate in the class. Teachers at the preservice level will be exposed to various aspects of the law as they progress in the student-teaching process.

Beginning teachers may be expected to demonstrate knowledge of the federal law from the first day of school.

1. Teachers in training may be involved in implementing and monitoring measurable annual goals, benchmarks, and short-term objectives of a student's educational program under the guidance of the directing classroom teacher. They may be asked to observe a classroom in which a student is being considered for special education. Their observational data may be used to monitor the student's progress in the general education curricula.

2. Beginning teachers may be asked to attend IEP conferences prior to the beginning of the school year and to begin implementing the special education program during the initial week of classes. First-year teachers may be involved in the screening and referral steps, formal or informal assessment processes, curriculum planning, or students' exit from special education services.

Major components of recent laws affect the developing teacher's roles with special needs students: (1) a full range of services, (2) incentives for the LRE, (3) IEP development, including access to the general education curriculum, (4) assessments, referral, evaluation, and placement guidelines, (5) participation in statewide and districtwide assessments, and (6) procedural safeguards.

Full Range of Services

Writers of EHA and IDEA stipulated that a continuum of special education placement options must be available to meet the needs of special students in the LRE, the placement closest to the general classroom environment. However, to make the intent of the law become real, teacher support is necessary for the LRE to have meaning. For instance, Rueda, Gallego, and Moll (2000) described the LRE employing a sociocultural basis. To these authors, LRE becomes a reality, not because of a particular physical placement of students, but because of social mediation and careful structuring of the activities in the setting. These authors suggested that the linking of education, play, and peer interaction, structured around individual student needs, represents a model of how inclusion in the LRE may be accomplished successfully.

Even though inclusion is a popular choice in which services are provided in the general education setting, inclusion is not a legal term. To ensure appropriate services, school personnel still must provide a continuum of alternative placements. Thus, students may need general education classrooms, special classes, special schools, home instruction, or education in residential facilities. (Chapter 1 illustrates the cascade of service delivery, one of the most common continua.) Federal law also makes preferable placement in the school the child would have attended if nondisabled unless participants in the educational process agree to some other arrangement. If a school district does not have a particular option, it may contract for the needed services.

Suspensions, Expulsions, and Alternative Interim Educational Placements

Due process protections must be extended to all students when applying short- and long-term suspensions and exclusions (including expulsions and alternative educational placements) (Yell et al., 2000). For instance, legally correct and educationally appropriate responses must be made when students with disabilities exhibit serious problem behaviors. In cases where students with disabilities violate school rules, IDEA permits school districts to remove a child from school for up to 10 days as long as there is not a pattern of removals. However, school personnel cannot implement long-term suspensions (i.e., those longer than 10 days) if the IEP team determines that the behaviors causing the consideration for long-term suspension are a manifestation of the student's disability. In cases where the behaviors are not a manifestation of the student's disability and the school district follows its discipline policy by suspending a student with disabilities for periods longer than 10 days, the school district must still provide special education services. Importantly, in cases where students with disabilities are found

1. to have brought a gun or dangerous weapon to school,

2. in possession of illegal drugs, or

3. to have sold or in the act of soliciting the sale of a controlled substance,

the school district may unilaterally place students in an interim alternative placement for up to 45 calendar days.

Incentives for the LRE

Currently, emphasis is on educating students demonstrating less severe mental, learning, or social disabilities in the general education class with normally functioning peers to the extent that the student can handle. General educators and special educators are working together in inclusion models, consultation, and teaming formats. New directions in service delivery expands the legal role of teachers (Chapter 3 provides details of inclusion settings; Chapter 11 expands on consultation and teaming themes). As teachers are encouraged to collaborate together and are supported to use known, effective practices to be more responsive to all students' learning characteristics, the focus for teaching and managing diverse students is shifting (1) from where interventions occur to which interventions are effective and (2) from viewing students as the problem to viewing teachers as the solution (Carpenter & McKee-Higgins, 1996). Thus, some educators view teachers' effective practices as the key to specially designed instruction in the LRE—no matter where students receive services.

In addition to being a direct-service provider to students with disabilities, new special education teachers may be asked to provide consulting help and assistance to new general education classroom teachers on instructional strategies, accommodations or modifications, behavior management, or classroom organization. Special education teachers may offer a combination of direct services and consulting assistance to make the general education classroom setting more appropriate to diverse students' needs. Special education teachers may help to develop, maintain, and evaluate prereferral strategies that general education classroom teachers implement. Teachers in both general education and special education may use a variety of effective instructional formats to plan, implement, and evaluate appropriate learning materials or specially designed curricula for diverse students. Importantly, specially designed strategies to help students remain in the LRE are legal safeguards and rely on teachers' good faith efforts to execute effective practices.

IEP Development and Access to the General Education Curriculum

A major component of the reauthorized IDEA is the emphasis on students with disabilities having access to the general education curriculum (Hehir, 1999). School professionals and families address this component in each student's IEP. The IEP's present education levels, annual goals, benchmarks or short-term objectives, and a new section dealing with participation in statewide and districtwide assessments are relevant. In the present education levels section, the IEP team must indicate how a student's disability affects involvement and progress through the general education curriculum. Annual goals and benchmarks/short-term objectives must reflect general education curriculum standards. Furthermore, the IEP must contain a statement of how progress toward annual goals will be measured and how parents will be regularly informed of student progress. Progress reports for students with disabilities must be at least as frequent as those provided to parents of nondisabled students.

To coordinate the IEP with the general education curriculum, a general education teacher must participate in the IEP team whenever a student is expected to participate in the general education environment. Also, the IEP team must include statements about the student's inclusion in statewide and districtwide assessments. Any accommodations or adaptations needed for the student to participate in the assessments must be delineated. If a student's participation in statewide or districtwide assessments is inappropriate, then an explanation must be provided and an alternative testing system must be used.

Further, transition issues must be addressed in the IEP for all students 14 years of age and older. For students 14 to 15 years old, the IEP must contain a statement of transition needs focusing on the individual student's course of study. For students 16 and older, the IEP must delineate interagency responsibilities and linkages and reflect programming that will affect postsecondary transitions. When the student is to reach the age of majority during the IEP cycle, the school district must notify the parents of the transfer of all parental rights to the student. (The age of majority varies from state to state.)

Referral, Evaluation, and Placement Guidelines

Federal regulations set up priorities for services given to those students who were unserved at the time of EHA's passage and to the most severely involved students within each area of exceptionality receiving inadequate services. IDEA continues to maintain Child Find, a referral system for locating students with special needs. The overall purposes of Child Find, and referral and screening services, are to determine whether or not a student has a disability and to identify the educational needs of each student.

Specific guidelines in the referral, screening, diagnosis, evaluation, placement, and reevaluation processes mandate steps that all teachers are required to follow to receive allocated funds. New teachers may be involved in every step—from referral to reevaluation procedures. Each must meet legal requirements within specific time frames of the local area and state to receive allocated funds and to provide the needed help to students. Figure 2.2 presents a description of the various steps in the process. (Chapter 7 describes the paperwork involved in the referral, evaluation, and placement process.)

IDEA mandates additional requirements for the evaluation and reevaluation of students with disabilities and those who are thought to have a disability. The multidisciplinary evaluation (MDE) team must address the individual student's ability to participate in and progress through the general education curriculum. In addition, the MDE

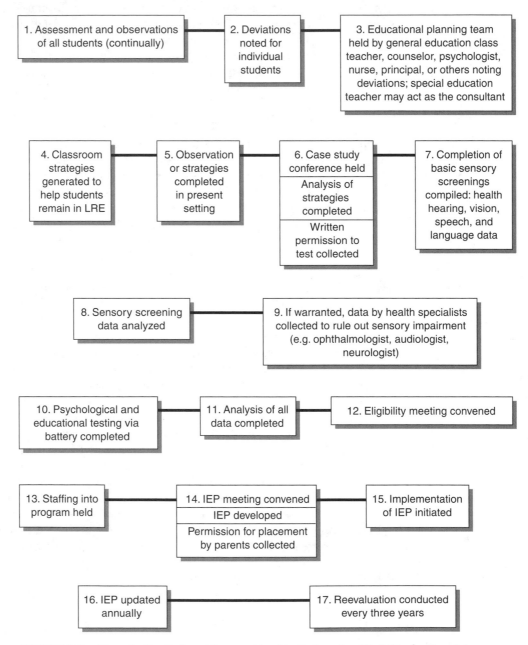

FIGURE 2.2   Steps in the Referral Process Used to Determine Eligibility for Special Education and to Plan Educational Programs

team needs to determine what, if any, modifications need to be made to the curriculum or instruction for the student to be reasonably expected to achieve measurable annual goals. The team must assess cognitive and behavioral factors as well as physical and developmental factors. A student cannot qualify as having a disability if the determinant factor is either a lack of instruction in reading or math, or limited English proficiency.

The reevaluation process has been changed significantly under the new IDEA. Informed consent must be obtained for reevaluations as well as initial evaluations. However, if the parents do not respond to reasonable attempts by the school district to obtain consent, the school district may proceed with the reevaluation.

The MDE team needs to determine first if there is a need to collect additional data to determine the student's continued eligibility in special education. If there is a need, then the team proceeds with any necessary testing or data collection. If not, then the team must provide notice to the parents specifying why the team does not believe additional testing is necessary and inform the parents of their right to request that assessments are done to determine continued eligibility. If the parents and school district personnel are in agreement that no additional information is needed for an eligibility determination, then the team should focus on gathering information on how to instruct or assist the student.

Procedural Safeguards

Every developing and beginning teacher will be involved to some degree in legal proceedings with students, parents, and professionals. Due process rights, also referred to as **procedural safeguards,** are afforded to participants of the educational process. Parents and classroom teachers are involved directly in the implementation of rights guaranteeing parents' active involvement in their child's educational program. These rights are afforded also to all professional personnel. Procedural safeguards are illustrated in Figure 2.3, including rights in programming decisions, hearings, and confidentiality of record keeping. A new requirement under IDEA is that states must develop a mediation

FIGURE 2.3 Procedural Safeguards Involving Rights in Programming Decisions, Hearings, and Record Keeping and Confidentiality

Evaluation
1. Written permission to evaluate (notice/consent)
2. Comprehensive battery
3. Nondiscriminatory practices
4. Independent educational evaluation
5. Informed results
6. Assessment by a multidisciplinary team

Educational Placement
1. Written permission to place (notice/consent)
2. Participation in educational decisions
3. Approval for proposed changes (notice/consent)
4. Input into creation, maintenance, and monitoring of IEP

Mediation and Hearings
1. Mediation
2. Prehearing conference
3. Due process hearing
4. Appeal process
5. "Stay put" policy until alternative placements

Records
1. Review
2. Explanations and interpretations
3. Copies
4. Challenge
5. Assurance of confidentiality

system that is available to parents and school districts. The intent is to reduce the number of due process hearings by providing a less adversarial process for resolving disputes.

Programming Decisions. The reauthorized IDEA requires all educators to follow specific notice, consent, evaluation, and placement procedures for programming to ensure nondiscriminatory evaluation and placement of students.

Notice/Consent. Despite an emphasis on the general education setting, today's professionals still must gain consent or provide written notice to parents before school officials can initiate or change, or refuse to initiate or change, the identification, evaluation, or placement of students. Although implementation of these rights varies according to individual school practices, developing teachers will be involved in the process (e.g., sending written notices home to parents, holding informal conferences prior to the student's formal testing). All notices must be in the parents' native language or other principal mode of communication. New teachers should work actively to ensure that notices are stated clearly and avoid teacher jargon. The notice must include a description of the proposed action, an explanation of the proposal, a summary of all options considered, and information as to why other options were rejected. Parents must be notified of each evaluation procedure, test, record, or report that teachers will use as a basis for any educational decision reached.

Parents must grant written permission prior to initial evaluations and placement into any special education program or related service. This includes the need for specially designed instruction provided in the general education classroom. IDEA extends the consent requirement to all reevaluations of students who are already receiving special education services. Beginning teachers should be aware that parents can change their minds at any time to revoke the consent. School officials, however, have the right to initiate a due process hearing in the absence of parental consent. A hearing officer, then, must determine whether the student should be evaluated or placed. In turn, parents have the right to protest at a hearing any evaluation or programming action by school officials.

Evaluation. Evaluation safeguards include the right to an independent assessment by an evaluator of the parents' choosing. Parents have a right to be told where and how the evaluation will be conducted and to be given a list describing any available low-cost or free legal aid in the geographic area in which they reside. Parents have the right to request that the LEA or SEA pay for the independent evaluation if the agency evaluation was done incorrectly or inadequately. School districts must inform parents that a hearing officer may be asked to order an independent evaluation at public expense and of the criteria for the examiner needed to secure payment by the LEA or SEA.

The student must be given a full and individual evaluation using a battery of tests. The testing cannot discriminate on the basis of the student's language or culture. The evaluator must ensure that all testing devices and materials are sensitive to individual needs, including differences of sensory, manual, or speaking abilities. Professionals should assess all aspects of the student's strengths and abilities.

Placement. Teachers must use more than one criterion when specifying the appropriate educational program based on a student's specific instructional or behavioral needs. The new IDEA mandates that parents be given the opportunity for input into all aspects of the proposed placement. The program must be evaluated and implemented by a multidisciplinary team. Preservice teachers and beginning teachers should note that the student's educational program must be updated annually and that areas of functioning must be reevaluated by a trained evaluator every 3 years, or more frequently if conditions warrant or if professionals or parents request it.

Individualized Education Program (IEP). The student's IEP is the most important document that teachers and parents will determine for the student together. The IEP is formulated from multidisciplinary team input and parents' suggestions. Every student with special needs is provided with an IEP that specifies, in writing, measurable annual goals, and benchmarks or short-term objectives proposed for the student during the school year. The IEP must be current and in effect at the beginning of every school year. For students identified during the year, teachers must still hold an IEP meeting within 30 calendar days from an eligibility meeting specifying the special education and related services to be provided. After parents give written consent for placement, the IEP goes into effect. (Chapter 7 describes the IEP in detail.)

Due Process Hearings. Due process hearings are part of the processes for dispute resolution mandated by law. They are intended to allow dissenting or aggrieved parties opportunities to question educational decisions. To receive federal monies allocated by IDEA, representatives of the SEA and LEA must guarantee federal authorities the adoption of appropriate due process procedures in their locale to present complaints relating to the student's identification, evaluation, or placement, or the right to FAPE. In addition, parties in litigation have the right of review (i.e., they may appeal to a higher court any decision that they believe requires further interpretation).

For example, a new teacher may teach a student in the general education class. In the teacher's opinion, the student is placed in an inappropriate program and requires a change in placement to a full-time special class. The parents disagree with the need for change and request a due process hearing. Until a final decision is reached, the student remains or "stays put" in the present educational setting (i.e., general education class) unless all parties agree to an alternative placement. The review process may continue until the case is heard before the U.S. Supreme Court. Figure 2.4 presents levels of the review process.

Mediation. Each professional, especially teachers in training and those new to the field, should strive for **mediation,** the process of solving disagreements and deciding issues of FAPE, before they escalate into a due process hearing. Mediation helps parents and professionals resolve differences prior to involvement of representatives of

FIGURE 2.4 Levels of the Review Process Used to Redress Disagreement Regarding the Education of Individual Students

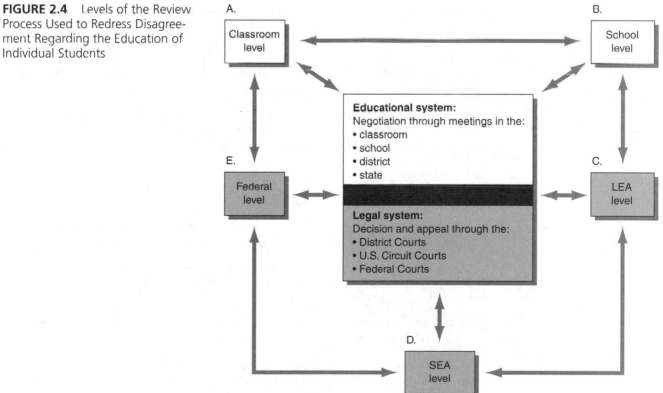

the legal system. Situations will arise in which agreement with others will not always occur. The following strategies may help professionals new to the field avoid problems in the mediation process or informal conferences with parents and other professionals:

1. Treat parents and other professionals with respect in all dealings. Consider both verbal and nonverbal messages of participants during all professional contacts. Record all pertinent messages evolving from mediation attempts.

2. Provide scheduled conferences to get things out in the open and on the table even prior to initial mention of legal action. Times should be scheduled, when students are not present, to review academic, behavioral, or social progress; answer questions; or discuss concerns of the administrator, evaluator, teacher, or parent.

3. Inform parents of their due process rights (i.e., procedural safeguards) in writing during every meeting in which evaluation or educational decisions are made for their child. The teacher, principal, or administrator may do this. Keep a copy of all written material presented during the meeting.

4. Keep on-task; confer about student progress in all structured conferences to discuss strengths observed, weaknesses of concern, or proposed changes in behavioral or educational goals and objectives.

5. Have a written agenda to share in each conference. An agenda will help in the smooth running of the conference and will provide data for the teacher's records if a hearing does follow the mediation process.

6. Always allow all participants a chance to speak at the meeting to question, seek clarification, or provide feedback on data presented. Demonstrate empathy, listening skills, and approachability.

7. In all mediation efforts scheduled with parents and professionals, come prepared. This will help to ensure that meetings will run smoothly and end on time.

8. Provide a copy of all written documentation to every member in attendance.

9. Listen to every concern at meetings and be open to all legitimate solutions to evaluation or programming options prior to a change in placement.

10. Always make officials of the LEA aware of potential problems with parents and other professionals. Report major outcomes of all meetings to those in authority.

11. Always include other school personnel in any potentially explosive conference. Always inform the principal and/or special education supervisor of all conferences when evaluation or placement decisions are to be made or when mediation is in progress.

12. Document meetings. Tell participants in advance that the meeting will be transcribed or recorded. Elicit their permission.

13. Encourage all participants to sign, date, and identify their relationship to the student on a conference participation form before the meeting gets underway.

14. Devise a written summary of the meeting as soon as possible after meetings conclude. The LEA representative or teacher may complete this. Be sure all data are accurate and dated.

15. Send a copy of the written summary to each participant and administrator in authority who may not have attended.

When many conferences are planned and professionals have the opportunity to discuss evaluation results or placement issues with parents and advocates, the need for involving judicial representatives may be lessened. At times, however, litigation will be unavoidable and legal authorities necessarily will participate in mediation, hearings, and reviews. During this stage, teachers may be asked to provide information they have collected on the student during the year. Mediation, the step prior to initiation of a hearing, often begins with a review of tangible data.

Record Keeping and Confidentiality. IDEA stipulates that all teachers must ensure students' and parents' rights to fair record-keeping procedures and confidentiality of all records. Records may include informal and formal assessments, anecdotal records, behavior lists, and checklists. Federal law provides that parents have the right to inspect and review all data about their child. They have the right to copy all information and to receive a list of all types and locations of records being collected, maintained, or in any way used by LEA or SEA members. A teacher's data on the student, thus, are important pieces of information and may be used as evidence in legal proceedings. Parents may ask for an explanation of any information in the records and may ask for changes if they believe the records are incorrect, misleading, or violate privacy rights. They also may initiate a hearing on the issue if school personnel refuse to change the data. Parents can restrict access to their child's records by withholding consent to disclose the data. School officials must inform parents about where and how information is to be used by others and before information in the student's file is to be destroyed.

MAJOR CHALLENGES OF IDEA FOR DEVELOPING TEACHERS

Areas of federal law identified by Abeson and Zettel (1977) and later reiterated by Zirkel (1995) and Yell et al. (2000) pose strong challenges for teachers of diverse students. These areas underscore major components that continue to be important. They bear directly on what new teachers provide to students with special needs: (1) fair and nondiscriminatory referral/assessment practices and procedures, (2) ongoing Child Find activities, (3) placement of all students in the LRE, (4) development of an IEP for each student requiring special education and related services, (5) confidential data collection and accurate record keeping, (6) assurances of equal protection and due process rights, and (7) ongoing involvement and input of parents and guardians in all aspects of the educational process.

Federal and state mandates can make the job of new teachers especially difficult. Paperwork, many hours of data collection and conferences, often difficult students or parents, and logistics of operating within a multidisciplinary team can be frustrating and stressful. New teachers, however, may consider the ramifications of legal components as a means of providing structure to their tasks. Federal and state mandates may help ensure consistency in the quantity and quality of the services provided. The more experience teachers have in implementing federal and state mandates, the easier teachers' jobs can be.

Related Legislation

Recent legislation has an impact on new teachers' roles as they serve students with disabilities. The following paragraphs briefly describe such legislation.

Americans with Disabilities Act (ADA). Currently, state officials are required to establish facilities so that students with disabilities have the opportunity to participate with others to the most possible extent. Importantly, the Americans with Disabilities Act (ADA) of 1990 requires that all facilities provide students the access they need, including accessibility in public accommodations (e.g., school cafeterias, school lavatories) and telecommunications (e.g., relay services for students with hearing impairments and speech impairments; National Loss Control Service Corporation, 1992).

Additionally, all special students have the right of access to supplementary services or aids. This means that the new teacher may provide prosthetic devices, assistive

Pause and Reflect 2.2

List with a partner five legal issues that have affected you or other professionals in your field placement, practica, internship, or student teaching site. Then, for each example, describe what might have been done at your site to make the situation less stressful for you, your host teacher, the students, and/or the parents or guardians.

Legal Issues	You	Host Teacher	Students	Parents/Guardians
1.				
2.				
3.				
4.				
5.				

technology, adaptive equipment, flexible scheduling, test modifications, and so forth to make it possible for the student to remain in the LRE. The key component is students' access to general education curricula, programs, services and opportunities to respond in learning settings that ensure students' FAPE. Box 2.4 presents major components of ADA.

Section 504 of the Rehabilitation Act of 1973. Section 504 of the Rehabilitation Act of 1973 is important in today's classroom (Katsiyannis & Conderman, 1994; Zirkel, 2000). It prohibits discrimination against individuals with disabilities under any program receiving federal financial assistance. The section arguably provides rights for school-age children with disabilities in addition to those provided by the reauthorized IDEA.

Section 504 and IDEA have certain significant differences and many similarities (Zirkel, 1995; Zirkel, 2000). Section 504 applies to recipients of any federal assistance, including all programs or activities that receive or benefit from the assistance. IDEA, however, applies only to those states and political subdivisions receiving payment under IDEA. Thus, to be protected from discrimination in a school setting, a student must be labeled as disabled and must also be of an age for which a state is required to provide FAPE. An amendment to Section 504 excludes students with disabilities who use or are in possession of alcohol or illegal drugs. Such students may still be protected though, under IDEA, if they otherwise qualify as disabled.

Box 2.4   **Major Components of the Americans with Disabilities Act (ADA)**

Accessibility Requirements

Title 1: Employment

Employers with fifteen or more employees may not discriminate against qualified individuals with disabilities.

Employers must reasonably accommodate the disabilities of qualified applicants or employees, including modifying work stations and equipment, unless undue hardship would result.

Title II: Public Services (Examples)

State and local governments may not discriminate against qualified individuals with disabilities.

Buildings must be accessible.

New buses and rail vehicles for fixed-route systems must be accessible.

One car per train must be accessible.

Title III: Public Accommodations (Examples)

Restaurants, hotels, theaters, shopping centers and malls, retail stores, museums, libraries, parks, private schools, day care centers, and other similar places of public accommodations may not discriminate on the basis of disability.

Physical barriers in existing public accommodations must be removed. If not, alternative methods of providing services must be offered if those methods are readily achievable.

New construction in public accommodations and commercial facilities must be accessible.

Title IV: Telecommunications

Telephone companies must provide telecommunications relay services for hearing-impaired and speech-impaired individuals 24 hours per day.

Source: Americans with Disabilities Act of 1990 (ADA), PL 101-336. (July 26, 1990). Title 42, U.S.C. 12101 *et seq.: U.S. Statutes at Large, 104,* 327-378.

The full impact of Section 504 is only now being felt because of the interest of the Office of Civil Rights and the Department of Education in (1) implementing the mandate of the LRE, (2) ensuring access to educational opportunities for students with acquired immune deficiency syndrome (AIDS), and (3) meeting the educational needs of the increasing at-risk and other students who qualify for services under Section 504 (Katsiyannis & Conderman, 1994).

Some school districts have moved from underdoing to overdoing Section 504. Where IDEA typically leads to services for 10 to 15% of a school district's population, Section 504 should account only for approximately another 1 to 2%. However, some school districts have trouble determining eligibility, relying on overidentification of students protected under Section 504 (Zirkel, 2000). To avoid overidentification, Zirkel suggested that the school district must have firm eligibility criteria. District personnel should determine that the student's impairment must limit a major life activity, and the limitation on the overall major life activity must be substantial. New teachers need to be cognizant of important determinations when their students qualify for Section 504 services.

How Can Teachers Demonstrate Implementation of Special Education Laws?

Preservice and beginning teachers can use and demonstrate a working knowledge of current trends and practices by adhering to processes and procedures. They can demonstrate professional standards that lessen the probabilities of legal action initiated by disagreeing parties. All teachers can do the following:

1. View education as a process that continually changes in the face of evolving federal and state laws and regulations. To survive legal challenges, teachers must be flexible and adaptable within acceptable professional guidelines of their locales.

2. Be articulate consumers of public policy by talking with parents, teachers, community leaders, administrators, and legal representatives. Teachers should be familiar with local philosophies and goals of educational programs. Reading district procedures and other legal policies published by the state or local education office may help new professionals become familiar with current issues affecting their classrooms.

3. Be familiar with legal and professional guidelines to ensure fairness and appropriateness of their programs and to facilitate program accountability. This includes awareness of prereferral strategies, referral steps, testing procedures, program criteria, and exit criteria for all special education and related services provided.

4. Demonstrate knowledge of the major components of special education law, including the new IDEA, ADA, and Section 504 of the Rehabilitation Act.

5. Seek to upgrade personal knowledge of legal changes that affect themselves or their students (e.g., legal issues related to teaching practices; research and services bearing directly on public policy) through in-service, professional development opportunities, recertification, and so forth.

Legal and Professional Responsibilities of New Teachers

Positive educational changes have occurred in recent years for students of all ages from infants to 21-year-old adults with special needs. Transitional needs of students in various life stages are examples of positive educational changes. These changes evolved with the help of dedicated teachers fulfilling their legal and professional responsibilities to students, parents, themselves, and their profession. When dedicated professionals critically analyzed past practices, inadequacies were tackled head on and the process of change helped initiate better practices in meeting students' needs.

Today's preservice and beginning teachers also share responsibilities, including (1) provision of FAPE through effective teaching practices and the application of pertinent laws and regulations, (2) efforts within the educational system to promote communication and teaming, (3) use of mediation and professional behaviors during litigation, and (4) advocacy for new and better legislation to promote educational progress of their diverse students. Figure 2.5 illustrates the major responsibilities of teachers today to guarantee required services to special students in a timely and effective manner.

Provision of FAPE

Understanding important regulations and laws and abiding by legal mandates may help promote progress of all students. New teachers need to modify their programs to meet current federal and state laws and regulations, to modify the program according to current teaching practices, and to display professionalism.

Effective Teaching Practices. Changes within individual classrooms may affect the quality and quantity of services provided in the school, LEA, or SEA. Teachers can effect changes in their own classrooms in a number of ways. (Consult later chapters for specific researched-based practices that have been found to provide positive changes.) However, all teachers should be skeptical of extraordinary claims about new methodologies to guard against charlatans (O'Shea, O'Shea, & Algozzine, 1998).

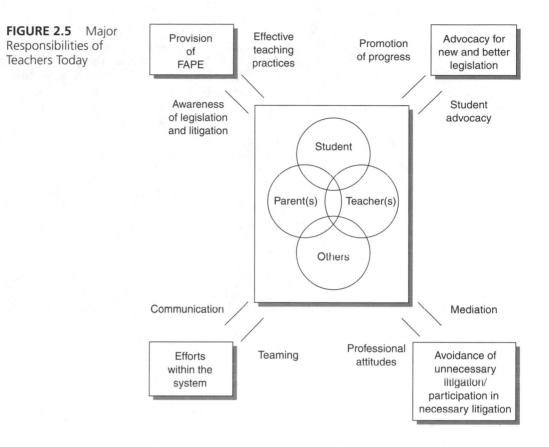

FIGURE 2.5 Major Responsibilities of Teachers Today

Awareness of Legislation and Litigation. All teachers have a legal and professional responsibility to display a working knowledge of legislation and litigation that affects students. Awareness of legislation and litigation can occur through a number of ways. Developing and beginning teachers can maintain knowledge of current practices, laws, and court cases through active participation in conferences, workshops, in-services, continuing education classes, and professional development opportunities. Subscribing to relevant journals and newsletters may help teachers obtain information on research-based teaching practices, technology advances, and service activities. Working actively in local, state, or national advocacy groups may widen the contacts that teachers have and may aid in political and legal awareness. Becoming an advocate may also provide new perspectives to the educational process occurring at the local level so that teachers may work effectively within the educational system.

Efforts Within the Educational System

To facilitate efforts to solve problems within the school, teachers should confer regularly with each other and parents about similarities and differences that they perceive of the student or any aspect of the FAPE provided. Energies can be directed toward a team model encouraging parental and professional involvement. The use of effective communication skills during all professional endeavors and the concept of *teaming* may enhance teachers' abilities to effect positive changes.

Communication. Communication is the foundation of all interpersonal relationships and the framework for every meeting with parents or professional contacts with peers. For teachers to be effective communicators, real effort is needed. Teachers new to the field can develop and enhance their interpersonal communication skills by setting priorities, demonstrating good rapport-building skills, and being flexible and adaptable.

Additionally, new teachers should consider their roles in sending or receiving messages during the communication process. They should speak clearly and correctly, with consideration given to the meaning behind discourse. Teachers should listen to what parents and other professionals say and be open to suggestions. They should consider their nonverbal messages, including body language, facial expressions, posture, and stance, and demonstrate empathy, positive regard, and nonjudgmental statements to peers and parents. All of these suggestions may aid in facilitating better communication. The need for legal action may be lessened when individuals closest to the student believe and demonstrate that they are working together.

Teaming. Involving others in the change process often helps if everyone perceives a team effort. Individuals may assume ownership of the functions of the team and often may work harder to lessen legal difficulties for the benefit of the student. Teaming helps parents and professionals work together to ensure FAPE to students and access to the general education curriculum. Some general tips to promote teaming can be used within the context of any functional relationship with parents and other professionals:

1. From the first day, capitalize on the personal strengths of the student and always demonstrate that the major consideration is the student's best interests.

2. Provide constructive criticism by sharing information and by eliciting from parents and other professionals targeted improvements in the student or ways to initiate improvements. Provide encouragement through a balance of positive statements and corrective feedback statements.

3. Aim criticism with the goal of improved performance. Although teachers should never gloss over individual weaknesses that need discussion, always mention some strength of the student at every meeting. It is wise to start and end all meetings with a positive statement. Even one small word of progress may aid in the teaming effort.

4. Strive for consistency in all team meetings by using verifiable data. Do not base information on personal opinion-provide facts. Communicate effectively, in speech and in writing, the data to parents, colleagues, administrators, and community members.

5. Get continual feedback from parents and other professionals to assess reasonableness of the type and amount of programming requirements and others' roles in facilitating the requirements. Ask parents and professionals continually for their suggestions to improve the student's performance.

6. Involve parents and professionals in every step of the educational process. Elicit their suggestions to provide more appropriate programming for the student. Be flexible and adaptive to their suggestions.

7. Always keep others informed of all records, evaluation results, or educational proposals. Keep a written, dated copy of all communication attempts for records. Keep the records where they can be located quickly.

Using Mediation and Professional Attitudes During Litigation

Even with the best efforts during the communication process or teaming, problems may still escalate over which the classroom teacher has little or no control. During this time, mediation efforts require help from other professionals, including administrators, peers, or even school attorneys.

Classroom teachers can frame positive steps during in-school mediation to solve disagreements of the student's evaluation or educational placement and plan. They can:

1. Provide many informal conferences to attempt to remediate differences within the student's current placement. Invite all significant individuals to the mediation conference.

2. Designate a leader to chair all mediation attempts. It may be the classroom teacher, principal, supervisor, or legal counsel. Have a written agenda to share in all conferences.

3. Encourage all participants to sign, date, and identify their relationship to the student on a conference participation form.

4. Listen to all suggestions to ascertain the student's LRE. Strive for a group opinion on new strategies and procedures to try first in the student's immediate classroom environment.

5. Implement all suggested new strategies, procedures, and modifications within 6 weeks of the mediation conference.

6. Collect baseline data on the student's present levels prior to the introduction of treatments or changes in strategies. Keep data on all progress over time.

7. Document all modifications of the usual classroom techniques and procedures. Observe the student under different conditions within the classroom (e.g., individual assignments, group tasks, peer tutoring) and record all observations. Observe the student in different settings and working or socializing with different individuals.

8. Ask various school professionals and parents to observe the modifications within the class and to document their observations on student progress. Compare professional and parental observations to determine interrater reliability.

9. Meet again in a structured conference to compare observation data and the student's progress to date. Strive again for group consensus on the next steps and "iron out" differences. Record the outcomes of all meetings.

10. Devise a written summary as soon as possible after the meeting concludes.

11. Send a copy of the written summary to each participant.

These suggestions will help the developing professional to document every attempt to ensure the LRE for the target student. Parties may still disagree, however, over best practices or specific treatment for individual students. Be assured that with dated, written data, new teachers need not fear legal actions. If litigation still results, preparation and professional attitudes may still provide relief.

Necessary Litigation. If repeated mediation attempts fail, the only resource may be a hearing in which the decision passes from parents and school authorities to an impartial hearing officer who determines the outcome of the case (Schrybman, 1982). It is vital that teachers in training and teachers new to the field not view litigation as an evil process. When seen in the context of past litigation resulting in new and better laws for students, litigation may be considered a healthy and necessary process. When inappropriate management occurs, when procedures need to be redefined or refined, or when public policies require clarification that cannot be agreed on by local participants of the educational process, litigation can and should be looked on as a legitimate step in the process of FAPE for students with disabilities.

Advocacy for New and Better Legislation

Professional attitudes can affect public policy encouraging beneficial changes in the educational system. As demonstrated by past efforts, new legislation can result that will help guarantee gains in special education and related services. It is beneficial for all teachers to remember that much litigation evolved during the past because individuals recognized and responded to inadequate services, poor practices, and unfair procedures occurring in schools. Past advocates were willing to work for changes within the system but realized that the power of political forces and legal influences were necessary. These individuals acted when data verified warranted changes. Today, new teachers should strive to work within established rules of the school, the district, and the state and strive for mediation first when disagreements arise. They can respond when changes are necessary through simple modifications in school policies or classroom procedures. All teachers need to formulate and follow a professional code of ethics and to assume inherent professional roles and responsibilities.

Professionals who care about students and use established methods of intervention can be confident that members of the educational and legal systems will protect appropriate educational programming. An effective role that beginning teachers can assume to protect the legal rights of their students is to recognize, implement, and monitor the best teaching practices in their classrooms. This role is the foremost assurance that all students are afforded legal justice in educational settings.

SUMMARY

In this chapter, we described how new teachers would be involved in legal issues from the moment they enter teaching. Among other essential dispositions, knowledge, and skills are the legal requirements providing the basis for special education practices. We emphasized that despite recurring changes in legal interpretations and procedural aspects of federal law (i.e., the shifting sands of special education), new professionals must have fundamental knowledge dealing with the definition and identification procedures for individuals with exceptional needs. Teachers also require an appreciation for assurances and due process rights related to assessment, eligibility, and placement for students. We indicated that teachers will implement, through their effective practices, actions upholding "rights and responsibilities" of parents, students, teachers, and schools as they relate to individuals with exceptional needs.

ACTIVITIES TO EXTEND YOUR KNOWLEDGE

1. Locate local school and community agencies, including Web sites, the library, advocacy centers, or legal aid offices, to list the names, addresses, telephone numbers, and specific activities of contacts/resources related to Section 504, ADA, and IDEA's reauthorization.

2. Ask for written school board policies on local assurances and due process rights related to access to the general education curricula, assessments, eligibility, and placements for students with disabilities.

3. Obtain a copy of your district's attendance, discipline, and suspension and expulsion policies. Ask your special education director or supervisor to clarify assessment and placement practices for students with disabilities when questions arise about students' infringement of such policies.

4. Interview local school board members; ask them to identify their personal philosophies of special education, including its relationship to general education. Compare

and contrast these statements with those of local advocacy groups and those of parents or guardians of students with disabilities.

5. Walk through a local shopping mall and visually inspect local restaurants and department stores. Try to determine from visual inspection any violations of accessibility for individuals with disabilities.

POINT AND CLICK

The following Web sites highlight the chapter's theme of legal issues in special education. Each of these listings can assist new teachers in complying with local, state, and federal legislation on behalf of students with disabilities.

CFR Titles on GPO Access—Part 300–399
http://www.access.gpo.gov/nara/cfr/waisidx_99/34cfrv2_99.html
Information: Part 300 (Part B Regulations) and Part 303 (Part C Infant and Toddlers)

A Web site to gain access on important federal regulations related to infants, children, and youth with disabilities.

CFR Titles on GPO Access—Part 1–99 and Part 101–299
http://www.access.gpo.gov/cgi-bin/cfrassemble.cgi?title=199834
Information: Education Department General Administrative Regulations (Part 76); Family Education Rights and Privacy Act Regulations (Part 99); and Rehabilitation Act of 1973, Section 504—Regulations (Part 104)

A Web site new teachers can use to gain access to important federal regulations related to confidentiality issues and discrimination practices.

Federal Register Daily
http://www.access.gpo.gov/su_docs/aces/aces140.html
Information: Daily publication of Federal Register; search back issues of Federal Register

A Web site that identifies the Federal Register. It disseminates important national legislation.

IDEA Practices
http://www.ideapractices.org/
Information: CEC Web page information and other links

A Web site that links new teachers to classroom and school practices underscoring legal mandates of IDEA.

IDEA Statute (PL 105–17)
http://www.access.gpo.gov/nara/index.html#pl
Information: Statute (PL 105-17) for IDEA—June 4, 1997; to select 105th Congress, scroll to find PL 105-17

A Web site where teachers can read the actual federal law guaranteeing students with disabilities their educational rights.

REFERENCES

Abeson, A., & Zettel, J. (1977). The end of the quiet revolution: The Education for All Handicapped Children's Act of 1975. *Exceptional Student, 44,* 114–128.

Amendment to the Education for All Handicapped Children's Act (EHA), PL 99-457. (1986). Washington, DC: Office of Special Education and Rehabilitation Services.

Americans with Disabilities Act of 1990 (ADA), PL 101-336. (July 26, 1990). Title 42, U.S.C. 12101 *et seq.: U.S. Statutes at Large, 104,* 327–378.

Ballard, J., Ramirez, B. A., & Weintraub, F. J. (1982). *Special education in America: Its legal and governmental foundations.* Reston, VA: Council for Exceptional Children.

Carpenter, S. L., & McKee-Higgins, E. (1996). Behavior management in inclusive classrooms. *Remedial and Special Education, 17* (4), 195–204.

Education for the Handicapped Law Report. (1977–1988). Alexandria, VA: CRR.

Hanley, T. V. (1995). The need for technological advances in assessment related to national educational reform. *Exceptional Children, 61* (3), 222–228.

Hehir, T. (1999). The changing roles of special education leadership in the next millennium: Thoughts and reflections. *Journal of Special Education Leadership, 12*(1), 3–8.

Hodapp, R. M. (1993, April). Comparison of families of children with mental retardation and families of children without mental retardation. *Mental Retardation,* 75–77.

Individuals with Disabilities Education Act of 1990 (IDEA). 20 U.S.C. S 1400 *et seq.*

Katsiyannis, A., & Conderman, G. (1994). Section 504 policies and procedures: An established necessity. *Remedial and Special Education, 15* (5), 311–318.

Maheady, L. (1988). An opportunity for developing instructional diversity. *Special Services Digest, 2,* 4–6.

McDonnell, J. (1993, March). Impact of community-based instruction on the development of adaptive behavior of secondary-level students with mental retardation. *American Journal on Mental Retardation,* 575–584.

McLaughlin, M. J. (1999). Access to the general education curriculum: Paperwork and procedures for redefining "special education." *Journal of Special Education Leadership, 12*(1), 9–14.

National Loss Control Service Corporation. (1992, Spring). *Americans with Disabilities Act: Whom does it cover?* Long Grove, IL: Author.

O'Shea, L. J., O'Shea, D. J., & Algozzine, B. (1998). *Learning disabilities: From theory toward practice.* Upper Saddle River, NJ: Prentice-Hall.

Pennsylvania Department of Education. (1995). *Pennsylvania 2000.* Harrisburg, PA: Author.

Rueda, R., Gallego, M. A., & Moll, L. C. (2000). The least restrictive environment. *Remedial and Special Education, 21*(2), 70–78.

Schrybman, J. (1982). *Due process in special education.* Rockville, MD: Aspen.

Tomlinson, C. A. (2000). Reconcilable differences? Standards-based teaching and differentiation. *Educational Leadership, 58*(1), 6–11.

Turnbull, H. R. (1993). *Free appropriate public education: The law and children with disabilities* (4th ed.). Denver, CO: Love.

Weintraub, F. J., Abeson, A., Ballard, J., & LaVor, M. L. (1977). *Public policy and the education of exceptional children.* Reston, VA: Council for Exceptional Children.

Yell, M. L., Katsiyannis, A., Bradley, R., & Rozalski, M. E. (2000). Ensuring compliance with the discipline provisions of IDEA. *Journal of Special Education Leadership 13*(1), 3–18.

Ysseldyke, J., & Olsen, K. (1999). Putting alternate assessments into practice: What to measure and possible sources of data. *Exceptional Children 65*(2), 175–185.

Zirkel, P. A. (2000). Over-identification: Not all IDEA-ineligible students are Section 504. *The Special Educator, 15*(12), 10.

Zirkel, P. A. (1995, May). *Special education law for regular educators.* Paper presented at Lehigh University Education Law Conference XXII, Bethlehem, PA.

Setting Up for Instruction

In this chapter, we will

✔ we will review the importance of being an organized manager of the instructional environment

✔ discuss alternatives for designing the physical classroom environment

✔ review the levels of instructional time and outline specific strategies for increasing the efficacy of time spent in school

✔ present approaches and strategies for scheduling activities and grouping students in both self-contained and inclusive classroom settings

✔ list methods that assist in the development, introduction, and maintenance of classroom rules and procedures

✔ outline strategies that assist in the coordination of resources

Classrooms for students with mild to moderate disabilities tend to be busy places. Whether one is student teaching in a self-contained classroom, resource room, or "co-taught" inclusive setting, many and varied instructional and noninstructional events occur simultaneously. While a student teacher may be conducting a remedial lesson on long division to a small group of students in one corner of the room, it would not be unusual for several other students to be completing seatwork assignments with peer tutors from neighboring classrooms or for still another group to be returning from their music class. If these events were not enough of a management concern, most special education teachers are also often asked to assume a variety of responsibilities that go beyond the boundaries of traditional classroom instruction. In addition to being charged with the usual array of diagnostic and teaching responsibilities, teachers of students with disabilities are frequently called on to (1) complete full-scale educational evaluations, (2) field-test new and existing learning programs and instructional procedures, (3) monitor students' progress through the curriculum, (4) coordinate the logistics involved in implementing inclusive programming, (5) initiate and maintain collaborative working relationships with general educators and related service personnel, and (6) develop outreach programs with parents and significant others in the community.

Not surprisingly, special education teachers, as with most education professionals, meet these often overwhelming demands with differing levels of success. Variation in degree of success is not, however, a function of magic or luck; those able to deal effectively with the multitude of demands involved in teaching students with mild to moderate disabilities succeed because they work hard to produce conditions that promote success. The lesson is short and relatively simple: *To successfully manage the daily demands of their busy classroom, special educators must be organized managers of their environments.*

All classrooms, regardless of whether they contain special, "at-risk," or normally achieving students, contain organizational pressures that influence the teaching/learning process. Table 3.1 presents Doyle's (1980) conceptualization of these complex organizational pressures typical of most classrooms. It is interesting to note that these six factors portray the classroom as a public forum requiring frequent and immediate teacher actions in the face of almost overwhelming and, in many cases, unpredictable environmental variables. The range and intensity of the six pressures can vary according to a teacher's level of experience, dedication, level of competence, and even the time of year. Whereas many veteran teachers are experienced in managing the busy classroom, preservice and beginning teachers face the challenge of managing the sensory overload of their first days in the classroom. This problem may be particularly evident in classrooms

TABLE 3.1   Organizational Pressures of Classrooms

Organizational pressure	Definition
Immediacy	Many events require immediate attention or action.
Publicness	Teacher is always on stage.
Multidimensionality	Classrooms are crowded and busy places in which limited resources are used to achieve a wide range of goals.
Unpredictability	Events in classrooms change daily, and many occurrences are difficult to predict.
History	Events that occur early in the school year set the tone for later happenings.
Simultaneity	Many things happen at the same time in classrooms.

Adapted from Doyle, W. (1980). *Classroom management*. West Lafayette, IN: Kappa Delta Pi.

serving students with disabilities where the unique learning and behavioral characteristics of such students often require explicit supports and additional external controls.

Fortunately, early recognition of the organizational pressures of the classroom can allow for the development of strategies to manage these ever-present demands. These strategies are best viewed as preventive—an approach in which the events of a busy classroom are anticipated and planned for by an organized and flexible professional who successfully manages multiple occurring events (Paine, Radicci, Rosellini, Deutchman, & Darch, 1983). In this chapter, we examine and provide guidelines for five interrelated preinstructional activities that will assist student and beginning teachers in preparing for successful teaching: (1) the design of the physical environment, (2) the management of instructional time, (3) the effective scheduling of classroom activities and the grouping of students, (4) the formulation of meaningful and relevant classroom rules and procedures, and (5) the coordination of available resources.

DESIGNING THE PHYSICAL ENVIRONMENT

The first of the many organizational challenges facing beginning, experienced, and to a certain extent, student teachers is to make effective use of the physical dimensions of the classroom. Whether one is working in a self-contained, resource, or inclusive setting, chairs, desks, bookcases, tables, room dividers, and countless other pieces of furniture must be arranged for accessibility and safety. Instructional equipment such as computers, tape recorders, and filmstrip projectors must be arranged for controlled student access and efficient teacher use. Seating patterns for instruction, independent work, and appropriate socialization must be considered in relation to their effects on discipline and transitions among activities. Finally, those aesthetic features that promote pride in one's classroom, such as displays, plants, and bulletin boards, must be infused appropriately into the existing physical structure of the room.

This monumental task of orchestrating the physical learning environment is critical because classroom designs are directly related to effective classroom management and student academic performance. This relationship among physical environmental variables and student performance variables is especially pronounced for students with mild to moderate disabilities. These students typically require added structure in all facets of their educational experience. For all students, however, the appropriate arrangement of the physical environment can decrease the rate of student disruptions, improve the quantity and quality of desirable social interactions among students, and increase the amount of time that students attend to their assignments (Paine et al., 1983).

Figures 3.1 and 3.2 illustrate a self-contained elementary and secondary resource classroom configuration. Each contains a common large-group area, room for small-group instruction, and study carrels for private study. General education settings that are adapted for the inclusion of students with disabilities often integrate some of the features (e.g., study areas, group instruction areas, study carrels) found in self-contained and resource settings. It should be cautioned, however, that the design of any physical classroom environment will vary according to a number of interacting variables, including (1) the actual physical layout and location of the classroom, (2) the number, age, and behavioral profiles of students in the class, and (3) the degree of disability or levels of supports required by students. Several generic factors, however, should be considered when arranging the physical layout of a special education classroom.

Public and Private Space

Regardless of the ages of or the types of problems exhibited by students with mild to moderate disabilities, classroom environments should provide opportunities for work, study, and free time in both public and private areas. Public areas used for group

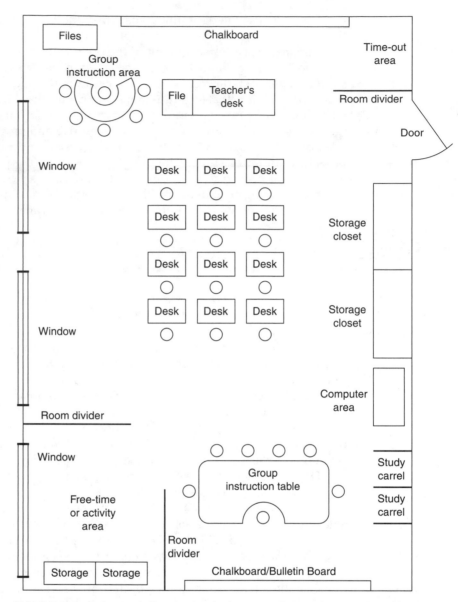

FIGURE 3.1 Primary Self-Contained Classroom for Students with Mild Learning and Behavioral Problems

instruction and the majority of independent practice activities should be arranged in such a way that all students can see the teacher's desk or the primary instructional area. Because students with mild to moderate disabilities have low rates of time-on-task under the best of conditions, exposure to potential distractors such as windows, free-time areas, and displays should be minimized.

Traditionally arranged student desks, class meeting tables, and large- or small-group instruction areas should be complemented with private quiet areas where students can work with limited distractions. Such areas can be easily designed through the creative arrangement of bookcases, filing cabinets, and study carrels. Partitions with greater portability and flexibility could be used as room dividers, providing privacy for small instructional groups, peer-tutoring activities, or counseling sessions.

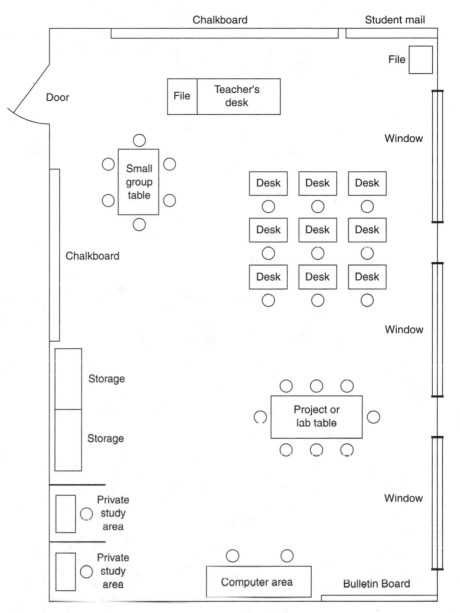

FIGURE 3.2 Middle School or Secondary Resource Room for Students With Mild Learning and Behavioral Problems

Furniture

It is critical that teachers consider patterns of movement typical of busy classrooms and plan furniture and seating arrangements to regulate such movement. Movement around the classroom can be facilitated by keeping high-traffic areas free of unnecessary congestion. Students should be able to move to high-traffic areas such as the teacher's desk, the pencil sharpener, and the front door without disturbing others. Moreover, these areas should be located in separate areas of the classroom so that students engaged in other activities are not overwhelmed or distracted by such activities. Open spaces that have no clear purpose should be avoided; such areas often become a breeding ground of problematic behaviors. Furniture should be used to regulate or channel movement in and around the room. Bookcases, room dividers, and filing cabinets can be used to limit movement in those areas that require regulation. For example, furniture can be arranged in such a way that movement around quiet or time-out areas can be easily monitored and regulated.

Easy Lines of Vision

In general, teachers should be able to monitor their students throughout the day. Because many of the instructional goals for students with learning and behavioral problems necessitate the direct observation of behavior, it is critical that their teachers have an unobstructed view of the entire classroom. A teacher's attention is a powerful reinforcer of appropriate behavior—easily used to manage minor instances of disruptive behaviors. In planning, teachers should also ensure that each student can easily see the key elements of daily lessons: the teacher, the teacher aide, the chalkboard, and so forth. Each key element should be in full view of students with minimal movement of their heads, desks, or chairs.

Storage of Instructional Materials

As observed by Evertson, Emmer, Clements, Sanford, and Worsham (1984), easy access to instructional materials and supplies increases the effectiveness of instructional procedures by minimizing the time needed for getting ready and cleaning up for individual lessons. Materials used frequently by teachers and students should be kept within easy reach at materials stations, activity centers, or other designated areas. Materials used on a more infrequent basis (e.g., overhead projector, craft supplies, seasonal decorations) should be stored in closets, storage bins, or bookcases.

Aesthetics

Similar to other work sites, classrooms that are pleasing to the senses can communicate a sense of pride to teachers and students. To contribute aesthetically pleasing elements to the classroom, teachers can use any of a number of items, including (1) displays of content or seasonally appropriate bulletin boards, (2) exhibits of students' work, and when appropriate, (3) plants and animals. Students can and will respond with respect to an aesthetically pleasing learning environment.

In summary, the structuring of the physical environment is a critical variable in the design of a successful classroom. The levels of structure and intrusiveness required in different settings, however, will vary according to the developmental levels, severity of disability conditions, and instructional goals of students being served. Teachers of young children or students with behavioral problems, for example, may find it necessary to assign seats to their students prior to the first day of school and to label desks, chairs, and lockers as belonging to specific students. In such situations, it may also be necessary to use discrete supports, such as markings on floors and tables, to prompt students where their chairs, desks, and materials are located during various parts of the day. In more inclusive settings, it may be useful to assign seating in a way that promotes social contacts among students with and without disabilities.

MANAGING INSTRUCTIONAL TIME

Effective teachers value instructional time and carefully control its allocation. Efficient use of instructional opportunities is critical if teachers are to maximize the effects of special education efforts. Fortunately, teachers of all experience levels—developing, beginning, and master—can become sensitive to and influence time-related factors that rob instructional opportunities. Two interrelated activities can increase the appropriate use of instructional time: (1) an awareness of the different levels of instructional time and how they differentially influence classroom events and (2) the implementation of generic and lesson-specific strategies designed to increase the effectiveness and efficiency of the time that students are in school.

Levels of Instructional Time

As noted in Figure 3.3, instructional time is broadly viewed as a variable that exists in four subsetting quantities: allocated time, actual instructional time, engaged time, and academic learning time. **Allocated time** is the amount of time that school systems or individual teachers set aside for the teaching of specific skills, concepts, units, or subject areas. Although school boards typically mandate how much instructional time students should receive in basic curricular areas, the individual teacher decides how much time is allocated to the various skills within the areas. A readily available measure of how time is allocated to learning is a teacher's planbook.

Actual instructional time is a measure of how much instructional time is actually delivered to students. Unfortunately, numerous unforeseen events (e.g., fire drills, visiting related-service personnel) can reduce the time allocated for instruction. Moreover, noninstructional activities such as secretarial chores, the organization of materials, and the management of disruptive behavior can spill over into planned instructional time. Actual instructional time is measured by timing the length of a lesson presented to a group of students regardless of how much time is allocated. In most special education settings, 80% of the time allocated for instruction is actually delivered (Wilson & Wesson, 1986).

Engaged time refers to how much students attend to the actual instructional time. Because engaged time accounts for the possibility that students can only learn material to which they attend, it is generally regarded as a sensitive measure of the effectiveness of how time is used in classroom settings.

However, **academic learning time** is the most meaningful measure of instructional time. This final level of instructional time is the amount of time students attend to work that is diagnostically and instructionally appropriate. Thus, in evaluating whether academic learning time is occurring, variables such as task difficulty, teacher diagnostic ability, and student success rate must be considered.

Strategies for Time Management

Strategies that can be used readily by student and beginning teachers to increase the effectiveness and efficiency of instructional time fall into two major domains: generic classroom initiatives and lesson-specific procedures.

Generic Classroom Initiatives. Three generic strategies can increase the amount of productive time in classrooms for students with mild disabilities. First, teachers should conspicuously demonstrate that attendance and punctuality are expected and valued

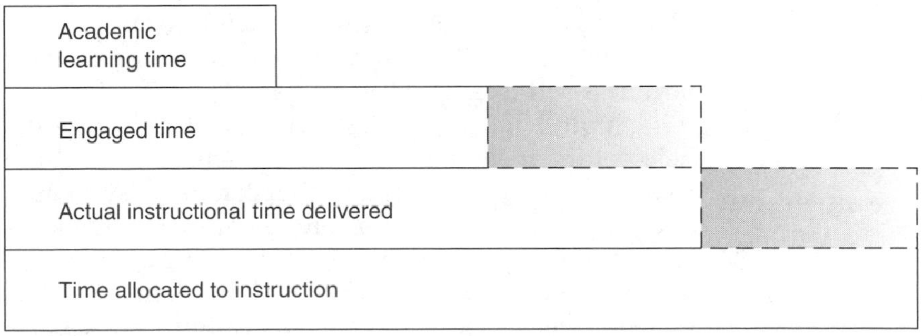

FIGURE 3.3 Subsetting or Vanishing Nature of Instructional Time

ℙ*ause and Reflect 3.1*

When real hours and minutes are plugged into the theoretical constructs of instructional time, it becomes readily apparent that, during the course of a typical school day, students receive a frighteningly small amount of instructional time. As illustrated in Figure 3.4, it is possible that a student could receive a mere *108 hours of academic learning time per year.* Clearly, instructional time is a valuable resource that can easily vanish.

	Hours per day	Hours per year
Academic learning time	0.6 – 1.5	108 – 270
Engaged time	1.5 – 3.5	270 – 430
Actual instructional time delivered	2 – 4	360 – 720
Allocated time to instruction	4.75	855
Typical attendance time	5.4	970
Total available time	6.0	1080

FIGURE 3.4 How Instructional Time Can Vanish

In response to these limited opportunities for learning, some policymakers have advocated that the length of the school day and year be extended. Is this the best alternative for addressing the issue of "vanishing" instructional time? What alternatives are available for increasing the amounts of instructional time that are delivered to students? How could you ensure that you are maximizing the effectiveness of the time that students are in school? What sorts of activities can groups of educators plan and implement to ensure that instructional time is viewed as a valuable resource?

behaviors. Truancy, absenteeism, and tardiness are insidious thieves of instructional time. In addition to highlighting a policy that encourages and prompts school attendance, intermittent rewards for consistent participation and punctuality should be administered. These rewards can fit within the framework of the general classroom management plan and need not be elaborate or expensive. Moreover, systematic follow-up plans should be made for students who are absent or tardy repeatedly. Telephone calls, letters to students' homes, and other types of parental contacts can reduce instances of tardiness and unexcused absences.

Unfortunately, some children come from home environments where parents need help getting their children ready for school. In such cases, teachers may need to be active resources for parents and to recommend strategies that could promote attendance and punctuality. For example, problems with school attendance can be avoided if teachers remind or prompt parents to establish a morning routine. This routine would involve (1) setting out appropriate school clothes that children would wear the next day, (2) using alarm clocks, (3) eating a healthful, relaxed breakfast, and (4) keeping the television off in the morning (Bleichman, 1985).

Routines for home/school preparation can be put into a motivating and reinforcing format. Figures 3.5 and 3.6 illustrate how one school developed the "Take It Easy; Be Happy" strategy and checklist. Using a mnemonic and self-monitoring checklist format, teachers from Marley Middle School in Glen Burnie, Maryland, articulated the specific behaviors required of a well-prepared student.

Once students are attending school regularly, consideration should be given to a second concern: increasing the amount of the school day that is devoted to academic or task-relevant activities. Research on effective teaching has demonstrated that academic performance thrives in special education settings where teachers maintain an academic focus. In such settings, effective teachers conduct more instructional activities and make more frequent use of directed questioning than less effective teachers. However, clear

---

TAKE IT EASY; BE HAPPY

(Homeroom/Advisory Checklist)

Take all materials to class: notebooks, paper, pencils, special supplies.

Ask yourself if it's A or B Day. P.E., music, foreign language, etc.

Know your schedule.

Expect a lot from yourself. Excel!

it

(Morning Checklist)

Eat a good breakfast?

A or B Day?

Supplies all ready?

Your lunch money?

Be

(Morning Checklist)

Homework: Complete it, check it, and pack it.

Ask for help if you don't understand.

Pack your bookbag.

Parents or guardians: Tell them about your school day.

Yawning? Get a good night's rest. You need 8 hours of sleep.

> This is our motto and checklist for success!

FIGURE 3.5   The "Take It Easy; Be Happy" Strategy

TAKE IT EASY; BE HAPPY

Planning ahead and being organized will help you to succeed academically. We, at Marley Middle School, would like to assist you in developing those skills. Post this checklist at home in a convenient location. Every evening, check off the "HAPPY" sections as you complete them. In the mornings, check off the "EASY" sections. Soon your planning and organization will be routine. Have a great year!

		Mon.	Tues.	Wed.	Thurs.	Fri.	Mon.	Tues.	Wed.	Thurs.	Fri.
E	Eat a good breakfast.										
A	A or B Day?										
S	Supplies all ready?										
Y	Your lunch money?										
H	Homework, completed, checked and packed?										
A	Ask for help if you don't understand.										
P	Pack your bookbag.										
P	Parents or guardians: Tell them about your day.										
Y	Yawning? Get a good night's sleep!										

FIGURE 3.6 The "Take It Easy; Be Happy" Checklist

danger signs of an environment at risk for a low-academic or task-relevant focus include the following:

- Excessive amounts of time in open-ended, undirected discussions about personal opinions and beliefs
- Too much time allocated for noncontingent recess or free activity periods
- Large amounts of time spent on the management and discussion of discipline problems and disruptions
- Exceedingly long periods of time spent on attendance and other housekeeping or organizational chores
- Unscheduled but regular discussions of sporting events, movies, and television programs during academic work periods

- More than 25% of the day devoted to nonacademic activities
- Many seemingly harmless, social interruptions from teachers' colleagues during academic periods

Planning and regularly scheduled monitoring of how time is used can ensure that appropriate amounts of time are delivered to academic or task-relevant activities. In terms of planning, it is important to be prepared for the teaching of lessons; instructional procedures should be mastered, and materials necessary for the entire lesson should be accessible. Teachers should regularly analyze how time is used in their own classroom settings. These continuous analyses can range from informal self-monitoring exercises to more systematic and precise observational regimens that require the help of peer observers. Regardless of the method chosen, it is critical that teachers determine how they use class time and, when necessary, consider alternative teaching methods that emphasize academics or task-relevant activities. A straightforward method for gathering data about instructional time during a typical school day is provided in the form found in Box 3.1.

The final generic classroom initiative to maximize the effectiveness of instructional time is to facilitate fluid transitions among activities. The great majority of classrooms for students with mild disabilities have many activity shifts, which typically require movement from one area of the classroom to another, or in settings where there is resource room programming or extensive mainstreaming, from one part of a school building to another. Transitions are unavoidable by-products of comprehensive educational programs; the greater the variety provided to students, the more they will need to switch locations and behavior. Because students are not working during transitions, valuable instructional time is lost. Transitions also tend to be disruptive and create circumstances that often require the use of planned instructional time for classroom management activities rather than teaching.

To facilitate efficient transitions, teachers need to arrange the physical environment appropriately, establish and enforce rules that encourage smooth transitions, and use signals to indicate clearly that activity shifts are to occur. To teach effective transitioning skills, teachers should (1) analyze tasks and model appropriate methods of shifting between activities or locations, (2) provide directed practice in activity and location changes, (3) use a variety of group and individual cues to signal transitions, and (4) frequently evaluate the effectiveness of the types of transition signals used. Twenty-four transition cues are listed in Box 3.2.

Lesson-Specific Procedures. The most productive method for maximizing the use of time during lessons is to ensure that students attend to diagnostically and instructionally relevant instruction. Monitoring systems and corresponding instrumentation are available for the observation of on-task behavior. Each available alternative can be adapted to the unique features of any classroom. Box 3.3 contains a generic form for the measurement and recording of on-task behavior; it can be adapted for use under varying instructional conditions. Specific strategies for increasing on-task rates during both teacher-directed instruction and practice sessions are summarized in Box 3.4.

SCHEDULING ACTIVITIES AND GROUPING STUDENTS

The complicated, interrelated tasks of scheduling activities and grouping students are typically completed when preservice teachers enter a student-teaching situation. Consequently, those preparing to be teachers rarely have supervised experiences in these frustrating activities. The following discussion is provided as an advance organizer for developing teachers who will be faced with scheduling and grouping responsibilities

Box 3.1   Monitoring Instructional Time

Directions: For each classroom activity, record the amount of instructional time allocated and actually delivered. Also, indicate whether the major use of the delivered time involved teacher-directed instruction (TDI), seatwork (SW), or a nonacademic activity (NA). Use the formulas to calculate how instructional time is used. An illustration is provided on the first line of the form.

Activity	Allocated Time	Time Started	Time Ended	Actual Minutes	TDI/ SW/NA	Comments
Check H.W.	15	8:33	8:43	10	TDI	Discipline Problems

Total TDI minutes _____

Percentage of instruction delivered $= \left(\dfrac{\text{Actual minutes}}{\text{Allocated time}}\right) =$ _____

Total SW minutes _____

Percentage of delivered instruction that is TDI $= \left(\dfrac{\text{TDI}}{\text{TDI} + \text{SW}} \times 100\right) =$ _____

Total TDI/SW minutes _____

Total NA minutes _____

and as a set of guidelines for beginning teachers who are faced with the task of organizing their first classrooms.

Scheduling Activities

Effective classrooms serving students with mild to moderate disabilities are places where (1) schedules of daily tasks are relatively fixed and (2) routines consistently facilitate the completion of assigned tasks. When planning activities, two tools can facilitate the development and implementation of effective schedules: a master schedule and individual schedule cards.

B ox 3.2   **Transition Cues**

1. Teacher gives verbal cues to group.
2. An appointed child gives verbal cues to group.
3. Teacher gives verbal cues to individuals.
4. An appointed child gives verbal cues to individuals.
5. Teacher touches children to dismiss.
6. An appointed child touches children to dismiss.
7. Lights blink, a bell rings, a piano sounds, a buzzer buzzes, and so forth to signal dismissal.
8. Teacher begins a song that routinely tells children to move.
9. Teacher makes a routine gesture or stands in a routine place to signal dismissal.
10. Teacher or an appointed child hands out individual necklaces or bracelets with a color, number, word, or symbol keyed to the children's intended destinations.
11. Teacher or appointed child distributes cards with symbols for the destinations printed on them.
12. Teacher calls for all children wearing a certain color, type, or pattern of clothing.
13. Teacher gives each child an object that will be needed in the next activity.
14. Teacher holds up something (e.g., coat, library book) for its owner to recognize and take to the destination.
15. Teacher tells children to go and find their names at the destination.
16. Teacher dismisses children by physical characteristics (e.g., brown eyes, red hair).
17. Teacher dismisses children by gender.
18. Teacher dismisses children by letters in name.
19. Teacher shows a letter, number, or word and asks for volunteers to identify it; correct answers earn dismissal.
20. Teacher dismisses children by tables at which they sit.
21. Teacher calls on all children who received stickers or "smiley faces" on this day to leave first.
22. Teacher calls first on those students who completed a valued task (e.g., remembered to clean out their cubbie yesterday, took a nap, said their telephone number).
23. Children look at a picture list on the chalkboard or cue card to learn where to go next after finishing an assigned activity.
24. Teacher dismisses using an if-then sentence (e.g., "If you have teeth in your mouth, then go ... "; "If you could be a father when you grow up, then go ... ")

Source: Rosenkoetter, S. E., & Fowler, S. A. (1986). Teaching mainstreamed children to manage daily transitions. *Teaching Exceptional Children, 19*(1), 20–23. Copyright 1986 by The Council for Exceptional Children. Reprinted with permission.

Master Schedule. The most difficult and logistically complex step in developing consistency and predictability in the learning environment is the development of an overall class schedule. This overall or **master schedule** is directly related to the allocation of instructional time; teachers must determine how much of the school day is to be devoted to specific skill instruction and other relevant activities. Obviously, much of this information is gathered from students' records, recent IEP data, and current diagnostic test information. The master schedule is, however, a direct reflection of the relative emphases that will be given to content-area instruction for each student in the class. The schedule also reflects the level of each student's participation in general education or mainstreamed activities, as well as the amount of related service activities received each week.

B ox 3.3 **Recording Rates of On-Task Behavior**

At 10-second intervals, record a plus sign (+) if the target student is on-task and a minus sign (–) if off-task. Operationally defined, **on-task** means that the student is looking at the appropriate individual or instructional stimulus. Alternate among the targeted students at the prearranged 10-second intervals. Use a tape recording of a low audible sound to signal an observation.

Name	1	2	3	4	5	6	7	8	9	10	11	12	13	14	15

Activity type _____ Time begin _____

_____ Time end _____

Note: To arrive at a percentage of the amount of time a student is on-task, use the following formula:

$$\frac{\text{number of plus signs } (+s)}{\text{number of plus signs} + \text{number of minus signs } (+s + -s)}$$

Master schedules should contain (1) the precise times the scheduled periods are to begin and end, (2) a general label representing the subject area or general activity to be covered, (3) the adult (teacher, paraprofessional, parent volunteer) responsible for leading or supervising the period, and (4) the location where the assigned task should be completed. These components are illustrated in Figure 3.7 for several students with mild disabilities attending a self-contained setting. This type of scheduling format can be adapted for resource placements as well. Any type of sturdy chart paper can be used for the construction of the master schedule, although large sheets of paper having preprinted rows and columns will result in a product that is neat and easy for students to read.

The master schedule should be posted in an area that is accessible in the classroom; smaller copies of the chart should be placed in the teacher's and instructional aide's planbooks. The master schedule should serve as a resource for (1) students who may have forgotten or misplaced their own personal schedules, (2) substitute teachers who need to ensure that quality programming continues when regular personnel are absent, (3) building administrators who may need to know where a student should be during a particular instructional period, and (4) parents and other interested visitors needing a guide to classroom activities.

Individual Schedule Cards. To personalize the master schedule, each student should receive a personal schedule card. The card should be small enough to fit into the student's pocket, purse, or wallet, or, when necessary, be attached to the student's desk. Activities related to the construction of student schedule cards should be started on the first day of a new school year.

Box 3.4

Strategies for Increasing On-Task Behavior During Teacher-Directed Instruction and Independent Practice

Teacher-Directed Instruction

1. **Teach more and test less.** Rather than replicate diagnostic testing and repeatedly ask students to tell what they already know about the instructional subject matter, devote time to instructing students in what they need to know.
2. **Question students frequently.** Frequent questioning increases opportunities for students to respond. Pose randomly sequenced questions on a frequent basis. Whenever possible, have students respond both in unison and individually.
3. **Ensure that all students participate.** Structure instructional tasks so that all students can be actively involved in responding to learning opportunities.
4. **Use signals and prompts** to indicate transitions and other attentional shifts within the lesson. Signals can ensure smooth movement between the various components of lessons.
5. **Be enthusiastic.** Students participate more when teachers are excited about what they are teaching. Ways to show enthusiasm involve a touch of the "ham" in all of us and can include humor, animation, and gimmicks.

Practice Sessions

1. **Reward correct student responses frequently.** Because students with learning and behavioral problems tend to have high rates of off-task behavior when assigned independent practice, teachers need to provide frequent reinforcement of appropriate behavior. Methods that can be used include *(a)* directed content-related praise; *(b)* tangible reinforcers such as pencils, books, and food; *(c)* generalized reinforcers such as tokens, points, and checkmarks; and *(d)* activity reinforcers such as computer time, library time, and free time.
2. **Develop clear and concise rules, procedures, and instructions for practice activities.** How and what students should do both during and after completion of practice activities should be highlighted as a classroom rule. Procedures for the correct method of obtaining assistance should also be clearly defined.
3. **Use interesting and motivating practice activities.** In addition to using traditional "ditto" pencil-and-paper seatwork activities, intersperse assignments that require the use of microcomputers, learning centers, language masters, and filmstrip or filmloop projectors.
4. **Have private study spaces available.** Highly distractible students may find a "private office" helpful in maintaining the sustained attention necessary for the completion of practice assignments.
5. **Use peer-mediated or cooperative-learning strategies.** Tutoring systems and cooperative-learning strategies are effective in increasing the number of opportunities that students have to respond, as well as in improving the academic achievement of students with mild disabilities.

Sources: Adapted from Rosenberg, M. S., & Baker, K. (1985). Instructional time and the teacher educator: Training preservice and beginning teachers to use time effectively. *Teacher Educator, 20,* 195–207; and Wilson, R., & Wesson, C. (1986). Making every minute count: Academic time in LD classrooms. *Learning Disabilities Focus, 2,* 3–19.

Scheduling Students in Inclusive Settings. When scheduling activities for students receiving instruction in inclusive general education environments, it is useful to use individualized scheduling matrices that explicitly operationalize how critical aspects of the students' educational program is to be delivered. Any type of scheduling matrix format can be used as long as educational goals, general class activities, educational supports, and necessary personnel are highlighted. Figure 3.8 is an example of such a

Name	Opening exercises 8:45 – 9:00	Period 1 9:00 9:35	Period 2 9:40 10:15	Period 3 10:20 10:55	11:00 – 11:20	Period 4 11:25 12:00	Period 5 12:05 12:40	Period 6 12:45 1:15	Period 7 1:20 1:55	Period 8 2:00 2:30	Dismissal at 2:35
Jane A.		Reading decoding group A Bk. group table w/Mrs. Fisk	M Art w/class 3-303 MTWTh Music – F Rm. 202	Math group A Fr. group table w/Mr. Ross	Recess	Lunch	Spelling w/peer tutor MWF TTh – PE	Reading compreh. group A Fr. table group w/Mr. Ross	Written expression Group A w/Mr. Ross	Social studies MW: Science; TTh: Free time; F: all	
Hector B.		Speech R Rm 302 MWF w/ Mr. Brooks TTh – PE	Reading group C Fr. group table w/Mr. Ross	Math group A Fr. group table w/Mr. Ross	Recess	Lunch	Spelling w/peer tutor TTh MWF – Art Rm. 202	Reading compreh. group B Bk. table group w/Mrs. Fisk	Written expression Group A w/Mr. Ross	Social studies MW: Science; TTh: Free time; F: all	
Dale C.		Reading decoding group A Bk. group table w/Mrs. Fisk	Math group B Bk. group table w/Mrs. Fisk	Spelling w/peer tutor MWF TTh – Art Rm. 202	Recess	Lunch	M Art w/class Rm 3-301 Music – F Rm. 202	Reading compreh. group A Fr. table group w/Mr. Ross	Written expression Group A w/Mr. Ross	Social studies MW: Science; TTh: Free time; F: all	
Louise Z.		Reading decoding group B Fr. group table w/Mr. Ross	Math group B Bk. group table w/Mrs. Fisk	Spelling w/peer tutor MWF TTh – PE	Recess	Lunch	M Art w/class 3-301 MTWTh Music – F Rm. 202	Reading compreh. group B Bk. table group w/Mrs. Fisk	Written expression Group B w/Mrs. Fisk	Social studies MW: Science; TTh: Free time; F: all	

Key: ▨ M ——→ Indicates a "mainstream" activity   Teacher: Mr. Ross
      ▽ R ——→ Indicates a "related service" activity   Aide: Mrs. Fisk

FIGURE 3.7   Master Schedule for a Self-Contained Setting

matrix from Giangreco, Cloniger, and Iverson's (1993), COACH (Choosing Options and Accommodations for Children) program.

Grouping Students

Grouping students for effective instruction is not an easy task; the process tests teachers' diagnostic, organizational, management, and decision-making skills. In special education, the process of grouping is tied directly to individualization of instruction. Individualization is based on the assumption that the adaptation of instruction to the individual characteristics or needs of students results in desired rates of learning. Individualization, however, must not be mistaken for one-to-one instruction; instruction appropriate to a learner's individual needs can be and often is presented in small and large groups.

Although compelling arguments can be made for most grouping alternatives (e.g., within-class ability grouping, learning-style approaches, specific-skill grouping), two preconditions must exist prior to the consideration of any such alternative. First, the alternative must result in success and achievement for all members of the group. Second, no stigma or negative feelings must be associated with group membership. To meet both of these preconditions, student and beginning teachers should keep in mind the following points:

- *Make grouping decisions based on the principle that each student possesses specific strengths and weaknesses.* It is possible that a student will be placed in an advanced group for writing instruction while requiring a slower pace for math, story problems, and measurement.

General Class Activities

Student's name _____

Grade _____

IEP Goals												
Breadth of Curriculum												
General Supports												

FIGURE 3.8   Scheduling Matrix

From Giangreco, M. F., Cloninger, C. J., & Iverson, V. S. (1993). *Choosing options and accommodations for children.* Copyright 1993 by Michael F. Giangreco. Reprinted with permission.

- *Assignment to groups should not be considered permanent.* As students progress through their programs, factors influencing group success may require changing a group's composition. Reassessment of student characteristics and, when necessary, reorganization of groups highlight that the ever-changing individual characteristics of students are regularly monitored and addressed.
- *Consider the necessity of grouping.* Content areas, such as science and social studies, that do not have the "building block" character of math or reading may be best presented in large-group settings (Slavin, 1986).
- *Program for the size of groups on the basis of student ability levels.* For average or high-performing students, groups of six to ten students may be appropriate. Low-performing students may require a group size of three to five, and very low achieving students may need tutorial groups consisting of no more than three students (Paine, 1982).

When grouping for instruction, students should be assigned to groups on the basis of (1) criterion-referenced or curriculum-based placement tests, (2) standardized test scores, (3) previous performance observations, (4) typical rates of acquisition, and (5) learning-style preferences. Attention should be paid to students' actual knowledge and skills, rather than to inappropriate behavior. Once students are grouped, instruction should be tailored to meet the needs of each group. This tailoring typically involves adjustments to the content level assigned, the pace of the lesson, and the dominant mode of presentation. For example, one group in an elementary class of students with and without identified disabilities may require three lessons to master the math content that

TABLE 3.2   Teacher-Centered Grouping Alternatives

Grouping Method	Description	Advantages	Disadvantages	Sources
Whole Class	Students spend class time being instructed by the teacher.	• Students less likely to go off-task • Special needs students not singled out • Less time spent transitioning/giving directions • More time for assessment and explanation	• Diverse needs of students may not be addressed	Friend & Bursuck (1996) Mason & Good (1993)
Small Group: Same Skill	Students are divided into groups on the basis of their ability to perform a skill. Teacher instructs each group separately.	• Overall academic achievement tends to increase • Diverse abilities can be addressed • Stimulation for high-ability students	• Low-performing students may be stigmatized • Increased time needed for transitioning/giving directions • Instruction may not be delivered equitably	Gamoran (1992) Hooper (1992) Kamps, Walker, Maher, & Rotholz (1992) Mason & Good (1993)
Small Group: Mixed Skill	Students are divided into groups randomly. Teacher instructs each group separately.	• Students observe positive peer role models • Opportunity for individualized instruction • Special needs students not singled out	• Acceleration of high-ability students slowed	Friend & Bursuck (1996) Mason & Good (1993)
One-to-One	Students work one-to-one with teacher or computer. Students proceed at their own pace on their own ability level.	• Appropriate for students' ability level and pace • Students receive individualized attention • Early one-to-one interventions can prevent future academic failure	• Extensive one-to-one instruction allows less overall instructional time for everyone • Unattended students may go off-task • Students encounter fewer peer models • Extensive one-to-one instruction is expensive	Kamps, Walker, Maher, & Rotholz (1992) Slavin (1993) Wasik & Slavin (1993)

another group of students can acquire in just one lesson. Moreover, the group requiring the additional instructional time may require substantially more visual cues or an explicit strategy for acquiring the necessary content.

In an inclusive secondary setting, it may be necessary to periodically group together students who require explicit instruction in how to develop and use **internally generated mediators** when engaged in processing content area instruction. As noted by Bulgren and Lenz (1995), these mediators are learning strategies that a student uses to process information on an independent level. Appropriately implemented grouping within the general education setting can allow for the acquisition of these important

TABLE 3.3 Peer-Mediated Grouping Alternatives

Grouping Method	Description	Advantages	Disadvantages	Sources
Peer Tutoring	Pairs of students, at the same grade level or at different grade levels, instruct one another.	• Students often increase in skill performance • Students often increase their social skills • General education students grow in their acceptance of special needs students	• Considerable time commitment is required to ensure properly trained tutors • Considerable time commitment is required to monitor and evaluate tutoring	Ezell, Kohler, & Strain (1994) Miller, Kohler, Ezell, Hoel, & Strain (1993) Garcia-Vazquez & Ehly (1992)
Classwide Peer Tutoring	Students are divided into two teams and assigned to tutoring pairs, in which tutor and tutee roles rotate; the two teams compete against each other for points.	• Students increase skills in subject areas • At-risk students increase performance • Individual differences are addressed	• Unattended students may go off-task • Considerable time commitment is required to monitor and evaluate pairs' progress	Maheady, Mallette, & Harper (1991) Simmons, Fuchs, Fuchs, Mathes, & Hodge (1995)
Cooperative Learning	Students work in small mixed-ability groups, each group with a shared learning goal.	• Students learn social and work-related skills • Student self-esteem and motivation may increase as students learn their strengths in mixed-ability setting	• Teacher may expend much energy trying to force cooperation between students of widely varying abilities • Gifted students may be forced to act as task-masters to peers less gifted or else to accept a lower grade	Fenton (1992) Jules (1992) Manning & Lucking (1991) Mills & Tangherlini (1992) Tomlinson (1994)

adaptations, as well as the necessary curricular material. (More specifics of strategy instruction and methods for developing effective instruction are provided in Chapter 6.) Still, it is generally recognized that students with special needs, regardless of grade level and placement type, can benefit from a wide variety of grouping arrangements. Friend and Bursuck (1996) have organized the menu of grouping alternatives under two major categories: *teacher centered* and *peer mediated*. As noted in the brief description of alternatives in Table 3.2, teacher-centered groups are groups in which the classroom teacher is primarily responsible for instruction; as noted in Table 3.3, in peer-mediated instructional alternatives, students are primarily responsible for instruction.

FORMULATING MEANINGFUL AND RELEVANT RULES AND PROCEDURES

Organization and management, two factors critical to the successful functioning of classrooms, produce much apprehension between students and beginning teachers. These concerns are well founded; a teacher's ability to organize and manage classrooms is related to a student's academic performance and social-emotional behavior and to both teachers' and students' attitudes toward school. Teachers demonstrate or present their organizational and management expectations through two general delivery systems: rules and procedures. **Rules** identify, define, and operationalize a teacher's specific principles of acceptable behavior. **Routines** and **procedures** specify a protocol of behaviors necessary for the appropriate completion of an activity, task, or classroom operation.

The need for clear, unambiguous, and concise rules and procedures for students with mild disabilities cannot be overstated. As a result of their unique learning and behavioral difficulties, these students tend to have difficulties in learning and/or complying with many of the more obvious standards of conduct typical of schools and classrooms. (In Chapter 8, you will see how these rules and procedures fit into a comprehensive behavioral management system.) Rules and procedures, however, also serve as discriminative stimuli, or antecedents, of appropriate situation-specific behavior. When used correctly, rules and procedures become the overt guides, models, and prompts for desired student (and teacher) behavior. They remind and motivate students to meet the standards of a specific learning environment. Finally, classroom rules and procedures, when used in a positive context, can serve as specific behavioral targets to which teachers can direct reinforcers such as attention, praise, and tokens. The success of rules and procedures depends on (1) how they are introduced and presented to students and (2) how teachers plan for maintaining the integrity of their stated expectations.

Introducing Rules and Procedures

Classroom rules and procedures should not be designed in a quick or frivolous manner. Considerable forethought and troubleshooting is necessary to ensure that stated procedures match a particular school's and teacher's expectations of student behavior. The following guidelines, adapted from a number of sources (Evertson et al., 1984; Paine et al., 1983; Rosenberg, 1986; Strain & Sainato, 1987), can assist developing and beginning teachers in planning and introducing rules and procedures.

- *Be aware of school district policies.* Have a working knowledge of the expectations for all students within the LEA. Design classroom rules and procedures to be congruent with the prevailing expectations.
- *Identify the specific behaviors and procedures expected of students.* Reconstruct these expectations into overt, behavioral, and measurable pinpoints. Ensure that agreement as to the occurrence or nonoccurrence of such expectations can be attained between teachers and students.
- *The first order of business on the first day of school should be to discuss and teach classroom rules and procedures.* Because rules and procedures govern how daily classroom activities and events should occur for the entire school year, it is important they be in place and reinforced as soon as possible.
- *Present a solid rationale as to why classrooms need well-defined rules and procedures.* Because a teacher's approach to the presentation of the need for structure can influence student compliance, discussions about rules and procedures should be conducted in a patient, businesslike, and sincere fashion.
- *Involve students in the development of the rules and procedures.* Solicit opinions as to what the consequences should be for both compliance and noncompliance. By promoting a sense of ownership in the classroom system, students will feel a greater sense of allegiance to the rules and procedures identified.
- *Keep the number of rules and procedures that students need to follow small.* For each rule generated, ensure that the wording is kept simple and to the point. Students often view stated rules and procedures literally, and verbiage should be avoided. When specifying procedures, such as what a student should do after completing a seatwork assignment, an easy-to-follow, step-by-step sequence of behaviors is most effective.

- *Phrase rules and procedures positively, rather than negatively.* Instead of accentuating what students should *not* do (e.g., "Do not call out during lessons"), highlight appropriate behaviors that students should engage in regularly (e.g., "Raise your hand if you wish to get the teacher's attention").

Maintaining the Integrity of Rules and Procedures

Unfortunately, the potency of classroom rules and procedures seems to diminish as the school year progresses. Factors as diverse as lapses in students' memories and lack of consistency in providing consequences for rule and procedure compliance and noncompliance account for this loss of effectiveness. The following guidelines, adapted from a number of sources (Evertson et al., 1984; Paine et al., 1983; Rosenberg, 1986), will assist in promoting long-term compliance to the stated behavioral expectations of classrooms.

- *Keep rules posted in an area visible to all students.* Prominently displayed rules and procedures can be powerful cues for appropriate student behavior and can prompt busy teachers to provide consequences for student compliance and noncompliance on a regular basis.
- *Ensure different rules for various situations.* One set of rules will not hold for the range and variety of activities typical of most special education classrooms. For example, during highly structured instructional activities such as directed reading and math lessons, rules and procedures should reflect the need for quiet, order, and a high degree of engagement to the task. In contrast, less ordered activities, such as art and discussions or debates of citizenship issues, would require a different, more relaxed set of rules.
- *Teach and provide practice for all rules.* Both overall classroom rules and activity-specific rules need to be taught and reviewed just like any other material that teachers wish students to acquire. Lessons scheduled early in the school year can ensure rapid acquisition of the various rules and procedures of the classroom; brief reviews of rules prior to lessons can remind students of the expectations for that specific lesson. The potency of brief reviews of rules should not be underestimated. Rosenberg (1986) found that brief reviews (1 to 2 minutes) of lesson-specific rules just prior to instruction increased rates of time-on-task and of the number of opportunities to respond over levels found when no such reviews were provided.
- *Model classroom procedures.* Most classroom procedures, whether involved with the correct way to behave during a fire drill or to line up for lunch, involve a complex series of behaviors. To ensure that students learn the correct way to comply with standard classroom procedures, it is recommended that teachers (1) model or demonstrate how specific procedures are to be performed, (2) provide opportunities for guided practice in the initial performance of the procedures, (3) reinforce correct performance of the procedures, and (4) provide corrective feedback immediately if procedures are not followed correctly.
- *Self-monitor performance with the documented rules and procedures.* Two major reasons for the lack of maintenance in classroom organization and management systems is failure of the teacher to be consistent in following class procedures and the lack of regular enforcement of the rules. To promote high levels of consistency in the administration of classroom management systems built on a foundation of stated rules and procedures, teachers should (1) regularly sample, through peer observation or self-recording, their performance in providing consequences for rule and procedure compliance and noncompliance and (2) develop a personalized system to prompt regular and consistent enforcement of the class rules.

Developing Routines and Procedures

Student attention to task is often lost when procedures associated with the successful completion of recurring classroom routines are not followed. The routines and procedures

Procedures for Morning Arrival
- Check if it is an "A" or "B" schedule day
- Go directly to your locker
- Take all supplies needed for your morning classes
- Put hats and other personal items in your locker
- If you eat breakfast in school, report directly to the cafeteria
- Report directly to homeroom by the warning bell
- Upon arrival to homeroom, complete your morning log
- Listen quietly to morning announcements

Cafeteria Procedures
- Walk quietly when entering the cafeteria
- Remain seated until the teacher invites you to proceed to the lunch line
- Use quiet voices when speaking to your friends
- Remain seated at your table until the teacher signals for you to dispose of trash
- Remain in your seat until dismissed

Arrival To and Dismissal From Class
- Be seated when bell rings and begin working on warm-up
- After completing warm-up, wait quietly for teacher to begin
- The teacher directs preparation for dismissal
- When given the signal, clean up your workspace and pack your bookbag
- When bell rings, wait for teacher to dismiss the class
- Walk safely, quickly, and quietly to your next class

FIGURE 3.9   Procedures from a Typical Middle School Program

of specific schools and classrooms will vary according to the age and developmental levels of students. It is clear, however, that explicit and consistent routines and procedures are tools that help teachers orchestrate their classrooms with greater efficiency and effectiveness. Successful teachers know how to successfully facilitate the completion of routine tasks such as morning arrival, dismissal from class, transitioning to and from the cafeteria, and checking homework assignments. They do this by having clear and explicit procedures that (1) guide the successful completion of the task and (2) preclude negative impact that can result from common yet annoying events that often interrupt the instructional flow of the classroom. These procedures are taught and practiced throughout the school year, and positive supports (e.g., self-monitoring procedures, buddy systems) are provided to assist those students who have trouble following the required steps. Figure 3.9 lists several typically troubling events, along with sample procedures designed to minimize disruptions.

P*ause and Reflect 3.2*

List the explicit rules and procedures that are in effect in your classroom setting. In your opinion, do these rules and procedures promote a sense of organization and management in the classroom? Do these rules and procedures correspond to best practices for developing and implementing rules, routines, and procedures? What additions or suggestions can you offer to improve the quality and long-term effectiveness of these behavioral standards?

COORDINATING RESOURCES

The final category of guidelines related to the successful organization of special education classrooms involves the coordination of the resources and personnel available to teachers. By creating or coordinating several key instructional resources and by using the strengths of other school personnel, developing and beginning teachers will find that much of the time typically spent searching for or organizing materials and information could be replaced with the more relevant activities of teaching or lesson planning. Five types of coordinating activities are considered: (1) using the IEP as a living and working document, (2) keeping files and materials organized and accessible, (3) appropriate use of technology-based resources, (4) preparing a substitute teacher's packet, and (5) being aware of school- and community-based support services. Using the strengths of other personnel in the school environment is discussed in later chapters.

Using the IEP as a Living and Working Document

In most programs that prepare individuals to teach students with disabilities, considerable time is devoted to individualized education plans (IEPs). As will be noted in Chapter 7, developing teachers require considerable practice in structuring the IEP document to ensure that it meets local, state, and federal standards. Sometimes overlooked in the activities related to technical and legal compliance is the notion that students' IEPs should be treated as working documents related directly to the ongoing instructional activities of the classroom.

Treating the IEP as a living and working document begins at the time of its preparation. When writing the document, the annual goals and short-term objectives should be treated as the foundation for the lessons that will be presented to students. When initially completed, IEPs should be placed in an accessible area close to the teacher's desk. An IEP should be monitored frequently regarding (1) the status of the goals and objectives listed and (2) the specific activities or instructional modifications necessary for successful attainment of the listed goals and objectives. When the teacher is communicating with parents or other professionals involved in the education of a student, the IEP should be used as the definitive record by which educational progress is measured and recorded.

Keeping Files and Materials Organized and Accessible

The time devoted to the organization and accessibility of files and resource material can pay rich dividends throughout a school year and, in many cases, a teacher's full career. Quick and easy access to student records, instructional materials, and test protocols is an example of how a systematic filing system can save time and stress. Student records should be close to the teacher's desk; in case of emergencies, it is essential to have parents' or guardians' addresses, places of employment, and telephone numbers. Curricular materials can be filed according to subject areas, specific skills, or instructional objectives. McCoy and Prehm (1987) recommend that teachers file their material by sequenced instructional objectives within broad content categories. Material related to each objective is coded according to a task-analytic hierarchy related to skill acquisition and the specific learning adaptations that each activity provides. Time devoted to the ordering of new instructional materials also can be saved if catalogs for instructional materials are filed according to this same system.

Appropriate Use of Technology-Based Resources

In addition to the countless benefits associated with "information on demand" technologies, our rapid ascent into the use of computer and Internet-based materials presents all educators with a number of challenges. As we enter the new millennium, our issues are no longer exclusively in the domain of access; it is likely that most beginning teachers and their students know how to operate a computer and retrieve information from a range of commercially available search engines. Today, it is the ethical and appropriate use of the computer and the Internet that is critical.

Most school districts have practices and policies that govern how technologies are to be used by teachers, administrators, and students. For example, most school districts employ software that restricts access to sexually explicit Web sites, images of violence and drug use, textual material that uses profanity and advocates racial/religious intolerance, as well as unmoderated and unpredictable chat rooms.

Still, student and beginning teachers should design a set of understandable policies and procedures involving the use of their classroom-based technologies and model ethical use of technology-based materials. Policies and procedures regarding the use of computers should, among other district-specific requirements, articulate that

- modification of the system without permission and supervision is not permitted
- only programs authorized for student use are allowed
- confidentiality is essential and accessing another's data or work is not permitted
- downloading copyrighted material is not permitted
- e-mails must have user identification (but not personal information) and that objectionable content and language is forbidden

Moreover, teachers should model appropriate conduct regarding the downloading, transmission, and copying of electronic materials (Brownell, Youngs, & Metzger, 1999). This starts with knowing how to effectively search for and evaluate Web-based materials as well as employing ethical, fair-use practices when encountering copyrighted materials.

Preparing a Substitute Teacher's Packet

Under the best conditions, the job of substitute teacher is difficult. Even the best students behave as if there is a lessening of standards when the regular teacher is absent. In special education settings serving students with disabilities, reports of disarray and confusion from substitute teachers are not uncommon. Consequently, many school districts have found it difficult to arrange for substitute teachers to fill in for ailing special education teachers.

All student and beginning teachers should plan ahead for the occasional need of a substitute teacher. Because there is no way to know for certain when sickness or emergencies will strike, a generic substitute teacher packet should be prepared at the beginning of the school year. The packet should contain all the information needed to teach and manage students left in the substitute teacher's charge. Platt (1987) has recommended that information be provided in six broad areas: policy information, schedules, specific student information, classroom procedural information, daily plans, and alternative activities. These six areas are further defined in Table 3.4.

Being Aware of School- and Community-Based Support Services

The needs of students with mild to moderate disabilities require the coordinated efforts of a team of professionals. Fortunately, most schools have a cadre of support personnel who can and do assist as part of their typical responsibilities. For example, it is not uncommon for counseling and guidance personnel to assist with family outreach services or for the school psychologist to offer social skills instruction groups. Student and beginning teachers should make the effort to be aware of all the services available in their buildings and school districts and to know the procedures to access needed services.

Unfortunately, school-based personnel are not nearly as knowledgeable about valuable community-based resources as they should be. Still, it has become increasingly clear that students with disabilities, particularly those with sustained and pervasive emotional or behavioral problems, require integrated and comprehensive services that involve education, mental health, social work, and family preservation personnel. It is

TABLE 3.4   Components of a Substitute Teacher's Packet

Major Areas	Specific Information to Be Included
Policy information	Floor plan or map of school. Names of individuals to contact in case of emergencies, problems, or questions. Entry, lunch recess, and discussion policies and procedures. Emergency and fire drill procedures.
Schedules	Master schedule of student activities. Teacher's duty schedule (e.g., lunch, recess, and so forth). Schedules of parent volunteers, aides, peer tutors, and related service personnel.
Specific student information	Seating chart and description of students. Medication needs of students. Names, addresses, and phone numbers of students' parents or guardians.
Classroom procedural information	Attendance, charting, and record-keeping procedures. Brief description of classroom management program. Location of instructional materials and equipment. Free-time activities.
Daily plans	Location of students' IEPs. Location and guide to teacher planbook or daily lesson plans.
Alternative activities	Bag of tricks containing fun and motivating student activities. Structured recess plans.

Adapted from Platt, J. M. (1987). Substitute teachers can do more than just keep the lid on. *Teaching Exceptional Children, 19*(2), 28–31.

critical that all of these human service professionals communicate and act in concert to meet the variety and multiplicity of needs presented by students and their families. The Child and Adolescent Service System Program (CASSP: National Institute of Mental Health, 1990; Stroul & Friedman, 1986) provides a framework for understanding the interrelatedness of services within an integrated system of care. As implied by the overlapping circles in Figure 3.10, interagency communication and cooperation are necessary if professionals are to deliver integrated services for students and their families.

FIGURE 3.10   Components of an Integrated System of Care

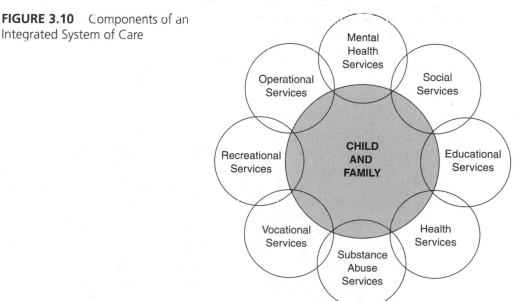

Preservice and beginning teachers should be aware of the range of services offered in their community and who in their school or district is responsible for agency access. Moreover, these teachers should be prepared to consult with and serve as liaisons among the many professionals involved in the lives of their students. Although specific liaison activities can vary from setting to setting, it is important for preservice and beginning teachers to (1) respect the belief systems and goals held by those in the other professions, (2) have a nonterritorial view of service provision, and (3) share both the responsibilities and the rewards for providing services (Coleman, 1996).

SUMMARY

We conclude this chapter with the same message with which we started: To manage busy classrooms successfully, special educators must be organized. In this chapter, we provided practical suggestions for improving the organization of classrooms serving students with learning and behavioral problems. A theme that emerged throughout the chapter was that organization required for successful teaching can be acquired, practiced, and mastered.

The first topic discussed was the challenging task of arranging the physical environment. Five interrelated preinstructional activities pertaining to classroom design were outlined, and specific illustrations related to the physical layout of special education environments were provided. Second, the management of instructional time was considered. The different levels of instructional time were operationally defined, and both generic and lesson-specific strategies were presented for using instructional time effectively and efficiently. Third, the logistically complex tasks of scheduling classroom activities and grouping students were discussed. Strategies for organizing the school day into manageable segments were reviewed, and guidelines for the grouping of students were examined. Fourth, the formulation and maintenance of meaningful and relevant classroom rules and procedures were examined.

The chapter concluded with ideas related to the coordination of resources. Included were suggestions regarding IEP use, the organization of files and materials, the appropriate use of technology, the preparation of a substitute teaching packet, and the development of a resource list of school- and community-based resources that can serve students and their families.

ACTIVITIES TO EXTEND YOUR KNOWLEDGE

1. Generate a series of strategies that you can use to organize your classroom environment. If you were to develop a checklist of things to consider in your "organizational strategy," which actions and items would you put toward the top of your priority list? What supports do you think you would need in order to maintain your level of organization?

2. What is the best way to group students? How children are grouped for instruction continues to be a most contentious issue. Is it best for high-achieving students to be grouped *heterogeneously*, with low-achieving students or students with disabilities? Or should students of similar abilities and instructional needs be grouped *homogeneously*? What available instructional approaches (e.g., cooperative learning, differentiated instruction) can guide teachers in their decisions of how to best group students for instruction? What does the available research tell educators about these approaches? How do these general approaches address the special needs of students with mild to moderate disabilities?

3. Create your own resource manual of school- and community-based resources. In the first section of this manual, list the in-school and in-district personnel who can

assist you in providing services to your students. Be sure to include each person's name, title, area of responsibility, and telephone number. In a separate section, begin to list the available community services that may be of use to your students and their families. You may also wish to begin a list of organizations and support groups that may be helpful to your students and their families. Keep these resources handy, especially when you have parent conferences. In some instances, parents are searching for support mechanisms to cope with or address many of the same issues that teachers face in school.

4. With several of your colleagues, create a meaningful substitute teacher packet. What information and items do you believe should be included in this packet? How could you ensure that the days you are absent will remain productive for your students?

POINT AND CLICK

These web sites have information and links to additional information related to how one can best set up for effective instruction.

McRel: Mid-continent Research for Edcuation and Learning
http://www.mcrel.org

Survival Guide for New Teachers
http://www.ed.gov/pubs/survivalguide

ERIC Digests
http://www.ed.gov/databases/ERIC_Digests/index/

School Psychology Resources Online
http://www.schoolpsychology.net/

Center for Effective Collaboration and Practice
http://www.air-dc.org/cecp/

Teacher Expectations and Student Achievement
http://education.indiana.edu/cas/tt/v2i2/tesa.html

Teachers Discuss
http://oeri3.ed.gov:8000/Teachers/

Ideas at Work
http://www.ed.gov/pubs/ideasatwork/

REFERENCES

Bleichman, E. A. (1985). *Solving child behavior problems at home and at school.* Champaign, IL: Research Press.

Brownell, G., Youngs, C., & Metzger, J. (1999). *A PC for the teacher.* Belmont, CA: Wadsworth.

Bulgren, J., & Lenz, B. K. (1995). Strategic instruction in the content areas. In D. D. Deshler, E. S. Ellis, & B. K. Lenz (Eds.), *Teaching adolescents with learning disabilities* (pp. 409–473). Denver: Love.

Coleman, M. C. (1996). *Emotional and behavioral disorders: Theory and practice.* Needham Heights, MA: Allyn & Bacon.

Doyle, W. (1980). *Classroom management.* West Lafayette, IN: Kappa Delta Pi.

Evertson, C. M., Emmer, E. T., Clements, B. S., Sanford, J. P., & Worsham, M. E. (1984). *Classroom management for elementary teachers.* Upper Saddle River, NJ: Prentice Hall.

Ezell, H., Kohler, F., & Strain, P. (1994). A program description and evaluation of academic peer tutoring for reading skills of children with special needs. *Education and Treatment of Children, 17,* 52–67.

Fenton, C. A. (1992). Cooperative learning: A view from the inside. *Contemporary Education, 63,* 207–209.

Friend, M., & Bursuck, W. (1996). *Including students with special needs.* Needham Heights, MA: Allyn & Bacon.

Gamoran, A. (1992). Is ability grouping equitable? *Educational Leadership, 50,* 11–17.

Garcia-Vazquez, E., & Ehly, S. (1992). Peer tutoring effects on students who are not perceived as socially accepted. *Psychology in the Schools, 29,* 256–266.

Giangreco, M. F., Cloniger, G. J., & Iverson, V. S. (1993). *Choosing options and accommodations for children.* Baltimore: Paul H. Brookes.

Hooper, S. (1992). Effects of peer interaction during computer-based mathematics instruction. *Journal of Educational Research, 85,* 180–189.

Jules, V. (1992). Cooperative learning: Student perceptions of the changing structure of learning. *Contemporary Education, 63,* 191–194.

Kamps, D., Walker, D., Maher, J., & Rotholz, D. (1992). Academic and environmental effects of small-group arrangements for students with autism and other developmental disabilities. *Journal of Autism and Developmental Disroders, 22,* 277–293.

Maheady, L., Mallette, B., & Harper, G. (1991). Accommodating cultural, linguistic, and academic diversity: Some peer-mediated instructional options. *Preventing School Failure, 36,* 28–31.

Manning, L., & Lucking, R. (1991). The what, why, and how of cooperative learning. *Social Studies, 82,* 120–124.

Mason, D., & Good, T. (1993). Effects of two-group and whole-class teaching on regrouped elementary students' mathematics achievement. *American Educational Research Journal, 30,* 328–360.

McCoy, K. M., & Prehm, H. J. (1987). *Teaching mainstreamed students: Methods and techniques.* Denver: Love.

Miller, L., Kohler, F., Ezell, H., Hoel, K., & Strain, P. (1993). Winning with peer tutoring: A teacher's guide. *Preventing School Failure, 37,* 14–18.

Mills, C., & Tangherlini, A. (1992). Finding an optimal match: Another look at ability grouping and cooperative learning. *Equity and Excellence, 25,* 205–208.

National Institute of Mental Health. (1990). *National plan for research on child and adolescent mental disorders.* Rockville, MD: Author.

Paine, S. C. (1982). Setting up for instruction. *Association for Direct Instruction News, 2,* 8–9.

Paine, S. C., Radicci, J., Rosellini, L. C., Deutchman, L., & Darch, C. R. (1983). *Structuring your classroom for academic success.* Champaign, IL: Research Press.

Platt, J. M. (1987). Substitute teachers can do more than just keep the lid on. *Teaching Exceptional Children, 19*(2), 28–31.

Rosenberg, M. S. (1986). Maximizing the effectiveness of structured management programs: Implementing rule-review procedures with disruptive and distractible students. *Behavioral Disorders, 11,* 239–248.

Rosenberg, M. S., & Baker, K. (1985). Instructional time and the teacher educator: Training preservice and beginning teachers to use time effectively. *Teacher Educator, 20,* 195–207.

Rosenkoetter, S. E., & Fowler, S. A. (1986). Teaching mainstreamed children to manage daily transitions. *Teaching Exceptional Children, 19*(1), 20–23.

Simmons, D., Fuchs, L., Fuchs, D., Mathes, P., & Hodge, J. (1995). Effects of explicit teaching and peer tutoring on the reading achievement of learning disabled and low-performing students in regular classrooms. *Elementary School Journal, 95,* 387–408.

Slavin, R. E. (1986). *Education psychology: Theory into practice.* Upper Saddle River, NJ: Prentice Hall.

Slavin, R. E. (1993). Preventing early school failure: What works? *Educational Leadership, 50,* 10–18.

Strain, P. S., & Sainato, D. M. (1987). Preventive discipline in early childhood. *Teaching Exceptional Children, 19*(4), 26–30.

Stroul, B. A., & Friedman, R. M. (1986). *A system of care for severely emotionally disturbed children and youth.* Washington, DC: Georgetown University, CASSP Technical Assistance Center.

Tomlinson, C. A. (1994). Gifted learners: The boomerang kids of middle school? *Roeper Review, 16,* 177–182.

Wasik, B., & Slavin, R. (1993). Preventing early school failure with one-to-one tutoring: A review of five programs. *Reading Research Quarterly, 70,* 178–200.

Wilson, R., & Wesson, C. (1986). Making every minute count: Academic time in LD classrooms. *Learning Disabilities Focus, 2,* 3–19.

Classroom Assessment Practices for Instruction

Stephanie L. Carpenter and Margaret E. King-Sears
Johns Hopkins University

In this chapter, we will

✔ discuss the importance of classroom assessment

✔ identify the purposes of classroom assessment and suggest activities that address student performance and instructional design in relation to each purpose

✔ present guiding/overarching principles of assessment that should characterize all classroom assessments

✔ describe approaches to classroom assessment and examine ways that different approaches may be used concurrently to provide different views of student performance

✔ outline a step-by-step framework (APPLY) for developing classroom assessments that both fulfills the purposes of classroom assessment and adheres to the guiding principles

✔ examine the relationship between assessments and grade assignment for student performance

*A*ccountability for instructional programs and services for students with and without disabilities is occurring at all levels of education. Globally, students in the United States are being compared with students in other countries. Nationally, statewide assessment practices yield results that allow comparison with students in other states, as well as comparisons of students within different counties or districts in that state. Locally, administrators are concerned about how well students in their schools are doing, compared with students in other schools. In the classroom, educators are focused on how each student is progressing within the local school curriculum. For students with mild to moderate disabilities, progress is also monitored on goals and objectives specified on the individualized education program (IEP). Moreover, the Individuals with Disabilities Education Act (IDEA 97) requires students with disabilities to participate in their state- or districtwide assessment of student achievement with no modifications *or* with individualized modifications as noted on the IEPs. If the state/district assessment is not appropriate for a student with mild to moderate disabilities, then the IEP content must note why that assessment is not appropriate and how the student will be assessed. Beginning teachers should consult their local and state guidelines to clarify how state/district assessments are conducted, guidelines for modifications for the assessments that would be appropriate for students' IEPs, as well as criteria for excluding a student from the state/district assessment *and* what alternative assessment will be used for that student.

Regardless of the level of accountability, the focus is on assessments that accurately portray how well students are progressing in critical curriculum areas. In the midst of pressures from different levels about accountability for students' progress, challenges facing developing teachers include using formal assessment reports and the IEP to plan instruction, deciding what to teach immediately, and linking assessment to both the IEP and the instruction (curriculum and methods). Beginning and developing teachers may find that their immediate concerns are as follows:

- What do I teach these particular students, starting tomorrow?
- How long should I spend on each area of instruction?
- How will I know whether students have mastered the required competencies?
- What should I do if students have not mastered the required competencies?
- What should I do if students seem to be making only minimal progress?
- What do I do when students seem to forget what they learned or don't continue to use new skills consistently in a variety of situations?
- How do I know what to teach next?

Although these questions will be addressed throughout this text, the answer to each begins with classroom assessments.

Beginning and developing teachers can demonstrate accountability by responding proactively and reactively to assessing students with mild to moderate disabilities in special and general education classrooms. Proactively, educators plan classroom assessments that effectively monitor both their students' response to instruction and their students' progress toward IEP goals and objectives. Reactively, educators make sound decisions about what to teach and how to teach on the basis of assessment results. In this chapter, we examine aspects of classroom assessment that will assist developing teachers in using classroom assessments proactively and reactively, including: (1) purposes for assessment as related to the IEP and instruction, (2) overarching principles that characterize meaningful classroom assessments, (3) various approaches to assessing students' performance competencies, (4) a framework for developing classroom assessments, and (5) the relationship between classroom assessments and grading practices.

PURPOSES FOR CLASSROOM ASSESSMENT

By understanding the purposes of assessment, beginning teachers are better prepared to develop and use assessments that will provide functional, reliable, and valid information that facilitates planning, guides instruction, and documents student progress. The type of assessment administered is related to the purpose of assessment. Salvia and Ysseldyke (1991) note the differences between norm-referenced tests and criterion-referenced tests. **Norm-referenced tests** measure a student's performance in relation to the performance of his or her peers. Eligibility teams often use norm-referenced tests to determine the presence of a disability and whether students qualify for special education services. **Criterion-referenced tests** measure a student's performance in terms of absolute mastery of particular skills. Classroom teachers use criterion-referenced tests to help in planning instructional programs and monitoring students' mastery of skills. These "classroom" assessments serve four primary purposes related to planning instruction and documenting students' progress: (1) to identify students' entry-level competencies, (2) to monitor students' performance during instruction, (3) to determine students' mastery of competencies at the conclusion of instruction, and (4) to monitor students' maintenance and generalization of competencies. Developing and beginning teachers can engage in a series of activities to accomplish these purposes as they begin the academic year or begin new units of instruction within the year for their students with mild to moderate disabilities.

Identify Students' Entry-Level Competencies

The first activity in classroom assessment is to identify students' entry-level competencies in order to plan for instruction. The domain of instruction must be known before students' current competencies can be assessed and before purposeful instructional planning can occur. This step in identifying students' entry-level skills is frequently overlooked in descriptions of classroom assessment and may cause confusion for beginning teachers. Beginning teachers may find that they are expected to teach, and that students are expected to learn, skills and content that are not specified on the IEP but are encountered by students during a school day. IDEA 97 requires the IEP team to address how the student's disability impacts involvement and progress in the general education curriculum. As a result, beginning teachers must familiarize themselves with the general education curriculum and ensure that instructional content (whether delivered by the special educator in a self-contained classroom or resource setting, or via co-teaching with the general educator) and, consequently, assessment includes general education curriculum. The challenge for developing educators is to integrate several sources of information, including the general education curriculum, to determine instructional domains or units and then to assess students' current performance to provide a basis for planning units of instruction (see Chapter 5 for detailed information on planning instruction).

The domain or content area that will be targeted for instruction is determined by considering a variety of information sources. Students with disabilities have IEPs with annual measurable goals that indicate domains for instruction and short-term objectives or benchmarks that indicate what students will do. Measurable IEP goals can be written a variety of ways; beginning teachers should follow their school systems' format, as the style and wording can vary within and across states. Two goal formats are described here. The first format contains five components that summarize expectations for student performance within given domains of instruction (see Table 4.1 for examples of this format for goal statements):

1. *Direction* of the desired gain (e.g., increase, decrease, maintain)

2. *Deficit area* from which the student is operating (e.g., reading, written language, social skills)

TABLE 4.1   Examples of Exemplary Goal Statements from IEPs

Direction	Deficit area	Starting Point	Ending Point	Resource
Increase	reading skills	from third-grade level as measured by Woodcock Reading Mastery test	to the fourth-grade level as measured by Woodcock Reading Mastery test	using direct instruction teaching methods.
Decrease	inappropriate behaviors	from an average of five tantrums per day	to appropriately dealing with frustrating situations without a tantrum	using functional analysis and social skills training.
Increase	reading skills	from reading seven words per minute from a fourth-grade reading list	to reading ninety words per minute from a fourth-grade reading list	using peer tutoring and direct instruction techniques.
Increase	task completion	from turning in no homework or classroom assignments per week	to turning in all assignments	using self-management techniques.

3. *Starting point for instruction* (typically, similar to the student's present level of performance)

4. *Ending point for instruction* (level of performance the student is expected to attain in a year)

5. *Resources* (instructional methods or techniques from which the student is most likely to benefit, given the student's individual learning characteristics)

The second format for writing measurable annual goals is similar to the format used for behavioral objectives, described later in this chapter. For example, Bateman and Linden (1998) recommend using verbs that are observable, a measurement guide, a timeline, and information that clearly references the general education curriculum when appropriate: "By the end of the school year, Jeremy will be able to complete 85% of multiplication and division problems correctly on the district math test" (p. 135).

When IEP goals are vague (e.g., increase written language) or do not contain measurable information (e.g., the student's current performance level in written language, how written language increases will be measured, how written language can be linked to general education curriculum), then teachers should use the available IEP information to further develop more complete goal statements that do contain all components for instructional information purposes. Teachers can conduct further assessments (typically, these are classroom-based assessments, such as those described in this chapter) to determine where to start accomplishing the IEP goals. The available IEP information can help in both narrowing the possible curriculum areas and emphasizing the relevant curriculum content.

Short-term objectives on IEPs are directly related to the goal statements in that the objectives represent incremental and observable behaviors related to students' deficit areas that will denote and promote progress and growth. In this chapter, short-term objectives are conceptualized similar to benchmarks in that each represents sequential endpoints for instruction; IDEA 97 requires that short-term objectives or benchmarks accompany each measurable goal on an IEP. Consequently, the terms are used interchangeably. Again, beginning teachers will need to find out how their school system prefers or requires short-term objectives or benchmarks to be written, as formats may vary.

Short-term objectives or benchmarks may be written so that the timeline they reference is a unit of instruction (caution: this is typically more detailed information than required for an IEP, but excellent for planning instruction), a grading period (which may be more realistic to find on an IEP, and also prompts teachers to review the IEP content at the same time that teachers are reporting progress for students without IEPs-which is another IDEA '97 requirement), or a semester/half-year. Typically, a minimum of two objectives are written per goal statement on the IEP. Objectives describe sequences, or benchmarks, from which progress toward accomplishing an IEP goal can be measured. Exemplary IEP objectives contain information related to a student's observable behaviors, the conditions under which the behaviors should occur, and the degree or criteria that indicate a mastery performance. Each objective is assumed to refer to the student, or "audience," for whom the IEP is written. Many teachers use "ABCD" as a reminder when writing behavioral objectives:

- *Audience:* The student (other components of the objective explicitly address the student's learning characteristics and instructional needs)
- *Behavior:* The observable action performed by the student (the performance represents proficiency with the "content," ranging from low-order skills such as direct recall [e.g., spelling words correctly in a list] to high-order skills such as applying the skill in a unique format [e.g., spelling words correctly in a story])
- *Conditions:* The circumstances and/or materials used during assessment (the condition describes what is given to the student to perform the behavior [e.g., the content of the materials or the type of instructional cues])
- *Degree:* The criteria that indicate a mastery performance of the behavior (criteria include such descriptors as percentage, number of steps/items/trials, and duration that directly relate to the behavior and conditions portion of the objective)

Each of these parts (ABCD) is not merely required in exemplary behavioral objectives; their match to each other must be evident for objectives to have internal congruence, or to make sense when used together (see Table 4.2 for nonexamples of behavioral objectives and why they are nonexamples).

TABLE 4.2   Poor Behavioral Objectives

Poor Behavioral Objective	Why
Given 25 problems, the student will write the correct answer with 80% accuracy.	80% accuracy is not available with the number of problems in the condition, which is 25; 82%, accuracy would be available. Clarify the content of the 25 problems.
The student will improve written language.	Does not contain observable behavior, conditions, or degree/criteria.
Given words to read in isolation, the student will answer comprehension questions appropriately.	The stated conditions do not relate to the behavior. Specify how the student will answer the questions: Writing is required in some classes, and verbal answers are required in others. The type of comprehension questions may also be important: recall, inferential, prediction?
The student will accurately define social studies terms.	The conditions are missing; the way in which degree/criteria is noted is ambiguous.

TABLE 4.3   Examples of Well-Written Short-Term IEP Objectives

Conditions	Observable Behavior	Criteria/Degree of Behavior
Given 25 math computations on basic addition and subtraction facts,	the student will write the correct answer	to 23/25 (92%) of the computations.
From memory when asked to define a biology science term,	the student will verbally identify a definition	that includes the term's function and relationship to the body system.
When given the opportunity to perform a seven-step task,	the student will perform* the task	accurately with 7/7 steps.
From memory,	the student will write the definition to terms	correctly.
When given choices of tasks to complete,	the student will identify sequences of task completion in priority order	so that the first task, second task, and so on are sequentially ordered.
Provided with a job to complete and a due date,	the student will perform each function	so that the assignment is completed by the due date.
When faced with situations in which criticism of performance may occur,	the student will perform*	in a socially acceptable manner.*

* NOTE: These behaviors need further description (refinement) to be accurately observed. In behavioral terms, this refinement is called an "operational definition of behavior" (ODB). An ODB allows teachers to provide a sequence of observable behaviors that either *exemplify* or *lead to* the objective; these ODBs provide educators with a terminology (e.g., the "observable behavior") for succinctly identifying a behavior in the objective and further describing the constellation of behaviors (e.g., the sequence of behaviors that ultimately leads to the observable behavior) that the objective is intended to communicate to others (e.g., the student, parents, educators, and support personnel).

Careful thought and analytic preparation of behavioral objectives are foundational to preparing assessments for students with mild to moderate disabilities. See Table 4.3 for examples of behavioral objectives that contain each component (e.g., ABCD) and in which the components make sense when used together.

Even when IEP goals and objectives are well written, they may not give sufficient information for beginning teachers to plan instruction because of the influence of other variables on day-to-day teaching. To have a comprehensive idea of the areas that

Pause and Reflect 4.1

Hypothetically, the goals and objectives on students' IEPs should serve as guides to providing instruction for students with disabilities. Beginning teachers may find, however, that the IEP document does not give them enough information to begin daily instruction for a number of reasons. First, during the time lapse between the writing of the IEP and the start of instruction, students may either lose previously acquired prerequisite skills or make unexpected performance gains. Second, the goals and objectives may not address all areas in which students are required to participate in school. Third, goal statements and objectives may not be written in a way that clearly communicates expectations for students' performance in specific, observable, and measurable terms. Any of these inconsistencies between the IEP and expectations for students' performance in the educational setting will result in teachers needing to gather additional information about their students' entry-level competencies in relation to units or domains of instruction. Examine your students' actual performance levels, the daily expectations for them in school settings, and the IEP goals and objectives. Have your students' skills changed since the IEPs were written? Are any expectations for what they must do in school not addressed in the IEPs? Do the IEP goals and objectives clearly communicate what students should do? Your answers will influence your choice of instructional domains or units that you will teach first and for which you will assess students' entry-level competencies.

should be targeted for instruction, developing teachers should also keep in mind desired life outcomes for all students (What do students need to be successful when they transition from school to adult life?); expectations for students in school settings (What basic skills do students need to be successful academically, behaviorally, and socially in school settings?); and the curricula (materials, procedures, scope and sequence) used in the school (What resources are readily available? What content do the same-age students without disabilities experience in their classes?). Identifying areas to target for assessment prior to instruction requires teachers to look at the "big picture."

Once the domain or content area for instruction has been determined, teachers can identify students' current performance competencies in the targeted domain prior to beginning instruction. Informal inventories survey a sampling of key knowledge or skills within the domain. Commercially prepared inventories are available for many core achievement areas, including language arts, reading, and mathematics. These criterion-referenced devices usually contain a wide range of developmentally based skill sequences that provide educators "with lists of mastered and unmastered skills from which strengths and weaknesses as well as potential instructional objectives can be inferred" (Salvia & Ysseldyke, 1991, pp. 373–374). Teachers may develop their own inventories that correspond to the targeted domain and the local curriculum. The inventories should still address a broad spectrum of skills, beginner and advanced, from each domain (see Table 4.4). Because inventories provide a broad overview of students' performance within the entire domain, pretests within specific areas provide the teacher with more detailed information immediately prior to beginning a particular unit of instruction. These pretests can later be used as posttests. Similar to inventories, detailed pretests are available for some commercially prepared curriculum materials, or teachers may develop their own. The important feature of pretests is that they correspond to the material that will be taught. Once assessment of students' entry-level competencies has occurred, teachers can plan instruction that addresses the levels at which students perform independently, require instruction, and are frustrated.

Monitor Students' Performance During Instruction

The second activity in classroom assessment is to monitor students' performance during instruction in order to guide instructional content and methods; it includes deciding how to measure performance and designing the assessment device, administering the assessments, and responding to assessment results during future instruction. Prior to beginning instruction, teachers should develop the assessment devices and determine the assessment schedule that will be used to assess students' performance during instruction for both short-term and long-term goals and objectives. **Short-term assessments** measure progress during a particular unit of instruction; they typically encompass all the individual competencies taught within the lessons that comprise the unit. **Long-term assessments** measure progress toward annual goals; they typically encompass the major competencies taught within the units that comprise the annual goals. The assessment device used for the pretest may be reused or adapted (shortened or present different stimuli for the same skill) for performance monitoring. Between the onset and conclusion of instruction for unit and annual goals, teachers should administer assessments several times. Teachers who assess their students' performance consistently and frequently receive timely indicators of whether students are making the desired achievement gains and whether changes in instruction are warranted. (Chapter 5 covers the diagnostic teaching model, which details possible explanations for students' lack of progress and strategies for adjusting instruction.)

Determine Students' Mastery of Competencies

The third activity in classroom assessment is to measure students' mastery of competencies at the conclusion of instruction in order to confirm the effectiveness of instruc-

TABLE 4.4   Assessment Components Within Core Achievement Areas

Content Domain	Assessed Skills
Reading	*Decoding (accuracy then fluency)* • letter recognition and letter sound correspondence • sight vocabulary, phonics, and morphology *Comprehension* • paraphrasing (retelling orally or in writing) the gist of the passage • recall and inference • rate of oral reading
Mathematics	*Skill topics* • readiness skills, vocabulary, and concepts • numeration and whole number operations • fractions and decimals • ratios and percents • measurement • geometry *Skill format* • problem sets requiring computation • word problems requiring selection and application algorithm *Skill difficulty variations* • number of steps in solution • amount of extraneous information • explicit versus implicit indicators of mathematical operation
Written Language	*Penmanship* • letter formation and rudimentary spelling *Content* • number of words written • quality, sequencing, or coherence of ideas • consideration of the audience *Style* • grammar (e.g., subject-verb agreement) • mechanics (e.g., punctuation or sentence structure) • word choice
Language Arts	*Skill topics* • alphabetization and spelling • reference skills (e.g., dictionary, phone book, newspaper) • correspondence skills and filling out forms

Compiled from information in Salvia, J., & Ysseldyke, J. E. (1991). *Assessment* (5th ed.). Boston: Houghton Mifflin.

tion and students' readiness to proceed to the next unit of instruction (for details, see the discussion of the diagnostic teaching model in Chapter 5). Again, posttests may be available with curriculum materials, may be developed by teachers, and may be a readministration or adapted version of the pretest; however, the "posttest" device should correspond to what was taught.

Monitor Students' Maintenance and Generalization of Competencies

The final activity in classroom assessment is to monitor students' maintenance and generalization of competencies in order to determine whether additional teaching is needed. **Maintenance** refers to whether students remember what they have learned after instruction for that content has stopped. For example, do students who demonstrate mastery of addition and subtraction facts during the first month of school remember them in the second, third, or seventh month of school? Beginning teachers may find, to their dismay, that students who performed at a mastery level on the posttest seem to have forgotten how to add and subtract when they begin a unit on measurement. **Generalization** refers to whether students use what they have learned in one setting or situation in other settings and situations that are different from the original instructional context. For example, do students who spell words correctly on a spelling test also spell those words correctly when they write paragraphs? Developing teachers are often disappointed to find that students who perform skills in one context will not transfer use of the skill or information to other appropriate situations. Thus, even after instruction has ended for a particular unit, teachers should conduct follow-up assessments of students' maintenance and generalization of previously mastered competencies.

PRINCIPLES OF ASSESSMENT

Educators can select from a variety of formats (paper-and-pencil tasks, spontaneous reactions, impromptu performances, writing samples) and systems (authentic, performance, portfolio, curriculum-based) in developing and using assessments. Assessments can cover a range of skills (word identification, concept formation, problem solving, self-help, vocational), and the skills can represent content from different curricula (reading, math, writing, social studies, science, social skills, work-related). Assessments can also occur in a number of settings (special education classroom, general education classroom, work site, community settings). Regardless of what skills are assessed, what curriculum is being taught, where assessment occurs, or the type of assessment system used, three principles guide assessment for students with mild to moderate disabilities:

1. Critical skills are selected for assessment.

2. Data are collected in a systematic manner.

3. Data on student performance are collected frequently.

Principle 1: Critical Skills Are Selected for Assessment

Given the wide variety of skills (or outcomes or standards) taught in educational settings, it is impossible to monitor each skill. Multiple student behaviors contribute to students' progress in reading; varied work behaviors are needed for employees to receive a satisfactory job performance rating; and several skills are executed when students problem-solve in math. Teachers feel responsible for teaching and assessing a wide range of skills, yet the logistics of conducting extensive assessments on *each* skill is prohibitive: There is not enough time. Consequently, the first principle of assessment is that items representing critical skills or skill areas (benchmarks) are selected for assessment to serve as indicators of progress for a student within an instructional unit.

Although multiple objectives *could be written* and multiple assessments *could occur* to monitor each instructional activity within a domain or unit, a more efficient use of instructional time occurs when teachers select the critical skills, or key final skills, to serve as guides or benchmarks. These benchmarks enable a teacher to note student progress *toward the original objective*. In math, benchmarks might be student proficiency and fluency with solving particular types of computations and solving multistep word problems. In reading, critical skills might be fluent identification of words with certain types of patterns and answering recall and inferential questions about reading passages containing those words. A social studies curriculum unit might have critical skills such as identifying and defining the vocabulary, recalling important sequences of events, and discussing causes and effects of situations. For any content area of curriculum or set of skills identified, it will be impossible to "micro-assess" every skill. Consequently, teachers—*as they apply their knowledge of and skills with pedagogy*—target more specific objectives that represent critical concepts or skills within the curriculum or unit of instruction. Critical objectives represent the *ending* skills or concepts the teacher is teaching toward during the unit of instruction, *not each* skill or concept the teacher is teaching.

Principle 2: Data Are Collected in a Systematic Manner

Systematic data collection consists of using a predetermined plan for assessing students' progress that produces reliable and valid indicators of students' mastery of instructional objectives. Predetermination of instructional objectives is critical to systematic collection of data. When behavioral objectives are specified in advance, teachers are able to plan relevant instruction *and* assessment. Although a variety of activities may be used to accomplish any objective, the focal point during assessment remains systematic collection of information on the objective, and not on extraneous or irrelevant information.

When teachers informally monitor students' involvement in academic activities during instruction and students successfully complete those activities, some educators claim that this form of observational information is sufficient for noting whether students are acquiring the targeted skills. Fuchs and Fuchs (1984), however, found that teachers' informal observation of students during activities does not necessarily provide reliable and valid information *related to the lesson's goals and objectives*; that is, some teachers note that the student enjoyed the lesson or participated in the activity or was able to get the answer correct when cues were given. Although this information is interesting and can help guide the teacher about some aspects of instructional content and contexts, it may not be an accurate or reliable indicator of students' mastery of the targeted skills. Reliable and valid assessments produce results that dependably measure the skills the teacher was intending to assess.

Reliability. **Reliability** refers to the extent to which assessment results are generalizable. In other words, reliable assessments provide similar information about students' performance competencies whether or not students are assessed with a different version of the assessment (alternate form or internal-consistency reliability), by a different person (interrater or interscorer reliability), or at a different time (stability or test-retest reliability). Although there are quantitative methods for determining the reliability of assessments, beginning teachers may find it helpful to ask themselves three questions related to the reliability of the classroom assessments they develop. Assuming no additional teaching or practice,

1. Will students perform similarly on a different version of the test that contains items within the target domain?

2. Will another person (an instructional assistant, another teacher, a parent volunteer) who scores the students' performance on the assessment device obtain the same results?

3. Will students perform similarly (with similar levels of mastery) in the assessed area if they are assessed again at a different time?

Each version of the test should contain a similar sampling of the skills being taught, but not necessarily identical items. For example, to assess students' mastery of addition operations that have two-digit addends requiring regrouping, teachers would provide different sets of math problems each time, but each set should require students to perform the targeted computation skill. In other words, the problem set, but not the computation skill, would vary from one test administration to the next. The extent to which the different versions of the assessment require students to use the same skills is an indicator of **alternate form reliability**.

The scoring guidelines for the assessment should be explicit enough that students' scores would be the same if two (or more) people were to evaluate students' performance. Interscorer reliability is easily obtained for factual items that have a clearly recognizable right or wrong response, as in spelling, decoding, mathematical computations, or direct recall of content. The more or less defined the range of acceptable responses, the greater the variability among scorers may be and the less students may understand what signifies a mastery performance. Explicit scoring guidelines are important so that students understand the performance expectations and teachers know whether students have mastered the objectives. The extent to which two people using the same guidelines evaluate students' performance in the same way is an indicator of **interrater reliability**.

The way assessment items or components are presented should require that students actually know the content or perform the skill in order to receive mastery scores. If students' performance is highly variable from one administration of the assessment to the next (in the absence of new teaching or practice), then variables other than the targeted skills may be responsible for the performance variations, and the teacher cannot be certain that students have attained mastery. The extent to which assessments require students to demonstrate a particular skill and reduce the opportunities for a "chance" performance is an indicator of **test-retest reliability**.

Beginning teachers may be most concerned with interscorer reliability. Overall reliability will be enhanced, however, when the content of assessments "is equivalent from test to test or probe to probe; [and] . . . test directions, kinds of cues or hints, testing formats, criteria for correct responses, and type of score (for example, rates or percentage correct) . . . [are] the same" (Salvia & Ysseldyke, 1991, p. 557).

Validity. **Valid assessment** means that the skills measured are indeed the skills purported to be measured. Salvia and Ysseldyke (1991) note that the validity of an assessment is inferred from a variety of information, and they identify three interrelated types of validity: content validity, criterion-related validity, and construct validity. **Content validity** will be the primary focus of beginning teachers for the assessments they develop. Salvia and Ysseldyke recommend evaluating three factors to determine content validity: "the appropriateness of the types of items included, the completeness of the item sample, and the way in which items assess the content" (p. 146). When assessments require students to respond to content taken directly from the materials used during instruction and to perform tasks similar to those encountered during instruction, content validity is seldom a problem. If students are taught strategies for solving word problems and if the assessment requires students to solve similar word problems for which the strategies are appropriate, then content validity should be satisfied. However, if students are taught strategies for solving addition and subtraction word problems only and if the assessment requires application of multiplication and division strategies to solve word problems, then content validity is not satisfied. Furthermore, the types of word problems selected need to include dimensions of content that are faithful to the types of word problems originally selected for the instructional objective. If the teacher intended the student to solve problems involving multiple steps and varied computational skills, then the word problems used to measure that objective need to include multiple steps and varied computations.

Gersten, Keating, and Irvin (1995) expand the technical features of validity to include social and instructional validity. To ensure that assessment is valid for informing instruction, they challenge researchers to "present evidence indicating that the assessment information is in fact used by teachers as intended and that it results in improved student learning" (p. 510). Teachers who develop sound assessment practices, yet do not use those results to make necessary changes in instruction, are not sufficiently fulfilling the *purpose* of the assessment process: to guide teaching.

Principle 3: Data on Student Performance Are Collected Frequently

Frequent collection of data encompasses, at the very least, the use of pretests and posttests. **Pretests** confirm that students know prerequisite information and do not yet know the targeted content. **Posttests** confirm that students have learned the targeted content. Yet, pretests and posttests do not inform the teacher how well students are learning while the instructional unit is in progress. Teachers who wait until the posttest to gather such critical information are missing timely opportunities to reteach content in different ways during the instructional unit. Thus, data should be collected on several occasions between the pretest and posttest dates, especially for students with special needs, who may benefit from alternative instructional strategies. Frequent data collection provides the teacher with information about how well students are acquiring the content while instruction is occurring.

APPROACHES TO CLASSROOM ASSESSMENT

Traditionally, educational services for students with mild to moderate disabilities have been delivered by special educators in resource rooms, self-contained classrooms, or special schools. Consequently, assessment practices in the past largely focused on students' individual academic or social achievements within a relatively controlled environment, with small groups of students present for instruction, and with specific educational materials and practices as the cornerstone for education. Recent emphasis on inclusion of students with all types and severities of disabilities, however, has resulted in more students, including those with mild to moderate disabilities, being educated in general education classrooms (Cullen & Pratt, 1992; IDEA 97). Additionally, emphasis has also been placed on the uses of community-based environments to promote students' opportunities to learn and practice skills in the authentic environment within which they are expected to perform. In short, educational classrooms for students with mild to moderate disabilities *used to be* primarily special education classrooms; now those classrooms may also be general education classrooms, work environments, community environments, and activities and locations around the school, such as recess, lunch, and homeroom. The expansion of where the classroom is for students may affect the assessment parameters that teachers use to monitor instruction, as well as the types of skills and strategies the teachers are teaching. **Authentic assessment** is one of several terms used recently in general education. Other new terms are **performance assessment** and **portfolio assessment**. In the next section, we define and describe each of these terms and provide examples of how each system can be used for students with mild to moderate disabilities. Next, we describe curriculum-based assessment. **Curriculum-based assessment (CBA)** is a system of assessment that has a solid research base for students with mild to moderate disabilities and can be directly linked to making instructional decisions to ensure that students are achieving instructional objectives regardless of the setting where instruction occurs.

Authentic, Performance, and Portfolio Assessment

Authentic Assessment. Archbald (1991) notes that the term **authentic assessment** has been used more frequently and recently to represent varied interpretations of what meaningful, valuable, and realistic assessments can provide. Elliott (1992) describes authentic assessment as involving assessment activities like those commonly used in the world outside the classroom. Authentic assessments occur in the real environment and consequently require the student to perform behaviors that will successfully allow him or her to meet authentic setting demands.

The practice of authentic assessments is not new to education, although the application of the concept and terminology has increased in recent years. Poteet, Choate, and

Stewart (1993) note that authentic assessments have traditionally been used in vocational education (consider on-the-job performance ratings), music education (e.g., participating in a recital), and sports programs (when students ultimately perform in competitions or games). Not only are students' behaviors assessed in these arenas by professionals who are typically evaluating individuals or teams according to exemplary standards, but there are also elements of students' self-evaluating their performance in the light of familiar standards for which they are striving. Authentic assessment occurs when student performance is measured both within realistic setting demands and in real-life contexts.

In special education, generalization of a student's target behavior occurs when the student uses the skill or behavior in a real-life setting. In a classroom setting, a student may be learning to read words that have varied sound patterns (e.g., consonant blends, digraphs). Generalization occurs when the student can automatically read words with those patterns whenever those words are seen: in another book, on a bulletin board, or in a magazine. The authentic assessment, or generalization, of the student's reading skill occurs when the student encounters a situation in which words with similar patterns need to be identified and the student can identify the words correctly.

Another example of an authentic assessment, or generalization, is when a student is learning to complete a series of tasks for a "job" and he or she accurately completes those tasks in a way that satisfies the "employer." The job could be clearing and cleaning a work area (e.g., the student's desk, the student's bedroom, the office area at a work site), and the employer may be the student's teacher, parent, or supervisor. The student receives instruction for identifying the tasks that need to be completed, putting them in sequential order, and making decisions on how well the job must be performed. The employer constructs a checklist with this information and teaches the student how to use the checklist. Assessment of the student's use of the checklist may initially occur during instruction using simulated situations. The authentic assessment, however, occurs when the student is able to accurately and satisfactorily complete the tasks on the checklist when the appropriate situation arises.

Authentic assessment links very well with special education's emphasis on teaching and assessing skills within the actual environments in which students must perform. In fact, the concept of *teaching for generalization* is directly connected to the concept of *authentic assessment*. If students can use their learned academic and social skills with specialized instruction only in artificial environments with controlled materials and cues (e.g., the therapy room, the special education classroom, with only small groups of students present, when given a cue from the teacher), then the specialized instruction is not yet completed. The true assessment of instruction occurs when students can automatically and proficiently use behaviors and skills in real settings and situations. Student performance in authentic situations, with authentic setting demands, and even with authentic

*P*ause and Reflect 4.2

Examples of authentic assessments for students with disabilities include (1) when a student with an emotional or behavioral disorder responds appropriately to classmates who are making fun of her during recess, (2) when a student with a learning disability in reading correctly pronounces words when verbally reading paragraphs from a science text during a lesson, (3) when a student with moderate mental retardation correctly follows verbal directions while participating in a cooperative group activity, and (4) when a student with a learning disability in mathematics is able to use a calculator in a grocery store to determine when he has overspent his budget. What authentic assessments are already occurring for your students? What additional opportunities do you have to structure authentic assessments? Would identifying opportunities for authentic assessment assist you in teaching your students to generalize skills and behaviors to functionally relevant situations?

consequences, is the ultimate aim of all instruction, whether the instruction is programmed and delivered by special educators, general educators, related service personnel, or employers. Educators should be teaching toward and measuring authentic results of instruction. It is also appropriate, however, that measurement of skills and behaviors occurs in nonauthentic situations during instruction. Performance assessment can be used when the demands, expectations, and behaviors are similar to, or simulated for, authentic situations.

Performance Assessment. When student behaviors occur in a simulated environment or in more controlled or "planned for" contexts, then the assessment may be identified as **performance assessment**. Note that when students' performance occurs in authentic situations, the accurate term is *authentic assessment*. Sometimes, however, authentic demands can be used within simulated situations so that the same or similar student performance is required but the situation has not occurred within the "true" environment.

Meyer (1992) describes aspects of performance assessments that are authentic in nature. She delineates multiple features of tasks that can be considered authentic: the stimuli presented, the complexity of the tasks, and the standards developed for performance (see Table 4.5).

The Office of Technology Assessment (U.S. Congress, 1992) defines *performance assessment* as students' creation or construction of knowledge, or what students do with

TABLE 4.5   Authentic Features of Performance Tasks

Task Feature	Question for Teachers	Example of Feature
Stimuli	Is the stimulus used identical to the stimulus encountered in real life?	Student can use a variety of vending machines to get a snack.
Task complexity	Does the task represent the difficultylevel encountered in real situations?	Student completes a job application that hasnot been redeveloped for his or her reading level.
Spontaneity	Can the student perform the task when the situation requires it?	Student interacts appropriately with peers and adults throughout the day.
Conditions	Are the conditions present during assessment similar or identical to the conditions present in real life?	Student reads independently without someone there to tell him or her the words.
Criteria	Is the performance standard required in actual situations also required in the assessment situation?	Student must complete all steps in the task of making coffee, not 80% accuracy.
Locus of control	Is the student responsible for initiating or completing a response?	When the bus door opens, the student boards the bus before it departs.
Resources	Is the availability of materials similar to actual situations?	Student must locate art supplies and bring them to the work area.
Consequences	Are the consequences for performance similar to the consequences in real life?	Student gets to drink the soda after putting the correct change in the vending machine.

Features derived from Meyer, C. A. (1992). What's the difference between authentic and performance assessment? *Educational Leadership, 49*(8), p. 40.

TABLE 4.6   Descriptions and Examples of Performance Assessments

Type of Performance Assessment	Description	Examples
Constructed-response items	Students produce or construct their own answers.	• Mathematics calculation • Geometry proofs • Drawing graphs • Fill-in-the-blank • Matching • Definitions • Short written answers • Essays
Essays and writing assessment	Students' writing ability, and knowledge and understanding of content, is assessed.	• Direct writing sample in response to a writing prompt or question
Interviews and direct observations	Students verbally respond to or actively demonstrate knowledge.	• Give spoken response on or discuss a given topic • Perform tasks that have been taught in a simulated situation and/or spontaneously in a real situation • Observe dialogue of students spontaneously engaged in an academic activity • Collect work samples
Exhibitions	Students produce comprehensive products, presentations, or performances for the public.	• Recital • Cumulation of activities, projects, or demonstrations is aggregated and displayed • Debate • Individual or group competitions • Dramatic presentation • Group project
Experiments	Students demonstrate the process of planning, conducting, and writing up experiments	• Hands-on manipulative skills tasks • May include teamwork and interpersonal skills
Portfolios	Students contribute work samples to files, folders that portray their learning profile through documenting their experiences and accomplishments.	• Drafts and final products • Self-reflection

Constructed from information in U.S. Congress, Office of Technology Assessment. (1992). *Performance assessment: Methods and characteristics*. In *Testing in American schools: Asking the right questions* (OTA SET-519, pp. 201–249). Washington, DC: Government Printing Office.

what they know. The Office identifies six types—and related examples—of performance assessment: (1) constructed-response items, (2) essays and writing assessments, (3) interviews and direct observations, (4) exhibitions, (5) experiments, and (6) portfolios (see Table 4.6). Examples include when the student is assessed (1) during a role-play situation in which the student practices appropriate responses to criticism from peers, (2) during an oral reading of material that is similar to grade-level material, (3) while following a specific set of directions during a contrived group activity, and (4) while solving a math problem on a worksheet. Regardless of which method is selected, educators must predetermine criteria for successful performance in order to (1) explain criteria to the student before and during instruction, (2) have a basis for dialoguing with the student during feedback sessions about his or her performance, and (3) develop valid and reliable assessment formats. Sarouphim (1999) notes that performance-based assessments must clearly and logically link to specific activities in order to be credible and effective. *Several features of performance assessment can resemble the real-life, or authentic, situation.* Teachers should be sure to incorporate those features into their assessment sequence even when the authentic situation cannot be used. Actually, many types of performances can serve as documentation of a student's progress. Teachers can use a portfolio format to assist them in documenting such performances.

Portfolio Assessment. **Portfolio assessment** can be conceptualized as an innovative notation of students' performances related to instructional objectives and can conceivably be an alternative "gradebook" for a teacher. The portfolio itself can be a folder, notebook, or some other "holder" of student work products. Paulson, Paulson, and Meyer (1991) describe a portfolio as

> a purposeful collection of student work that exhibits the student's efforts, progress, and achievements in one or more areas. The collection must include student participation in selecting contents, the criteria for selection, the criteria for judging merit, and evidence of student self-reflection. (p. 60)

Paulson et al. emphasize the importance of *what type of information* the portfolio is intended to communicate. A folder that merely holds a student's work does not represent portfolio assessment; decisions about what type of work can be placed into a portfolio and how that work relates to curriculum (or IEP) goals and objectives must be clearly identified and discussed with the student. Paulson et al. suggest that teachers clearly identify the purpose of the portfolio, the type of content that can be included in it, the goals the student is working toward, and the standards for determining the quality of the content (see Table 4.7 for examples of these and other related questions for portfolio content).

TABLE 4.7   Questions for Determining Portfolio Content

Question	Recommendation
1. Is the portfolio's purpose identified?	Clarify how the portfolio will be used in determining grades, guiding instruction, deciding content for instruction, and so on.
2. How closely will the portfolio content parallel the IEP/curriculum?	Link the content of the portfolio directly to the IEP and curriculum.
3. What type of content can be included in the portfolio?	Discuss with the student ways to make decisions about what goes into the portfolio. Content may also include alternative assessment formats such as projects and results from a role-play.
4. What are the standards for lthe content in the portfolio?	The teacher and student should be well aware of what an excellent product, or project, looks like. The criteria for selecting content may parallel the criteria statement of a behavioral objective.
5. How much student involvement will be elicited, and when?	Inform the student at the beginning of instruction what his or her choices are for including portfolio content. Guide the student initially in portfolio selection of content. Allow the student to make independent choices as he or she demonstrates more proficiency with making decisions.
6. How many purposes can the portfolio serve?	Use fewer purposes that coincide, rather than more purposes that may fragment, isolate, or confuse the critical instructional objectives. The portfolio can inform the teacher about the student's progress, thinking processes, and preferences for demonstrating proficiency.
7. To what extent should growth and progress be evident in the portfolio content?	Growth and progress should be evident to a great extent. Furthermore, the teacher may want to include (for his or her future use) what methods were used to more consistently promote growth and progress.

Work products in a portfolio can represent either work in progress (e.g., writing outlines, drafts of a report being written) or the final sample of work completed (e.g., the report that was turned in for a grade or for teacher evaluation). Work contained in a portfolio may be chosen by the teacher independently or by the student and teacher together. Teacher and student collaboration—about deciding what goes in the portfolio, and why, and how that work represents student growth and progress related to instruction—is desired, and in some cases is required, so that the portfolio represents assessment content decided *with* the student, not *for* the student. Duffy, Jones, and Thomas (1999) describe how portfolios can be used to promote independent thinking with students because they are encouraged to learn and use self-evaluation skills.

In addition to work products directly related to an academic area, *the information in a portfolio may also contain the student's comments and reflections on how well he or she is learning and what he or she is learning from the academic content.* More extensive content from a wide variety of sources can also be used in portfolios. For example, Viechnicki, Barbour, Shaklee, Rohrer, and Ambrose (1993) describe portfolio content that teachers developed for each student that included teacher anecdotal accounts of student learning, observations from lessons that were designed to elicit evidence of exceptional potential and performance, information from parents and/or peers, and examples of products produced by the student.

Nolet (1992) discusses portfolio assessment as a process that can be used for *either instructional or assessment* purposes, and his points can help guide teachers in clarifying their purposes for portfolio assessment. He distinguishes between *uses* of a portfolio that make it appropriate for assessment purposes versus instructional purposes. For example, if the purpose of the portfolio is assessment, then teachers need to ensure the reliability and validity of the portfolio contents in relation to instructional goals and objectives. In other words, teachers must view the content selected for inclusion in the portfolio in relation to technical adequacy for assessing students' performance competencies. For an instructional portfolio, in contrast, teachers may be less concerned with technical features of the student work included in the portfolio; indeed, the student may select work to include that he or she believes reflects progress and performance but that the teacher knows does not represent reliable or valid measures (e.g., the student had much assistance in completing the work vs. completed the work independently).

Student involvement in determining content is desired. By including the student's reasons for *why* he or she selected a particular piece of work to include in the portfolio, the teacher can use the portfolio assessment process as an opportunity to gain insight into what the student is thinking about his or her learning experiences. Including the student's preferences for demonstration of knowledge (e.g., writing a report, constructing a model, developing a timeline, reflecting on his or her work) not only encourages student involvement and decision-making but also is an excellent method of increasing student motivation and responsibility in the learning process.

Authentic, performance, and portfolio assessments represent relatively recent initiatives in general education. At this time, however, the research base on how well these assessments work for students with disabilities is relatively scarce, although some research is beginning to emerge (Nolet, 1992; Poteet et al., 1993; Sarouphim, 1999). Certainly, the basic premises of these assessment systems apply to the performance demands for students with mild to moderate disabilities, and flexibility for differentiated performance standards (e.g., the standard for a student with learning disabilities may be different from that of a student who is gifted) is available. Creative special educators can develop parallel and appropriate formats for students with mild to moderate disabilities that allow students to participate in assessment formats similar to those used by general educators. An assessment system that does have a research base for teaching and assessing students with mild to moderate disabilities is CBA (Deno, 1985; Deno & Fuchs, 1987; Fuchs & Fuchs, 1985; Salvia & Hughes, 1990). We describe CBA next, with suggestions for incorporating aspects of authentic, performance, and portfolio assessment systems.

FIGURE 4.1   APPLY as a Framework for Developing and Using CBA

King-Sears, M. E. (1994). *Curriculum-based assessment in special education* (p. 17). San Diego: Singular. Reprinted by permission.

1. **A NALYZE** the curriculum.
2. **P REPARE** items to meet the curriculum objectives.
3. **P ROBE** frequently.
4. **L OAD** data using a graph format.
5. **Y IELD** to results—revisions and decisions.

Curriculum-Based Assessment

Elliott (1992) refers to **curriculum-based assessment (CBA)** as observation techniques of student's behavior that link assessment results to instructional interventions. CBA can be used as a formative assessment technique during instruction. Fuchs and Fuchs (1984) found that teachers who (1) conducted formative assessments during instruction, (2) used results from those assessments to change their teaching, and (3) graphically displayed those results to assist them in decision-making were able to increase their students' academic achievement and to use instructional time more productively than teachers who did not conduct and use formative assessments. Although a variety of definitions and interpretations of CBA are used in the literature (e.g., Blankenship, 1985; Fuchs & Deno, 1991; Salvia & Hughes, 1990), the definition of CBA used for this chapter is based on the following principles of effective instruction:

* Observable behavior of critical student performances related to the curriculum being taught is used.
* Frequent and brief measurements of student behavior occur prior to, during, and after instructional units.
* Measurements are graphically displayed.
* Students and teachers use the graphic displays to make instructional decisions.

Systematically observing key student behaviors related to instructional content includes two of the principles of assessment presented earlier in this chapter: Critical skills are selected for assessment, and data are collected in a systematic manner. Methods for teachers' development and use of CBA have been described in as many as 11 and as few as 4 steps (e.g., Blankenship, 1985; Salvia & Hughes, 1990). *APPLY* is a mnemonic that synthesizes the steps for teachers' development and use of CBA (Jorden & Haube, 1995; King-Sears, 1994; King-Sears, Burgess, & Lawson, 1999). In the next section, we describe APPLY as a framework for developing and using CBA (see Figure 4.1). We also provide case studies about students with mild to moderate disabilities in elementary and secondary grades to illustrate varied examples of CBA in different content areas.

APPLY FRAMEWORK FOR DEVELOPING CLASSROOM ASSESSMENTS

Before using the APPLY framework to develop a CBA, teachers acquire critical information about the student from a variety of sources (e.g., IEPs, confidential files, parents, other teachers, standardized assessments, informal assessments, other CBAs, the student him- or herself). These sources provide indicators of the curriculum from which the student should be working and a general idea of the curriculum level in which the student can satisfactorily perform. APPLY can be used as an initial diagnostic framework for determining a student's instructional curriculum and level. It can also be used as an ongoing diagnostic framework throughout the year when a student is progressing from unit to unit within a curriculum area.

Analyze the Curriculum. Target from the curriculum the critical objectives that will serve as benchmarks or indicators that the student is learning the content. For reading or social studies, for example, the new vocabulary throughout a unit of instruction and the types of comprehension questions used may represent benchmarking. Social studies curriculum might also include definitions of key terms or foundational concepts. Mathematics curriculum could include specific types of computations and word problems. Vocational curriculum could be comprised of a checklist of tasks to perform on a work site. A social-emotional curriculum might target specific verbal and nonverbal behaviors related to interpersonal skills.

Regardless of which curriculum is used, the teacher needs to predetermine the areas of the curriculum that can serve as critical markers *across* the instructional unit. Those markers can comprise low- and high-order thinking skills. A CBA cannot assess all information taught or anticipated for a student to learn; key objectives need to be specified in advance. Consider that the key objectives are critical to a student's further understanding and use of the major information in the unit or domain.

Nolet (1992) notes that validity of portfolio assessments increases when teachers clarify the goals of instruction in a particular skill or knowledge area, design tasks that representatively sample those goals, administer the tasks reliably, and aggregate those data to arrive at conclusions about student performance. Teachers clarify the goals of instruction by analyzing the curriculum, determining the important goals, and specifying the behavioral objectives that will be used to monitor student progress related to the goals.

As has already been described, behavioral objectives specify observable student behaviors, the conditions under which the behaviors occur, and the criteria that indicate mastery of the objective (refer to Table 4.3 for examples of behavioral objectives that could guide the development of CBAs). After each component of the objective is determined, the method for assessing the objective can be developed more easily and clearly.

Prepare Items to Meet the Curriculum Objectives. Once the key objectives are targeted, the teacher develops short assessments, or probes, that can be used throughout instruction to elicit student responses. (Note: *Probe* is used both as a noun and a verb in CBA terminology. *Probe* is a noun when it represents the format used to elicit student responses; *probe* is a verb when it represents the act of eliciting student responses on a CBA.)

The item format is constructed so that it is brief in duration. It is useful to place a time limit on how long the student will be given to respond. In developing—and, ultimately, administering—the CBA probe, teachers should address several time-related issues. First, the time limit can help teachers note both students' acquisition and performance fluency of content. For example, students may be able to compute math problems when given enough time to count the facts by using blocks, an indication that acquisition of the math concepts is occurring at a concrete level. Also important, however, is how quickly the student can compute math at the abstract level. A CBA that allows only a brief amount of time can provide that information. Second, a time limit is used to maximize the gathering of critical information in a minimal amount of time so that instructional decisions can be made more frequently. Allotting 20 minutes 3 days per week to gather CBA data may not be the best use of instructional time; 2 minutes on three occasions during the week is more realistic and manageable for teachers. Third, the time limit is not used to increase students' anxiety for an assessment; prior to administering the CBA, teachers should discuss with students that the CBA is not for a test grade, but rather to get indicators of student progress. See Table 4.8 for examples of brief CBAs.

Teachers should consider, when preparing items related to key curriculum objectives, how quickly relevant information can be acquired. Moreover, teachers need to consider the correlation between key learning that is representational of, or foundational to, more comprehensive learning. For example, students who are able to identify words quickly and correctly are better able to understand the reading passages they read. Consequently, CBA probes on the correct words per minute are helpful. Students

TABLE 4.8   Examples of CBA Brief Probes with Time Limit for Noting a Student's Acquisition and Fluency Rates

Content Area	Time	Description of CBA
Reading	1 minute	The probes are reading passages, which may be selected from any content area. The student reads aloud for 1 minute. Conduct CBA two times per week with each individual. Graph the number of words read correctly and incorrectly.
Math	2 minutes	The probe is a worksheet of math computations. The student solves as many problems as possible in 2 minutes. Conduct CBA three times per week by using group administration. Graph the number of digits computed correctly and incorrectly.
Spelling	2 minutes	The probe is an oral or audiotaped dictation of spelling words. Conduct CBA four times per week by using group administration. Graph the number of correct letter sequences or the number of words spelled correctly or incorrectly.
Written Language	3 minutes	The probe is a story opener, which may be a topic or a brief story starter situation. The student elaborates on the story opener by writing for 3 minutes. Conduct CBA one time per week by using group administration. Graph the total number of words written, number of words spelled correctly, or other salient aspects.

King-Sears, M. E. (1994). *Curriculum-based assessment in special education* (p. 21). San Diego: Singular. Reprinted by permission.

who can identify the correct steps to solve a problem are better prepared to use those steps in solving a problem; a CBA might probe their ability to correctly identify the steps. Another CBA probe might elicit information on the correct application of the steps to a novel problem.

When preparing items to meet the targeted curriculum objectives, teachers can consider (1) providing a prompt for writing a response, (2) developing a checklist of behaviors required for completing a task, (3) listing words to identify, (4) designating words to define, and (5) describing a set of requisite behaviors. Regardless of the item format, teachers must consider the validity and reliability of the items in relation to the curriculum and instructional objectives. For example, listing steps in a problem-solving process can be used as a CBA when the objective is that the student can correctly list those steps. That CBA will not indicate, however, whether the student can apply the steps to novel situations. A CBA that provides a situation and requires the student to demonstrate using the problem-solving process to arrive at a solution would be more appropriate. Although the ultimate goal of instruction may be that the student independently applies problem-solving processes and uses an appropriate solution when faced with varied situations (an excellent example of generalization or authentic assessment), the initial CBA may have a more limited focus, such as the student's recall of the problem-solving steps, or the student's ability to provide examples of how to use the problem-solving sequence when given a situation, or the student's identification of appropriate solutions for solving a problem.

Probe Frequently. Teachers should conduct brief CBAs two or three times a week. This frequency cannot be maintained if the CBAs require extensive instructional time to conduct. For that reason, brief CBAs are more desirable, manageable, and practical for teachers to use with consistency. Some teachers are able to use CBA probes daily (which is the most desirable frequency); other teachers are able to conduct CBA probes weekly (which is less desirable, but better than not conducting any probes during instruction).

Consider the time lapse between a pretest and a posttest: CBA occurs between the pretest and the posttest and lets the teacher and students know that progress is occurring. Teachers who assess students' performance only at the end of instructional units are not able to make changes during instruction; by the time they know that the student or students are not "getting it," the end-of-unit test has already occurred—it's too late to make teaching changes. CBA functions as a frequent formative assessment that helps guide instruction for the teacher and learning for the student. Periodic assessments, or probes, during instruction ensure that teachers are gathering information that allows them to make teaching changes while instruction is occurring.

Load Data Using a Graph Format. After each probe is administered and evaluated, the score is plotted on a graph. The date of the assessment or the session number of the probe is identified on the horizontal axis. The assessed skill or competency, with its corresponding measure (e.g., percentage or number correct, number per minute), is identified on the vertical axis. It is important to plot the data point on the graph as soon as possible after the CBA is administered so that a timely and accurate performance line can be drawn. A delay in plotting students' data points reduces the usefulness of the CBA for making instructional decisions.

The graphic format of recording data accomplishes multiple purposes. First, the visual depiction provides teachers with a means to analyze students' performance and to make instructional decisions. Second, the visual depiction provides students with a concrete representation of their actual performance. Third, graphs provide parents with a visual representation of their child's progress. Fourth, the performance graphs provide other teachers with a quick comparison of individual students' current and previous progress and a guide for grouping students for instruction. When data are graphed, students can more efficiently note their progress (e.g., an ascending progress line), teachers can more readily know when to make changes in instruction (e.g., a stable or descending line indicates that teaching changes are needed), and others can more fully note ongoing performance (e.g., parents can see the results of their child's performance related to IEP objectives over time). Some teachers find computer-graphing applications to be an excellent time-saver for graphing.

Yield to Results—Revisions and Decisions. The visual depiction of a student's performance is used to make decisions about instruction. Wesson, Skiba, Sevcik, King, and Deno (1984) found that some teachers require extensive training or continuing support in order to use data to make ongoing changes in their instruction. Hasbrouck, Woldbeck, Ihnot, and Parker (1999) found that one teacher who was initially resistant to using curriculum-based measurement became convinced of its value after seeing the impact on student performance *and* receiving technical support and assistance. King-Sears, Burgess, and Lawson (1999) describe how the use of CBA in general education classrooms can more actively involve students in decision-making discussions and subsequent actions (e.g., students decide how they'd like to study information they still need to learn). In other words, for developing teachers, the issue may be how to make decisions based on the data, not how to collect and graph data. As Gersten et al. (1995) note, social and instructional validity of assessments does not occur unless the teacher uses assessment results to improve a student's future performance. Several techniques can be used to evaluate data: the 3-day rule, aimline performance, and quarter-intersect.

The **3-day, or three-session, rule** refers to any set of three consecutive connected data points on the graph. If the trend (direction) of the line connecting the three most recent consecutive data points is in the desired (either increasing or decreasing) direction, then the student is making progress, current instructional procedures seem to be effective, and instruction should continue in the present manner. However, if the trend of the line connecting the most recent three data points is not in the desired direction or plateaus, then "it's time for a teaching change," and subsequent revisions of instruction should be planned.

Aimline performance is a modification of the 3-day rule in which a line is drawn on the graph to connect the student's initial (sometimes considered baseline) data point and the desired data point *and* session in which the teacher anticipates the student will have mastered the objective. Decisions using the aimline are made when data points fall below the aimline for three consecutive sessions; that is, progress may be occurring, but the progress is not at the anticipated rate. Instructional changes made when aimline is not being met include revising teaching methods, dialoguing with the student about how to improve the performance, intensifying the amount of practice, and reteaching major concepts. In some cases, a decision may be made to revise the aimline and set a more reasonable aim for that student, although a decision to do this should be preceded by instructional alternatives to enhance performance toward the original aimline.

The **quarter-intersect method** can be used when seven or more data points are plotted and teachers use the following procedure to develop a line of progress:

1. Divide the number of data points in half by drawing a vertical line down the graph (midsession).

2. On the left half of the graph, find the midsession and draw a vertical line (middate).

3. On the left half of the graph, find the midperformance point and draw a horizontal line (midrate).

4. Repeat steps 2 and 3 on the right half of the graph.

5. Draw a line connecting the intersections (the intersection of the horizontal [midrate] and vertical [middate] lines from steps 2 and 3) of both halves of the graph. This is the quarter-intersect trend line.

6. Teachers may wish to further refine the line of progress by using the split-middle method so that an equal number of data points fall above and below the line; start by counting the number of data points that fall above and below the line.

7. If the same number of data points are on and above the line as are on and below the line, then stop. The trend line is accurate.

8. If an unequal number of data points are on and above the line as are on and below the line, then move the line up or down until there is a balance of points above and below the line.

The resulting trend line may be ascending, descending, or stable. The trend line can be compared with the slope of the aimline to determine whether the aimline should be raised or lowered. The quarter-intersect trendline can be especially helpful when developing long-range goal data because the teacher can use consistent performance on CBAs from the current year to develop realistic goals for the following year on the basis of current rate of performance.

The case studies presented next describe how teachers have used CBA in a variety of settings and with students who have a range of mild to moderate disabilities. Throughout the case studies, note how teachers have used CBA for themselves to make instructional decisions and revisions and how they have used CBA to benefit their students by (1) showing progress and performance in a more concrete manner, (2) encouraging goal setting, (3) sharing responsibility for learning, and (4) increasing motivation.

APPLY Case Study 1: Fractions and Decimals

Analyze the Curriculum. Ms. Joseph is teaching in a self-contained classroom of fourth- and fifth-grade students with emotional or behavioral disorders. She is responsible for delivering math instruction to each student (according to IEP goals and objectives), and during the math period, she is responding to varied levels of knowledge related to decimals and fractions. The school year has just begun, so she is determining what students know already about this area of mathematics. Her curriculum objective is:

> Given fractions to convert to decimals and decimals to convert to fractions, the student will correctly convert each problem.

Prepare Items to Meet the Curriculum Objectives. Because Ms. Joseph is surveying her class for a variety of learning levels in math, she develops a probe sheet featuring single items pertaining to benchmark math objectives from all curricula. The CBA probe shown in Figure 4.2 was used to determine each student's skill level related to a synthesis of decimal and fraction math objectives at varied grade levels. From that probe, she was able to graphically depict skill areas for students that led her to instructional groupings and starting points (see Figure 4.3 for the class profile).

Note that Ms. Joseph's class profile not only allows her to determine who needs instruction in specific skills but also indicates students who already know the information for this math unit. Three groups for instruction are developed according to the data

FIGURE 4.2 CBA Probe for Fractions and Decimals

1. 9/10 =
2. 47 5/10 =
3. 3 2/10 –
4. 7.1 =
5. 13.4 =
6. 28.8 =
7. Draw a picture to show 6/10:

8. Write a decimal to show 6/10:

BONUS: Develop your own question and answer that shows your knowledge of this information.

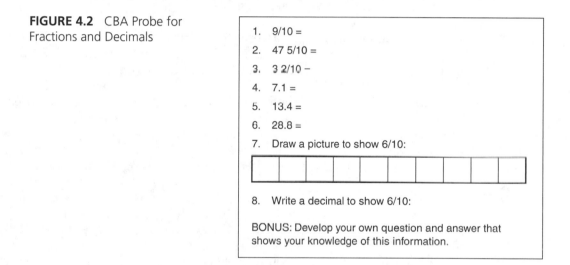

	MW	ME	BA	AS	DR	JI	JF	BK	DL	CE	BH	BI	ST
# 1.	X	X	X	X	X	X	X	X	X	X	X	X	X
# 2.				X		X	X	X	X	X	X	X	X
# 3.					X	X	X	X	X	X	X	X	X
# 4.										X	X	X	X
# 5.										X	X	X	X
# 6.										X	X	X	X
# 7.	X	X	X	X	X	X	X	X	X		X	X	X
# 8.	X	X	X	X	X	X	X	X	X	X	X	X	X
BONUS			X							x			

FIGURE 4.3 Class Profile of Decimal and Fraction Conversions

from this CBA: Group 1 needs instruction on converting decimals to fractions and fractions to decimals, group 2 needs instruction on converting decimals to fractions, and group 3 already knows the information probed on this CBA. Group 3 needs to be probed on a different CBA that assesses the next set of math skills; students from group 3 would be involved in repetitive instruction for concepts they already know if Ms. Joseph were to erroneously include them in this particular math unit.

In essence, this CBA has also served as a pretest for students in determining who needs instruction in these math skill areas and who does not. Although one could argue that avoiding repetitive instruction is important for any group of students, some might emphasize the added importance of focusing on pertinent instruction for students who have emotional or behavioral disorders, because these students may be more likely to display inappropriate behaviors when they are bored with academic content. Conversely, when Ms. Joseph targets accurate academic skill levels, she is using a method to minimize the likelihood of academic frustration or boredom, to motivate students to focus on academic material they are capable of doing, and to increase the opportunities for time-on-task with relevant instructional concepts that can lead to enhanced academic achievement. The remaining portion of this APPLY case study focuses on students in groups 1 and 2, whose initial CBA results indicate they need further instruction in converting fractions and decimals.

Probe Frequently. Ms. Joseph can use varied forms (that feature similar items) of the CBA to conduct brief probes at the beginning of math instruction on several days during the week. Because Ms. Joseph is interested in what concepts students have remembered (e.g., from the previous day's instruction, from their homework assignments), she selects the beginning of the math sessions for CBA probes, instead of the end of the math sessions. She has built into her math lesson plans for Mondays, Tuesdays, and Thursdays a 2-minute period for students to complete a CBA probe. She wants to quickly gather the information at the beginning of the class session and briefly review the results to note what she may need to emphasize during the class session.

Ms. Joseph has several options for reviewing the CBA probe results: She can informally glance at the probes as she collects them at the end of 2 minutes, she can put them aside and review them at the end of the day, she can put them aside and have an instructional assistant or volunteer score them and then she can review them at the end of the day, or she can have students correct their papers at the end of 2 minutes. She decides to have students correct their own papers at the end of 2 minutes; then she has the students themselves graph their correct responses on their progress graphs, which is the next step in the APPLY framework.

Load Data Using a Graph Format. Ms. Joseph has each student correct his or her own CBA probe, count the total number of correct responses, write that number at the top of the probe, and then graph the number correct on his or her progress graph. Initially, this procedure took about 15 minutes because Ms. Joseph wanted to ensure that students understood that the CBA probes were *not the same as a test*. On the CBA probes, students were trying to make progress on answering the CBA items correctly, but their correct responses were to indicate progress over the instructional sessions, not to make 100% correct for each probe administration (note that group 3 students, who did make 100% correct, were eliminated from the instructional math concepts because they already knew the information). Figure 4.4 shows the progress for one student across 2 weeks of instruction.

Yield to Results—Revisions and Decisions. Ms. Joseph uses the "3-day/session rule" for deciding about student progress. She routinely reviews all student progress graphs on Fridays when she is writing lesson plans for the next week's instruction. When students have not made sufficient progress on their CBAs during the week, she knows she

Student: Michael	Teacher: Ms. Joseph	Subject: Math
Objective: Given fractions and decimals (whole numbers and tenths), the student will correctly (1) convert the fraction to a decimal, (2) convert the decimal to a fraction, and (3) draw a picture to represent the fraction or decimal.	**Goal:** 8 out of 8 points earned. **Bonus:** The student includes something different than was asked for on the probe sheet.	

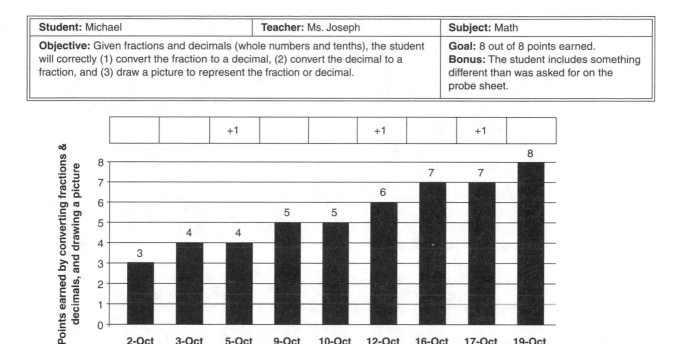

Student Goal: I plan to get 8 out of 8 points by (write a date here): October 19

FIGURE 4.4 CBA Graph for Math (note bonus points awarded October 5, 12, and 17)

needs to work more on those concepts. Revisions may entail (1) reteaching using more concrete examples, (2) more guided practice activities using a variety of examples, (3) more demonstration examples using real-life situations that deal with fractions and decimals, (4) peer tutoring as an activity, and (5) instructional games to provide more practice opportunities. The CBA data provide Ms. Joseph with instructionally relevant information that helps her in deciding about how well students are learning and when revisions in instruction may need to occur.

Extensions or Variations.

- Use newspaper advertisements of sale products to determine the amount of money saved on a sale item.
- Use a recipe for a favorite meal item to identify how the same denominator could be used in all ingredients. Provide a variety of measuring items so that equivalent measurements can be concretely seen.
- Use metric packages that are prevalent in products sold in stores (e.g., soda containers) to make connections to the decimal system.
- Identify everyday items or situations in which students may use the fraction/decimal conversion skills. Students who are using portfolios to document their instructional progress may be responsible for adding items to their portfolio that illustrate how they see fraction/decimal conversion skills in their life. For example, one student may insert in his portfolio the following items to document his progress in this math area: (*a*) a copy of the probe sheet, (*b*) the progress graph that depicts his learning performance during instruction, and (*c*) a narrative that he has written that describes how he can use these fraction/decimal conversion skills when cooking and shopping for items.

APPLY Case Study 2: High School Essays

Analyze the Curriculum. Ms. Rodriguez is a general education teacher who teaches 10th-grade English. A series of curriculum objectives emphasize written language skills. All students in her fifth-period class, which includes three students with learning disabilities and one student with emotional or behavioral disorders, have an assignment to write an essay related to a contemporary topic. Ms. Rodriguez specifies the following objective for all students:

> After selecting a contemporary topic and reading information related to that topic, the student will write an essay that (1) is well-organized, (2) uses accurate and varied sentences, (3) uses correct vocabulary, (4) uses correct mechanics of writing, and (5) is presented in an appropriate format.

Prepare Items to Meet the Curriculum Objectives. Ms. Rodriguez has done some research on what other professionals use to assess students' writing proficiency. One article by Archbald (1991) displays a scoring rubric for essays that she has adapted for her use (see Figure 4.5). Ms. Rodriguez's "probe" is the rubric itself, which students received at the beginning of the instructional unit and can use as a self-assessment prior to turning in their essay drafts to Ms. Rodriguez.

Probe Frequently. Ms. Rodriguez views students' drafts on an average of three occasions before the final essay is turned in for a grade. Students who have particular difficulty with written language, which includes all students with learning disabilities and several other students in the class who are not labeled to receive special education services, will require more feedback sessions. Ms. Rodriguez meets with one student, Maria, on five occasions to provide her with feedback by using the rubric's scoring criteria. On each occasion, Ms. Rodriguez has had an opportunity to review Maria's essay in a formative manner and to emphasize/reteach those areas that Maria needs to improve. Maria's essay is formatted correctly from the very first draft; she receives the highest score (5), which is multiplied by the value for that criterion (format value is 1), to receive a total of 5 for format. In organization, Maria initially earns a 3 for performance (multiplied by the value of 6 equals 18); sentence structure is a 3 (multiplied by the value of 5 equals 15); usage is 3 (multiplied by the value of 4 equals 12); mechanics is 4 (multiplied by the value of 4 equals 16). All totaled for the first draft, Maria has earned 66 of a possible 100 points. In subsequent feedback sessions, Maria and Ms. Rodriguez review Maria's draft and determine a performance score. As Maria's writing improves, her score improves.

Load Data Using a Graph Format. Maria totals each rubric's score to find the cumulative number of points she has earned on each draft of her essay. Maria plots the total number on a graph and also sets a goal for herself about the areas she needs to concentrate on in her next draft to improve her score (see Figure 4.6).

Yield to Results—Revisions and Decisions. Ms. Rodriguez has drawn an aimline on Maria's graph to show how many points Maria should be accruing throughout the unit. By comparing Maria's performance to the aimline, Ms. Rodriguez and Maria are able to determine whether Maria is progressing toward satisfactory completion of the essay assignment.

The rubric also provides Ms. Rodriguez with information about common areas in which she needs to reteach or reemphasize written language skills. Sometimes this instruction occurs with small groups, sometimes it occurs individually, sometimes peers can help edit each other's work, and sometimes there is content on which the whole class needs to work. Ms. Rodriguez is acquiring information about how well students in her fifth-period English class are progressing on their essay assignment while they are completing the assignment. Using the scoring rubrics in both a formative and summa-

	1	2	3	4	5	Value	Total
O	Little or nothing is written. Essay is disorganized and poorly developed. Does not stay on topic.		Essay is incomplete. It lacks an introduction, well-developed body, or conclusion. Coherence and logic are attempted but inadequate.		The essay is well-organized. It is coherent, ordered logically, and fully developed.	X 6	=
S	The student writes frequent run-ons or fragments.		Occasional errors in sentence structure. Little variety in sentence length and structure.		Sentences are complete and varied in length and structure.	X 5	=
U	Student makes frequent errors in word choice and agreement.		Occasional errors in word choice and agreement.		Usage is correct. Word choice is appropriate.	X 4	=
M	Student makes frequent errors in spelling, punctuation, and capitalization.		Occasional errors in mechanics.		Spelling, capitalization, and punctuation are correct.	X 4	=
F	Format is sloppy. There are no margins or indents. Handwriting is inconsistent.		Margins and indents have inconsistencies. No title or inappropriate title.		The format is correct. The title is appropriate. The margins and indents are consistent.	X 1	=
						TOTAL	=

The essays are scored using a 1-5 scale. The numbers in the boxes to the right indicate the relative importance of each factor in the overall grade. Thus, organization is valued the most and counts 30% of the grade; format counts 5% of the grade.

O = Organization
S = Sentence structure
U = Usage
M = Mechanic
F = Format

FIGURE 4.5   Scoring Rubric for Essays

Adapted from Archbald, D. A. (1991). Authentic assessment: Principles, practices, and issues. *School Psychology Quarterly, 6*, p. 284. Adapted with permission of the publisher.

tive manner is more likely to result in each student's successful completion of the assignment, student awareness of what they will be scored on, what each score on the rubric means, and how the score will be assigned.

APPLY Case Study 3: Sight Word Recognition

Analyze the Curriculum. Mr. Jones is a special education teacher working with elementary students who have learning disabilities. Students are reading at different levels: Some are working on basic sight vocabulary, some are working on decoding skills, and all are working on comprehension skills. For his CBAs, Mr. Jones identifies the following objectives:

Given a listing of 45 words from the Dolch word list, the student will read the words at a rate of 25 correct words per minute.

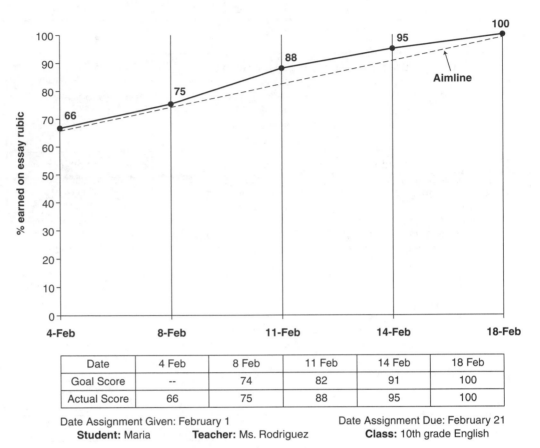

Date	4 Feb	8 Feb	11 Feb	14 Feb	18 Feb
Goal Score	--	74	82	91	100
Actual Score	66	75	88	95	100

Date Assignment Given: February 1   Date Assignment Due: February 21
Student: Maria   **Teacher:** Ms. Rodriguez   **Class:** 10th grade English

FIGURE 4.6 Curriculum-Based Assessment for Essays

Given a 400-word reading passage, the student will read the passage, pronouncing each word correctly at a rate of 60 correct words per minute.

Given reading passages of factual information containing five to seven paragraphs each, the student will state the main idea and two details for each paragraph correctly.

Prepare Items to Meet the Curriculum Objectives. Mr. Jones prepares a series of probe sheets he can use with individual students when they reach certain levels of proficiency with each objective. Mr. Jones spends substantial time initially developing the probes for the reading curriculum area, but then he has a variety of probes readily available throughout the year (see Bui, Hlass, & Reda, 1995, for a compilation of probes and graphs that can be used for the Dolch words).

Mr. Jones can use two probe formats for the Dolch words. One format is flash cards, and he has a "deck" of flash cards for each set of words from the Dolch word list (e.g., preprimer level, primer level). The second format is a listing of the words on a worksheet, with the same words used repeatedly and each line precounted so that he can score the probe quickly after a student reads from it (Figure 4.7).

Probe Frequently. Three times a week, Mr. Jones conducts 1-minute probes with each student working on this unit of instruction. He conducts the probe sessions at the beginning of the reading period, and he sets aside 10 minutes each day for the probes. Although it took more time when he first began using the probes, now he and his students are well acquainted with the CBA probe routine. Students begin seatwork when they begin the period, and Mr. Jones calls each student to a "CBA Center" in the classroom. Mr. Jones provides each student with a probe sheet, sets the timer for 1 minute, and

kind	fall	seven	about	laugh	far	shall		7
better	light	full	show	bring	long	got		14
six	carry	much	grow	shall	clean	myself		21
hold	start	cut	never	hot	ten	done	only	29
hurt	today	draw	own	if	together	drink	pick	37
keep	try	eight	warm	kind	fall	seven		44
about	laugh	far	shall	better	light	full		51
show	bring	long	got	six	carry	much		58
grow	shall	clean	myself	hold	start	cut		65
never	hot	ten	done	only	hurt	today		72
draw	own	if	together	drink	pick	keep		79
try	eight	warm	kind	fall	seven	about		86

DOLCH WORD LIST LEVEL 3 (Probe Form A)

FIGURE 4.7 CBA: Dolch Sight Word Probe

marks on his laminated probe sheet any errors a student makes when orally reading the words. The student counts his or her number of correct and incorrect responses and gets ready to transfer those data to a graph.

Load Data Using a Graph Format. When Mr. Jones first began using the graph, he showed students how to figure out and write their correct and incorrect rates on the graph. Now each student is able to record his or her own data (see Figure 4.8) to record numbers of correct and incorrect word identifications.

Yield to Results—Revisions and Decisions. Students are able to "see" their progress when they connect the sessions' data points across days of administration. Students

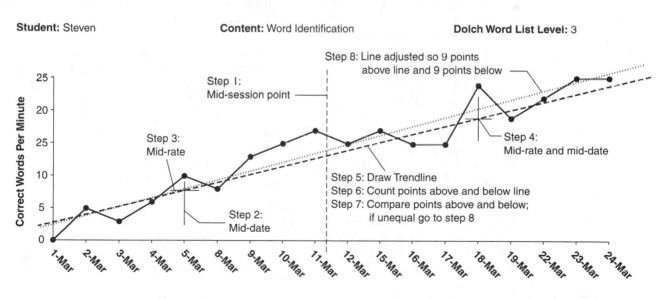

Objective: Given words from level __3__ of the Dolch Word List, the student will verbally identify the words at a rate of __25__ correct words per minute.

FIGURE 4.8 CBA for Dolch Words: Equal Interval Graph

can select individual goals for themselves by predicting the number of correct or incorrect words they want to get the next time they use a CBA probe. Some students are encouraged by the rising slope of their progress line, which documents that they are learning the words. Other students discuss with Mr. Jones ways to increase their progress line, such as reviewing the words more often by using the Language Master, using flash cards with a peer to study, finding the words in the school newspaper, or tracing the words on the bulletin board. Mr. Jones used to direct students in ways that they can increase their performance; now students formulate ideas to help themselves and each other.

Mr. Jones also uses the quarter-intersect and split-middle methods of assessing student performance. Once seven data points are gathered, Mr. Jones applies the quarter-intersect and split-middle methods to predict future performance rate.

Extensions and Variations. Mr. Jones could use similar CBA formats for different IEP objectives: "Given words with different phonetic patterns, the student will verbally identify the word correctly." "After silently reading a brief passage that contains words the student already knows, the student will correctly answer five comprehension questions that are recall and inference level questions."

GRADING PRACTICES

The guiding principles for developing assessments described earlier in this chapter should also guide grading practices for students with mild to moderate disabilities. Whether those grades are determined for general classes or for special education classes does not change the fact that the nature of the grading is individualized for students—according to directions and directives on each student's IEP. *Data still need to be collected in a frequent, systematic manner on critical instructional objectives.* Much of the data collection described so far in this chapter may be used formatively to guide instruction; however, grades are usually derived from summative evaluations. **Summative evaluations** include homework scores, quiz grades, and test percentages that collectively comprise a student's final grade in a course. Effective teachers are able to present to students, at the onset of a course, those assessments and their relative value that will ultimately determine a student's grade in a course.

Ornstein (1994) notes several reasons that teachers use grades: (1) to indicate mastery of specific content at a predetermined level, (2) to determine grouping of students, (3) to diagnose or plan instruction, or (4) to motivate students toward learning objectives. Wiggins (1988) notes the arbitrary nature that teachers sometimes employ when determining grades for students when he states, "Students see that even teachers next door to each other, teaching different sections of the same course, employ different standards. . . . A grade is usable by students only if the criteria behind it are explicit and put in descriptive terms" (p. 23). To that end, several guidelines from Ornstein (p. 64) are applicable:

- Explain your grading system to students.
- Base grades on a predetermined set of standards.
- Base grades on the student's degree of progress.
- Base grades on a variety of sources.

SUMMARY

In this chapter, we discussed how teachers who follow three principles of assessment are able to develop and use *frequent assessments* in a *systematic manner on critical curricu-*

lum objectives to make sound decisions about instruction. Furthermore, we described how involving students during their assessment process can promote responsible, motivationally oriented, and meaningful learning of instructional content and progress. We pointed out how decisions that teachers make about student progress can be gathered by using a variety of assessment systems, including authentic, performance, portfolio, and curriculum-based systems. Effective teachers use the information gained from assessments to guide their teaching methods, materials, and techniques throughout instruction, not just on a pretest or posttest basis. Furthermore, encouraging student involvement by teaching students how to set goals for their learning and to self-evaluate their performance can increase students' achievement. We discussed how students with mild to moderate disabilities benefit educationally when their teachers involve them in their assessment practices. Insightful educators develop meaningful ways throughout the instructional process to assess students frequently and systematically on critical skills. By collaborating with students during the assessment process, developing and beginning teachers can enhance achievement gains and improve learning opportunities for students with mild to moderate disabilities.

ACTIVITIES TO EXTEND YOUR KNOWLEDGE

1. Develop an inventory that samples a broad spectrum of students' skills or knowledge within an identified instructional domain or unit.

2. Identify a unit of instruction.
   a. Write a measurable goal and at least two corresponding objectives or benchmarks for student performance.
   b. Design a pretest to measure students' entry-level skills on the identified objectives.
   c. Compose an alternate form of the pretest you developed.
   d. Answer the following questions for the pretest and alternate form you developed:
      • Does each form of the assessment contain different items that require students to perform the same skills?
      • Are the scoring criteria for each form of the assessment explicit enough for different people to obtain the same scoring results?

3. An assortment of performance-assessment methods are available to assess students' competencies in targeted areas. For your students, identify a domain or unit of instruction for which performance assessment could be used. Choose a method of performance assessment and predetermine the criteria for successful performance. What will you say to explain the criteria? When you dialogue with students during feedback sessions, what will the focus of your discussion be?

POINT AND CLICK

IDEA 97. Several Internet sites provide paraphrases of IDEA 97 content, as well as access to the law itself. Because there are important elements that guide instruction and assessment for students with IEPs, beginning teachers may find these sites useful not only for themselves, but also for some of their general education colleagues.

http://www.ideapractices.org/idea97a.htm

http://www.ldonline.org/ld_indepth/iep/idea97.html

General Education Curriculum Standards from National Organizations Beginning teachers may use local, state, or national curriculum standards to guide them when developing instructional and assessment content (check whether your state or school system posts its standards on the Internet). The following Internet sites identify different general education curriculum standards for national organizations. Special and general educators can use these or similar sites (e.g., their local school system) to assist in determining instructional and, subsequently assessment items.

Curriculum Standards for Social Studies, National Council for Social Studies
http://www.ncss.org/standards/1.1.html

National Standards in Foreign Language Education;
http://www.actfl.org/htdocs/standards/index.htm

National Council of Teachers for Mathematics
http://www/nctm.org/

National Council for Music Education
http://www.namm.com/mktdv_ncme.shtml

National Geography Standards
http://www/cadgis.lsu.edu/lagea/natgeostand.html

National Standards for Arts Education
http://www.amc-music.com/srfact.htm

National Standards for Civics and Government: ERIC Digest
http://ericae.net/db/digs/ed380401/htm

National Standards for United States History
http://www.sscnet.ucla.edu/nchs/us-toc.htm

Standards for Science and Mathematics
http://ssdoo.gsfc.nasa.gov/education/standards.html

Assessment The following Internet sites can be especially helpful for beginning teachers if the instructional and assessment content is a good match for their local school curriculum as it pertains to IEPs. If there is not a good match, some teachers may be able to adapt the content to achieve a good fit. Moreover, some sites contain generic information (e.g., literacy rubrics, math portfolios, CBA probes) that can easily be used for noting progress across many curricular and IEP areas regardless of what curriculum is used.

http://www.uvm.edu/~mhock/standards/rubric/altmath.html

http://www.aea1.k12.ia.us/transition/goalexamples/html

http://brt.uoregon.edu/rctp/rctpcim/annweb/orfrationale/html

http://www.cse.ucla.edu/CRESST/pages/Rubrics/htm

REFERENCES

Archbald, D. A. (1991). Authentic assessment: Principles, practices, and issues. *School Psychology Quarterly, 6*, 279–293.

Bateman, B. D., & Linden, M. A. (1998). *Better IEPs: How to develop legally correct and educationally useful programs* (3rd ed.). Longmont, CO: Sopris West.

Blankenship, C. S. (1985). Using curriculum-based assessment data to make instructional decisions. *Exceptional Children, 52*, 233–238.

Bui, X., Hlass, J., & Reda, M. (1995). *Curriculum-based assessment and reading.* Unpublished manuscript, Johns Hopkins University at Rockville, MD.

Cullen, B., & Pratt, T. (1992). Measuring and reporting student progress. In S. Stainback & W. Stainback (Eds.), *Curriculum considerations in inclusive classrooms* (pp. 175–196). Baltimore: Paul H. Brookes.

Deno, S. L. (1985). Curriculum-based measurement: The emerging alternative. *Exceptional Children, 52*, 219–232.

Deno, S. L., & Fuchs, L. S. (1987). Developing curriculum-based measurement systems for data-based special education problem solving. *Focus on Exceptional Children, 19*, 1–16.

Duffy, M. L., Jones, J., & Thomas, S. W. (1999). Using portfolios to foster independent thinking. *Intervention in School and Clinic, 35*(1), 34–37.

Elliott, S. N. (1992). Authentic assessment: An introduction to a neobehavioral approach to classroom assessment. *School Psychology Quarterly, 5*, 273–278.

Fuchs, L. S., & Deno, S. L. (1991). Paradigmatic distinctions between instructionally relevant measurement models. *Exceptional Children, 58*, 488–500.

Fuchs, L. S., & Fuchs, D. (1984). Criterion-referenced assessment without measurement: How accurate for special education? *Remedial and Special Education, 5*(4), 29–32.

Fuchs, L. S., & Fuchs, D. (1985). Effectiveness of systematic formative evaluation: A meta-analysis. *Exceptional Children, 53*, 199–208.

Gersten, R., Keating, T., & Irvin, L. K. (1995). The burden of proof: Validity as improvement of instructional practice. *Exceptional Children, 61*, 510–519.

Hasbrouck, J. E., Woldbeck, T., Ihnot, C., & Parker, R. I. (1999). One teacher's use of curriculum-based measurement: A changed opinion. *Learning Disabilities Research & Practice, 14*, 118–126.

Jorden, J., & Haube, A. (1995). *A guide to using curriculum-based assessment: Do you know what your students know?* Unpublished manuscript [videotape & guide], Johns Hopkins University at Rockville, MD.

King-Sears, M. E. (1994). *Curriculum-based assessment in special education.* Belmont, CA: Wadsworth.

King-Sears, M. E., Burgess, M., & Lawson, T. L. (1999). APPLYing curriculum-based assessment in inclusive settings. *Teaching Exceptional Children, 32*(1), 30–38.

Meyer, C. A. (1992). What's the difference between authentic and performance assessment? *Educational Leadership, 48*(8), 39–40.

Nolet, V. (1992). Classroom-based measurement and portfolio assessment. *Diagnostique, 18*(1), 5–26.

Ornstein, A. C. (1994). Grading practices and policies: An overview and some suggestions. *NASSP Bulletin, 78*(561), 55–64.

Paulson, F. L., Paulson, P. R., & Meyer, C. A. (1991). What makes a portfolio a portfolio? *Educational Leadership, 48*(5), 60–63.

Poteet, J. A., Choate, J. S., & Stewart, S. C. (1993). Performance assessment and special education: Practices and prospects. *Focus on Exceptional Children, 26*(1), 1–20.

Salvia, J., & Hughes, C. (1990). *Curriculum-based assessment: Testing what is taught.* New York: Macmillan.

Salvia, J., & Ysseldyke, J. E. (1991). *Assessment* (5th ed.). Boston: Houghton Mifflin.

Sarouphim, K. M. (1999). Discovering multiple intelligences through a performance-based assessment: Consistency with independent ratings. *Exceptional Children, 65*, 151–161.

U.S. Congress, Office of Technology Assessment. (1992). Performance assessment: Methods and characteristics. In *Testing in American schools: Asking the right questions* (OTA SET-519, pp. 201–249). Washington, DC: Government Printing Office.

Viechnicki, K. J., Barbour, N., Shaklee, B., Rohrer, J., & Ambrose, R. (1993). The impact of portfolio assessment on teacher classroom activities. *Journal of Teacher Education, 44*, 371–377.

Wesson, C., Skiba, R., Sevcik, B., King, R. P., & Deno, S. (1984). The effects of technically adequate instructional data on achievement. *Remedial and Special Education, 5*(5), 17–22.

Wiggins, G. (1988). Rational numbers: Toward grading and scoring that help rather than harm learning. *American Educator, 12*, 20–25, 45–58.

Planning for Instruction

In this chapter, we will

✔ provide reasons for lesson planning

✔ discuss the developmental aspect of lesson planning and its relationship to the diagnostic teaching model

✔ define strategic and tactical planning

✔ identify components of successfully planned lessons, including instructional activities and materials in planned lessons

✔ examine methods to evaluate lesson implementations, follow-up, and self-evaluation

✔ review unit and lesson plan formats, including those for inclusive programming

*I*n any systematic approach to a task, planning is central. Consequently, effective teachers spend significant amounts of time planning for instruction in a variety of ways. The purpose of this chapter is to provide developing teachers with a rationale for planning, to show how planning relates to systematic teaching, to specify the components of well-designed plans, and to provide suggestions for writing unit and daily lesson plans. Many teachers are skeptical about the need for written lesson plans. Some argue that the time spent writing plans could be better used developing or adapting materials, thinking through lessons, or consulting with other teachers.

All of these activities are important elements of instruction, and certainly there never seem to be enough hours in the day to complete all the planning and teaching functions expected of teachers. However, written plans that specify objectives of a lesson and that detail the instructional activities that will be used to attain the objectives have been shown to be attributes of effective teaching (Archer, 1991; Hofmeister & Lubke, 1990; Rosenshine, 1986). In the following paragraphs, we explain reasons why written plans are valuable teaching tools.

Pause and Reflect 5.1

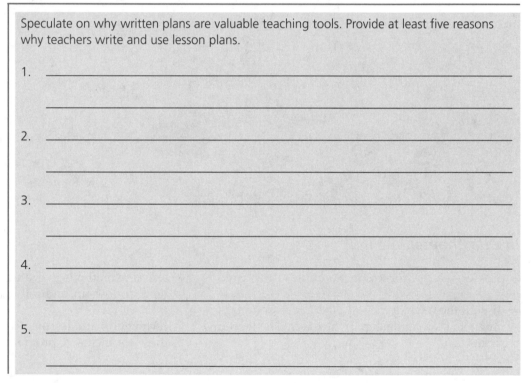

Speculate on why written plans are valuable teaching tools. Provide at least five reasons why teachers write and use lesson plans.

1. _____

_____

2. _____

_____

3. _____

_____

4. _____

_____

5. _____

_____

REASONS FOR PLANNING

There is a number of reasons for planning. These include the increased probability of effective teaching; the increase in teachers' confidence, security, and direction; and the establishment of good habits.

Planning Increases the Probability of Effective Teaching

As an old axiom applies to travel—if you don't know where and how you are going, you won't be able to get there—it applies to instructional planning as well. Specific goal statements provide a destination for teachers and students and the basis for evaluating the effectiveness of instructional activities and materials in aiding students to arrive at some prescribed skill level. Detailing through activity descriptions the means by which students are to attain objectives is necessary as well. Researchers have found that teachers who set specific objectives and write more detailed lesson plans are more effective than those teachers who write broadly stated goals and superficial lesson plans (Algozzine, Ysseldyke, & Elliott, 1997; Cooper, 1986; Hudson, 1996; Mager, 1996; Williams & Fox, 1996).

An important distinction needs to be made between written and mental planning. Many hours of mental planning precede the act of writing plans. Thoroughly thinking through instructional objectives and activities is often a necessary, but insufficient, means of planning. Mental planning alone still leaves a high probability that objectives and activities will be vague and loosely structured. Preparing a written document increases the chances that objectives will be clearly stated and that activities will be thoroughly organized. Mager (1996) found that when teachers write out clear lessons, they make instruction work. Written plans help teachers derive appropriate learning outcomes and develop the instructional techniques to enhance their students' learning. Written plans can help teachers anticipate and solve students' performance problems in advance of delivery. Plans can assist teachers in creating instruction that matches student needs. Plans help in the development of more effective instructional evaluations.

Planning Increases Confidence, Security, and Direction

Plans remind teachers what they are to do during a lesson. Considering the range of variables that teachers deal with during instruction, having a plan they can refer to tends to increase teachers' confidence and sense of security. Effective teachers know that when uncertainty strikes, they can glance quickly at their notes, respond in an appropriate direction, and continue with their lesson (Clark & Yinger, 1979; McCutcheon, 1980).

Planning Helps Establish Good Habits

Being consistent in writing lesson plans helps developing teachers establish a systematic approach to instruction (Algozzine et al., 1997). Using a particular format for sketching out what and how to teach forces teachers to examine each element of a lesson, to sequence activities more carefully, and to organize materials more thoroughly. Once this routine is established and followed, it should be maintained and used when planning to teach any new content. And with changes in teacher roles to include increased teaming models (discussed in Chapter 11), lesson plans can be approached creatively and collaboratively in traditional class settings or in cooperative teaching models, whereby teachers help each other adapt and deliver instruction (Rutherford & Warger, 1995; Thousand, Villa, & Nevin, 1994; Wood, 1991). Dieker (2000) reported that special education and general education teachers can coplan instruction for students with disabilities as they reflect on the value and impact of their coteaching experiences. Darch, Miller, and Shippen (1998) found that professionals who plan in advance of lesson presentation are proactive and can prevent learning and behavior problems before a problem occurs instead of reacting to problems. However, a teacher must set the stage by how he or she thinks about lessons; how he or she talks to students, teachers, parents, and school administrators; and how he or she anticipates and responds to problems in the classroom and the general school environment. These actions are core to effective lesson planning.

DEVELOPMENTAL ASPECT OF LESSON PLANNING

Novice teachers will have more extensive written plans than more experienced teachers. This is a function of beginning teachers' unfamiliarity with students, materials, and content.

Written lesson plans provide the first steps for developing teachers to learn to manage and carry out daily instructional activities. Although a time-consuming and often tedious activity, writing out plans helps developing teachers structure their thinking about teaching, which results in a more systematic course of action (Whitaker, 2000). Eventually, beginning teachers gain sufficient experience so that the need to write down detailed daily lesson plans diminishes (a point is reached at which teachers can taper off the amount of written planning they do). On the basis of interviews with experienced teachers, researchers have found that, ultimately, teachers covertly think through, rather than write down, their daily plans (Clark & Yinger, 1979; McCutcheon, 1980). To get to this point, however, it is necessary to practice writing out detailed plans in an efficient manner. Over time, developing teachers will spend more time mentally planning lessons and attending to broader, long-term planning needs than focusing on writing out details of individual lessons.

RELATIONSHIP OF PLANNING TO THE DIAGNOSTIC TEACHING MODEL

The **diagnostic teaching model (DTM)** is a framework for conceptualizing teaching as a hypothesis-testing process. Teachers systematically examine the variables (e.g., students' present skill levels, available teaching materials, strategies for presenting content, practice activities) associated with learning and how they apply to their students. They then construct a hypothesis in the form of an instructional plan. The plan is implemented, and student performance is monitored. If the plan to manipulate learning variables in certain ways changes the performance of students, then the hypothesis is supported. If the plan does not manifest the intended effects, then teachers are able to analyze their plan to determine where changes are needed. Consequently, instruction is approached in a systematic way that acknowledges teaching as an inexact science and teachers' limited ability to determine the cause-and-effect relationship of the numerous variables in any learning environment (Cartwright, Cartwright, & Ward, 1981).

The DTM contains five core steps that teachers follow in planning for instruction:

1. Identifying attributes

2. Specifying objectives

3. Selecting strategies

4. Selecting materials

5. Testing strategies and materials

Step 1 involves the collection of information about the classroom setting, the behavioral and learning attributes of students, and any other relevant variables. Teachers first collect baseline data prior to intervention, allowing them to form a picture of what is occurring in the classroom under existing conditions. Next, they determine what skills or behaviors they want to decrease, maintain, or increase by specifying clear and behaviorally stated objectives that reflect how the target students are to respond (e.g., see-say, hear-write, see-write) and what criterion level they are to attain (e.g., 90% accuracy, 60 movements per minute) (step 2). Teachers then select alternative strategies (e.g., self-monitoring, semantic webbing, concept induction) and any accompanying materials (e.g., tangible reinforcers, reading books, concrete examples) for accomplishing the stated objectives (steps 3 and 4). Once implemented by the teacher, the strategies and materials are tested through subsequent observations and data collection (step 5).

On the basis of the information gathered, teachers analyze students' performance on daily or weekly measures and determine whether the objectives have been reached. Accordingly, the sequence is repeated in one of two ways (see Figure 5.1). If objectives

FIGURE 5.1   The Diagnostic Teaching Model

Adapted from Cartwright, G. P., & Cartwright, C. A. (1972). Gilding the lily. *Exceptional Children*, 39, 231–234.

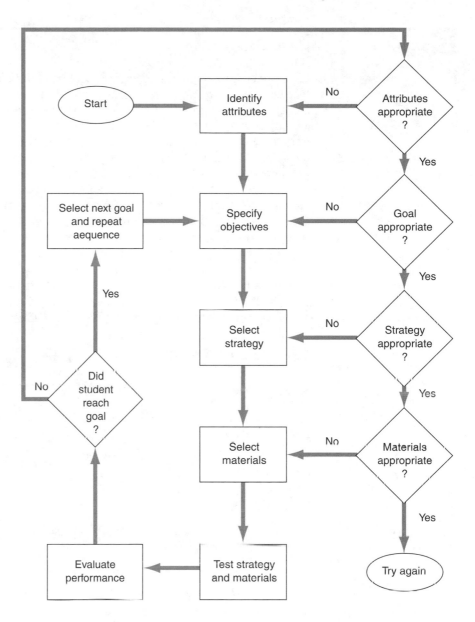

have been reached, the teacher moves the students on to the next objective in the curriculum hierarchy (step 2) and continues through the other steps as described. If objectives have not been reached, the teacher reexamines the accuracy and appropriateness of the baseline data, stated objectives, strategies, and materials. If modifications in any of these areas are necessary, the teacher makes the changes and the sequence is continued. When all steps seem to be accurate and appropriate, the teacher implements the strategies and materials again and retests (see Box 5.1).

One other point requires consideration. Often, teacher-training programs prepare their preservice teacher trainees to follow the steps in the sequence provided here. Researchers who have surveyed actual planning patterns followed by teachers in the field, however, suggest that teachers typically plan in a different sequence. Often, the first steps involved in planning focus on activities, content, materials, or resources (Peterson, Marx, & Clark, 1978) instead of on specifying goals and objectives. In other cases, planning may not be a sequential process. Instead, teachers go back and forth among these steps, simultaneously working on each step. Regardless, the steps within the DTM are considered to be critical despite variations in the sequence with which they are carried out.

Box 5.1   **Case Study**

Christopher, a sixth-grade student, has just been referred to Ms. Theodore, a learning support teacher in an elementary school. Christopher has been having difficulties responding to comprehension questions. Ms. Theodore has decided she wants to confirm his reported reading level by administering an informal reading inventory based on words, passages, and questions from the reading materials in the learning support class. In addition, she has collected interview data from Christopher's classroom teacher and parents regarding the reading environment in the general education classroom and at home. She also asked Christopher what he does while he reads. From the information gathered, Ms. Theodore concludes that Christopher can recognize words by using phonic and semantic cues and can fluently read material written on a fourth-grade level but that he can answer comprehension questions with only 60% accuracy. He is provided with opportunities to read in the general education class, and his parents appear to provide a good reading environment at home (both parents read magazines and newspapers daily and encourage Christopher to read as well). When he was asked what he thinks about during reading and how he reads, Christopher reported that he reads the words and that sometimes he thinks about other things. He apparently does not correctly review what he has read, ask himself questions, or try to predict what will happen in the passages he reads.

Pause and Reflect 5.2

See whether you can determine how Ms. Theodore used steps of the DTM in the example with Christopher.

1. What are relevant classroom attributes in Ms. Theodore's class?
2. What are important teaching considerations, given Christopher's reading comprehension skills?
3. What are appropriate reading objectives for Christopher, based on Ms. Theodore's use of the DTM?
4. How can Ms. Theodore use appropriate strategies to improve Christopher's written comprehension answers?

On the basis of the attributes derived from her assessments (step 1 of the DTM), Ms. Theodore specified the following objectives (step 2 of the DTM):

- When given a passage at the fourth-grade reading level, Christopher will paraphrase the content after each paragraph read with 100% accuracy.
- When given a passage at the fourth-grade reading level, Christopher will see-write answers correctly for seven of eight comprehension questions.

To improve Christopher's written answers to comprehension questions, Ms. Theodore decides to teach Christopher to paraphrase the content of each paragraph read during daily 15-minute sessions of small-group instruction (step 3 of the DTM). She selects a set of passages and accompanying comprehension questions written at the fourth-grade level to use for practice and as evaluation probes (step 4 of the DTM). Ms. Theodore then implements her teaching strategy and records Christopher's performance in using the paraphrasing strategy and writing answers to comprehension questions (step 5 of the DTM). If Christopher's performance increases at an acceptable rate (he increasingly uses the paraphrasing strategy and answers more questions correctly), then Ms. Theodore will continue with her intervention program. If not, she will have to reevaluate each step of the DTM process and make necessary modifications.

STRATEGIC AND TACTICAL PLANNING

Planning has two basic levels: strategic and tactical (Algozzine et al., 1997). **Strategic planning** refers to the broad, overall rationale for providing instruction to particular students. It includes justification for the content, activities, materials, and objectives that are included in the day-to-day operations of a classroom. Typically, at the strategic level, teachers reflect on their philosophy of instruction and the ultimate outcomes that should result from sound instructional programs. An example is that teachers consider what the needs of students will be once they leave school and enter some vocation, how those needs can be most effectively met, and how the curriculum can be structured to provide the highest probability that those needs will be met. Thus, teachers planning functional skill activities help students reach adult-life goals and objectives (Gable, Laycock, Maroney, & Smith, 1991). When teachers are well-planned, schools, community service agencies, private organizations, and family members can work together to help students make a smooth transition to adult life. Effective planning supports students' transitioning and individualized education program (IEP) processes (West, Corbey, Boyer-Stephens, Jones, Miller, & Sarkees-Wircenski, 1999).

On the basis of strategic considerations, teachers then consider how, on a day-to-day, week-to-week basis, they can provide instruction that builds on the bits and pieces of previous learning to attain the long-range goals of a program. These daily operational considerations, which take the form of daily lesson plans or unit plans, are the essence of tactical planning. **Tactical planning** includes determining prerequisite skills acquired by students, setting short-term objectives (e.g., what the teacher will teach the next day), describing specific teaching activities and related materials to present particular concepts or skills, and designing daily evaluation procedures.

An example of strategic and tactical planning is reflected in the preparation for the implementation of curricular interventions in learning strategies programs (Carnine, 1991). A group of content-area secondary teachers and the special education resource and consulting teachers meet to discuss how they can better facilitate the needs of students with learning problems (strategic planning) in the general education setting. After discussion of observational data, they conclude that these students appear to have few or no skills in monitoring and regulating their own learning. The teachers decide to set up a learning strategies course to be offered by the learning support teachers, cotaught with content instructors in the general education setting. In addition, the content-area teachers (e.g., science, mathematics, economics) will modify their demands for content mastery, particularly during the first term of the school year, and provide opportunities for students to practice using the strategies they have learned. The expectation is that, with improved learning processes, students will be able to master more content.

With the overall plan sketched out, the teachers identify specific objectives to be mastered and learning strategies that they believe need to be taught. In addition, they identify the strategies intervention model (Deshler & Schumaker, 1986) as the set of procedures to be used. They then begin work on unit plans for the courses on learning strategies and plans for content-area teachers to facilitate the use of strategies in their classrooms (tactical planning). Accordingly, as teachers approach planning lessons systematically, they can diagnose and use differentiated instruction to meet the needs of many students who have individual needs (Pettig, 2000).

In sum, planning occurs at a variety of levels, moving from more global to more specific considerations. It is important for new teachers to realize that the process of strategic and tactical planning is not necessarily sequential, whereby teachers make strategic plans and then move on to tactical planning. Teachers often move back and forth between global and specific considerations until both levels of planning are complete.

COMPONENTS OF SUCCESSFULLY PLANNED LESSONS

Effective planning is characterized by definable components that contain information on where and how students will reach some specified goal. These components include prerequisite skills, instructional objectives, instructional activities and materials to be used, methods to evaluate lessons, adaptations and modifications, anticipated problems, and self-evaluation of lesson plans.

Prerequisite Skills

To provide effective instruction, teachers must determine the present educational levels of their students; that is, they must determine what each student can and cannot do vis-à-vis the curriculum hierarchy. If one envisions a skill hierarchy for a given content area (e.g., reading, math, language) organized in some rational sequence, then determining students' present educational levels entails teachers pinpointing which skills students have mastered and which skills they must learn or continue to practice. In some cases, published skill hierarchies may not be available, and so teachers must determine the subskills for a given task.

Determining the current educational levels of students entails collecting some baseline data. Depending on the target skills, baseline data may be derived from probe sheets, teacher observation, curriculum-based assessments, rubrics, formal assessment devices, task analyses, and so forth. In any case, these assessments enable teachers to specify the target skills that will form the basis for instructional objectives.

Instructional Objectives

Effective teachers know where they want to take their students. They have explicit goals and make students aware of them. Differences in how they guide students to reach those goals may not be as important as the need to specify where students are going. By setting clear and specific goals, developing and new teachers can more easily determine what types of activities will better facilitate students achieving their goals. Without specific goals, teachers and students may flounder, completing one activity after another yet not making any progress toward the mastery of some predetermined skill or concept.

Writing instructional objectives in well-planned lessons relates to teacher effectiveness. For example, Mager (1996) found that when teachers identify, select, and write well-stated objectives, they create the foundation necessary to reach their instructional goals. Well-stated lesson plans include objectives that describe performances that teachers expect to achieve. Lesson objectives can be benchmarks to help teachers identify the conditions under which they expect the performance to occur. Objectives can set criteria within lessons.

Hudson (1996) suggested that although planned prelesson activities can be found in the literature under a variety of names, including "lesson opening" (Archer, 1991) and "learning sets" (Hudson, Lignugaris-Kraft, & Miller, 1993), planning is a necessary component to link past and new sets of knowledge. Plans can be organized into two categories: review and introduction. The teacher plans anticipatory sets or review techniques, including oral and written questions and lesson activities permitting students to practice content knowledge. Planning for reviews (Rosenshine, 1986) includes considering actively involving all students in response opportunities, telling students when they are correct, and informing students when they make errors. Teachers plan to introduce lesson activities when they set the stage for the upcoming content and tasks. They plan for statements of lesson objectives and task objectives. To introduce new information, teachers plan on telling students how the new skill or knowledge benefits the students.

Characteristics. Behaviorally stated instructional objectives contain phrases identifying the target students, the behavior they will demonstrate, the conditions under which they will demonstrate the behavior, and the criterion for mastery. They are written in clear and concise language that makes it easy for others to understand the focus of instruction. The behavior is stated in observable, measurable terms indicative of the response mode the students will use (e.g., see-write, hear-say). Behavioral objectives are student-focused (reflect what students will do or accomplish, not what the teacher will do). For example, the following statement contains all the attributes of a behavioral objective:

> When given a probe sheet with words beginning with *bl, cl,* and *fl* consonant blends, Calvin, Tony, John, and Tanya will see-say the words at a rate of 60 words per minute with two or fewer errors.

Often, teachers run into problems when they make unclear statements such as, "The teacher will work on decoding." It is unclear because "work on" connotes numerous possible activities. The same statement is flawed because it does not indicate a desired outcome; instead, it refers to the process of "working on." Also, the statement does

Pause and Reflect 5.3

- During cleanup time, Perry begins to talk loudly. Ms. Martin looks at him sternly and tells him to "settle down and clean quietly."
- Both Jane and Freida complete work quickly and accurately.
- Five minutes before math class is over, Joan tells Aaron that if he completes his math assignment correctly, he may use her computer for the next 20 minutes.
- When asked to be Bill's partner for soccer practice, Andy responds that he doesn't want to be Bill's partner.
- Joe warns his friends: "Watch your language—there are small children here."
- Marsha fidgets, squirms, or seems restless whenever history class begins.
- Lorenzo often shifts from one uncompleted task to another and rarely completes his assignments on time.
- Using a fifth-grade math book, Betsy will complete 10 fraction problems daily, with no more than two errors on each occasion.
- Sally often loses things necessary for class.
- Yasmine seems to have difficulty sustaining attention during school assemblies.
- Hillary often displays strong self-management skills.
- When Athena wanted to telephone her parents, she put in the quarter and dialed the number. She talked with her mother for 2 minutes.
- "I worked very persistently on my class readings and assignments. When the instructor gave an examination on Tuesday, I received a score of 95%."
- Given 5 minutes during class to complete her handwriting, Martha will form the letter *c* five times without errors.

1. What are student behaviors in each of the above examples?
2. Which of these examples contain all of the attributes of good behavioral or instructional objectives?
3. After identifying the student behaviors, specify appropriate conditions and criterion level for each example.

not mention students. The most common error is the lack of an observable, measurable behavior that indicates specifically how the students will respond to a stimulus.

Behaviorally stated objectives are focused on some desired outcome of instruction. This does not limit the utility of objectives to the end product of an academic task. Processes (e.g., metacognitive strategies, verbal rehearsal, self-instruction) used in attaining some end product (e.g., reading faster, comprehending more, writing better essays) can also be the targeted behavior(s). For instance, a student with writing difficulties may be asked to employ a learning strategy such as TOWER (*t*hink, *o*rder, *w*rite, *e*rror monitor, and *r*evise) in generating an essay (Mercer & Mercer, 1985). The objective could be stated in terms of the strategy, not the end product (the characteristics of the essay). The following objective is an example:

> When asked to write an essay, the student will show evidence of using each step of the TOWER strategy with 100% accuracy for 3 consecutive days.

A second objective could also be written to reflect the intended effect of using the TOWER strategy (to be able to write a more coherent essay). Such an objective may read:

> When asked to write an essay, the student will think-write topics and supporting material that are coherently ordered as judged by the teacher in three consecutive essays.

Functions. Once teachers determine where students are functioning in a skill hierarchy, they determine how far up the hierarchy students should go over some period of time. With the objectives of instruction identified, teachers can begin to select activities and materials that will help students attain the objectives. Like a Sunday driver, a teacher without specific objectives may take a winding path in some unknown direction and never reach the appropriate destination (instructional objective).

Selection of Activities and Materials. Activities and materials act as vehicles for reaching some objective. They are generated from a sense of purpose; they must help students to acquire an understanding of a concept or to remember the steps of an academic rule and provide sufficient practice to develop mastery. For instance, if, on the one hand, the objective of instruction is for students to discriminate between squares and rectangles, then the instructional activities and materials should focus on students identifying the attributes that make one shape different from the other. These activities would involve the teacher stating or having students discover the attributes of each figure, listing them on the chalkboard, and having students methodically examine examples and check to see that all the attributes are present. If, on the other hand, students can already discriminate between a square and a rectangle but the discrimination responses are slow, then the activities and materials should focus, not on what the attributes are, but rather on a quick and accurate response to examples and nonexamples of each. These activities and materials may involve students quickly naming shapes by using flash cards. Consequently, the activities and materials change as the objectives change.

Assistance to Tracking Student Progress. Clearly stated objectives indicate what students should be learning (Mager, 1996). All those with an interest in students' progress—teachers, administrators, parents, and students themselves—can draw conclusions about the effectiveness of instruction on the basis of whether students are reaching their objectives. Consequently, objectives form the basis for evaluation of instruction and accountability.

Task Analysis and En Route and Terminal Objectives. Objectives are generated from analyzing the components of a superordinate task or skill. Once a task or skill is selected for instruction, teachers or curriculum specialists often break down the task into steps. Instruction is then focused on students mastering individual steps and sets of steps leading to mastery of the entire task or skill.

Depending on the complexity of the target task or skill and the existing skills of students, the number of steps (en route objectives) leading to mastery of the task (terminal objective) will vary. Another factor in determining the number of steps or en route objectives used to master a terminal objective depends on who makes the distinction between a task being the terminal objective or being an en route objective leading toward the mastery of some greater objective. One person may call mastery of consonant blends a terminal objective, whereas another may identify it as an en route objective leading to the mastery of phonics. Both persons may be right. The point is that teachers determine what they want to call en route or terminal.

In any case, the skill needs to be mastered. A rule of thumb for developing and new teachers is to break down tasks or skills to the largest unit appropriate for the instructional situation. Some students can master multiple steps at once, whereas others will have to focus on each step individually. Again with the example of consonant blends, some students can master a set of blends containing the /L/ sound, whereas others may have to work on *bl, fl,* and *cl* separately.

Curriculum specialists and publishers of instructional materials have already done task analysis of many basic academic tasks. These skill hierarchies are lists of sequentially ordered subskills that lead to some terminal objective. Consequently, new teachers need not spend as much time analyzing the components of a task or skill. Hierarchies or

Pause and Reflect 5.4

Practice the process of task analysis in the following academic skills. Sequence each of the following into component skills. Put each step in order, starting from the smallest step.

Reading
Names alphabet letters
Discriminates letter sounds
Uses dictionary skills
Sequences a story read
Finds a main idea in the written paragraph
Names the time, setting, characters, and story plot

Mathematics
Solves a division problem
Makes change for a dollar
Writes a check
Uses a calculator

Self-Help
Brushes teeth
Ties shoes
Dresses self
Feeds self
Takes care of personal needs
Makes a bed
Cooks a hamburger

Leisure
Gets a strike in bowling
Completes a word search puzzle
Bats a ball
Uses a jump rope
Plants a vegetable garden
Checks out a library book
Watches a home video

curricula may not be available for a particular content area, however. In those cases, teachers must complete their own task analysis. Even when skill hierarchies or curricula are available, some task analysis may be needed to fit them to the learners' needs.

The benefit of following skill hierarchies is that planning is guided in a logical or sequential fashion. Teachers know where students are and where they need to go; they can see both the trees and the forest. This allows them to anticipate where instruction is going, to make adaptations, and to better assist students in reaching some terminal objective.

Instructional Activities and Materials to Be Used

Instructional activities are designed to assist students in the realization of targeted objectives. Designing instructional activities requires that teachers consider the stage of learning to which the activity is directed. The simple four-stage model (acquisition, fluency building, maintenance, and generalization) illustrated in Figure 5.2 can be used to show how learning proceeds. Stage 1 of learning, acquisition, is characterized by high rates of inaccurate responses. Students have little or no skill at this stage. With careful teacher-directed instruction, however, the rate of accurate responses rises and the rate of inaccurate responses declines.

When the responses reach 90% accuracy, students are moving into stage 2, fluency building. At this stage, instructional time involves students practicing their newly acquired skill to increase the speed of responding accurately. For instance, instead of solving computational math problems at a rate of 40 digits per minute with five or fewer errors, students practice building their speed to a rate of solving 60 digits per minute with zero errors.

Once students respond fluently, instructional time for the target skill can be gradually reduced, but students must be provided with practice at stage 3, maintenance. During the maintenance stage, students are largely engaged in periodic independent practice to ensure that they can still perform previously taught skills at an acceptable rate of speed and accuracy.

Stage 4, generalization, involves preparing students for using newly developed skills in settings and times different from those used during acquisition and fluency building. Generalization is accomplished by reducing the level of prompting and rein-

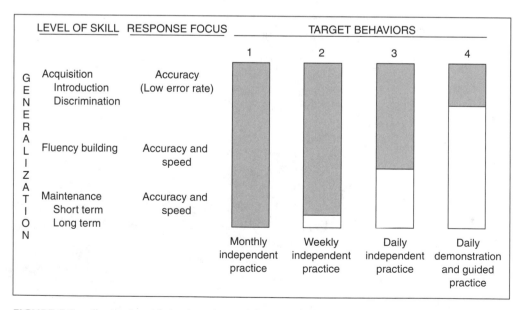

FIGURE 5.2 Illustration of the Interface of Stages of Learning, Response Focus, and Instructional Activities

forcement used by the teacher so that the students can demonstrate the behavior independently.

Instructional activities will be different at each of the four stages. Activities at the acquisition stage require intense teacher-student interaction in which the teacher models a response and students imitate. The teacher explains the steps to a skill or the definition and characteristics of a concept. Numerous cues are used to assist students in responding accurately. Fast responding is not the focus of instruction; the numbers of correct responses and errors are the important measures. During the fluency-building stage, teacher-student interactions continue, but the interactions are largely a function of providing corrective feedback as students work on daily independent practice activities. These activities require less teacher supervision than at the acquisition level. The supervision entails periodic checks of student work and reminders to students of the need to respond quickly and accurately. Maintenance stage activities are much the same type of independent practice activity used at the fluency-building stage, except that more review may be required beforehand and the practice is distributed over intervals of a week or month. Generalization stage activities are embedded into activities at all the previous stages and therefore do not occur necessarily as discrete independent activities. Further description of these stages and the types of strategies and learning activities used are provided in Chapter 6.

Regardless of the stage of learning, a lesson contains a beginning, a middle, and an end. This not-so-novel concept is surprisingly absent from the conceptualization of many developing teachers. The beginning of a lesson for effective teachers usually entails telling students what they will be doing during the lesson and linking previous lessons with the content of the current lesson. This often takes the form of a lesson-initiating review. Next, teachers provide some demonstration of a concept or academic skill and appropriate practice activities for students. Finally, the lesson should end with some form of closure that indicates to students the transition from one session to another. A lesson-ending review often fills this need. The following sections detail the various sections of a lesson.

Lesson Initiation. It is necessary to prepare students for a lesson by telling them what activities they will do and how these fit in with previous and future lessons. Consequently, the first step in lesson description should be to note the activities of the lesson. For example, an advance organizer may be used: "Today, we will discuss nouns and verbs. Then, we will look at some magazine ads to find nouns and verbs. Finally, I have a worksheet for you to complete." To link this lesson with the previous lesson, a teacher may say, "Yesterday, we talked about nouns. We defined them and came up with some examples. Today, we will do the same, but we will discuss verbs too." What may follow is a review of the definition and examples of nouns either by the teacher simply stating this information or, preferably, by students responding to teacher questioning. The latter strategy provides students with an additional practice activity, as well as a link to the previous lesson.

Demonstration. Once an initial review is conducted, instruction on new content begins (Hofmeister & Lubke, 1990; Hudson, 1996; Nolet & Tindal, 1993). Instruction initially involves a demonstration of target concepts, facts, skills, principles, or value judgments. The demonstration entails the teacher either providing a model or inducing the model from students. For instance, in teaching the concept of *square*, the modeling strategy would begin with the teacher presenting a diagram of a square and telling students what it is. Next, the teacher would write the definition of a square on the chalkboard: "A square is a quadrilateral with four congruent sides and four congruent angles." Using a diagram of a square, the teacher would then show how the example has four congruent sides and four congruent angles. In contrast, if using an induction strategy, the teacher would present a diagram of a square without naming its shape and proceed to ask students leading questions about the number of sides and angles and other attributes that distinguish a square. Using that information, the teacher may have students write a definition and give a name to the diagram. In either of these two cases, the target content is explicitly provided to students in a systematic fashion.

Although lecturing is a primary way of presenting information in content classes, effective teachers use demonstration, guided practice, and independent practice (Hudson, 1996). Nonetheless, Nolet and Tindal (1993) found that teachers actively lecture, demonstrate, and direct students through a task 70% of the time and that often students are expected to listen 57% of the time. Effective teachers may realize that although students often need listening comprehension and note-taking skills during demonstrated lectures, students with disabilities often lack such skills.

Another dimension to the demonstration phase of a lesson is the type of subject matter that students are learning. When teaching academic rules, the teacher needs to expose students to a stated rule (e.g., *bl* makes the /bl/ sound). Then students must apply the rule (e.g., sounding /bl/ in the word *blue*). When teaching concepts, teachers need to expose students to the definition or attributes (e.g., a square is a quadrilateral with four congruent sides and four congruent angles) and give examples and nonexamples. In cases where the concept is too abstract to define for students, the teacher may simply use examples and nonexamples to teach the concept (e.g., in teaching the concept of *square* to children functioning at the preschool level). Special types of concepts are called laws and lawlike principles. **Laws** and **lawlike principles** refer to cause-and-effect relationships usually found in the sciences. They are taught by explicating the causal agent and the effect and by linking the two together. For example, the cause-and-effect relationship between temperature and moisture and the formation of rain is illustrated in Figure 5.3.

Teachers need to specify whether they will provide a teacher model or use an inductive strategy and to indicate what type of subject matter will be taught. Clear statements of the facts, academic rules, concepts, and principles, along with examples and nonexamples, should be written in the plan (see Figure 5.3).

Guided Practice. Once the target subject matter has been demonstrated, the teacher engages students in guided practice activities. **Guided practice** is characterized by teacher-student interactions involving many teacher cues and prompts in a closely supervised activity. Examples of guided practice are asking students to state in unison the definition of a checking account, asking students about the attributes of a checking account, and asking students to evaluate examples and nonexamples of checking accounts. During guided practice, teachers model responses, lead students in practicing responses, and test students' skills in making responses with decreasing amounts of cues and prompts.

Often the shift from demonstration to guided practice is indistinguishable, especially when teachers use an inductive teaching approach. Being able to discern exactly when a lesson moves from demonstration to guided practice is not of primary concern. What is important is that the subject matter be clearly and explicitly presented and that students be given numerous opportunities to respond with high rates of accuracy (Greenwood, Delquadri, & Hall, 1984).

Independent Practice. When students respond accurately during guided practice, they are ready to work for fluency through independent practice activities such as seatwork (Hudson, 1996) or homework (Jayanthi, Sawyer, Nelson, Bursuck, & Epstein, 1995). **Independent practice** refers to activities in which students engage in repeated responding and require scant teacher supervision. **Fluency** refers to fast as well as accurate responding. Therefore, the focus of independent practice activities is on attaining a high rate of correct responding. Students are ready to work independently on a target skill after they have attained 90% accuracy. If a teacher asks students who are unable to re-

FIGURE 5.3   Teaching Steps for Explicating the Cause-and-Effect Relationship Between Rising Moist Air and Cold Air in the Atmosphere in the Formation of Rain

1. The teacher demonstrates the effect of rising moist air by reviewing a previously taught concept of *evaporation* (the sun's heating effect on bodies of water and atmosphere).

2. The teacher uses the diagram above to illustrate.

3. The teacher explains to students that the air high in the atmosphere is much colder, as illustrated in the diagram.

4. The teacher explains that as the heated, moist air rises up into the cold air, the little droplets of water begin to join and make bigger and bigger drops of water. When they are big and heavy enough, they begin to fall through the air down to the ground, in the form of rain.

5. The teacher shows students the following and explains:

   Cause ⟶ Effect

   heated, moist air rising
   +
   cold air in the upper
   atmosphere
   = Rain

6. The teacher next demonstrates the cause-and-effect relationship by heating a pot of water on a hot plate and holding an aluminum tray filled with ice above the pot of water. Soon steam (hot, moist air) begins to rise, and as the steam reaches the tray, drops form on the bottom of the tray. As the drops get larger or condense, they begin to "rain" down.

Variation: Instead of the teacher "explaining" each step, the teacher may ask a series of probing questions to *induce* the steps in the cause-and-effect relationship.

spond accurately to practice independently, students will either make numerous errors or constantly ask for assistance while the teacher attempts to work with others. In the case of homework, parents begin to wonder about the effectiveness of instruction if their children cannot respond accurately and require parental assistance.

Demonstration and guided practice are used to prepare students for independent practice. It may take one or several lessons involving only demonstration and guided practice on a target skill before students are able to work independently. Consequently, for a particular group of students, an instructional period may include either demonstration and guided practice; demonstration and guided and independent practice; or demonstration and guided practice plus independent practice on another previously acquired skill.

Teachers designing independent practice activities need to consider two points for students with special needs. First, practice sessions should be massed (daily practice) at the early stages of fluency building and then distributed on weekly or monthly intervals to facilitate short- and long-term maintenance. Second, practice activities should be considered in terms of the number of opportunities to respond provided for the learner. Some gamelike activities are highly motivating, but students only get a few chances to respond after waiting for other students to take their turns. Other activities, such as worksheets, require students to make many responses in a relatively short period of time. Consequently, teachers working with special needs students need to balance their practice activities so that they are exciting and motivational and provide the opportunity for students to make a sufficient number of responses.

Lesson Review. The final step of a lesson should be a summary review of the content being taught or practiced (Good, Grouws, & Ebermeier, 1983). A review allows a teacher to highlight the major points of the lesson, which helps students organize material. A review becomes practice when the teacher asks students to respond to questions about the major points of the lesson. Review provides a sense of closure to the lesson, gives students a sense that the lesson has an explicit ending, and helps prepare them for the transition into the next lesson.

Methods to Evaluate Lessons

Effective teachers monitor and evaluate their instruction. Measuring instruction gives a teacher the power to (1) determine when instructional results have been achieved, (2) demonstrate that instructional results match the teacher's intended outcomes, (3) improve instruction, and (4) increase the value of the instruction the teacher creates (Mager, 1996). Teachers must identify a behavior or academic task, set goals, collect data to establish a baseline, introduce an intervention, and record the results over time until the goal has been reached or until no further progress has been demonstrated. A technique frequently used is the direct measurement and recording of student performance using data charts or graphs (Fuchs & Fuchs, 1986).

Graphing Performance. Graphs allow data organization and visual analysis of the effects of an intervention on behavior or academic achievement. In addition, the use of a pictorial rather than a narrative form saves time and space (Deno & Mirkin, 1977). Two basic types of graphs may be used by developing teachers to record data on a daily, weekly, or monthly basis: performance graphs and progress graphs.

Performance graph. A performance graph depicts a regular, frequent measure of a student's performance and behavioral changes on a specific task over time (Figure 5.4).

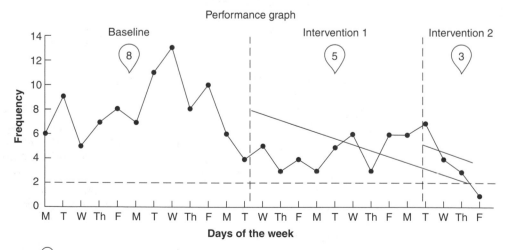

FIGURE 5.4 A Decrease in the Frequency of Targeted Behavior

An example is the number of times a student interrupts during a 30-minute interval. Plotted on the abscissa is the time interval during which the observations are recorded; plotted on the ordinate is the level of performance on that particular task. Vertical lines indicate periods of time or phases when specific instructional strategies are implemented. The **baseline** phase is first and shows that no instruction occurred or that current instructional procedures remained the same. Data from this phase are used to identify the student's current level of functioning and to set instructional objectives. Next, a **goal line** is plotted (horizontal dotted line). Based on the median performance of a target student (represented by the number inside the teardrop shapes on the graph), the estimated time of intervention available, and the goal, a **decision line** is plotted (the diagonal line beginning at the end of the baseline and running until the estimated ending data for intervention).

After the baseline phase, **intervention** phases are implemented as needed. Each of these phases represents implementation of a different strategy or mix of multiple instructional strategies. Student performance is monitored and continuously compared with the pattern of performance displayed during baseline. Data points are plotted until the goal is reached or until no further progress is made.

As the data points are plotted, the teacher decides to continue or to modify an intervention. Specific decision-making rules are used to make these determinations:

1. If for three consecutive sessions the data points fall above the decision line (when attempting to decrease a behavior) or fall below the decision line (when attempting to increase a behavior), then the treatment phase is terminated and a new or modified treatment is initiated.

2. After 3 weeks (fifteen sessions) of the same treatment, modify or change the treatment (to maintain interest and performance levels).

When necessary, additional intervention phases are introduced, with goal lines and decision lines reformulated. The teacher evaluates the effectiveness of instruction on the basis of changes in the level of student performance (how much higher or lower the student's current performance level is than the baseline performance) and the rate of change in student performance (how quickly the student's performance is improving).

In the example, the first intervention was the teacher talking with the target student about his behavior. Talking appeared to be effective, as indicated by the data points falling below the decision line. This decrease in the frequency of the behavior changed, however, as indicated by the last three data points of this phase, which fall above the line. This result prompted the termination of the first intervention and the implementation of a second intervention of planned ignoring. A new decision line was constructed by using the median performance level as the endpoint and drawing a line parallel to the first decision line. Ultimately, the target student did reach his goal during the second intervention phase. In fact, all three data points during this phase fall below the adjusted goal line for phase two.

Progress graph. A progress graph (or chart) is intended to measure the time it takes a student to master a set of instructional objectives. The abscissa indicates the time, and the ordinate expresses the series of objectives. Data points are plotted sequentially on the relevant intersection of the vertical (objective) and horizontal (time) lines and connected with a straight line, thereby illustrating graphically the student's progress in achieving the desired objectives. Unlike a performance graph, a progress graph is cumulative; that is, the data points never descend: They either remain at the same level or ascend. Regardless, the same decision rules are used in both performance and progress graphs.

The progress graph example provided in Figure 5.5 is based on a districtwide primary-level mathematics curriculum goal of mastering three objectives per week. LaShonda, a first-grade student, mastered only one objective after 6 weeks of instruction (not shown on the graph). The teacher referred LaShonda to the resource teacher,

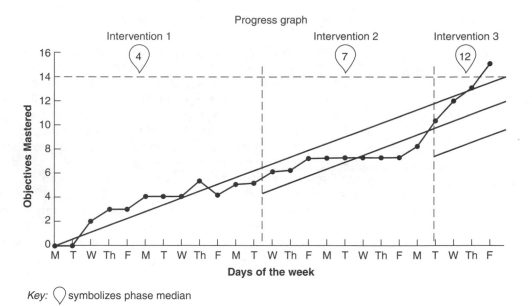

Key: ⬭ symbolizes phase median

FIGURE 5.5 Cumulative Mastery of Curriculum Objectives

and in consultation it was decided that a goal of three objectives per week was appropriate even though LaShonda would be functioning slightly below grade level at the end of the school year. Initially, a trained fifth-grade student tutored LaShonda on her arithmetic skills for 15 minutes daily. This extra practice proved insufficient, and individual work with the resource teacher for 15 minutes daily was added to the intervention. In the third phase, LaShonda was given 25 minutes of daily practice with the resource teacher.

Graphs are an effective means of monitoring student performance on specific instructional tasks and progress through sets of curricular objectives. The choice of a performance graph or a progress graph depends on the type of data to be charted. If the rate of mastering a set of instructional tasks is of greater importance, the use of a progress graph is recommended. If change in the level of performance on a specific task is to be highlighted, then the preferred medium is the performance graph. In both cases, the graphs provide a means for succinctly displaying the achievements of students and, consequently, the effectiveness of instruction. This conciseness can motivate students, teachers, parents, and other individuals interested in the student's attainment of educational goals. It should also be remembered that, in addition, graphs provide a vehicle for clear communication among teachers, administrators, and parents.

Adaptations and Modifications

An increasing concern as more and more diverse students spend time in the general education setting is the issue of adaptations and modifications (Lenz & Schumaker, 1999; Schumm, 1999; Simmons & Kameenui, 1999). When teachers adapt or modify the planned lesson, they help students acclimate to the task or activity through a change in the task, task presentation, or task evaluation. Or, teachers make changes by reworking the task, often making the task easier for students to do. Teachers rely on adaptations and modifications when they use prosthetic devices, adaptive equipment, flexible scheduling, test modifications, and so forth to enable students to remain in the least restrictive environment (LRE).

Planning for adaptations and modifications allows teachers to identify adaptations to enhance student outcomes. Teachers can determine in advance such factors as other student outcomes for the activity, including outcomes from such content areas as social skills, communications, and problem solving. Teachers can determine whether those activity outcomes would benefit the students and the type of lesson format (e.g., large group, small group, teacher-directed, independent work) best suited to students. Decisions can be made regarding current materials used, materials that students need to use, and necessary changes in materials for individual students. Teachers also can pinpoint such factors as current response modes for the group (e.g., making choices, writing short answers, expressing thoughts and feelings), the students' modes for responding, and whether the response modes should be changed (Williams & Fox, 1996).

Planned adaptations and modifications for students with disabilities often entail teachers adapting and modifying (1) social interactions between and among students and teachers, (2) the learning setting, (3) the teacher's lesson plans, (4) the instructional format and delivery, (5) equipment and materials, or (6) instructional evaluations. Box 5.2 illustrates adaptations and modifications that teachers have at their disposal for use with students with disabilities in the general education setting.

Box 5.2   Adaptations and Modifications for Students with Disabilities

1. Social Interactions

Use a "communication booklet" to allow students to write about positive experiences or to express grievances and frustrations. Assign students in the classroom to be "peer buddies" or mentors for the at-risk students. Reduce the emphasis on social competition. Give students preferred responsibilities. Reduce distracting stimuli. Maintain consistency in daily routine. Limit students' independent movement in the classroom environment. Provide students with choices and behavioral options. Avoid physical contact with students. Avoid arguing with students. Have students avoid crowded areas. Provide students with predetermined signals (e.g., hand signals, verbal cues). Model appropriate social behaviors for students. Provide positive feedback. Use a positive behavioral support system in the class. Teach problem-solving skills and social skills.

2. Learning Setting

Furnish students with their own personal spaces for belongings. Provide visual displays of progress (e.g., bulletin boards, charts). Post rules in various places throughout the classroom. Equip the classroom with a carrel for private study or time-out.

3. Lesson Plans

Initially state the objectives, purpose, and relevance of the lesson. Review prerequisite information; define key terms for understanding the main points. Explain the relationship between the new material and previously covered material.

4. Instructional Format and Delivery

Use ordinal numbers and temporal cues (first, second, finally) to organize data. Emphasize key concepts by varying voice quality and by using cue words—speaking them with emphasis, writing them on the chalkboard, and repeating them. Reduce extraneous information and stimuli. Discuss and summarize all main points. Ask factual and analytic questions throughout the presentation. Use cooperative learning techniques. Use collaborative discussion teams and sharing formats in place of lectures. Assign students shorter tasks; gradually increase the number of problems over time. Allow alternative assignments; gradually introduce more components of the regular assignments until these assignments are routinely performed (e.g., if the student feels uncomfortable giving an oral presentation, allow him or her to tape the assignment and play it for the class). Provide students with choices in selection of assignments. Use peer tutoring. Vary the schedule so that students are not passive for long periods of time. Select students randomly to respond. Vary response modes of instructional presentations. Integrate popular characters, items, and trends into classroom assignments. Offer students time at the end of class to review, summarize, and organize notes.

5. Equipment and Materials

Use examples, illustrations, charts, diagrams, advance organizers, and maps to make material more concrete. Provide visual clues, including overhead transparencies, charts, graphs, and lists. Provide advance organizers to define lesson objectives and responsibilities. Make periodic appointments with students to discuss their academic progress. Underline correct responses. Highlight main points. Organize notebooks and work areas. Place students close to the speaker. Assign hands-on materials. Provide students with a list of necessary materials for each activity. Use structured study guides, information organizers, or skeletal outlines. Allow peer note takers and audiocassettes.

6. Instructional Evaluations

Present oral tests for students with reading problems/learning disabilities. Encourage students' portfolio assessments. Use oral debates to check for student knowledge. Attempt to simplify responses to questions on tests to avoid frustration. Make certain that tests or quizzes measure knowledge of content and not related skills such as reading, spelling, or writing. Teach students to ask questions of their peers. Expand on and use student responses to questions. Allow students to create study guides for tests and quizzes. Teach test-taking strategies. Give shorter tests or quizzes more frequently. Allow students to take tests in alternative settings. Remove the threat of public knowledge of results. Use test alternatives (e.g., computer usage, models, drawings). Modify question formats when necessary. Simplify the response level (e.g., develop a separate test form). Modify test procedures with regard to length, frequency, and content.

Anticipated Problems

An important step before implementing a lesson plan is to anticipate potential instructional and behavioral problems that might arise during the lesson. Regardless of how well teachers prepare materials and activities, they may still have to deal spontaneously with glitches in the subject presentation, learning needs, or disruptive behavior by individual students. Such problems frequently can be addressed on the spur of the moment. Planning ahead, however, can help in either avoiding these problems before they occur or dealing with them with a minimal loss in instructional time. For example, developing teachers often have difficulties determining how long activities will take to complete and do not prepare backup activities when students complete the primary activity sooner than expected. By preparing a contingency plan, teachers can quickly move students into another activity and avoid the potential behavioral problems associated with students not being engaged in constructive activities (see Box 5.3.)

| **B**ox 5.3 | ## Case Study |

Mr. Sarason, the teacher of an elementary learning support service, uses a theme approach to teach units of concepts and skills. During one term, the theme was zoo animals. Students receiving learning support services for reading and language arts read about animals, listened to stories about zoos and jungles, and wrote compositions about the circus, the rain forest, and the desert. During math instruction, word problems and computation skill development were set in the context of animals' habitation needs, food supplies, and survival rates. With from 5 to 15 students working at different skill levels and on different types of activities at the same time, Mr. Sarason designed activities to fill in any "dead time" between activities. He used learning centers that involved activities that students could complete with scant or no assistance from him or his aide. (When activities required instruction, Mr. Sarason appropriated a specific time to teach the necessary skills.) So when students finished an instructional activity, they could spend time completing the papier-mâché zoo animal or sit at the listening post with a storybook and read along with a tape-recorded story.

Pause and Reflect 5.5

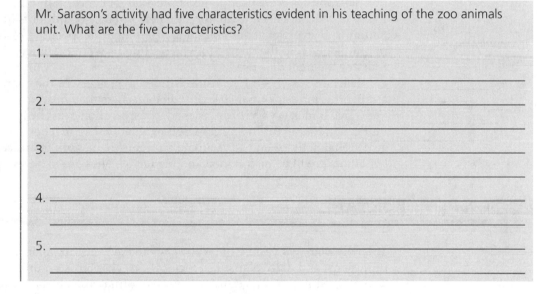

Mr. Sarason's activity had five characteristics evident in his teaching of the zoo animals unit. What are the five characteristics?

1. _____
2. _____
3. _____
4. _____
5. _____

Importantly, the activities had five characteristics:

1. "Dead time" was reduced.
2. Independence was promoted.
3. The learning of theme concepts and skills was enriched.
4. The teacher was able to work with other students.
5. The activities served as a reward for completing previous activities (Premack principle).

Self-Evaluation of Lesson Plans

To benefit fully from the experience of carrying out each instructional plan, teachers must spend time during and after the lesson, analyzing and evaluating what occurred. Teachers who use responsive instruction evaluate their instruction (Englert, Tarrant, &

Mariage, 1992). Thus, when they evaluate, teachers imbue instruction with new procedures or strategies at the point where students are likely to experience confusion. Teachers who evaluate adjust lessons on a moment-to-moment basis as they reflect on students within the lesson. Teachers accept and incorporate student ideas, examples, and experiences into the lesson content. They provide students with alternatives and opportunities to engage in decision-making. They continually tie new data to those that students already know (before, during, and after the lesson). When students make errors, reflective teachers use self-evaluation to link what students know and what they need to know (e.g., teachers bridge new knowledge to familiar knowledge). When teachers self-evaluate as a follow-up to lesson implementations, they respond to student mistakes as opportunities for students to gain new knowledge and meanings. Teachers who use self-evaluation can decrease their own behaviors that may be contributing to learning or behavior problems in the classroom (Allinder, Bolling, Oats, & Gagnon, 2000). Teachers who self-evaluate often are reflective, thereby personifying master teachers.

Thus, the self-evaluation process affords teachers the opportunity to determine the strengths and weaknesses of the lesson. The foci of the postlesson evaluation are teacher and student performance. In evaluating their own performance, teachers may analyze their organizational and lesson development, presentation of concepts or skills, or management of classroom behaviors. For example, they may determine whether sufficient examples were used to illustrate a target concept. In addition to their own effectiveness, teachers need to analyze the performance of students in terms of their participation in instructional activities and attainment of specified objectives. Consideration might be given to the degree to which students were motivated by an instructional activity or the materials used.

Teachers also need to consider students' mastery of the content. If students do not attain criterion performance levels, then teachers may need to recycle students through the DTM. If mastery has been reached, consideration must be given to the next objective in the skill hierarchy. In any case, self-evaluation of a teacher's ability to conduct an instructional activity and to facilitate students' behaviors is critical if effective teaching behaviors are to be maintained and ineffective ones are to be reduced or eliminated.

LESSON-PLAN FORMATS

Teachers plan at a variety of levels: They make year-long plans, semester or term plans, unit plans, and daily plans. The focus of this chapter is on unit and lesson plans. Selection of the unit plan or a daily lesson-plan format must be based on classroom variables and individual needs at any given time.

Daily Lesson Plans

The most commonly used format for writing lesson plans is the **traditional group instructional plan**. Such a plan lists objectives and provides a relatively detailed description of the materials, activities, and evaluation procedures for multiple small-group or single large-group instruction. Teachers using this format write down when and how they will provide instruction. An alternative format is the **daily activity schedule,** a succinct list designating when instruction will occur, with scant reference to how instruction will be carried out. Often this format is used in conjunction with a unit-plan format or in resource rooms where students work predominantly on their own, with their assignments for each day listed in a work folder.

Traditional Group Instructional Plan. Traditionally, preservice teacher trainees have been taught to construct daily lesson plans with the assumption that, at any given time, they would be working with a single large group or two to four small groups simultaneously. The generic format of a lesson plan includes a statement of the lesson objective and a description of the materials, activities, and evaluation procedures to be used. This format continues to be used extensively because of its ease of use and applicability. In many classrooms for students with disabilities, large and simultaneous small-group instruction and practice are provided. In those classrooms where students are individually placed at different points in the curriculum, however, the traditional lesson-plan format is not feasible.

In fact, the chapter section entitled "Components of Successfully Planned Lessons" contains the categories used in the traditional daily lesson plan. Box 5.4 illustrates how the categories are laid out in the traditional lesson plan. Sections 1 through 6 are the contents of the actual plan; the remaining sections are used to self-evaluate the lesson after the plan has been implemented. The following steps are needed to complete the lesson plan:

1. Provide the teacher's name, the date, and the students' or group's name in the header.

2. Write behaviorally stated objectives that indicate how students will respond to demonstrate mastery.

3. In the activities description section, write step-by-step procedures for each activity. Content information such as definitions of concepts and academic rules should be included as well.

4. List all materials to be used in the lesson.

5. List evaluation tools/measures and indicate whether the measures will be taken at daily, weekly, or monthly intervals. The evaluation tools selected should be designed to assess the mastery of the objectives, not the activity.

6. List any special adaptations and modifications needed for individual students.

7. Describe anticipated instructional or behavioral problems, along with strategies to deal with any problems if they arise.

8. After the lesson has been implemented, note any problems that occurred and the strategies used to resolve them. Provide information that will be helpful in dealing with problems in the future. Note any other information that would be helpful in preparing for the same lesson.

B ox 5.4   **Traditional Lesson-Plan Format**

Lesson Preparation and Analysis Form

Name: Ms. Baldwell   Date: 5/12/02
Student(s) or Group: Cary, Carlos, Bill, Su-Lee, and Trone

1. Behavioral objectives of activity

When given a passage to read, students will be able to underline two important words or phrases for each paragraph with 90% accuracy.

When given a passage to read, students will be able to see-write answers to seven of eight comprehension questions for three consecutive passages.

2. Description of activity

Demonstration

Explain the purpose of the underlining strategy (to help the student identify and recall important information). Tell students that the teacher will show them how to use the underlining strategy. Model the strategy by reading the first paragraph of the passage aloud. Verbalize the steps to the strategy:

"I need to underline two important words or phrases."

"Important words or phrases tell me about the main idea or details."

"Underline."

"Ask myself, why is this important?"

"Go on to the next paragraph."

Guided practice

Have students read the second paragraph.

Lead students through verbalizing the steps above.

Repeat the guided practice with paragraphs 3 and 5.

Lead students in summarizing the content of each paragraph by using the underlined key phrases.

After finishing the passage, lead students in using underlined phrases to read-write answers to comprehension questions.

Independent practice

None.

3. Measurement

Note each student's use of self-instruction statements.

Note each student's underlining of two words or phrases per paragraph.

Tally the number of comprehension questions correctly.

4. Materials

Story "Animals With Pouches"

Highlighter pens

5. Adaptations

Engage students in choral practice on self-verbalizations.

6. Problems that might be encountered

Students may not be able to discriminate important from unimportant words or phrases. If so, ask students to justify the importance of the words and phrases they underlined. Provide feedback on selections and justifications.

7. Problems that actually arose

Students had difficulty identifying important words and phrases. Feedback was provided, and student selections were shaped into more appropriate responses.

8. Behavioral techniques used during activity

Strategy modeling and specific academic praise for accurate self-verbalizations and underlining

9. What you learned from this activity

Students respond well to modeling strategy steps. The model and lead steps provide sufficient support to students so that they can respond accurately and enjoy their success.

Daily Activity Schedule. The daily activity schedule replaces the traditional daily lesson plan with a daily timeline depicting when instruction will occur. Teachers list the sequence of activities and document who will supervise each activity (teacher, aide, or students). The activities listed on the schedule are derived from either (1) a unit plan, which contains a list of instructional objectives, materials to be used, a description of the activities, and evaluation procedures that monitor progress toward attaining the objectives or (2) a set of materials from an individual student's work folder. The daily activity schedule provides planned activities without the details for each day of instruction.

A daily activity schedule is designed to achieve the following:

1. Provide consistent, accurate, and meaningful planning for each student

2. Provide a written record of previous activities to facilitate future planning, monitoring, and record keeping

3. Provide a plan of action for the implementation of the unit plan.

Alternative Forms: Option A.
Instructions for completing daily activity schedule Option A (see Figure 5.6):

1. Enter your name and date.

2. According to the time blocks that you determine, enter each student's name in the appropriate column:

    Activity with teacher: Teacher-directed activities are typically used to introduce, continue development, or review acquisition and/or provide guided practice.

    Activity with aide: These can be teacher-directed activities used by the teacher aide as above to introduce, continue development, or review acquisition skills.

ACTIVITY SCHEDULE

Teacher: Ms. Ley   **Date:** Wednesday, April 19

Groups:
G1: Willie, Brett, Jose, Errol & Juanita
G2: Barb, Sam, Myron, Amal & Robert
G3: Lindsay, Kelly & Chris
G4: Conor, Patrick, Kevin & Shannon
G5: Mike, Maria & Bo
G6: Greg, Jack, Carol & Paul

Time	Activity with teacher	Activity with aide	Independent practice
8:30–9:30	**G1** Flash card drill (sums to 10)	**G2** Language master: fluency building on phrases to 100 wpm	**Kevin & Conor** computer (Spell Blaster)
9:30–10:30	**G2** Reading comprehension, pp. 42–48: underlining strategy training with explicit text questions	**G1** Handwriting: copy and edit last week's language experience sentences	**G5 & 6** Peer tutoring, 2 digit x 2 digit multiplication w/regrouping
10:30–11:30	**G3** Oral repeated reading, pp. 31–36; fluency building to 120 wpm	**G4** Mastery test: fractions G6 Probe: 2 x 2 multiplication	**G1** Listening post: spelling quiz **G2 & 5** Sustained silent reading
12:15–1:15	**G4** Reading comprehension, pp. 98–107: paraphrase strategy training with explicit text questions	**G5** Handwriting: copy and edit last week's language experience stories	Lindsay: Implicit text questions from passage Chris: Listening post: Main idea from "Over the Fence"
1:15–2:00	**G3, 4, & 5** Written expression topic: fossils (based on field trip)		

FIGURE 5.6   Completed Daily Activity Schedule for Option A

Independent activity: These are practice activities to help the students maintain or develop fluency on previously acquired skills. They are characterized by the students' abilities to complete the activity with little or no teacher assistance once the directions for the activity have been overviewed.

3. Beside the student's name, list each activity. Be specific as to page number, cassette, filmstrip, disk, and so forth. Also indicate whether the activity entails demonstration, guided, or independent practice.

Helpful hints

1. If your schedule remains the same on a daily/weekly basis, fill in students' names, time periods, and so forth. Then make a master copy of the activity schedule. As a result, you will only have to complete the activity columns from day to day or week to week.

2. A student can be a group, if consistent and clearly labeled initially.

3. A code may be developed to correspond to your unit plan. For example: In the unit plan, reading activities can be numbered such as R-1, R-2, and so forth; math activities as M-1, M-2, and so forth. Then, when entering activities on the activity schedule, R-1 or M-2 could be used to refer to specific items on your unit plan.

Alternative Forms: Option B.
Instructions for completing daily activity schedule Option B (an advantage to this format is that each student and teacher can readily see daily routines and expectations; see Figure 5.7):

1. Use one sheet for each day of the week.

2. Fill in students' names across the top. Arrange by classes/grade levels to facilitate groupings. If pencil is used and space on the schedule is a priority, new students can replace those who leave your program.

3. Enter time (standard time) notations down the left side (e.g., 8:00, 8:30, 9:00, 9:30).

4. Enter each student's daily schedule (including lunch, recess, regular classroom activities, other specialists, and so forth). If desired, use consistent color coding for each different activity.

5. Block out periods in your classroom setting.

6. Record specific daily activities (e.g., reading, math, language, spelling) directly on the sheet. If a plastic or separate sheet is used, the master schedule can be reused each week/day.

Unit Plans

Individualized programming is not exclusive to special education services, but it is a more predominant practice than in general education. In addition, the heterogeneity of many special education services is more extreme than in many general education class programs. As a result, many special education teachers provide multilevel instruction to students who are functioning within a broad range of skills. Often this means that separate instructional activities must be prepared for each student. Because of these factors, preparing daily lesson plans can be an enormous task. To ask developing teachers to write traditional lesson plans for each student or small sets of students at each skill level each day is unrealistic. The unit-plan format is a viable option to accommodate the need to write effective lesson plans within the context of special education service locations.

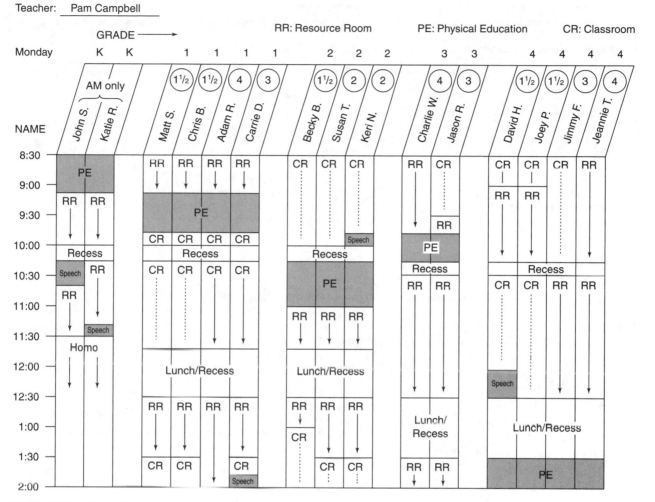

FIGURE 5.7   Completed Daily Activity Schedule for Option B

The **unit plan** is the vehicle whereby the specific objectives are translated into and correlated with specific activities, materials, and evaluation methods. A unit plan is designed to achieve the following:

1. Provide a comprehensive plan for curriculum implementation

2. Provide a foundation and rationale for all instruction

3. Develop creative planning from determination to implementation and evaluation of instructional objectives.

Alternative Forms: Option A.
Instructions for completing unit plan Option A (see Figure 5.8):

1. Enter the student's or group's name, subject, major goal, dates of initiation and completion, and charting method (progress or performance graphs).

2. Enter specific objectives that correspond to a major objective.

3. List all materials that might be used.

4. List activities that will help students reach the stated objectives. Under each activity, describe the specific step-by-step procedures. Content information such as definitions

Students: Groups 1 & 2		**Annual Goal:** Students will improve reading comprehension	
Date of Initiation: September 18		**Date of Completion:**	

Objectives	Materials	Activities	Evaluation
1. When given passage at their instructional level, SWBAT see-write correct answers to seven out of eight comprehension questions related to text explicit and implicit information for three consecutive sessions.	Stories from basal and supplemental reading series.	**Semantic Web (SW)** 1. Set purpose for reading (e.g., predicting events, main ideas, related facts). 2. Discuss theme of story and relate to students' background experiences. 3. Have students read first and second paragraphs. 4. Assign third paragraph. Have students predict what will happen next in the story. 5. Formulate a core question and write on the board. 6. Elicit possible answers to core question and write in list separate from web. 7. Ask students to accept, reject, or modify answers. 8. Draw web. 9. Build support for web strands. Ask students to examine them and accept, reject, or modify. (Students may reread prior to doing this.) 10. Guide students to relating strands (two or three relationships maximum).	Probe containing eight comprehension questions will be completed at the end of each passage. 

FIGURE 5.8 Unit Plan Format for Option A

of concepts and academic rules should be included as well. The activity description will have to be entered only at the initial entry point in the unit plan. If you wish to use the same activity to reach another objective, you need only list the activity title in the activity column next to subsequent objectives.

5. List evaluation tools/measures and indicate whether they are daily, weekly, or monthly. The evaluation tools selected should be designed to assess the mastery of the objectives, not the activities.

Helpful hints

1. Be as broad-based as possible. Build and adapt objectives, activities, and materials across groups and skill levels.

2. Be creative and flexible. Design a mixture of creative high-interest activities, along with less elaborate drill activities.

Alternative Forms: Option B.
Instructions for completing unit plans Option B (see Figure 5.9):

1. Develop a card file of successful activities. Code activities according to skill area.

2. Activity cards might include name of activity, identifying code, materials needed, objective, appropriate and instructional level.

3. Copy several cards onto one sheet of paper to be included with your unit plan.

FIGURE 5.9 Activity Card for Unit Plan Format Option B

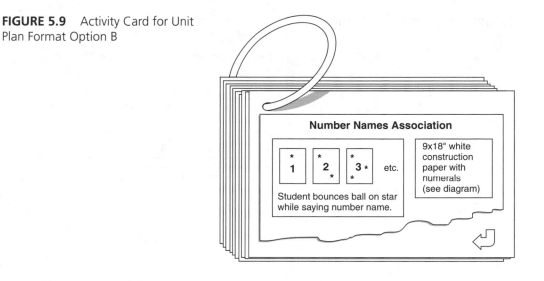

This technique permits using the same activity with several skill levels without re-copying the same information. In addition, the card file will be an invaluable resource.

STRATEGIC PLANNING FOR INCLUSIVE PROGRAMMING

With a growing number of students with disabilities being educated in the general education setting, planning strategies have been developed to address the diverse needs of all students. The Joint Committee on Teacher Planning for Students with Disabilities (1995) highlighted specific routines based on the premise that teachers in inclusive classrooms require plans that focus on specific students' needs and (1) the skills and content to be acquired and (2) the activities that students will engage in to learn the skills and content.

One such method is the **lesson planning pyramid** (see Figure 5.10). Developed by Schumm, Vaughn, and Leavell (1994), the pyramid is a planning process in which teachers use a mental template or graphic image to focus on the content of a lesson that will be learned by all students, most students, and some students and how the learning will be directed. The advantage to using the pyramid is that it focuses on the entire range of learners in the content-based class yet does not necessitate extensive paperwork. To use the pyramid, teachers first identify the concepts to be taught and then differentiate what all, most, and some students are to learn from the lesson. Second, teachers structure an agenda for the lesson. In developing the agenda of activities, teachers are to consider the unique aspects of their classroom, such as (1) class size, (2) how well their students work together in small groups, (3) resources available, (4) possible instructional adaptations, and (5) events that may distract students or alter instructional time. Finally, the teacher lists the materials to be used, specifies in-class and homework assignments, and identifies how student learning will be evaluated.

Another method, the **lesson planning routine** (Bulgren & Lenz, 1996), is an explicit planning process that requires teachers to reflect on the content and outcomes of a lesson and to create a graphic road map for the lesson (see Figure 5.11). When completing the graphic organizer, teachers use the acronym SMARTER to guide their reflective planning. The seven steps involved in the SMARTER prompt are described in Table 5.1. This type of lesson planning is most effective when used in conjunction with other strategic routines, such as reflective course planning and reflective unit planning. For additional information and specific implementation procedures regarding these tech-

FIGURE 5.10 The Lesson Planning
Pyramid Form

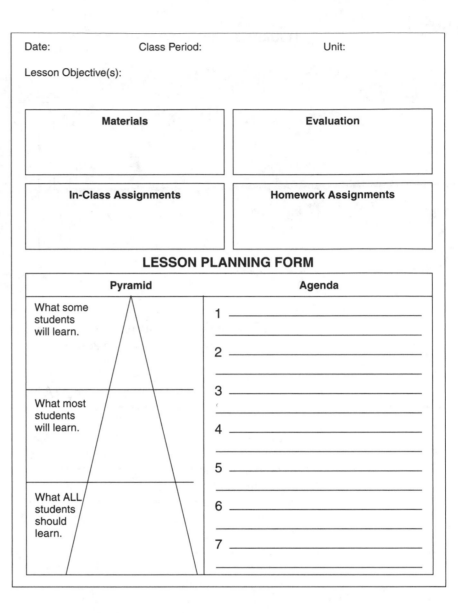

niques, we recommended that developing and beginning teachers consult Deshler,
Ellis, and Lenz (1996).

Lesson Plans and Computer Technology

Some school districts across the country are beginning to plan the use of computer technology to complement specially designed instruction. In addition to providing computers, districts are establishing local area networks that connect classroom computers to
one another electronically and wide area networks to connect schools. Increasingly, districts are enhancing their connectivity by providing access to the Internet through on-
line and access service providers. Consequently, teachers are able to plan ideas, share
methods, and disseminate lesson plans locally or globally. For example, America Online
(AOL) has an education area that allows users to download or upload lesson plans devised for a variety of subjects and student populations. Information lesson plans on the
Internet are appearing in local areas and on "teacher pages" in which teachers can share
instructional strategies and tactics.

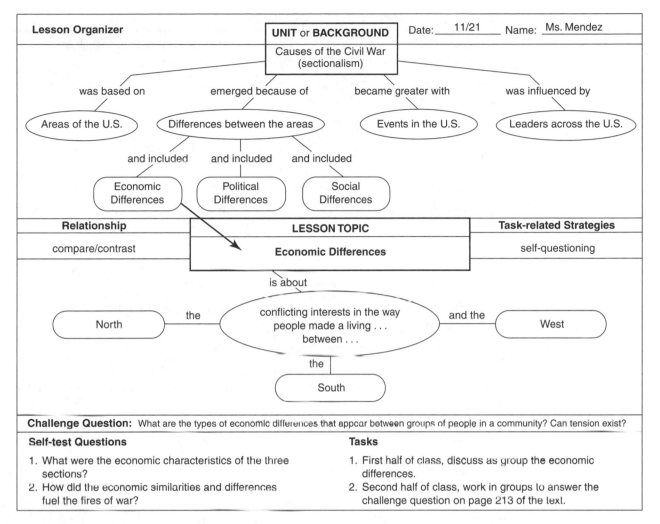

FIGURE 5.11 Lesson Planning Routine Graphic

Additionally, the laptop computer has been reported by some school officials to improve the quality of other aspects of the instructional process, including special education referral-to-placement procedures, school-based conferences, and staff meetings (Johnston, Proctor, & Corey, 1995). Paperwork, including lesson plans and required procedures for special education services, can be retrieved, modified, and stored more effectively. Staff can use their time and materials more efficiently. Data files can present an immediate visual display that helps teachers make informed decisions and track longitudinal progress. Teachers can easily generate data when reporting lesson results to parents in documenting progress for school records. Data can be easily compiled to help administrators and teachers make informed decisions about curriculum and instruc-

𝗣 *ause and Reflect 5.6*

How are your planning skills? Write a reflective summary indicating why writing out specific lesson plans will help you with your students. Include in your reflective summary five specific teacher behaviors you want to do/increase to provide effective lesson plans to your students. What can you do now to get started to do these five behaviors?

TABLE 5.1   SMARTER Reflective Planning

1. **Select** the critical content outcomes and develop a set of critical questions that all students should be able to answer by the end of instruction.

2. **Map** the organization of the critical content in a way that will show the structure of the content and that will be meaningful to all students.

3. **Analyze** why the critical content might be difficult to learn, based on:
   amount   complexity
   interest   student background
   relevance   organization
   abstractness   external conditions (e.g., interruptions)

4. **Reach** decisions about how the content will be taught and how the content might be enhanced during instruction to reduce potential learning difficulties through specific teaching devices.

5. **Teach** students about the enhancements in ways that will inform them about how to use the devices, routines, strategies, or curriculum revision, and explicitly guide students to become actively involved in exploring and using the enhancements to improve learning.

6. **Evaluate** mastery of the critical content and related processes for high achievers, average achievers, low achievers, and others.

7. **Reevaluate** planning and teaching decisions for the next step in learning.

Adapted from Bulgren, J., & Lenz, K. (1996). Strategic instruction in the content areas. In D. D. Deshler, E. S. Ellis, & B. K. Lenz (Eds.), *Teaching adolescents with learning disabilities*. Copyright 1996 by Love Publishers. Reprinted with permission.

tion. Smith (2000) reported that technology is now integrated into teacher preparation programs.

Importantly, effective teachers can have an impact on students' educational placement decisions through the use of technology and lesson planning. For instance, some teachers now are planning and organizing assistive technology resources into lessons in order to make it possible for students with disabilities to attend neighborhood schools and be successfully included in general education classes (Webb, 2000). Milone (2000) also described a total inclusion program in which teachers planned lessons using technology in order to ensure that special needs students were fully integrated into general education classrooms. Computer technology is a major component of the 21st century that will affect the quality of both the content and presentation of lesson plans and other relevant classroom documentation.

SUMMARY

The bottom line for effective teaching is that teachers need to invest a substantial amount of time in preparing to teach. Although many developing and beginning teachers would like to think there must be a shortcut, there is none. To be effective, teachers have to work hard to develop their lessons and revise and polish them continuously.

This chapter provided beginning teachers with an overview of the rationale and principles of planning that set the foundation for effective teaching. Plans help teachers identify clearly what they hope to accomplish and specify the means for accomplishing their goals. They help foster confidence and security. Plans provide the basis for an organized educational direction that ensures the success of students in developing academic, behavioral, and functional skills. To derive these benefits, plans must contain objectives, sound instructional and practice activities, and a method for evaluating attainment of the objectives (Garland, 1982).

Several suggested formats were presented that provide a starting point in developing a system of planning. Teachers need to examine the generic principles of effective planning and examine some possible formats for writing out their plans. Then they can devise a system that fits their own needs.

ACTIVITIES TO EXTEND YOUR KNOWLEDGE

1. Plan a science lesson on the weather involving a diverse group of five learners, two of whom require assistive technology. Use at least two of the Point and Click Web sites listed in this chapter to assist in locating creative lesson plan themes.

2. Work in groups to task-analyze the following skills. Be sure to sequence each component skill (put the task into small, ordered steps): tying shoes; using tense, pronouns, and possessives; using dictionary skills; naming numbers 0 to 20; counting objects 0 to 20; solving simple addition and subtraction problems; telling time; using money skills.

3. Using one of the task analyses above, determine a learning outcome or behavioral outcome for students at the grade or ability level you teach. Practice writing instructional objectives for the learning outcome. Practice writing behavioral objectives for the behavioral outcome.

4. Use the instructional objectives or behavioral objectives above to practice planning appropriate equipment and materials you will need to implement the objective.

5. Plan one modification to an instructional objective or behavioral objective. The modification may be (*a*) social interactions between and among students and teachers, (*b*) the learning setting, (*c*) the teacher's lesson plans, (*d*) the instructional format and delivery, (*e*) equipment and materials, or (*f*) instructional evaluations.

6. Write out a teacher-student(s) script to implement the planned objective. Include demonstration, guided practice, and independent practice scripts as appropriate for students in your class.

7. Write out how you will evaluate the objective while/after it is implemented. How will you link the objective to the next lesson? How will you review the lesson the next time it is taught? How will you evaluate student outcomes?

8. Share your results with your instructor and colleagues for each of the activities listed above. Discuss new ideas with your host teacher or university supervisor in terms of how you can implement your new ideas in your field site. How will you self-reflect your own teacher behaviors?

POINT AND CLICK

The following Web sites highlight the chapter's theme of lesson planning. Each of these listings can assist new teachers in their use of carefully-developed instructional activities and materials in planned lessons.

Council for Learning Disabilities
P.O. Box 40303
Overland Park, KS 66204
www.1wintrop.edu/cld
A Web site devoted to helping teachers of students with learning disabilities share strategy planning and tactics for effective instruction.

The Gateway
Syracuse University
Syracuse, NY
http://www.thegateway.org
http://www.ed.gov/
http://www.ed.gov/NLE/index.html
http://www.askeric.org/ithome/
A Web site devoted to offering lesson plans, prekindergarten through adult education, that are free to educators. The National Library of Education and the ERIC Clearinghouse, Syracuse University, created this Web site.

Big Chalk Corporation
1-800-521-0600, ext. 3304
fax: 734-973-9145
www.bigchalk.com
A Web site devoted to helping students select resources needed to conduct research, access the curriculum, and collaborate with peers. Teachers can receive data on instructional planning for curriculum integration of various topics. Additionally, teachers can access resources for parents to link school instruction with home activities.

Family Education Network
1-800-927-6006
fax: 617-542-6564
Family eduction.com
www.myschoolonline.com
A Web site for teachers to share ideas and inspiration on planning activities and resources for timely events and school features.

CompassLearning
1-800-521-8538
fax: 858-587-1629
www.compasslearning.com
A Web site promoted to helping teachers create, explore, and achieve more comprehensive lesson plans and lesson integration. CompassLearning, formerly Jostens Learning, is part of the educational divisions of Ripplewood Holdings, LLC.

REFERENCES

Algozzine, B., Ysseldyke, J. E., & Elliott, J. (1997). *Strategies and tactics for effective instruction.* Longmont, CO: Sopris West.

Allinder, R. M., Bolling, R. M., Oats, R. G., & Gagnon, W. A. (2000, July/August). Effects of teacher self-monitoring on implementation of curriculum-based measurement and mathematics computation achievement of students with disabilities. *Remedial and Special Education, 21*(4), 219–226.

Archer, A. (1991, June). *Design of instruction: Lesson structure.* Paper presented at the Fourteenth Annual Intervention Procedures Conference, Logan, UT.

Bulgren, J., & Lenz, K. (1996). Strategic instruction in content areas. In D. D. Deshler, E. S. Ellis, & B. K. Lenz (Eds.), *Teaching adolescents with learning disabilities* (pp. 409–474). Denver: Love.

Carnine, D. (1991). Curricular interventions for teaching high-order thinking to all students: Introduction to the special series. *Journal of Learning Disabilities, 24,* 261–269.

Cartwright, G. P., & Cartwright, C. A. (1972). Gilding the lily. *Exceptional Children, 39,* 231–234.

Cartwright, G. P., Cartwright, C. A., & Ward, M. (1981). *Educating special learners.* Belmont, CA: Wadsworth.

Clark, C. M., & Yinger, R. J. (1979). *Three studies of teacher planning* (Research Series No. 55). East Lansing: Michigan State University, Institute for Research on Teaching.

Cooper, J. M. (1986). *Classroom teaching skills* (3rd ed.). Lexington, MA: Heath.

Darch, C., Miller, A., & Shippen, P. (1998). Instructional classroom management: A proactive model for managing student behavior. *Beyond Behavior, 9*(3), 18–27.

Deno, S., & Mirkin, P. (1977). *Data-based program modification: A manual.* Reston, VA: Council for Exceptional Children.

Deshler, D. D., Ellis, E. S., & Lenz, B. K. (1996). *Teaching adolescents with learning disabilities.* Denver: Love.

Deshler, D. D., & Schumaker, J. B. (1986). Learning strategies: An instructional alternative for low-achieving adolescents. *Exceptional Children, 52,* 583–590.

Dieker, L. A. (2000). *Co-teaching lesson plan book 2000.* Reston, VA: Council for Exceptional Children.

Englert, C. S., Tarrant, K. L., & Mariage, T. V. (1992). Defining and redefining instructional practice in special education: Perspectives on good teaching. *Teacher Education and Special Education, 15*(2), 62–87.

Fuchs, L. S., & Fuchs, D. (1986). Effects of systematic formative evaluation: A meta-analysis. *Exceptional Children, 53,* 199–208.

Gable, R. A., Laycock, V. K., Maroney, S. A., & Smith, C. R. (1991). *Preparing to integrate students with behavioral disorders.* Reston, VA: Council for Exceptional Children.

Garland, C. (1982). *Guiding clinical experiences in teacher education.* New York: Longman.

Good, T., Grouws, D., & Ebermeier, H. (1983). *Active mathematics teaching.* New York: Longman.

Greenwood, C. R., Delquadri, J. C., & Hall, R. V. (1984). Opportunity to respond and student academic performance. In W. L. Heward, T. E. Heron, D. S. Hill, & J. Trap-Porter (Eds.), *Focus on behavior analysis in education* (pp. 58–88). New York: Merrill/Macmillan.

Hofmeister, A., & Lubke, R. (1990). *Research into practice: Implementing effective teaching strategies.* Needham Heights, MA: Allyn & Bacon.

Hudson, P. (1996). Using a learning set to increase the test performance of students with learning disabilities in social studies classes. *Learning Disabilities Research & Practice, 11*(2), 78–85.

Hudson, P., Lignugaris-Kraft, B., & Miller, T. (1993). Using content enhancements to improve the performance of adolescents with learning disabilities in content classes. *Learning Disabilities Research & Practice, 8,* 106–126.

Jayanthi, M., Sawyer, V., Nelson, J. S., Bursuck, W. D., & Epstein, M. H. (1995). Recommendations for homework-communication and problems: From parents, classroom teachers, and special education teachers. *Remedial and Special Education, 16*(4), 212–227.

Johnston, S. D., Proctor, W. A., & Corey, S. E. (1995). A new partner in the IEP process: The laptop computer. *Teaching Exceptional Children, 28*(1), 46–49.

Joint Committee on Teacher Planning for Students with Disabilities. (1995). *Planning for academic diversity in America's classrooms: Windows on reality research, change, and practice.* Lawrence: University of Kansas Center on Research and Learning.

Lenz, K., & Schumaker, J. (1999). *Adapting language arts, social studies, and science materials for the inclusive classroom.* Reston, VA: Council for Exceptional Children.

Mager, R. F. (1996). *Preparing instructional objectives.* Atlanta: Center for Effective Performance.

McCutcheon, G. (1980). How do elementary school teachers plan their courses? *Elementary School Journal, 81,* 4–23.

Mercer, C. D., & Mercer, A. R. (2001). *Teaching students with learning problems* (6th ed.). Upper Saddle River, NJ: Merrill/Prentice Hall.

Milone, M. (2000). Special teachers for special needs. *Technology & Learning, 20,*(9), 40–44.

Nolet, V., & Tindal, G. (1993). Special education in content area classes: Development of a model and practical procedure. *Remedial and Special Education, 14*(1), 36–48.

Peterson, P. L., Marx, R. W., & Clark, C. M. (1978). Teacher planning, teacher behavior, and students' achievement. *American Educational Research Journal, 15,* 417–432.

Pettig, K. L. (2000). On the road to differentiated instruction. *Educational Leadership, 58*(1), 14–18.

Rosenshine, B. (1986). Synthesis of research on explicit teaching. *Educational Leadership, 43*(7), 60–69.

Rutherford, R., & Warger, C. (1995). *A collaborative approach to social skills instruction: An inclusionary ap-*

proach. Reston, VA: Foundation for Exceptional Innovations.

Schumm, J. S. (1999). *Adapting reading and math materials for the inclusive classroom.* Reston, VA: Council for Exceptional Children.

Schumm, J. S., Vaughn, S., & Leavell, A. (1994). Planning pyramid: A framework for planning for diverse student needs during content area instruction. *Reading Teacher, 47,* 608–615.

Simmons, D., & Kameenui, E. J. (1999). *Toward successful inclusion of students with disabilities: The architecture of instruction.* Reston, VA: Council for Exceptional Children.

Smith, S. J. (2000). Graduate student mentors for technology success. *Teacher Education and Special Education, 23*(2), 167–182.

Thousand, J. S., Villa, R., & Nevin, A. (Eds.). (1994). *Creativity and collaborative learning: A practical guide to empowering students and teachers.* Baltimore: Paul H. Brookes.

Webb, B. J. (2000, March/April). Planning and organizing assistive technology resources in your school. *Teaching Exceptional Children, 32,*(4), 50–55.

West, L. L., Corbey, S., Boyer-Stephens, A., Jones, B., Miller, R. J., & Sarkees-Wircenski (1999). *Integrating transition planning into the IEP process* (2nd ed.). Reston, VA: Council for Exceptional Children.

Whitaker, S. D. (2000). What do first year special education teachers need? Implications for induction programs. *Teaching Exceptional Children, 33,* 1, 28–36.

Williams, W., & Fox, T. J. (1996). Planning for inclusion: A practical process. *Teaching Exceptional Children, 28*(3), 6–13.

Wood, J. W. (1998). *Adapting instruction to accommodate students in inclusive settings* (3rd ed.). Upper Saddle River, NJ: Merrill/Prentice Hall.

Delivering Instruction

In this chapter, we will

- ✔ identify elements of delivering instruction effectively

- ✔ describe generic procedures of direct instruction (DI) and guided discovery learning (GDL)

- ✔ provide applied examples of DI and GDL

- ✔ examine procedures for presenting concepts and academic rules in subject material

- ✔ analyze students' learning stages and teachers' behaviors during the learning process

- ✔ discuss the TEAL model—Teaching: Explicit Activation of Learning

- ✔ illustrate applications of various instructional strategies

O ur purpose of this chapter is to describe for developing teachers a set of instructional elements related to effective instruction. These instructional elements derive from two instructional models prominent in classrooms today: direct instruction (DI) and guided discovery learning (GDL). These models form the conceptual and procedural basis for a variety of other instructional approaches. For example, DI steps underscore the strategies intervention model (Deshler & Schumaker, 1986) and the classwide peer tutoring model (Greenwood, Delquadri, & Hall, 1984). The GDL steps form the basis of propletic teaching and scaffolding (Bruner, 1973; Rojewski & Schell, 1994; Vygotsky, 1978), cooperative learning (Johnson, Johnson, Holubec, & Roy, 1984; Slavin, 1990), language experience approaches, and process writing (Graves, 1994).

Then, we provide specific procedures for presenting concepts and academic rules in subject material. All content areas in special education and general education reflect both concepts and academic rules to varying degrees.

Next, we describe learning stages that students pass through as they develop mastery of the subject matter that teachers present. Our lesson development section presents teacher behaviors and instructional elements associated with initiating instruction, engaging students, and ending a lesson.

Finally, we synthesize the above material as represented in the TEAL model—*Teaching: Explicit Activation of Learning* (O'Shea & O'Shea, 1997). The TEAL model is used to present the chapter content in an integrated form. Also, we discuss teachers' use of particular instructional elements. We illustrate a variety of different content area examples to show how teachers apply the suggested strategies across different contexts.

INTRODUCTION

The central function of teachers is to deliver instruction to their students in the most efficient and effective manner possible. Developing teachers need to take into account the various instructional elements, weaving them into a form that will communicate clearly to students what target responses teachers expect.

To deliver instruction effectively, new teachers must be aware of and act on a number of complex factors that define how and to whom they instruct in classrooms. For instance, teachers are confronted daily with an increasingly diverse student population, and they are expected to assist these students in meeting increasingly high standards. However, in order to instruct diverse students effectively, teachers must implement a growing range of instructional strategies that responds to the differentiation of students' needs (Holloway, 2000).

Additionally, increasing numbers of students in American schools are affected by environmental, familial, educational, and interpersonal risk factors, all of which may interfere with students' needs being met and their ability to profit from instruction (Prater, Sileo, & Black, 2000). Teachers implementing effective instruction reach students at risk for and with identified problems because these teachers are aware of how students learn and how to organize, implement, and manage instruction geared toward student needs.

Effective teachers want to know specifically what to do with students, and teachers use a structured and organized way to get specific ideas across to students. There is research on linking the principles of learning and the principles of teaching to strategies and tactics for effective instruction (Algozzine, Ysseldyke, & Elliott, 1997).

Accordingly, teachers involved in implementing instruction while delivering effective strategies and tactics rely on identified ways to instruct diverse students

(Johns, 2000). A teacher planning to deliver instruction might focus on the following questions:

1. Is the amount of work appropriate for my students?

2. Is the work at the appropriate instructional level for my students?

3. Have I considered my students' specific learning needs when providing the instruction?

Algozzine et al. (1997) suggested that the most important aspects of effective teaching are tactics that bring broad components, general principles, and specific strategies of effective instruction to life. Appropriate instructional delivery relies on what works in instruction. Factors that contribute to instructional outcomes for students relate to implementing appropriate plans, management, delivery, and evaluation processes.

When teachers plan instruction, they are concerned with the degree to which teaching goals and teacher expectations of student performance and success are stated clearly and are understood by students. Teachers who manage instruction promote an effective and efficient learning setting. There is a sense of positiveness in the class. Such teachers deliver instruction by seeking an appropriate instructional match with their students, present lessons clearly, and follow specific instructional procedures. They provide instructional support to individual students. They allocate sufficient time to academic and instructional time and ensure each student's opportunity to respond. When teachers evaluate their instruction, they actively monitor student progress and understanding, and evaluate student performance appropriately and frequently. Thus, teachers applying principles of effective instruction as they deliver planned goals and objectives are able to reach their diverse students in significant ways.

DIRECT INSTRUCTION AND GUIDED DISCOVERY LEARNING: PRINCIPLES FOR EFFECTIVE INSTRUCTION

The two most broadly applicable models of instruction, which are often thought to be diametrically opposed, are direct instruction (DI) and guided discovery learning (GDL). DI proponents often focus on the need for students to master specific curriculum content; GDL proponents focus on the importance of students learning procedures for problem solving and for learning how to learn. In the former case, the instructional outcome is viewed as the demonstration of specific skills and knowledge about reading, math, social science, science, and so forth (e.g., being able to sound out words, knowing facts about state capitals). In the latter case, the instructional outcome is viewed as the demonstration of skills and knowledge about the process of learning (e.g., how to implement steps for solving problems, how to use study skills).

Although the philosophical underpinnings may be accurately thought of as in opposition, the procedural applications deriving from these models can be seen as complementary. Each model has its strengths and weaknesses, and the weaknesses of one are compensated by the strengths of the other. Therefore, to counter any shortcomings of DI, teachers can use GDL techniques in appropriate situations and vice versa.

In the following section we describe both models and the key components of each. We provide examples of how lessons are taught by using each model. Importantly, instructional procedures attributed to either DI or GDL are not so precise that variation in their implementation will lead to significant reductions in their effectiveness. Developing teachers should instead consider the procedures outlined as guidelines from which they can vary to meet their needs on the basis of content being presented and students' educational states.

Direct Instruction

In the areas of special and remedial education, a DI methodology has grown in popularity like no other instructional approach. Its roots date back to the mid-1970s, when Rosenshine (1976) coined the term *direct instruction,* in reference to effective teaching behaviors. By extensive classroom observation, Rosenshine (1971) and others (Anderson, Evertson, & Brophy, 1979; Fisher et al., 1980) identified critical teacher behaviors that correlated positively with student academic gains. Englemann and associates (Becker, Englemann, & Thomas, 1971; Carnine & Silbert, 1979; Englemann & Carnine, 1982) expanded the term *direct instruction* to include not only specific teaching procedures but also the use of highly structured curriculum materials. Direct instruction also has been viewed as a positive behavioral support strategy, in that teachers focus on the integration of well-designed curriculum materials and effective instructional delivery to help in management of student behaviors (Stein & Davis, 2000).

The purpose of direct instruction curriculum materials is to help a teacher systematically direct students in making accurate responses. The teacher uses scripted lesson plans to ensure that precise communication occurs between teacher and students. During instruction, the teacher models target responses, leads students in making the response, and periodically tests students' skills to respond without teacher cues.

Direct Instruction Defined. DI refers to teacher-guided instruction directed toward the mastery of specific skills and includes students working in small groups with high rates of engagement. Teachers facilitate success through the use of fast-paced, structured lessons. They use structured curricula, corrective feedback procedures, and performance monitoring. The critical aspect of the DI model is that teachers control instruction. They determine what and how subject matter content is presented (they demonstrate target responses and lead students in making responses). As a teacher gradually fades cues, students increasingly are able to respond independently. The teacher gives extensive practice so that students have sufficient opportunities to respond and thus master the target skills. Practice activities are done in a fast-paced mode to allow for a high density of responses during instructional periods. During initial learning, the teacher works with students in small groups to monitor the accuracy of their responses, ensuring that students engage in academic tasks. When students err, the teacher responds to provide corrective feedback that entails taking students through the model-lead-test sequence.

Principal Components of Direct Instruction. The three principal components of DI are the demonstration, guided practice, and independent practice stages of lesson development. During each of these stages, teachers execute instructional behaviors in a standard, systematic manner. If teachers use predictable steps in lesson development, students are able to participate in activities and perform responses in a more consistent manner.

Demonstration. The demonstration stage of lesson development entails the teacher modeling target responses for students. The responses relate to the performance of **academic rules** (sets of procedures for performing academic tasks such as solving computations with regrouping) or the formation of **concepts** (well-defined categories of information used for classification, such as types of plants). For instance, if the target response for students is to see-say a set of words containing the medial short vowel sound /a/, then the teacher would point to each target word and sound out the letter sounds contained in the words (e.g., c-a-t, m-a-t, r-a-t). If the target response being taught were to state a concept name and say the definition, the teacher would model the response by stating the target word and its definition (e.g., a square is a quadrilateral that contains four congruent sides and four right angles).

Guided Practice. The second stage of lesson development is supervised practice that entails the teacher using cues and prompts to emit target responses. The teacher leads groups of students in making the desired response (teacher and students perform the response simultaneously). As students demonstrate accurate responses, the teacher gradually fades the degree of leading. Instead of making the response with the students, the teacher presents the stimulus and has the group of students respond. **Unison responding,** groups of students making responses simultaneously, allows students more opportunities for responding during a period of time. The teacher must monitor the response of individual students in the group during unison responding to determine whether all students are responding accurately. In addition, the teacher tests students by calling on individual students to respond on their own.

As students become more accurate in their responding, the teacher shifts the performance criterion to fast and accurate responding. The teacher concentrates on asking for as many responses as possible during a guided-practice session. This focus increases the opportunities to respond and helps ensure skill mastery.

If the teacher were continuing the lesson on see-say words with medial short vowel sounds, after the sounding out demonstration the teacher would have students sound out the words with him or her simultaneously. Similarly, in teaching the hear-say response for the concept of square, the teacher would demonstrate the response and then lead students in stating the definition with him or her.

During the interactive process of instruction, these two stages of lesson development often overlap, with little discernible differentiation where one stage ends and the next begins. Making such a differentiation when implementing these procedures is much less important than the teacher ensuring that responses are demonstrated and that students have numerous opportunities to practice the responses while the teacher leads.

Independent Practice. Once students have performed responses accurately without cues or prompts, the third stage of lesson development is initiated to provide students the opportunity to practice response accuracy and speed. **Independent practice,** therefore, is minimally supervised practice in which students respond with a 90% or better response accuracy.

Two important and closely related features of independent practice assist in skill development and efficient management of classroom activities. First, the teacher can work with other groups of students while one group practices independently. Second, students must be making accurate responses so that they can truly work independently of the teacher (without a constant parade of students moving over to the teacher to ask questions about their seatwork).

The most frequently used form of independent practice is seatwork. **Seatwork** typically involves independent reading and writing tasks that can be performed without direct and immediate teacher supervision. In general, students with and without disabilities spend up to 70% of their instructional day in assigned seatwork activities. Consequently, a major management concern for preservice and beginning teachers involves keeping "seatwork students" on-task so that they can benefit from the independent work and not interrupt the other students who are receiving direct teacher instruction. To ensure that seatwork serves its function as an effective independent practice activity, teachers should ensure the following:

1. The assigned exercises and activities are directly related to the objectives being taught.

2. Instructions are clear and concise.

3. Multiple stimulus and response formats are provided.

4. The appearance of the assignments are age-appropriate, attractive, and organized.

5. Students can complete the activity with a high degree of success and can check the accuracy of their responses (Gaffney, 1987).

To manage students involved in seatwork practice activities effectively, it is recommended that teachers (1) circulate and provide feedback and reinforcement for appropriate seatwork behavior, (2) arrange desks for easy monitoring of the instructional groups and those students assigned to independent seatwork, and (3) develop a seatwork routine so that all students understand the rules regarding seatwork and procedures for obtaining assistance.

In addition to independent seatwork, independent practice activities can be programmed for at-risk students or those identified with disabilities in a number of other ways, including instructional games and cooperative, peer-mediated activities (see later sections of this chapter). For students with persistent problems, particularly in the areas of basic skill acquisition and organizational skills, computer-assisted instruction may be especially potent. As noted earlier by Schiffman, Tobin, and Buchanan (1984), the microcomputer is both user-friendly and nonjudgmental. It is especially suited to give the student who needs additional opportunities to respond the undivided attention that most teachers (and peer groups) cannot physically deliver to individual students. Furthermore, the computer, along with its powerful CD-ROM diagnostic and graphics capabilities, can be programmed rather easily by teachers to recognize immediately, diagnose, and correct errors as soon as they are made. In more recent applications, Dawson, Venn, and Gunter (2000) evaluated the effects of reading previews, comparing models provided by a teacher to models provided by a computer. Their findings demonstrated that reading rates and accuracy increased when computers read information. In the absence of a teacher model, the computer model appeared to be a viable tool for increasing fluency. The computer model assisted in exposing students to repeated reading of a story and in scanning reading materials. Thus, technology can enhance students' independent practice activities.

Importantly, independent practice does not have to occur only during the school day; once students are proficient with the relevant task, independent activities can be given as **homework assignments.** By adhering to several basic "rules for homework," these additional practice activities can assist with the retention and integration of academic material. Friend and Bursuck (1996) offered some general guidelines for preparing and assigning homework assignments. First, preservice and beginning teachers should realize that the assignment of homework has different purposes at different grade levels. For younger students, a major goal of homework is to foster positive attitudes toward school and to build good work habits; at higher grades, the main goal is to reinforce knowledge acquisition. Similarly, the frequency and intensity of the assignments should vary according to student age. Students in primary grades should receive no more than one to three assignments per week, lasting no more than 15 minutes per assignment. In sharp contrast, students in the secondary grades should receive assignments four or five times per week, each lasting 75 to 120 minutes each. Assignments for the intermediate and middle-school grades should fall within appropriate places along this continuum. Second, in terms of composition, homework assignments should contain both mandatory and voluntary components, and the teacher should provide clear consequences for both homework completion and the failure to turn in the assignment. However, it is important to remember that homework is not to be used as a punishment or to teach complex skills directly; nor should teachers expect that parents play a formal *instructional* role in the completion of their child's assignment. Parents can, however, be asked to create a home environment that fosters the completion of independent work.

Even when following these general guidelines, it is possible that preservice and beginning teachers will find that students with disabilities encounter difficulties completing their homework assignments. Patton (1994) reviewed the available literature on the use of homework for students with learning disabilities and developed a comprehensive list of recommended homework practices (see Figure 6.1).

Other Components. Other components of DI have been developed for use during the different stages of lesson development. They are used by teachers to ensure that instruction is systematic and that students are engaged in academic tasks to the maxi-

Management Considerations

Assess student homework skills
Involve parents from the outset
Assign homework from the beginning of the year
Schedule time and establish a routine for assigning, collecting, and evaluating homework
Communicate the consequences for not completing assignments
Minimize the demands of teacher time
Coordinate with other teachers
Present homework instructions clearly
Verify the assignment given
Allow students to start homework in class
Use assignment books and/or folders
Implement classroom-based incentive programs
Have parents sign and date homework
Evaluate assignments

Assignment Considerations

Recognize the purpose of the homework assignment
Establish relevance
Use appropriate stage of learning demands
Select appropriate type of activity
Keep assignments from getting too complex or novel
Ensure reasonable chance of completion and high rate of success
Adapt assignment as needed
Avoid using homework as punishment
Consider nonacademic assignments

Student Competencies

Demonstrate minimum levels of competence
Possess academic support skills
Promote interdependent learning
Develop self-management skills
Foster responsibility

Parent Involvement

Serve in a supportive role
Go through training, if available
Create a home environment that is conducive to doing homework
Encourage and reinforce student effort
Maintain ongoing involvement
Communicate views regarding homework to school personnel

FIGURE 6.1   Recommended Homework Practices

Patton, J. R. (1994). "Practical recommendations for using homework with students with learning disabilities" *Journal of Learning Disabilities, 27*(a), p. 573. Copyright 1994 by PRO-ED, Inc. Reprinted by permission mum extent possible and are evaluated continuously for their progress toward skill mastery (Carnine & Silbert, 1979).

Small-Group Instruction. In an ideal world, there would be one teacher for every student. Such an instructional arrangement is hardly practical, however. A ratio of one teacher for 100 students would provide excellent economic efficiency but is not an effective instructional strategy. The practical compromise is to have 10 to 15 students in a special classroom or 20 to 30 students in a general education classroom. Under these conditions, the most efficient and effective arrangement is to work with students in small groups when engaging in demonstration and guided practice. For those teaching exclusively in special education settings, three to five students would be considered a small instructional group; for those teaching in a general education classroom, five to eight students would be a small group.

Small-group instruction allows teachers to fulfill the criteria for effective instruction (discussed later in the chapter). A teacher can keep students engaged more easily, have students respond in unison, monitor group and individual performance, and provide corrective feedback. The close proximity of the teacher to students in small-group situations is a controlling force. Students are more likely to engage in desired tasks and to be responsive to teacher cues and prompts.

Engaged Time. **Engaged time** is the amount of time students spend actively performing the academic tasks presented to them. The concept of engaged time is simple: The greater the proportion of engaged time to allocated instructional time, the greater the academic performance of students. When students are off-task, overtly or covertly performing nonacademic tasks, they are not working toward mastery of target responses. Teachers maximize engaged time by efficiently using instructional time, monitoring the rates of engagement in their classrooms, and avoiding dead time. **Dead time** occurs when teachers delay the start of instructional periods or do not have materials ready and close at hand, when students take unnecessary time to make transitions from one activity to another, and when discussions go off on tangents unrelated to the responses being taught. Developing teachers can minimize all these by being aware of the importance of engaged time and by monitoring the rates of engagement in their classrooms.

Unison Responding. During small-group instruction, teachers seek to maximize the number of opportunities students have to perform target responses. **Unison responding,** a technique used to maximize the efficiency of practice time, is the simultaneous performance of a response by a group of students. A synonymous term is *choral practice.* Each student is provided with more practice under unison responding than if individual students were asked to respond one after the other. The result is more efficient use of instructional time, which increases the likelihood of students mastering the response in the shortest amount of time (Greenwood et al., 1984).

Signaling. **Signaling** is used during unison responding. The teacher visually or auditorially prompts students to make the desired response to ensure that the responding is truly unison. Without signaling, some students will lag behind and wait for another student to begin the response before they join in. For example, if a teacher has the word *mate* written on the chalkboard and does not teach students to react to a signal, some students will wait for others to begin sounding out the /ma/ sound before starting their response. It is difficult for teachers to determine who is capable of making a response independently without cues.

When teachers begin to use unison responding, they must teach students to respond to their signal. Without explicit training in responding to signals, some students will persist in delaying responses.

Pacing. DI lessons are also characterized by fast-paced practice sessions. Not only does a fast rate of stimulus presentation facilitate the efficient use of instructional time, but it also helps maintain interest and decrease off-task behavior.

Monitoring. To ensure appropriate instructional decisions, developing teachers need to know how well students are progressing toward skill mastery. Direct and continuous monitoring of students' rate and accuracy of responding allows developing teachers to determine the daily instructional needs of each student. Daily monitoring better ensures that students will not proceed through an extended series of lessons with high error rates before instruction is modified to improve response accuracy. Monitoring can take the form of simply tallying the number of correct and error responses that students make during an oral practice session or on a paper-and-pencil seatwork assignment. These frequencies can be kept in a daily log or bulletin board chart or can be plotted on a graph. Chapter 4 contains a discussion on charting techniques for monitoring student performance and progress.

Corrective Feedback. The teaching precision under the DI model is designed to increase the probability that students will respond accurately. Accordingly, ideal instruction occurs when instructional procedures are so carefully designed that students make no errors; however, students invariably err regardless of the teaching precision. In such cases, the following set of corrective feedback procedures is to be used with the DI model in small groups: (1) Praise students making correct responses, (2) model the correct response, (3) lead students in the correct response, (4) test students by asking them to respond on their own, (5) alternate between erred example and other examples, and (6) give a delayed test later in the lesson.

For high-level responses, restate or ask students to restate the rule or strategy used to arrive at the correct response. For instance, in teaching the spelling rule "i before e except after c," students can state this rule and then spell the word.

Box 6.1 contains excerpts from a DI lesson that includes the primary components—demonstration, guided practice, and independent practice.

Box 6.1   **Example DI Lesson**

The target skill being taught is two digit plus two digit addition with regrouping. This lesson has been preceded by instruction on prerequisite concepts (e.g., place value, regrouping) and skills (e.g., basic math facts, procedures for regrouping).

Demonstration

Ms. van Noord **models** the procedures for example problems by writing the computations and vocalizing the steps as she completes them:

"We begin with the ones column and add the two digits, 7 ones + 6 ones = 13 ones."

$$\begin{array}{r} 2\ 7 \\ +4\ 6 \\ \hline 13 \end{array}$$

"Thirteen ones can be regrouped into 1 ten and 3 ones."

"So we can replace the 1 ten in the tens column and leave the 3 ones in the ones column."

$$\begin{array}{r} ^1 27 \\ +46 \\ \hline 3 \end{array}$$

continued

"Next we add the digits in the tens column including the 1 ten we regrouped. 1 ten + 2 tens = 3 tens; 3 tens + 4 tens = 7 tens."

$$\begin{array}{r} {}^{1}27 \\ +46 \\ \hline 73 \end{array}$$

"Our complete sum is 7 tens and 3 ones or 73."

Ms. van Noord then introduces a second example problem, and, depending on the attentiveness of her small group of students, she may begin to include them in verbalizing parts of the computation or steps for completing the computations.

"Let's look at another example of two digit plus two digit addition with regrouping."

"We begin with the ones column and add the two digits. Let's say the addition together." **(Unison responding)**

$$\begin{array}{r} 53 \\ +29 \end{array}$$

Ms. van Noord **signals** the students to respond together by pointing to the 3 and says, "Begin." The teacher and group respond:

"3 ones + 9 ones = 12 ones."

$$\begin{array}{r} 53 \\ +29 \\ \hline 12 \end{array}$$

Ms. van Noord continues with the demonstration.
"Twelve ones can be regrouped into 1 ten and 2 ones."

$$\begin{array}{r} {}^{1}53 \\ +29 \\ \hline 2 \end{array}$$

"So we replace the 1 ten in the tens column and leave the 2 ones in the ones column."

"Next we add the digits in the tens column, including the 1 ten we regrouped. Let's say the addition together."

Ms. van Noord signals by pointing to the regrouped 1 ten and says, "Begin." The teacher and group respond:

"1 ten + 5 tens = 6 tens; 6 tens + 2 tens = 8 tens."

$$\begin{array}{r} {}^{1}53 \\ +29 \\ \hline 82 \end{array}$$

Ms. van Noord continues:

"Our complete sum is 8 tens and 2 ones, or 82."

Guided Practice

During guided practice, Ms, van Noord **leads** students in completing the computations and vocalizing the steps as **they** complete them. Students write the computations on their worksheets, and together with the teacher they vocalize the steps.

As more examples are completed, the teacher fades her vocalizations until students "talk through" the computations and steps by themselves. Together the teacher and group of students complete the computations in the right column and vocalize the steps in the left column:

"Start with the ones column and add the two digits; 8 ones + 7 ones = 15 ones."

$$\begin{array}{r} 28 \\ +37 \\ \hline 15 \end{array}$$

"Fifteen ones can be regrouped into 1 ten and 5 ones."

$$\begin{array}{r} {}^{1}28 \\ +37 \\ \hline 5 \end{array}$$

"Replace the 1 ten in the tens column and leave 5 ones."

"Add the digits in the tens column, 1 ten + 2 tens = 3 tens; 3 tens + 3 tens = 6 tens."

"The sum is 6 tens and 5 ones or 65."

$$\begin{array}{r} {}^{1}28 \\ +37 \\ \hline 65 \end{array}$$

These procedures are continued with other examples in **unison.** Ms. van Noord intermittently has the members of the group complete an example individually **(tests).** When an individual student (Travis) errs, then Ms. van Noord initiates the **corrective feedback procedure.**

"Everyone is adding the ones column correctly and stating the steps."	Step 1—Praise students making correct responses.
"Let's make sure that we replace the tens in the tens column."	Step 2—Model correct response.

Ms. van Noord **models** the steps to example emphasizing the replacement steps. She continues with the corrective feedback procedures:

"Let's complete the same example problem together. Add the ones column…"	Step 3—Lead students in correct response.
"Travis, say the steps that you followed to complete this example."	Step 4—Test students individually.
"Do the next example problem by yourselves. As you write the additions, say the steps quietly to yourselves."	Step 5—Alternate between erred example and other examples.

Ms. van Noord **monitors** students as they complete the examples.

"Travis, write the additions and say the steps for the last problem we did . . . "	Step 6—Give delayed test later in the lesson.

Independent Practice

Once students have demonstrated 90% accuracy in responding during guided practice, the teacher can have the group practice example problems on their own in the form of seatwork. Independent practice on the target skill two digit plus two digit addition with regrouping may not occur during the first few lessons. Instead, independent practice on the target skill is delayed until students are firm on the procedure. The first lessons usually involve demonstration and guided practice only.

Teaching Models Related to Teacher-Directed Instruction

There is a number of teaching models related to teacher-directed instruction. These include the strategies intervention model and classwide peer tutoring. Each is described in the following sections.

Strategies Intervention Model. A widely applied example of the combination of DI methodology with metacognitive-based strategies is the **strategies intervention model (SIM),** conceptualized at the University of Kansas (Deshler, Schumaker, Lenz, & Ellis, 1984). Teachers can attempt to determine what setting demands their students need to meet, whether students have the skills to meet demands, and then, if students do not have the skills, teach them through SIM to use learning strategies students need to meet the demands (Rogan, 2000).

Early research by Alley and Deshler (1979) was based on the theory that educational delivery systems and curriculum at the secondary level were ineffective because they failed to address the underlying needs of students with learning disabilities. The researchers held that students could succeed in high school if the delivery system and curriculum focused on teaching students learning strategies—"techniques, principles, or rules that will facilitate the acquisition, manipulation, integration, storage, and retrieval of information across situations and settings" (Alley & Deshler, 1979, p. 13). Deshler and his colleagues have either revamped earlier strategies (e.g., the SQ3R method developed by Robinson, 1941) or developed new ones. For instance, RAP, a three-step strategy, helps students in summarizing what they have read by following the mnemonic:

- *R*ead paragraph.
- *A*sk self questions.
- *P*ut it in own words. (Schumaker, Denton, & Deshler, 1984)

Other strategies are the word identification strategy (DISSECT), test taking strategy (PIRATES), sentence writing strategy (PENS), first-letter mnemonic strategy (FIRST), error monitoring strategy (COPS), and visual imagery strategy (RIDER).

The SIM includes structures for what to teach and how to teach. Specifically, the "what to teach" component draws from the metacognitive needs of adolescents with learning disabilities; that is, teachers promote awareness and regulation of the information-processing demands of the secondary-school setting. The SIM curriculum consists of learning strategies designed for three processes: acquisition of information, storage of information, and expression and demonstration of competence (see Table 6.1).

The "how to teach" component is based on the behaviorally oriented DI model, involving teachers modeling, leading, and testing students through the acquisition stage of learning. The strategy acquisition procedures consist of eight steps:

1. Teacher pretests and obtains student commitment to learn.

2. Teacher describes the new strategy.

3. Teacher models the new strategy.

4. Teacher and students verbally rehearse strategy steps.

5. Student practices on controlled materials.

6. Student practices on grade-appropriate classroom materials.

7. Teacher posttests and obtains student commitment to generalize.

8. Student generalizes.

During step 1, motivation to learn and use the strategies is developed by pointing out the inefficiencies or ineffectiveness of students' present strategies. In addition, the pretest step is conducted to ensure that the student can perform all the preskills prior to the strategy being taught. In step 2, the teacher describes the procedures for executing the strategy. These procedures include the major behaviors in which the student will sequentially engage to complete the strategy correctly. In step 3, the teacher then models

TABLE 6.1 Strategies Intervention Model (SIM)

Acquisition of Information	Storage of Information	Expression and Demonstration of Competence
Word identification	First-letter mnemonic	Sentence writing
Paraphrasing	Paired associates	Paragraph writing
Self-questioning	Listening and note taking	Error monitoring
Visual imagery		Theme writing
Interpreting visual aids		Assignment completion
Multipass		Test taking
SOS		

the strategy through a "think aloud" process. In step 4, students are then led through a verbal rehearsal process designed to prompt the self-instruction process. Verbal rehearsal progresses from stating the steps aloud to stating the steps to yourself. So that students may focus attention on learning the strategy without having to deal with new or difficult materials, initial practice, in step 5, is done with less demanding materials. Once students have demonstrated skill in executing the strategy in these materials, they then practice in their grade-level materials (step 6) to further develop generalization of strategy use to general education classroom content. In step 7, students are provided with a posttest to determine whether mastery has been achieved, and a behavioral contract is used to gain a commitment to use the strategy in their general education classrooms (Deshler & Schumaker, 1986).

Generalization (step 8) is facilitated during and after the acquisition stage. Ellis, Lenz, and Sabornie (1987a, 1987b) describe the process of teaching generalization in terms of four stages:

1. *Antecedent:* Teacher changing negative student attitudes that might ultimately affect generalization behaviors

2. *Concurrent:* Student acquiring the skill well enough for it to become generalized

3. *Subsequent:* Student applying the skill to various contexts, situations, and settings

4. *Independent:* Student using self-instruction to mediate generalization

Antecedent steps are taken to encourage generalization by changing negative student attitudes that might ultimately affect students' efforts to generalize. In planning for instruction, teachers select or are provided with, in the SIM materials, extensive and diverse examples of the application of strategies. During strategy acquisition, concurrent steps are taken to facilitate generalization by having students learn strategies well enough to become generalized. By practicing strategies in controlled materials, students can attend to the steps for executing the strategy without having to focus their attention on reading material that requires attention to decoding or on comprehending complex semantic relationships. After students have demonstrated mastery of strategy use in controlled materials, they are subsequently taught to apply the strategy to various contexts, situations, and settings. Less emphasis is placed on students completing the strategy steps in the regimented manner used in earlier stages. Instead, teachers vary formats, procedures, and examples as students gain mastery of a strategy in order to promote generalization. Ultimately, independence (executive functioning)

Pause and Reflect 6.1

Try challenging your peers to use the strategies intervention model.

1. Without referring to notes or the text narrative, have peers list the eight SIM strategy acquisition steps listed above in the proper sequence.
2. Have peers try to sequence the SIM strategy storage steps.
3. Have peers try the SIM expression and demonstration of competence steps

is generated by teaching students to use self-monitoring procedures to mediate generalization and cue other teachers to provide reinforcement (Ellis et al., 1987a).

Other characteristics of SIM include explicit delineation of treatment outcomes, their importance, and techniques to be employed; use of self-verbalization; active participation by students in training; and an emphasis on generalization at all stages of learning (Deshler & Schumaker, 1986; Deshler, Schumaker, Alley, Warner, & Clark, 1982; Deshler et al., 1984).

Classwide Peer Tutoring. Classwide peer tutoring (CWPT) is a system of instruction in which students tutor peers in basic academic responses by using prescribed tutoring procedures that enhance the ecobehavioral interactions between classroom antecedents and overt student responses (Delquadri, Greenwood, Whorton, Carta, & Hall, 1986). The underlying principles include increasing students' opportunities to respond through practice activities. Often, when teachers are working with other groups, students outside the instructional group tend to engage in off-task behavior. By having peers work with each other, they are more apt to stay on-task and to make responses related to academic learning. For example, during a second period, a fourth grader's oral reading performance was observed. Monitors observed that the student read for less than 10 seconds and was actively engaged in work for only 8 of 60 minutes of reading instruction. During reading instruction, the student typically sat alone at his desk while the teacher worked with reading groups. When his group was called for reading with the teacher, often the period was nearly over and the group had to move to another activity.

Additionally, the responses targeted for peer tutoring are functional and have high utility in the classroom; that is, they are skills the students can use often and in a variety of situations. The strategy is to select those responses that are more likely to be practiced and maintained in the classroom environment, such as the following:

- Textual oral reading
- Answering comprehension questions
- Reading workbook practice
- Math fact practice
- Vocabulary practice involving meanings and definitions

Responses reflect teacher outcome measures as much as possible. Outcome variables are the focus, not the process variables (e.g., rules for carrying out academic tasks or gaining meaning such as metacognitive strategies). Textual oral reading, for instance, focuses on such measures as sentences read, words written, and comprehension questions answered, not on phonetic rules or decoding skills, studying definitions, or comprehension rules.

A system for *reinforcement of correct responding* is designed so that the teacher reviews daily or weekly performance, giving the opportunity for the teacher to monitor and recognize student gains. The reinforcement system is viewed by participating teachers as a critical component to CWPT. Tutors and teams distribute reinforcement;

tutors provide individual contingencies, and teams group contingencies (team of the week). Daily and weekly team totals are posted on a classroom bulletin board (Delquadri et al., 1986).

Student Training. Students are trained in three 20-minute sessions. The teacher explains how the "game" works. Students are paired, and a variable number of pairs comprise a team. Each student functions as a tutor for 10 minutes and a tutee for 10 minutes, and the final 5 to 10 minutes are used to add and total points for correct responses. Therefore, the entire practice period is a 30-minute block. The teacher then demonstrates the tutoring procedures by acting as the tutor with one student. Next, two students act as tutor and tutee while the rest of the class watches and the teacher gives feedback. A few more demonstrations are provided as needed, followed by a whole-class practice. After students have demonstrated mastery of the procedures, the teacher assigns partners and teams.

The CWPT daily procedures are initiated with a reminder about tutoring partners, and then students are signaled to pair up. A timer is set for 10 minutes. The first tutee in each pair responds to materials while the tutor observes, rewards, and gives feedback. At the end of 10 minutes, the students switch roles and begin the second tutoring session. After the end of the second session, the points are added and totaled. Each correct response earns two points, and each successful correction of an error earns one point. Bonus points are awarded for working immediately and cooperatively with the tutor. The winning team is applauded for their performance, and the losing team is applauded for their effort.

Guided Discovery Learning

From a philosophical perspective, the antithesis of DI is the pure form of discovery learning, of which guided discovery is a derivation. Barlow (1985) defined **discovery learning** as a process of presenting students with problem situations and encouraging them to identify solutions through group interactions or individually. Assumptions are made regarding the learners' psychological state (learners are viewed as processors of information and problem solvers who are curious and motivated to learn and who want to make sense of a situation).

Discovery learning methods emanate from a child-centered view of learning in which students decide what they learn and how learning proceeds. Teachers provide little structure for students. The tight control that teachers maintain under a DI model is largely absent in GDL. There are few specific teaching behaviors to be followed, and the content and materials are not prearranged or tightly structured.

Jerome Bruner is the leading proponent of the discovery model. In his conceptualization of "cognitive structure," Bruner (1966) emphasized the importance of students learning the structures and relationships of structures of a field of study. By teaching them generic problem-solving and information-processing techniques, students can learn how to learn independently. Bruner identified this "heuristic economy" as a means for accommodating the vast amounts of information that individuals must manipulate. School curricula should contain courses that transcend subject matter content and teach critical thinking skills.

Bruner's early work led to continued work by cognitive psychologists and special educators to develop **cognitive routines,** or strategies for developing internal processes for storing, manipulating, and retrieving information. These approaches are referred to as *self-regulation, cognitive training, strategic learning, metacognitive learning,* and a host of other related terms. The connection among these variations on a theme is that curricula are designed to help students learn about learning (Reid & Stone, 1991). They learn when and how to use cognitive routines that enable them to process information better. Instruction revolves around students learning how to process **declarative knowledge** (factual information including concepts), **conditional knowledge** (knowledge about when to use strategies), and **procedural knowledge** (steps to follow to complete a cognitive task) (Paris & Winograd, 1990). Students learn to set goals, apply strategies, monitor their progress, and subsequently modify goals or strategies or both (Butler, 1995; Kirby, Booth, & Das, 1996). The learning strategies from the strategies intervention model and the skills for success program (Archer, 1991) are examples of strategic learning applications. The overall purpose is to provide students with the cognitive tools to be able to learn independently. These cognitive routines, or tools, are examples of what we refer to later in the chapter as academic rules.

The foundational principles of discovery learning have been shared in the social constructivistic paradigm. The basic tenets of **social constructivism** are based on the assumption that students are *self-directed, meaning-constructing, meaning-seeking individuals* who act on their environments accordingly. Students' knowledge bases are shaped by contextual conditions and meaningfulness, as well as by their individual interests and purposes. Self-directed learning is more motivating than teacher-directed learning that imposes the problem and the solution. Academic programs designed without considering the context of purpose, use, and desired social relations fail to provide motivating and meaningful environments conducive to self-directed learning (Heshusius, 1986, 1989; Poplin, 1987, 1988; Smith & Heshusius, 1986). Curricula and instructional techniques are developed so that learning is functional, genuine, and authentic. Curricula are integrated so that the focus of the content is real-life problem solving and skill development; that is, students study problems as they occur in nature or society, not as separate subject areas. Content area curricula are integrated to include problem solving that reflects knowledge structures across social studies, science, literature, art, music, and mathematics. For example, students may study the problem of balanced ecosystems; they may have to read narrative and expository prose, examine scientific principles, and use mathematical algorithms in order to show how an ecosystem works. The integrated curriculum approach is modeled after the British infant school tradition and the project approach of Kilpatrick (1918).

From a discovery learning perspective, the purpose of instruction is to teach students to be independent problem solvers, to learn the generic steps to scientific inquiry and logical thinking. By learning the generic process of problem solving, it is believed that information from other content areas can be readily learned. Instruction is directed toward transferring the use of problem-solving strategies to new material and situations. Specific content information is learned incidentally, through the introduction of novel problems requiring similar problem-solving strategies and involving new but similar information. The bottom line is that the process of problem solving supersedes any learning of content material (Ausubel, Novak, & Hanesian, 1978; Biehler & Snowman, 1986).

Proponents of discovery techniques argue that DI techniques are too simplistic and authoritarian. It is believed that DI methods are effective for low-level cognitive tasks but that discovery techniques using induction better facilitate the use of high-level cognitive skills. Also, the tight control that DI teachers exercise over content and instructional activities is criticized because students are taught to be passive and overly dependent on teachers and extrinsic rewards. With discovery techniques, students learn to be more independent learners, able to determine their own instructional needs.

Guided Discovery Learning Defined. Gagne (1980) has developed a variation of the pure form of discovery learning. Under Gagne's GDL model, curricular content and structure are integrated with a bottom-up, inductive approach to learning. Gagne asserts that learning is most effective when content is presented by starting with the specific and moving to the general (bottom-up). Concepts or rules are learned by assembling the examples, making comparisons, identifying patterns, and then identifying the concept or rule that links the examples. A teacher's cues or hints and structured curricula are used to assist students in inducing the concept or rule identification. Curricula are to be analyzed and hierarchy developed from the top-down, but instruction begins at the bottom and moves to the top (Belkin & Gray, 1977).

Guided discovery methodology focuses on gaining specific content, as well as on teaching generic problem solving skills. Instead of solely focusing on teaching students to be independent problem solvers, as is the case with the general format of discovery learning, GDL focuses on teachers guiding students through a logical series of problem-solving steps to better facilitate learning specific content.

Principal Components of Guided Discovery Learning. Several components of GDL are the foundation of its effectiveness. Proponents of the guided discovery model, however, do not delineate these components as clearly as the proponents of DI delineate its components. From what can be discerned, a set of identifiable components that characterize GDL follows (Ausubel et al., 1978).

Contrasts. Contrasts are emphasized throughout this process by identifying and comparing the distinctive features of like concepts. These distinctive features determine the relationship among concepts and help students in discriminating concepts, such as a square from a rectangle. For instance, teachers guide students to identify the features of a square, such as the length of the sides, comparative length of different sides, the inside angles formed by each set of perpendicular sides, and its two-dimensionality. Other nonrelevant features also may be examined, such as size and color. The distinctive features are then compared with those of other figures with square characteristics used as the comparison basis (Figure 6.2).

Example Selection. Example selection is critical for contrasts to be made. Examples are carefully selected and grouped by distinctive features so that when they are presented, void of a classification scheme, to students, the students will be able to identify the relationships themselves. By presenting numerous examples applicable to the target skill or concept, the teacher adds further cues as to the relationship shared by the concepts. For instance, in teaching the concept of chair, a kitchen chair would be a good first example. It contains the standard features of a chair, and it is a form of chair that students would see frequently and in different settings. Providing other examples of chairs with some variations from a kitchen chair, such as a living room chair (different

FIGURE 6.2 At early stages of concept development during preschool and primary grades, students learn to discriminate by using examples and nonexamples; later, in a spiral curriculum, concepts are further developed through formal definitions, examples, and nonexamples.

Early development of concept *square*

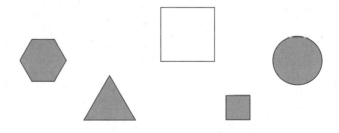

Advanced development of concept *square*

Square – a square is a closed figure with four equal sides and four right angles

shape and material) or a secretary's chair (different shape with wheel bases), would help students in forming a concept set that accommodates varieties of form and that enables students to identify distinctive features (e.g., the seat) and irrelevant features (e.g., wood, material). Gradually, less typical forms, such as a bean bag chair, can be introduced to elaborate the concept set further.

Informed Guessing. Students are encouraged to make informed guesses by using information they have identified as the basis for asking questions that lead to further information about the concepts. In reading a story, for instance, a student may use a self-questioning strategy that entails writing and answering questions about the content of each paragraph read, based on the information gained from previous paragraphs. The questions are used to aid in identifying and analyzing the concepts presented in the passage. Consequently, students are being taught to reflect on their state of understanding at any given time and to use questions to guide their acquisition of new information.

Awareness of the Underlying Problem-Solving Process. If students are asked to focus on the process steps they use to solve problems, they can form their own self-regulating strategies for problem solving. An obvious example is solving math word problems. Students are given problems to solve and are asked to state the steps used to determine the operation and to identify the variables and constants.

Active Participation. Participation is encouraged by arranging students to work in various capacities as part of a group. In a group assignment, for example, students may be assigned or volunteer to record answers to questions or to research other sources of information. The purpose of active participation is to ensure that students are actively involved in the process of solving problems, classifying information, or establishing rules.

The concept teaching model (Gregory, 1985) provides an example lesson format that incorporates the components of guided discovery:

1. Three to five well-chosen examples of the concept are presented one at a time. As they are presented, the teacher states, "This is an example of [concept name]."

2. Three to five well-chosen nonexamples are presented one at a time. The teacher states, "This is not an example of [concept name]."

3. Other stimuli representing the target concept or other concepts from the same form class are presented to students. Students are to answer yes or no when asked, "Is this an example of [concept name]?"

4. The teacher, using leading questions, asks students to list the attributes of the examples and the nonexamples.

5. The teacher has the students construct a definition of the concept, based on a list of attributes.

6. The teacher provides practice by pointing to examples and nonexamples of the concept and having students answer the question "What is this an example of?"

Pause and Reflect 6.2

Which statement best illustrates the role of teacher effectiveness in a GDL framework?

1. Give me better students, I'll give you better results.
2. Teach slowly, and students will absorb the information.
3. How well I teach = How well they learn.
4. Students will not learn until they are ready to learn.

Why did you choose the item above?

Box 6.2 contains excerpts from a GDL lesson that includes the steps from the concept teaching model.

Teaching Models Related to Guided Discovery Learning

There is a number of teaching models related to guided discovery learning. These include proleptic teaching and scaffolding, cooperative learning, language experience approach, and the process-writing model. Each is described in the following sections.

Box 6.2   **Example GDL Lesson**

The target concept being taught is story setting, a story grammar that describes the context in which a story takes place.

Example and Nonexample Presentation

Mr. Elkins presents three examples, listed on the chalkboard, excerpted from narrative prose that illustrate story settings. Students are asked to read each silently.

"This is an example of a story setting from the story 'Back of Burke.'"	The small Western town was at the base of a range of steep mountains. Most people in Burke owned cattle ranches that surrounded the town.
"This is an example of a story setting from the story 'Letter to the Editor.'"	Before he got dressed for school, Alan sat in his room with dirty clothes everywhere. Posters of his favorite sports players hung on all four walls. Alan typed quickly on his new computer.
"This is an example of a story setting from the story 'The Guilty Witness.'"	The sirens grew louder in the hot summer night's heat as the ambulance approached. Pat stood dazed by the sight of the bloody victim. Her mind raced back through the visions of what had just happened.

Mr. Elkins points to an adjacent chalkboard and has students silently read three nonexamples of story settings.

"This is *not* an example of a story setting."	It was all over. Adrian's cattle were back, and the town was a safe place to live.
"This is *not* an example of a story setting."	Alan wasn't going to let that stop him. He was determined to interview his hero.
"This is *not* an example of a story setting."	The jury returned their verdict to the judge. Pat knew, from the expressions on their faces, what they had found.

Mr. Elkins proceeds to have students open their textbooks to specific pages and read brief excerpts from several stories. After reading each, he asks, "Is this an example of a story setting?" The students respond either yes or no (**informed guessing and active participation**).

continued

Definition or Rule Induction

Next, Mr. Elkins asks a series of questions about the attributes of the examples and nonexamples in order to explicate **contrasts,** and the students respond.

"Let's look at our examples and non-examples of story settings. What did you learn about the story in the first example?"

"The story is in a little town."

"The name of the town is Burke."

"People raise cows and stuff."

Mr. Elkins lists the students' responses on the chalkboard and continues to ask more leading questions.

"By learning these kinds of things, what does the story setting do for the reader?"

"Tells us things about the story."

"Yes, it does, but what kinds of things does the story setting tell us?"

"Where the people live."

"If it's day or night."

"Yes, good thinking. The story setting tells us information about where and when the story takes place."

To confirm this conclusion, Mr. Elkins directs the students to look at the nonexamples to confirm that the statement "story setting tells us information about where and when the story takes place" adequately distinguishes examples from nonexamples (**contrast, informed guessing, and active participation**).

"Let's look at the nonexamples and see whether they tell us where and when the story takes place. Read the first nonexample. Does this statement allow us to answer the questions *where* or *when* the story takes place?"

"Sort of, it says the town."

"But that could mean any town."

"What about telling us *when* the story takes place?"

"Well, I guess it really doesn't tell exactly where."

"No."

After reviewing a few more nonexamples, Mr. Elkins induces students to **construct a definition** of story setting.

"How can we complete the following sentence beginning— 'Story settings tell us . . . .' "

"Where the story happens."

"When it takes place."

"Good, you've figured out the pur-pose of story settings. When in the story do we usually find the story setting?"

"In the first couple of pages."

"Yes, the story setting tells us where and when a story takes place and is usually found at the beginning of the story."

Mr. Elkins posts this definition of a story setting on a bulletin board and uses it in subsequent lessons when asking students to identify story settings in their reading passages.

Proleptic Teaching and Scaffolding. Another model of instruction that carries many of the general features of guided discovery learning is that of **proleptic teaching,** the anticipation of competence (Vygotsky, 1978). Accordingly, the teacher provides a model of a strategy or skill being taught through a natural dialogue with students and gradually allows the student to take over the steps and procedures involved in applying the strategy or skill (Paris & Winograd, 1990; Rosenshine & Meister, 1992). As needed, the teacher provides the necessary support structures, or **scaffolding** (Bruner, 1973; Rojewski & Schell, 1994). The analogy is made to the tutelage that occurs between a master crafter and an apprentice; the master crafter provides that support so that the apprentice can carry out some simple aspects of the task with the aid of the tutor (Rogoff, 1990). In the instructional context, neophytes are asked to perform a task before they really have the skills to do it. Parents or teachers then guide students through a particular activity and gradually relinquish the responsibilities for completing the activity to students as they become more and more skilled in the task at hand.

This concept is closely related to Goodman's (1989) conceptualization of child-centered learning whereby teachers **"lead from behind"**; that is, as students demonstrate needs and seek out assistance, the teacher provides the guidance and support structures to allow students to learn what they need to complete a particular task. The teacher does not establish and follow a preset curriculum sequence, but rather follows the sequence dictated by each student's naturally developing needs.

Additionally, a reciprocity occurs between teacher and student in what is termed a **community of learners.** Teacher and students learn from each other, and students learn from each other. Approaches to tasks often involve collaboration by groups of learners. Cooperatively, learners study and seek to solve problems. Students and teacher plan and develop curricular activities that are integrated across subject areas to facilitate growth and each student's emerging repertoire of skills. The teacher monitors student progress by *kid watching,* a term popularized by Yetta Goodman (1989). The social aspect of learning is heavily emphasized.

Cooperative Learning. **Cooperative learning** involves sets of techniques that have students working together in groups to practice and master prescribed skills. Different approaches usually entail some form of student-to-student interaction, individual accountability, and positive student interdependence (Maheady, Mallette, Harper, Sacca, & Pomerantz, 1994). Students are sorted into teams, and their individual and team performances are evaluated. The most dominant approaches are **student learning teams,** developed by Slavin (1990) and the **learning together approach,** developed by Johnson et al. (1984). Following are specific applications of cooperative learning.

Jigsaw. Perhaps the most widely used and best example of cooperative learning is the **jigsaw** (Aronson, Stephan, Sikes, Blaney, & Snapp, 1978). Heterogeneous groups of three to five students are formed. All groups are given the same assignment that is divided into the same number of parts as there are members on each team. Each team member is assigned a part (piece) of the assignment (puzzle). Students from the different groups who are assigned to the same part form "expert groups." The expert groups meet to review information regarding their part, determine the most important information, and then return to their teams. The teams then review the important information from each part and synthesize the information (put the puzzle pieces together). Students are expected to master the information for all parts. Ultimately, students are individually quizzed on all parts of the topic.

Student Teams—Achievement Divisions (STAD). Students are arranged into heterogeneous teams of four to six. A pretest is provided on the lesson or unit content. Concepts, principles, and/or procedures are presented or elicited. The teams work together on worksheets, study guides, or other practice activities. After students have mastered the content, they take individual tests on the material. Their scores are compared with their pretest scores to derive a gain score. The gain scores are averaged for a team gain score. Points are awarded for individual and team gains.

Teams-Games-Tournaments (TGT). Students are arranged in groups, and lesson content is presented in the same way as with STAD. However, students participate in weekly games and tournaments, rather than take weekly quizzes. After practice sessions, students are arranged on the basis of ability levels into three-person tournament tables. The homogeneous grouping allows students with comparable skills to compete with each other and to have an equal probability of success as higher functioning students.

Team-Assisted Individualization (TAI). TAI is designed to assist students in learning various math algorithms and problem-solving strategies. Students' skill levels are determined and are placed within an individualized skill sequence. Students complete worksheets daily and progress through the curriculum at their own pace. Other team members help check responses on the worksheets. At the end of each unit of individualized instruction, students take a final unit test. Points are awarded for passing the unit tests, completing multiple units, and completing homework assignments.

Language Experience Approach. A narrower application of guided discovery is the language experience approach. **Language experience approaches** involve students and teachers collaborating on story construction. Students unable to use all the technical conventions of written language (e.g., spelling, punctuation) dictate to the teacher their construction of a story, and the teacher writes down the oral statements. The stories are used as the stimulus for learning language in written and oral forms and for learning about the content communicated within the story. Through constant exposure to their own writing and the writings of others (books), students begin to use vocabulary that they would find in written discourse they have written, heard, or read. They tell stories, create, and convey information (Holdaway, 1979). Readers construct their own interpretations of the text that authors have written. Meaningfulness and functionality are

Pause and Reflect 6.3

Devise a cooperative learning activity for use with a set of students at the grade level in which you are instructing now.

List and describe the student grouping format for the content area (e.g., reading, science, mathematics) in which you are employing the cooperative learning activity.

Assign all students a group assignment for a 30-minute time period.

Describe each student's role in the cooperative learning time frame.

Consider: What materials and equipment will students need to complete this activity?

individualized, and there really is no teacher-directed interpretation. It is up to individuals, with their own experiences and what they bring to a task, that guides their interpretation. This student-centered prospective on the construction of knowledge implies that a teacher's job is to understand what a student's interpretation is and how it came to be, not one of trying to correct and point the student to some single convergent response or interpretation.

Depending on students' needs, the teacher uses the student-constructed stories as the basis for leading students to recognize and understand principles of word recognition, spelling, grammar, story structure, and strategies for comprehending written and oral language. Guided discovery techniques such as contrasting and informed guessing are used to identify principles or procedures that students can apply to different stories.

Process-Writing Model. **Process writing** involves a teacher guiding students through a series of steps that include *planning, drafting, conferencing/consultation, revising,* and *publishing.* Although the degree of teacher directiveness can be high, the process-writing model is more often associated with student-directed approaches. The degree of teacher directedness is most controversial in the conferencing step. The fundamental concern is the difference between *consultation* and *conferencing.* The teacher's interaction with students is much more directive under the consultation mode than it is under the conferencing mode.

During **planning,** students collect information about the topic and begin to outline the content. Brainstorming is often used to map out information regarding the basic

Pause and Reflect 6.4

Defend or refute each of the following statements. Why did you choose the position that you did for each?

The overriding issue associated with metacognition and strategies instruction is to help students become more knowledgeable of content.
Why did you choose the position?

The overriding issue associated with metacognition and strategies instruction is to help students become independent learners.
Why did you choose the position?

The overriding issue associated with metacognition and strategies instruction is to help students become responsive to cognitive demands.
Why did you choose the position?

The overriding issue associated with metacognition and strategies instruction is to help students become well-rounded students.
Why did you choose the position?

questions of who, what, where, when, and how. The structure or sequence of the content is also listed. For a narrative story, the author maps out ideas about the setting, the problem encountered by the protagonist, the protagonist's goal, the order of actions taken by the characters to solve the problem, and how the problem is ultimately resolved (Zipprich, 1995). For expository prose, the author begins organizing the concepts and points to be presented. Next, the author begins **drafting** the initial version of the prose. During the **conferencing** step, students share their work with others. Often, the draft is shared with others by using the "author chair" (Graves & Hansen, 1983) or a "sharing conference" (Milem & Garcia, 1996). The author shares his or her story with classmates, who in turn ask questions and give constructive suggestions that can be used for the revising. Next is **revising** of the initial draft; the author takes into consideration the suggestions of others and his or her own reflections about the work. In addition to revising the content, students edit their work for spelling, capitalization, and grammar. After the revision, the author may then conference a second time. This cycle may be repeated until the author is ready for **publishing** the work. Publication involves reviewing the work to polish details and the visual presentation of the work (e.g., title page, accompanying pictures or graphics). Publication also provides students with opportunities to gain skills in proofreading. They must also learn to conform with the formal correctives of written discourse. With continued process-writing experiences, children become very comfortable with sharing their work with others, discussing it with others, and receiving some assistance (Englert, Raphael, Anderson, Anthony, & Stevens, 1991; Graves, 1994; Richardson, 1991).

PROCEDURES FOR PRESENTING SUBJECT MATTER

In addition to concerns about how to teach, developing and beginning teachers often worry about what to teach. Although the scope of this chapter does not include specific curricular content, we present a description of the type of subject matter taught by most teachers. In most classrooms, two basic forms of subject matter—concepts and academic rules—are the focus of teaching and learning during any given day. These types of subject matter necessitate the use of specific steps that can be included within the more general procedures involved in using either DI or GDL. For instance, in using a DI format, what the teacher models, leads, and tests will be somewhat different when teaching concepts, as opposed to teaching academic rules. Nonetheless, the same general DI procedures are used regardless of subject matter. This is equally true when using a GDL approach. Therefore, the relationship between the DI and GDL models and the presentation of concepts and academic rules is that the latter dictates more specific steps within the general framework of the former. Following is a description of how these two types of subject matter are presented effectively.

Presentation of Conceptual Knowledge

Concepts are the basis for categorizing and organizing one's understanding about the world. They provide a hierarchical structure for superordinate and related subordinate categories of ideas or information. Before students can master academic skills, such as in mathematics or reading, they need to have grasped the basic underlying skills (Stanger, Symington, Miller, & Johns, 2000). By categorizing information, students are better able to understand similarities and differences among various ideas or events and to use information in more efficient ways. To describe conceptual structure, the analogy of a file cabinet is often used. Superordinate categories are the file drawers, and within each drawer are file folders, the subordinate categories, and within the file folders are sets of papers, the second tier of subordinate categories.

Conceptual knowledge is the basis for all content areas. Language arts involve a seemingly infinite set of concepts about the human experience and the world. These concepts deal with the struggle among people, nature, and even supernatural powers. The foundation of mathematics comprises a set of fundamental concepts about numbers and their manipulation. The natural and social sciences also deal with a host of concepts used to categorize plants and animals and people and places. The sciences even have special cases of conceptual knowledge called laws and principles. Both involve cause-effect relationships that explain natural and social phenomena. In the physical sciences, for instance, Newton's third law of motion is an explanation of the equilibrium of forces acting on each other. In the social sciences, principles are used in explaining causal relationships such as the economics of supply and demand. Laws differ from principles in that they carry a greater certainty about their ability to account for what happens in nature. Natural laws are absolute, but principles are only guidelines that have exceptions. Although concepts differ from subject to subject and there are special categories of concepts such as laws and principles, teachers of conceptual knowledge can use a common set of principles to guide instruction.

How to Teach Concepts. Presentation of conceptual knowledge is centered on definitions of the concepts being taught. To teach students the category of information subsumed by the concept name, developing teachers must set the limits for what fits and what does not fit. This can be thought of as a conceptual basket. A determination must be made as to what will fit in one basket and not another, just as though the concept of sorting as applied to clothes washing were being taught in a secondary daily living skills class for students with mild mental retardation. Initially, the hierarchical structure of the categories must be determined (Figure 6.3). With reference to the selector dial on the washing machine, Mr. Gunn, the teacher, might plan to start with three categories: permanent press, heavy duty, and regular. Next, remembering his bachelor training, the teacher separates whites from colors. So now Mr. Gunn has planned a two-tier system of sorting clothes requiring six baskets. To set limits, the teacher has to state the characteristics of the clothes that go into each basket, so he lists the essential attributes of the clothes for each basket. For example, to define white permanent press clothes, the teacher might say it is those clothes that are 90% or more white (when clean) and made of a permanent press material. He now has a definition of white permanent press clothes that can be used to classify the heaps of filth piled up in the laundry room.

FIGURE 6.3 Hierarchical Structure of the Categories of Clothing Used as Analogs for the Hierarchical Structure of Superordinate and Subordinate Concepts

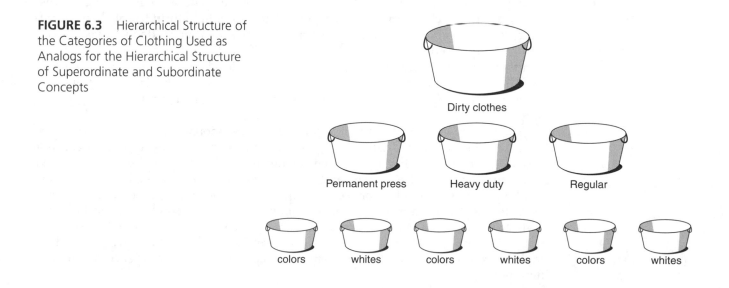

The definition has three components: concept name (e.g., white permanent press), class term (e.g., clothes), and essential attributes (e.g., 90% or more white when clean and made of a permanent press material). The **concept name** simply serves as a label for the concept. The **class term** links the target concept to a broader, superordinate conceptual category to which it belongs. The **essential attributes** define the parameters of the target concept and help in distinguishing it from other related concepts (e.g., dark permanent press clothes, white heavy-duty clothes).

Definitions alone are insufficient for presenting conceptual knowledge. They are abstractions that need to be translated into more concrete examples. To do so, the class term and the essential attributes are used to identify those items that fit in the conceptual basket and those that do not. In examining the clothes pile, the students are taught to place each item of clothing into its appropriate basket by examining the item and first asking themselves whether or not it is a piece of clothing (the broad class of items) or some other item found in the dirty clothes pile. If it is a piece of clothing, then the students examine it more closely to determine the match between the essential attributes of conceptual baskets and the characteristics of the piece of clothing. If the piece of clothing is a white shirt (90% or more white when clean) and made of a permanent press material, then it would be a good example of clothes that go into the white permanent press basket.

To complete the process of conceptualizing, the teacher needs to determine what does not fit in the baskets (nonexamples). The critical item for selecting nonexamples is the class term because it serves as a screening device for two types of nonexamples. Those items that are not members of the broader class are between-class nonexamples. They do not possess the essential attributes to even be a member of the broad class, let alone a member of a subclass. On the one hand, a wallet found in the middle of the clothes pile would be a gross nonexample of clothing. On the other hand, a pair of blue jeans would fit the class of clothing but would not share either of the essential attributes for the white permanent press basket. Consequently, it would be a within-class nonexample. Within-class nonexamples have varying relations to the target concept (the more essential attributes an item of clothing shares with the target concept, the more alike it is and the finer the discrimination needed to sort it). For example, in the white permanent press category, clothing must have only two essential attributes in order to fit. So the degrees of fineness are limited to two—those pieces of clothing that have none of the essential attributes, and those that share one essential attribute but not the other (see Figure 6.3).

These distinctions are important because the use of examples and varying degrees of nonexamples is critical in teaching students to discriminate among related concepts. If they are given clear examples that possess the essential attributes of the concept, students can more efficiently construct a stimulus set. After students have worked with a group of good examples and are firm on what fits in the conceptual basket, then they can effectively use clear nonexamples in deciding what fits and what does not. This confirmation process is aided by moving from between-class to within-class nonexamples. It enables students to shape and fine-tune their understanding of the target concept.

The presentation of conceptual knowledge is operationalized in one of two ways. First, teachers may use a definition, examples, and nonexamples to teach a concept (Box 6.3). On the one hand, they may model the concept by defining it and then show students a set of examples and nonexamples to form a more concrete understanding. This sequence is congruent with the DI teaching method. On the other hand, teachers may introduce a set of examples and nonexamples and induce students to formulate a concept definition based on common characteristics. This approach is more typical of a GDL approach commonly used at the upper elementary grades and above when complex related concepts are taught in science, math, and literature.

Box 6.3　　　　　　**Procedural Options for Teaching Concepts**

Define (give concept name, class term, and essential attributes) and give examples and non-examples.

OR

Give examples and nonexamples.

Second, a teacher may choose to give (DI) or to induce students to give (GDL) examples and nonexamples without stating a formal definition. This strategy is applicable to situations in which a formal definition may be too complicated to be of value to the learner (e.g., teaching the concepts of *redness* and *blueness* to preschoolers) or at the early stage of a spiral curriculum where a concept is developed at progressively higher levels throughout students' educational careers (e.g., the concept of *square* when taught to preschoolers as a visual discrimination of shape vs. teaching the concept to an elementary school child as a geometrical plane with essential characteristics involving sides, angles, and closedness; Figure 6.2).

Presentation of Academic Rules

A second type of subject matter that is taught on a large scale is the academic rule. **Academic rules** are procedures that are followed to complete an academic task. Academic rules contain two elements: (1) a situation or condition that denotes when or where a procedure is to be used (conditional knowledge) and (2) a command that pinpoints what is to be done (procedural knowledge) (Box 6.4). For example, students are taught, when writing a paragraph, to indent the first line. The situation or condition is "when writing a paragraph," and the command is "indent the first line." More complex academic rules contain a situation or condition and a series of commands that represent the steps needed to complete a task. For instance, students being taught to use **multipass** (Alley & Deshler, 1979), a study-skill strategy, are instructed that when they set out to read a passage, they must first do a survey pass, then a size-up pass, and finally a sort-out pass. Learning strategies like **multipass** and self-regulation routines referenced earlier are forms of academic rules.

Academic rules also operationalize the application of conceptual knowledge. A prime example is mathematics. Numerous procedures for doing computations and problem solving entail the use of conceptual knowledge. An example is the concept of *place value,* the idea that, in a base-10 system, the placement of a number in a right-to-left progression determines the factor of the units it represents. For students to understand what it means to "carry" or "regroup" a number from one column to another,

---

Box 6.4　　　　　　**Steps for Teaching Academic Rules**

1. State the academic rule.
   Condition or situation.
   Procedural step(s).

2. Apply the rule to examples.

ℙause and Reflect 6.5

Try to determine *academic rules* that teachers can teach, given the following examples:

a.)	b.)	c.)
book	stash	ax
look	cash	an
took	bash	at
hook	lash	as
Academic Rule:	Academic Rule:	Academic Rule:

d.)	e.)	f.)
replace	washing	ape
review	helping	cake
retake	fixing	place
rerun	spelling	brake
Academic Rule:	Academic Rule:	Academic Rule:

g.)	h.)	i.)
5,10,15,20	2,4,6,8	10, 20, 30, 40
Academic Rule:	Academic Rule:	Academic Rule:

j.)	k.)	l.)
$0 \times 1 = 0$	$6 \times 1 = 6$	$(3 \times 2) + 1$
$0 \times 4 = 0$	$77 \times 1 = 77$	$(5 \times 2) + 1$
$0 \times 9 = 0$	$42 \times 1 = 42$	$(15 \times 2) + 1$
$0 \times 7 = 0$	$10 \times 1 = 10$	$(92 \times 2) + 1$
Academic Rule:	Academic Rule:	Academic Rule:

they must learn the concept of *place value*. Then, the academic rule for "carrying" or "regrouping" makes sense to students (they recognize that the digit they are regrouping represents sets of 10, 100, and so forth).

How to Teach Academic Rules. The principles for teaching academic rules are relatively simple. A teacher needs to state (DI) or induce students to formulate (GDL) the rule, including the condition or situation and the command(s). Next, the rule must be applied to examples, and ultimately students need to be able to distinguish when and where the rule is used appropriately. For instance, when the academic rule for decoding CVCe words is being taught, the rule must be stated or discovered and applied to words that fit the pattern. Students then practice decoding the sounds of example words. Using a DI procedure, the teacher points to the chalkboard and states the academic rule as written:

"When a consonant, vowel, consonant is followed by a final e (CVCe), the vowel is long and the final e is silent" (model).

"All right, when I signal, say the rule with me. 'When a consonant . . . .'" (lead).

"What is the rule, Sondra?" (test).

After several opportunities to practice, the teacher demonstrates the application of the rule and provides guided practice.

After students have accurately stated and applied the rule by using examples, then nonexamples would be introduced in this or a subsequent lesson so that students learn when the rule is appropriate (examples) and not appropriate (nonexamples).

LEARNING STAGES

Another consideration in using either a DI or GDL approach is the progression of students through the stages of skill development. As students' conceptual knowledge and academic skills improve, the DI and GDL procedures are modified to accommodate mastery. When initially learning a new concept or skill, students characteristically make numerous mistakes, require cues and prompts, and need corrective feedback. But with instruction and practice, students gradually become able to conceptualize information or execute the skill. This is clearly evident when they are learning to decode and recognize words in print. At first, they read each individual word slowly, often saying the wrong sound or leaving out a sound. Teachers have to model letter-sound correspondence and sounding-out procedures. Gradually, young readers decode or recognize words with greater speed and accuracy as a result of instruction and practice. Ultimately, they are able to read fluently many varied types of reading material at school and home. Learning to read exemplifies the stages of learning through which students pass when learning a new concept or skill. These stages are concept or skill acquisition, fluency building, maintenance, and generalization (Figure 6.4).

Acquisition (Introduction and Discrimination)

Naive learners and the precision of developing teachers characterize the **acquisition stage** of learning. Students at this stage typically make frequent errors when attempting to use a target concept or skill but gradually respond more and more accurately. Teachers provide effective instructional antecedents, which are characterized in this stage of learning by extensive direction or guidance, prompts, and cues that assist students in responding accurately. Through careful selection of examples and clear definitions of concepts or clear rule statements, teachers structure learning in ways that decrease the complexity of the learning environment and increase the probability that students will respond in a desired fashion.

The key principle associated with instructional antecedents at the acquisition stage is clear communication (Englemann & Carnine, 1982). This is accomplished by the teacher either providing directly or guiding students in developing clear concept **definitions** or academic rules. A definition contains distinctive attributes that set the target concept apart from other similar concepts. An **academic rule** effectively describes the situation in which the rule is appropriate and provides clear steps to execute the skills. Additionally, clarity of communication is provided through the selection of effective examples. During the acquisition stage, examples should contain the prototypical dimensions of the concept or provide an easy stimulus for executing an academic rule. Our earlier reference to using a kitchen chair as a prototypical example is applicable here. Similarly, using the word *mat* would be a good example for introducing the CVCe sounding-out rule, whereas the multisyllabic word *material* would not.

1. **Acquisition Stage—Introduction**
   a. **Advance Organizer**—Outline the activities to be completed during the lesson.
   b. **Linkage**—Review related concepts, rules, or skills from previous lessons.
   c. **Demonstration**—Target concept, rule, or skill is demonstrated or induced. *Examples* are demonstrated or induced.
   d. **Guided Practice**—Target concept, rule, or skill is practiced with extensive prompting using *examples only.*
      1) Lead child in stating definition, attributes, rule, or skill
      2) Lead child in identifying concept examples or applying rules to examples
         a) use signalling to lead choral responses
         b) pose question, wait 3 to 5 seconds, call on reciter
         c) recognize student response
            1. give specific praise
            2. probe, amplify, restate student response
            3. ask peer for response
         d) follow corrective feedback steps as needed
      3) Test student's response
   e. **Independent Practice**—Target concept, rule, or skill is practiced daily without prompting using *examples only.*
      1) Give directions to complete activity tasks
      2) Lead students in completing example tasks
      3) Indicate deadline for completing activity
      4) Circulate and assist students
      5) Review student responses to activity tasks
   f. **Ending Review**—Review target concept, rule, or skill.
2. **Acquisition Stage—Discrimination**
   a. **Advance Organizer**—Outline the activities to be completed during the lesson.
   b. **Linkage**—Review related concepts, rules, or skills from previous lessons.
   c. **Demonstration**—Target concept, rule, or skill is demonstrated or induced. **Examples and nonexamples** are demonstrated or induced.
   d. **Guided Practice**—Target concept, rule, or skill is practiced with extensive prompting using *examples and nonexamples.*

FIGURE 6.4   Teaching: Explicit Activation of Learning (TEAL)

The acquisition stage can be divided into two levels: introduction and discrimination. The differences between these two levels are minimal but significant. The **introduction level** entails the use of examples only; the **discrimination level** entails the use of examples and nonexamples. During the introduction level, the examples-only format helps in establishing a pattern of accurate responding. When students respond accurately, those responses are reinforced by students' sense of success and by teacher praise. During the discrimination level, learning is solidified by having students distinguish between examples and nonexamples (they are able to determine whether the stimulus fits the concept category or fits the situation for using an academic rule).

1) Lead student in stating definition, attributes, rule, or skill.
2) Lead student in identifying concept examples and nonexamples or applying rules to examples and nonexamples
   a) use signalling to lead choral responses
   b) pose question, wait 3 to 5 seconds, call on reciter
   c) recognize student response
      1. give specific praise
      2. probe, amplify, restate student response
      3. ask peer for response
   d) follow corrective feedback steps as needed
3) Test student's responses

e. **Independent Practice**—Target concept, rule, or skill is practiced daily without prompting using *examples and nonexamples.*
   1) Give directions to complete activity tasks
   2) Lead students in completing example tasks
   3) Indicate deadline for completing activity
   4) Circulate and assist students
   5) Review student responses to activity tasks

f. **Ending Review**—Review target concept, rule, or skill.

3. **Fluency-Building Stage**—Target concept, rule, or skill is practiced *daily* with high rate of speed and accuracy.
   1) Review target concept, rule, or skill
   2) Give directions to complete activity tasks
   3) Lead students in completing example tasks
   4) Indicate deadline for completing activity
   5) Circulate and assist students
   6) Review student responses to activity tasks

4. **Maintenance Stage**—Target concept, rule, or skill is practiced *weekly or monthly* with high rate of speed and accuracy.
   1) Review target concept, rule, or skill
   2) Give directions to complete activity tasks
   3) Lead students in completing example tasks
   4) Indicate deadline for completing activity
   5) Circulate and assist students
   6) Review student responses to activity tasks

The two levels occur sequentially in DI procedures but are presented in a more simultaneous fashion in GDL procedures. Students move from the introduction to the discrimination level when they respond accurately to examples of the target concept or rule. The time spent at the introduction level varies with the complexity of the response being taught. On the one hand, the presentation of three or four examples during 5 minutes of instruction may be sufficient. On the other hand, instruction at the introduction level may require numerous examples being presented over 3 or 4 days before nonexamples are introduced. Similarly, several lessons may be needed at the discrimination level before mastery is attained.

Teaching the reading strategy of skimming can be used to exemplify instruction of an academic rule at the acquisition stage of learning. Using a DI approach, the teacher lists the steps for the procedure on poster board and uses it as the focus of a bulletin board in the front of the room (permanent model). Before reading a passage, the teacher first demonstrates the steps. Later, the teacher leads students in reading the steps and applying these to their daily reading passage. The skimming procedure, to this point, is applied to appropriate passages for which skimming is suited (introduction level using examples only). As students respond by accurately following the steps, the teacher gives them very short passages, for which skimming is not necessary (discrimination level using examples and nonexamples).

If a teacher uses a GDL approach to teach skimming, he or she would demonstrate by using appropriate example passages and say, "This is an example of skimming." Then the teacher would fully read the short passages (nonexamples) and say, "This is not an example of skimming." The next step would be to ask a series of guiding questions to induce students to identify the steps for skimming and to determine when it is appropriately used. Under the GDL approach, the presentation of examples and nonexamples is done in more of a simultaneous, rather than sequential, manner.

Fluency Building

Students maintaining high rates of accuracy and increasing the speed with which they respond characterize the second stage of learning, **fluency building.** Once students have demonstrated consistent accurate responding, the focus of instruction changes to speed and accuracy. Instructional activities at the fluency-building stage involve the students in fast-paced drill. Use of 1-minute timings to measure a student's rate of performance, as done in precision teaching (see References for address), is an example of a fluency-building activity. Guided and independent practice sessions are scheduled on a daily basis to provide massed or concentrated practice. Once a prescribed level of fast and accurate responding is attained, the skill is considered to be mastered. A number of instructional strategies for building fluency through modeling have been evaluated empirically, such as repeated reading, peer mediation, computer-guided practice, and previewing (Dawson et al., 2000).

During the fluency-building stage and continuing through the maintenance stage, the basic strategy is to wean students from their dependence on the teacher and the structures that have been built into the learning environment, such as demonstrations of the skill, instructions to perform the skill, and prompts to perform the skill (Wollery, Bailey, & Sugai, 1988). **Fading out** means that developing teachers monitor student progress and, as appropriate, decrease the intensity and frequency of instructional antecedents. In the skimming example, for instance, the teacher moves students through the introduction and discrimination levels with elaborate and frequent demonstrations, prompts, and praise for accurate responding. As students are able to discriminate when and when not to use skimming, the teacher begins focusing on fast and accurate responding in the fluency-building stage. At this time, the teacher reminds students intermittently of the steps and instructs them to use the poster on the bulletin board as a reference.

The same fading procedure is necessary for those events that follow the use of a target skill (consequences). Teachers diminish the intensity of positive reinforcement. By moving from a continuous schedule to an intermittent schedule, the frequency of positive reinforcement is reduced. Initially, students are praised every time they successfully implement the skimming steps. As they become more accurate, the teacher praises them every two instances, then every six.

Maintenance

Maintenance is the third stage of learning during which previously acquired concepts or skills are practiced for retention. Further fading of antecedent procedures and consequences continues the weaning process.

For example, once students demonstrate fluent skimming, the teacher begins implementing maintenance strategies. First, the poster board containing the skimming steps is replaced with a poster containing a simple prompt—"Skim before you read." The poster is moved from a prominent position in front of the room to the side of the room. Second, the teacher intermittently reminds students to skim when they appear not to be using the strategy.

These steps are taken to help students in adapting to the use of skimming in a more natural environment. The teacher transforms the antecedents from contrived instructional techniques (demonstration and leading) to more naturally occurring events (the poster prompt and intermittent verbal reminders to skim). Importantly, it is necessary to recognize that the beginning steps for maintaining skills are initiated from the first stages of instruction (Wollery et al., 1988).

As in the fluency-building stage, speed and accuracy are emphasized in maintenance activities. The practice sessions, however, are spaced apart in intervals ranging from 1 week to 1 month. They may take the form of an end-of-the-week or end-of-the-month review. As with the instructional antecedents and consequences for skimming, the regularity of explicit practice and review of the procedures is gradually faded. Maintenance is based on the axiom "What you don't use, you lose."

Generalization

The ultimate educational outcome that underlies every instructional activity is to have the students function better in the world outside the school, either during or after their school years. This is achieved by fostering generalization of what is learned to other situations and times. Exhibiting learned responses in places other than where they were taught is referred to as **setting generalization.** For responses learned in a resource room, setting generalization occurs when the responses are performed in the general education classroom or at home. When responses are made after teaching conditions have been faded completely, then a second form of generalization, **time generalization,** has occurred. For example, a month after a unit of instruction on skimming, a student uses the strategy when reading a magazine during free reading time.

In the facilitation of both forms of generalization, three sets of variables need to be considered: antecedent, response, and consequence (Wollery et al., 1988). As previously mentioned, instructional **antecedents** take the form of teachers demonstrating for, leading, and prompting students in making a conceptual or academic rule response. To facilitate maintenance, the intensity and frequency of antecedents need to be faded out gradually, with the aim of using naturally occurring antecedents to trigger a response. The objective is to maintain the response, but an additional objective is to facilitate setting generalization. **Naturally occurring antecedents** are operationally defined as those antecedents that occur in the setting to which the child needs to generalize the response. If resource room teachers want to prepare students to generalize a concept or rule to the general education classroom, they need to observe how the general education classroom teacher triggers responses. Using the skimming example, if the general education classroom teacher uses a verbal prompt (e.g., "Remember to skim your passage before reading"), then the resource room teacher should use the same prompt so that the student can make a setting generalization. Often, though, simply matching the antecedents will not suffice. The resource room teacher may need to tell students to use the procedure in the general education classroom and vice versa. Ultimately, both teachers should fade out their prompts completely.

Behavioral variables are attributes of the responses that students are taught. Generalization is more likely to occur if the behaviors selected for instruction have a high degree of utility in the target setting or over time. Students must be able to recognize that exhibiting the target academic behavior will be beneficial in some way. The benefits may be in the form of gaining reinforcement or the independence derived from learning new skills. These benefits should be conveyed explicitly to students so that they are made aware of why they are learning a concept or academic rule.

Careful structure of *consequence variables* can aid generalization significantly. The first strategy for manipulating the consequences of behavior to promote generalization is to develop the use of social reinforcers. Social reinforcers are important because they are naturally occurring and are used most frequently in classrooms as the primary means of reinforcement. **Social reinforcers** come in a variety of forms, including smiles, verbal praise, pats on the shoulder, eye contact, and teacher attention. The second strategy is to prepare students for the usually thin schedule of reinforcement that occurs in most classrooms. In remedial and special classrooms, students are often systematically or arbitrarily put on a very dense schedule of reinforcement. Without thinning to levels equivalent to those in the general education classroom, the behavior may not generalize at all or will extinguish after a short period of time. The third strategy is to increase systematically the gap between the occurrence of the target response and the introduction of reinforcement. Such delays are designed to acclimate students to classrooms with larger numbers of students and fewer adults. In such environments, teachers and paraprofessionals or volunteers are unable to get to every student as often as in a remedial or special classroom, where the adult to student ratio is lower. The fourth strategy also helps students in adjusting to thin reinforcement schedules or delays in reinforcement by others. Teach students to self-reinforce for appropriate use of conceptual knowledge and academic rules. Self-verbalizations such as, "You did it, big guy," a discrete little dance around the desk, or "low-fiving" themselves are effective ways in which students can self-reinforce.

LESSON DEVELOPMENT

The discussion to this point has focused on the principal elements of effective instruction for the sake of identification and analysis. Of course, practicing teachers soon realize that instruction is never a neat little prescriptive package with totally distinct and separate parts. Delivering instruction is an integrated mass of interactive elements that vary in their form and sequence. In the section below, we present this integrated whole in the context of a sequence of lesson delivery. We describe three very general sequential elements of a lesson: initiating a lesson, engaging students during instruction, and closing a lesson. The section on lesson formats that follows later is more detailed, providing the specific sequence for lessons that incorporate direct instruction or guided discovery techniques for teaching concepts and academic rules at different stages of learning.

Initiating a Lesson

The beginning of a lesson should accomplish three basic objectives: gain students' attention, orient students to the lesson content and format, and initiate lesson review (see Box 6.5).

Gaining Students' Attention. Learning is characterized by active participation in the manipulation of concepts and rules, either covertly through mental activity, or overtly through responses like talking or writing. Regrettably, to those looking for an easy way to learn, unconscious, inattentive activities such as listening to foreign language audiotapes while sleeping do not result in learning. The first step in lesson development is to gain students' attention before engaging them in conscious efforts to manipulate concepts or rules.

Box 6.5   **Example of Lesson Introduction**

Mr. Ketcher is in the middle of a unit plan on home budgets. During the past few weeks, he has covered concepts and academic rules related to using a checking account. Mr. Ketcher has already introduced such concepts as *current balance, check charges, debits,* and *credits*. Also, he has introduced the academic rules for filling out checks and maintaining a running record of transactions. Today, he will introduce the concept of *automated teller machine (ATM)* and the procedures for its use. Mr. Ketcher uses the following discourse to introduce the lesson, including gaining attention, orienting, and a lesson-initiating review:

"OK, class, park it and eyes on the front of the class-that includes you, James." **(gaining attention)**

"Remember that we have been discussing home budgets for the past few weeks; in the last few days, we have focused on checking accounts. Today, we are going to discuss automated teller machines and the procedures for using them. We are going to practice using an ATM by using our computer, and next week we are going to apply for ATM cards." **(orienting)**

"Let's review first what we have covered so far relating to checking accounts. First, we discussed the concept of current balance and said that it is the amount of money that remains in your account to date." **(lesson-initiating review with teacher statements)**

"We also talked about the concept of a *running record*. How did we define the term *running record*?"

"It is the part of the checkbook where we write down how much checks were and any money we put in."

"Yes, Clyde, the running record is the section in the checkbook where we enter the amount of withdrawals, deposits, and current balance.

"Hey, I have used some of those fancy banking terms like *withdrawal* and *deposit*. What is the difference between withdrawals and deposits?" **(lesson-initiating review with teacher question)**

"We take out money, that's a withdrawal. When we put in money, that's a deposit."

"Good, Henry, withdrawals are the amounts of money we take out of the account, and deposits are the amounts we put into the account."

Mr. Ketcher continues the review of major points by asking students additional questions about how to keep the running record and so forth and then moves into the new material on ATMs. Students should now be aware of the important concepts and rules they have already covered and be ready to use that content in conjunction with the discussion of ATMs.

This can be done in some very simple and easy ways:

1. Start lessons on time so that students come to expect that a schedule is in place and will be followed.

2. Cue students—by sounding a bell or buzzer, by making a statement like, "Let's get started," or by switching the lights on and off—that the lesson is to begin.

3. Become more creative in your lesson initiation by using more elaborate techniques that spur student interest and curiosity. For example, a pet snake placed in a conspicuous location in the classroom is sure to get students to focus their attention on the upcoming lesson on reptiles.

4. Solicit students to participate in an exciting lesson-initiating activity, such as playing word bingo.

5. Wear an article of clothing that is unusual and related to the lesson topic to stir interest.

Orienting Students to the Lesson. Orienting students by providing a brief overview of the lesson sequence will make them aware of the content to be covered and the activities they will engage in during the lesson. Revealing the anticipatory set directly to students helps to orient students to the lesson. For instance, in orienting students to a reading lesson, a teacher may say, "Today we are going to read a story about a pirate ship manned by a crew of ghosts. First, we are going to talk about pirates and ghosts, and then we are going to review the self-questioning procedures we have been using during silent reading. Then we will read and discuss the story." In addition to telling students about the lesson to follow, the teacher has established a bridge among what has been taught in previous lessons, the self-questioning strategy, and what is to take place during the present lesson. This tactic helps students in recognizing the link among successive lessons by cueing them to the fact that concepts and rules taught earlier will be used in subsequent lessons.

Initiating Lesson Review. To establish further the links among a set of lessons, teachers often engage students in a lesson-initiating review. The review is a connector between information already introduced in previous lessons and information to be introduced in the new lesson. Teachers strategically integrate information across lessons to demonstrate the connections and to assist students in understanding the new information at a deeper level (Baker, Simmons, & Kameenui, 1994).

During a block of time, usually between 2 and 10 minutes, teachers highlight pertinent information in one of two ways. In one, they may simply state for students the relevant information for the upcoming lesson, emphasizing critical information. In a second form, the teacher may ask a series of questions to have students rehearse information about concepts and academic rules. This form of review has the added benefit of providing an overlapping practice session: Not only is information reviewed, but students also practice verbalizing or applying the content.

Engaging Students During Instruction

Teaching at any stage of learning entails a varying degree of interaction between student and teacher. Two critical features of teacher-student interactions are the teacher's questioning skills and the teacher's treatment of students' responses.

Questioning Students. The teacher's questioning skills are important because the questions frame the responses received from students. They determine the complexity of students' responses in terms of the level of cognitive processing required and the degree of elaboration. For instance, teachers may ask students questions that require knowledge, comprehension, application, analysis, synthesis, or evaluation of information (see Box 6.6). It is important that teachers know the type of cognitive processing and response desired and are able to form questions that emit the desired response (Martin, 1979). In teaching a lesson on the concept of *helping*, for example, a teacher may want students to recall some basic facts from a story about a mouse, an elephant, and a lion, and therefore asks, "Which two animals helped each other?" This query requires a

Box 6.6 **Hierarchy of Questions Ranging from Low-Level to High-Level Cognitive Processing Related to Social Studies**

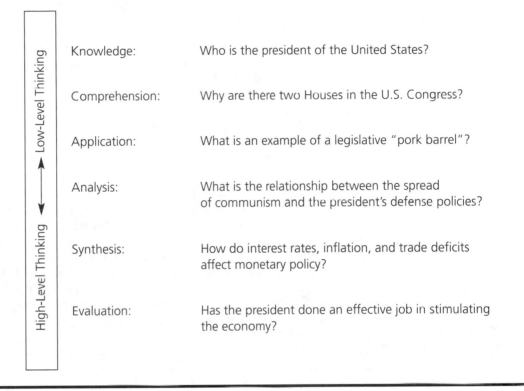

Low-Level Thinking	Knowledge:	Who is the president of the United States?
	Comprehension:	Why are there two Houses in the U.S. Congress?
	Application:	What is an example of a legislative "pork barrel"?
	Analysis:	What is the relationship between the spread of communism and the president's defense policies?
High-Level Thinking	Synthesis:	How do interest rates, inflation, and trade deficits affect monetary policy?
	Evaluation:	Has the president done an effective job in stimulating the economy?

relatively low level of cognitive processing and a brief response. In contrast, the teacher asks the class, "Why is it so odd that a mouse saved the elephant?" Here students are asked to analyze the relationship between the animals, which requires a more complex level of cognitive processing and a more elaborate verbal response.

A related strategy for questioning is *mixing* the types of questions so that a variety of responses are required (Dunkin & Biddle, 1974; Rosenshine, 1971). Often, developing teachers fixate on low-level recognition and recall questions. These are certainly the easiest types of question to ask, but the content of academic instruction should require students to do more than recognize and recall. Once basic factual information is presented or developed, teachers should require students to make responses that involve comprehension, application, analysis, synthesis, evaluation, and judgment.

The previous questioning example involving the helping relationship between the elephant and the mouse illustrates how teachers can take basic factual information (recall of who the animals were) and build on that base to the level of analyzing this relationship to determine why animals—and for that matter, people—help each other.

In addition to knowing what types of questions to ask, developing teachers need to know *how to ask* questions. Two strategies need to be applied. In the first strategy, the teacher poses a question first and then calls on a student to respond, rather than calls a specific student's name and then asks the question. For instance, the more effective strategy would be to ask, "Why did the mouse help the elephant?" . . . (pause) . . . "Yes, Miguel," rather than, "Miguel, why did the mouse help the elephant?" One benefit of the first strategy is that it enables teachers to get more "bang for their buck" (all students must covertly process a response because they do not know who will be called on to make the overt response). Consequently, a teacher can emit an overt response and several covert responses with a single question. A second benefit is that students are less likely to engage in off-task behaviors because they are less able to predict who will be called. When a student's name is called before the question is posed, other students are inclined to believe they are off the hook and do not need to attend to the question that follows.

The second strategy is called **wait time** (Rowe, 1974). One form of wait time, **wait time I,** refers to the gap in time between the presentation of a question and when a student is called on to respond. By waiting 3 to 5 seconds after posing the question, the teacher provides students with time to formulate a response. Use of wait time I results in a greater frequency of accurate responses. Wait time I is used at the early stages of skill acquisition and when desired responses entail higher levels of cognitive processing. During fluency-building drills and practice activities, however, when speed and accuracy are being developed, wait time is not desirable.

A second form of wait time, **wait time II,** refers to the gap in time between the completion of the student's response and the teacher's subsequent response. Using the preceding story of the helpful mouse, wait time II would occur following Miguel's response to the teacher's question, "Why did the mouse help the elephant? . . . (wait time I) . . . "Yes, Miguel." Miguel replies, "Because the elephant had helped the mouse." . . . (wait time II) . . . Miguel continues, "When the lion was going to eat the mouse, the elephant scared him away and the mouse was saved." Wait time II provides students with time to contemplate their responses and subsequently elaborate or modify them. This provision results in increased accuracy and more elaborate responses. Wait time II is used more often when teachers ask questions that require responses generated from higher levels of cognitive processing.

Providing Feedback. Once questions have been asked and responses made, teachers evaluate students' responses and provide feedback. For accurate responses, teachers usually praise students, but often they do not inform students as to what was praiseworthy about their responses. Statements that praise students and provide information that indicates how they can receive praise in the future is referred to as **specific academic praise.** Such statements refer to the cognitive processes, strategies, or behaviors used to formulate the response. For example, the statement, "Excellent answer, Caitlin. You made the connection between the two important events in the story," contains a praise component and indicates to the student that "making the connection" is what was praiseworthy. In contrast, by simply saying, "Excellent answer, Caitlin," the focus is on the response, not on the process by which it was derived. The process is important because it provides generalizable guidelines for making similar excellent responses in the future.

Other ways that teachers can treat students' accurate responses include feedback statements that paraphrase, elaborate, or clarify students' responses. **Paraphrasing** entails restating what the student said or did; **restatement** emphasizes the responses and ensures that other students observed the response. An example from the reading lesson above would be the teacher stating, "That nasty lion did try to eat the poor little mouse," following a student's response, "That bad lion was going to eat 'em." **Elaboration** is feedback that uses students' responses as a core to which the teacher adds further information. For example, a student responds to the question, "Why do lions have such big claws?" by stating, "They need them to climb trees." The teacher then states, "Yes, they often hide in trees, wait for animals to walk nearby, and then jump on them." A **clarifying response** is used to either confirm what students have said or reformulate the response in a more comprehensible way. For instance, when asked to state why people (or the mouse and elephant) become friends, a student responds, "Well, because they sort of think they're cool and they do stuff together, you know, like that." A teacher's clarifying response would be, "So you are saying that people become friends because they are interested in doing the same kinds of things, like going to concerts or playing basketball, and enjoy doing those things with each other."

These forms of positive feedback are important because they provide information about students' responses without providing any explicit praise. Keep in mind that gradual thinning of reinforcement is important for the maintenance and generalization of behaviors; the systematic use of combinations of academic praise and other feedback techniques is an important teacher strategy.

When students' responses are inaccurate, teachers can use the steps for corrective feedback associated with teaching low-level content by using the DI model. Another set of options is to rephrase the question or request, provide additional cues to guide a student's responses, or indicate to students that a response is inaccurate and help them identify the nature of the inaccuracy. **Rephrasing** entails presenting the stimulus question in a slightly different form that may clarify the desired response or refocus students' attention. If a teacher asks, "How did the elephant use his trunk?" and the student responds, "He eats peanuts with it," the teacher may rephrase the question: "Let me ask that question a different way. In the story, when the lion was coming closer, how did the elephant use his trunk?" **Providing additional cues** is synonymous with giving "hints." For example, a teachers asks, "How did the lion sneak up on the mouse?" and when the student's response is inaccurate, the teacher adds, "Remember the tall grass."

A third option for teachers is to *indicate that the response is inaccurate* and help students determine what the correct response is. This may be done by telling students the response is inaccurate and then redirecting the question to another student or by telling students why the response does not fit the question. For instance, in the case where a teacher asks students to state the characteristics of someone who is helpful, and a student responds, "They leave other people alone," the teacher may redirect the same or a rephrased question to another student (e.g., "What do helpful people do to help other people?") or tell the student the response is incorrect and why (e.g., "Being helpful is judged by the things you do for others, not by the things you don't do").

Closing a Lesson: Ending Review

The **closing review** provides an end point and summary of what occurred during the lesson. The review cues students to the impending transition from one lesson to another. In addition, it is an opportunity for the students to conceptualize the relationships among the discrete content elements of the lesson. For instance, as part of a written expression lesson, the teacher can guide students in restating the rule for writing a complete sentence and showing two or three examples and nonexamples of the rule application.

The review component proceeds in the same way as a lesson-initiating review, either by the teacher making verbal summary statements or physical demonstrations of the target responses or by asking a series of guiding questions to elicit the responses from students. The latter is the preferred format because it increases the opportunities for students to practice responses actively. With the sentence-writing lesson, the teacher might say, "When writing a complete sentence, a subject and predicate must be included. Examples are 'The dog barked' and 'The cow jumped over the moon.' 'The black angry dog' is not an example because it doesn't have a predicate." A guided review, however, would entail the teacher asking, "What is the rule for writing complete sentences?" Subsequently, examples and nonexamples would be induced.

LESSON FORMAT FOR DIRECT INSTRUCTION AND GUIDED DISCOVERY LEARNING APPROACHES

To summarize the elements of this chapter, we designed the following section to show in outline form how the principles of DI and GDL can be overlaid with the procedures for presenting concepts and academic rules at each stage of learning. The integrated format is represented in Figure 6.4 as the TEAL model—Teaching: Explicit Activation of Learning (O'Shea & O'Shea, 1997). This integrated format can be used in structuring the development of lessons in a manner that incorporates the critical elements of effective instruction.

Acquisition Stage—Introduction

As described earlier, this initial stage of learning requires significant teacher time and attention directed toward planning and monitoring students' responses to target concepts and academic rules. The introduction phase of the acquisition stage is characterized by precise demonstrations and guided practice using examples only. The following sequence exemplifies this and other features of lesson development at this stage of learning:

1. Gain students' attention and orient students with an outline of the activities to be completed during the lesson.

2. Link the present lesson with previous lessons by reviewing related concepts or academic rules previously taught.

3. During the demonstration, model or induce through questioning the target concept or academic rule. Use examples only.

4. During guided practice, provide extensive opportunities to respond through practice activities involving the target concept or academic rule. Use extensive prompts and cues to emit responses involving examples only.

   a. Lead or induce students in stating definition, attributes, or rule.

   b. Lead or induce students in identifying concept examples or applying rules to examples by using signaling to lead choral responses when appropriate.

      • Pose a question, wait 3 to 5 seconds, and then call on a student for a response.

      • Recognize a student's response by giving academic praise, paraphrasing, amplifying, clarifying, or redirecting to another student.

   c. Provide corrective feedback as needed.

5. For independent practice, provide daily activities involving examples of the target concept or academic rule that students can perform with minimal prompting or cues. Students should be able to perform tasks with 90% accuracy or better.

   a. Give directions to complete activity tasks.

   b. Lead students in completing example tasks.

   c. Indicate the deadline for completing activity.

   d. Circulate and assist students as needed.

   e. Review students' responses to activity tasks.

6. Engage students in an ending review to summarize the content covered in the lesson and to signal the transition to the next lesson.

Acquisition Stage—Discrimination

The acquisition stage continues with the introduction of nonexamples used to teach students to discriminate between the target concept or academic rule and other similar concepts or academic rules. Accurate discrimination responses are indicators that students are solidifying their skills. The steps are identical to those under the acquisition-introduction stage except that examples and nonexamples are used during instruction.

Fluency-Building Stage

Lessons at the fluency-building stage entail independent practice activities. Teachers simply introduce the activity and monitor students' responses to a few example stimuli to ensure that they are responding with relative degrees of speed and accuracy. To ensure that students use their time productively and that fluency is built, the following steps are suggested:

1. Gain students' attention and orient students with an outline of the activities to be completed during the lesson.

2. Link the present lesson with previous lessons by reviewing related concepts or academic rules previously taught.

3. Provide daily independent practice activities that engage students in responding to examples and nonexamples of the target concept or academic rule. The focus of practice is on high rates of speed and accuracy. Students should be able to perform tasks with 90% accuracy or better.

   a. Give directions to complete activity tasks.

   b. Lead students in completing example tasks.

   c. Indicate the deadline for completing the activity.

   d. Circulate and assist students as needed.

   e. Review students' responses to activity tasks.

4. Engage students in an ending review to summarize the content covered in the lesson and to signal the transition to the next lesson.

Maintenance Stage

The primary characteristic of the maintenance stage is that practice schedules are distributed over longer intervals of time. These weekly or monthly practice activities are geared to assist students in retaining appropriate levels of fast and accurate responding. As the time interval between sessions increases, the need to conduct a brief review of the target concept or academic rule increases. Additionally, instructional antecedents and reinforcement should be thinned. The following steps are guidelines for lesson development:

1. Gain students' attention and orient students with an outline of the activities to be completed during the lesson.

2. Link the present lesson with previous lessons by reviewing related concepts or academic rules previously taught.

3. Provide weekly or monthly independent practice activities that engage students in responding to examples and nonexamples of the target concept or academic rule. The focus of practice is on high rates of speed and accuracy. Students should be able to perform tasks with 90% accuracy or better.

   a. Give directions to complete activity tasks.

   b. Lead students in completing example tasks.

   c. Indicate the deadline for completing the activity.

   d. Circulate and assist students as needed.

   e. Review students' responses to activity tasks.

4. Fade out the frequency and intensity of response antecedents and consequences by using intermittent schedules.

5. Engage students in an ending review to summarize the content covered in the lesson and to signal the transition to the next lesson.

Generalization Stage

Unlike the earlier stages of learning, the steps for teaching generalization outlined as follows are not taught in separate discrete lessons. Instead, these steps are incorporated, to varying extents, into lessons at all previous learning stages. The primary characteristic of generalization instruction is that students are encouraged to use their skills in other settings and at different times. The following suggestions are means to set the occasion for generalization: (1) use instructional antecedents and consequences that occur in other settings, (2) use materials found in other settings for practicing target concepts or academic rules, (3) use delayed and intermittent reinforcement schedules, (4) teach students to self-reinforce fast and accurate responding, (5) encourage other teachers to reinforce students' use of target concepts and academic rules, and (6) tell students to use concepts and academic rules in other classrooms.

WHEN TO USE SPECIFIC ELEMENTS OF EFFECTIVE INSTRUCTION

The lesson-format outline and overall discussion in this chapter deal primarily with what effective teachers do when they deliver instruction. The classroom examples provided throughout the chapter are aimed at illustrating how effective teachers operationalize the principles of effective instruction. Another important aspect of effective teaching deals with knowing when to use certain key elements. Following are some guidelines to assist developing teachers in deciding when they implement specific elements of effective instruction provided in the lesson-format section above.

Teaching Concepts and Academic Rules by Using the DI and GDL Models

First, developing teachers must decide when to use either of the two general models of instruction presented in the chapter. The DI model can be used with either concepts or academic rules. It is more often used with content that entails rote learning of basic facts and skills. It can also be used, however, with content and learning tasks that involve high-order cognitive processes such as synthesis, analysis, and application. In the latter case, the teacher gives the concept definition and examples and nonexamples but the students are asked to apply the concept to novel situations, thus requiring high-order cognitive processes. The GDL model, in contrast, can be used with both concepts and academic rules but is more frequently used with concept induction. GDL is more often used with high-order content and learning tasks than for rote learning.

Second, developing teachers must decide when to treat content as concepts or academic rules. Concepts are ubiquitous; they are a part of all content area material, including basic tool skills such as reading and math, social science, science, vocational subjects, and daily living skills. When the developing teacher is teaching categories of information, the material should be treated as conceptual knowledge. Academic rules are not so pervasive; they are associated more with basic tool skills and, to some extent, other content areas, such as auto mechanics, in which a set of procedures must be followed to complete a learning task. When the subject matter entails students learning how to complete a learning task either covertly (e.g., learning strategy) or overtly (e.g., compute a math sum), the content should be treated as academic rule knowledge.

Third, developing teachers must decide the degree of precision with which they must follow the prescribed steps. In first learning to implement either model, developing teachers should start out with careful precision until they automatically carry out the steps. Then they can begin to focus more on students' responses to specific aspects of a lesson. At this point, developing teachers can make decisions about varying things, such as the number of examples presented or asking students to volunteer examples, rather than the teacher giving them. Such decisions will be based on students' familiarity with the steps in instruction, as well as their interest and prior knowledge of the content.

Stages of Learning

Decisions concerning when to move students through the different stages of learning should be based on the accuracy and rate of students' independently made correct responses. In a very general sense, a criterion of 90% accuracy is a sound basis for moving students from the acquisition stage to the fluency-building stage. Movement into the other stages should be based on speed as well as accuracy.

The rate criterion can be derived from one of two sources. The first source, peer medians, is readily available regardless of content area and grade level, but it may take a little advance work. To determine the rate for a particular response, developing teachers must sample the rate of responding of a peer group that has mastered the target response. The median rate of responding (responses per minute or some other unit of time) for the peer group is used as the criterion for mastery. The second source, published proficiency rates, can be obtained for most tool skills in reading, math, and spelling but may not be available for other content areas. Table 6.2 is a sample of rate criteria from a variety of sources.

Lesson Development

The two decision areas in lesson development most often of concern to developing teachers are frequency of reviews and mixing of low- and high-order questions. Some teachers are concerned that overdwelling on reviews may cause boredom and impede students' progress in mastering the full range of skills needed to be completed in a school year. Both are legitimate concerns that can be the dysfunctional effects of reviewing too frequently or for too long a period of time. To help avoid these potential problems, developing teachers need to remember that the review need only deal with the major points of the lesson and not all the details. Also, developing teachers can use lesson-initiating reviews judiciously. When making an important conceptual bridge between two closely related concepts or academic rules, they should engage students in a thorough review at the beginning of the lesson. When the lesson is a continuation of work on a concept or rule that was introduced earlier, developing teachers can spend less time reviewing at the beginning of the lesson. Ending reviews appear to be more crucial. Developing teachers should be less willing to cut back on these reviews.

The second area of concern deals with the mix of low- and high-order questions. To begin with, developing teachers need to be aware of a trap into which many teachers fall: When working with academically low-functioning students, many developing teachers fixate on asking low-order rote questions, believing that such students are not capable of handling high-order questions. The trap is that, without instruction and practice in answering high-order questions, these students will surely be limited in their ability to respond to questions involving comprehension, application, analysis, synthesis, evaluation, or judgment. Therefore, developing teachers should start units or segments of instruction with low-order questions but should plan in advance the introduction of high-order questions for students at all levels of ability once accuracy of rote responding reaches criterion. Effectively using cues and prompts can help students in responding accurately to high-order questions.

TABLE 6.2 Criterion Levels for Corrects and Errors per 1-Minute Sample for Reading, Math, and Spelling Skills

PROFICIENCY RATES FOR READING SKILLS

	Says isolated sounds (K–3)		Says Words in List (2–4)		(5–6)		(Adult)		Says Words in Text (1–3)		(4–6)		(Adult)	
	Cor.	Err.[a]	Cor.	Err.	Cor.	Err.	Cor.	Err.	Cor.	Err.	Cor.	Err.	Cor.	Err.
Koenig & Kunzelmann (1980)			140	0	120–130	0								
Starlin & Starlin (1973)									50–70	2	100–200	2	100–200	2

PROFICIENCY RATES FOR MATH SKILLS

	Addition Facts 0–9 Gr. 2–3		Sub. Facts (1–5) and Facts Top Numb. 2–9 Gr. 2–3		Add. Facts Sums and Sub. Facts Top Numb. 6–9 Gr. 3–4		Two-Column Addition with Re-grouping Gr. 4–5		Two-Column Subtraction with Re-grouping Gr. 4–6		Multiplies Facts Through x9 Gr. 5–6		Divides Facts Through Divisor of 9 Gr. 6	
	Cor.	Err.	Cor.	Err.	Cor.	Err.	Cor.	Err.	Cor.	Err.	Cor.	Err.	Cor.	Err.
Koenig & Kunzelmann (1980)	60	—	60	—	90	—	60	—	60	—	90	—	60	—
Precision Teaching Project (Montana)	70–90	—	70–90	—	70–90	—	70–90	—	70–90	—	70–90	—	70–90	—

PROFICIENCY RATES FOR SPELLING

	Gr. 2		Gr. 3		Gr. 4		Gr. 5		Gr. 6	
	Cor.	Err.	Cor.	Err.	Cor.	Err.	Cor.	Err.	Cor.	Err.
Koenig & Kunzelmann (1980)	60–90	—	90–100	—	100–120	—	110–130	—	120–140	—

	K–Gr. 2 Instructional Level		K–Gr. 2 Independent Level		Gr. 3–Adult Instructional Level		Gr. 3–Adult Independent Level	
	Cor.	Err.	Cor.	Err.	Cor.	Err.	Cor.	Err.
Starlin & Starlin (1973)	15–29	3–7	30–50	≥2	25–49	3–7	50–70	≥2

[a]Letters correct and errors

Adapted from Mercer, C. D., & Mercer, A. R. (2001). *Teaching students with learning problems* (6th ed.). Upper Saddle River, NJ: Merrill/Prentice Hall.

SUMMARY

This chapter presented a variety of elements found in the effective delivery of instruction. These elements are very complex and are intricately interwoven into the fabric of teaching. They were artificially separated and described here for purposes of analysis, but when put into practice, they can be difficult to identify as discrete elements.

Nonetheless, developing teachers who continuously analyze the instructional environment of their classrooms and their role in that environment can benefit from the application of these elements to their own instructional repertoire.

Educational researchers and philosophers continually strive to explain what makes effective instruction work. They have devised and revised a variety of instructional models. Two prominent models of instruction are direct instruction (DI) and guided discovery learning (GDL). Often, these models are viewed as diametrically opposed, but in another light they can be viewed as complementary. DI offers developing teachers a set of procedures for presenting subject matter by having teachers model components of concepts or academic rules and then present examples and nonexamples. GDL generally entails presenting strong examples first and then having students deduce the concept or academic rule through a series of guided questions. Many other features of these two models are similar, such as the importance of guided practice, the development of content mastery through extensive practice, the selection of strong examples, and the need to identify essential attributes of concepts and steps for academic rules. Selecting which model to use can be guided by applicability of subject matter to the instructional steps in each model and the need to mix instructional techniques to enhance student interest. As Dixon and Carnine (1994) concluded, the divisions in beliefs about instruction between proponents of different models may not be as deep when the respective practices are compared.

Another important element of instruction is the type of subject matter being presented. Two categories of content and the steps for presenting them were outlined: concepts and academic rules. Concepts are pervasive subject matter that are central to all content areas. They provide a means by which students can categorize and classify information and understand the relationships of various superordinate and subordinate levels. Academic rules are procedures used to complete academic tasks that involve covert and overt responses by students. They are also found in a variety of content areas that require problem solving and the application of conceptual knowledge.

The third element of instruction discussed in the chapter is the stages of learning. Developing teachers can benefit in recognizing that students first acquire skills in responding to concepts and academic rules through careful presentation of examples and nonexamples. Once they have acquired a degree of accuracy in working with target subject matter, fluency is built through daily practice sessions. For acquired skills to be maintained and not degenerate, practice sessions need to be distributed over longer intervals of time. The final stage of instruction, generalization, is focused on having students use their acquired skills in different settings and times.

The final section of the chapter was an outline of the integration of the above elements. This lesson-development format is designed for developing teachers to use in guiding students to the ultimate goal of instruction: students independently using subject matter in appropriate setting at appropriate times.

ACTIVITIES TO EXTEND YOUR KNOWLEDGE

1. Select two of the five components of academic and cognitive interventions (motivation, acquisition, generalization, communication, and transition). Describe their contribution and importance to effective instruction.

2. Conduct a literature review on the use of strategies by students with learning disabilities. Describe how teachers can assist students with problems in attention during reading and mathematics instruction.

3. Take a position on each of the following issues: The purpose for having students practice learning strategies in controlled materials is to increase

    a. setting generalization

    b. readability of materials

    c. opportunities to use strategies

    d. skill maintenance

      Discuss your responses with peers.

4. List three advantages of peer tutoring, one of which should refer to work with culturally diverse populations.

5. Identify and describe strategies that facilitate learning in a specific academic situation by participating in workshop presentations with peers. Discuss, in roundtable fashion, strategies that will take into account students' memory, attention, verbal mediation, visual imagery, rehearsal, relaxation, and/or subject-oriented instruction. Provide all class members and the instructor an up-to-date reference list and a two-page summary of important points on the chosen strategy presented.

6. Practice the classwide peer tutoring model throughout your academic semester with peers in your university class. Use the topics of lesson planning and delivering instruction. Assign tutors and teams to distribute reinforcement. Tutors are to provide individual contingencies. Work with your university instructor and other class teams to provide group contingencies. Work with your instructor in posting the daily and weekly team totals. Compare and contrast the totals with those of your peers.

7. Consider your field setting and briefly list five ways in which you have been an effective teacher who has integrated instructional strategies for your students. Give specific examples of what you have done in your field site.

8. After the announcement of your selection as Outstanding Rookie Teacher of the Year, your principal has asked you to describe for the rest of the faculty in your school the secret of your success—TEAL. Outline your presentation to the faculty. Give examples to illustrate your points; that is, select a concept, law or lawlike principle, academic rule, or value judgment and apply it to the TEAL model.

POINT AND CLICK

The following web sites highlight the chapter's theme of delivering instruction effectively. Each of these listings can assist new teachers in their delivery of instructional activities.

I-Mind Education Systems
104 Tiburon Blvd.
Mill Valley, CA 94941
415-380-4667
Fax: 415-380-4660
www.i-mind.com
I-Mind is an educational systems group devoted to providing teachers with instructional delivery and management tools, educational resources, student data, and on-line communications through a single, convenient access point. This system can help teachers to correlate lesson plans to state curriculum standards. It provides listings of educational resources, including software titles and Web sites.

Riverdeep Interactive Learning
125 Cambridge Park Dr.
Cambridge, MA 02140
1-800-564-2587
www.logal.net
info@riverdeep.nt.
This Web site provides teachers software correlated to state and national standards. It gives easy-to-follow lesson plans and instructional strategy guides. It provides student handouts and on-line tools to check student progress and performance. Students can experience lesson simulations and tool-based activities, including Web-based news programs and an on-line student community.

Blackboard
1111 19th St. NW Ste. 600
Washington, DC 20036
202-463-4860
www.blackboard.com
The Blackboard Web site is a member of School Tone Alliance and provides a wide range of education access and services to schools. It is part of a Web-based portal system for content, communication tools, applications, and professional development activities for teachers.

VTECHSoft, Inc.
714-734-4800
Fax: 714-734-4801
1-800-742-1050
www.vtechsoft.com
VTECH lists for elementary and middle-school teachers the names of educational toys and educational software used in effective instructional delivery. It covers content areas such as history, reading, science, and spelling.

wwwrrr
1-877-999-771
Fax: 651-686-5501
www.wwwrrr.net
wwwrrr is an on-line training, communication, and education company that helps teachers to use the Internet more effectively in their instructional delivery. It focuses on helping teachers to integrate communication tools, educational products, and training into the classroom.

REFERENCES

Algozzine, B., Ysseldyke, J., & Elliott, J. (1997). *Strategies and tactics for effective instruction.* Longmont, CO: Sopris West.

Alley, G. R., & Deshler, D. D. (1979). *Teaching the learning-disabled adolescent: Strategies and methods.* Denver: Love.

Anderson, L. M., Evertson, C. M., & Brophy, J. E. (1979). An experimental study of effective teaching in first-grade reading groups. *Elementary School Journal, 79,* 193–222.

Archer, A. (1991, June). *Design of instruction: Lesson structure.* Paper presented at the Fourteenth Annual Intervention Procedures Conference, Logan, UT.

Aronson, E., Stephen, C., Sikes, J., Blaney, N., & Snapp, M. (1978). *The jigsaw classroom.* Beverly Hills, CA: Sage.

Ausubel, D., Novak, J., & Hanesian, H. (1978). *Educational psychology: A cognitive view*. New York: Holt, Rinehart & Winston.

Baker, S. C., Simmons, D. C., & Kameenui, E. J. (1994). Making information more memorable for students with learning disabilities through the design of instructional tools. *LD Forum, 19*(3), 14–18.

Barlow, D. L. (1985). *Educational psychology: The teaching-learning process*. Chicago: Moody Press.

Becker, W. C., Englemann, S., & Thomas, D. R. (1971). *Teaching: A course in applied psychology*. Chicago: Science Research Associates.

Belkin, G. S., & Gray, J. L. (1977). *Educational psychology: An introduction*. Dubuque, IA: William C. Brown.

Biehler, R. F., & Snowman, J. (1986). *Psychology applied to teaching* (5th ed.). Boston: Houghton Mifflin.

Bruner, J. S. (1966). *Toward a theory of instruction*. New York: Norton.

Bruner, J. S. (1973). *The relevance of education*. New York: Norton.

Butler, D. L. (1995). Promoting strategic learning by postsecondary students with learning disabilities. *Journal of Learning Disabilities, 28,* 170–190.

Carnine, D., & Silbert, J. (1979). *Direct instruction: Reading*. New York: Merrill/Macmillan.

Dawson, L., Venn, M. L. & Gunter, P. L. (2000). The effects of teacher versus computer reading models. *Behavioral Disorders, 25*(2), 105–113.

Delquadri, J. C., Greenwood, C. R., Whorton, D., Carta, J. J., & Hall, R. V. (1986). Classwide peer tutoring. *Exceptional Children, 52,* 535–542.

Deshler, D. D., & Schumaker, J. B. (1986). Learning strategies: An instructional alternative for low-achieving adolescents. *Exceptional Children, 52,* 583–590.

Deshler, D. D., Schumaker, J. B., Alley, G. R., Warner, M. M., & Clark, F. L. (1982). Learning disabilities in adolescent and young adult populations: Research implications (Part I). *Focus on Exceptional Children, 15*(1), 1–12.

Deshler, D. D., Schumaker, J. B., Lenz, B. K., & Ellis, E. S. (1984). Academic and cognitive interventions for LD adolescents (Part II). *Journal of Learning Disabilities, 17*(3), 170–187.

Dixon, R., & Carnine, D. (1994). Ideologies, practices, and their implications for special education. *Journal of Special Education, 28,* 356–367.

Dunkin, M., & Biddle, B. (1974). *The study of teaching*. New York: Holt, Rinehart & Winston.

Ellis, E. E., Lenz, B. K., & Sabornie, E. J. (1987a). Generalization and adaptation of learning strategies to natural environments: Part 1. Critical agents. *Remedial and Special Education, 8*(1), 6–20.

Ellis, E. E., Lenz, B. K., & Sabornie, E. J. (1987b). Generalization and adaptation of learning strategies to natural environments: Part 2. Research into practice. *Remedial and Special Education, 8*(2), 6–23.

Englemann, S., & Carnine, D. (1982). *Theory of instruction: Principles and applications*. New York: Irvington.

Englert, C. S., Raphael, T. E., Anderson, L. M., Antony, H. M., & Stevens, D. D. (1991). Making strategies and self-talk visible: Writing instruction in regular and special education classrooms. *American Educational Research Journal, 23,* 337–372.

Fisher, C. W., Berliner, D. C., Filby, N. N., Marliave, R., Cahen, L. S., & Dishaw, M. M. (1980). Teaching behaviors, academic learning time, and student achievement: An overview. In C. Denham & A. Lieberman (Eds.), *Time to learn*. Washington, DC: Government Printing Office.

Friend, M., & Bursuck, W. D. (1996). *Including students with special needs: A practical guide for classroom teachers*. Needham Heights, MA: Allyn & Bacon.

Gaffney, J. S. (1987). *Seatwork: Current practices and research implications*. Paper presented at the 64th Meeting of the Council for Exceptional Children, Chicago.

Gagne, R. M. (1980). *The conditions of learning* (2nd ed.). New York: Holt, Rinehart & Winston.

Goodman, Y. (1989). Roots of the whole-language movement. *Elementary School Journal, 90,* 113–127.

Graves, D. H. (1994). *A fresh look at writing*. Portsmouth, NH: Heinemann.

Graves, D. H., & Hansen, J. (1983). The author's chair. *Language Arts, 60,* 176–183.

Greenwood, C. R., Delquadri, J. C., & Hall, R. V. (1984). Opportunity to respond and student academic performance. In W. L. Heward, T. E. Heron, D. S. Hill, & J. Trap-Porter (Eds.), *Focus on behavior analysis in education* (pp. 58–88). New York: Merrill/Macmillan.

Gregory, J. (1985). *The concept teaching model*. Unpublished manuscript.

Heshusius, L. (1986). Pedagogy, special education, and the lives of young children: A critical and futuristic perspective. *Journal of Education, 168*(3), 25–38.

Heshusius, L. (1989). The Newtonian mechanistic paradigm, special education, and contours of alternatives: An overview. *Journal of Learning Disabilities, 22,* 403–415.

Holdaway, D. (1979). The foundations of literacy. Sydney: Aston Scholastic.

Holloway, J. H. (2000). Preparing teachers for differentiated instruction. *Educational Leadership 58,* (1), 82–83.

Johns, B. (2000). Reaching them through teaching them: Curriculum and instruction for students with E/BD. *Beyond Behavior, 10*(1), 3–6.

Johnson, D. W., Johnson, R. T., Holubec, E. J., & Roy, P. (1984). *Circles of learning.* Alexandria, VA: Association for Supervision and Curriculum.

Kilpatrick, W. H. (1918). The project method. *Teachers College Record, 19,* 319–335.

Kirby, J. R., Booth, C. A., & Das, J. P. (1996). Cognitive processes and IQ in reading disability. *Journal of Special Education, 29,* 442–456.

Maheady, L., Mallette, B., Harper, G. F., Sacca, K., & Pomerantz, D. (1994). Peer-mediated instruction of high-risk students. In K. D. Wood & B. Algozzine (Eds.), *Teaching reading to high-risk learners.* Needham Heights, MA: Allyn & Bacon.

Martin, J. (1979). Effects of teacher higher-order questions on student progress and product variables in a single classroom study. *Journal of Educational Research, 72,* 183–187.

Mercer, C. D., & Mercer, A. R. (2001). *Teaching students with learning problems* (6th ed.). Upper Saddle River, NJ: Merill/Prentice Hall.

Milem, M., & Garcia, M. (1996). Student critics, teacher models: Introducing process writing to high school students with learning disabilities. *Teaching Exceptional Children, 28*(3), 46–47.

O'Shea, L. J., & O'Shea, D. J. (1997). *Teaching: Explicit activation of learning.* Unpublished manuscript.

Paris, S. G., Cross, D. R., & Lipson, M. Y. (1984). Informed strategies for learning: A program to improve children's reading awareness and comprehension. *Journal of Education Psychology, 76,* 1239–1252.

Paris, S. G., & Winograd, P. (1990). Promoting metacognition and motivation of exceptional children. *Remedial and Special Education 11,* 7–15.

Patton, J. R. (1994). Practical recommendations for using homework with students with learning disabilities. *Journal of Learning Disabilities, 27*(a), 570–578.

Poplin, M. (1987). Self-imposed blindness: The scientific method in education. *RASE, 8,* 31–37.

Poplin, M. (1988). The reductionistic fallacy in learning disabilities: Replicating the past by reducing the present. *Journal of Learning Disabilities, 21,* 389–400.

Prater, M. A., Sileo, T. W. & Black, R. S. (2000). Preparing educators and related school personnel to work with at-risk students. *Teacher Education and Special Education, 23*(1), 51–64.

Precision Teaching Project. Available from Skyline Center, 3300 Third Street Northeast, Great Falls, MT 59404.

Reid, D. K., & Stone, C. A. (1991). Why is cognitive instruction effective? Underlying learning mechanisms. *Remedial and Special Education, 2,* 8–19.

Richardson, P. (1991). Language as personal resource and as social construct: Competing views of literacy pedagogy in Australia. *Educational Review, 43*(2), 171–190.

Robinson, R. P. (1941). *Effective study.* New York: Harper & Row.

Rogan, J. (2000). Learning strategies: Recipes for success. *Beyond Behavior, 10*(1), 18–22.

Rogoff, B. (1990). *Apprenticeship in thinking: Cognitive development in social context.* New York: Oxford University Press.

Rojewski, J. W., & Schell, J. W. (1994). Cognitive apprenticeship for learners with special needs: An alternative framework for teaching and learning. *Remedial and Special Education, 15,* 234–243.

Rosenshine, B. (1971). *Teaching behaviors and student achievement.* London: National Foundation for Educational Research.

Rosenshine, B. (1976). Academic engaged time, content covered, and direct instruction. *Journal of Education, 160*(3), 38–66.

Rosenshine, B., & Meister, C. (1992). The use of scaffolds for teaching higher-level cognitive strategies. *Educational Leadership, 49*(7), 26–33.

Rowe, M. (1974). Wait-time and rewards as instructional variables, logic, and fate control: Part 1. Wait-time. *Journal of Research in Science Teaching, 11,* 81–94.

Schiffman, G., Tobin, D., & Buchanan, B. (1984). Microcomputer instruction for the learning disabled. *Annual Review of Learning Disabilities, 2,* 134–136.

Schumaker, J. B., Denton, P. H., & Deshler, D. D. (1984). *Learning strategies curriculum: The paraphrasing strategy.* Lawrence: University of Kansas.

Slavin, R. E. (1990). *Cooperative learning: Theory, research, and practice.* Upper Saddle River, NJ: Prentice Hall.

Smith, J. K., & Heshusius, L. (1986). Closing down the conversation: The end of the quantitative/qualitative debate among educational inquirers. *Educational Researcher, 15,* 4–12.

Stanger, C., Symington, L., Miller, H., & Johns, S. (2000). Teaching number concepts to all students. *Teaching Exceptional Children, 33*(1), 65–69.

Stein, M., & Davis, C. A. (2000). Direct instruction as a positive behavioral support. *Beyond Behavior, 10*(1), 7–12.

Vygotsky, L. S. (1978). *Mind in society: The development of higher psychological processes.* Cambridge, MA: Harvard University Press.

Wollery, M., Bailey, D. B., & Sugai, G. M. (1988). *Effective teaching: Principles and procedures of applied behavior analysis with exceptional children.* Needham Heights, MA: Allyn & Bacon.

Zipprich, M. A. (1995). Teaching web mapping as a guided planning tool to improve student narrative writing. *Remedial and Special Education, 16,* 3–15.

The Paperwork

In this chapter, we will

- ✔ discuss a rationale for useful paperwork in special education services

- ✔ review prereferral and referral procedures through paperwork usage

- ✔ review the use and interpretation of testing for determining eligibility and need for special education services

- ✔ delineate the required components of individualized education programs

- ✔ reiterate the importance of writing reports to parents and other professionals

*A*lthough there may be some local differences in format and content, required documentation and paperwork involved in special education are similar nationwide. We summarize typical documentation in this chapter.

When asked to complete paperwork, developing and beginning teachers typically react with disdain and signs of stress. Most experienced members of the profession, however, can confirm that managing classrooms successfully entails careful, written records on students and on actions demonstrated by teachers. Effective paperwork is one key to survival and success for many teachers.

Accordingly, in this chapter, we identify the documentation necessary for ensuring an appropriate team effort in all aspects of specialized services. Documentation is necessary: from activities initiating the screening-prereferral process for students who may be at risk because of ability, learning, or behavioral problems, to data-collection procedures necessary to exit students from special education.

As we discuss in other chapters, current special educators function as consultants or coteachers when students with disabilities receive their education in inclusive classrooms. Other teachers continue to be direct-service providers when students meet the criteria for formal direct placement in specialized educational services. All special education roles, however, necessitate professional skills in developing and maintaining paperwork.

There can be no doubt that when teachers enter the classroom in their first years, many hours are spent in developing and maintaining written data. Long hours are used in recording student behaviors or in planning classroom events. Special education paperwork often reflects the types of assessment and instructional activities that school professionals conduct. Such activities, described by Choate, Enright, Miller, Poteet, and Rakes (1995), entail screening, eligibility steps for special education placement, and instruction to provide appropriate services based on students' needs and strengths. Teachers' paperwork reflects the quantity and quality of data, including (1) screening-prereferral documentation; (2) written records of individual student progress; (3) observation records; (4) assessment results; (5) eligibility placement information; (6) cumulative school files; (7) health and sensory notations; (8) annual individualized education programs (IEPs), including transition components; (9) written inquiries and responses to parents, guardians, general education teachers, or others; and (10) lesson plans, or unit teaching summaries.

The effective use of paperwork requires time, effort, and patience. There is a bright note: As experience develops, teachers may find demands minimized considerably. Once teachers are in the habit of completing paperwork, stressful tasks will be made easier. Access to or investing in a laptop computer is worth the effort. Electronic management and storage of written data can save hours of time.

SIMULATED CASE EXAMPLE

A fictitious student named Lindsay Christopher, age 9, is followed throughout the chapter by using examples of required paperwork. Starting with pertinent data from her general education setting, examples of the kinds of data that professionals may collect are illustrated. Beginning and developing teachers will be able to note the types of data useful to families and professionals as Lindsay progresses through the screening-prereferral process. Background information (Box 7.1) is included to help beginning and developing teachers gain insights into Lindsay's needs and strengths.

Box 7.1   Background Information on Lindsay Christopher

Lindsay is a well-mannered, attractive youngster currently attending a third-grade classroom in a large urban school. Lindsay recently transferred from another school district in the state. As of this time, few prior school records are available. School officials from her previous school did send an incomplete cumulative record of her kindergarten experience. Former professionals indicated her normal progress in kindergarten. However, no data were received describing her school progress during the last 2 years when she attended grades one and two.

During the current school year, Lindsay is considered a potential candidate for special education because of problems in reading comprehension and study skills. On the Cromer Achievement Test, given by her current teacher, Ms. Marshall, Lindsay performed at 3.7 in mathematics, 1.9 in reading, and 3.3 in spelling. Chapter tests from the Universal Reading Series, level 3, were provided by her teacher. Lindsay had not mastered the first group of objectives from Chapter 1 of this reading series, suggesting to Ms. Marshall some of Lindsay's difficulties in reading comprehension.

Lindsay's speech and language development appear to be adequate for a child of Lindsay's age. Ms. Marshall reported also that Lindsay's motor development is adequate for a child in the third grade: She is able to run, jump, skip, and hop as most children her age; and she competes satisfactorily in physical education with her classmates and performs exceptionally well in swimming. Lindsay's medical history is unnotable.

In the classroom, Lindsay neither begins on time nor completes assignments in reading. Other subject area requirements do not appear to pose problems to her. She continues to perform well in mathematics and spelling although assignments in social skills and science are beginning to contain more required reading skills than previously. Ms. Marshall reported to her principal that she fears Lindsay is falling farther and farther behind her classmates as the school year continues.

DEVELOPING USEFUL PAPERWORK: A RATIONALE

Although tedious and time-consuming, written products are important for a compelling reason: Federal law requires written documentation by professionals on students at risk for and with identified disabilities (Individuals with Disabilities Education Act, 1990). Individuals viewing burdensome procedures criticize the amount of time and effort that professionals must devote to paperwork ("CEC Leads IDEA Testimony," 1995). Additionally, researchers report that hassles over legal procedures and paperwork contribute to stress and burnout increasingly experienced by special education personnel (Billingsley, 1993; Billingsley & Cross, 1992; Cooley & Yovanoff, 1996). Involvement in legal responsibilities of paperwork continues to be stressful to teachers and is sometimes seen as a detriment to collaboration efforts with parents and other professionals. However, the importance of documenting step-by-step adherence to federal and state mandates cannot be overemphasized. The paperwork guides all parties through the special education process. Without documentation, teachers and administrators are unable to substantiate their actions, which can result in additional monetary and time costs to a school district.

Some stress and conflict may be inevitable; nonetheless, the time spent developing and using paperwork should not be considered wasted time. Accurate, written information helps in creating a conducive learning environment for students and a more organized workplace for adults. The development and maintenance of paperwork can

$\mathbf{P}$*ause and Reflect 7.1*

Describe what you believe are relevant reasons that paperwork helps in professional decision-making. List at least three reasons why beginning teachers would want to participate in paperwork activities.

1. _____

   _____

   _____

   _____

   _____

2. _____

   _____

   _____

   _____

   _____

3. _____

   _____

   _____

   _____

   _____

also sharpen teachers' planning, instructional, management, evaluation, communication, and partnership skills. Maintaining paperwork helps professionals in making educational decisions about students and about classroom happenings.

Paperwork has multiple uses for professionals working with students with diverse needs:

- Professional observations, analyses, and judgments to make educational decisions for students
- Varied explanations of variables, trends, and patterns appearing in students' past schooling, home, or community, providing clues to current behaviors
- Determination of the most effective and efficacious way to instruct and manage students in the least restrictive evnironment (LRE)
- Modifications of curricula, strategies, or programs when students are served in inclusion classrooms

- Explanation of links between the general education placement and special education placement based on students' strengths and needs
- Continual verification of students' needs to remain in or exit from special education and related services
- Accounts of actions in the classroom (e.g., lesson planning and unit planning as discussed in Chapter 5)
- Documentation in transition planning, implementation, and monitoring as students progress toward mastery of learning outcomes, graduation, and preadult life activities
- Communication efforts with other professionals and parents

Examples of potential problems confronting the teacher in completing paperwork and solutions to these problems are presented in Box 7.2. If implemented early in the novice teacher's career, these suggestions may reduce the time, effort, and stress associated with completion of paperwork.

Box 7.2   **Problems in Completing Paperwork and Potential Strategies to Prevent or Remediate Problems**

1. **Unawareness of required forms, data collection, paperwork, and so forth**

   Potential strategy: Take the time to become familiar with the content on forms prior to completion. Read directions in advance of completion. Be aware of and plan for required due dates, necessary signatures, and so forth.

2. **No plan for handling paperwork**

   Potential strategy: Develop a plan to screen, consolidate, and prioritize the completion of forms. Use trial-and-error strategies in the implementation process. If problems arise, revise the plan with input from administrators, experienced special education teachers, and general classroom teachers. Use self-evaluation techniques.

3. **Unavailability of factual information**

   Potential strategy: Be prepared. Study past cumulative files, grade records, health histories, and attendance files of students. Talk with parents. Obtain information from the home, community, and former teachers. Store obtained facts in an accessible location for later use during school-based committee meetings, case conferences, and so forth.

4. **Lack of time to complete paperwork**

   Potential strategy: Find the time. Complete a daily schedule, doing paperwork in a specified time slot. Work as a team. Elicit help from others (e.g., more experienced colleagues) to complete paperwork. Ask paraprofessionals to complete demographic information or any data not requiring confidentiality. Write down and make only written decisions that paraprofessionals can't.

5. **Inadequate notice to/from others contributing to written product**

   Potential strategy: Ask for a written request for expected contributions and materials. Request written due dates if not given. Encourage others to specify notices in writing at all times. Provide an outline of required information when soliciting data from others.

6. **Unrealistic priorities**

   Potential strategy: List what needs to be done first, second, and so forth. Put first things first. Resist unnecessary change.

continued

7. **Overplanning**

   Potential strategy: Monitor paperwork continually. Plan less (e.g., allow transition time for teachers and paraprofessionals). Write down only essential data. Use a tape recorder in lieu of writing whenever possible.

8. **Lack of policies and procedures for completion**

   Potential strategy: Clarify your role with administrators and other teachers for completing paperwork. Ask many questions. Persist. Be diligent.

9. **Lack of skills for improving paperwork**

   Potential strategy: Set and realize deadlines. Use cues to remind yourself when paperwork is due (e.g., write out short, daily to-do lists to yourself). Self-monitor progress. Solicit feedback from others. Attend workshops and professional conferences for updated information.

10. **Lost data**

    Potential strategy: Keep in an accessible location a copy of all written data turned in to others. Initial and date all copies. Throw out all unnecessary, outdated copies.

11. **Lack of motivation to complete paperwork**

    Potential strategy: Become aware of the impact of your own teacher effectiveness on students, parents, peers, and so forth. Seek individual causes for lack of motivation and self-correct.

12. **Inadequate maintenance and storage of paperwork**

    Potential strategy: Keep a copy of all written data in an accessible location. Set up a realistic filing system. File important documentation immediately. Computerize as much as possible. Use a tape recorder in lieu of written documentation whenever possible.

TYPICAL PROCEDURES USED FOR SCREENING— PREREFERRAL, REFERRAL, AND CLASSIFICATION

Legal procedures for special education often structure the types and content of paperwork that teachers will produce and maintain. Before a student may receive special services, many screening and prereferral data are necessary.

Screening-Prereferral Process

Prereferral consists of screening procedures for problem solving (consultation) and intervention as the first step of special education referral. It provides assistance to students and their teachers in the general education class, where the problems first arise. The actions of prereferral initially were identified by Graden and coworkers (Graden, Casey, & Bonstrom, 1985; Graden, Casey, & Christenson, 1985) as a logical first step in professional efforts to help students remain in the LRE. Today, with the promotion of increased services in general education classes, professionals must still collect data and the necessary paperwork on the student's individual skills and abilities in the LRE, the setting closest to the general education class (IDEA, 1997).

Important questions, based on the work of Cartwright, Cartwright, and Ward (1981) and posed by current multidisciplinary team members, continue to be helpful to new teachers. The answers to such questions may help teachers in determining appropriate prereferral strategies for students exhibiting learning or behavioral problems.

These questions can help guide the types of data and written products that teachers will collect. Examples include the following:

- Under what conditions does the student seem to have the most trouble?
- What specifically are the student's problem areas?
- What specifically are the student's strengths?
- How does the student learn best (e.g., independently, in small groups)?
- Does the student display both academic weaknesses and problem behaviors?
- What have professionals tried thus far?
- Are current approaches successful? Why or why not?

Written documentation can be collected to help professionals in specifying students' strengths and weaknesses. Effective beginning and developing teachers will consult with general education class teachers and other professionals in prereferral attempts. In the case example, prereferral questions were posed to Lindsay's classroom teacher, Ms. Marshall (Box 7.3). Ms. Marshall provided important clues in specifying some of Lindsay's strengths and weaknesses in the general education class setting.

Box 7.3   **Prereferral Questions on Lindsay Christopher**

Lindsay's teachers were asked to answer prereferral questions about her classroom progress. This is what her teacher, Ms. Marshall, wrote:

1. **Under what conditions does the student seem to have the most trouble?**

   Lindsay demonstrates problems during independent study periods and unstructured class time. She also has difficulties with reading, especially when asked to complete read-and-answer sheets.

2. **What specifically are the student's problem areas?**

   Lindsay's main problem appears to be self-management. She just doesn't seem to want to try in reading. However, I'm not sure whether she has the ability to comprehend the tasks required of her or she does not employ any cognitive strategy to aid comprehension. She lacks many reading comprehension skills for a child in the third grade.

3. **What specifically are the student's strengths?**

   Lindsay demonstrates strong skills in basic mathematical operations. She has excellent abilities in spelling. However, none of these tasks have required much reading so far. Another strength I notice is how well she gets along with peers and adults. I think she really does try to please others.

4. **How does the student learn best (e.g., independently, in small groups)?**

   Lindsay appears to learn best in small groups. I've noticed that she does well when she works with a classmate. She also works well in one-on-one situations with adults. I just can't always have someone there to work with her.

5. **Does the student display both academic weaknesses and problem behaviors?**

   Her main problem areas appear to be reading comprehension and completion of independent work.

6. **What have professionals tried thus far?**

   Lindsay has worked with minimal success with our classroom paraprofessional. School volunteers have tried also to tutor her. It seems she would rather socialize with them than complete her tasks.

7. **Are current approaches successful? Why or why not?**

   Unknown at this time.

Box 7.4   Data of the Completed Referral Process

Present Educational Setting Documentation

- Data of the student's deviations from the norm of classroom behaviors
- Data collection by professionals and parents from the home, school, or community
- School-based planning meeting results
- Prereferral strategy-implementation results
- Professional observations
- Case study conference results

Testing Data

- Prereferral sensory-screening results (vision and hearing assessments)
- Consent for individualized testing by parents
- Complete battery of tests
- Explanation and interpretation of formal testing in a written report
- Written results of eligibility meetings determining educational placement

Individualized Education Programs

- Consent for placement by parents
- Initial placement IEPs
- Annual updated IEPs
- Results and implications of reevaluations

Paperwork in the Referral Process

The **referral** process includes a comprehensive collection of documentation from many sources, including data of progress in the present educational setting, prior school records, sensory screening results, both formal and informal observations, assessments, and past health records. Among relevant data required to refer a student for a change in educational placement is evidence that the student was provided with the full opportunity to remain in the LRE (IDEA, 1997). To remove a student from instruction with general education students for even part of the day, professionals must collect written evidence establishing the need for a change in placement and the type of instruction the student receives.

Written documentation of prereferral attempts to remediate problems is actually the first step in the formalized referral process of special education (Gloeckler & Simpson, 1988). The completed referral process should include information related to (1) the present educational setting, (2) testing, and (3) IEPs. Box 7.4 delineates components of the completed referral process. Each area of the completed referral process is explained below through typical actions of school professionals. Examples of required paperwork are provided in each section.

Beginning and developing teachers should note that the forms and content of required paperwork may differ slightly from school district to school district. Names of meetings and professional teams (e.g., school-based committee meetings, educational-planning teams) may differ from locale to locale. However, professional team members completing effective paperwork share the common theme: providing evidence that the student is served in the educational setting best suited to his or her needs.

Pause and Reflect 7.2

Locate copies of the special education paperwork used in your local school district. Below, provide the specific name of the form and determine the form's purpose. Compare and contrast purposes with the paperwork listed in this chapter.

Paperwork Area	Form Name/Purpose	Local Form Name/Purpose
Present education setting		
	Data collection on deviations from the norm	
	Multiprofessional data	
	Prereferral strategies	
	Professional observations	
	Case study conference results	
Formalized testing		
	Sensory screenings	
	Consent for individualized testing	
	Individualized battery protocol	
	Testing requirements	
	Formal testing results	
	Eligibility meetings	
IEPs		
	Consent for placement by parents or guardians	
	Initial placement IEP forms	
	Results of IEP meeting	
	Notice of recommended assignment	
	Annual updated IEP	

continued

*P*ause and Reflect 7.2 continued

Paperwork Area	Form Name/Purpose	Local Form Name/Purpose
Special Education Continuation or Exit		
	Consent for reevaluation	
	Reevaluation results	
	Continuation or exit	
	Meeting notification	
	Consent for continuation or exit from services	
	Notice of recommended assignment	

Present Educational Setting

Most students with mild to moderate disabilities are in the general education setting. However, many students at risk for problems differ from other students in cognition, language, self-help, motor, behavior, social-emotional skills, or other areas. The teacher's task is to begin to discern whether students who display differences require assistance through specially designed instruction and/or related services.

Classroom Diversity

In many school systems, teachers complete similar tasks as they go about the daily challenges of implementing instruction and managing the behaviors of students. Most teachers observe students and measure progress through curriculum-based assessments, teacher-made materials, chapter tests, portfolio assessments, student-made products, commercially prepared assessment devices, academic rating scales, or behavioral checklists.

Teachers observe and assess students daily either by formal methods (e.g., checklists, rating scales, tests) or by informal methods (e.g., discussions with past teachers, unstructured comments based on task analysis). Effective teachers are able to discern their students' patterns of normal behaviors (Choate et al., 1995). Through assessment and observations of all students, teachers begin to note those displaying some variations from others in learning tasks, social behaviors, organizational skills, attention to tasks, study skills, developmental milestones, or cultural expectations. When teachers are familiar with students' backgrounds, they use data that are continually being generated in the classroom, home, and community to identify and screen out students suspected of low ability, learning difficulties, or problem behaviors.

Concerned teachers often examine data in a student's cumulative folder to discern grade levels repeated, school achievement, past test results, anecdotal information, and attendance patterns (Gloeckler & Simpson, 1988). Some teachers talk with parents and other school personnel involved with the student. Individuals whose behaviors differ greatly from the norm may require more formalized observations and evaluations. When deviations are noted frequently over time and to such an intensity that the

Home		School		Community	
Complies with parental demands?	yes	Displays academic needs?	yes	Frequents social organizations?	yes
Demonstrates good rapport with siblings?	yes	Has problem behaviors?	no	Demonstrates leisure-time activities?	yes
Completes chores routinely?	no	Demonstrates adequate organizational skills?	no	Uses community resources?	yes
Displays self-help skills?	yes	Demonstrates adequate study skills?	no	Complies adequately with neighborhood peers?	yes
Are developmental milestones on time?	yes	Displays adequate socio-emotional development?	yes	Complies with community norms?	yes
Demonstrates adequate health/nutrition?	yes	Displays adequate speech/language skills?	yes	Has and uses a support system?	yes
		Has adequate motor abilities?	yes		

Comments: Parents' report: Lindsay does not always fulfill her family responsibilities at home. She sometimes completes household chores haphazardly. She will complete adequately if offered a reward. She needs to be reminded often. She doesn't always remember what her home chores are.

School social worker's report: Lindsay appears to function adequately in her community setting. She demonstrates no major problems with peers, neighborhood organizations, and community groups.

Darby Olsen, Social Worker
1/7/02

Teacher's report: Lindsay's organizational and study skills are of concern. She doesn't complete required assignments and rarely brings in homework papers.

Mr. Thompson, Counselor
1/7/02

FIGURE 7.1   Home, School, and Community Data of Lindsay

teacher believes that the student is in danger behaviorally or academically, other professional judgment is required. More data need to be generated on the targeted student so that appropriate educational decisions may be made. As an example, Figure 7.1 shows paperwork collected from Lindsay's home, community, and school that are useful in educational screenings.

Data Collection by Multiple Professionals

An **educational planning team (EPT)** is typically necessary when evidence indicates that a student stands out from his or her peers. The team may be called by a host of titles, but the intent of these professionals is to discover more information on the target student who differs in important ways from other students. The team of multidisciplinary professionals may include principals, counselors, school psychologists, educational diagnosticians, content area teachers, nurses, therapists, special education teachers, and other school professionals. The purposes of an EPT meeting are twofold: (1) to generate classroom strategies (prereferral strategies) to help the student remain in the present setting and (2) to determine observation schedules needed to verify the student's progress toward the general education class goals and prereferral objectives.

Prereferral Strategy Implementation

The general education class teacher, with consulting help by the special education teacher, psychologist, administrator, clinician, counselor, or other professionals, often implements the prereferral strategies. A functioning multidisciplinary team, however, shares rights and responsibilities in the efforts to help the student succeed with prereferral strategies. Rights pertinent to general education teachers and special education teachers (as based on Schulz & Turnbull, 1984) continue to be relevant in today's classrooms and include the following:

- The opportunity to attend all meetings in which educational decisions are made that affect the student and professionals involved with the student
- A chance to select appropriate content, methodology, or objectives from a program to use in assessment or instructional activities implemented in prereferral attempts
- Access to all specialized materials, equipment, and curricula that would make instruction and management easier in the general education class setting
- Participation in baseline data collection, strategies implementation, and teaching modification monitoring
- Input and feedback into all learning strategies and behavioral management steps devised as prereferral strategies
- Assistance in acquiring resources and extra classroom helpers, including parents, volunteers, aides, specialized itinerant help, and peer tutors

Responsibilities of professionals to prereferral implementation should also be recognized and include the following:

- Demonstrated competency in given specialization areas
- Display of effective organization of the learning environment
- Ongoing observation of and data collection on strategies and management steps
- Continual and objective assessment
- Individualization based on students' needs
- Attempts to make baseline data collections, prereferral strategies, observations, and other teaching modifications relevant so that students with diverse needs are a part of all general education class activities
- Monitoring of students' academic and social-emotional requirements over time
- Consultation efforts including input of parents and professionals

Together with other team members, the special education teacher helps determine the success of attempts to remediate within the present setting. A team approach means that special educators, general education teachers, principals, counselors, school psychologists, librarians, therapists, paraprofessionals, students, parents, community volunteers, and professional/consumer organizations all have opportunities in planning and implementing strategies to help students remain with their normally functioning peers. Emphasis is directed to coordinating and monitoring all involvement carefully to maximize the ultimate benefit to students. Coordination, communication, and cooperation are keys to shared strategy implementation and successful programming.

The developing special education teacher and other team members may be called on to assist the general education class teacher in devising and implementing strategies such as those listed in Box 7.5. Examples of applied activities of the teacher are listed under each strategy.

Examples of components of the paperwork used in prereferral strategies are illustrated In Figure 7.2. On this form, modifications in prereferral strategies are planned, with implementers collecting data on Lindsay's baseline level. There is a space to monitor modifications every day of the week for 6 weeks. Professionals at Lindsay's school discovered the necessity to review her educational program at the end of the 6-week period. Prereferral modifications of teaching strategies were not enough to remediate her problems in independent study skills and reading comprehension. Teaming efforts must be intensified for her, and more formal data are required. As in Lindsay's and other students' cases, observations of the strategies by professionals other than the general education class teacher (e.g., special education teacher, psychologist, counselor, principal) help in providing evidence of objective modifications in teaching or changes

Box 7.5   **Prereferral Implementation Strategies**

1. Special modifications in teaching strategies

- Team teach with peers often, especially in individual areas of expertise.
- Write homework assignments on the chalkboard and have students copy them into their notebooks. Make sure the directions are clear.
- Team students (peer tutoring) who have complementary strengths and weaknesses. The entire class can begin independent study at the same time, using this buddy system.
- Let some students listen to taped reading assignments while others work on computerized assignments or read from texts. Change groups so that all students experience a variety of teaching modes.

2. Changes in classroom materials

- Break the work into short assignments. Place a marker over distracting pictures or other stimuli.
- Use audiovisual equipment with students as often as possible.
- Raise the stimulus value of elements to be learned: Any novel emphasis will help (e.g., color coding, emphatic use of voice, animation of materials).
- Block off sections of work the student has completed so that he or she is aware of where the assignment is on the page.
- Encourage the use of a typewriter or computer for students whose writing is slow and labored.
- Prerecord the classroom material to assist the slow reader.

3. Varying evaluation/schedules to be used

- Adjust grades so that the student is not constantly experiencing failing marks.
- Consider alternatives to grades, such as rewards for conduct and effort.
- Count intermittent scores on academic tests.
- Eliminate lowest and highest scores occasionally and go with average scores.

4. Modified curricula

- If students are required to take notes in class, provide an outline of general topics so that students can keep notes in order.
- Allow slow learners to complete work at their own pace.
- Integrate subject areas in which students succeed (e.g., let students draw the answer, rather than write it, if art is a strong subject for students).

5. Identification of effective assessment techniques for learning weaknesses and problem behaviors

- Consider that spelling and grammar need not be the basis for grading if mastery of the content is the objective.
- Draw lines on or fold worksheets and tests to divide them into various sections by types of questions or problems.
- Use a variety of formal and informal assessment techniques.
- Consider curriculum-based assessment, rather than standardized assessment.

6. Behavioral management plans specific to the student's observed problems

- Set up contingency contracting: the completion of X before the student is able to do Y.
- Devise a token economy or point system: Students earn tokens that are exchanged for specific rewards.
- Use time-out: the removal of the student from an apparently reinforcing setting to a presumably nonreinforcing setting for a specified and limited period of time.

Student's Name <u>Lindsay Christopher</u>   Teacher <u>Ms. Marshall</u>

School <u>Howard Elementary</u>   Birthdate <u>May 14, 1993</u>

Date <u>February 25, 2002</u>   Subject area <u>Reading</u>

Modification(s) in (circle):   (Teaching strategies)   Classroom materials
     Evaluation schedules   Curriculum
     Assessment   Behavior management
     Other

Describe modification(s):   <u>*Peer tutoring with another student to aid in</u>
<u>Lindsay's reading skills.</u>

Reason for prereferral: <u>*Lindsay cannot complete classwork</u>
<u>independently.</u>

Target student's baseline level in problem area: <u>*4/5 times Lindsay does not turn in reading</u>
<u>comprehension materials when asked to do so.</u>

Student progress (describe):   <u>Lindsay's progress has been minimal. Tom W.</u>
<u>(peer) has been assigned to help her complete</u>
<u>reading comprehension papers.</u>

Modifi-cation	Week 1	Week 2	Week 3	Week 4	Week 5	Week 6	Comments
M	R = 62% P	R = 59% P	—	—	—	R = 60% P	Papers turned in on Monday with teacher's cue. (Accuracy is low—≤60%.)
T	R = 40% P	absent	R = 60% P	R = 50% P	—	—	Accuracy is low, x = Papers turned in 3/6 times.
W	R = 10% P	—	R = 5% P	—	—	—	Comprehension problems noted.
T	—	—	—	R = 62% P	—	—	Low turn-in rate; 62% accuracy rate.
F	R = 50% P	—	—	—	absent	—	Lindsay has not responded to peer tutoring strategy/ less work requirements.

Professional's name/title   <u>Ms. Marshall—Teacher, Mr. Thompson—Counselor,</u>
<u>Ms. New—Special Education Teacher</u>

P = Paper completed and turned in
R = Accuracy rate (percentage of correct comprehension questions) for independent work

FIGURE 7.2 Prereferral Strategies Implemented in Lindsay's General Education Classroom

in procedures. Observations may also indicate that students require more help by specialists than can be provided in the present setting.

Professional Observations

Professionals who observe students with learning and behavioral problems highlight data on the appropriateness of the present setting. After many strategies have been tried, professionals familiar with the student in question can help determine the success

Pause and Reflect 7.3

Briefly describe two observations that Lindsay's teacher might conduct to help Lindsay in the LRE. What should the school professionals observe? How should they observe? Who should do the observation?

1. What? _____

   _____

   How? _____

   _____

   Who? _____

   _____

2. What? _____

   _____

   How? _____

   _____

   Who? _____

   _____

Reflect on educational objectives that you believe teachers and other professionals should focus on to help Lindsay remain in her present educational setting.

_____

_____

_____

of prereferral planning. These individuals can provide an objective perspective to the student's opportunities to meet the classroom teacher's or parents' expectations. An appropriate observer may be an administrator, school psychologist, school counselor, or another teacher familiar with the target student.

In each observation, the selection of a valid data-collection procedure should be matched to the student's needs. Data should be collected through systematic procedures ensuring replicability and use of discrete behaviors. This means that areas of strengths and problem behaviors of the student are specified (defined in observable terminology for use by professionals). Efficient and consistent observation procedures ensure that the behaviors are actually observed. To increase the likelihood of interrater reliability, two or more observers must agree on the behaviors that occurred (Cartwright et al., 1981).

The use of a stopwatch or clock to time observations and a graph of the results may help in producing evidence of strategy effectiveness. Tangible products can also be observed and measured systematically for clues to the target student's strengths or problem areas, including the student's organization or study skills, appropriateness of the teacher-made product, or the student's approach to problem solving. Methods of observations include (1) a record of the student's permanent products, (2) anecdotal records, (3) frequency counts, (4) duration recordings, and (5) time samplings (Ysseldyke & Algozzine, 1984).

The use of paperwork, such as that shown in Box 7.6, helps teachers in defining steps to each of these methods of observations. Developing and beginning teachers of special education may be asked to observe and/or help other members of the multidisciplinary team observe the student's progress. Box 7.6 is used to highlight Lindsay's data. Ms. Marshall's suggestions to operationalize the methods of observation are delineated in the box. Both Lindsay's teachers and her counselor, Mr. Thompson, collected data and examined written products to verify Lindsay's strengths and weaknesses in the general education class setting. Ms. New, the school's special education teacher, participated actively in Lindsay's observations.

Case Study Conference Results

After observations are completed, professionals meet with parents in a case study conference or similarly titled meeting to analyze the data and to discuss the student's current functioning. Parents should be involved in all meetings when educational decisions are made (IDEA, 1997). It is important that they are aware of educational conferences when evidence is provided that promotes their child's progress in the present educational setting. The purposes of this updated team meeting are to (1) analyze the prereferral strategies, (2) discuss the results of all classroom instructional strategies and observations, (3) review new data collected since the initial multidisciplinary team meeting, (4) elicit the parents' perceptions of their child's functioning and needs, (5) decide whether the student is to be provided with individualized testing and continue in the formal referral process, (6) secure the parents' written permission if the student is to be a candidate for formal testing, and (7) complete the formal referral application as warranted for the student's testing, signed and dated by referring professionals and/or parents.

Examples of collected data relevant to the case study conference are illustrated in Figure 7.3. School academic documentation is highlighted, as are behavioral data from the school, home, and community.

An example of the paperwork used for a formal referral application is illustrated in Figure 7.4. On this application, referring individuals and their titles should be described. The reason for referral and the results of prereferral strategies and observations are summarized. Additionally, recommendations for follow-up and testing must be targeted. In Lindsay's case, information from prereferral strategies and results of professional observations verify the need to test her further by professionals, including the school psychologist and/or the educational diagnostician.

Summary of Present Educational Setting Documentation

Much paperwork is required before students with disabilities may leave the general education class. Necessary steps of comprehensive data collection, initial parental contact, and completion of the referral form must be accomplished (Gloeckler & Simpson, 1988). During the student's time in the present setting, the special education teacher assumes the role of consultant, assisting in prereferral strategies and observations. Many students with disabilities are provided instruction with their normally functioning peers. When students still require more specialized help, the collection of comprehensive information helps professionals in initiating a change in educational placement for students requiring the direct service model of special education. These students continue

Box 7.6   **Methods of Observations on Lindsay**

A.   Record of student's permanent products (e.g., worksheets, artwork, and so forth):
  ✔ 1. Collect and keep a record of these products.
  ✔ 2. Systematically analyze the quality of the student's products.
  ✔ 3. Engage in error analysis (systematic analysis of the kinds of errors students make).

Comments: During a 6-week period, work samples were collected 10 of 64 times (30% of total work required). Accuracy rate, reported by Ms. Marshall, was in the low range (62%). Most errors were reported to be careless errors, although reading comprehension problems were noted. Ms. Marshall suspected that the reading material may be too difficult for Lindsay. Motivation may also be a problem.

B.   Anecdotal records:
  ✔ 1. Write down recollections of the occurrence of specific behaviors.
  ✔ 2. Keep a log of teacher's comments.

Comments: Ms. Marshall keeps a daily log of Lindsay's progress. Lindsay appears to socialize during peer-tutoring sessions, rather than attend to assignments. She is reported to be off-task for more than 70% of the independent reading time. When given one-on-one instruction, she often completes the reading assignments accurately (if instruction provided by her teacher is a direct instruction format). This last observation of successful direct instruction was observed by Ms. New, special education teacher.

C.   Frequency counts:
  ✔ 1. Record the frequency of observable behaviors.
  ✔ 2. Record the extent to which other students exhibit the same behaviors.
  ✔ 3. Compare target student's behaviors with those of others.

Comments: Relative to other students, Lindsay's independent study skills are off-target (average observation was 8 of 12 times she did not complete and organize work). Independent reading assignments completed only 4/14 trials. Accuracy rates reported to be 85% when direct instruction was provided by Ms. Marshall. (Observations were reported by Ms. New, special education teacher.)

D.   Duration recordings:
  ✔ 1. Gather data on the occurrence of the behavior by recording the length of time it persists.
  ✔ 2. Indicate initiation time and ending time of the behavior.

Comments: Off-task behavior during peer-tutoring sessions averaged 28 minutes of 35 minutes during a 6-week period. Lindsay was observed to be off-task for group reading instruction 73% of the time and 90% of independent seatwork. She was observed to be on-task 85% of time during one-on-one instruction with her teacher. Initiation ation and ending time for direct instruction reading was reported by Ms. New, special education teacher.

E.   Time samplings:
  ✔ 1. Measure the number of times a behavior occurs after a preset observation period.
  ____ 2. Measure the number of times a response occurs after a preset observation period.

Comments: Lindsay appears to complete reading tasks 85% of the time during a direct-instruction format by Ms. Marshall. She cannot work independently on these same reading tasks. Apparently, she has begun to recognize some of the required vocabulary, but as observed by Ms. New, she cannot apply vocabulary words to independent reading tasks.

Source: Adapted from Algozzine, B., Ysseldyke, J., & Christenson, S. L. (1983). An analysis of the incidence of special class placement: The masses are burgeoning. *Journal of Special Education, 17,* 141–147.

SCHOOL DATA

Academic Documentation	Behavioral Progress Data
Prereferral data	Behavioral ratings
Classroom strategy results	Socioemotional progress reports
Observations by multiple professionals	Observation reports of attention-to-task
Previous formal/informal assessments	Data reports of rapport with others

FAMILY DATA

Parental observation notations	Family member observations
Interaction with other reports	Child behavior scale ratings by parents, siblings, other family members

COMMUNITY DATA

Interaction with neighbors' observations	Involvement in community reports
Access to community functions data	Habilitation plans
	Social worker's checklists

FIGURE 7.3 Data Relevant to the Case Study Conference

in the formal referral process because evidence indicates that the general education class setting may not be the LRE for that student. Through an initiation of formalized testing, the student continues to be monitored for specialized help. Test results provide additional evidence of the need for special education and related services.

FORMALIZED TESTING

Relying on the analysis of general education class data discussed during a student's case study conference, professionals may indicate the success of prereferral strategies; that is, educators, psychologists, counselors, or others may be able to document mastery of academic objectives or a decrease in inappropriate behaviors. Parents may confirm the success of prereferral attempts through home observation. In such cases, the student does not need to continue in the formal referral process. Despite prereferral strategies and observations, however, another student may continue to demonstrate low ability, problem behaviors, or academic difficulties. At this point, professionals should acquire the parents' written permission to test the student formally. With parents fully aware of the decision to test, the formal referral process of special education is in operation. (If parents refuse to sign their permission, school officials can resort to the mediation and hearing procedures as detailed in Chapter 2.) An example of the required paperwork for permission to test Lindsay is included in Figure 7.5. As can be seen, Lindsay's parents were involved in the decision to test her formally. The reasons for testing Lindsay and the names of specific tests to be used with her are marked clearly on the form for her parents' perusal and consent.

Collection and Results of Sensory Screenings

Prior to official testing by the school psychologist or other evaluator, sensory data on the student are collected, including health, hearing, vision, or speech and language screenings (IDEA, 1997). If the student fails any of the sensory or health screenings,

Name <u>Lindsay Christopher</u>   Birthdate <u>May 14, 1993</u>

Class <u>3</u>   Parents <u>John & Mary Christopher</u>

Address/Phone <u>62 Sandlewood Dr. / 472-0765</u>

Teacher <u>Ms. Marshall</u>

Referring individuals:

Name	Title	Date
Jane Marshall	Classroom Teacher	February 25, 2002
Terri Thompson	Counselor	February 25, 2002
Betsy New	Special Education Teacher	February 25, 2002

Reason for referral:

<u>Lindsay demonstrates problems in following directions, motivation, and</u>

<u>independent study skills. She may have a reading problem—especially</u>

<u>comprehension of third grade material.</u>

Results of prereferral strategies:

Strategy

1.   <u>Peer tutoring was unsuccessful. During a 6-week period, she turned in only 10</u>

<u>assignments completed independently (highest accuracy rate = 62%).</u>

Strategy

2.   <u>Amount of reading assignments required was reduced—she still did not turn in</u>

<u>organized, completed work.</u>

Results of observations:

<u>Work may not be motivating for her, or assignments may be too difficult. Her read-</u>

<u>ing level may be too low to complete requirements. She can comprehend, apparently,</u>

<u>in a direct instruction, one-on-one format with her teacher.</u>

Recommended follow-up and testing:

<u>It is recommended that she be tested by Dr. Weiss, the psychologist, to</u>

<u>determine whether Lindsay has a learning problem (especially in reading).</u>

FIGURE 7.4   Lindsay's Formal Referral Application

more data must be obtained from health professionals (e.g., if the student fails the hearing screening, an audiometric report by a certified audiologist is pertinent; if the student fails the vision screening, such as the Snellen Chart screening, a report from an ophthalmologist or optometrist is in order). These data are important for a number of reasons: (1) Evaluators must give the correct test matched to student needs; (2) sensory impairments may be the major reason for the student's difficulties, suggesting a different interpretation and explanation of test results; (3) the discovery of a sensory impairment as the student's primary disability condition may yield different educational placement options; and (4) the discovery of a sensory impairment may suggest different goals/objectives on the IEP.

Student's name <u>Lindsay Christopher</u>

Parent/guardian's name <u>John & Mary Christopher</u>

Parent/guardian's address <u>62 Sandalwood Dr.</u>

Birthdate <u>May 14, 1993</u>   Parent's phone   <u>492-0765</u>

Class <u>3</u>   Teacher <u>Ms. Marshall</u>   Date <u>February 25, 2002</u>

Reason for testing

<u>Level of class assignments may be too difficult for Lindsay. Teacher suspects a</u>
<u>learning problem in reading (reading comprehension may be too low to complete</u>
<u>assignments). Classroom strategies reported to be unsuccessful. Observations</u>
<u>verified low accuracy rates and incomplete assignments; off-task behavior observed</u>
<u>to be high. On-task behavior and higher accuracy rate during direct instruction with</u>
<u>teachers.</u>

Check all test types to be given/name of tests

	Types	Name
Ability	✓	Wechsler Intelligence Scale for Children–Revised
Achievement	✓	Woodcock Johnson Psychoeducational Battery
Socioemotional	✓	Achenbach Behavioral Scales
Process	✓	Developmental Test of Visual Perception
Adaptive behavior		
Others	✓	Brigance Diagnostic Inventories (Reading)
		Gates-McKillop Reading Diagnostic Test

Other comments   <u>*Only the educational component of the Woodcock Battery</u>
                        <u>will be given.</u>

Student's name   <u>Lindsay Christopher</u>

<u>✓</u>   I give permission to test my child <u>Lindsay</u>. I understand I will be informed of all
           results. I have been given procedural safeguards.

_____   I do not give permission to test. I have been given procedural safeguards.

_____   I wish to have another meeting prior to granting my permission to test my child.

Parent/guardian's signature <u>John Christopher</u>   Date <u>February 25, 2002</u>

FIGURE 7.5   Permission to Test Lindsay

An example of the paperwork used in the collection of Lindsay's sensory data is found in Figure 7.6. On close examination of this required paperwork, the teacher is able to confirm that Lindsay has no sensory impairment. This information now is used to substantiate Ms. Marshall's data from previous reports. Vision, hearing, speech and language, and overall health appear to be in the normal range.

Consent for Individualized Testing

Prior to their child's testing, parents must be assured of procedural safeguards (explained in detail in Chapter 2). After all pertinent sensory data are collected and parents have signed the necessary paperwork giving their permission to test, the evaluator provides the student with the individually administered battery.

Student's name <u>Lindsay Christopher</u>   Class <u>3</u>
Birthdate <u>May 14, 1993</u>   Teacher <u>Ms. Marshall</u>

1. Vision screening
   Distance acuity results <u>20/20 (l)</u>   <u>20/30 (r)</u>
   Measure <u>Snelling</u>   Given by <u>Ms. Parkens (nurse)</u>   Date <u>Oct. 2, 2001</u>
   Field vision results <u>Adequate</u>
   Measure <u>n/a</u>   Given by _____   Date _____
   Follow-up required <u>no</u>   Reason <u>Vision adequate.</u>
   Ophthalmologist/Optometrist: Name _____
                               Address _____

   (Enclose copy)   Phone _____
   Recommendation <u>Follow-up is not necessary at this time. Distance vision</u>
   <u>appears to be within the normal range in both eyes.</u>

2. Hearing screening
   Auditory acuity results: Left ear <u>Pass</u>   Right ear <u>Pass</u>
   Measure <u>Conversational speech</u>   Given by <u>Ms. Parkens (nurse)</u>
   Date <u>Oct. 22, 2002</u>   Follow-up required <u>no</u>
   Reason <u>Hearing (conversational speech) adequate.</u>

   Audiologist   Name _____
                       Address _____

   (Enclose copy)   Phone _____
   Recommendation <u>Follow-up is not necessary</u> at this time. Both ears
   responded to stimuli (given conversational speech).

3. Speech/language screening
   Clinician <u>Jan Jenkins</u>   Date <u>Oct. 14, 1997–Oct. 22, 2001</u>

Test name	Results	Recommendation
Articulation TOLD; VCS	Passed	
Voice TLD	Passed	No follow-up
Fluency TOLD; VCS; PSLT	Passed	necessary at
Language PSLT	Passed	this time

   Goldman Fristoe-Woodcock Test of Auditory Discrimination; Vocabulary Comprehension
   Scale; Test of Language Development; Picture Story
   Language Test
   Follow-up required? <u>No</u>

FIGURE 7.6   Lindsay's Health/Sensory Screening Results   *continued*

Reason for speech/language placement option:

At this time, speech and language training not recommended.
Lindsay's articulation, voice, fluency, and language skills appear to be
within the normal range.

4. Overall health

Physician's name Dr. Joseph Charles

Address 1608 Fairway Circle

Phone number 451-3928

Date of last physical December 18, 2001

Comments: Lindsay appears to be in excellent health

5. Sensory/health screening comments: No notable sensory and/or health
deviations to report at this time.

Ms. Parkens (nurse)

Jan Jenkins (Clinician)

FIGURE 7.6 continued

Individualized Battery

The purpose of the formalized testing situation is to link identification and intervention. Teachers need specific data to describe students' strengths and to help refine appropriate instructional strategies and techniques (Cartwright et al., 1981; Ysseldyke & Algozzine, 1984). Assessment must be multifactor, examining all areas of functioning. Through assessment, the guidelines for appropriate instruction begin.

Testing Requirements

Testing is to be completed in the student's native language, with all testing materials sensitive to the student's abilities. Examples of tests that may be included in an individualized battery are included in Box 7.7. Teachers may be asked to complete part of these instruments (e.g., to complete a behavioral rating, to write down anecdotal information used by the psychologist in the test interpretation), or the instruments may be given solely by the educational diagnostician or school psychologist. Many various assessment devices are used by personnel in different school systems. Box 7.7 is a partial listing of assessment devices used by psychologists and educational diagnosticians.

Explanation and Interpretation of Formal Testing

After testing is completed, all data are condensed into a written, psychological report, which is to be shared with parents and professionals. Testing results must be interpreted and explained by the evaluator. Implications for instruction are generated from results, and assessment should link the student's current abilities to teaching strategies and procedures used by general education class or special class teachers. An example of Lindsay's psychological report is included in Box 7.8. On this report, the psychologist provided evidence of Lindsay's above-average intelligence and her lack of severe behavioral and sensory problems. Data support the claim that although she displays learning problems, her difficulties are not severe enough to remove her from the general class setting. Data from the present educational setting and the formal testing

Box 7.7   **Examples of Tests in a Battery**

Ability Measures

- Kaufman Assessment Battery for Children (K-ABC)
- Stanford-Binet Intelligence Scale
- Wechsler Adult Intelligence Scale (WAIS)
- Wechsler Intelligence Scale for Children (fourth edition) (WISC-4)

Achievement Measures

- Brigance Diagnostic Inventories
- Gates-McKillop Reading Diagnostic Test
- Gray Oral Reading Test
- Inventory of Elementary Reading Skills
- Key Math
- Metropolitan Achievement Test
- Peabody Individual Achievement Test
- Wide Range Achievement Test
- Woodcock Johnson Psychoeducational Battery

Process Measures

- Auditory Discrimination Test
- Auditory Sequential Memory Test
- Bruininks-Oseretsky Test of Motor Proficiency
- Developmental Test of Visual Perception
- Frostig Test of Visual Motor Integration
- Purdue Perceptual-Motor Survey
- Wepman Auditory

Socio-emotional Measures

- Achenbach Behavioral Scales
- Burke's Behavior Rating

Adaptive Behavior Scales

- American Association on Mental Deficiency (AAMD) Adaptive Behavior Scales
- Adaptive Behavior Inventory for Children
- System of Multi-Cultural Pluralistic Assessment
- Vineland Social Maturity Scale

Self-Report Techniques

- Bower-Lambert Screening Scales
- California Test of Personality
- Children's Apperception Test
- Piers-Harris Self-Concept Scale

Source: Based on Salvia, J., & Ysseldyke, J. E. (1991). *Assessment in special education* (5th ed.). Boston: Houghton Mifflin.

Box 7.8   Psychological Report on Lindsay Christopher

Name: Lindsay Christopher

Birthdate: May 14, 1993

Parents: John and Mary Christopher

School: Howard Elementary School

Grade: 3

Teacher: Ms. Mary Marshall

Evaluator: Betty Weiss, Certified School Psychologist

Date: 3/20/02

Background Information: Lindsay has been reported by her teacher, Ms. Marshall, to be a well-mannered, attractive youngster attending third grade at Howard Elementary School. Lindsay recently transferred from Pelton School, Bowersville, another school district in the state. At the time of her entry into Howard, few prior school records on her were available. School officials from Pelton did send an incomplete cumulative record of her kindergarten experience. Former professionals indicated her normal progress in kindergarten. However, no data were received describing her school progress during the last 2 years when she attended grades one and two.

During the current school year, Lindsay has been experiencing problems in reading comprehension and study skills. On the Cromer Achievement Test, given by Ms. Marshall on September 22, 2001, Lindsay performed at 3.7 in mathematics, 1.9 in reading, and 3.3 in spelling. Chapter tests from the Universal Reading Series, level 3, were provided by her teacher. Lindsay had not mastered the first group of objectives from Chapter 1 of this reading series, suggesting to Ms. Marshall some of Lindsay's difficulties in reading comprehension. Mr. and Mrs. Christopher have reported also that Lindsay has problems reading homework assignments and completing household chores and family responsibilities at home. The parents indicated, however, that she does not seem to have any difficulties in making and keeping friends in and around the neighborhood. She appears to get along well with her younger brother, Larry, age 4.

Ms. Marshall also reported Lindsay's near-perfect handwriting and her love of drawing. Lindsay's motor development is adequate for a child in the third grade. She is able to run, jump, skip, and hop as most children her age. She competes satisfactorily in physical education with her classmates and performs exceptionally well in swimming. Lindsay's medical history is unnotable.

Lindsay's speech and language development appear to be adequate for a child of her age. She was screened by the school nurse, Mrs. Parkens, on October 2, 2001, for vision and hearing. Both vision and hearing screenings were unremarkable. Mrs. Jenkins, the speech and language clinician at Howard, screened Lindsay on October 14, 2001, in areas of articulation, voice, fluency, and language by using the Test of Language Development, Goldman-Fristoe-Woodcock Test of Auditory Discrimination, Vocabulary Comprehension Test, and Picture Story Language Test (refer to the completed screening report, dated October 22, 2001). On the basis of the results of these speech and language assessments, no speech/language training appears necessary at this time.

In the classroom, Ms. Marshall reported Lindsay's difficulty to begin on time and complete assignments in reading. Other subject area requirements do not appear to pose problems to her. She continues to perform well in mathematics and spelling, although assignments in social skills and science are beginning to contain more required reading skills than assignments previously. Ms. Marshall reported her fears of Lindsay falling farther and farther behind her classmates as the school year continues. For these reasons, prereferral strategies were proposed by an educational planning team on January 14, 2002. Teaching modifications applied in the general classroom were suggested and implemented by Ms. Marshall. The school's counselor, Mr.

Thompson; special education teacher, Ms. New; and I, psychologist, participated in prereferral strategies. After completion of 6 weeks, however, peer tutoring with a classmate during reading comprehension time was not successful. Lowering the amount of work required for her was also reported to be an unsuccessful strategy. For a majority of the time, Lindsay continues to display problems in completing her work and in comprehending the assignments. Her papers continue to contain many errors (62% accuracy was the highest reported score). Observations by Ms. Marshall, Mr. Thompson, Ms. New, and myself included an analysis of Lindsay's work samples (during a 6-week period, work samples were turned in 10 of 64 times; problems in reading comprehension were noted); anecdotal records (Ms. Marshall's daily log continued to verify problems specific to reading comprehension); and a frequency count of observable behavior during reading instruction (relative to peers, Lindsay was on-task during independent reading instruction only 4 of 14 times; Lindsay was off-task for 73% of reading instruction and off-task for 90% of seatwork during two independent observations by the counselor and psychologist). She appears to respond well to direct-instruction strategies when working one-on-one with her teacher. When she was provided with direct-instruction strategies geared to her level of learning (e.g., acquisition stage for reading comprehension), she improved in reading attention and level.

Testing:

Between March 4 and March 14, 2002, Lindsay was given the following tests and obtained these scores:

- Wechsler Intelligence Scale for Children (fourth edition): Lindsay obtained a full scale of 114 (verbal: 110, performance: 116) on the WISC-4, including raw scores on picture completion, picture arrangement, block design, object assembly, coding, and mazes. All are within the average or above raw-score range.
- Woodcock Johnson Psychoeducational Battery: Only the educational component was given to Lindsay, and she scored 2.5 in reading, 3.7 in math, and 3.2 in language.
- Gates-McKillop Reading Diagnostic Test: On this measure, she obtained a score of reading comprehension grade level 2.4.
- Brigance Diagnostic Inventories: This measure was given to determine more specific information about Lindsay's reading abilities. An overall score of 2.3 was obtained with the breakdown of the subsets as follows:

Word recognition	3.1
Oral reading	2.7
Reading comprehension	2.3
Functional word recognition	2.4
Word analysis	2.4
Reference skills	2.0
Writing	2.1
Spelling	2.1
Forms	2.4

- Achenbach Behavioral Scales: The ABS was completed by both Lindsay's parents and Ms. Marshall, her classroom teacher, with no significant behaviors reported in any areas of the behavior-rating scale. Her socioemotional development appears to be adequate for a child of her age.
- Developmental Test of Visual Perception: To determine whether Lindsay displays problems in visual processing, the DTVP was given. Lindsay appears to have adequate functioning in all areas of the DTVP.

Summary of Data:

Lindsay was given testing in areas of ability, achievement, socioemotional development, processing, and reading-diagnostic skills. Classroom strategies and observations of her progress in Ms. Marshall's class were conducted prior to testing. Peer tutoring and lowered rates of homework/seatwork requirements (teaching modifications) did not appear to aid Lindsay in skills in which she needs to succeed in the general class.

On the current testing, Lindsay performs at the above-average range of intelligence (ability results of the WISC-4 are one standard deviation above the norm). Reading scores range from a low of 2.1 to 3.1 on reading diagnostic testing. Overall reading comprehension is reported currently at the 2.3 level. There is no discrepancy between achievement and ability. Processing and sociomotional ratings are unnotable for a child of her age. Tentative strategies that may prove to be helpful to Lindsay are suggested by Ms. New, Ms. Marshall, Mr. Thompson, and me:

1. Have Lindsay repeat directions to assignments prior to the initiation of independent work problems.
2. Cue Lindsay orally to read for facts before she starts reading comprehension assignments.
3. Work with Lindsay to use underlining strategies (important details of assignments).
4. Teach Lindsay self-questioning strategies so that she can ask herself whether she comprehends tasks.
5. Paraphrase important details to her in a variety of ways (e.g., orally say directions in two different ways).
6. Highlight assignments (color-code important information in each paragraph she is to read).
7. Set time limits on and monitor her completion of tasks.
8. Reward Lindsay with tangibles, special class privileges, and so forth when she hands in assignments on time and follows classroom suggestions.
9. Post a record of her accomplishments for assignments and for successful completion of reading comprehension tasks (chart or graph).
10. Consider her stage of learning and plan instructional methods accordingly. If in the acquisition stage, consider direct instruction methods. Use independent and practice activities only when she demonstrates mastery or near mastery of the skills.
11. Continue to use, over time, peer tutors, student interns, and volunteers/paraprofessionals as warranted to assist her.
12. Plan for consultation time among her parents, the special education teacher, and the general class teacher to consider Lindsay's individual progress.

---

completed by Dr. Weiss, the school psychologist, have been summarized on the written psychological report. All information is explained and interpreted to parents and professionals by evaluators.

Eligibility Meeting

After completion of all formal testing, parents and professionals decide whether the student qualifies for specialized help. This decision occurs at an **eligibility meeting.**

An eligibility decision to determine an appropriate placement and to discuss the results of all written data must be made (IDEA, 1997). All data generated to date are compiled and synthesized during an eligibility meeting. For many students, the explanation and interpretation of the psychological report are completed during this meeting.

The purpose of the meeting is to match the needs of the student to the most appropriate setting available. If an appropriate setting is unavailable, the school district may contract for the needed services. In all cases, a placement must be found for the student (placement options are described in Chapter 1). A representative of the assessment team, often the school psychologist or educational diagnostician who conducted the assessment, is a member of the eligibility meeting. Other members include a school administrator, the referring teachers, the special education teacher, parents or guardians, and if warranted, the student. An example of the paperwork used in Lindsay's eligibility meeting is included in Figure 7.7.

Pause and Reflect 7.4

Briefly summarize the data that you believe Lindsay's school professionals and family members will need during the eligibility meeting. Compare and contrast data collected during the prereferral strategy and observation processes with those accumulated in Lindsay's formal testing. Can any relevant indicators of Lindsay's needs and strengths help in determining her current strengths and needs for an IEP?

Eligibility Data Summary

_____

_____

_____

_____

Relevant Prereferral and Observational Summary

_____

_____

_____

_____

Formal Testing Summary

_____

_____

_____

_____

Strengths and Needs Summary

_____

_____

_____

_____

Student's name <u>Lindsay Christopher</u>　　　Teacher <u>Ms. Marshall</u>　　Class <u>3</u>

Problem area defined <u>Lindsay appears to lack motivation. Her reading</u>
<u>comprehension and study skills are reported as low.</u>

Reason for referral <u>She was referred for testing because prereferral</u>
<u>strategies of the general education class were not successful. Multiple</u>
<u>observations provided evidence of off-task behaviors and low accuracy</u>
<u>rates in performance.</u>

Prereferral strategies <u>Peer tutoring and lower rates of homework/seatwork</u>
<u>requirements have not aided Lindsay in completion of tasks and reading</u>
<u>comprehension.</u>

Results <u>Assignments over a 6-week period continue to be incomplete and</u>
<u>to have low accuracy rates.</u>

Observation <u>4 completed</u>　　　Name(s) <u>Thompson</u>　　Date(s) <u>3/1/02</u>
　　　　　　　　　　　　　　　　　　　<u>Thompson</u>　　　　　　<u>3/5/02</u>
　　　　　　　　　　　　　　　　　　　<u>New</u>　　　　　　　<u>3/13/02</u>
　　　　　　　　　　　　　　　　　　　<u>Weiss</u>　　　　　　　<u>3/19/02</u>

Results <u>Off-task in group reading 73% of the time (4/17 times off-task).</u>
<u>Does not keep up with others (28/35 minutes off-task 70% of time).</u>

Test results <u>Lindsay's test results include: WISC-R (verbal, 110; performance,</u>
<u>116; full scale, 114); Woodcock Johnson (reading, 2.5; math, 3.7; language,</u>
<u>3.2); Gates-McKillop (reading comprehension, 2.4); Achenbach (no significant</u>
<u>problem behaviors); DTVP (adequate in all areas) Brigance reading</u>
<u>(2.3). Although her reading comprehension appears to be low (2.3 level),</u>
<u>results of testing indicate she is beginning to comprehend grade-appropriate</u>
<u>material but is not ready for independent assignments at this time.</u>
<u>Motivation may be a problem.</u>

Recommendation for placement <u>Continue in general education class.</u>

Reason <u>Lindsay does not meet the requirements for special education.</u>
<u>Teachers should continue to provide small-group and tutorial help on a one-to-one</u>
<u>basis in the acquisition of reading comprehension skills. Tentative strategies as</u>
<u>listed on the psychological report of 3/20/02 should be implemented. Team</u>
<u>meeting should reconvene to update general class strategies on 8/20/02</u>
<u>to provide direction for the coming school year. Continue to emphasize direct</u>
<u>instruction.</u>

	Participants' signatures	Date
LEA	<u>Thomas Smart, Principal</u>	<u>4/5/02</u>
Evaluator	<u>Betty Weiss, School Psychologist</u>	<u>4/5/02</u>
Teachers	<u>Jane Marshall, Teacher</u>	<u>4/5/02</u>
Others	<u>Betsy New, Special Education</u>	<u>4/5/02</u>
	<u>Terri Thompson, Counselor</u>	<u>4/5/02</u>
Parent/Guardian	<u>Mary/John Christopher, Parents</u>	<u>4/5/02</u>

FIGURE 7.7　Lindsay's Eligibility Meeting

The results of the eligibility meeting for Lindsay are used to determine whether she has a disability and is in need of a special education program. Lindsay will remain in general education: She is not a candidate for special education because her formal test results, along with prereferral information and formal observation data, were found to confirm the appropriateness of the general education program for her. Lindsay does display learning problems, but she is not a student with severe enough problems to necessitate her removal from her present educational setting. She responds well to small groups, direct instruction techniques, and some modifications in the general education curriculum. Her achievement levels are low to moderate and not severe enough to require special education. An important recommendation by her eligibility team members is that a team meeting reconvene at the start of the school year to update potential general class strategies. At this point, the special education teacher may continue to be a consultant to Lindsay's general education class teachers.

Pertinent Questions of Formal Testing Results

If the purpose of formal testing is a change in placement, important questions that developing and beginning teachers should ask during the eligibility meeting might include the following:

- What other information is relevant about the student's functioning that test results may not provide?
- Does the written report present a complete and accurate picture of the student's ability in cognitive, language, social, motor, or other forms of development?
- Do test results conflict with previous data collected?
- What are the implications for instruction and management, based on the test results? That is, do the results provide a framework to instruct or manage the student in the special education situation?
- If a change in placement is not warranted, do test results imply other strategies, materials, or evaluation systems that may help the student in the general education curriculum setting (Cartwright et al., 1981)?

Box 7.9 presents the types of responses that professionals at Lindsay's school gave in answering these questions. One key element not to be overlooked is Lindsay's opportunity to remain in the general education curriculum class and be provided with consultative services by a team, including her school's special education teacher. Even after formal testing is completed, many students may continue to display problems in the general education curriculum but not be candidates for specialized programming. When this happens, the role of the special education teacher continues to be as a consultant to the general education class teacher. However, all students with individual differences in learning or behavioral needs are not removed from instruction with normally functioning peers. As in Lindsay's case, many students can remain in inclusive classrooms when professionals are provided with comprehensive data and work as a team to facilitate the LRE.

Summary of the Formalized Testing Situation

After securing parents' permission to test and obtain all sensory information about their child, a complete battery of testing is given. Each educational decision for the student should be based on comprehensive information. Because data have been collected by many professionals over time and in a variety of settings, much is now known about the student. An objective decision is more likely to be made on how best to offer instruction and management. Some students, like Lindsay, may have undergone the formal testing situation but are ineligible for special education and related services. These students may be provided with remedial help through general inclusive classroom education courses, with consulting help by the special educator. An emphasis by professionals on teaching

---

Box 7.9   **Pertinent Questions and Answers on Lindsay Christopher**

These questions were answered by Ms. Marshall, the general education classroom teacher.

- What other information is relevant about the student's functioning that test results may not provide?

Other information that may be helpful for us to consider include readability level of the classroom material; distractions from peers, paraprofessionals, or volunteers; and expectations of parents and professionals. More emphasis on direct instruction techniques and less requirements on independent assignments (for Lindsay's learning stage) are important.

- Does the written report present a complete and accurate picture of the students' ability in cognitive, language, social, motor, or other forms of development?

The written report provides data about Lindsay's functioning in the domains listed above, but the question still remains: How do we best instruct Lindsay? No matter what the psychologist and educational diagnostician diagnose, we still must find strategies and techniques to teach and help Lindsay succeed.

- Do test results conflict with previous data collected?

Lindsay's parents have reported her lack of initiation to study independently at home and to complete home chores, so there is some reliability across individuals and settings concerning the data. I really believed, however, that Lindsay's reading scores would have been much lower than she actually obtained on the formal achievement test given by our school psychologist.

- What are the implications for instruction and management based on the test results? That is, do the results provide a framework to instruct or manage the student in the classroom situation?

How can we teach Lindsay best if she remains in the general education class? Should we change her reading assignments? Should we provide another formal reading program? Should we allow her to attend reading class with second graders?

- If a change in placement is not warranted, do test results imply other strategies, materials, or evaluation systems that may help the student in the present educational setting? (Cartwright et al., 1981).

Other strategies may include a change in her reading curriculum, more time alone with the teacher, additional small-group instruction, direct instruction for reading comprehension, and study skills.

---

behaviors (e.g., use of modified materials, direct instruction techniques, management using tokens and rewards) will allow many students opportunities to remain in general education classrooms. Other students, however, may have undergone the formal testing situation and are eligible for special education and related services. The special education teacher's role for students requiring formal special education (removal from the general education class placement for at least part of the school day) is the direct service model.

INDIVIDUALIZED EDUCATION PROGRAMS

Prior to a new educational placement, the individualized education program (IEP) must be developed for every student entering special education and related services (IDEA, 1997). All paperwork collected to date can be very useful in determining goals and objectives of the new educational setting. All data are linked to the student's IEP.

Students' IEPs are the most important documents that teachers, school officials, and parents develop cooperatively. Important aspects of the IEP process that developing and beginning teachers should recognize include (1) the necessity of parents' or guardians' consent for placement, (2) requirements of initial placements, (3) requirements of annual updated IEPs, and (4) results and implications of reevaluations.

Consent for Placement by Parents

Each student placed into a special education program is provided with an IEP. Programs must be current and in effect at the initiation of every school year or within 30 calendar days from eligibility meetings specifying the special education and related services provided (IDEA, 1997). Prior to initial placement, parents or guardians must give and date their written permission for their child's program. If parents refuse, mediation and due process hearing procedures (as described in Chapter 2) are initiated.

Also, consenting parents or guardians are given the opportunity to attend the IEP meeting at a time and place convenient for them. Federal authorities have mandated school officials to give parents two types of notices of the upcoming IEP meeting. One notice must be written and a copy saved for school records. The other notice may be a written request, personal correspondence, telephone call, or other means. Figure 7.8 illustrates the paperwork used in securing parents' permission to place their child. Lindsay's example is a reminder that she will continue in her general education curriculum program. Although an IEP is not required for her, an IEP is required for all students who receive special education and related services.

Requirements of Initial Placement IEPs. Federal requirements are very specific for students entering special education and related services for the first time. Documentation must be provided by school personnel in two major areas: (1) the legal participants at IEP meetings and (2) the required components of the IEP written document. Because developing and beginning teachers must demonstrate knowledge of the IEP from the first day of school, it is very important to be familiar with all requirements during preservice training.

IEP Participants. Federal requirements specify the presence of various individuals when an IEP meeting commences. Box 7.10 lists the title and function of required participants. IDEA 97 extends participant requirements to a general education teacher in cases in which students will be receiving some or all of their educational services in a general education classroom. An IEP should never be written prior to the actual meeting, but rather must be developed during the meeting, with all participants providing insights to meet the student's needs best. Each participant should be given the opportunity to (1) provide information on the student, (2) suggest IEP goals and objectives, (3) question interpretations and explanations, (4) examine educational alternatives, and (5) disagree with proposed actions.

Specific Components of the IEP. IDEA 97 mandated specific IEP sections. Seven areas must be specified in writing for every student:

1. A statement of the student's current level of educational performance, including to what extent the child's disability affects the child's involvement and progress in the general curriculum

2. A statement of measurable annual goals, including benchmarks or short-term objectives, related to meeting the child's needs that result from the child's disability

3. A statement of the particular special education and related services and supplementary aids and services to be provided to the child, or on behalf of the child, and a statement of the program modifications or supports for school

---

Student's name <u>Lindsay Christopher</u>   Class <u>3</u>

Present setting <u>Sandling Howard Elementary</u>   Teacher <u>Ms. Marshall</u>

Type of setting <u>General education classroom</u>   Date <u>June 20, 2002</u>

Results of tests <u>Results of ability, achievement, processing, and socioemotional</u> <u>testing were discussed by the eligibility team. Motivation appears to be a major</u> <u>problem for Lindsay. Learning, ability, achievement, socioemotional, and processing</u> <u>appear to be in at least the average range.</u>

Recommended program name <u>General education classroom placement.</u>

Reason for recommendation <u>Lindsay meets the criteria for general education</u> <u>classroom placement continuation. Lindsay does display learning problems (she</u> <u>appears to be at the three-level acquisition stage of reading comprehension—</u> <u>rather than generalization as most of her peers). She appears to need extrinsic,</u> <u>tangible motivation and small-group instruction to help her succeed. Direct</u> <u>instruction in a small-group format should be highlighted.</u>

Delivery service provided <u>Lindsay will continue to receive her educational</u> <u>placement in the general education classroom, with consulting help provided by the</u> <u>instructional support.</u>

Recommended school name <u>Continue in Sandling Howard Elementary</u>

Address <u>230 Haystack Court Road, Maimlee, Florida</u>

<u>Continue in general education class, summer school, June 24, 2002–</u> <u>July 23, 2002 J.C. M.C.</u>

Placement to begin on <u>August 8 2002</u> (30 calendar days from eligibility determination).

___<u>✓</u>___ I have been given a copy of "Procedural Due Process".

___<u>✓</u>___ I give permission to place my child _____<u>Lindsay</u>_____ in the recommended program.

_____ I do not give permission to place my child _____ in the recommended program.

_____ I request another meeting prior to making a decision.

Parent/guardian's name <u>John Christopher/Mary Christopher</u>

LEA representative <u>Thomas Smart, Principal</u>

Date: <u>4/5/02</u>   Evaluator <u>Betty Weiss, Psychologist</u>

Teacher: <u>Jane Marshall (General Education Classroom)</u>

Others <u>Betsy New (Special Education Certified)</u>

FIGURE 7.8 Lindsay's Parents' Permission to Place

personnel that will be provided for the child (a) to advance appropriately toward attaining the annual goals, (b) to be involved and progress in the general curriculum, (c) to participate in extracurricular and other nonacademic activities, and (d) to be educated and participate with other children with disabilities and nondisabled children

4. An explanation of the extent, if any, to which the child will not participate with nondisabled children in the regular class and in other activities

Box 7.10   **Required IEP Participants and Their Functions**

1. *LEA representative:* The local education agency (LEA) representative provides meeting participants with pertinent data about available programs of the local area. The individual must be available to discuss service delivery options, transportation methods, and district procedures of program implementation. The LEA representative is usually a district administrator of special education or the principal of the local school attended by the student.
2. *Member of the evaluation team:* Someone knowledgeable about psychological and educational testing must be available to discuss, interpret, and explain all test results to those in attendance at the meeting. Usually, this person is the school psychologist or educational diagnostician who provided the testing to the student.
3. *Special education teacher:* A professional who is knowledgeable about the special education program to be provided to the student must be present. The person answers any questions posed by group participants and guides the writing of student-oriented goals and objectives on the written documents.
4. *General education teacher:* At least one general education teacher of the child (if the child is, or may be, participating in the general education environment) who is knowledgeable about the general education curriculum.
5. *Other participants* of the IEP meeting may include the parent, guardian, or surrogate parent, and when appropriate, the student. Also, any other person the student, parent, guardian, or surrogate parent wishes may attend. Lawyers, therapists, physicians, or other advocates may represent parents or school officials at meetings. Their functions are to provide input and feedback on goals and objectives proposed for the IEP.

5. A statement of any individual modifications in the administration of state- or districtwide assessments of student achievement that are needed in order for the child to participate in the assessment, or if the IEP team determines that the child will not participate in a particular state- or districtwide assessment of student achievement (or part of an assessment), a statement of why that assessment is not appropriate for the child and how the child will be assessed

6. The projected date for the beginning of the services and the anticipated frequency, location, and duration of those services

7. A statement of how the child's progress toward the annual goals will be measured and how the child's parents will be regularly informed (through such means as periodic report cards), at least as often as parents are informed of their nondisabled children's progress, of (a) their child's progress toward the annual goals and (b) the extent to which that progress is sufficient to enable the child to achieve the goals by the end of the year

Also, the transition services for students who are 14 years of age or older must be delineated. Students' transitions operate within an outcome-oriented process that promotes movement from school to postschool activities, including postsecondary education, vocational training, integrated employment (including supported employment), continuing and adult education, adult services, independent living, and community participation. School professionals work with family members to identify pertinent transition activities in students' services.

For each student with a disability beginning at age 14 (or younger, if determined appropriate by the IEP team), the IEP must include a statement of the transition service needs of the student under the applicable components of the student's IEP that focuses on the student's courses of study (such as participation in advanced-placement courses or a vocational education program). For each student beginning at age 16 (or younger, if determined appropriate by the IEP team), a statement of needed transition services for the student, including, if appropriate, a statement of the interagency responsibilities or any needed linkages. Also, in a state that transfers rights at the age of majority, beginning at least 1 year before a student reaches the age of majority under state law, the student's IEP must include a statement that the student has been informed of his or her rights under part B of the act, if any, that will transfer to the student on reaching the age of majority (IDEA, 1997). Box 7.11 details information that IEP planning meeting participants would analyze and discuss in the development of the written program.

Figure 7.9 illustrates the component parts of IEPs. Written examples of required components are also illustrated. Beginning and developing teachers may be involved in every step shown in Figure 7.9, either as a consultant to some students (e.g., Lindsay) in the general education class placement or as a direct service provider to others requiring specialized programming.

The IEP as a Working Document

As described earlier, specific written statements provide (1) a destination for teachers, parents, and students to strive for and (2) the basis for evaluating the effectiveness of the instructional activities and materials in helping students arrive at some prescribed skill level. An IEP helps parents and teachers to describe annual plans for students with diverse needs. Some teachers may view the IEP process as a dreaded chore. The IEP is a true opportunity to plan with parents and other professionals. The IEP is the focal point for planning a student's program and coordinating services received to provide for the student's needs. Developing and beginning teachers are wise to recognize that the IEP will be only as useful as the individuals employing them in schools. Employability of IEPs is a concept significant to every teacher. Only by actually devising, monitoring, and continually revising IEPs for students requiring special education and related services can the true intent of federal and state laws be implemented.

Effective IEP Meetings

Professionals and parents who work together and can agree on a common set of objectives can share in the decisions regarding the nature of a student's programs. The legal intent was for parents to be equal partners in decision-making; unfortunately, several researchers have painted a rather bleak picture of parental participation (Goldstein, Strickland, Turnbull, & Curry, 1980; Lynch & Stein, 1982; Morgan, 1982). General education class teachers, too, may have concerns over their involvement in the IEP process and the guarantee that they will receive the assistance they need to instruct students with diverse needs. The thinking is that if classroom teachers are required to provide specially designed instruction to students with learning or behavioral problems, they have both the right as well as the responsibility to share in decisions regarding the nature of students' programs ("CEC Leads IDEA Testimony," 1995; Cooley & Yovanoff, 1996; O'Shea, Stoddard, & O'Shea, 2000).

Ms. Marshall, Lindsay's general education class teacher, expressed legitimate concerns about instructing Lindsay effectively after the formal testing situation (as represented from her statements in Box 7.8). Special educators and general education class teachers must continue to work on teaming ideas for all students requiring support from school personnel. School professionals in the 21st century must reaffirm that the input of parents, special educators, administrators, psychologists, counselors, and general education class teachers is valued and that their concerns for students and their educational programming are legitimate. Effective special educators continue to offer

Box 7.11   **Critical Information for the IEP Team to Review**

1. *Present educational levels:* This is a statement of the strengths and needs of present levels of functioning. The present educational levels may be derived from teachers' informal or formal observations, classroom assessments, prereferral strategy analysis, or case studies. Present educational levels are the bases for annual goals.

2. Measureable *annual goals:* These are broad statements of students' anticipated educational outcomes and behavioral outcomes for the year. Annual goals may include generic statements of subject or performance areas that students will encounter during the year. Annual goals should be linked to both the present educational levels and the short-term objectives.

3. *Benchmarks, or short-term objectives:* These are very specific statements of students' educational areas and behavioral programs anticipated for the year. Benchmarks, or short-term objectives, should be written concisely and clearly in concrete terminology. It is best to use behavioral terminology observed easily by objective observers. Benchmarks, or short-term objectives, are statements that teachers and parents anticipate students will master within the year. All benchmarks, or short-term objectives, specify conditions (circumstances under which objectives are presented to students) and behavior (specifically, what students must do or how students are to act or behave).

4. *Statement of special services needed:* This statement must reflect the specific special education program and related services provided for students. Usually, this is written in the form of the category assigned to students (e.g., specific learning disability, physical impairment, to designate special education programs; or specialized transportation, specific counseling, social services to designate related services). The special services noted should be based on the results of assessment reports and data collected from case studies during prereferral or referral. All information can be reported to the multidisciplinary team at the eligibility meeting or continuation placement meeting.

5. *Programs to be followed:* Participants of the IEP meeting must agree to all educational programs provided to special students. This component specifies the degree to which students are integrated with general students. Writers of IEPs must specify the amount of general education (basic education), special education, and in some areas, vocational education. The need for adaptive physical education or general physical education should be determined for each student.

6. *Initiation date and expected duration:* These dates must specify when programs are to take place and how long they will last. Most expected duration dates run 1 year from the date of the initiation of programs when parents first give written consent. IEPs can be updated and rewritten, however, anytime during the school year.

7. *Criteria to assess objectives:* Every short-term objective written for students should be assessed continually to monitor progress made toward goals and objectives. Mastery levels for objectives should be specified. Specification is done usually in terms of duration (e.g., for two minutes), trials to criterion (e.g., four of five trials), or percentages (e.g., 80% mastery level for acceptable performance). All materials, evaluation procedures, and schedules used to monitor should be specified. When students have obtained the duration or criterion level or reached the number of trials specified, the person responsible for implementing the program area should write the date of mastery by the objective. If objectives are not mastered by the ending duration date of the IEP, objectives may be eliminated or revised for continuation on the next IEP. During periodic monitoring of the IEP, teachers may write progress reports on students' completion of objectives (e.g., On January 24, 1998, Mun-Hee mastered three of five trials for decoding skills. On March 16, 1998, Mun-Hee mastered four of five trials for decoding skills).

FIGURE 7.9 Individualized Education Programs

ASSESSMENT RESULTS

A. Prereferral strategies
B. Observations
C. Data of classroom teachers
D. Psychological testing using battery of tests

PRESENT EDUCATIONAL LEVELS

A. Academic strengths and needs
B. Sociobehavioral strengths and needs

MEASURABLE ANNUAL GOALS

A. Yearly academic outcomes
B. Sociobehavioral expectations
C. Transition goals

BENCHMARKS, OR SHORT-TERM OBJECTIVES
A. Conditions
B. Behavior
C. Criteria

ANNUAL UPDATE

Reevaluation for program continuation

EXAMPLES OF ASSESSMENT RESULTS

A. Tim completed 3/5 chapters in the Global Reading Series at level 6. He was observed by his reading teacher to be struggling with oral reading skills. He could not answer any comprehension questions after reading a paragraph aloud.

B. Ruby was assessed by the school psychologist with the WISC-R and received 98 verbal, 109 performance, and 104 full scale. Her behavior ratings by the classroom teacher and parent yielded no significant problems. She received a 4.0 in reading, a 3.6 in mathematics, and a 4.1 in spelling, revealing average achievement for a student of her age.

---

consulting services when students exit from the referral process and/or exit from placement in special classes.

Rights and Responsibilities of All IEP Participants. IEP members share rights and responsibilities that are valid today. Every member must believe that he or she can contribute to the written product and should work to reach a consensus agreement of what is in the best interests of students. Participants should be able to provide input into determining responsibility for instruction, curriculum planning, scheduling, roles in implementing the IEP, and specifying reasonable expectations for students to master goals and objectives.

The rights of IEP participants that developing and beginning teachers will share with all other team members include (1) the opportunity to attend all IEP meetings, (2) a chance to determine appropriate goals and objectives for the students they serve, (3) access to all specialized materials, equipment, and curricula, (4) input and feedback related to all learning and behavioral management strategies devised for the student, (5) the opportunity to call additional IEP meetings as indicated by the student's mastery of goals and objectives, and (6) assistance in implementing individualized instruction from other multidisciplinary team members.

The responsibilities of IEP participants are also pertinent and include (1) demonstrated preparedness for all meetings, (2) display of professionalism during every meeting, (3) demonstrated organization and timeliness for every meeting, (4) display of empathy, positive regard, and nonjudgmental statements of other team members, (5) concerted effort to actually implement the written IEP, (6) continual attempts to evaluate the appropriateness of the IEP, and (7) ongoing collaborative efforts underscoring the importance of parents and other professionals.

If personnel new to school systems take the rights and responsibilities of IEP team members seriously, IEPs can remain vital documents to ensure the appropriateness of students' education in the LRE.

Behaviors of New Teachers. New teachers should focus on a few behaviors to facilitate the involvement of others in the IEP process. These behaviors, listed below, occur prior to, during, and after the IEP meeting. Many of these behaviors are vital to students who continue to receive a majority of their educational services in the general education class after formal testing and/or exit from specialized programs, as well as students pinpointed for special education and related services.

Prior to the IEP Meeting

- Observe confidentiality, report objectively, and qualify subjective judgments whenever possible. Always demonstrate this attitude when working with others.
- Be sensitive to the attitudes of other professionals involved with the student. Try to display empathy for their situation while still seeking appropriate solutions for the student with diverse needs.
- Try to anticipate potential problems that could arise during the meeting. Write down possible solutions prior to the meeting's initiation.

During the IEP Meeting

- Be sure a leader is present to organize the meeting.
- Make sure introductions are completed prior to starting the formal meeting. Participants should sign and identify their relationship to the student.
- Determine in advance the length of the meeting. The leader should state the purpose of the meeting, provide a brief outline of the expectations of the meeting, and guide the meeting according to appropriate timelines.
- Encourage the administration to keep the number of professional participants to the fewest possible. Consider the professional/parent ratio and the special education/general education curriculum ratio. Realize that some may feel awkward when outnumbered.
- In speech and all written statements, avoid the use of teacher jargon that may be confusing or too technical for some participants' use. Speak and write in a clear, understandable level of discourse but never miscalculate any participant's ability to understand and use data.
- Ensure that the evaluator summarizes all testing done and that parents are provided with a copy of the evaluation.
- If disagreements arise over any components of the evaluation, ensure that the leader asks participants to specify their disagreements in writing. Secure a copy of the disagreements for administrators not in attendance.
- Ensure that the leader states the placement-delivery system most appropriate for the student's needs (e.g., resource room, special class). Be sure that parents understand placement options by asking questions and encouraging their questions.
- Develop and write the IEP during the meeting. Never have a completed form for participants merely to sign.

- Develop complete IEPs before requesting participants' signatures and dates.
- Select and specify in writing any goals, objectives, and instructional procedures that are appropriate to the student on the basis of identified strengths and weaknesses.
- Link interventions to assessments. Ensure that the present educational levels are tied to the psychological report and other pertinent classroom data. Link present educational levels to annual goals, annual goals to short-term objectives, and so forth.
- Write verifiable objectives for the student in all areas of concern, specifying conditions, behaviors, and criteria.
- Solicit input from parents and all participants during the meeting. Actively encourage the input and feedback of others through display of visual cues, communication, and appropriate questioning and responses as warranted. Use empathy, positive regard, and nonjudgmental statements in all communication efforts.
- Encourage the leader to summarize the meeting and to plan for follow-up strategies during future meetings. The leader should write down all follow-up plans and promise all participants a copy of the plans.
- Discuss the tentative date for the next IEP meeting. Ensure participants that it is at least within one year's time.

After the IEP Meeting

- Implement all goals and objectives devised at the meeting.
- Strive to match the written plan to actual programming for the student.
- Monitor goals and objectives consistently. Date all monitoring efforts.
- If changes need to be made, hold another IEP meeting to revise.
- Continue to solicit input and feedback from all participants, including parents and general education class teachers. Demonstrate a team approach.
- Continue to keep written records and reports affecting students, parents, and other professionals and of all educational decisions made about the student.

Specific behaviors of teachers before, during, and after the meeting are included to represent the continuing process of a useful IEP. Effective IEPs are implemented by concerned teachers who know their students well, who will continually collect and maintain useful written data on the students, and who respect and implement their rights and responsibilities in the IEP process.

Requirements of Annual Updated IEPs

IEPs must be updated yearly for students in special education and related services (IDEA, 1997). This means that school professionals must ask parents to attend an annual IEP meeting to reconsider all goals and objectives. Again, parents must be notified twice. One notice must be in writing and a copy saved for school records. Attempts for a mutual time and place should be set. If the parents then refuse to attend the updated IEP meeting, school officials may continue with the meeting as planned without the parents. It is the responsibility of multidisciplinary team members to initiate additional meetings when a student's IEP no longer matches needs as the school year progresses.

Results and Implications of Reevaluations

It is a professional responsibility to reevaluate students every 3 years (IDEA, 1997). However, some states may require more frequent reevaluations. Just as eligibility meetings are held to determine whether students meet entrance criteria into programs, a decision for exit criteria is also important. Figure 7.10 is an example of an observation-recording form that may be used to help verify a student's exit from specialized programming.

Student's name __Jenny Wain__   Grade __6__   School __Fiddler Middle__

Date __4/14/02__   Level __–__   Teacher __Mr. Metan__

Subject area/class __ESE (English/Math)__

Dates of observation __April 1, 2002__ to __April 4, 2002 (3rd period)__

Number of students present __12__   Teaching format used __Small group; independent self-management__

Target student's behavior (description prior to observation) __During functional English and math classes, Jenny continues to be on-task for 95% of total allocated time.__

Important antecedents __Observation of 90% to 100% on-task compliant behavior reported by Mr. Metan for 6 weeks during the last 3 months.__

✓ = mastery   X = absent

Behavior	1	2	3	4	5	6	7	8	9	10	11	12	13	14	15	Comments
1. Describe: Functional English: Followed teacher's directions 90% of time after given oral instructions.	✓	✓	✓	✓	✓	✓	✓	✓	X	✓	✓	✓	✓	✓	✓	1. 100% compliance (except 1 day due to absence)
2. Functional math: Completed math assignment with 80% accuracy in self-instructional format.	✓	✓	✓	✓	✓	✓	✓	✓	X	✓	✓	✓	✓	✓	✓	2. Met criterion level for every day (except due to absence).
3. Functional English: Was able to read and complete homework during study time.	✓	X	✓	✓	✓	✓	✓	✓	X	✓	✓	✓	✓	✓	X	3. 12/15 days completed required assignment with 90% accuracy.
4. Functional math: On-task at least 75% of small-group math instruction.	✓	✓	✓	✓	✓	✓	✓	✓	X	✓	✓	✓	✓	✓	✓	4. Exceeded criteria (to 90% time on-task)
5.																
Days	1	2	3	4	5	6	7	8	9	10	11	12	13	14	15	

Important consequences __Demonstrated continued self-help, self-management, and self-evaluation skills in functional English and math class. Responded well in small-group format.__

Comments _____

Reevaluation focus __Jenny may be a good candidate for consideration of exit from specialized programming. She has been able to keep up with her required assignments in both the special class and her mainstreamed class for the past 3 months, as reported by Mr. Metan.__

Observer's Name/Title __Mr. Chew, Counselor__

FIGURE 7.10   Observation Recording Form Useful for Exit Criteria

Reevaluations determine whether a student's program should change. Developing and beginning teachers should become familiar with local and state procedures for exit requirements when a change in educational placement is warranted for a student. Box 7.12 lists four phases of an exit process to remove a student from special education. These steps are important aspects of placing students back into a general education class. Many data are required to verify the general education class as the LRE for the student. Again, the role of the special educator is as a consultant to the general education class teacher when the student exits from special education. Professionals continue to team together to implement the exit process steps of Box 7.12.

Box 7.12   **Four Phases of an Exit Process**

Phase 1: Plan (prior to reevaluation/exit conference)

- Identify a systematic data-collection procedure for exit from special education programming.
- Identify pertinent strategies based on the student's needs.
- Determine how information is to be observed and collected.
- Identify data gatherers in the special education class and, as necessary the general education class.
- Develop a time frame and schedule for data collection.

Phase 2: Data collection (prior to reevaluation/exit conference)

- Identify student demographic attributes.
- Collect background data on mastery of general education goals/objectives.
- Provide observational data, including teacher-made tests and behavioral ratings in the general class and special class.
- Compare and contrast past standardized test results with past and present criterion-referenced tests.
- Collect work samples from the general class and special class.
- Analyze personal health and sensory data.
- Compare past prereferral strategies with current strategies.
- Collect individual interest surveys and goals.

Phase 3: (data analysis (prior to/during exit meeting)

- Provide comparison with norms after individualized reevaluation.
- Analyze strengths and needs within the individual.
- Note patterns of behaviors and changes across time.
- Determine goals and objectives for the mainstream class.
- Determine timelines for mainstream transition.
- Develop consultation teaming strategies and schedules of observation to implement during mainstream transition.

Phase 4: Mainstream Implementation (student returns to general programming)

- Continue to observe and modify practices as needed.
- Collaborate with other professionals.
- Consult with parents.
- Implement goals and objectives in the mainstream class.
- Monitor progress and continue to collect data.
- Evaluate continually appropriateness of the new LRE.

WRITING REPORTS TO PARENTS AND TO OTHER PROFESSIONALS

Reports to parents and to other professionals should be a continuous process that all teachers undertake. As discussed earlier, progress reporting to parents of students with disabilities must occur with at least the same frequency of reports for nondisabled students. Developing and beginning teachers must realize the importance of communication. Special educators, general educators, other professionals, and parents need a continual communication process—more than can be provided through yearly IEP meetings or case conferences and school-based committee meetings. Reports may be formal statements of a student's progress, or they may be informal notes on the day's events or the student's reactions to them. Teachers may do simple tasks to complete the communication process with parents and other team members. Such things as writing down expectations, teacher's roles, and anticipated study units to share with parents and professionals is a good method to implement at the start of the school year. Special education teachers may also try to elicit from others how they perceive their role in the student's development. In an informal planning session, teachers may write down ways of working together. A suggestion to establish and maintain a continual positive rapport with the student's family is to initiate the first written contact with the parents or guardians during the beginning of the school year. Sharing responses intermittently will establish a positive rapport with others.

Also, a plan could be devised at the IEP meeting to maintain communication throughout the year. Such a plan could schedule updated review meetings for parents and teachers to discuss the student's progress or set up a notebook the student could take back and forth from the general education class teacher to the special education teacher (Schulz & Turnbull, 1984). Getting together on a consistent basis with parents and other teachers may help the novice teacher in understanding the importance of continual communication with all individuals significant to the student.

Developing and beginning teachers should work to send written data home to parents on an informal basis. For example, the teacher may send home periodic newsletters or class happenings to keep parents informed of units of instruction, to target special activities, to announce special events, or to request inexpensive resources or household items from home. It's a good idea to send a copy of all newsletters and class happenings to the general education class teachers to keep them updated as well. Some school systems provide server space for their teachers to maintain a home page on the Internet. This is an excellent medium for two-way communications with parents who have the means to access the Internet. Another example is sending home notes of progress and specific praise for tasks accomplished. (Try to accent the positive, rather than contact parents only when negative behaviors occur. Again, do the same positive correspondence with the general education class teachers to alert them when students have had a particularly productive day.) Still another idea is to have a suggestion box available for use by parents and professionals to demonstrate active solicitation of their written feedback.

In all written correspondence with parents and with other professionals, special educators should remember to translate all technical information. Write notes, e-mails, letters, and information sheets in short, clear, uncluttered language. In all contacts with parents, consider the discourse used. Try to communicate respect for the family's values, ideas, cultural background, and needs in all written correspondence.

Finally, all teachers should strive to establish and maintain a positive rapport with parents and other professionals by meeting formally and informally throughout the year. Providing a written invitation to all get-togethers and following up with a letter of thanks for their attendance at functions coordinated by the teacher are effective ways to help maintain positive communication throughout the year.

Pause and Reflect 7.5

Use the following checklist to reflect on your communication methods with significant individuals in your students' lives. Check all the methods you used within the past 7 days. Reflect on these points: Were these methods effective for you? What would you continue if you were to use them again with the same student(s)? How would you change the methods?

Communication Methods	How/When Used with Families	How/When Used with School Professionals	How/When Used with Community Professionals
Formal statements or reports of student progress			
Informal notes on the day's events and students' reactions to them			
Written expectations, teachers' roles, and anticipated study units to share with others			
Statements from others about how they perceive their role in student development			
Informal written ways of working together			
Written ways devised at the IEP meeting to maintain communication throughout the year			
Scheduled review meetings for parents and teachers to discuss students' progress			
Notebook feedback or written progress reports that students take back and forth from the general education class to the special education class			
Periodic newsletters or class happenings to keep parents informed of units of instruction, special activities, or announcements of special events			
Requests for inexpensive resources or household items from home			
Home notes of progress indicating specific praise for tasks accomplished			

Pause and Reflect 7.5 continued

Communication Methods	How/When Used with Families	How/When Used with School Professionals	How/When Used with Community Professionals
Suggestion box available in the classroom for use by parents and professionals to demonstrate active solicitation of their written feedback			
A written invitation to all informal/formal school get-togethers			
Written follow-up letters of thanks for attendance at functions coordinated by the teacher			

Who Can Help the Novice Teacher Understand the Ins and Outs of Paperwork?

This chapter stresses the importance of paperwork in the special education process. After reading it, developing and beginning teachers should recognize the link between updated, accurate paperwork and effectiveness in teaching.

Teachers must understand the crucial role that paperwork plays in the communication process and in ensuring an appropriate education to students with diverse needs. Effective paperwork will pinpoint those students who need to be removed from general class programming and those who can function adequately in the general education class. Professionals should strive to implement effective teaming ideals. Developing and beginning teachers must not view either the vast amount of documentation needed for prereferral, referral, and the IEP process, or the less formal means of communication with parents and other professionals as busywork.

Complying with Monitoring and Evaluation Procedures

Just as it is important to recognize the value of paperwork and be aware of potential strategies to alleviate pitfalls of stress and conflict associated with paperwork, teachers new to the profession must also realize that they are not alone in generating, collecting, and maintaining quality paperwork and instruction for their students. When new teachers comply with local, state, provincial, and federal monitoring and evaluation requirements documented through effective paperwork as representative of quality services to students, teachers help ensure a free and appropriate public education (FAPE) to every student they serve. Colleagues can help. Peer teachers can answer many questions about the realities of paperwork. General educators and special educators can share documentation ideas, as well as effective teaching strategies. Administrators may provide critical feedback about the proper procedures of using paperwork efficaciously. Parents and students can provide valuable clues to the content and types of data that teachers will find necessary on forms or other documentation. The teacher's own experience during meetings can help in making sense of the necessity of and logic behind paperwork requirements. The novice teacher will function best by asking many questions. By using some of the strategies and teaming suggestions offered throughout this textbook, developing and beginning teachers may begin even to like using paperwork and to value the utility of well-written documentation.

In Lindsay's case example, a well-documented set of data was vital in continuing her in the appropriate LRE—the general education class. The special education teacher can provide assistance to her general education class teacher through continual teaming efforts and support. Teachers in the 21st century can continue to team together to ensure all students the best educational opportunities available in the public school setting.

SUMMARY

This chapter provided developing and beginning teachers with an overview of data collection involved in special education. The theme of the chapter, paperwork, is central to the role of the special educator. Initially, a rationale for the importance of writing tasks was provided, as was comprehensive documentation required for referral and communication tasks.

Additionally, IEPs and IEP meetings were discussed. Specific behaviors of classroom teachers before, during, and after the IEP meeting were listed.

Finally, the chapter ended with suggestions to help teachers in writing reports and in informing parents and general education class teachers of classroom activities and student progress. The role of teachers maintaining effective paperwork is to facilitate teaming efforts to ensure the most appropriate educational setting for all students.

ACTIVITIES TO EXTEND YOUR KNOWLEDGE

1. Set up a panel presentation on the theme of "the importance of conducting instruction and other professional activities consistent with the requirements of law, rules and regulations, and local district policies and procedures." How would you present the panel to your students' families?

2. Conduct a literature review to determine your role in preventing behavioral management problems and/or academic difficulties in students who are culturally and/or linguistically diverse. What important data collections would help in the prevention process?

3. Given a variety of observation and data-recording systems during your term or semester, select appropriate observation and data-recording systems when presented with common classroom problems or set of problems (e.g., calling out, teasing, name calling, swearing, not following directions, not completing class assignments). What important written data will you glean when you match the observation and data-recording systems to the problem behaviors? How can these data help your students in the LRE? How can these data be used in a prereferral process?

4. Apply the behavioral diagnostic protocol to a problem or cluster of problems presented by students in your field site to determine whether active intervention is appropriate. What are important written data that you will share with your host teacher and university supervisor when you use the intervention?

5. Describe in a written essay the essential ethical and practical issues that must be considered if teachers are to respect the rights of families when applying

confidentiality of record-keeping and data-collection procedures on infants, children, and youth with disabilities.

POINT AND CLICK

The following web sites highlight the chapter's theme of special education paperwork. Each of these listings can assist new teachers in their compliance with local, state, and federal mandates on behalf of students with disabilities.

National Center for the Dissemination of Disability Research
http://www.ncddr.org/
This Web site offers new teachers important information on special education research, publications, and other information.

OSERS IDEA 97 Home Page
http://www.ed.gov/offices/OSERS/IDEA/
New teachers can access relevant information from the home page of the U.S. Department of Education, Office of Special Education.

U.S. Department of Education Publications and Products
http://www.ed.gov/pubs/index.html
New teachers can access the Web site of the U.S. Department of Education for a wealth of information.

U.S. Government Printing Office
http://www.gpo.gov/
The U.S. Government Printing Office offers information on relevant governmental documents and service. It can be used as a general site for individual research on selected topics important to teachers.

InfoHandler.com Electronic IEPs
http://www.infohandler.com/
InfoHandler.com produces electronic IEP, child accounting, medical assistance billing, and other data management software. The software is cross-platform and in some cases Web-based. The use of electronic media can decrease paperwork time significantly.

REFERENCES

Algozzine, B., Ysseldyke, J., & Christenson, S. L. (1983). An analysis of the incidence of special class placement: The masses are burgeoning. *Journal of Special Education, 17*, 141–147.

Billingsley, B. S. (1993). Teacher retention and attrition in special and general education: A critical review of the literature. *Journal of Special Education, 72*(2), 137–174.

Billingsley, B. S., & Cross, L. H. (1992). Predictors of commitment, job satisfaction, and intent to stay in teaching: A comparison of general and special education. *Journal of Special Education, 25*(4), 453–471.

Cartwright, G. P., Cartwright, C. A., & Ward, M. (1981). *Educating special learners.* Belmont, CA: Wadsworth.

CEC leads IDEA testimony at congressional hearings. (1995, June/July). *CEC Today*, p. 1.

Choate, J. S., Enright, B. E., Miller, L. J., Poteet, J. A., & Rakes, T. A. (1995). *Curriculum-based assessment and programming.* Needham Heights, MA: Allyn & Bacon.

Cooley, E., & Yovanoff, P. (1996). Supporting professionals-at-risk: Evaluating interventions to reduce burnout and improve retention of special educators. *Exceptional Children, 62*(4), 336–355.

Gloeckler, T., & Simpson, C. (1988). *Exceptional students in regular classrooms: Challenges, services, and methods.* Mountain View, CA: Mayfield.

Goldstein, S., Strickland, B., Turnbull, A. P., & Curry, L. (1980). An observational analysis of the IEP conference. *Exceptional Children, 46,* 278–286.

Graden, J. L., Casey, A., & Bonstrom, O. (1985). Implementing a prereferral intervention system: Part 2. The data. *Exceptional Children, 51,* 487–496.

Graden, J. L., Casey, A., & Christenson, S. L. (1985). Implementing a prereferral interventional system: Part I. The model. *Exceptional Children, 51,* 377–387.

Individuals with Disabilities Education Act (Public Law No. 101–476). (1990, October). Washigton, DC: U.S. Office of Special Education and Rehabilitation.

Individuals with Disabilities Education Act, Public Law No. 105–17 (1997). 20 U.S. Code Section 1400 et seq. Washington, DC: U.S. Office of Special Education Programs.

Lynch, E., & Stein, R. (1982). Perspectives on parent participation in special education. *Exceptional Education Quarterly, 3*(2), 73–84.

Morgan, D. P. (1982). Parent participation in the IEP process: Does it enhance appropriate education? *Exceptional Education Quarterly, 3*(2), 33–40.

O'Shea, L. J., Stoddard, K., & O'Shea, D. J. (2000). IDEA '97 and educator standards: Special educators' perceptions of their skills and those of general educators. *Teacher Education and Special Education, 23,* 2, 125–141.

Salvia, J., & Ysseldyke, J. E. (1991). *Assessment in special education* (5th ed.). Boston: Houghton Mifflin.

Schulz, J. B., & Turnbull, A. P. (1984). *Mainstreaming handicapped students A guide for classroom teachers* (2nd ed.). Needham Heights, MA: Allyn & Bacon.

Ysseldyke, J., & Algozzine, B. (1984). *Introduction to special education.* Boston: Houghton Mifflin.

Classroom Management

Promoting Discipline and Self-Control

In this chapter, we will

- ✔ review the importance of having comprehensive school and classroom management programs

- ✔ discuss alternatives for prevention of problem behaviors

- ✔ specify how to develop rules, procedures, and behavioral supports that can facilitate the development of well-ordered instructional environments

- ✔ present alternatives for effectively responding to instances of student misbehavior

- ✔ present functional behavioral assessment and intervention alternatives for addressing student misbehavior

- ✔ discuss procedures that assist students in developing internal self-control and problem-solving protocols

- ✔ demonstrate a protocol for designing and implementing individual behavior-change interventions

When asked what concerns them most about upcoming student-teaching assignments, developing teachers typically identify apprehension and anxiousness about classroom behavioral management. Specifically, many preservice (and, unfortunately, many in-service) teachers worry about losing control of students in their charge and about possible encounters with students who do not comply with implicit and explicit behavioral standards. Most developing teachers find that they are able to apply management skills learned in their university-based training programs. Feelings of apprehension persist, however, when student teachers move on to their own first classrooms. Surveys of beginning teachers indicate that management and remediation of student misbehavior are among the most pressing problems reported. In a review of studies concerned with the perceived problems of beginning elementary and secondary teachers, Veenman (1984) found that classroom discipline and student motivation ranked 1 and 2 among a listing of 24 problems. These concerns are also shared by the general public: In almost all of the past 2 decades of Gallup Polls of Public Attitudes About Public Schools, lack of discipline in schools has ranked among the top major concerns facing the public schools.

Because students with mild to moderate disabilities tend to engage in a wider range and higher rate of problem behaviors than most other students in educational settings, it is essential that prospective special education teachers become effective classroom managers and be able to share successful approaches with general education colleagues. In most university-based training programs for special educators, issues and strategies related to discipline and the management of classroom behavioral problems receive considerable attention. Prospective special educators typically complete course work and projects on (1) the characteristics of child and adolescent behavioral problems, (2) applied behavioral analysis, and (3) classroom management alternatives. The lesson that emerges is that there are no "magic bullets," formulas, or recipes to ensure appropriate student behavior.

On the positive side, however, are a series of general and specific strategies that, used correctly, can increase the probability of a successfully managed classroom. These general strategies provide the organizational structure for our discussion of effective classroom management. Because it is generally recognized that schoolwide comprehensive management programs form the foundation for successful management programs (e.g., Dwyer, Osher, & Hoffman, 2000), we first discuss the major components of successful schoolwide comprehensive management programs. Unfortunately, it is not always possible (or prudent) for developing and beginning teachers to advocate for, initiate, or organize important schoolwide reform efforts. Therefore, we provide specific techniques and basic teacher attitudes, consistent with the schoolwide approach, that can be used in the prevention, management, and resolution of problem behaviors in individual classrooms. We also provide guidelines for the completion of formal behavior-change efforts for individuals and groups of students.

*P*ause and Reflect 8.1

Discipline in the schools continues to be a major concern of the general public. Many claim that today's children and youth are more difficult to manage than those of the past and that schools are spending more time on discipline than on instruction. In your opinion, are these assertions true? If so, what factors are contributing to the breakdown in order in our schools? If these assertions are false, why is it that so many people believe that schools are failing to manage the troubling behaviors of students? Be prepared to back up your opinions!

COMPREHENSIVE SCHOOL AND CLASSROOM MANAGEMENT PROGRAMS

As it should be with all students, the development of effective management procedures for students with mild to moderate disabilities is a team effort. Although the ultimate responsibility for the maintenance of order in the special education setting rests with the classroom teacher, active support and participation from building administrators, general education colleagues, and related service personnel are essential for the maintenance of successful management programs. Because most students with mild to moderate disabilities will have contact with members of the school staff, it is critical that management plans, classroom rules, and special interventions designed to foster inclusive programming be developed with input from all relevant personnel. A prerequisite to successful collaborative and supportive working relationships within schools is clear and open communication. Unfortunately, open communication and cooperation in school settings do not automatically happen. As with most complex social systems, schools sometimes become places where individual and immediate concerns take precedence over activities that promote communication and teamwork. Successful cooperative efforts require hard work, persistence, diplomacy, flexibility, and a genuine belief that the efforts of a team can enhance the delivery of educational services to students. Box 8.1 provides some generic guidelines for how beginning teachers can facilitate open communication and teamwork in their schools.

A number of models (e.g., Dwyer & Osher, 2000; Lewis & Sugai, 1999; Rosenberg & Jackman, 1997) for comprehensive school and classroom management have appeared in the literature. Rosenberg and Jackman (1997), for example, developed and implemented an approach that promotes the development of positive, schoolwide, comprehensive management plans. Adapted from the work of Curwin and Mendler (1988) and other researchers, this process-based, operational model has collaborative teams of teachers, school administrators, and related service personnel work together within a prescriptive format to come to consensus on plans and strategies to (1) PREVENT the occurrence of troubling behavior, (2) ACT, or respond to instances of rule compliance and noncompliance in a consistent fashion, and (3) RESOLVE many of the issues that underlie or cause troubling behavior. In essence, using the PAR model (signifying the emphases on *prevention*, *action*, and *resolution*), building-based teams design their

---

Box 8.1   **Three Strategies for Facilitating Open Communication and Teamwork in School**

1. Meet with the school administrator responsible for student disciplinary actions prior to the start of the school year. The agenda for this meeting should include *(a)* the correspondence between schoolwide discipline policies and the behavioral management programs to be implemented as part of students' IEPs, *(b)* the proposed classroom rules, procedures, and consequences for noncompliance, and *(c)* suggested strategies to ensure consistency in instances when a student's behavior necessitates removal from the classroom.
2. Meet, both formally and informally, with other teachers in the building. The nature of the academic and classroom management program within the special education setting should be discussed, and issues related to the mainstreaming of eligible students should be highlighted. Arrange a mutually satisfying mode for communicating student progress throughout the academic year.
3. Alert the school support staff (e.g., psychologists, therapists, lunch aides, custodians) to the unique character and demands of your classroom. Discuss provisions that will enable easy access to support services.

own unified plan of action based on data-based procedures that have been documented to work. Figure 8.1 illustrates the specific components of the PAR model that team members design for implementation.

As part of the collaborative process, each team completes a structured, jargon-free PAR management plan that is readily understood by all involved in the education and treatment of students (e.g., parents, students, related service personnel, bus drivers). Participants begin by agreeing on rules, expectations, and procedures that can preempt problem behaviors. This is followed by the development of specific procedures for the implementation of positive consequences to promote rule compliance. An intervention hierarchy for negative consequences (for noncompliance) and specific crisis procedures are also developed. Finally, specific resolution interventions and logistical concerns regarding implementation are discussed.

In the sections that follow are suggestions on how developing and beginning teachers can apply these processes in their own schools and classrooms.

PREVENTING PROBLEM BEHAVIORS

The key to successfully managing the high-activity learning environments that serve students with mild to moderate disabilities is prevention. It is essential for developing and beginning teachers to be aware of the antecedent events related to student behavior that they as teachers can influence. **Antecedent events** include any expectations, attitudes, environmental conditions, or teacher behaviors that typically precede a student's response. As noted in Chapter 3, many antecedent events are associated with increased academic achievement, especially those related to the planning of instruction and the organization of a learning environment. Therefore, it is not surprising that many factors

FIGURE 8.1 Comprehensive Management for All Students: PAR Model Components

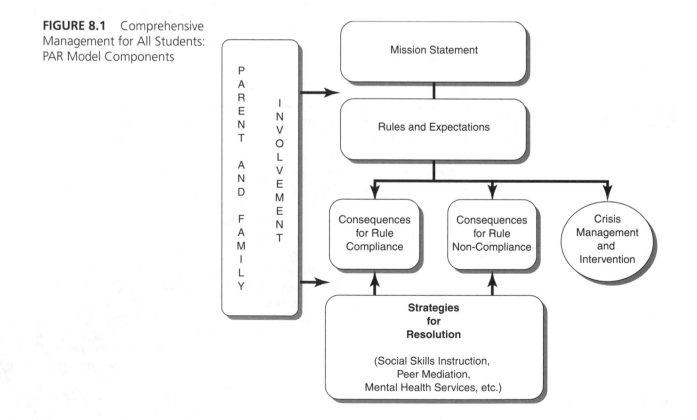

associated with the effective planning for instruction overlap with those associated with effective classroom management.

Effective Instruction

A major prerequisite to the success of any behavioral management system is that effective, motivating instruction is taking place. To that end, it is critical that developing and beginning teachers view their instructional behaviors as being central to the management process. Effective instruction that is both challenging and structured for student success can be the biggest factor in reducing problem behaviors. In many settings, a major cause of troubling behavior is student frustration with academic content and how it is presented. Students who encounter repeated failure find it easier to "act out" rather than to "act dumb." It is far easier to explain being the tough guy or class clown to one's peers than it is to explain that one does not know how to organize and integrate the material from a social studies or science lesson.

The implication for developing and beginning teachers is clear: Instructional adaptations and accommodations are the first line of action in developing comprehensive management plans. Students who are successful in meeting motivational academic challenges will be less likely to act up; they will be too busy garnering the internal and external reinforcers that accompany a job well done.

An Appropriate Management Perspective

The management of student behavior is not a cut-and-dried technical activity devoid of the human touches of empathy and emotion. Although systematic, scientifically validated techniques are applied for the purpose of maximizing student learning and social adjustment, management techniques are delivered through a series of interpersonal exchanges between teacher and students. Close examination of these exchanges reveals that several intangible (difficult to operationalize) behaviors, personal qualities, and attitudes are essential prerequisites for the teacher in successfully managing students with mild to moderate disabilities.

Respect for Students. Successful classroom managers generally like their students and respect them as individuals (Good & Brophy, 1987). Demonstrations of this affection and respect, however, need not be presented in a superficial or overly dramatic fashion. Genuine concern for the welfare of each student is demonstrated through (1) regular private interactions that exude warmth and a desire for knowing students individually, (2) facial gestures and body language that indicate acceptance and respect, (3) a vocal tone that shows patience and understanding, and (4) the use of enthusiasm and humor to ease tension in anxiety-filled situations. Even in the face of frequent misbehavior, effective classroom managers make it clear that students are differentiated from their behaviors. Students are shown that they are valued even when their instances of inappropriate behaviors are not given approval.

Appropriate Expectations. Researchers investigating teachers' expectations of their students have found that students tend to live up to the expectations their teachers have for them. The professional literature is replete with examples of how such negative self-fulfilling prophecies influence academic performance. Similarly, negative expectations can have a direct influence on rates of student misbehavior. Students considered to be behavioral problems are more likely to act out if expectations regarding the continuation of these types of behaviors are communicated with strength and consistency. In many instances, identified problem students have little incentive to change their behavioral patterns and typically conform to the negative expectations presented by significant others in their environment.

In several implicit and explicit ways, developing and beginning teachers can communicate positive expectations of behavior. First, similar to academic programming, reasonable goals related to how students should behave must be developed. This entails knowing what behaviors are expected of students during school and class activities. Second, expectations must be communicated to students in a no-nonsense, straightforward fashion. This communication can take several forms, including (1) the formulation of positively stated classroom rules, (2) the design of an overall classroom management system in which all students are treated equally, and (3) the delivery of consistent consequences for both compliance and noncompliance to the components of the management system. Furthermore, teachers need to convey that a student's acting-out history or "teachers' lounge hearsay" has nothing to do with how consequences will be applied under the current management system. Each student should be made aware that his or her current behavior is evaluated in relation to current standards, rather than to past years' rule infractions or subjective behind-the-scenes gossip.

Credibility, Dependability, and Assertiveness. Effective classroom managers are models of appropriate behaviors. They practice what they preach and can be counted on to be consistent and reliable in the enforcement of classroom rules and procedures. Teachers' credibility is established when (1) instances of their verbal behavior coincide with their instrumental behavior and (2) they respect and adhere consistently to their daily responsibilities within the classroom. Once correspondence between words and actions is established, students will come to depend on teachers' verbal intentions and will test limits less frequently. Credibility and dependability will not develop, however, if a teacher chats sociably with other teachers during planned activities, makes empty threats, or enforces rules selectively rather than consistently (Good & Brophy, 1987).

Effective classroom management, like effective teaching, requires that a teacher convey strong leadership qualities. This does not mean that classes of students with mild to moderate disabilities need to be taught by power-hungry, harsh, or "in your face" dictatorial men and women. Strong leaders convey authority with subtlety, tact, and diplomacy, rather than through intimidation and intrusiveness. Developing and beginning teachers can convey a strong leadership presence by (1) using clear, calm, controlled, and defined statements when requesting student compliance; (2) being self-assured, confident, and consistent when delivering the consequences of a student's misbehavior; (3) not arguing with students; and most important (4) conveying to students that any problems and concerns that may arise will be addressed in an empathic and constructive manner (Weber & Roff, 1983; Westling & Koorland, 1988).

Withitness. **Withitness** refers to a teacher's ability to be aware of students' actions and a proficiency in communicating that awareness to students (Kounin, 1970). Teachers possessing withitness position themselves so that they can readily monitor the multitude of events occurring in their classrooms. They seem to have a sixth sense or "eyes in the back of their heads" and can deal successfully with more than one matter at a time. The heightened sensitivity to the events in a classroom allows a "with it" teacher to prevent disruptions before they grow into serious management problems.

*P*ause and Reflect 8.2

It is relatively easy to say that we as teachers respect students or have high expectations for their continued growth and achievement. It is much more difficult to actually *demonstrate* that we hold these beliefs. How can teachers actually demonstrate to their students that they hold them in high regard and believe that they can have continued success in the school environment? Be sure that these are tangible things that students will be able to recognize.

Although withitness, per se, cannot be directly taught in methods courses, beginning and developing special education teachers can enhance their development of this important skill by (1) arranging their classrooms to allow for easy observations of all instructional activities, (2) regularly monitoring their classrooms, (3) responding to those small events and minor disruptions that often precede major behavioral problems, (4) attempting to handle multiple classroom situations simultaneously, and (5) communicating to students an awareness of what is going on in and around the classroom.

Preparation

A sure way to promote disruption among students is to be unprepared for lessons or activities. Most students, particularly those with mild disabilities, are likely to act out if they are not engaged in purposeful activities. Moreover, teachers who appear unprepared for the day's events present a poor model for their students. Lack of readiness on the part of a teacher signals to students that planned classroom activities are not valued and that preparation for academic work is unimportant. Not surprisingly, teachers who are consistently unprepared for lessons have difficulties motivating and managing their students.

Thorough preparation is a difficult, time-consuming task, particularly for developing and beginning teachers. Nonetheless, time spent in preparation saves both time and anguish in the long run: Prepared teachers spend less time dealing with student behavior problems. Effective classroom managers prepare for their lessons and know how to keep their students on-task with productive and educationally relevant work. Prepared teachers (1) have well-developed and organized lesson plans, (2) start lessons promptly and keep to a consistent schedule, (3) have student assignments ready for distribution and board work prepared prior to the scheduled start of the lesson, (4) keep the materials necessary for a planned activity close at hand, and (5) take care of grading and record-keeping responsibilities promptly and efficiently. Teachers highlight the importance of class activities by preparing for them and by not wasting lesson time on clerical or organizational tasks.

Physical Environment

As discussed in Chapter 3, the physical design of the classroom environment can influence students' academic and social behavior. It is especially important to consider the relationships between physical environmental variables and behaviors of students with mild to moderate disabling conditions. Such students are easily influenced by events that are often regarded as merely neutral in most learning situations. Teachers of highly distractible students, for example, often find it essential to arrange group lesson tables in such a way that students' lines of vision are narrowly focused in the direction of a chalkboard. As a general rule, the proper arrangement of the classroom can assist teachers in managing their students by preventing student discomfort, decreasing opportunities for disruptive behavior, increasing levels of task-oriented behavior, and facilitating the quality and quantity of social interactions among students (Paine, Radicci, Rossellini, Deutchman, & Darch, 1983). What follows is a brief description of what teachers should consider when arranging the physical environment to prevent inappropriate behavior.

Ensure Student and Teacher Safety and Comfort. Students, particularly those with a low tolerance for frustration, may act out if they perceive a threat to their safety or experience physical discomfort. Teachers also affected by the physical conditions of a school or classroom may overreact to student behaviors if faced with persistent discomfort. The physical comfort of individuals in classrooms depends on such factors as lighting, temperature, ventilation, and noise level. Smith, Neisworth, and Greer (1978) recommend that, to ensure physical comfort in learning environments, (1) lighting be warm, free from glare, and at least 100A-candles where reading and other visual tasks are required; (2) room temperature be controlled to fall within a moderate range (68-74°F) with adequate humidity; (3) circulated fresh air be available at all times; and (4) noise levels of classrooms be controlled so that the ongoing activities of one room do not disturb others.

Provide Security in and Around School. It is often said that events that occur in schools are a direct reflection of happenings in society at large. In the case of crime and the fear and anxiety associated with such violations, this is an unfortunate reality. Many students possess legitimate fears about attending certain schools. To many students, schools are not places of learning, but rather are places where they must contend with repeated threats to their safety, property, and psychological well-being. Obviously, the fear of injury or loss of property can deleteriously influence students' behaviors in the classroom. Safe learning environments are possible, however, if school administrators, teachers, parents, and students work together to promote a security-conscious philosophy.

Developing and beginning teachers can do their part by (1) following duty assignments related to monitoring student entry, movement in, and exit from school; (2) ensuring that parents are made aware of safe avenues for students to travel to and from school; (3) closely monitoring students during recess activities and reporting any strangers who may be loitering either in or around the building; (4) securing school's, teachers', and students' valuables and reporting instances of theft, vandalism, and property destruction; and (5) delivering immediate and potent consequences to those students who break the rules. Most important, however, teachers should educate students to be security conscious both inside and outside school. Furthermore, specific school and class policies regarding security should be developed and transmitted to students, parents, and the community.

Arrange Furniture to Minimize Disruptions. Classroom furnishings should be safe, comfortable, durable, and age- and size-appropriate for students in the class. Available classroom space should be organized to promote prosocial behavior and to facilitate academic achievement. In Chapter 3, several effective classroom configurations were presented, along with specific guidelines for the placement of furniture for students with mild to moderate disabilities. Important design considerations include (1) provisions for both public and private student work spaces, (2) the availability of a convenient and unobstructed view of the entire classroom, and (3) easy access to instructional materials.

Teachers of students with greater tendencies toward overactivity, distractibility, and aggression should also attend to traffic patterns within their classrooms. First, students' desks should be spaced adequately, ensuring that each student can work independently without disturbing others. Second, access to high-action or -activity areas (e.g., the work "in-box," the pencil sharpener) should be designed to facilitate an easy flow of traffic. Paths to such areas should be away from major group and independent work centers, and teachers should try to limit the number of students moving to such areas at the same time. Movements within and between activities should be smooth, with little loss of positive momentum. Most important, the major high-traffic areas should be located in different quadrants of the room to limit the oversaturation of one part of the room and allow for the maximum use of available space.

Keep Classrooms Neat and Trim. There are four good reasons for keeping learning environments neat and picked up. First, by taking care of and storing instructional materials in their assigned containers or areas, preparation time for lessons can be minimized. Students and teachers can begin their tasks with little need for frustrating "search" activities. Second, unsupervised high-interest materials can sway student attention from an assigned task. By storing materials, teachers limit these potential distractors that often start instances of misbehavior. Third, the storage of personal belongings prevents minor and nagging disturbances involving lost and stolen possessions. By providing adequate and secure storage of personal belongings, conflicts involving personal property losses can be minimized. Finally, students with mild to moderate disabilities tend to be unusually hard on both the hardware and consumable supplies of their classrooms. Highlighting and modeling procedures that promote respect for property can result in students demonstrating increased levels of care with instructional materials.

DEVELOPING RULES, PROCEDURES, AND BEHAVIORAL SUPPORTS

Rules and procedures allow teachers to communicate the behavioral standards and expectations of the classroom environment to their students. **Rules** identify, define, and operationalize a teacher's specific conceptualization of acceptable behavior; **procedures** delineate the steps necessary for the successful and appropriate completion of an activity, task, or operation. Concise and unambiguous rules and procedures serve as discriminative stimuli for appropriate classroom behavior. When planned and implemented correctly, both rules and procedures can guide, motivate, and remind students to adhere to stated standards. The research literature is clear in its support of the use of rules and procedures: Teachers who establish reasonable, definable, and clearly understood rules are effective classroom managers (Smith & Rivera, 1995; Weber & Roff, 1983).

As was discussed in more detail in Chapter 3, rules and procedures need to be introduced correctly and adequately maintained throughout the school year. In regard to introducing rules and procedures, developing and beginning teachers should (1) identify the specific behaviors and procedures expected of students, (2) discuss and teach rules and procedures beginning on the first day of school, (3) present students with a solid rationale for the rules and procedures, (4) involve students in the formulation and development of these classroom standards, (5) phrase rules and procedures positively rather than negatively, and (6) keep the number of rules and procedures to a minimum.

By following several guidelines, the strength and integrity of agreed-on rules and procedures will be maintained. First, rules and procedures should be posted in areas visible to students. Second, rules and procedures should be taught and practiced throughout the school year. Like any skill or concept, rules and procedures need to be taught in a complete and systematic fashion. Lessons should be designed that contain relevant exemplars, role-playing demonstrations, and opportunities for guided and independent practice. Brief reviews of lesson-specific rules can prompt students to adhere to the behavioral expectations specific to a particular activity. Third, teachers should model and demonstrate the correct way of adhering to school and classroom procedures at regular intervals throughout the school year. Finally, because the failure of many classroom-management systems stems from less than consistent adherence to and compliance with the management system, teachers should monitor their own performance on whether they follow the stated rules and procedures and provide consequences consistently. We further explore the development of effective consequences in the next section of this chapter.

It is also critical that positive behavioral supports be provided for students who have trouble complying with the rules. Rather than a change in the expectations for rule and procedural compliance, positive behavioral supports are proactive adjustments that assist a student in meeting success with a particular rule or procedural expectation. If a middle school student with an attentional problem repeatedly has difficulty getting to a particular class on time, the teacher can choose to make a proactive accommodation (a buddy-system, a self-monitoring plan) that will increase the probability that the student will have the expected level of success complying with the stated rule or procedure. Figure 8.2 provides a format for the development of school and classroom rules,

Rules Development Worksheet

General Case Rule	Meaning of Rule in My Class	Teaching the Rule	Available Supports
The students will be prepared for class.	The students will be in their seat at the ringing of the bell with books, writing tools, drill, and homework.	• Role playing "The Prepared Student" • Display prepared materials	• Have pencils available for borrowing • Praise to those who are prepared. • Provide visual and verbal reminders. • Checklist of supplies needed to be prepared.

FIGURE 8.2   Rules Development Worksheet

as well as positive behavioral supports. The format provides a place for the general case of a schoolwide rule, what the rule means in each teacher's individual classroom, how the teacher will teach the rule to students, and what supports are available for promoting rule compliance. Figure 8.3 provides a listing of support strategies adapted from the work of Topper, Williams, Leo, Hamilton, and Fox (1994) that can be used to prevent the occurrence of troubling behaviors.

Increase Students' Control and Choices

- Ask students what they need to have a better experience at school.
- Include students in planning and problem solving.
- Increase the number, variety, and importance of the decisions that students make.
- Support students having flexibility in their daily schedules.
- Grant students legitimate power—involve students in leadership roles.
- Support students to transition to the next class/activity at a different time.
- Add interesting activities and experiences matched to students' individual needs.
- Support students to self-evaluate their work.
- Support students to leave class when needed.
- Support students to choose testing methods.
- Develop assignments that emphasize students' strengths and talents.

FIGURE 8.3   Support Strategies for Preventing Problem Behavior

Increase Opportunities for Positive Attention

- Assign students to teacher advisor/mentors.
- Increase the number of friends or allies who know and spend time with students.
- Engage family, friends, faculty, students in supporting the students.
- Identify an adult mentor within the community.
- Increase the number of community activities to which students have access to.
- Support students to join after-school groups/clubs/teams.
- Use teaching assistants to help all students in the class, rather than an assistant paired directly with one student.
- Speak and react to students in ways that model respect and friendship.
- Develop a peer buddy system for students.

Increase Students' Status, Self-Esteem, Image

- Support students to be peer mentors/tutors.
- Support student involvement in community service activities.
- Give students assignments that will "guarantee" success.
- Add prosocial skills to students' curricula.
- Give students high-status classroom/school jobs/roles.
- Increase the amount of time that students spend in roles that offer the best opportunities to express their natural abilities or strong interests (e.g., drawing, music, drama, pottery, sports, reading, math).

Match Expected Responses/Testing Methods to Student Strengths

- Support students in communicating ideas and demonstrating learning in a variety of ways (art, music, dance, poetry, oral presentations).
- Avoid requiring students to respond in ways that are likely to produce extreme stress or anxiety (e.g., reading aloud for a nonreader, essay exam for a poor writer).
- When anxiety-producing situations (e.g., oral presentation, final exams) cannot be avoided, provide additional support tailored to students' needs.
- Provide extra practice in nonthreatening, supportive situations.
- Read the test to students.
- Test students in private.
- Give students extra time.
- Break tests into short segments.

Physical Arrangement and Classroom Management

- Sit students in the classroom in a position that will best meet their needs (e.g., near the front of the classroom, near the teacher, near the door, near a window, near a supportive peer, away from unsupportive peers).
- Arrange the classroom to prevent problems from occurring, facilitate cooperative interactions, and the sharing of materials and ideas between students and adults.
- Support students to leave the classroom (e.g., on a mission to the office, to run an errand, to go to the guidance counselor) when anxious, angry, or fearful.
- Limit student access to peers or adults who tend to set them off.
- Model appropriate ways of interacting with students for peers and other adults.
- Make sure all materials are handy and set up in advance.

Adapted from Topper, K., Williams, W., Leo, K., Hamilton, R., & Fox, T. (1994). *A positive approach to understanding and addressing challenging behavior.* Burlington: University of Vermont.

TAKING ACTION: RESPONDING TO STUDENT MISBEHAVIOR

When we speak of **taking action,** we are referring to those preplanned initial responses to student behavior. These responses include (1) surface management of minor annoyances, (2) conducting a functional behavioral assessment, (3) consequences for rule and procedure compliance and noncompliance, and (4) crisis management.

Surface Management Techniques

Surface management techniques (Long & Newman, 1965) are commonsense "stop-gap" methods for dealing with minor instances of troubling behaviors. Most teachers use some surface techniques intuitively. For example, it is not unusual to see effective classroom managers using the technique of *proximity control,* moving close to a student who may be approaching a level of frustration to preempt a blowup.

One of the most frequently used surface management techniques is **planned ignoring.** Similar to the behavioral technique of *extinction,* planned ignoring is the conscious attempt to not feed into the child's need for immediate gratification; this technique works best for minor behaviors that are likely to fade away if they are not reinforced. **Signal interference** is the use of nonverbal gestures, eye contact, noises, and body postures that a teacher uses to communicate to students that their behaviors are inappropriate; these actions signal to students that their behavior needs to change. **Proximity control** is when the adult uses his or her close presence as a deterrent to troublesome behavior. Because a teacher is typically regarded as a source of protection, strength, authority, and identification, students will tend to stop their impulsive actions without the need for any type of verbal cue or prompt. As observed by Long and Newman (1965), the three techniques of planned ignoring, signal interference, and proximity control are positive alternatives for dealing with troubling behaviors because they do not embarrass or even identify the student who is misbehaving but still have the potency to get the student back into the flow of the lesson.

Interest boosting is a direct intervention to reenergize a student's interest in the assigned activity. If a student's attention to an activity is diminishing, it is often helpful for an adult to demonstrate some genuine interest in the assignment. This interest can be operationalized by asking how challenging the assignment is or by indicating one's own personal interest in the content areas being explored. **Tension decontamination through humor** is the diplomatic use of humor to reduce a tense or anxiety-filled situation. In most situations, this tactic should be in the form of teacher-based "self-deprecating" comments and should not be done at the expense of one or two vulnerable students. As with the use of humor in public-speaking situations, a good rule to follow here is "When in doubt, don't!" Finally, **antiseptic bouncing** is a technique used to safely remove a student from a potentially serious behavioral event in a nonpunitive fashion. Some students just need some time away from the situation if they are to regain control over themselves. With antiseptic bouncing, the teacher can ask the particular student to deliver a message, wash up, or complete a task that requires movement to another part of the school. This intervention is characterized as "antiseptic" because the intent is to redirect the behavior, rather than to provide a negative consequence. Developing and beginning teachers should be cautioned that the overuse of this technique can be quite detrimental: With too much "bouncing," students will see that they can get out of their responsibilities by merely acting up.

These are just a sampling of the more common surface management techniques used by successful veteran teachers. For a more complete discussion, readers are urged to review the classic work by Long and Newman (1965). These techniques are by no means a substitute for a well-designed, comprehensive management program; they do, however, assist in getting students back in the flow of the classroom with minimal intrusiveness.

P ause and Reflect 8.3

Refer to the brief descriptions of the surface management techniques provided in the text and reflect on how you have either observed or used these techniques. For each of the techniques listed below, specify the type of behavior to which it was applied. Also evaluate the effectiveness of each technique in managing the presenting behavior.

Technique	Type of Behavior	Efficacy
Planned ignoring		
Signal interference		
Proximity control		
Interest boosting		
Tension decontamination through humor		
Antiseptic bouncing		

Conducting a Functional Behavioral Assessment

IDEA 97 calls for schools to implement specific disciplinary procedures when working with students who are identified or suspected of having disabilities and who exhibit significant behavior problems. A major component of these provisions is to conduct **functional behavioral assessments (FBA)** and to implement behavioral support plans. According to the Center for Effective Collaboration and Practice (1998), the logic behind FBAs is that most behavior occurs within a particular context and serves a specific purpose. As with most of us, students with behavior problems behave in ways that satisfy a need or result in a desired, purposeful outcome. In most cases the desired outcomes are not inappropriate; it is the ways of getting to those goals and outcomes that are typically problematic. Changes in behavior will only occur when it is clear that a different pattern of behavior will result in the desired outcome. FBA is a problem-solving process that helps to identify the purposes of individual student behavior patterns and allows for the introduction of alternative and appropriate ways for students to attain their goals. In general, students engage in problem behavior for one of two reasons: to get something (e.g., attention, tangible object, etc.) or to avoid something such as a difficult task or an embarrassing situation (Lewis & Sugai, 1999).

To conduct an FBA one first reviews information from a variety of sources, including questionnaires, structured interviews, and most importantly, direct observations of a student in various settings. Forms that can assist in the collection of these information sources are readily accessible in easy-to-use formats from a number of print sources (e.g.,

---

Box 8.2   **10 Steps for Conducting a Functional Behavioral Assessment**

To complete a useful functional assessment it is necessary to identify the challenging behavior and to gather information that will allow for a determination of the probable purposes of the behavior. McConnell et al. (1998) have recommended that the following 10 steps be used in conducting the FBA.

Step   1: Identify the student's behavior.

Step   2: Describe the problem behavior.

Step   3: Collect baseline data.

Step   4: Describe environmental and setting demands.

Step   5: Complete a functional assessment interview form.

Step   6: Develop a hypothesis.

Step   7: Write a behavioral intervention plan.

Step   8: Implement the plan.

Step   9: Collect data.

Step 10: Follow up and evaluate.

Demchak & Bossert, 1996; McConnell, Hilvitz, & Cox, 1998; O'Neill et al., 1997) and Web-based resources funded by the U.S. Department of Education (see Point and Click section for specific sites). Once the data are collected, hypotheses regarding the context and possible purposes of the misbehavior are generated. These hypotheses are testable propositions as to why the problem is occurring and include descriptions of antecedent and/or consequent events associated with the behavior. Finally, a behavior intervention plan is designed that can include either one or all of the following strategies: (1) antecedent and setting event modifications (see Figure 8.3), (2) consequence interventions, or (3) the teaching of alternative or replacement behaviors, problem-solving, and self-control procedures (Bambara & Knoster, 1998). McConnell et al. have outlined 10 steps that educators can use to conduct a functional assessment. These steps are listed and explained in Box 8.2.

Development of Consequences

The development of consequences is an essential component of successful management programs. Three important skills are needed for the development of effective consequences: creativity, the ability to provide recognition for rule compliance, and the ability to see the logical extension of rule violations (Curwin & Mendler, 1988; Rosenberg & Jackman, 1997). In short, good consequences (1) are clear and specific, (2) are not always punishments, (3) are natural and related directly to the rule, (4) preserve the student's dignity, (5) increase the student's motivation, and (6) promote an internal locus of control within students.

Thinking of effective consequences can be problematic, however, for developing and beginning teachers. Fortunately, four generic consequences can be effective for any rule. According to Curwin and Mendler (1988) these are (1) a reminder of the rule, (2) a warning, (3) developing an action plan for improving behavior, and (4) practicing appropriate behavior. Still, it takes considerable skill and practice to develop effective consequences that are not aversive. Strategies to assist developing and beginning teachers in creating good consequences are found in Table 8.1.

In providing recognition for rule compliance—consequences for appropriate behavior—many large-group or whole—class alternatives are available. Three such procedures—token economies, class contingencies, and level systems—are described below.

TABLE 8.1 **Creating Effective Consequences: Five Strategies for Developing and Beginning Teachers in Special Education Settings**

Strategy	Putting It to Practice
Reread and visualize the classroom rule	Close your eyes and imagine a student breaking a rule; consider the possible scenarios resulting from the various natural consequences.
Collect effective consequences	Observe master teachers. Ask them how they respond to specific instances of rule breaking.
Ask the students	Early in the school year, have students provide input as to what they believe would be effective consequences. At the end of the year, ask students to comment on the effectiveness of each consequence.
Ask parents	At IEP meetings or parent conferences, ask parents what consequences have been effective at home.
Ask yourself	Remember your own days as a student and consider what consequences helped you (1) stop misbehaving, (2) learn from the experience, (3) cooperate, and (4) not feel embarrassed, angry, or resentful.

Adapted from Curwin, R. L., & Mendler, A. N. (1988). *Discipline with dignity.* Alexandria, VA: Association for Supervision and Curriculum Development.

Token Economies. A system that employs tokens is referred to as a **token economy.** In such a system, tokens function in ways very similar to currency in the national economy. Tokens are used to purchase available backup reinforcers, which can include treats, trinkets, activities, and privileges. Token economies have been implemented in special education, remedial, and general classroom environments and have been successful in changing a variety of inappropriate classroom behaviors. Token systems have also been successful in improving academic performance and in raising standardized test scores.

Unfortunately, it is beyond the scope of this chapter to provide all the specifics necessary to design and implement a successful whole-class token economy. It would be useful, however, to review several general guidelines prepared by Slavin (1986).

First, the specific behaviors that will be targeted for reinforcement need to be determined and articulated clearly. In general, these targeted behaviors should be similar in content to the stated rules, procedures, and behavioral standards of the classroom.

Second, a logistically appropriate point system must be developed. A range of alternative schedules for the systematic delivery of points is available. In some environments, teachers can wait until the end of an instructional period before awarding earned points; in other settings, the behavioral characteristics of students require that points be awarded more frequently. Similarly, there are alternatives for the recording of points. In some instances, students are able to keep track of their own points, whereas in others, record keeping must be the responsibility of the teacher.

Third, a selection of backup reinforcers must be developed. Each selection should be assigned a price, with many items being small enough that a student can earn a tangible backup in one day. A number of highly desirable big awards should require the saving of points over time.

Fourth, a response cost system that deducts points for specific instances of misbehavior should be considered. Although such a system is not necessary for routine and minor instances of misbehavior, it could be very effective in reducing instances of disruptive and aggressive behaviors.

Finally, plans must be made for the eventual fading of the extrinsic controls. The outcome of a behavior modification program is considered successful only when appropriate behaviors occur without artificial points and nonnormative backup reinforcers.

Class Contingencies. Although they are less systematic than token economies, class contingencies can be used to promote and maintain appropriate classroom behavior. In **class contingency** situations, the entire class receives consequences based on the behavior of its group members. Several types of informal, whole-class contingencies can be used. For example, the teacher can put marbles, chips, or paper clips into a canister whenever he or she catches students engaging in a targeted appropriate behavior or remove one of the objects if a rule is violated (Mastropieri & Scruggs, 1987). When the receptacle is filled, the whole class could share in a group reward, such as a party or field trip. In a second type of whole-class program, an individual disruptive student could be made responsible for the earning of reinforcers for the entire class of students on the basis of his or her performance alone (Kazdin, 1975). In such an instance, all members of the class would share in the benefits when one troublesome student behaves appropriately.

The Good Behavior Game, originally formulated by Barrish, Saunders, and Wolf (1969), is a formal group contingency program that has a long history of reducing disruptive behaviors. The game is implemented in four steps.

1. The classroom rules are stated, and the class is divided into two teams.

2. The teacher awards negative marks whenever any member of a team engages in a prespecified inappropriate behavior.

3. The team with the lowest number of marks is declared winner for the day and is given some form of reinforcement.

4. The losing team is required to do some extra work and/or forfeit a privilege.

It is generally believed that group contingencies work because group members encourage one another to do the things required to earn the reward. Overenthusiastic encouragement can, in some cases, get out of hand. Developing and beginning teachers who employ group contingencies should ensure that peers do not use coercive or threatening means to pressure others into behaving appropriately.

Level Systems. A **level system** is a group management alternative that accommodates the differing entry-level behavioral skills of students within a learning environment. The system is an organizational framework within which varying intensities of management alternatives are applied. At each level of a particular system, specific expectations and corresponding privileges can be earned for meeting the expectations. Students' points of entry into a system and their progress through the levels depends on the intensity of their presenting problems, as well as on progress through the various levels of the system (Bauer, Shea, & Keppler, 1986). The system shapes student behavior gradually by providing opportunities for movement through varying intensities of expectations and management alternatives. The ultimate goal of most level systems is self-management.

Level systems are flexible and can be applied in resource, self-contained, day-school, and residential settings (e.g., see Braaten, 1979; Mastropieri, Jenne, & Scruggs, 1988). Developing and beginning teachers can employ these systems with both elementary and secondary students. Bauer et al. (1986) have provided guidelines for the planning and implementation of levels systems (Box 8.3).

Crisis Management

Crisis is one of those terms that is often used yet difficult to define. We can all relate to how we have felt—physically, emotionally, and cognitively—when we have been in what we describe as crisis situations. Although signs and symptoms vary across indi-

| **B**ox 8.3 | Guidelines for the Planning and Implementation of Levels Systems |

Step 1: Determine the entry-level behaviors of the students with whom the system is to be applied.

Step 2: Determine the terminal behavioral expectations for the students.

Step 3: Formulate at least two but no more than four sets of behavioral expectations that seem to be appropriately graded steps between those expectations described in steps 1 and 2. Label each of the steps level 1 through level "x".

Step 4: Consider the inclusion of a transition level. This would allow for part-time placement at a higher level for a portion of the school day.

Step 5: Determine the privileges appropriate for students at level 1 and for students ready to terminate the program.

Step 6: For each of the levels developed in step 3, list corresponding privileges that would be appropriate. Ensure an equal distribution among the levels and remember to reduce the amount of direct supervision as students progress through the levels.

Step 7: Consider the following logistical concerns:

a. How, when, and at what frequency will a student's level status be reviewed?

b. Who will review a student's status?

c. How will self-monitoring procedures be implemented?

Step 8: Determine how to facilitate communication among the many individuals (e.g., parents, administrators, related service personnel) involved in the student's education in the levels system.

Source: Bauer, A. M., Shea, T. M., & Keppler, R. (1986). Levels systems: A framework for the individualization of behavior management. *Behavioral Disorders, 12,* 28–35. Reprinted with permission.

viduals, typical descriptions of crisis responses from adults include (1) physical signs and symptoms such as headaches, rapid breathing, muscle tension, and nausea; (2) emotional responses such as tension, depression, extreme anxiety, and panic; and (3) behavioral indicators such as a withdrawal from regular activities and an inability to attend or concentrate. Although most events that precipitate a crisis are beyond the control of school personnel, it is critical that educators be aware of what a child is experiencing when he or she is in crisis, what specific steps can minimize crisis responses, and how to manage such situations when they occur.

The physical and emotional by-products of a crisis situation are not pleasant. In many cases, the student in crisis has little or no control over his or her behavior. Therefore, the delivery of consequences for misbehavior or noncompliance to rules or procedures will have little or no effect. Steps must be taken to help the student though the crisis situation in a nonthreatening and nonpunitive fashion. Formal crisis intervention is an involved process that requires considerable efforts from trained counselors, psychologists, and crisis personnel. Nonetheless, developing and beginning teachers should be prepared with a fixed set of steps or procedures in the event that a crisis situation emerges in their classroom. Figure 8.4 lists several steps adapted from Alpert (1989) for defusing crisis situations. However, all personnel should develop a mechanism to access psychological support personnel when necessary. For example, some schools have a code system that signals crisis personnel to report to areas of the school where a crisis is believed to be occurring.

FIGURE 8.4 Steps for Avoiding and Defusing Crisis Situations

Adapted from Alpert, L. (1989). *A teacher's guide to cooperative discipline: How to manage your classroom and promote self-esteem.* Circle Pines, MN: American Guidance Service.

Focus on Behavior, Not the Student.
- Describe, rather than evaluate, the presenting behavior.
- Deal in the present, not the past.
- Be firm, direct, and professional.

Take Charge of Emotions.
- Be in control of your own emotions and actions.
- Respond reasonably, rather than react impulsively, to student verbalizations and actions.
- Provide for a negative release or venting of student emotions.

Exercise Caution and Avoid Escalating the Situation.
- Be aware of your own body language.
- Avoid unsubstantiated accusations, hearsay, and generalizations.
- Do not back a student into a corner.
- Model appropriate "resolution" behaviors.

Make Plans to Discuss the Crisis Fully at a Later Time.
- Stress that people respond more rationally when they are calm.
- Stress the need to actually "hear" each other's points.

*P*ause and Reflect 8.4

Develop a crisis plan for your setting. In your plan, be sure to identify how you can be reasonably confident that a student is in crisis and the steps that you will take to secure assistance and to manage the crisis. How can you ensure that the crisis will be handled in a nonpunitive fashion?

RESOLVING STUDENT MISBEHAVIOR

Although the key to successful classroom management is prevention and action, many students, particularly those with mild to moderate disabilities, present problem behaviors that necessitate thoughtful and effective interventions for problem resolution. In this section, we review techniques that can be employed to intervene when students engage in problematic behaviors. First, we describe generic strategies for influencing students' inappropriate behaviors. Then, we discuss specific individual and group management alternatives.

Generic Behavioral Strategies

In most cases, interventions that are successful in managing and remediating student misbehavior involve both the strengthening and reducing of different behaviors. Management programs designed to reduce or eliminate problem behaviors alone may be ineffectual because they do not directly teach or strengthen appropriate behaviors. Because a student may not be aware of, or proficient enough in, a correct mode of functioning in the classroom, the reduction or elimination of one series of problematic behaviors may lead to a situation in which other negative behaviors replace the initial problem behaviors. Clearly, dynamic management interventions are needed that simultaneously strengthen and weaken specific student target behaviors. Although techniques that increase and decrease student behavior are presented separately, it is critical that they be applied in a logical and dynamic fashion.

Increasing Behavior. When we speak of **increasing behavior,** we are referring to the process of reinforcement. **Positive reinforcement** occurs when the contingent presentation of a positive environmental consequence results in corresponding increases in the frequency or intensity of a target behavior. **Negative reinforcement,** sometimes confused with punishment, occurs when the contingent removal of an unpleasant or aversive event results directly in the increased frequency of a targeted behavior. Whether positive or negative, **reinforcement,** by definition, always refers to an increase in a behavior's frequency or intensity. Therefore, praise, tokens, and free activity time will not always function as reinforcement. To be a reinforcer, an item, event, or activity must increase the strength or intensity of a behavior. For new and developing teachers, this functional definition of reinforcement highlights the need to identify potential items and events that have the greatest likelihood of increasing an individual student's appropriate behaviors.

According to Kazdin (1975), the effectiveness of reinforcement depends on several major factors: (1) the delay between the performance of a behavior and the delivery of a potential reinforcer, (2) the magnitude of a reinforcer, (3) the quality of a reinforcer, and (4) the schedule for reinforcer delivery. In delivering positive reinforcers, developing and beginning teachers should ensure that reinforcers are delivered in close proximity to the target behavior. If the delivery of a reinforcer does not closely follow the target behavior, the risk is that behaviors other than the target behavior will be reinforced inadvertently. The magnitude, or amount, of reinforcement also influences the level of change in a target behavior. Quite simply, the greater the amount of a reinforcer delivered for the presentation of a behavior, the more frequent that response will be on future occasions. This relationship between amount of reinforcement and behavioral intensity is limited, however. Too much reinforcement can easily lead to **satiation,** a condition whereby reinforcers lose their potency. Teachers can combat satiation by using a variety of potential reinforcers in their classroom settings.

When we speak of **reinforcement quality,** we are referring to a student's reinforcer preference. In general, students will work with greater intensity if their efforts are recognized with items, behaviors, or events they value. Developing and beginning teachers can determine students' reinforcer preferences through direct observation or by administering a reinforcer preference survey. A complete listing of items that may be included on a preference survey are found in Box 8.4.

Schedule of reinforcement refers to a specific arrangement by which reinforcers are delivered. **Continuous reinforcement** is an arrangement in which reinforcers are delivered after each instance of a target behavior. When reinforcement is delivered after only some instances of a target behavior, the schedule is considered to be **intermittent reinforcement.** The nature of classroom events necessitates the use of intermittent reinforcement schedules because they reduce the risk of reinforcer satiation and promote long-term behavioral maintenance.

The most common types of intermittent reinforcement schedules are *fixed-interval (FI), variable-interval (VI), fixed-ratio (FR), and variable-ratio (VR)*. On FI schedules, reinforcers are delivered at prearranged, unvarying intervals of time. On VI schedules, reinforcers are delivered at prearranged, varying intervals that average a certain number of minutes. On a VI:15 schedule, for example, an average of 15 minutes would pass prior to the delivery of a reinforcer. For any given occasion, the interval would be more or less than the specific 15-minute interval. An FR schedule delineates the precise number of behaviors a person must perform to receive a reinforcer. In an FR:20 schedule, a student would earn a certain number of minutes on the computer for every 20 problems completed during a seatwork activity. With the VR schedule, the number of responses necessary to receive reinforcement would vary from occasion to occasion and reflect an average number of responses desired of the student.

Alternative procedures for increasing students' levels of appropriate behaviors are as diverse as the contingent delivery of edibles and the contingent awarding of tokens or

---

B ox 8.4 **Possible Items for a Reinforcer Preference Survey**

Job reinforcers

- Handing out paper, pencils, and so on
- Taking a note to the office
- Erasing the chalkboard
- Helping the teacher with a project
- Managing the class store
- Helping in the cafeteria
- Assisting the custodian
- Distributing and arranging reinforcers
- Watering the plants
- Running the copy machine
- Stapling papers together
- Feeding the fish or other animals
- Giving a message over the intercom
- Taking the class roll
- Serving as secretary for class meetings
- Raising or lowering the flag
- Carrying the wastebasket while other children clean out their desks
- Using the overhead projector
- Recording own behavior on a graph
- Teaching another child
- Helping the librarian
- Telling the teacher when it is time to go to lunch
- Sharpening the teacher's pencils
- Adjusting the window shades

Tangible Reinforcers Other Than Food

- Tickets to games or movies
- Personal grooming supplies
- Toys and games from the class store
- Colored chalk, pencils, or felt-tipped pens

Social Reinforcers

- Receiving verbal praise
- Having photograph displayed
- Getting personal time with the teacher, aide, counselor, or principal
- Having work and projects displayed
- Participating in show-and-tell
- Clapping and cheering by others when successful
- Being leader or organizer of an event
- Getting a hug, handshake, or pat on the back
- Sitting next to the teacher at lunch
- Playing with a classmate of choice
- Sitting and talking with a friend (adult or child)

Consumable Food Reinforcers

- Raisins
- Crackers
- Cookies
- Popcorn
- Potato chips

- Peanuts
- Gumdrops
- Jelly beans
- Small candies
- Juice
- Soda
- Ice cream
- Lollipops

Reinforcing Activities

- Reading books, magazines, and comic books
- Writing on the chalkboard with white or colored chalk
- Getting free time for self-selected projects
- Making things, such as kites, model cars, and airplanes
- Making bead jewelry
- Playing games (e.g., Monopoly)
- Doing puzzles
- Singing
- Finger painting
- Playing with puppets
- Drawing
- Reading with a friend
- Studying with a friend
- Tutoring younger children
- Eating lunch at a restaurant
- Decorating a designated area of the room in own style
- Taking field trips
- Going on outdoor walks
- Watching a movie
- Watching television
- Listening to music
- Doing a project of own interest
- Using the tape recorder or phonograph
- Getting extra recess
- Going home early
- Taking a class pet home for the weekend
- Going on a trip to a fair or museum
- Using a typewriter
- Doing "special," "the hardest," or "impossible" teacher-made arithmetic problems
- Reading the newspaper
- Reading or drawing a road map
- Listening to the radio with earplugs
- Going to the library
- Doing a science experiment
- Weighing or measuring various objects in the classroom

---

free activity time. Because students with mild to moderate disabilities have individual and often unique needs, it is important that teachers apply the procedures with the knowledge that outcomes will typically vary from student to student. Table 8.2 presents a summary of the more common procedures for increasing appropriate student behavior.

Decreasing Behavior. Students with mild to moderate disabilities present a number of problematic behaviors that need to be reduced or eliminated. Three types of procedures

TABLE 8.2   Procedures for Increasing Appropriate Behaviors

Type	Definition	Advantages	Disadvantages
Edible	A primary reinforcer. Potency varies as a function of deprivation and satiation.	Potency with students who possess severe handicaps. Useful in establishing reinforcing properties of other events (e.g., praise, smiles).	Delivery disrupts classroom functioning. Difficult to dispense in busy classroom settings. Need to be constantly aware of student allergies.
Praise and attention	Conditioned social reinforcers that can be delivered verbally and nonverbally (e.g., smiles, winks, physical contact).	Easily and quickly administered. Unobtrusive during classroom activities. Little preparation required.	Because the reinforcement value of praise and attention need to be learned, some individuals may not respond. Limited potency with inappropriate behaviors that have high secondary reinforcing properties (e.g., theft, substance abuse).
High-probability behaviors	The preferred activities of students can be used as reinforcers for low-probability behaviors. Using the knowledge of progress or results to reinforce a target behavior.	Schools have many desirable activities available. Powerful and cost free. Low probability of satiation.	Difficulty in delivering activity reinforcers immediately. Disruptions may occur during transitions between activities. Delivery mode tends to be all or none; little opportunity to portion out activities.
Performance feedback	Conditioned, generalized reinforcers whose strength is derived from items, activities, and desirable consequences they present.	Easily initiated in settings where performance criteria are explicitly stated. Low cost and motivating.	Effectiveness of feedback alone has been equivocal.
Tokens		Combat satiation in that a number of backups can be employed. Easily dispensed. Serve to bridge the period of time between the occurrence of a behavior and the delivery of a primary reinforcer. Allow for gradations of reinforcement.	Require effort in record keeping and other management activities. Fading of tokens often neglected.

exist for the systematic reduction of problematic behaviors: extinction, differential reinforcement, and punishment. **Extinction** is a process that decreases the strength and intensity of behavior by withholding reinforcement previously given to the behavior. The most common and productive application of extinction is the planned ignoring of minor inappropriate behaviors (e.g., the tapping of a pencil on a desk) that had been reinforced previously through teacher attention. High-intensity problematic behaviors such as tantrumming, fighting, and noncompliance require the use of stronger behavior-reduction techniques.

Inappropriate classroom behaviors can be reduced indirectly by the creative use of reinforcement contingencies. By employing **differential reinforcement of low rate of**

TABLE 8.3   Three Commonly Used Punishment Techniques

Type	Definition	Advantages	Disadvantages
Reprimand	A verbal statement or nonverbal gesture that expresses disapproval.	Easily applied with little or no preparation required. No physical discomfort to students.	Sometimes not effective. Can serve as positive reinforcement if this is a major source of attention.
Response cost	A formal system of penalties in which a reinforcer is removed, contingent upon the occurrence of an inappropriate behavior.	Easily applied with quick results. Does not disrupt class activities. No physical discomfort to students.	Not effective once student has "lost" all reinforcers. Can initially result in some students being more disruptive.
Time-out	Limited or complete loss of access to positive reinforcers for a set amount of time.	Fast acting and powerful. No physical discomfort to students.	Difficult to find secluded areas where students would not be reinforced inadvertently. May require physical assistance to the time-out area. Overuse can interfere with educational and prosocial efforts.

behaviors (DRL), teachers can reduce the frequency of a problem behavior by reinforcing a student for keeping the targeted problem at or below a particular level. Another technique, **differential reinforcement of other behavior (DRO),** involves the reinforcement of any behavior except the behavior to be reduced. To receive a reinforcer under a DRO schedule, the student must refrain completely from performing the behavior targeted for reduction. Thus, other behaviors are developed to replace the problematic behaviors being reduced or eliminated. The most stringent differential reinforcement technique is **differential reinforcement of appropriate behaviors incompatible with a targeted behavior (DRI).** The power of DRI is that students cannot engage in problematic behaviors if those behaviors are operating under contingencies to promote behaviors contradictory to the problem behavior. Because a behavior such as correctly completing seatwork cannot occur simultaneously with running around the classroom, the reinforcement of seatwork completion could result in the reduction of the room-running behavior.

Punishment, the manipulation and delivery of consequences designed to decrease the strength or intensity of a target behavior, typically takes one of two forms: (1) the presentation of an aversive consequence or (2) the removal of a previously earned reinforcer. Three common punishment techniques are reprimands, response cost, and time-out. These techniques are described in Table 8.3.

PROMOTING SELF-CONTROL AND PROBLEM SOLVING

Self-Control

The ultimate goal of any classroom management effort should be the development of student self-management. Students who are able to control their own behaviors independent of external agents in situations requiring delays in gratification, problem-solving skills, and conflict resolution are better prepared to meet complex societal demands. Self-control procedures allow students to assume a larger role in many aspects of their classroom behavioral management programs. According to Hallahan, Lloyd, and Stoller (1982), most self-control programs include three major components: self-assessment, self-recording, and self-determination of reinforcement. First, in **self-assessment,** a student examines his or her own behavior and decides whether a target behavior (or series of target behaviors) was performed. This is followed by **self-recording,** a process in which a student records objectively the results of the self-assessment. Finally, in the process of **self-determination** of reinforcement, a student determines the nature and amount of reinforcement he or she should receive for the performance of the target behavior.

Self-monitoring, a combination of self-assessment and self-recording, should be employed regularly by developing and beginning teachers. Its use increases the probability that maintenance of intervention efforts will occur. According to Hallahan et al. (1982), materials needed for a self-monitoring program include (1) a self-monitoring cuing tape, (2) a self-monitoring card, and (3) an assigned task that a student can work on while self-monitoring. The procedure is introduced by informing an individual (or small group of students) that it is important to keep track of the occurrence and nonoccurrence of a target behavior. The student is then introduced to the cuing tape, tape recorder, and self-monitoring card. Every time the student hears the tone of the cuing tape, he or she is to ask covertly, "Was I engaging in the target behavior?" and to mark the monitoring card appropriately. The procedures should be modeled and practiced initially to ensure that students can reliably differentiate between occurrence and nonoccurrence of the target behavior. Once the procedure succeeds in teaching students to monitor and record their own behavior, procedures designed to teach the self-determination of reinforcement can begin.

On reaching an acceptable level of performance, it will become necessary to wean the student from the external aspects of the procedure. Hallahan et al. (1982) recommend that the process begin by removing either the tape or the self-monitoring card. If student performance begins to deteriorate, however, there should be no hesitation to resume using the external prompts as part of a modified maintenance strategy.

Problem Solving

Many students possessing mild to moderate disabilities are deficient in their ability to solve interpersonal problems. The goals of problem-solving programs are to teach children (1) to be sensitive to interpersonal problems, (2) to develop the ability to generate alternative solutions to problems, and (3) that one person's behavior affects the behavior of others.

Successful problem solving consists of several components, each of which can be taught directly to students who exhibit inappropriate patterns of behavior. The following list of these components has been gleaned from several sources, including D'Zurilla and Goldfried (1971) and Spivack and Shure (1982). Suggestions on how to apply these components are also provided.

1. **Develop a general sensitivity or orientation to the problem.** Students need to be instructed and given the opportunity to practice recognizing that interpersonal problems exist. This can take the form of role playing or examination of case studies in which problems appear.

2. **Articulate the specifics of a problem.** Students need to practice identifying the specific troublesome aspects of problem situations. For example, this could involve task analysis of hypothetical conflict situations.

3. **Develop step-by-step procedures for solving the problem.** Students require models and practice opportunities in the ordering of events that could lead to a problem's solution. For example, case studies and hypothetical problem situations that require several steps for possible resolution can be practiced through role playing and group discussion activities.

4. **Generate a set of alternative strategies to approach a problem.** Using the ordered steps necessary for problem resolution, students must be able to generate alternative solutions to the presenting problem. Through brainstorming sessions, students should be encouraged to think of all types of possible strategies that could result in problem resolution. This component of the process should not be neglected; considerable evidence suggests that the capacity to generate alternative solutions to problems is positively related to increased problem-solving ability and social adjustment throughout the life span.

5. **Consider the consequences of each generated alternative.** Once the set of possible alternatives has been listed, students should be encouraged to identify the possible consequences for each. This task can be structured by having students relate what the worst and best scenarios could be for each. This is a critical step. It requires students to project beyond the presenting problem and to determine what might happen if a particular alternative is chosen.

6. **Decide on a course of action.** On the basis of a thorough consideration of alternatives, students are to choose the best alternative for solving the presenting problem.

7. **Verify whether the selected alternative achieved the desired outcome.** Students should be made aware that the initial choice of a solution may not always resolve the problem as anticipated. It may be necessary to consider another alternative.

In terms of efficacy, self-monitoring and interpersonal problem-solving techniques show great promise for teaching appropriate behaviors to students with mild to moderate disabilities. These proactive activities can be employed for intervening with problem classroom behaviors.

ℙause and Reflect 8.5

What are some specific problem-solving deficiencies that your students present? What specific curricular alternatives can you use to facilitate the development of problem-solving skills? How can such instructional alternatives be integrated into other aspects of your curriculum?

DESIGNING AND IMPLEMENTING INDIVIDUAL BEHAVIOR-CHANGE INTERVENTIONS

When a student's inappropriate behavioral patterns cannot be prevented, many teachers use data gathered from FBAs and employ individual behavior-change procedures. Although these often involve considerable time for planning and monitoring, the initial effort is usually rewarded by increases in appropriate classroom functioning. A step-by-step sequence of activities for implementing individual behavior-change procedures follows.

Rationale and Current Intervention Efforts

Two important concerns should be addressed before the implementation of formal behavior-change procedures. First, the teacher should know why a formal change procedure is necessary. Second, the teacher should know details of previous (and presumably unsuccessful) behavior-change efforts involving the student. In addressing concerns related to the rationale, developing and beginning teachers should be able to readily cite why changing the observed problem behavior is necessary. If the change procedure is to be implemented, the benefits of the effort should be readily interpreted as being of social and educational relevance to the student. A listing of previously unsuccessful behavior-change efforts is necessary to assist in planning for intervention; there is no need to repeat strategies found to be unsuccessful.

Pinpointing a Target Behavior

Educators frequently characterize the inappropriate behaviors of their students in general (e.g., hyperactive, lazy, aggressive) rather than in specific terms. These general descriptions are not especially useful for individual behavior-change programs. Specific valid and reliable behavioral pinpoints are necessary. The pinpointing process involves moving from general to specific descriptors of behavior. For example, hyperactivity (a general descriptor that would vary from observer to observer) is not a good pinpoint; out-of-seat behavior would be a more useful and reliable descriptor of the problem behavior. A good rule of thumb when developing behavioral pinpoints is to ensure that targeted behaviors (1) are overt, (2) are easily observed, and (3) contain movement. Several individuals observing a student should be able to agree on whether a target behavior did or did not occur.

Selecting an Observation and Recording Procedure

Once an appropriate target behavior has been pinpointed, a convenient method for observing and recording the behavior should be selected. Alternatives range from labor-intensive, continuous-recording systems to more time-efficient systems such as behavior sampling (Table 8.4).

Obtaining Baseline Measures of Targeted Behavior

Once decisions have been made on the pinpointing and recording of behavior, a baseline measure of a targeted behavior must be obtained. **Baseline** refers to the level or intensity of a behavior prior to the introduction of an intervention procedure. Data recorded under subsequent intervention phases are compared with the baseline data. There are no general rules as to how long baseline data should be collected. The amount of time will vary according to the behavior pinpointed. Baseline data should continue to be collected until a stable trend is noted. **Stability** is characterized as the lack of a significant slope in the data and only moderate variability in daily observations. It should be remembered, however, that many aggressive and destructive behaviors require rapid intervention. In such cases, short baseline periods are the only practical course of action even though they lack the predictive power of longer baseline periods.

Setting Goals

Once the presenting problem has been pinpointed and the baseline data have been recorded, a goal or set of goals for the intervention should be set. Without goals, teachers would be unable to ascertain whether, when, or how well their interventions succeeded. Two of the more common methods for setting behavioral management goals are the use of normative data guidelines and consulting previous performance records.

Normative Data Guidelines. Normative data guidelines attempt to bring students' problem behaviors into line with least restrictive or general environmental expectations. Therefore, social-emotional goals for students with mild to moderate disabilities should, in most cases, approximate or even match behavioral frequencies found in chronological age-appropriate general classroom settings. To obtain such data, developing and beginning teachers can observe general classrooms and collect behavioral frequencies of

TABLE 8.4 Alternatives for Observing and Recording Behavior

Format	Purpose	Advantages	Disadvantages and Cautions
Continuous recording	Narrative description of behavior allows specification of conditions in which behavior occurs. Can provide general information that will assist when seeking a more formal and objective recording alternative.	Provides a broad-based subjective account of a problem behavior's antecedent and consequent conditions. A useful diagnostic approach to determine the possible environmental interactions that elicit and maintain behavior.	Requires continuous attention and considerable time. Subjective nature can result in reduced accuracy.
Permanent product	A physical product of a behavior can be translated into numerical terms and provide a direct measure of an effect of a behavior. Examples include student worksheets, time-clock records, and videotapes.	Direct observation of student not necessary. Typical practice in most classroom settings. Tangible product allows for review at varying intervals.	Not practical for many behaviors in the socioemotional domain.
Event recording	A simple frequency count of discrete behaviors (e.g., number of swear words, number of times talking-out) during a predefined period of time.	Useful with behaviors that have clear beginning and ending parts. Easily recorded with a checklist, bead counter, or pencil-stroke procedure.	Not useful for long or varying duration behaviors. Requires considerable attention during the predefined observation period. Lower accuracy with very high-rate behaviors.
Duration recording	A record of how long a behavior occurs within a given time period. Can be used to record the total length of time for each occurrence of a behavior, as well as response latency.	Most useful for low-frequency behaviors of moderate to long duration.	Usually used with only one student. Not useful for high-rate behaviors of short duration. Requires continuous attention during observation period and the use of a stop-watch.
Interval recording	A determination of whether or not a behavior occurred within specified time intervals (observation period is divided into smaller, equally sized intervals).	Applicable to a wide range of behaviors and can be used with multiple students. Provides estimates of both frequency and duration of behaviors. Provides information about student behavior across time intervals.	Difficult for teachers to use while instructing students. Length of interval must be appropriate for the behavior targeted.
Momentary time sampling	An on-the-spot determination of whether or not a behavior occurred immediately following specified time intervals.	Allows teaching and data collection to occur simultaneously. Applicable to a wide range of behaviors and can be used with multiple students.	Length of interval must be appropriate for the behavior targeted. Not useful for low-frequency and short-duration behaviors.

various prosocial and inappropriate target behaviors. These frequency counts can be used as terminal goals for students in the special education settings. Such an approach to goal setting is consistent with the goal of normalization and can facilitate the process of returning students to least restrictive educational settings.

Previous Performance Guidelines. For certain behavioral problems, it is reasonable to expect student performance to match previous intervention outcomes. For example, if a student reduced the rate of hitting others by 80% under a particular contingency management program, it would be reasonable to expect that the same goal could be attained with another target behavior (e.g., out-of-seat behavior) under the same or slightly modified management program.

Administering the Intervention

When selecting one or a set of intervention procedures, it is important to record all components of the program and to note all environmental changes that accompany the implementation of the procedures. Such precision will produce a resource bank of possible treatment alternatives and facilitate the replication and use of successful approaches.

To facilitate the precise recording of a program's components, many educators use behavioral contracts to specify joint agreements between themselves and their students. These **contingency contracts** list the specific behaviors the contracting parties should emit and the consequences that will result. Contracts are advantageous in individual behavior-change programs because they allow students to work at individualized rates and involve students in the planning of interventions. According to Hall and Hall (1982), contracts should always (1) be stated in positive terms, (2) be designed to promote success (e.g., reward small gradations of change), (3) provide frequent and immediate reinforcement, and (4) be the result of mutual negotiation between teacher and student. The physical body of the contract should contain the following:

- The dates on which the contract is to begin, end, and/or be renegotiated
- A clear specification of the behavior or behaviors targeted for intervention
- The consequences (rewards) for meeting the terms of the contract
- A listing of who is to provide the consequences
- A signature of all parties involved in the contract

A sample contract is found in Figure 8.5. For more details on the construction of contracts, consult Hall and Hall (1982), Homme (1977), or Kazdin (1975).

Analyzing Results Continuously

Because data are collected throughout the intervention period, evaluation and interpretation of results are relatively straightforward. By merely "eyeballing" the continuously measured performance of the student in contrast to the goal of the intervention, an assessment of the treatment program's effects can be completed. If the treatment is on a successful course, then it should be continued; if it seems unsuccessful, then it should be modified or alternative intervention procedures should be considered.

Completing Follow-Up and Maintenance Procedures

Once a treatment goal has been achieved, two interrelated programming activities need to be completed to ensure that the positive outcomes maintain and generalize to non-treatment settings. First, there should be a gradual removal or fading of all external and artificial treatment components. Rapid and unsystematic removal of external treatments will usually result in the return of inappropriate behaviors. Second, there should be the scheduling of maintenance probes at regular intervals to assess the success of the

This is a contract between _____ and _____ .

Student's name   Teacher's name

The student _____ agrees to work on the following behaviors:

1. _____

2. _____

3. _____

If I meet the above conditions, I will get from the teacher:

_____

_____

_____

_____

as a special reward. If the terms of the contract are not met by the student, all rewards will be withheld.

Signatures and date

_____	_____
Student	Date
_____	_____
Teacher	Date
_____	_____
Witness	Date

We will review this contract on _____ to reevaluate it.

Date

FIGURE 8.5 Sample Behavioral Contract

fading procedure. If the probes indicate a significant loss of treatment gains, intervention procedures with modified maintenance plans will need to be reintroduced.

SUMMARY

This chapter covered a range of issues related to the area of classroom management. Our goal was to provide a series of strategies that could be used to promote discipline and self-control. We began by noting that there are no magic bullets, formulas, or recipes that guarantee appropriate student behaviors in classrooms for students with mild to moderate disabilities. The management of classrooms involves strategies and procedures designed to increase the probability that classrooms run effectively and efficiently.

The following strategies to prevent discipline problems were presented: (1) the development and maintenance of an appropriate management perspective, (2) teacher readiness, (3) the design of the physical environment, (4) the development of rules and procedures, and (5) the coordination of schoolwide cooperation. Procedures for intervening with student misbehavior were presented, with special emphases on methods for conducting a functional behavioral assessment, as well as increasing and decreasing behavior. Strategies for promoting self-control were also provided and step-by-step guidelines were provided for the completion of individual behavior-change efforts.

ACTIVITIES TO EXTEND YOUR KNOWLEDGE

1. How would you go about involving colleagues, both general and special educators, to join you in the development of a comprehensive behavioral management system? What advantages of this approach would you like to highlight? What collaborative skills would you use to ensure that the others would likely stay involved?

2. Set up a system to monitor your own performance in classroom management. What specific behaviors would you monitor in your presentation and implementation of the management system? What behaviors would you look for in the behavior of your students?

3. Some educators claim that providing students with positive consequences for appropriate behavior is nothing short of bribery and that such actions preempt the natural development of an intrinsic sense of right and wrong in many children. In your view, what, if any, are the differences between positive reinforcement and bribery? Is it possible for a teacher to develop a positively based management system that recognizes appropriate behavior without the use of tangible rewards?

4. Every once in a while, a teacher will require the services of a substitute teacher. How would you direct a substitute to implement your behavioral management procedures? What directions and materials would be necessary for the substitute to implement your well-developed plans?

5. Gather and organize the materials you will need to conduct an FBA on a troubling behavior in your classroom. These materials can be readily downloaded from several Web sites (see Point and Click section). Develop a plan for conducting the assessment. How much time will you need? Who will you need to interview? When and where should you conduct your direct observations? Once you have mapped out your plan, complete the FBA. After several weeks, evaluate the usefulness of the FBA.

POINT AND CLICK

These Web sites have information and links to additional information related to classroom management.

Addressing Student Problem Behavior: Functional Assessment Materials
http://www.air-dc.org/cecp/resources/problembehavior/

Center on Positive Behavior Interventions and Supports
http://www.pbis.org/english/index.html

Behavior Home Page
http://www.state.ky.us/agencies/behave/ebs3.html

Johns Hopkins University PAR Project
www.par.project.org

Virginia Youth Violence Project
http://curry.edschool.virginia.edu/curry/centers/youthvio/

School Psychology Resources Online
http://www.schoolpsychology.net/

Center for Effective Collaboration and Practice
http://www.air-dc.org/cecp/

REFERENCES

Alpert, L. (1989). *A teacher's guide to cooperative discipline: How to manage your classroom and promote self-esteem.* Circle Pines, MN: American Guidance Service.

Bambara, L. M., & Knoster, T. (1998). *Designing positive behavior support plans.* Washington, DC: American Association on Mental Retardation.

Barrish, H. H., Saunders, M., & Wolf, M. M. (1969). Good behavior game: Effects of individual contingencies on disruptive behavior in the classroom. *Journal of Applied Behavior Analysis, 2,* 119–124.

Bauer, A. M., Shea, T. M., & Keppler, R. (1986). Levels systems: A framework for the individualization of behavior management. *Behavioral Disorders, 12,* 28–35.

Braaten, S. (1979). The Madison School program: Programming for secondary-level severely emotionally disturbed youth. *Behavioral Disorders, 4,* 211–218.

Center for Effective Collaboration and Practice. (1998). *Addressing student problem behavior: An IEP teams introduction to functional behavioral assessment and behavior intervention plans.* Washington, DC: Author.

Curwin, R. L., & Mendler, A. N. (1988). *Discipline with dignity.* Alexandria, VA: Association for Supervision and Curriculum Development.

Demchak, M. & Bossert, K. W. (1996). *Innovations: Assessing problem behaviors.* Washington, DC: American Association on Mental Retardation.

Dwyer, K. & Osher, D. (2000). *Safeguarding our children: An action guide.* Washington, DC: U.S. Department of Education.

Dwyer, K., Osher, D., & Hoffman, C. C. (2000). Creating responsive schools: Contextualizing early warning, timely response. *Exceptional Children, 66*(3), 347–365.

D'Zurilla, T., & Goldfried, M. (1971). Problem solving and behavior modification. *Journal of Abnormal Psychology, 78,* 101–126.

Good, T. L., & Brophy, J. E. (1987). *Looking into classrooms* (4th ed.). New York: Harper & Row.

Hall, R. V., & Hall, M. C. (1982). *How to negotiate a behavioral contract.* Lawrence, KS: H & H Enterprises.

Hallahan, D. P., Lloyd, J. W., & Stoller, L. (1982). *Improving attention with self-monitoring: A manual for teachers.* Charlottesville: University of Virginia, Learning Disabilities Research Institute.

Homme, L. (1977). *How to use contingency contracting in the classroom.* Champaign, IL: Research Press.

Kazdin, A. F. (1975). *Behavior modification in applied settings.* Belmont, CA: Dorsey Press.

Kounin, J. S. (1970). *Discipline and group management in the classroom.* New York: Holt, Rinehart & Winston.

Lewis, T. J., & Sugai, G. (1999). Effective behavioral support: A systems approach to proactive school-wide management. *Focus on Exceptional Children, 31*(6), 1–23.

Long, N., & Newman, R. G. (1965). Managing surface behavior of children in school. In N. Long, W. Morse, & R. Newman (Eds.), *Conflict in the classroom: The education of emotionally disturbed children* (pp. 233–240). Belmont, CA: Wadsworth.

Mastropieri, M. A., Jenne, T., & Scruggs, T. E. (1988). A level system for managing problem behaviors in a high school resource program. *Behavioral Disorders, 13,* 202–208.

Mastropieri, M. A., & Scruggs, T. E. (1987). *Effective instruction for special education.* Boston: College-Hill.

McConnell, M. E., Hilvitz, P. B., & Cox, C. J. (1998). Functional assessment: A systematic process for assessment and intervention in general and special education classrooms. *Intervention in School and Clinic, 34,* 10–20.

O'Neill, R., Horner, R., Albin, R., Sprague, J., Storey, K., & Newton, J. S. (1997). *Functional assessment and program development for problem behavior: A practical handbook.* Pacific Grove, CA: Brooks/Cole.

Paine, S. C., Radicci, J., Rossellini, L. C., Deutchman, L., & Darch, C. R. (1983). *Structuring your classroom for academic success.* Champaign, IL: Research Press.

Rosenberg, M. S., & Jackman, L. A. (1997). Addressing student and staff behavior: The PAR model. *The Fourth R, 79,* 1–12.

Slavin, R. E. (1986). *Educational psychology: Theory into practice.* Upper Saddle River, NJ: Prentice Hall.

Smith, D. D., & Rivera, D. P. (1995). Discipline in special education and general education settings. *Focus on Exceptional Children, 27*(5), 1–16.

Smith, R. M., Neisworth, J. T., & Greer, J. G. (1978). *Evaluating educational environments.* New York: Merrill/Macmillan.

Spivack, G., & Shure, M. B. (1982). The cognition of social adjustment: Interpersonal cognitive problem solving. In B. B. Lahey & A. E. Kazdin (Eds.), *Advances in clinical child psychology* (Vol. 5). New York: Plenum.

Topper, K., Williams, W., Leo, K., Hamilton, R., & Fox, T. (1994). *A positive approach to understanding and addressing challenging behavior.* Burlington: University of Vermont.

Veenman, S. (1984). Perceived problems of beginning teachers. *Review of Educational Research, 54,* 143–178.

Weber, W. A., & Roff, L. A. (1983). A review of the teacher education literature on classroom management. In W. A. Weber, J. Crawford, L. A. Roff, & C. Robinson (Eds.), *Classroom management: Reviews of the teacher education and research literature* (pp. 7–43). Princeton, NJ: Educational Testing Service.

Westling, D. L., & Koorland, M. A. (1988). *The special educator's handbook.* Needham Heights, MA: Allyn & Bacon.

Student and Family Transitions

Coauthored by Janeen M. Taylor
Johns Hopkins University

In this chapter, we will

✔ introduce transitions faced by students with disabilities and their families

✔ identify transition components of individualized family service plans (IFSPs) and IEPs

✔ discuss linkages in school opportunities, including interagency coordination

✔ review teachers' roles as students age

*I*n this chapter, we provide an overview of transition issues related to very young children with disabilities and the effects on children's families. We review early intervention services and transitions that students and their families face. We help new teachers examine evaluation and assessment needs of young children and explore various medical or development, implementation, and monitoring of a child's individualized family service plans (IFSPs). We explore these in relation to teachers' roles in providing quality services to young children and families.

Next, we identify services offered to school-age children and youth with disabilities. Such services have undergone dramatic changes since the enactment of IDEA in 1990. We explore teachers' work with diverse families of school-age students involved in IDEA and other federal initiatives. The influx of diversity variables is changing the shape and milieu of elementary-, middle-, and high-school services.

A necessary prerequisite to school programs is interagency coordination. We identify helpful teacher roles as students age and as their families become increasingly involved with adult agencies. We view strategies to facilitate transitions in high-school years and beyond. Because new teachers will help in linking high school to postschool services, we offer ideas on how school curricula can entail a range of options in career planning (e.g., college-bound training, technical schools, vocational training, supported work, paid employment). Many high-school teachers will focus on a curriculum model for high-functioning students that encourages students' job training; postsecondary education requirements; self-advocacy, self-management, and awareness of learning strengths and weaknesses; and individual decision-making related to their leisure-time pursuits, marriage and living arrangements, and other adult considerations. Teachers providing a curriculum model for low-functioning students will stress experiences that are community referenced, integrated, longitudinal, and community based.

New teachers will be involved in making meaningful decisions regarding students' transitions (adjustments to change) and family concerns affected by students' transitions. Today, new teacher roles and responsibilities are related to linking services within and between agencies. New service views, or what has been termed "life-long transition planning," entail the anticipation, planning, implementation, and analysis of systematic timeline procedures to prepare infants, children, and youth for adult roles and services (deFur, Getzel, & Kregel, 1994; deFur & Taymans, 1995; Karge, Patton, & de la Garza, 1992; Kolher, 1993; Martin, Marshall, & Maxson, 1993).

Importantly, preparing for transitions begins early in a child's life. Early and sequential planning increases the chances of successful adjustments for the child and the family. Developing and beginning teachers working with students of all ages and ability levels will be called on to assist in students' transitions and to help families in various transitions.

TRANSITIONS FACED BY STUDENTS AND FAMILIES

Students and families face many transitions: beginning and coping with the daily demands of school as a very young child; advancing in school grades and interacting with different teachers; leaving parents' homes, marrying, and having children; getting jobs and being promoted; and moving to new homes or cities. When students and families make transitions, professionals can help. They can assist by offering coordinated and functional services: concrete, everyday skills that allow students to achieve the kind of life they and their families want (Lambie & Daniels-Mohring, 1993). Importantly, functional skills learned in school are the foundation of students' adult success. When teachers link their functional skill instruction with services offered by other professionals, teachers are helping students and families face and adjust to transitions.

Effective teachers focusing on functional skills need to consider real-life experiences that students will encounter as they age. Adult preparation increases in importance as students age. Changes are especially complex and difficult because, as students get older, they and their families must interact with various private and public agency personnel. For instance, young children and parents often spend an enormous amount of time in hospitals. Families may interact with countless numbers of doctors, nurses, therapists, or other health care personnel. Criteria for determining eligibility for services delivered to children in health care settings is usually medically based. By the time young children enroll in preschool- or school-age services, the professionals with whom families interact come from a different background; educational personnel usually deliver services in preschool and school settings. Additionally, the eligibility requirements for receiving services, pertinent contact personnel available, and types and quantity of services provided differ from those in a health care facility. Such changes represent stressful adjustments for many young students and their families.

When students reach middle and high schools, more changes occur in services, personnel, locations, and requirements. Families must interact with personnel from new agencies. In addition to medical and educational agencies, families may be involved with family support systems, legal services, counseling programs, social services, or welfare agencies. Often, agencies vary in the quality of services they provide. In addition, the focus of the interventions offered may vary from agency to agency. Some may continue to stress health or educational services, whereas others may be oriented toward social well-being and family interactions. Others may offer legal, community, or welfare supports. Nonetheless, students, families, and professionals must work together to

Pause and Reflect 9.1

Are you well prepared to discuss with families, your host teacher, or your university supervisor the following transition and family issues regarding students in your field placement? Circle Yes or No for each of the following in terms of your level of preparation to deal with the issue.

A. Early Life and Preschool Years

1. Transition types	Yes	No
2. Early services	Yes	No
3. Evaluation and assessment	Yes	No
4. Medical/physical issues	Yes	No
5. Teaming issues	Yes	No
6. Family-centered services	Yes	No
7. Individualized family service plans (IFSPs)	Yes	No

B. School-Age Years

1. Family participation	Yes	No
2. School-age transitions	Yes	No
3. Diverse family strategies	Yes	No

C. Adult Preparation

1. Linking schools and communities	Yes	No
2. Individualized education plans (IEPs)	Yes	No
3. Interagency coordination	Yes	No
4. Adult issues	Yes	No
5. Facilitating the transition process	Yes	No

address the changes in the activities, resources, and schedules. As time moves on and people adjust to the vast array of personnel, services, restrictions, and resources offered, working as a team is essential.

Teachers can help children, youth, and families make healthy adjustments to changes by support and information. Two life periods receiving particular attention are the transitions from preschool to public school and from school to work. Teachers providing services to students in or receiving students from both early and adult services assist students and families when they target planned activities, anticipate time frames, and help coordinate integrated services and appropriate follow through to the child and family.

Transition Issues in Families of Young Children

Ideally, transition planning is a process; it is not a point in time. **Transitions,** to young children and their families, mean a variety of individual and family movements and accompanying stressful events as children and families enter into, or initially change, service systems. Teachers need to recognize the importance of families as decision-makers in the transition process and work toward the common goal of successful treatments and programs for young children and their families.

Transitions mean change and adjustment as infants and toddlers enter and exit various levels of service delivery systems (Kilgo, 1990). Transitions may entail a change from no services (e.g., students with mild disabilities typically are not identified until they reach school age) or multiple systems (e.g., health and social services provided to students with more severe problems) to a unitary system (education).

Typical transition issues that teachers working with young children will confront are the adjustments and associated stresses that children and families encounter when changing to and from various service delivery systems. These changes include the switch from physicians to teachers as families' primary informational sources. New teachers may be called on to help families make the change from a program offered through a clinical or home setting to one that is provided in a preschool or school setting. Teachers may be the parents' or guardians' main resource for acquiring information on the scope of preschool offerings or additional legal requirements for services in a school setting.

Some teachers must assume different roles with family members, based on such factors as the child's degree of disabling condition, parents' desires for and level of involvement in their children's programs, variations in local offerings of infant/family intervention programs that may or may not match families' expectations, children's and parents' coping strategies, residential placement options, respite care needs, or independent functioning expectations. Nonetheless, adjustment and stress are evident in most children and families as they change faculty, staff, programming, adult-to-student ratios, service locations, schedules, communication methods, transportation methods, and service goals or objectives. Teachers can help families survive such adjustments.

Teachers can also help young children and families make changes across service delivery systems by initiating the transition process. For example, teachers can provide a bridge across various program elements by collaborating with other service providers. Teachers can use effective communication techniques when children transition from such locations as a neonatal nursery to home, and from home to school. Teachers can seek input from other relevant service providers when children change from child care centers to public school/preschool programs. Initial communication attempts by teachers are important because researchers have confirmed that a lack of communication between physicians, health care workers, social workers, speech and language therapists, physical therapists, or preschool staff can jeopardize the years of careful training and education provided to, or anticipated for, children in early childhood special education programs (Hanline & Knowlton, 1988). Important communication strategies include a focus on listening to family members' concerns, answering their questions honestly and promptly, and being a good resource to assist them with their child and family concerns.

Some researchers (Bailey, Simeonsson, Yoder, & Huntington, 1990; Craig & Leonard, 1990) suggest that teachers offering family-specific data on local contacts, program purposes, transportation information, times, and cost factors help families become more involved and responsive to services. When teachers act collaboratively with other professionals, they help families address the myriad of issues that define how families learn to live with and support their children. By working actively and assisting families, teachers pick up important home data on families' backgrounds, cultures, expectations, differences in coping styles, need for family support programs, parent training interests or accessibility, and teachers' influence on home environments. All of this information can be important when designing individualized treatments for children their and families.

Additionally, when teachers work well with other professionals, such as the medical and school services personnel also assessing families of young children, they help families enormously. They model for families how team building and group processes work. Teachers operating in effective professional teams with others support cross-disciplinary communication skills. They recognize how best to incorporate the basic terminology of other disciplines; they accumulate data about the roles, academic preparation, clinical experiences, and expertise of other professionals; they seek out the principles and procedures underlying team building and the group process; they discuss family needs across settings; and they work together to facilitate students' school or community entrance or exits. Special problems of students' preschool years relate to teachers' abilities to collect information on future skills and program requirements of the next school environment, while embedding training into current programming (O'Shea & Caldwell, 1990). Talking with other professionals and obtaining resources on new programs helps families while the child receives existing services. Transition coordination works when professionals cooperate and offer coordinated services.

Early Intervention and Early Childhood Special Education

Today, there are substantial differences between strategies for special instruction of very young children with disabilities (birth to age 6) and older children and youth with disabilities (ages 6 to 21) (Smith & Luckasson, 1995). The U.S. Congress recognized these differences by including Part H in the Individuals with Disabilities Education Act (IDEA) and by modifying sections related to preschool special education (Section 619).

Pause and Reflect 9.2

Discuss at least four specific ways that teachers can help young children and their families when families are transitioning from physicians to teachers as primary informational sources.

1. _____

2. _____

3. _____

4. _____

Part H and its accompanying regulations specify special instruction for infants and toddlers with disabilities as one of a long list of early intervention services. For children and youth ages 3 to 21, the terms *special education* and *related services* are used and addressed in Part B of IDEA. One section of Part B, Section 619, focuses on preschool children with disabilities and their special instruction and related services. Part H and Section 619 of IDEA entail unique features. These features, described as follows, hold importance for new teachers in their knowledge and skills and their roles with family members.

Teachers' Roles in Early Transitions. There are three important transitions for children in early intervention or preschool special education programs. The first involves the transition from a hospital-based setting to the community in which a family lives. Hospitals usually have discharge coordinators who work with families to develop a plan for treatment after hospitalization. New teachers can help in the transition from hospital settings by obtaining a list of the names and telephone numbers of area discharge coordinators. Teachers might call discharge coordinators to make a family's move from hospital to home a smooth one. Working with the referring hospital's discharge coordinator can help in collecting follow-through data, such as medical appointments, prescriptions, and/or therapies begun in the hospital. Teachers can ensure a smooth adjustment from a health care setting to an early intervention setting by linking medical and educational services.

The second major transition for young children is from an early intervention program to a preschool or preschool special education program. Any transition can be stressful, especially to families who have grown accustomed to the staff and routines of their child's program (Nelson, Bennett, & Lingerfelt, 1992). An important role for beginning personnel continues to be in assisting the family's receipt of accurate and timely information regarding the child's developmental strengths and needs. To do this properly, beginning teachers can help in initially judging the likelihood of each child's eligibility for preschool special education or for a particular community-based program. It may be helpful to schedule regular information sessions for families of 2- and 3-year-olds. For example, Box 9.1 offers a list of possible program options for 3-year-olds.

The third transition is from a preschool or preschool special education program to a primary (i.e., grades one, two, and three) education or primary special education program. Families need a head start on the planning process, so having current written information about special education and community-based program availability is vital. As appropriate, handouts with registration cutoff dates, income eligibility requirements, geographic boundaries of programs, transportation availability, age restrictions,

---

Box 9.1   **Community Programs for 3-Year-Olds**

_____ Before- or after-school care

_____ Child care facility

_____ Day camp

_____ Family child care (in-home)

_____ Head Start

_____ Play group

_____ Private lessons (e.g., gymnastics)

_____ Recreation center

_____ Residential camp

_____ Tutoring

degree of parental participation required, and other program-specific criteria may help in the transition process (Governor's Office for Children, Youth, and Families/ Maryland Infants and Toddlers Program, 1992).

Teachers work throughout the year to assist families in identifying the appropriate program(s) for their children. An important task is to orient families to the types of early services that are available locally. For example, teachers can provide accurate information on program eligibility criteria, resources, services, and contacts. Teachers' knowledge and skills regarding unique family needs or priorities can make this a time of growth for families and children alike.

Evaluation and Assessment of Young Children with Disabilities. Determining the developmental strengths and needs of infants, toddlers, and preschoolers is critical to successful programming (Bagnato, Neisworth, & Munson, 1989; Taylor & Fleming, 1997). Although some controversy surrounds specific terms used to describe developmental testing of young children, **evaluation** refers to instruments or procedures used to determine a child's (1) developmental diagnosis, (2) initial eligibility for a program, or (3) ongoing eligibility for a program (Campbell, 1991). **Assessment** refers to the process of monitoring or checking a child's developmental status for purposes of program adjustment (Fewell, 1991). For older students with disabilities, the terms *evaluation* and *assessment* are often used interchangeably (Henley, Ramsey, & Algozzine, 1993).

Developmental testing during the birth to age 3 years can be a time of crisis for many families (Fewell & Vadasy, 1986). Families are in the early stages of grappling with their child's disability. Tests results often confirm a serious problem that may carry long-term consequences (Turnbull & Turnbull, 1986). For families of premature infants, developmental testing can be especially difficult. Parents often spend days, weeks, or months visiting their child in the neonatal intensive care unit, watching their child struggle for survival. Many interact with a host of medical personnel, including doctors, nurses, technicians, and therapists. During this period, developmental testing can confirm or alleviate parental fears of permanent disability (Krajicek & Tompkins, 1993; VandenBerg & Hanson, 1993).

Professionalism during the process of evaluating an infant or toddler is critical for many families (Brown, Thurman, & Pearl, 1993; Katz, Pokorni, & Long, 1989). Teachers can take a number of steps to ensure evaluation and assessment preparation and professionalism. First, it is essential to determine the kinds of evaluation and assessment instruments or procedures operating in early childhood services that will help families move from hospital or home-care support to educational support.

Given the inherent stress in the evaluation or assessment process, teachers can begin to explore with parents the effects an exceptional condition may have on a person's life. They might provide written information to families on differential characteristics of children and youth with disabilities (including levels of severity, where applicable) and potential implications for parents, siblings, or other family members. They can assist families in understanding similarities and differences in children's development. They can become competent examiners of children's development (Bricker, 1989). Thus, new teachers can offer valuable information to parents on the child's developmental status and normal or exceptional milestones.

Box 9.2 presents suggested steps that teachers can take to become familiar with evaluation or assessment procedures. A beginning teacher's confidence in using a specific instrument or procedure will be transmitted to families whose infants may be under his or her care for months to come (Linder, 1993a).

For the preschool environment, however, an evaluation and assessment scenario is somewhat different. Curriculum-based assessment (King-Sears, 1994) is a common approach to initial and ongoing assessment of a child's developmental status (McLean, Bailey, & Wolery, 1996). It is important to determine the specific curriculum approach required by the child. If the school system or program does not have a standard

---

Box 9.2

Steps for Choosing and Using the Appropriate Evaluation and Assessment Tools for Infants and Toddlers

——— 1. Examine the scoring form.

——— 2. Read the manual carefully.

——— 3. Jot down questions you have.

——— 4. Ask experienced examiners the questions you've formulated.

——— 5. Observe an experienced examiner administer the instrument or procedure.

——— 6. Obtain the test kit or assemble appropriate materials.

——— 7. Practice using the instrument or procedure on children of friends or relatives.

——— 8. Have someone videotape your efforts, and ask colleagues for suggestions on improving your test administration.

——— 9. Reflect on the procedures and process.

——— 10. Develop a plan to correct deficiencies.

——— 11. Implement the plan.

---

curriculum, beginning teachers might choose a curriculum with an accompanying evaluation or assessment tool. At this time, teachers can begin to discuss curriculum options in relation to the child's educational strengths and needs. Teachers can discuss with parents or guardians similarities and differences among the cognitive, language, physical, social, and emotional needs of infants and toddlers who are developing in a typical fashion and those developing in an atypical fashion. Box 9.3 lists some commonly used curricula with accompanying evaluation or assessment materials. These early childhood special education curricula are in wide use throughout the United States and may be a helpful starting point for teachers' collaborations with family members. Box 9.4 lists criteria for choosing a curriculum.

Medical/Physical Issues Related to Working with Young Children with Disabilities. Advances in health care technology and practice underscore increased survival rates for many infants born prematurely and for newborns with formerly lethal congenital conditions (Bond et al., 1990). Many children born prematurely have special health care needs (Batshaw, 1997). Nonetheless, beginning teachers can take steps to make sure that the educational experience of children with special health care needs is positive and healthy. First, it is helpful to complete a pediatric CPR course from the local Red Cross

---

Box 9.3

Early Childhood Special Education Curricula with Accompanying Evaluation or Assessment Instruments or Procedures

* *Assessment, Evaluation, and Programming System for Infants and Children: Vol. 2* (Cripe, Slentz, & Bricker, 1993)
* *The Carolina Curriculum for Preschoolers with Special Needs* (Johnson-Martin, Attermeier, & Hacker, 1990)
* *HELP for Special Preschoolers Ages 3 to 6* (Santa Cruz County Office of Education, 1987)
* *Transdisciplinary Play-Based Assessment: Guidelines for Developing a Meaningful Curriculum for Young Children* (Linder, 1993b).

Box 9.4   **Criteria for Curriculum Selection**

In determining the appropriateness of a curriculum for use in an early intervention or early childhood special education program, consider the following:

1. Do you think children would like these curricular activities?
   Yes _____   No _____

2. Are these activities family-friendly (easy to use, attractive, appealing)?
   Yes _____   No _____

3. Is the curriculum teacher-friendly (logically formatted, understandable)?
   Yes _____   No _____

4. Would this curriculum be consistent with community values?
   Yes _____   No _____

5. Is the curriculum appropriate developmentally?
   Yes _____   No _____

6. Are the criteria for success in the accompanying evaluation or assessment instrument or procedures clear and measurable?
   Yes _____   No _____

7. Is there a range of opportunities for family members or caretakers to participate in (or lead) curricular activities?
   Yes _____   No _____

8. Can these curricular activities be adapted for use with children who have a range of abilities and disabilities?
   Yes _____   No _____

9. Does the curriculum require specialized or costly materials or equipment?
   Yes _____   No _____

10. Does the curriculum have guidelines for staffing patterns (caretaker-child ratios)?
    Yes _____   No _____

11. Are curricular activities suited for a child's natural environment?
    Yes _____   No _____

12. Are all developmental domains addressed?
    Yes _____   No _____

13. Are curricular activities sequenced appropriately?
    Yes _____   No _____

14. Is the curriculum appropriate for individual children, as well as groups of children?
    Yes _____   No _____

---

chapter (Urbano, 1992). Red Cross courses are relatively short and are especially important for pediatric health emergencies.

Second, it is important to read the medical files on each student as soon as possible. Files often contain valuable information about a student's health status and relevant implications for educational intervention. Third, by asking the program director, principal, or supervisor for information concerning local policies related to children with special health care needs, new teachers may be able to gather a wide range of local support services and resources for families and children affected by medical conditions.

Fourth, reading relevant materials on special health care needs can help new teachers stay abreast of current medical practices affecting a child's educational needs. Two very good books about children with special health care needs are *Children with Disabilities* (Batshaw, 1997) and *Preschool Children with Special Health Care Needs* (Urbano, 1992).

Another critical health issue is minimizing the transmission of communicable diseases in educational settings. Taylor and Taylor (1989) advise decreasing the incidence of infectious disease through specific guidelines for handwashing. Anderson, Bale, Blackman, and Murph (1994) advise: "Handwashing is the most important means of controlling infections. Staff and children should wash their hands upon arrival . . . after using the toilet or changing diapers . . . or assisting with toilet use, after wiping a child's or their own runny nose . . . before serving or eating food, and any time hands may be contaminated with a body fluid" (p. 62). A 50% reduction in the incidence of diarrhea was noted in centers where careful handwashing procedures were instituted (Donowitz, 1993).

Washing classroom surfaces, instructional materials, and toys is a useful strategy for minimizing infection (Taylor, 1995). The school nurse or local health department official can suggest an effective cleaning solution. Teachers and classroom aides can wash boxes, shelves, counters, and other surfaces. Older children can help rinse them thoroughly with clean water. Work and play surfaces can be air dried. If the program does not have guidelines for handwashing and keeping materials cleaned, it is important that new teachers establish their own written directives. Guidelines should be placed in appropriate room locations where, on daily arrival, teachers, classroom aides, volunteers, parents, guardians, and/or classroom visitors can read the listings.

The Expanded Multidisciplinary Team. Early intervention and preschool special education continues a strong emphasis on serving children from a coordinated team perspective (Smith & Luckasson, 1995). A multidisciplinary team typically includes representatives from three to five disciplines, including the physical therapist, occupational therapist, speech-language pathologist, and adaptive physical education teacher. Teachers work with other professionals daily and share data regarding young children's progress.

Further, teachers can offer families coordinated services with a variety of professionals. Communication and sharing with families and colleagues are vital if the expanded multidisciplinary team is to be successful. Early intervention entails a greater range of disciplines than special education for older students. The size of the team for younger children can be large, as illustrated in Table 9.1. The need for effective communication and collaboration increases in direct proportion to the number of individuals involved (Kroth, 1975).

Family-Centered Services. According to the Task Force on Recommended Practices (Council for Exceptional Children, 1993), early intervention and special education services for young children with disabilities must be family centered. Family-centered services entail teachers' knowledge and skills about individual and family needs and strengths. Teachers must practice functional instruction relevant to student diversity and family dynamics. They must respond to typical family concerns while individualizing appropriate student strategies. Further, implementing family-centered services means that teachers work with other team members to identify quality-of-life issues important to each family (e.g., leisure-time and recreation activities) and incorporate issues into students' educational programs.

Part H of IDEA is designed to be family centered in recognition of the importance of the family to a child's developmental well-being (Brazelton & Cramer, 1990; Fewell & Vadasy, 1986; Johnson-Martin, Attermeir, & Hacker, 1990; Singer & Irvin, 1989). The ability to interact positively with a wide range of family members and to understand children and disabilities within a cultural context is a key factor in a successful career as an early interventionist or preschool special educator. Teachers demonstrate successful family-centered services when they focus on implementing strategies for preparing students to live harmoniously and productively in a multicultural world.

TABLE 9.1   Possible Team Members for Part B and Part H of IDEA

Part B	Part H
Parents	Parents
Audiologist	Audiologist
Counselor	Counselor
Medical service provider (for diagnostic purposes)	Medical service provider (for diagnostic purposes)
Physical therapist	Physical therapist
Occupational therapist	Occupational therapist
Orientation and mobility specialist	Orientation and mobility specialist
Special education teacher	Special education teacher
Speech-language pathologist	Speech-language pathologist
Recreation specialist	Health care provider (e.g., pediatrician, dysmorphologist, neurologist)
Psychologist	Psychologist
Social worker	Social worker
	Child care provider
	Service coordinator
	Nurse
	Nutritionist
	Vision specialist
	Assistive technology specialist

Unfortunately, a lack of family knowledge and skills can be problematic for teachers unfamiliar with students' ethnic backgrounds, cultural heritage, and/or family living arrangements. Teachers need accuracy on students' family diversity, lifestyles, cultures, and the many contributions that family diversity can offer in classrooms.

Lambie and Daniels-Mohring (1993) and Lynch and Hanson (1998) offer the following suggestions for facilitating team functioning such that diverse family members believe they are integral to functioning multidisciplinary teams. First, the family must be involved in all aspects of decision-making regarding their child and the child's services (Jeppson & Thomas, 1995). Parents or guardians need a say in their child's services. Family members have a lifelong relationship with their child and are central to their child's development and well-being. Family involvement in decisions regarding their child's program is extremely important to program success (McLean, Bailey, & Wolery, 1996; O'Shea, O'Shea, & Nowocien, 1993).

Second, teachers must work toward developing an understanding of the cultural context necessary for communication and the importance of culture and community to verbal and nonverbal communication. If all team members have the same cultural identity, this may not be an issue. It is common, however, for teams to be comprised of individuals from diverse backgrounds. Effective communication strategies for one cultural framework may not work in a different cultural context. Teachers need to be alert to communicating appropriate messages to families and students.

New teachers can use their observational skills to determine how best to communicate with diverse family members. Teachers can talk with parents or guardians about services that family members would like stressed in their child's program. Teachers can

---

Box 9.5   **Considerations for Multidisciplinary Team Meetings**

When preparing for a multidisciplinary team meeting, remember to:

____ Consider the cultural context when communicating with team members.

____ Take careful notes about concerns and suggestions.

____ Put ideas about each child in writing before the meeting.

____ Know the rationale for each of your suggestions.

____ Take paper and pencils (or pens) for careful note taking.

____ Focus on each child and family.

____ Maintain confidentiality with regard to the discussions.

____ Follow up, when appropriate.

---

ask parents or guardians to provide input regarding priorities for the child's cognitive, language, physical, or social emphases. Teachers can help even the youngest child accept diversity by modeling appropriate acceptance behaviors when interacting with families or coworkers.

When new teachers take the time to acquire skills and competencies in cross-cultural communication, they maximize their group effectiveness. In the middle of fast-paced educational discussions, it might be easy to lose sight of important individual issues. Having written priorities based on each family's unique concerns before a meeting can facilitate team involvement in decisions. A written agenda even may help meetings run more smoothly.

If a team has a difficult time with task completion, conflict resolution and group problem-solving strategies are available. For instance, Turnbull et al. (1993) and Turnbull and Turnbull (1986) offer useful ideas for successful team meetings and collaboration. Noonan and McCormick's (1993) recommendations for effective team functioning involve a multicultural context with wide applicability to many family or community needs. Suggestions listed in Box 9.5 may be useful prior to team meetings. This list offers strategies for increasing a beginning teacher's effectiveness as a contributing team member who is cognizant of unique family strengths and needs.

Parents often value practitioners who build rapport (Dinnebeil & Rule, 1994), take time to listen (Turnbull & Turnbull, 1985), are respectful (Harry, Allen, & McLaughlin, 1995), and demonstrate that they understand the incredible time and service demands necessary in effective early intervention and preschool services (Brotherson & Goldstein, 1992). To support families as they parent young children with disabilities, effective teachers take time to reflect on family encounters. Box 9.6 presents reflection questions that may help new teachers in developing and refining skills in their family efforts (DeGangi, Wietlisbach, Poisson, & Stein, 1994).

Individualized Family Service Plans (IFSPs)

Federal and state guidelines mandate active family participation in the transition process. As previously implied, even for the youngest child with disabilities, early intervention entails professionals working with families to document a family's resources, concerns, priorities, and interventions. The documentation results in a child's individualized family service plan (IFSP). A number of federal IFSP requirements are listed in Box 9.7. New teachers should also query the program director to discover any additional state or local requirements. Figure 9.1 illustrates a sample IFSP.

Development of the IFSP continues to indicate the degree to which professionals and parents plan, implement, and evaluate appropriate programs. Input from families,

---

Box 9.6   **Reflecting on Family Interactions**

_____ What went well during the session?

_____ What was awkward or uncomfortable for me or the family?

_____ Did I really understand the family's concerns for their child? If I'm not sure, a follow-up telephone call is in order.

_____ Did I avoid professional jargon and use lay terms?

_____ Did I go slowly when offering suggestions and allow time for new information to sink in?

_____ Was I nonjudgmental of the family and their parenting style?

_____ What do I need to know to support this family?

_____ How will I acquire the needed information (e.g., telephone call, consult a colleague, read texts or journal articles)?

---

professionals, and agency personnel helps in the design and implementation of the IFSP. An IFSP focuses on child-related outcomes and supports the family-centered nature of early intervention services.

Given the number of agency providers involved in early intervention, service coordination is critical to success. **Service coordination** is the process of linking families with the services documented on the IFSP, monitoring child-related outcomes, and advocating on behalf of the child and family (Bennett, Nelson, Lingerfelt, & Davenport-

---

Box 9.7   **Federal Requirements for an Individualized Family Service Plan (IFSP)**

Have I met all of the federal requirements for this IFSP? Have I included a statement about the:

_____ Child's present level of development in:
- Cognition
- Communication
- Social or emotional development
- Adaptive skills
- Physical status (including vision, hearing, health status)

_____ Family's resources, concerns, and priorities

_____ Projected completion date for major outcomes

_____ Criteria, procedures, and timelines for determination of progress toward or achievement of each outcome

_____ Specific early intervention services

_____ Frequency and intensity of services

_____ Child's natural environment

_____ Location of services

_____ Payment for services

_____ Linkages with services not required (under Part H or Section 619 of Part B of IDEA)

_____ Transition planning

_____ Signatures for participants

Individualized Family Service Plan
Chesapeake County, MD

PART I: BIOGRAPHICAL INFORMATION AND SIGNATURES

Child: Date of Birth:
Address: Chronological Age:
Name of Parent/Guardian/Surrogate: Adjusted Age:
Address: Current Date:
Phone:
This is an: _____ Interim IFSP
                   _____ Initial IFSP
                   _____ Annual IFSP

Service Coordinator: Agency:
Address: Phone:

I (We) have had the opportunity to participate in development of this IFSP and have been provided with reasonable notice of the IFSP meeting. I (We) have been informed of my (our) rights under this program, understand the plan and parents' rights, and give permission to implement this plan.

_____
Parent/Guardian/Surrogate's Signature   Date

Each agency or person who has a direct role in the provision of early intervention services is responsible for making a good-faith effort to assist each eligible child and family to achieve outcomes listed on the child's IFSP.

_____
Service Coordinator   Date   Evaluator/Assessor   Date

_____
Lead Agency Representative   Date   Other Participant   Date

_____
Interpreter (if needed)   Date   Other Participant   Date

PART II: CHILD'S DEVELOPMENTAL STATUS

Child's Present Level of Development in:

LEVEL	CA	DA
Cognition		
Communication		
Socioemotional		
Adaptive		
Gross Motor		
Fine Motor		
Hearing		
Vision		
Health (including immunizations status)		
Primary Health Care Provider:	Phone:	

FIGURE 9.1 Sample Individualized Family Service Plan (IFSP)

Ersoff, 1992). Some services designed for children and families are easily available at the early intervention site. Other services may take time to identify or access. Creativity, perseverance, and ability to communicate will increase the likelihood of children and families meeting outcomes identified on the IFSP.

Box 9.8 offers a list of questions to help beginning teachers build resource files. To build resource files, new teachers can start with materials and information available at their own programs. It is also important to update notes about specific professionals

PART III: CHILD/FAMILY INFORMATION

A. Please describe the child's developmental strengths and needs.

B. Please describe the family's resources, concerns, and priorities as they relate to their child.

C. Please describe the settings in which this child spends most of his/her time.

D. What strategies will enable the child and family to participate in early intervention in the desired settings?

PART IV: CHILD/FAMILY OUTCOMES

Directions: Complete one page per outcome.

OUTCOME:

TYPE OF EARLY INTERVENTION SERVICE TO MEET THE OUTCOME:

LOCATION/FREQUENCY/INTENSITY:

STRATEGIES/ACTIVITIES:

CRITERIA/TIMELINES:

PERSON[S] RESPONSIBLE:

AGENCY/ADDRESS/PHONE:

FINANCIAL RESPONSIBILITY:

INITIATION DATE:

ANTICIPATED DATE OF ACHIEVEMENT:

PART V: TRANSITION CHECKLIST

_____ By the child's second birthday, transition planning is initiated.

_____ Families have been given descriptive information about their child's options at age 3.

_____ The local child-find coordinator for special education has been contacted (for children who are likely to be eligible for preschool special education).

_____ Site visits for parents are scheduled.

_____ Evaluation/assessment results are reviewed and appropriate additional testing is scheduled.

_____ Parents are given copies of federal and state laws, regulations, and policies related to preschool special education.

_____ Parents are given information about advocacy groups in the state or region.

_____ Appropriate meetings are scheduled with school/community personnel.

_____ Other (please specify)

_____ Other (please specify)

_____ Other (please specify)

FIGURE 9.1 *continued*

who are especially helpful. Documenting procedures for obtaining their services can help. A comprehensive resource file of local, state, and national services is one of the most important tools a service coordinator can offer to families and peers. Table 9.2 offers a list of national resources for young children with disabilities. Teachers can use it as a starting point for their resource file on national organizations. Relevant information should be kept in a central location and updated regularly.

| **B**ox 9.8 | **Checklist for a Comprehensive Resource File** |

- Where are resource directories kept in my center?
- Have I asked veteran colleagues (including parents) for suggestions regarding resources for families?
- Whom shall I call for help in obtaining immunizations for a family's child?
- Whom shall I call for an audiologic examination for a child?
- Who are the key contacts at relevant agencies or programs?
- Is there a file cabinet with relevant resource materials?
- Where are the resource files located?

TABLE 9.2 National Organizations for Families of Young Children With Disabilities

Resource	Address	Phone
Alliance of Genetic Support Groups	35 Wisconsin Circle, Suite 440 Chevy Chase, MD 20815	(301) 652-5553
Association for the Care of Children's Health	7910 Woodmont Avenue, Suite 300 Bethesda, MD 20814	(301) 654-6549
Beach Center on Families and Disabilities	Bureau of Child Research 3111 Haworth Hall Lawrence, KS 66045	(913) 864-7600
Family Resource Coalition	200 S. Michigan Avenue, 16th floor Chicago, IL 60604	(312) 341-0900
Institute for Family-Centered Care	7900 Wisconsin Avenue, Suite 405 Bethesda, MD 20814	(301) 652-0281
NEC*TAS (National Early Childhood * Technical Assistance System)	Frank Porter Graham Child Development Center CB#8040, 500 NCNB Plaza Chapel Hill, NC 27599	(919) 966-2622
National Information Clearinghouse for Infants with Disabilities and Life-Threatening Conditions	Center for Developmental Disabilities University of South Carolina Benson Building Columbia, SC 29208	(800) 922-9234, ext. 201
NICHY (National Information Center for Children and Youth with Disabilities)	P.O. Box 1492 Washington, DC 20013-1492	(202) 884-8200
National Maternal and Child Health Clearinghouse	8201 Greensboro Drive, Suite 600 McLean, VA 22102	(703) 821-8955, ext. 254 or 256
National Organization for Rare Disorders	P.O. Box 8923 New Fairfield, CT 06812-1783	(203) 746-6518
Zero to Three/National Center for Clinical Infant Programs	2000 14th Street N. Suite 380 Arlington, VA 22201-2500	(703) 528-4300

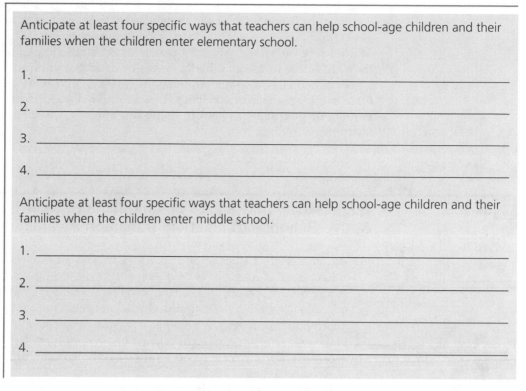

Pause and Reflect 9.3

Anticipate at least four specific ways that teachers can help school-age children and their families when the children enter elementary school.

1. _____

2. _____

3. _____

4. _____

Anticipate at least four specific ways that teachers can help school-age children and their families when the children enter middle school.

1. _____

2. _____

3. _____

4. _____

School-Age Years and Adult Preparation. Important to adult preparation needs are necessary program elements and supports affecting older students. Teachers are instrumental in linking school opportunities across learning settings. The linkage occurs through students' IEPs. Thus, we examine changes in IEPs as students and their families prepare for school progressions and students move toward adult services.

Program Elements and Supports Affecting School-Age Students. The U.S. Department of Education (1996) reported that approximately 4,800,000 individuals with disabilities, ages 6 to 21, were served under IDEA. Germane to all students with disabilities is federal legislation encouraging their early preparation for adult roles and responsibilities. Accordingly, IDEA ensures a collaboration impetus for interagencies involved in service provisions to older students and their families. In essence, family-centered services are also becoming priorities for school-age children. Family practices now link funding provisions, inclusion, participatory school-based management, and school reform (O'Shea et al., 1993) to educational accountability. Teachers' family practices are made more meaningful when teachers encourage active school participation of families.

Family Participation. Family participation with teachers of school-age students proliferated during the 1980s (O'Shea et al., 1993; Turnbull & Turnbull, 1986). As such, parents participated not only in educational planning for their school-age children with disabilities but also more fully in the development of home-to-school, within school, and school-to-community policies. Today, such family involvement includes parents' or guardians' participation on federal, state, and local interagency coordinating councils; their involvement in community-based decision-making; and their formations of local and state parent advocacy groups affecting family policies and program decisions.

Family members of school-age children often participate in local educational services by attending open houses or "back to school nights." They attend parent-teacher conferences. Together with faculty and staff, they often plan and implement parent organization activities, such as fund-raising events or organized speaker presentations. Many serve on school advisory panels or on strategic planning commissions. Often, they are active in school athletic events or in school volunteer projects.

Families of school-age students, in essence, are fast becoming more of a driving force in the provision of services to their children. Box 9.9 presents suggestions aimed at parents or guardians to help in increasing their active school participation-transition awareness.

Box 9.9   **Suggestions for Parents or Guardians to Help Them Increase Their Active School Participation-Transition Awareness**

1. Ask your child's teacher whether he or she uses a variety of resources in planning now for future needs of your child (e.g., does the teacher share information with you on a future school class or appropriate teaching materials?). Find out what is involved in the next educational setting by visiting your child's future class now or by asking now for concrete information from next year's teacher. In this way, you know what is in store for your child in the next program and can help prepare your child currently.
2. Ask your child's current teachers how the current educational program contains features of next year's class.
3. Ask yourself whether your school professionals are available to meet with you and your child often, but especially before your child's entry into new school programs.
4. Does your child's current teacher offer you information on community programs available now or ones in which your child can enroll next year?
5. Prior to your child's entrance into a new program or class, get the name of a school contact who can explain to you differences in programming requirements, legal issues, schedules, adult-to-child ratios, transportation, communication methods, and so forth. Ask for an appointment so that your questions may be answered concerning your child's specific needs.
6. Ask your child's present teacher how last year's goals and objectives on the IEP are related to this year's goals and objectives. Does your child's new teacher gradually introduce new information and match instructional or management goals and objectives to new program features on the basis of your child's needs? Seek written assurance from school personnel that this is happening for your child.
7. Prior to your child's placement in programs, visit the school and community programs and classrooms while they are in session.
8. Help your child's teacher write education and transition plans early enough so that your child has adequate opportunities to achieve goals. Realize that school professionals should be actively asking you for your input into your child's educational program.
9. Be willing to share information with others. Be open to help as much as possible before, during, and after your child's attendance in programs. Give teachers information on your child's behavior at home. If appropriate, share information from your child's doctor or recreational program personnel.
10. Ask professionals to provide you and other parents with workshops, meetings, reading materials, and so forth on expected stress and school adjustment difficulties. Ask them to talk with you and other parents about expected differences for children with various disabilities at home or in the community. Share with them your sources of stress with your child at home. Let them know when you can't find a baby-sitter to watch your child. Ask them to help you seek resources when your child's medical care is more than you can

handle. Discuss how your other children at home include your child with disabilities in play and other activities. Discuss the impact of your child on grandparents, neighbors, and so forth. Also ask professionals to share with you and other parents information on expected similarities of your child to others. Ask to be provided with specific implications about resources, services, and programs beyond your child's immediate future so that you can help your child learn to adjust now.

11. Respect information on those involved in the transition process. Become familiar with the backgrounds, experiences, training, philosophical orientations, languages, communication styles, and expectations of your child's teachers. Share similar information about yourself as well when in formal meetings, informal get-togethers, or through written communications. Let the teachers know you and your child so that better programming is offered.

12. Ask how your child's IEPs, ITPs, or IFSPs and programs are changed on the basis of your child's needs for a particular service. Ask for, and keep a copy of, all records on your child. If you don't understand information in your child's records, know that you have a right to have a professional explain all information. You may write down your concerns about any information with which you and professionals disagree, and your disagreements should be placed in your child's records.

13. Ask your child's school administrator or teacher to give you information in a variety of forms (e.g., books, materials) to help you, your child, siblings, and your family anticipate changes in your child's needs.

14. Try to locate information on local services that will be available when your child is no longer of school age. Share, and ask others to share, resources and information.

15. Acknowledge stress and adjustment difficulties openly. Share your concerns with your child's teacher and with other parents and families. At all times, expect school and community professionals to treat you and your child with dignity. Demonstrate a willingness to listen to professionals and a common goal of solving problems together.

16. Realize your own coping levels and abilities without condemning yourself when you can't handle every situation with your child. Be willing to give help to others. Just as important is the willingness to receive help from others. Recognize your own strengths and weaknesses as a parent. Remember that your decisions about your child with disabilities will always be challenging despite the best intentions and planning. Also realize, however, that you are not alone and that you can receive some help for you and your child when you let others into your life.

17. Speak openly with school professionals often. Send notes to school about your child's progress at home. Let the teacher know when your child had a bad weekend, as well as about a toy or book your child especially likes. If teachers request it, let them share reports with you, have face-to-face contacts, or visit your home. Let them set up with you a scheduled time to talk about your child, the future, and your concerns.

18. Be open to working with your child's teachers and community helpers. Work from a team approach and expect that you should be treated as a contributing member to your child's team. When you disagree with professionals about your child, don't be afraid to speak up about your concerns. Remember that you will be with your child longer than any professional will, so your input about the future is vital. All your questions are appropriate, no matter how small. All your issues are of importance.

19. Include your child in future decision-making as much as possible to enhance choices, emphasize independence, and consider your child's likes and dislikes, if appropriate. Changes in your child's life will be easier for all involved when your child believes that he or she is, and truly is, a part of the decision-making process.

20. Discuss with school personnel your ethnic and cultural customs, celebrations, and traditions. Help families and professionals work together in the change process through awareness, teaming, and action planning with others. Your child will benefit when you work together productively with professionals.

Teachers' Work with Families

Teachers of school-age students will be involved actively with diverse families. Recognition of and skills with American family diversity is a necessary competency for new teachers. For example, information on families' backgrounds, home experiences, priorities, and expectations for their children contributes to students' school success and teachers' effectiveness. Prerequisite skills in work with families include teachers' effective listening, written expressions, teaming skills, consensual decisions, problem solving, mediations, and compromises. By taking the first steps to establishing and maintaining a good rapport with students' families, teachers can build long-lasting foundations that help children at school and at home. Seeking family support for school projects and soliciting families' active participation in schools are ways of sending messages that teachers care and are responsive to family input.

Teachers can employ varied strategies to encourage families' active and productive participation in their children's school services. For example, new teachers can demonstrate flexible hours to meet family needs (e.g., meet before or after the workday to increase parental participation, conduct a home visit). They can communicate with families "in attitude more than in hours" by inquiring often on what parents do at home to help their children. Teachers can send home age-appropriate parent-child activities to supplement school objectives. They can directly ask families how the teachers can include parents or guardians as part of their children's team. They can use interest surveys, telephone calls, newsletters, or group forums.

Pause and Reflect 9.4

Put a check mark on your three top indicators, below, of diverse family strategies in your field site. Discuss your indicators with a peer. Compare and contrast the reasons why you and your peer chose the indicators.

_____ 1. Endorse and support parents or guardians by making time for each other, share contributions, problem solve, and collaborate.

_____ 2. Offer written ideas to encourage family-friendly school programs, improve existing programs, and extend the opportunity for involvement of parents, siblings, or grandparents.

_____ 3. Participate in school advisory committees and programs charged with identifying family needs, developing plans, and assessing family-school outcomes.

_____ 4. Contact families regularly by using group meetings, written reports, letters, notes and notices, telephone contacts, and family-class newsletters. Consider families' primary language needs.

_____ 5. Work collaboratively with coalition groups, parent advocacy groups, and parent support systems to link home, school, and community practices. Empower each other through communication. Recognize that compromise is essential to communication.

_____ 6. Attend and actively participate in family programs and family in-service programs. Share experiences and collaborate with families in the identification of local home, school, and community improvement plans.

_____ 7. Strive to implement diverse family suggestions and new ideas into the curriculum. Make opportunities to share resources related to disabilities, family issues, school programming, community services, or family life.

_____ 8. Be willing to accommodate family diversity. Be open to family input that initially may not appeal. Use a variety of family involvement methods (e.g., parent questionnaires, family attendance at school functions, home visits and observations, family behavioral change, student performance systems).

Teachers demonstrate acceptance of family participation, a positive attitude, and diverse family input through interpersonal communication skills and behaviors. They might identify and employ the strengths and interests of family members to participate actively in their child's education. For example, teachers can learn more about diverse family backgrounds, traditions, and priorities by inviting family members to demonstrate cultural traditions and family customs in open class discussions. They might ask family members to describe the family's traditions on national events or holidays (e.g., Independence Day, Valentine's Day). They then might ask students to compare and contrast their family customs with those of other class members.

New teachers can help students understand and accept individual differences and commonalties by directly supporting and sharing various ethnic celebrations, food, clothing, religious holidays, or special community celebrations. They can teach components of diverse family and community traditions in the curricula. By so doing, they give the message to students, families, and peers that they recognize family diversity as a strength. Again, communication strategies (e.g., teaming, display of empathy, openness, information sharing, dealing with conflicts) have a huge impact on teachers' success with individual families.

Elementary- and Middle-School Students' Transitions

Teachers, students, and family members face various transition issues when children enter school-age services. These issues, however, often differ from those of younger children (George & Lewis, 1991; Stewart, 1989). Students exit single educational programs offered in early intervention services to enter new situations in larger, elementary schools. The concept of *least restrictive environment (LRE)* implies learning opportunities across varied settings.

For example, important to students entering primary and middle schools, adjustments now entail teachers' provision of alternative management systems within classrooms; opportunities with specialized teachers, such as media specialists, computer technologists, and reading specialists; teachers' and students' maintenance of academic momentum and flow between classroom events; and/or movement across special and integrated learning environments offered in the home, school, or community.

Teachers' transition involvement during the elementary- and middle-school years, hence, includes planning for students' involvement with peers, community personnel, and extended family members (e.g., parents, siblings, grandparents, neighbors) (George & Lewis, 1991; Stewart, 1989). Curricula often focus on maximizing the participation, independence, and productivity of students in varied learning domains.

New teachers will participate in planning activities that emphasize students' coping strategies within the home, school, or community setting. For example, the curricula and service delivery demands for many new teachers will relate to students' inclusion needs, available resources, and the "flow" implications occurring between classroom events when students change classes or teachers. Teachers may provide direct services to students and families or may offer consultation and team-teaching options with other personnel. Curriculum offerings will target, for many students, their preparation for adult life. Teachers may offer training for work or discuss in class students' home and family adjustments. "Functional academics" may center on such skills as independent living needs, students' leisure-time and recreational pursuits, and students' community involvement.

In addition to the basics of reading, writing, and arithmetic, curriculum content such as self-management, independent study skills, social skills, and organizational skills may highlight the activities of many elementary- or middle-school teachers. Effects of students' disabilities and levels of independence on families' abilities to function also pose challenges to teachers. Teachers will use their knowledge of students and families to plan and collect information on future skills and program requirements of the next learning environment (e.g., high school, job site) while embedding appropriate curricula into current programming.

Important to elementary- and middle-school students are teachers' preparation for transition events such as changes within and between schools and class programs; students' effects on family members; initiation of independence training; and implications of students' inclusive opportunities, including academic, behavioral, social, and learning adjustments in the home, school, or community settings.

Thus, as students grow, their learning environments expand from school boundaries to include opportunities in the community setting, vocational training sites, family units, and alternative educational instructional sites. Teachers' transition activities necessitate coordination throughout the school years. Most often, students' IEPs document the coordination. Important transition issues entail goal specificity, concrete timeline planning, and cross-categorical focus on the varied needs of those served (Getzel, 1990).

LINKING SCHOOL OPPORTUNITIES

Implementing services for older students includes the coordinated efforts of many home, school, and community professionals involved with school-age children and their families. IDEA is very specific concerning educational services and family involvement for school-age students with disabilities. For example, the law continues to mandate that an IEP be drawn up for every child or youth found eligible for special education or related services, pinpointing what kinds of services the student will receive. It reaffirms parents' right to participate in every decision related to the identification, evaluation, and placement of their child or youth with a disability. It calls for annual planning; assessment of students' strengths, needs, and interests; and programming by interagency personnel.

Importantly, the law also promotes the linkage of school and community experiences, development of postschool adult living objectives, and the development of daily living skills and functional vocational evaluations. Activities occur starting long before a student exits high school.

IEPs and Students' Transitions

IDEA identifies "transition services" as a coordinated set of activities. Students' transitions must be designed within an outcome-oriented process that promotes movement from school to postschool activities, including postsecondary education, vocational training, integrated employment (including supported employment), continuing and adult education, adult services, independent living, or community participation.

IDEA encourages students, teachers, and families to coordinate school programming with businesses and transition service agencies, beginning early in students' careers. As such, the law now mandates that the IEP must include a statement of transition services, including, if appropriate, a statement of the responsibilities or linkages or both of each public agency and each participating agency before the student leaves the school setting. Hence, IEPs must now include a statement of transition services needed by students who are age 16 or over, and when individually appropriate, for students who are age 14 or over.

The most substantive amendment in IDEA transition plans specifies a statement of interagency responsibilities and linkages. The agency, purpose, contact persons, and time by which the linkage occurs are paramount to professionals and families. Importantly, when teachers and other professionals work together with families in planning and implementing linkages, they assist students' long-term gains. Figure 9.2 provides an example of the transition component to school-age students' IEPs.

INDIVIDUAL TRANSITION PLAN SECTION OF THE IEP

Transition services required for students with disabilities moving from school to adult life (beginning no later than age 16, and when determined appropriate, beginning at age 14 or younger). The IEP team addressed planning for transition services in the outcome areas checked below: (If an outcome area or instructional area is not needed, state and federal law requires a statement to that effect and the basis upon which the determination is made.)

I.   EXPECTED POSTSCHOOL OUTCOMES:

    [ ] Postsecondary Training/Education:

    _____

    _____

    [ ] Employment:

    _____

    _____

    [ ] Community Living:

    _____

    _____

    [ ] Recreation/Leisure:

    _____

    _____

    [ ] Residential:

    _____

    _____

I.   INSTRUCTIONAL AREAS NEEDED TO SUPPORT EXPECTED POSTSCHOOL OUTCOMES:

    [ ] FUNCTIONAL VOCATIONAL ASSESSMENT:

    _____

    _____

    [ ] INSTRUCTIONAL AREAS: (may include, but not be limited to):
    [ ] Academic Instruction
    [ ] Career Education
    [ ] Community-Based Experiences and Instruction
    [ ] Community-Based Vocational Training
    [ ] Functional Living Skills
    [ ] Preparation for Postsecondary Education/Training
    [ ] Vocational-Technical Education
    [ ] Vocational-Technical Program Assistance
    [ ] Work Experience
    [ ] Other:

Instructional areas should support expected postschool outcomes. Instructional areas should appear in the IEP as annual goals, short-term objectives, and specially designed instruction.

FIGURE 9.2   An Example of the Transition Component to Older Students' IEPs   *continued*

IIII. PERSON(s) RESPONSIBLE FOR IMPLEMENTING TRANSITION ACTIVITIES.

_____

_____

IV. INTERAGENCY RESPONSIBILITIES, OR LINKAGES, OR BOTH THAT WILL
BE PROVIDED BEFORE THE STUDENT LEAVES THE SCHOOL SETTING:

_____

_____

Agencies or individuals who may provide services support:

Agency: _____ Contact Person: _____

Address: _____ Phone: _____

Agency: _____ Contact Person: _____

Address: _____ Phone: _____

Agency: _____ Contact Person: _____

Address: _____ Phone: _____

FIGURE 9.2 *continued*

High-School Students' Transitions

Although IDEA's transition definition slants toward students' vocational needs, the federal definition also implies many functional adult living skills taught long before high-school students enter the adult world. Vocational training and employment opportunities, daily living skills, independent survival skills, and community participation skills, initiated earlier in elementary- or middle-school programs, now become necessary high-school curriculum components requiring sequential placement in school programming (Tindall & Gugerty, 1989).

Professionals targeting high-school transition help plan to-and-from programs through the individualized transition plan (ITP) portion of a student's IEP (Getzel, 1990). Teachers' use of a "top-down" curriculum can address longitudinal domains (Hawaii Transition Project, 1987), including school survival skills; "functional management"; self-help skills; "follow-along" support programs in the school, home, or community settings; home and family training; family adjustment; self-fulfillment and self-advocacy training; integration realities after leaving school; recreation/leisure skills; financial support; emotional/physical well-being; health awareness; community awareness; and citizenship (guardianship/advocacy) rights and responsibilities. Additionally, secondary-school personnel may focus on students' and families' preparation for post-secondary adjustment, when teachers and school support are no longer available.

Accordingly, to teachers of older students with disabilities, transition implies a variety of changing events: movement from a unitary system (education) to multiple service systems or, sometimes, a nonsystem; from education to job setting; within the parental or natural home; from the parental or natural home to other living arrangements; and from relative dependence on professionals and parents to relative independence from them (O'Shea et al., 1993; Turnbull & Turnbull, 1985). New teachers can help prepare their students when they work to coordinate services for their students with family

Box 9.10   **Examples of Linkage Component Activities to Promote the School-to-Work Opportunities Act of 1994**

Hold monthly meetings to address local collaboration and problem-solving initiatives espoused by the Departments of Education and Labor.

Initiate partnership models between school-based and employment-based sites at the local level.

Hold quarterly sessions for schools and employment site personnel to plan, implement, and evaluate integrated school-based and work-based learning. Invite families, students, and educational and business leaders.

Have bimonthly meetings with teachers and employers to match students with employers.

Plan student and family orientations or conferences on career education, career development programs, and work-based linkages. Invite guidance counselors, local college or university personnel, and educational and business leaders.

Plan transition-coordinating councils to develop and implement interagency agreements, technical assistance, and services to employers, educators, case managers, and others.

Prior to IEP meetings, send home surveys to parents or guardians and students to ascertain, in advance, postschool options and assistance anticipated for training, vocations, residence, recreation, and so forth.

Share written resources with family and community services on youth development activities, academic and vocation learning, and employer strategies for upgrading worker skills.

members and important interagency personnel. See Box 9.9 for suggestions for increasing parents' or guardians' active school participation-transition awareness.

Interagency Coordination Efforts

Today's schools require a high level of interagency coordination of frontline service providers, including teachers. Teachers increasingly work with other professionals and parents or guardians in a broader, community-oriented, service delivery context. For example, the School-to-Work Opportunities Act of 1994 also focuses on services linking students to adult life activities. It promotes collaboration and problem solving by the Departments of Education and Labor. The act encourages partnership models between school-based and employment-based sites at the local level and encourages schools and employment site personnel, along with family members, to plan, implement, and evaluate integrated school-based and work-based learning.

Among other components in the act are school-based learning components encouraging students' career awareness and exploration. However, components also target counseling to identify students' career interests and goals, as well as their integration of academic and vocational learning. Work-based learning components include workplace mentoring and instruction in general workplace competencies. Connecting activity components include provision of technical assistance to school and employers to integrate school-based and work-based learning. Linkage of youth development activities with employer strategies for upgrading worker skills are also relevant in program initiatives. Box 9.10 presents examples of linkage components that new teachers may find beneficial when they apply home input with school and employment opportunities inherent in the School-to-Work Opportunities Act.

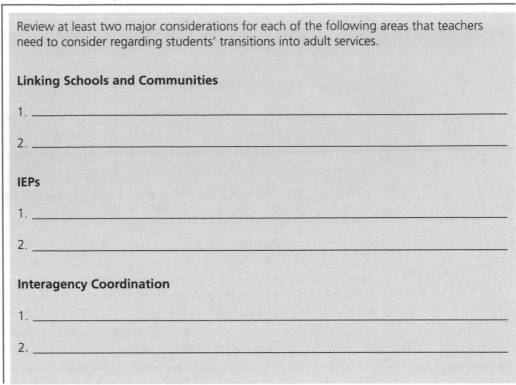

TEACHERS' ROLES AS STUDENTS AGE

As students transition across school-age programs and enter into adult services, professionals and families must continue to work together to plan, implement, and evaluate program services. New teachers will continue to help coordinate services through students' IEPs. Team members again consider students' varied needs and strengths as the students grow toward adult roles. For example, beginning teachers may work with others to determine location and accessibility of local community-based service delivery systems. They may work with parents and business leaders on securing appropriate jobs with the degree of integrated opportunities that families want for their children. They may work with other professionals and families on matching students' needs to available housing resources when students are ready to leave their parents' home, marry, or move to a new home or city. They may help evaluate curricula as students leave school, enter the service, and/or enter jobs or training opportunities.

Examples of the roles that teachers may play as students age include teachers' cooperative work with job coaches, employment trainers, supported employment personnel, and other vocational personnel at local vocational training sites or jobs. Teachers might be sharing data related to students' opportunities in community-based vocational training, vocational-technical education, or program assistance or students' work experiences offered through the armed services. Importantly, many teachers may be reorienting their school curricula from academic outcomes to adult outcomes and experiences.

Facilitating the Transition Process for Older Students and Their Families

As was the case with early intervention services, teachers can help older students and their families make adjustments in new settings. They can help families secure advance written information about training requirements and community-based program availability in the local area. They can help arrange students and families' visits to new programs before the students exit high-school programs. Teachers can help organize orientations. They can obtain necessary resources (e.g., handouts with registration cutoff dates, income eligibility requirements, geographic boundaries of programs, transportation availability, age restrictions, degree of parent participation required). These activities will continue to help in transitions to adult services.

Teachers' involvement with their students' families and communities, thus, is vitally important to the continuing success of older students. Unfortunately, educational, social, and medical professionals with whom teachers work often have various family conceptualizations (e.g., views of administrators, counselors, family legal advocates, family therapists, health care workers, psychologists, teachers, and social workers may clash in IEP meetings). Nonetheless, understanding the views of others is vital.

As new teachers integrate their students' family knowledge with what they can do to help students' successful transitions, they will be in a better position to value, respect, and/or accept the perspectives of others. Teachers can select, with families and other professionals, student assessment and instructional strategies that are age and ability appropriate. They can offer functionally based curricula geared to meeting daily and long-term needs. Family expertise can be targeted as a valued and recognized variable in school services. Families, as allies, can help increase resources important to students, schools, and communities.

As teachers gain information on the unique experiences of families, they are in better positions to offer realistic programming. Successful adjustments occur when individuals guide program and service options based on needs and strengths of their individual students and families. Box 9.11 provides a checklist to help teachers facilitate the transition process for school-age children.

Box 9.11

Checklist to Help Teachers Facilitate the Transition Process for School-Age Children

_____ Encourage families, students, and significant professionals in the students' lives (e.g., therapists, social workers, health workers, coaches, employers) to visit programs and classrooms while in session prior to students' placement in the program.

_____ Use a variety of formal and informal assessment devices to gather and determine goals and services for the existing program and to plan for the future program.

_____ Plan, teach, and evaluate relevant skills required of students in the next setting (an appropriate number of weeks before leaving the existing program). Consider the impact on the home, school, and community setting for the students and their families. Write education and transition plans early enough so that students have adequate opportunities to achieve goals.

_____ Devise educational plans with families and significant professionals in the children's lives (e.g., therapists, social workers, health workers), describing specific skills students will need to be successful in the home, school, or community.

_____ Include a clear description of what students will gain from the current programming with respect to future functioning in the home, school, or community setting. Specify in writing the potential gains and expectations across settings for the future.

_____ Be specific in sharing information with others. For example, teachers in sending and receiving programs need to be aware of the necessity of initiating and maintaining contacts as long as necessary for individual students and families. Be open to help as much as possible before, during, and after students' attendance in programs.

_____ Provide families and significant professionals with workshops, meetings, and reading materials about expected stress and adjustments in developmental ages.

_____ Talk about expected differences for students with disabilities. Include specific information about resources, services, and programs beyond the immediate future.

_____ Be available to meet with families, students, and significant professionals prior to students' entry into new programs.

_____ When students are ready to exit from current programs, visit the new program with students and families to act as a familiar link and support system to them.

_____ Provide families and significant professionals with specific details about the current program's components (e.g., curriculum, transportation, meals, therapies, job training, job placements) prior to students entering the programs.

_____ Provide students, families, and significant professionals with information on placement and service options available in the home, school, and community settings. Collect as many data as are pertinent to the local programming options. Share information continually and ask others to share.

_____ Initiate and maintain ongoing contact with families and significant professionals throughout students' involvement in the current program. Actively encourage program input from families and other professionals at all times.

_____ Invite others to express their questions, comments, and concerns through open communication methods such as letters home, progress reports, face-to-face contacts, and home visits.

_____ Demonstrate empathy, congruence, and availability to students, families, and significant professionals before, during, and after students attendance in programs.

_____ Facilitate parent-to-parent contacts and information sharing throughout students' involvement in the program. Encourage the same with other service providers.

_____ Observe and obtain information on the new learning environment, prior to students' exit from the existing program, so that current programming contains features of the next setting.

_____ Provide information in a variety of forms (e.g., books, materials) to help families and other professionals anticipate changes in students' needs.

_____ Provide students with the skills and training required in the next environment to reduce adjustment difficulties and associated stress of the "unknown."

_____ Match instructional goals and objectives to new program features as soon as possible for students' needs in the current setting.

_____ Modify IEPs, ITPs, and programs on the basis of student and family needs for a particular service. Continually collect data on program effectiveness. Document all attempts. Make adjustments when changes are r equired.

SUMMARY

This chapter emphasized that collaboration with families must start in the early years of a child's life, not just in the months before students enter the adult world. Teachers must be aware of relevant transitional periods and accompanying activities for children, youth, and families. Additionally, the individual developmental and educational needs of students and families should be foremost in teachers' professional planning and conduct.

Next, the chapter offered an overview of the need for new teachers to have a realistic base to match planning, programming, and evaluating. Present and future environmental conditions must be considered in relation to school programming. By assuming transition responsibilities related to both students and families in a wholehearted manner, teachers help ensure an effective education to all students.

ACTIVITIES TO EXTEND YOUR KNOWLEDGE

1. Interview several families of young children with disabilities. You can get names of families from the local chapter of Associations for Retarded Citizens (ARC) or other agencies with a focus on children with disabilities. Ask families to share their impressions of important issues surrounding their child's transitions from the hospital to home, home to early intervention services, early intervention services to preschool special education, and preschool special education to elementary-level special education. Be sure to ask the families to indicate which people and transition strategies were helpful and which were not. Ask whether families have suggestions for improving the transition process.

2. Read books or articles written by parents of children with disabilities to better understand families' perspectives. Visit your local library or bookstore and ask for guidance at the reference desk. Ask staff members of professional organizations (e.g., ARC) to suggest reading material.

3. Explore computer programs and/or library resources to locate more information related to the influence of students' diverse learning, behavioral, linguistic, and cultural characteristics on home, school, and community opportunities. How does this information help students in your field site?

4. Interview a social worker or family community worker on age-appropriate rules and reinforcers necessary for students' transitions from preschool to adult services. What are additional curriculum implications for students in your field site? What can you begin teaching your students now?

5. Visit various potential job sites for your students. Ask employers and employees about specific ideas for improving student motivation and cooperation on job sites. Share your findings now with your students and school personnel.

6. Discuss group problem-solving techniques within the context of students in your current site. Find out more on conflict resolution techniques and related social skills that can help your students transition into a relevant new setting. What can you begin teaching your students now?

7. Complete a log on successful assessment instruments and transition techniques appropriate in identifying and meeting needs of your students. Target specific ways that you can communicate assessment and transition results with parents.

8. Develop a transition management plan that will address specific academic, behavioral, social, vocational, and other functional needs of students in your site. Ask parents or guardians for their input.

9. Offer to provide a few hours of respite care for parents of more severely involved children. Respite care is often difficult for families to find. As you provide respite care, you'll not only provide a break for families from caregiving routines, but you'll also learn about the strengths and needs of the children in your care. The old saying about walking a mile in someone else's shoes is especially relevant when a child has a disability.

POINT AND CLICK

http://www.eparent.com/default.htm
This is the Web site for *Exceptional Parent* magazine. In addition to information for parents of children with disabilities, there are links to other relevant sites such as the Disability Network, an Internet directory, financial planning, mobility, and appropriate toys.

http://www.cec.sped.org
This Web site is the home page for the Council for Exceptional Children (CEC), the leading professional organization pertaining to the education of individuals with disabilities. There are also divisions (e.g., the Division for Early Childhood) with a specialized focus. CEC's Web site has numerous links to other Web sites related to disability issues.

http://www.nectas.unc.edu
This site offers a wealth of resources related to young children with disabilities and their families. The National Early Childhood * Technical Assistance System (NEC*TAS) is housed at the University of North Carolina in Chapel Hill. Of particular interest are the links to information about service coordination, an important component of many transitions for young children and their families.

http://www2.edc.org/NCIP/Default.htm
The Web site of the National Center to Improve Practice in Special Education Through Technology, Media, and Materials (NCIP) offers a wide variety of resources related to the education of children and youth with disabilities. The site's links are especially helpful in finding information on specific kinds of disabilities.

REFERENCES

Anderson, R. D., Bale, J. F., Blackman, J. A., & Murph, J. R. (1994). *Infections in children: A sourcebook for educators and child care providers.* Rockville, MD: Aspen.

Bagnato, S. J., Neisworth, S. J., & Munson, S. M. (1989). *Linking developmental assessment and early intervention: Curriculum-based prescriptions.* Rockville, MD: Aspen.

Bailey, D. B., Simeonsson, R. J., Yoder, D. E., & Huntington, G. S. (1990). Preparing professionals to serve infants and toddlers with disabilities and their families: An integrative analysis across eight disciplines. *Exceptional Children, 57*(1), 26–35.

Batshaw, M. L. (1997). *Children with disabilities* (4th ed.). Baltimore: Paul H. Brookes.

Bennett, T., Nelson, D. E., Lingerfelt, B. V., & Davenport-Ersoff, C. (1992). Family-centered service coordination. In T. Bennett, D. E. Nelson, & B. V. Lingerfelt (Eds.), *Facilitating family-centered training in early intervention.* Tucson, AZ: Therapy Skill Builders.

Bond, N., Farquahar, B., Hentz, P., Luckenbill, D., Prumo, M., Ralabate, P., Santelli, J., Taylor, J., Trice, C., & Weintraub, F. (1990). *Guidelines for the delineation of roles and responsibilities for the safe delivery of specialized health care in the educational setting.* Reston, VA: Council for Exceptional Children.

Brazelton, T. B., & Cramer, B. G. (1990). *The earliest relationship: Parents, infant, and the drama of early attachment.* Reading, MA: Addison-Wesley.

Bricker, D. D. (1989). *Early intervention for at-risk and handicapped infants, toddlers, and preschool children* (2nd ed.). Palo Alto, CA: VORT.

Brotherson, M. J., & Goldstein, B. L. (1992). Time as a resource and constraint for parents of young children with disabilities: Implications for early intervention services. *Topics in Early Childhood Special Education, 12*(4), 508–527.

Brown, W., Thurman, S. K., & Pearl, L. F. (Eds.). (1993). *Family-centered early intervention with infants and toddlers: Innovative cross-disciplinary approaches.* Baltimore: Paul H. Brookes.

Campbell, P. H. (1991). Evaluation and assessment in early intervention for infants and toddlers. *Journal of Early Intervention, 15*(1), 36–45.

Council for Exceptional Children, Task Force on Recommended Practices. (1993). *DEC recommended practices: Indicators of quality in programs for infants and young children with special needs.* Reston, VA: Author.

Craig, E. R., & Leonard, C. R. (1990, April). P.L. 99-457: Are speech-language pathologists trained and ready? *ASHA, 32,* 57–61.

Cripe, J., Slentz, K., & Bricker, D. (1993). *Assessment, evaluation, and programming system for infants and children: Vol. 2. AEPS curriculum from birth to three years.* Baltimore: Paul H. Brookes.

deFur, S., Getzel, E. E., & Kregel, J. (1994). Individual transition plans: A work in progress. *Journal of Vocational Rehabilitation, 4,* 139–145.

deFur, S., & Taymans, J. M. (1995). Competencies needed for transition specialists in vocational rehabilitation, vocational education, and special education. *Exceptional Children, 62*(1), 38–51.

DeGangi, G. A., Wietlisbach, S., Poisson, S., & Stein, E. (1994). The impact of culture and socioeconomic status on family-professional collaboration: Challenges and solutions. *Topics in Early Childhood Special Education, 14*(4), 503–520.

Dinnebeil, L. A., & Rule, S. (1994). Variables that influence collaboration between parents and service coordinators. *Journal of Early Intervention, 18*(4), 349–361.

Donowitz, L. G. (Ed.). (1993). *Infection control in the child care center and preschool* (2nd ed.). Baltimore: Williams & Wilkins.

Fewell, R. R. (1991). Trends in the assessment of infants and toddlers with disabilities. *Exceptional Children, 58*(2), 166–173.

Fewell, R. R., & Vadasy, P. F. (Eds.). (1986). *Families of handicapped children: Needs and supports across the life span.* Austin, TX: PRO-ED.

George, N. L., & Lewis, T. J. (1991). Exit assistance for special educators: Helping students make the transition. *Teaching Exceptional Children, 23,* 35–38.

Getzel, E. E. (1990). Entering postsecondary program: Early individualized planning. *Teaching Exceptional Children, 23*(1), 51–53.

Governor's Office for Children, Youth, and Families/Maryland Infants and Toddlers Program. (1992). *Transition at age three: Guidelines for implementing policies and procedures.* Baltimore: Author.

Hanline, M. F., & Knowlton, A. (1988). A collaborative model for providing support to parents during their child's transition from infant intervention to preschool special education public school programs. *Journal of the Division for Early Childhood, 12*(2), 116–125.

Harry, B., Allen, N., & McLaughlin, M. (1995). Communication vs. compliance: African American parents' involvement in special education. *Exceptional Children, 61*(4), 364–376.

Hawaii Transition Project. (1987). [Transition resources]. Honolulu: University of Hawaii, Department of Special Education.

Henley, M., Ramsey, R. S., & Algozzine, R. (1993). *Characteristics of and strategies for teaching students with mild disabilities.* Needham Heights, MA: Allyn & Bacon.

Individuals with Disabilities Education Act (Public Law 101–476). (1990, October). Washington, DC: U.S. Office of Special Education and Rehabilitation.

Jeppson, E. S., & Thomas, J. (1995). *Essential allies: Families as advisors.* Bethesda, MD: Institute for Family-Centered Care.

Johnson-Martin, N. M., Attermeier, S. M., & Hacker, B. (1990). *The Carolina curriculum for preschoolers with special needs.* Baltimore: Paul H. Brookes.

Karge, P. D., Patton, P. L., & de la Garza, B. (1992). Transition services for youth with mild disabilities. Do they exist, are they needed? *Career Development for Exceptional Individuals, 15,* 47–68.

Katz, K. S., Pokorni, J. L., & Long, T. M. (1989). *The chronically ill and at-risk infant: Family-centered intervention from hospital to home.* Palo Alto, CA: VORT.

Kilgo, J. (1990). Early intervention. *Research Forum: DEC-CEC, 17*(1), 4.

King-Sears, M. E. (1994). *Curriculum-based assessment in special education.* San Diego, CA: Singular.

Kohler, P. D. (1993). Best practices in transition: Substantiated or implied? *Career Development for Exceptional Individuals, 16,* 107–121.

Krajicek, M., & Tompkins, R. (Eds.). (1993). *The medically fragile infant.* Austin, TX: PRO-ED.

Kroth, R. (1975). *Communicating with parents of exceptional children.* Denver: Love.

Lambie, R., & Daniels-Mohring, D. (1993). *Family systems within educational contexts: Understanding students with special needs.* Denver: Love.

Linder, T. W. (1993a). *Transdisciplinary play-based assessment: A functional approach to working with young children* (Rev. ed.). Baltimore: Paul H. Brookes.

Linder, T. W. (1993b). *Transdisciplinary play-based assessment: Guidelines for developing a meaningful curriculum for young children.* Baltimore: Paul H. Brookes.

Lynch, E. W., & Hanson, M. J. (1998). *Developing cross-cultural competence: A guide for working with young children and their families* (2nd ed.). Baltimore: Paul H. Brookes.

Martin, J. E., Marshall, L. H., & Maxson, L. L. (1993). Transition policy: Infusing self-determination and self-advocacy into transition programs. *Career Development for Exceptional Individuals, 16,* 53–61.

McLean, M., Bailey, D. B., & Wolery, M. (1996). *Assessing infants and preschoolers with special needs* (2nd ed.). Upper Saddle River, NJ: Merrill/Prentice Hall.

Nelson, D. E., Bennett, T., & Lingerfelt, B. V. (1992). Facilitating transitions between settings. In T. Bennett, D. E. Nelson, & B. V. Lingerfelt (Eds.), *Facilitating family-centered training in early intervention.* Tucson, AZ: Therapy Skill Builders.

Noonan, M. J., & McCormick, L. (1993). *Early intervention in natural environments: Methods and procedures.* Pacific Grove, CA: Brooks/Cole.

O'Shea, D. J., & Caldwell, L. (1990, Fall). *Transition services for students with mental handicaps* (University Internal Research Grant). Boca Raton: Florida Atlantic University.

O'Shea, D. J., O'Shea, L. J., & Nowocien, D. (1993). Parent-teacher relationships in school renewal and educational reform. *Learning Disability Forum, 18*(3), 43–46.

Santa Cruz County Office of Education. (1987). *HELP for special preschoolers ages 3 to 6: Activities binder.* Palo Alto, CA: VORT.

School-to-Work Opportunities Act of 1994 (Public Law 103-239). (1994, May 4). Title 20, U.S.C. 6101 *et seq.: U.S. Statutes at Large,* 108-568–608.

Singer, G. H. S., & Irvin, L. K. (Eds.). (1989). *Support for caregiving families: Enabling positive adaptation to disability.* Baltimore: Paul H. Brookes.

Smith, D. D., & Luckasson, R. (1995). *Introduction to special education: Teaching in an age of challenge* (2nd ed.). Needham Heights, MA: Allyn & Bacon.

Stewart, D. (1989). *A curriculum framework for secondary-aged handicapped students designed for use in the state of Georgia under Technical Assistance Activity-03-GA-88-06* (Transition). Washington, DC: OSERS.

Taylor, J. M. (1995). Staying healthy. In V. Y. Rab & K. I. Wood (Eds.), *Child care and the ADA: A handbook for inclusive practices.* Baltimore: Paul H. Brookes.

Taylor, J. M., & Fleming, J. A. (1997). *Guidelines for the evaluation or assessment of three-year-old children transitioning from early intervention services to preschool special education.* Baltimore: Maryland State Department of Education.

Taylor, J. M., & Taylor, W. S. (1989). *Communicable diseases and young children in group settings.* Boston: Singular.

Tindall, L. W., & Gugerty, J. J. (1989). Collaboration among clients, families, and service providers. In D. E. Beckell & J. M. Brown (Eds.), *Transition from school to work for persons with disabilities* (pp. 127–160). New York: Longman.

Turnbull, A. P., Patterson, J. M., Behr, S. K., Murphy, D. L., Marquis, J. G., & Blue-Banning, M. J. (Eds.). (1993). *Cognitive coping, families, and disability.* Baltimore: Paul H. Brookes.

Turnbull, A. P., & Turnbull, H. R. (1986). *Families, professionals, and exceptionality: A special partnership.* Upper Saddle River, NJ: Merrill/Prentice Hall.

Turnbull, H. R., & Turnbull, A. P. (1985). *Parents speak out: Then and now.* Upper Saddle River, NJ: Merrill/Prentice Hall.

Urbano, M. T. (1992). *Preschool children with special health care needs.* San Diego, CA: Singular.

U.S. Department of Education, Office of Special Education Programs. (1996, February 7). *Seventeenth annual report to Congress.* Washington, DC: Author.

VandenBerg, K. A., & Hanson, M. J. (1993). *Homecoming for babies after the neonatal intensive care nursery: A guide for professionals in supporting families and their infants' early development.* Austin, TX: PRO-ED.

Collaborative Programming and Consultation

In this chapter, we will

✔ discuss the beginning teacher as the recipient and provider of consulting services

✔ provide a collaborative model for consultative processes

✔ examine important interpersonal communication skills and general procedures for collaborative consultation

✔ analyze basic procedures in the conference model and how to operationalize conference procedures

*O*ne area often overlooked or given only superficial attention in teacher-training programs is professional interaction. In this chapter, we discuss how communicating with other professionals embodies a set of critical skills that will enable developing teachers to use the resources available in a school more effectively. Developing teachers new to a school are given greater than usual attention. Other professionals, paraprofessionals, parents, and students observe and begin to make decisions about the kinds of persons new teachers are and whether or not the teachers believe they will be effective teachers, helpful associates, or even personal friends. Consequently, there is a need to be cognizant of how individuals come across to others.

By verbal and nonverbal actions, developing teachers can manipulate the perceptions of others. On the one hand, if they want to be viewed as aggressive, they can make demands about what they will and will not do and what resources they expect to have available. On the other hand, they may act passively by being very acquiescent and giving in to the demands of everyone else. And, of course, there are myriad degrees of aggressive/passive behavior between these extremes. The point is that developing teachers have a degree of control over how they are perceived by others within this continuum. Consequently, the perceptions of others determine how cooperative they will be and what human and other resources will be made available.

We discuss roles that developing teachers will assume. In the first chapter section, we offer common sense ideas about interacting with consultants (consulting teachers, supervisors, or principals). Then, we include more technical information regarding interpersonal communication skills and procedures for conferring with others. Developing and beginning teachers should be well versed in playing the roles of recipient and provider of consultative or supervisory services. Therefore, they must look at the discussion from both points of view and envision how they would apply principles of interpersonal communication and collaborative problem solving from any one of the roles they may play at any given time. Their ability to function effectively in these roles will help shape the perceptions of others toward them.

INTRODUCTION

Developing and beginning teachers take on a variety of roles in professional relationships with other school staff (see Figure 10.1). Obviously, they will take on the role of a beginning teacher and therefore be the consultee (recipient of consultative services)

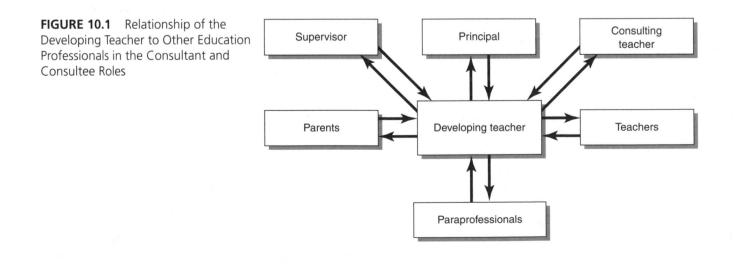

FIGURE 10.1 Relationship of the Developing Teacher to Other Education Professionals in the Consultant and Consultee Roles

from supervisory personnel (e.g., principal, program supervisor, consulting teacher). It is also likely that they will have paraprofessionals in their classrooms whom they will manage (e.g., assign instructional tasks, train in different teaching techniques). Thus, in this capacity, their role will be that of a consultant (provider of supervisory services).

In addition, with the emphasis on special education service provisions in general education classrooms and diverse students' access to the general education curricula, many special education teachers will be asked to assume educational consultant roles for other teaching staff in their school, as well as for parents. Because of the increased emphasis on educating students with disabilities with normally functioning peers, in addition to being a direct-service provider, special educators are providing increased consulting assistance to their general education peers.

Expanding roles and responsibilities entail teamwork and communication skills essential to meeting the challenge of diverse educational opportunities (Glatthorn, 1990; Villa, Thousand, Nevin, & Malgeri, 1996). Importantly, when teachers consult with others, they often use coaching models to support the communication process. In fact, the Council for Exceptional Children (CEC) defined the CEC standards for the preparation and licensure of new special educators (CEC, 2000a). Special educators who collaborate with families and other professionals recognize and acknowledge the competencies and expertise of others. They strive to develop positive attitudes among others. They cooperate with families and other agencies involved in serving persons with exceptionalities. They provide consultation and assistance, where appropriate, to both general and special educators as well as other school or nonschool personnel. They maintain effective interpersonal relations.

New teachers often rely on coaching models to support their proficiency in collaborating and consulting with others. New teachers profit from mentorships (Council for Exceptional Children, 2000b). CEC (2000a) found that each new special educator should receive a minimum 1-year mentorship during the first year of professional special education practice. The mentor should be an experienced professional in the same or a similar role as the mentee and can provide expertise and support on a continuing basis.

New teachers can develop greater practical competence and maintain enthusiasm for teaching when they engage in consultative mentoring experiences with novice and veteran teachers (Boyer & Gillespie, 2000; Caccia, 1996; McCaffrey, 2000; Whitaker, 2000). For instance, peer coaching entails seminars in which teachers instruct teachers in knowledge of content practices and implementations they are learning from each other. Peers help each other analyze their teaching skills, especially students' responses (Showers & Joyce, 1996). New teachers may consult with fellow teachers in local means to create and evaluate prereferral strategies for students' learning support. They may ask more experienced teachers for implementation tips in the general education classroom. Teachers in both general education and special education may use a variety of management strategies implemented together through peer coaching and assistance consultations. In some schools, teachers use consultative formats to modify and adapt learning materials, evaluations, or specially designed curricula.

When new teachers work with consulting teachers, they are involved in collaborative planning and data collection. Collaborate planning and data collection increase the time and the cost of staff development activities. To the extent that such activities result in greater clarity about means and ends, more thorough implementation of planned changes, and more immediate information about effects on students, the additional effort is well worth the investment. Teacher induction programs are beginning to use consultation formats to help new personnel learn the ropes of the system. The formation of supervisory assistance and peer coaching teams produces greater faculty cohesion and focus and, in turn, facilitates more shared decision-making. Some new personnel may be fortunate enough to work in a system where initial orientations, administrative consultations, and ongoing mentoring opportunities are the rule, rather than the exception. Other new teachers may experience informal staff development meetings, such as those that occur in faculty lounges. Regardless of the informal or formal basis to help new members learn to accept how the system operates, a skillful staff development program results in a self-perpetuating process for change, as well as new knowledge and skills for teachers and increased learning for students (Showers & Joyce, 1996).

CEC (2000b) suggested that school administrators and school directors provide opportunities for teachers to pursue actively professional growth activities that include collaboration. Because planning and preparation time are essential, administrators and directors can organize the school day and week so that school professionals have time to work collaboratively.

Thus, through peer coaching from new and experienced peers, new teachers receive help to implement their teaching effectiveness. In turn, new teachers receive administrative and peer assistance to help refine communication, management, and teaching behaviors. Consulting in supportive contexts is one key to successful professional growth and role development and to subsequent teacher change (Bos, 1995; Caccia, 1996; Showers & Joyce, 1996). In fact, opportunities for administrative support and peer collaboration, along with stress management, show promise as interventions for reducing burnout in special education and related services personnel (Cooley & Yovanoff, 1996; Westling & Whitten, 1996). Nonetheless, effective consultation and collaboration often rely on developing teachers' skills in recognizing how they are affected by and affect others through the use of consulting services.

THE BEGINNING TEACHER AS THE RECIPIENT OF CONSULTING SERVICES

Preservice teacher trainees and developing teachers are invariably the recipients of consulting services. **Consulting services** are activities or interactions provided by other professionals to help novice teachers improve their teaching performance. They may include a consulting teacher or supervisor formally assisting with setting up a classroom program on an ongoing basis, another teacher informally taking on the role of mentor and assisting as needed, or a principal evaluating teaching performance and providing corrective feedback. Team support from others, including university and district collaborators, often helps beginning teachers make strides in instructional practices, classroom management, and curriculum modifications (Karge, Lasky, McCabe, & Robb, 1995).

More experienced teaching personnel can assist with problem solving in more efficient ways by helping new teachers avoid mistakes and bureaucracy. They have gone through the process and have, more than likely, learned a lot that can be passed on to new personnel. For instance, teaching materials that would be of interest may be tucked away in some remote closet, or the school system may have a library of CD Roms that requires reserving far in advance. Often, asking the right person may better ensure receipt of some needed materials. More experienced teachers know how the school system really works and ways of getting around potential roadblocks.

Interactions with consulting teachers, supervisors, or principals can give developing teachers insights as to what is important in the eyes of key school personnel. Accordingly, new teachers can learn where to focus their time and attention. Administrators, for instance, may place more emphasis on classroom management and presentation of content than on having attractive bulletin boards. They may implicitly indicate hidden agendas, such as the expectation that teachers handle discipline problems in their rooms and not send students to the principal for reprimanding.

Pause and Reflect 10.1

What are potential roadblocks to "getting around the system" when you enter a school for the first time? Identify at least two areas of concern for college or university students initially entering a field site. Then, determine two different areas that may be potential roadblocks for student teachers. Next, list two avenues of concern for first-year teachers. Last, discuss with a peer one way to overcome each identified roadblock in your examples.

Students	Student Teachers	First-Year Teachers
Potential roadblock 1	Potential roadblock 1	Potential roadblock 1
A way to overcome potential roadblock 1	A way to overcome potential roadblock 1	A way to overcome potential roadblock 1
Potential roadblock 2	Potential roadblock 2	Potential roadblock 2
A way to overcome potential roadblock 2	A way to overcome potential roadblock 2	A way to overcome potential roadblock 2

Appreciating the Competence of Other Professionals

A large part of learning from experienced teachers and administrators is accepting that others are skillful and willing to be helpful when asked. Other teachers have refined their teaching skills so well that they make the act of teaching and classroom management look simple. They have developed styles that may or may not be congruent with the style of teaching that developing and beginning teachers wish to emulate. Nonetheless, developing and beginning teachers can learn a great deal about why specific teachers use certain styles and may find that what experienced teachers do can be modified to fit their concept of teaching and management. For example, a new teacher may observe that a teacher has excellent control of her students but seems to be verbally rough with them. This style may not be appealing, but beyond the surface the new teacher may notice that this teacher is very consistent in reinforcing appropriate behavior and in punishing inappropriate behavior. For the new teacher's own development, the rough tone may be dispensed and the consistency incorporated into his or her approach to student-behavior management.

Another point to consider is developing and beginning teachers' evaluation of and interaction with individuals of authority. Supervisory and administrative personnel are granted a degree of authority simply by the positions they hold. On the one hand, new teachers are expected, if nothing else, to respect the positions of such individuals in the organizational hierarchy. On the other hand, new teachers will make judgments about the competence of supervisory and administrative personnel and accordingly afford them varying degrees of respect for their professional competence. In either case, developing and beginning teachers will have to subordinate their views in order to survive in a hierarchical organizational system. If they find that a person with whom they work warrants respect for his or her competence, they can acquiesce to the dominant view with little or no resentment. If they only respect a person for the position he or she holds, it may at times be exceedingly difficult to subordinate their own views. Developing and beginning teachers, then, must make judgments for themselves, based on their level of confidence and whether others will perceive their views as having more merit. They also must depend on their willingness to jeopardize their continued employment in the system, on their perceptions of another person's power, and on the degree of support they believe they have among others in positions of power. An analysis of these variables is difficult, especially for developing teachers, who have not been a part of the system long enough to know its intricacies or to have established friends in high places who will look after them.

The safest strategy for developing teachers is to concede to authority in the early stages of induction into the school system unless such a concession entails committing an immoral, unethical, or illegal act. As developing and beginning teachers become more familiar with the system and demonstrate their own professional competence, they may become more assertive and challenge the system. Also, it should be remembered that new teachers are not necessarily alone; professional organizations and teachers' unions may be of great help, especially when an issue at hand is a serious one.

Often, developing and beginning teachers find that the consulting teachers, supervisors, and principals with whom they work have a different training background or teach different types of students or subject matter. Ideally, those professionals who are assisting with a developing teacher's growth have direct experience teaching the same content area, material, and category of students. But that may be a luxury that new teachers will not experience. Accordingly, they may be inclined to underestimate the quality and relevance of the assistance that teaching professionals in other areas can lend.

The fact remains, however, that the principles of effective instruction and behavioral management used by skilled teachers are, by definition, generalizable rules that guide teacher behavior (Box 10.1). They are appropriate for most populations and content (albeit, the application of those principles to different populations and content would have to be modified). Teachers unfamiliar with the specific content of instruction, however, may not be able to assist with issues of content accuracy and structure. But teachers in other content areas and with different types of students and age groups can demonstrate techniques or help developing and beginning teachers recognize effective or ineffective techniques they are using in their instruction. Nonetheless, developing and beginning teachers must be able to apply principles and good examples in their own classrooms.

Making the Most of Consultative Services

If developing and beginning teachers view the supervision process as a service being provided by their employer, then they can view their role in the process as that of a consumer receiving a service. Consequently, they should take advantage of supervision by making full use of the process. The consultative service should entail a systematic approach to the supervision process whereby conferences and observations are conducted on a regularly scheduled basis. Conferences and observations target specific performance objectives. Critiques of developing teachers' instructional or management behaviors are presented in conjunction with constructive suggestions for alternative teaching behaviors. Novice teachers should also be given increasing responsibility for identifying their own strengths and weaknesses and for devising prescriptions for their improvement.

Box 10.1   Effective Instructional and Behavioral Management Principles

Instructional Organization and Development

- Uses instructional time effectively
- Provides reviews of subject matter frequently
- Signals the initiation of lesson and lesson transitions
- Varies levels of questioning
- Provides numerous opportunities to respond
- Uses wait time to mediate question presentation and signal to respond
- Acknowledges and elaborates student responses
- Provides specific academic feedback
- Provides and monitors guided and independent practice

Presentation of Subject Matter

- Defines and gives examples and nonexamples of concepts
- States cause and effect for laws and lawlike principles
- States and applies academic rules
- Establishes criteria and assembles facts to make value judgments

Management of Student Conduct

- Sets, monitors, and enforces classroom rules
- Is aware of student behavior
- Manages multiple activities simultaneously
- Uses positive reinforcement
- Uses contingent punishment

Communication: Verbal and Nonverbal

- Presents discourse clearly and logically
- Emphasizes important information
- Makes academic tasks attractive and challenging

Source: Adapted from the Florida Coalition for the Development of a Performance Measurement System. (n.d.). *Domains: Concepts and indicators of effective teaching—Florida Performance Measurement System.* Tallahassee: Florida Department of Education.

If developing and beginning teachers tactfully indicate to supervisory personnel that these are their expectations for the consultation process, then they communicate to others that they are knowledgeable about the process, are serious about developing their skills as a teacher, and want some control over their own professional development.

Accepting Constructive Criticism

The most difficult aspect of consultation is being critiqued. When partaking in a collaborative consultation conference, the first priority for developing and beginning teachers is to maintain objectivity to the greatest extent possible. They need to suppress their desires to defend their performance, listen to what is being conveyed, and objectively present their rationale for their actions. If developing teachers are experiencing such a strong emotional response that they are on the verge of losing self-control, they should say as little as possible, allow the supervisor to finish, and then indicate the need to think over the points that were made and schedule another conference. During this cooling-down period, the developing teachers can vent any anger and then spend time carefully analyzing the supervisor's or consulting teacher's comments. In most cases, the new teachers will find that the feedback is not as terrible as first thought and that it is valid.

Before reconvening with the consulting teacher or supervisor, the developing teachers should reflect on how they could have approached instruction in a different, more effective way. Making some notes about what they think went wrong and how they can avoid the same mistakes in the future is a helpful strategy. In contrast, if the developing teachers believe that the feedback was invalid, then they need to reflect on what occurred during instruction and build a case to defend their performance. Again, they should make notes that can be taken to the next conference. (The conference planning guide, Figure 10.2, may be helpful to record notes.)

Regardless, keep in mind that effective teachers are made, not born, and that no one should expect developing and beginning teachers, and that includes themselves, to walk into a classroom and do a flawless job of managing classroom behavior and providing instruction. Developing effective teaching skills takes years of practice and conscious effort. Developing and beginning teachers should be patient and work toward the goal of becoming effective teachers.

Developing teacher _____	Clinical professor _____	
Clinical teacher _____		
A. Behaviors to continue/maintain	Specific examples	
1. _____	_____	
2. _____	_____	
3. _____	_____	
B. Behaviors to increase	Specific examples	Specific prescriptions
1. _____	_____	_____
2. _____	_____	_____
3. _____	_____	_____
C. Behaviors to reduce/eliminate	Specific examples	Specific prescriptions
1. _____	_____	_____
2. _____	_____	_____
3. _____	_____	_____
D. Responsibilities		Owner
1. _____	_____	
2. _____	_____	
3. _____	_____	
Date of next conference _____	Date of next observation _____	

FIGURE 10.2 The Conference Planning Guide Can Be Used in Planning and Documenting Strategies and Responsibilities for Solving Problems

ℙ*ause and Reflect 10.2*

How Well Do You Take Constructive Criticism?

    1 = Would listen quietly and comply with the feedback
    2 = Would sense a degree of panic but would comply with the feedback
    3 = Would not be affected by the feedback and would do nothing
    4 = Would sense a degree of panic but would not comply with the feedback
    5 = Would react emotionally (e.g., cry, scream, argue) and reject the feedback

Directions: Use the above scale to rate your behaviors in the following:

_____ 1. Your university supervisor asks you to redo your paper on classroom management strategies for lack of recent citations.

_____ 2. Your consulting teacher asks you to redo your science lesson plans for lack of specific instructional objectives.

_____ 3. Your university supervisor and your consulting teacher tell you to use a softer voice.

_____ 4. Students tend to avoid you in mathematics class, as indicated to you by your peer mentor.

_____ 5. Parents have noted that you spell many words incorrectly. They inform your consulting teacher, who in turn tells you to check your spelling before sending notes home.

_____ 6. Your university supervisor informs you that although your lesson plan was written neatly, you should spend more time on analyzing why your students did not meet the history objectives.

_____ 7. Your principal asks you to change your attire so that you are dressed more professionally for the job.

_____ 8. You overhear your consulting teacher tell another teacher that although you have been a help this semester, she can't wait to get her class back. It seems that the students pay you more attention.

_____ 9. Your university supervisor and consulting teacher indicate that they would like you to spend more time on assessing your students' writing skills before giving increased written expression assignments.

_____10. Your principal tells your consulting teacher that your students tend to act up (e.g., get out of their seats, become noisier) when you take over lunchroom duty).

Is there a way to turn constructive feedback around in these examples? What would you do if this feedback were given to you? Discuss a possible course of action that could turn these constructive critiques into positive actions.

THE DEVELOPING AND BEGINNING TEACHER AS THE PROVIDER OF CONSULTING SERVICES

Now that these great expectations have been built up for exemplary consultative services to be provided to the developing and beginning teacher, consideration must be given to how these teachers can do the same for other teachers and paraprofessionals.

When they have to be the consultants, developing and beginning teachers quickly realize how much work, frustration, and skill is involved. The kinds of skills needed are outlined in the next section and are categorized as interpersonal communication skills. A description of these skills is provided in some detail, but before reading about that, the developing teacher should consider a few simple concepts when acting as a consultant.

Novice teachers have a great deal of potential to become effective teachers and consultants, but they have to accumulate a great deal of experience in both roles before becoming effective in either. In working with others during the early stages of their careers, developing and beginning teachers need to accept that they know some things but that they have a great deal more to learn. They need to consider the sensitivity of others to constructive criticism. Again, they need to use the skills outlined in the sections that follow, always being aware that the feedback they provide may not be the information that others want to hear. They need to tune into the verbal and nonverbal reactions to what is being said.

COLLABORATIVE MODEL FOR CONSULTATIVE PROCESSES

As recipients of consultative services (consultees), or as providers of consultative services (consultants), new teachers are active participants in a collaborative consultation process. As consultees, developing and beginning teachers need to assist in scheduling conferences and observations. They have to prepare lesson plans and present them to their supervisor in advance. They are expected to reflect on their own teaching performance and to analyze their strengths and weaknesses. During conferences, they are asked to communicate their perceptions of their own teaching in an honest and uninhibited way and to assist in devising strategies for improving their teaching. Follow-up responsibilities are devised, and tasks must be completed before the next conference (e.g., practicing new techniques, observing other teachers demonstrating alternative teaching behaviors, reading reference texts).

As a consultant to other teachers, paraprofessionals, or parents, a developing and beginning teacher has to schedule conferences, direct the conferences toward achieving some set of goals, analyze information related to the situation at hand, determine a strategy for resolving target problems, and determine the procedures and responsibilities for consultant and consultee (Warger & Aldinger, 1984).

Consensual Decision-Making

The overall goal of collaboration is agreement on what is to be accomplished and how it is to be accomplished (Bos, 1995; Glatthorn, 1990; Karge et al., 1995; Villa et al., 1996). Individuals working on a problem need to feel a part of the problem-solving process. To accomplish this, the consultant and consultee in a working relationship need to participate actively in the process. This concept of active participation to achieve group consensus is referred to as **consensual decision-making.** Consensual decision-making requires a commitment of individuals within a working group to three principles (Chandler, 1982):

1. A belief that others understand their point of view

2. A belief that they understand others' points of view

3. Committed support for decisions made, whether or not they prefer the decisions, because they were arrived at in an open and fair manner

Consensual decision-making relies on individuals working as a cohesive group, perceiving the process as fair and worthwhile, and committing to the outcome of the efforts made. As consultees, developing and beginning teachers want to know that they have contributed to the problem-solving process, instead of being criticized on how they should improve their teaching skills. As consultants, they will want to help others (e.g., teachers, paraprofessionals, parents) develop ownership and commitment to the decisions.

Balance of Control

In successful collaborative consultation, the balance of control typically moves away from the consultant and toward the consultee. Early in the consulting relationship, consultees tend to be more reliant on others to provide them with information and directions on how to complete job-related activities. They do a lot of asking and a lot of listening. Consultants, in contrast, usually have a great deal of information about the school and views as to how the system should work. In the early stages of the process, consultants typically do a lot of telling and a lot of directing. Researchers like Blumberg (1980) refer to this as a **directive style of behavior.** Conversely, as the consultees become more knowledgeable and confident in what they are doing, they ask fewer questions and seek less direction. They begin to do more talking in a conference and asking consultants to confirm their suspicions about a situation. Consultants do more listening and ask leading questions to guide consultees in analyzing their own teaching performance. This consultative behavior is referred to as an **indirective style of behavior** (Figure 10.3).

The directness or indirectness of a consultant's style is related to the degree of emphasis given to the task at hand (improving the consultee's performance) or to the interpersonal relationship between the consultant and the consultee. A directive consultant tells developing consultees what their strengths and weaknesses are and how to

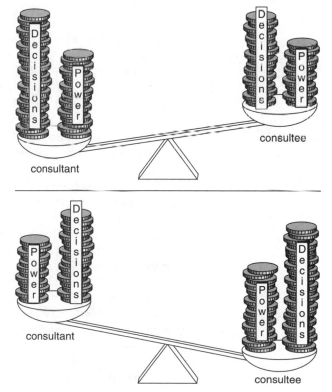

FIGURE 10.3 Decision-making and power are balanced between consultee and consultant, although, at different points in the process, the consultant or consultee may have more or less of each.

TABLE 10.1   Styles of Behavior Applicable to Consulting

Style A	High direct, high indirect	The consultee (teacher) sees the consultant (supervisor) emphasizing both direct and indirect behavior—he or she tells and criticizes but also asks and listens.
Style B	High direct, low indirect	The consultee perceives the consultant as doing a great deal of telling and criticizing but very little asking or listening.
Style C	Low direct, high indirect	The consultant's behavior is rarely direct (e.g., telling, criticizing); instead, he or she puts a lot of emphasis on asking questions, listening, and reflecting back the consultee's ideas and feelings.
Style D	Low direct, low indirect	The consultee sees the consultant as passive, not doing much of anything. Some consultants may appear passive as they try to engage in a rather misguided democratic role.

From Blumberg, A. (1980). *Supervisors and teachers: A private cold war.* Berkeley, CA: McCutchen.

improve their performance. Telling is usually a more efficient means of identifying problem areas and strategies to remediate them. With direct consultation, however, little attention is given to a consultee's self-esteem or the development of his or her self-evaluation skills. An indirective consultant, in contrast, asks the developing consultees questions to lead them to recognizing problem areas and deducing possible solutions. Under this indirect style, consultees tend to feel more in control of their performance, accept ownership for the diagnosis and intervention strategies, and develop self-evaluation skills.

Productive interpersonal work seems to be achieved best by maintaining an overall balance between energy directed toward improving the consultee's teaching and energy directed toward establishing a good interpersonal relationship among team members. Effective consultation is a combination of both direct and indirect approaches. The results of at least one study (Copeland, 1982) indicate that teachers (consultees) positively evaluate their supervisory interpersonal relations when they perceive their supervisor's (consultant's) behavior as being high direct, high indirect (style A) or low direct, high indirect (style C) (Table 10.1).

In sum, the collaborative model for consultative processes involves the consultant and consultee actively participating in decision-making and problem solving. The two people understand that the purpose of the process is to improve instruction and that they must agree about the goals of consultation and the means for attaining them. Consensual decision-making helps facilitate a commitment to the consultation process and ownership of the responsibilities associated with the goals and strategies agreed on by the team. For a true consensus to occur, the process requires a balance of control. That is not to say that, at each conference, there will be an equal distribution of control between consultant and consultee, but over the course of a series of conferences, each will equally contribute to the decision-making process. Early in the process, the consultant will usually dominate, but this will shift to the consultee as the relationship develops.

*P*ause and Reflect 10.3

Below are examples of activities that new teachers will engage in as active participants in a collaborative consultation process. For each of the following examples, analyze how you and others will operate as consultees or consultants. Provide a brief script for what you, your consultant teacher, the principal, your university supervisor, or parents might say or do.

1. Identifying discrepancies in a student's academic progress within general education content areas

2. Planning and using a variety of assessment strategies for a serious problem behavior

3. Observing students in the special education, learning-support program

4. Collecting and reporting social skills data on students' peer-tutoring sessions

5. Adapting specialized equipment to help a small group of students in the physical education class

6. Modifying one part of the general education language arts curriculum to make it easier for a student to remain in the grade-level curriculum

7. Creating an individualized behavioral support plan for one student displaying signs of attention deficit disorder

8. Locating for parents some resources on normal developmental milestones in language and social domains

INTERPERSONAL COMMUNICATION SKILLS

Some constructs taken from the work of Carl Rogers (1965) may be helpful to developing and beginning teachers in building a cooperative rapport with those with whom they work. Developing and beginning teachers must keep in mind that they will apply these constructs primarily in their role as consultants but that these constructs are also applicable to their role as consultees. There will, however, be differences in how the constructs are operationalized, depending on whether the new teachers are acting as consultants or consultees.

The first construct is **positive regard** for others. This is the ability to maintain a degree of respect for others simply because they are fellow human beings. Although developing and beginning teachers may respect others as individuals, this does not mean they necessarily agree with or condone the actions of others. In essence, the person is separated from his or her actions. For instance, a fellow teacher may photocopy copyrighted material in a way that violates the law and a new teacher's own moral values. The new teacher does not condone the behavior but can still maintain a degree of respect for the individual as a skilled teacher. The benefit of developing a positive regard for others is that greater objectivity is gained in dealings with others.

Positive regard for others can be shown by providing honest feedback and by offering encouragement. **Honest feedback** describes frankly what the target behavior is, the perceptions that the speaker has of the listener's attitudes and behaviors, and the response that the speaker has to the listener's behavior. For example, rather than say to the classroom paraprofessional who was obviously not prepared, "Well, I thought the tutoring went fairly well . . . considering," the developing teacher might provide honest feedback by saying, "This lesson did not go well because you were not fully prepared. You didn't have any visuals ready, and you weren't organized. Can we talk about why you weren't prepared?"

Encouragement is the acknowledgment that another person has the skills and behavioral repertoire to overcome problems and to extend existing skills to higher performance levels. Behaviors that express encouragement help in building and maintaining self-esteem and should increase the probability that similar positive behaviors will be demonstrated in the future. Importantly, statements of encouragement need to include specific, descriptive praises. Such statements describe the observed behavior and the observer's response to it. When a consultant observes that a consultee has displayed an effective behavior and comments on the behavior and her impressions of its effect, then descriptive praise is being used. For instance, the consultant might say, "I thought it was very effective when you stopped the talking by walking over to the student yet continued to discuss regrouping of numbers without a moment's interruption."

A second construct is **empathy**. Empathic responses indicate an understanding about what another person is going through. In everyday life, individuals often make empathic statements regarding both the positive and negative experience of others. For instance, in acknowledging a colleague's successful instruction of a student, a new teacher might say, "Oh, you must have been thrilled to see that Darius finally was able to conquer regrouping." When unpleasant experiences occur, teachers often console friends or colleagues with empathic statements such as, "Getting a parking ticket first thing in the morning is aggravating." Being empathic toward the experiences of others often helps convey the fact that individuals are concerned and can appreciate the emotional responses of others to situations or events.

Burke (1984) describes responding behaviors as skilled expressions reflecting an empathic attitude for another person. Empathy for another person as described by Rogers (1965) is not an overt behavior. The attitude of empathy, however, can be expressed through outward behavior in the form of active listening. Active listening entails the following:

1. *Using open-ended responses* that focus on the other person, are nonjudgmental, seek further information, and are uncomplicated utterances

   Example: "How do you think the lesson went today?"

2. *Using paraphrasing/clarifying responses* to help the other person hear his or her own words, help the listener understand what the speaker's concerns are, and relate back to the speaker that the listener has carefully considered the statements

   Example: "You said they didn't understand the concept very well. Do you mean they had difficulty with the follow-up activity?"

3. *Focusing on emotions* so that the component of a person's message is objectively and openly acknowledged as existing and not ignored

   Example: "I can see that you're upset with this situation. Let's talk it over."

The third construct, **congruence,** refers to the degree of accuracy between individuals' perceptions of their behaviors or experiences and the actual pattern of behaviors and experiences. Developing and beginning teachers in a state of congruence are psychologically well adjusted (comfortable about what they do and about their experiences). Consultants and consultees in a state of congruence are genuine and sincere when interacting with each other. They project the impression that they are honest and express their true impressions of a targeted problem area. Burke (1984) refers to statements with these characteristics as **attending skills,** which involve the use of **self-disclosure statements.** Such statements are characterized by three criteria (O'Shea & Hoover, 1986):

1. Taking responsibility for thoughts, behaviors, and emotions

   Example: "If I had planned that transition a little better, we wouldn't have lost so much time."

2. Making concrete rather than vague or abstract statements

   Example: "I find that my school day goes so much better if I get a good night's sleep, eat a full breakfast, and arrive half an hour before the students."

3. Referring to conditions in the immediate environment

   Example: "I plan the math lesson for late morning, before the music teacher comes in. After she leaves, the students are so excited that spelling is more easily accomplished."

Statements with these characteristics objectively convey the position of the consultant or consultee, specify the exact subject of the statement, and put the subject into the immediate context. One subset of self-disclosure statements is that of **I statements** (Gordon, 1974). These statements involve three components (O'Shea & Hoover, 1986):

1. The description of the consultee's target behavior is in nonjudgmental terms.

   Example: "I heard you ask 12 literal-level recall questions and 2 evaluation questions."

2. The effect of the target behavior on the speaker is described in concrete terms.

   Example: "I can't keep my roll book up to date when you fail to give me the weekly test results for your students on time."

3. The emotional response of the speaker to the other person's behavior is specified.

   Example: "I am delighted to have a developing teacher who is as interested and as willing to put forth effort as you are."

These kinds of statements convey that the speaker is a clear, honest, and sincere communicator.

FIGURE 10.4 Rogers's (1965) Constructs of Interpersonal Communication and the Overt Behavior Used to Exhibit Them

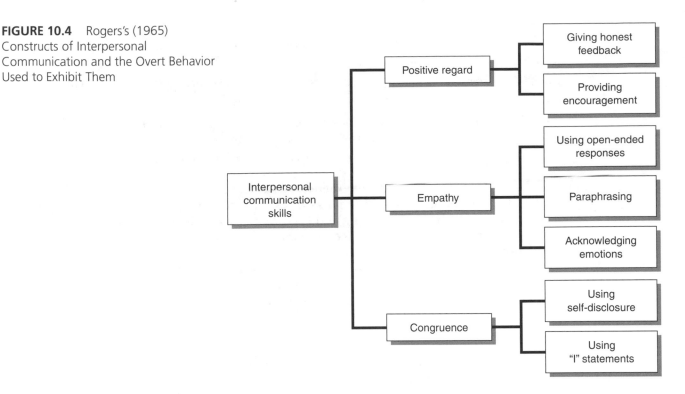

Again, these interpersonal communication skills are applicable to both consultant and consultee. When individuals in both roles use positive regard, empathy, and congruence, communication is clear and effective. Without clear communication, collaborative consultation used for problem solving will be muddled by ineffective attempts to communicate ideas, instead of attempts to resolve targeted instructional problems (Figure 10.4).

Pause and Reflect 10.4

Review the three major interpersonal communication skills applicable to both consultant and consultee. For each, name a person you observed who demonstrated the skill this past week in your class or school. Describe a specific example that indicated to you that clear and effective communication was occurring.

Interpersonal Communication Skill 1:

_____

Person demonstrating the skill:

_____

Specific example that indicated clear and effective communication was occurring:

_____

_____

Interpersonal Communication Skill 2:

_____

Person demonstrating the skill:

_____

Specific example that indicated clear and effective communication was occurring:

_____

_____

Interpersonal Communication Skill 3:

_____

Person demonstrating the skill:

_____

Specific example that indicated clear and effective communication was occurring:

_____

_____

GENERAL PROCEDURES FOR COLLABORATIVE CONSULTATION

The focal point of interpersonal relations in collaborative consultation is the series of conferences among members of the consultation team (consultee, consulting teacher, supervisor, or principal) that occur throughout the consultation process. In addition to spending energy and attention on the interpersonal relationships between consultant and consultee, an equal amount of energy needs to be directed at identifying and resolving instructional problems. An important facet of collaborative consultation, therefore, is the systematic implementation of procedures for conducting conferences. Whereas interpersonal communication skills aid in establishing a positive relationship among members of the collaborative consultation team, the procedures for conducting conferences focus on the activities that need to be accomplished. Initially, the procedures for conferences involve discussing team members' roles, scheduling conferences and observations, and identifying important classroom variables (e.g., types of students, classroom rules and schedules). After the first few weeks, however, conferences focus on diagnosing problems and testing strategies to resolve them (Garland, 1982; Goldhammer, Anderson, & Krajewski, 1980).

Three Basic Procedures

Many of the procedures incorporated into the collaborative consultation process are derived from behavioral principles and decision-making systems. These procedures are designed to help developing teachers in defining roles, functions, and goals of the collaborative consultation team (Bos, 1995; Caccia, 1996; Cooley & Yovanoff, 1996; Karge et al., 1995; Westling & Whitten, 1996). The three general procedures described as follows underlie the entire conference process and are designed for use by both consultant and consultee in collaboratively solving instructional problems.

The first general procedure is to formulate behaviorally descriptive statements related to the targeted instructional problem area. **Behaviorally descriptive statements** are those that operationally identify a behavior in specific, accurate, and concise terms. They refer to quantities or frequencies of behavior occurrences. Behavioral statements do not contain subjective descriptions that imply a judgment of the behavior. A statement like "The developing teacher is not enthusiastic" is imprecise and may lead to poor communication. Vague statements should be avoided or backed up with a more objective statement of observable behaviors to indicate clearly the basis for the statement.

In addition to behaviors, the conditions of behaviors need to be stated. These elements provide a clear reflection of the context in which behaviors occur. For instance, the consultation team may have agreed that the consultee should praise students each time they provide an accurate response to a question (condition) and not when they simply respond with any answer (noncondition). When a change in a specific teaching behavior is targeted, the desired level (greater or lesser) or direction (increase or decrease) of the change should be clarified. Behaviors must be referenced in clear, quantifiable, and observable terms. In this way, documentation and monitoring of changes in behavior are made easier and more objective (Piper & Elgert, 1979).

The second general procedure is to develop and maintain schedules for consistency and to routinize collaborative consultation procedures. In addition to their roles as consultants, developing and beginning teachers often have their own classroom responsibilities. Direct instructional services to students take a priority over consultations with other teachers. As a result, new teachers fail to make time available for conferences with consultees, be they other teachers, paraprofessionals, or parents. Unless consultants and consultees make the time by setting goals and scheduling observations and conferences, they are likely to defer these activities in favor of others. Following through with schedules establishes, over time, distributed practice of the procedures for various collaborative activities, which in turn better ensures that consultation activities occur.

To ensure that schedules are maintained, it is important not only to write down the series of activities to be completed but also to set a time and date to engage in each of the activities. Each subsequent conference should end with the confirmation of the next interaction, as well as of projected meetings that are to follow in the near future. Following this strategy ensures that the schedule is constantly used, reviewed, and modified throughout the consultation program.

Another general procedure involves the problem-solving process: to solve problems collaboratively. During collaborative consultations, the principal activity is that of identifying relevant classroom variables, identifying instructional program strengths and weaknesses, and formulating alternative strategies to improve student performance. These steps are delineated by the diagnostic teaching model (Cartwright & Cartwright, 1972) discussed in Chapter 5. The steps in the model are (1) identify attributes, (2) specify objectives, (3) select strategies and materials, and (4) test strategies and materials.

The first step, as applied to consultation, involves the collection of information about the classroom setting, the behavioral and learning attributes of students, the teaching style and behaviors of the teacher, and any other relevant variables. Consultants and/or consultees collect baseline data prior to any systematic intervention, allowing team members to form a picture of what is occurring in the classroom. Next, team members must determine what they want to maintain or modify by specifying clear and behaviorally stated objectives that reflect the desired outcomes of the instruc-

FIGURE 10.5 Three Basic Principles That Underlie the Collaborative Consultation Process

Use behaviorally descriptive statements

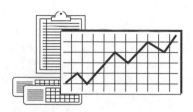

Write down schedules and keep appointments

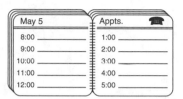

Solve problems collaboratively

tional program (step 2). Team members then select alternative strategies for accomplishing the stated objectives (step 3). Once implemented by the consultee, the strategies and materials are tested through subsequent observations and data collection (step 4). On the basis of the information gathered, team members analyze the feedback and determine whether the objectives have been reached. Accordingly, the sequence is repeated in either one of two ways. If objectives have been reached, the team forms new ones (step 2) and continues through the other steps as described. If objectives have not been reached, the team reexamines the accuracy and appropriateness of the baseline data, stated objectives, strategies, and materials. If modifications in any one of these areas are necessary, the team makes the changes and the sequence is continued. When all steps seem to be accurate and appropriate, then the clinical team implements the strategies and materials again and retests.

Behaviorally descriptive statements, schedules, and problem-solving procedures are used in conferences to identify and remediate instructional problems (Figure 10.5).

OPERATIONALIZING CONFERENCE PROCEDURES

During the preobservation conference that occurs at the beginning of the consultation experience, the consultant and the consultee focus on obtaining a baseline measure of salient situational variables involving the students, teacher aides, or a new teacher. At this point, the team members will discuss anecdotal observations of the members, the most important being those of the consultee. Areas of possible concern to the consultee may set the agenda for the initial observation by the consultant. Any additional areas dealing with planning, student conduct, management of classroom procedures, presentation of instructional material, building rapport, and so forth that the observer will attend to should be overviewed with the consultee.

Next, the means for collecting data on these areas need to be devised or selected. In systematic observation models, some form of data recording is used to monitor behavior and to provide feedback. Recordings of teacher behavior can take a variety of forms: (1) continuous event recording, (2) time sampling, and (3) interval recording.

Judgments about the situation and type of information sought from an observation dictate the type of recording system used. In any case, the recorded data provide the basis for discussion between the observer and the new teacher.

Used in conjunction with specific operational definitions of behaviors, observation records effectively communicate by providing a clear, quantifiable picture of the consultees' and/or students' behaviors. Observation records also serve as a prompt in follow-up conferences. For instance, after having observed and conducted a postobservation conference using a systematic observation record, consulting teachers can use the record in the subsequent preobservation conference to remind consultees of behavioral patterns and to guide the consultees in varying the patterns during the upcoming observation.

If a predesigned recording instrument is to be used (e.g., COKER, Flanders Interaction Analysis), then the team members should simply review the target behaviors on the instrument and the recording method to be used (e.g., continuous-event recording, time sampling). If an informal instrument is to be designed and used, the team should design the form and recording method together, incorporating the principles of interpersonal communication and participative decision-making outlined in previous sections.

During the postobservation conference, feedback on earlier observations is provided. This critical step involves providing consultees with objective data reflecting environmental variables, including student and teacher behavior in the classroom. Observers should present the data and explain how they were collected but should avoid making any value judgments about the performances of the students, the teacher aide, or the developing teacher. Both the consultant and the consultee should then discuss the data and analyze it to discern any recognizable patterns that reflect when a specific behavior occurs in the context of any antecedent or consequent events. For instance, every time a new teacher sits at his or her desk during seatwork assignments, the class noise level may begin to rise. This may become evident to the consultant and consultee when a recurring pattern is noted on the data record.

As consultees become more skilled at analyzing data, more responsibility should be shifted to them for identifying patterns with increasingly less direction from the consultant. This gradual fading process will help consultees in developing self-evaluation skills. In addition, by analyzing the data with consultees and by helping them identify salient patterns, consultants create an atmosphere that is less defensive and more productive in locating problems and devising solutions.

Once patterns of behaviors have been identified, team members need to specify those student, teacher aide, or new teacher behaviors to maintain or increase and those behaviors to reduce or eliminate. Here, again, the emphasis is on behaviorally stated target behaviors that the consultant and the consultee will focus on in the future. In addition, the team members should determine alternative strategies for modifying the behavior of the students, teacher, or aide. These strategies may also involve modifications to the classroom setting (e.g., rearranging the physical space) or the curriculum (e.g., moving students to more appropriate points in the curriculum, changing curricula).

Finally, the responsibilities of each member for the next observation and conference should be documented. For instance, if the strategies for changing the consultee's behavior include the consultant modeling a specific teaching technique, then arrangements for the consultee to observe the consultant should be made. If the consultees are to review some reference books, then arrangements for getting those books to them need to be made. This documentation helps in ensuring that the activities identified by

Pause and Reflect 10.5

Hold mock collaborative consultation conferences (include preconference and postconference sessions) for the following. Role-play what you, your consultant teacher, the principal, and/or your university supervisor might say or do.

1. Planning assessment strategies for a student's memory and retention problems in reading
2. Observing a student in a learning strategies classroom; devising generalization tips for the student's mathematics and science teachers
3. Modifying a penmanship lesson plan to accommodate a student with physical support needs
4. Devising a group management game for whole-class participation during art class
5. Designing, with fellow teachers, plans to prevent calling out disruptions during a schoolwide assembly
6. Using positive behavioral management strategies in biology instruction
7. Encouraging students' self-evaluations during computer science instruction

the team are carried out. Included within this step is the scheduling of the next observation and conference. The conference planning guide (Figure 10.2) can be used to document the decision made in the postobservation conference and to provide a permanent record of the process.

SUMMARY

This chapter described how developing and beginning teachers are involved in the consultation process in two ways: as recipients and providers of consultative services. In the first case, as consultees, their role is to assist in the process of developing their own teaching and classroom-management skills. They need to accept the consultant's assistance and, to some extent, acquiesce to their control and authority. In the latter case, as consultants, developing and beginning teachers will be required to direct others carefully in their development. This will entail being sensitive to the perceptions of those with whom they work. For both of these roles, the following principles and procedures of a collaborative consultation model have been suggested.

The chapter described the critical facet of collaborative consultation as the establishment and maintenance of productive interpersonal relationships between consultants and consultees. This can be accomplished through the application of the constructs of positive regard, empathy, and congruence. These constructs are displayed through verbal and nonverbal communication techniques during systematically implemented conference procedures. Consultants and consultees can operationalize these constructs through facilitating, responding, and attending. By facilitating, team members provide honest feedback regarding instructional variables but encourage continued professional development as well. A consultant responds to consultees' concerns by recognizing the effective elements of the learning process and by exploring and clarifying consultees' perceptions of their situation. Team members attend to the situation at hand by making concrete, nonjudgmental statements about the behaviors and emotions of the people within the instructional environment (e.g., teachers, paraprofessionals, students).

Facilitating, responding, and attending are the elements of the indirect style whereby consultants ask questions of consultees and attentively listen to their responses. Although, under a direct consultation style, active listening is replaced by telling and criticizing, facilitating and attending still can be employed. There is a time and place for both indirect and direct approaches as long as team members are aware and strive to maintain a complementary mix.

An important element that appears to influence consultees' responses to varying styles is their level of skill and confidence. During the early stages of consultation, more directive approaches by consultants may be necessary. As skills and confidence grow, consultees are better prepared to participate in the decision-making processes during conferences. Under these circumstances, consultees are able to self-evaluate more objectively and to commit themselves to decisions made by the consultation team.

ACTIVITIES TO EXTEND YOUR KNOWLEDGE

1. Plan a presentation in your student teaching or field placement seminar on consulting with general education teachers, administrators, and other school personnel. Use the theme of characteristics of students with specific exceptional learning or management needs. List 10 specific teaching or management strategies concerning ways that professionals in your area can consult to assist your students.

2. Revisit issues in the development of teachers' feedback and consultation skills by reviewing recent articles on these themes. Summarize at least five new important reflections that you gained regarding your own feedback and consultation skills.

3. Describe ways in which technology can assist with planning and managing the consultative environment. Plan and present one workshop activity with peer mentors on the use of technology as a consultation strategy.

4. Demonstrate proficiency in oral and written communication by researching a topic relevant to consultative services. Prepare overhead transparencies to provide a guided discussion on local and state consultative services to parents and fellow professionals at your school site. Include a handout with five anticipated questions that parents and professionals may have. Include the answers that you will provide regarding consultative services in your area.

POINT AND CLICK

The following Web sites highlight the chapter's theme of collaborative programming and consultation. Each of these listings can assist new teachers in their collaborative roles as consultees or consultants.

Council for Exceptional Children
1920 Association Drive
Reston, VA 20091
www.cec.sped.org
The nationally recognized organization in supporting teachers' work with families and students served in special education, this Web site offers the latest updates on collaboration and consulting roles for all professionals dealing with individuals with disabilities and their families.

Federation for Students with Special Needs
95 Berkeley Street, Suite 104
Boston, MA 02116
617-482-2915
Fax: 617-695-2939
www.fesninfo@fesn.org
This Web site offers to new teachers access to the federation that provides technical assistance for grassroots consortia.

National Association of Developmental Disabilities Councils
1234 Massachusetts Avenue NW, Suite 103
Washington, DC 20005
202-347-1234
E-mail: naddc@igc.apc.org
http://www.igc.apc.orc/NADDC/
This Web site provides a wealth of information that can assist new teachers in their collaboration and consultation knowledge and skills.

Parents Place
http://www.parentsplace.com/index.html
This Web site is a parenting resource center that can support new teachers' work with parents or guardians. When families request ideas in supporting their child at home, this site can offer important insights and ideas on teachers' positive regard, empathy, and congruence.

President's Committee on Employment of People with Disabilities
1111 20th Street NW
Washington, DC 20036
www.50.pcepd.gov/pcepd
New teachers' collaborative roles include their consultative skills with business associations. This Web site can offer important teaming skills on employment opportunities for individuals with disabilities within the workplace and ways teachers can provide insights into consultee roles for students.

REFERENCES

Blumberg, A. (1980). *Supervisors and teachers: A private cold war.* Berkeley, CA: McCutchen.

Bos, C. S. (1995). Professional development and teacher change. Encouraging news from the trenches. *Remedial and Special Education, 16*(6), 379–382.

Boyer, L., & Gillespie, P. (2000). Keeping the committed. The importance of induction and support programs for new special educators. *Teaching Exceptional Children, 33*(1), 10–15.

Burke, J. B. (1984). Interpersonal communication. In J. M. Cooper (Ed.), *Developing skills for instructional supervision.* New York: Longman.

Caccia, P. F. (1996). Linguistic coaching: Helping beginning teachers defeat discouragement. *Educational Leadership, 53*(6), 17–22.

Cartwright, G. P., & Cartwright, C. A. (1972). Gilding the lily: Comments on the training-based model for special education. *Exceptional Children, 39,* 231–234.

Chandler, T. A. (1982). Can Theory Z be applied to the public schools? *Education, 104,* 343–345.

Cooley, E., & Yovanoff, P. (1996). Supporting professionals-at-risk: Evaluating interventions to reduce burnout and improve retention of special educators. *Exceptional Children, 62*(4), 336–355.

Copeland, W. D. (1982). Student teachers' preference for supervisory approach. *Journal of Teacher Education, 33,* 32–36.

Council for Exceptional Children (2000a). *What every special educator must know: The standards for the preparation and licensure of special educators* (4th ed.). Reston, VA: Author.

Council for Exceptional Children (2000b). *Bright futures for exceptional learners: An action plan for quality conditions, teaching, and results for every exceptional learner.* Reston, VA: Author.

Florida Coalition for the Development of a Performance Measurement System. (n.d.). *Domains: Concepts and indicators of effective teaching—Florida Performance Measurement System.* Tallahassee: Florida Department of Education.

Garland, G. (1982). *Guiding experiences in teacher education.* New York: Longman.

Glatthorn, A. A. (1990). Cooperative professional development: Facilitating the growth of the special education teacher and the classroom teacher. *Remedial and Special Education, 11*(3), 29–50.

Goldhammer, R., Anderson, R. H., & Krajewski, R. J. (1980). *Clinical supervision: Special methods for the supervision of teachers* (2nd ed.). New York: Holt, Rinehart & Winston.

Gordon, T. (1974). *T.E.T.: Teacher effectiveness training.* New York: Peter H. Wyden.

Karge, B. D., Lasky, B., McCabe, M., & Robb, S. M. (1995). University and district collaborative support for beginning special education intern teachers. *Teacher Education and Special Education, 18*(2), 103–114.

McCaffrey, M. E. (2000). My first year of learning. Advice from a new educator. *Teaching Exceptional Children, 33*(1), 4–9.

O'Shea, L. J., & Hoover, N. L. (1986). *Conferring with teachers about teacher performance.* Tallahassee: Florida Department of Education.

Piper, T. J., & Elgert, D. B. (1979). *Teacher supervision through behavioral objectives: An operationally described system.* Baltimore: Paul H. Brookes.

Rogers, C. (1965). *Client-centered therapy.* Boston: Houghton Mifflin.

Showers, B., & Joyce, B. (1996). The evaluation of peer coaching. *Educational Leadership, 53*(6), 12–16.

Villa, R. A., Thousand, J. S., Nevin, A. I., & Malgeri, C. (1996). Instilling collaboration for inclusive schooling as a way of doing business in public schools. *Remedial and Special Education, 17*(3), 169–181.

Warger, C. L., & Aldinger, L. E. (1984). Improving student teacher supervision: The preservice consultation model. *TEASE, 7*, 155–163.

Westling, D. L., & Whitten, T. M. (1996). Rural special education teachers' plans to continue or leave their teaching positions. *Exceptional Children, 62*(4), 319–335.

Whitaker, S. D. (2000). What do first year special education teachers need? Implications for induction programs. *Teaching Exceptional Children, 33*(1), 28–37.

The Master Teacher

In this chapter, we will

- discuss professional teaching standards

- identify tips in conducting job searches and writing résumés

- examine typical job interview procedures

- explore the preparation of professional portfolios

- discuss how master teachers work effectively in partnerships with other professionals, parents and guardians, and paraprofessionals

- elaborate on the signs and symptoms of, and strategies to reduce, teacher stress and burnout

- articulate how continual professional growth and active involvement are components in a "teacher career cycle"

- challenge developing teachers to analyze their personal philosophies as they develop into master teachers

*T*his chapter is written to provide direction to beginning or developing teachers who are determined to make teaching a long-term career. Our goal is to increase awareness of the necessity of continual professional growth and active involvement. Professional growth and active involvement are vital steps in becoming and remaining master teachers.

We open the chapter with a discussion on the push for teaching standards in professional preparation programs. More and more pressure is being applied to novices to enter the field with appropriate knowledge, skills, and dispositions in order to reach an increasingly diverse student population. However, while a consensus is emerging about beginning or developing teachers needing to meet standards for practice that will attest to their grasp of essential skills (National Commission on Teaching and America's Future, 1996), there is a shortage of teaching personnel nationwide, especially in special education (Otis-Wilborn & Winn, 2000).

In spite of the push for increased professional standards and the need for more teachers, teachers seeking initial employment must be prepared to face the reality of school-to-job transitions. Accordingly, the chapter offers tips in conducting job searches and writing résumés. Teachers seeking employment present themselves well on paper initially. They articulate their past work experiences, professional qualifications, and career goal expectations during face-to-face interviews.

We also discuss the professional portfolio development process. All teachers must begin early to create well-developed professional portfolios, providing evidence that contributes to their professional expertise.

Further, partnership strategies to move from a student teaching viewpoint to a master teacher orientation frame the next portion of the chapter. We discuss cooperation and the necessity of teaming. Practical strategies for observing peers and other professionals in mentor-protege opportunities underscore the master teacher process. We also delineate strategies appropriate to working with parents or guardians. Master teachers daily face typical parental or guardian concerns and apply their professional expertise to help parents or guardians deal with these concerns.

The next portion of the chapter we devote to management approaches for dealing with paraprofessionals (or paraeducators, instructional assistants, and/or volunteers). Increasingly, teachers no longer work in isolated settings. Today, many classrooms operate with paraprofessionals to run successfully. Many students served in new service delivery systems require the attention of dedicated paraprofessionals. Teachers' ability in managing paraprofessionals is evolving into a key standard for the successful classroom performances of master teachers.

All teachers must be able to recognize and deal with stress and burnout, factors that impede the master teaching process. We provide a discussion on sources, signs, and signals of stress and burnout in teachers, and strategies to lessen negative effects.

Finally, we review steps in facilitating the master teacher process. Professionals making teaching a career articulate a personal philosophy of special education and field advancements. They remain committed to their profession. They help promote appropriate education for all students by being involved in professional organizations, participating in professional development activities, obtaining advanced degrees, and renewing teacher certifications and credentials.

PROFESSIONAL PREPARATION STANDARDS

Initiatives establishing national standards of teacher performance, such as the National Board for Professional Teaching Standards (NBPTS) and Interstate New Teacher Assessment and Support Consortium (INTASC), gained fast-paced momentum in professional circles. Beginning in the last portion of the 20th century, the "standards" movement caught on nationally. According to Diez (1998), as the end of the 20th century neared, more than 30 states had adopted the INTASC standards as a framework for new teacher licensure and certification. While most of NBPTS and INTASC activity focused on using national standards in program development and teacher assessment initiated in general education, program planners also explored the potential of standards for preparing all new teachers. For example, within the INTASC organization, national standards of performance and assessment practices for special education began to circulate (INTASC, 1994).

Importantly, the standards setting efforts of the Council for Exceptional Children (CEC) provided a structure that helps new teachers understand their move toward a master teacher process. New teachers preparing to instruct diverse students need a solid grounding in:

- professional, ethical, legal, historical, and philosophical aspects of the field
- human development, the characteristics of exceptional students, and the way these characteristics may interact with a student's culture and environment
- assessment procedures that contribute sound information for individualized educational decision-making and program improvement
- effective instruction practices that support successful access to challenging curricula and enhance self-advocacy and independence
- effective programs that assist exceptional students in using social skills to enhance learning and independence
- collaborative partnerships skills that are characterized by mutual and reciprocal respect and responsibility
- communication skills that enable the professional to be sensitive, culturally competent, and effective (CEC, 2000a)

In addition to articulating its knowledge and skill standards that all new special educators should possess, CEC collaborated with other national programs, projects, and agencies in its work to develop national teacher standards for experienced educators working with diverse students. For example, CEC worked with NBPTS in efforts to advance the teaching profession and to improve student learning. NBPTS approved standards for exemplary teachers of students with "exceptional needs" (NBPTS, 1999). Standards for accomplished practice for an "exceptional needs specialist" were designed so that accomplished teachers demonstrate what they know and are able to do in providing exemplary support for students in a broad range of settings and roles (O'Shea, Hammitte, Mainzer, & Crutchfield, 2000).

INTASC also pinpointed a knowledge base and performance measures for beginning educators that aligned with CEC's recognized standards for beginning special educators. That is, CEC's recent work highlighted its collaboration with INTASC in developing standards and performance assessments for beginning educators regarding the knowledge, skills, and dispositions needed for teaching students with exceptionalities in general classrooms (O'Shea, Hammitte, et al., 2000).

As these national standards movements emphasize, expectations are such that all beginning and developing teachers must develop practices that can bring their students to high standards, but doing so requires preservice and inservice programs to be based on clear expectations that define the concept of high-quality teaching. Clear standards also establish a blueprint that all new teachers and their mentors can use to gauge new teachers' development (National Association of State Boards of Education [NASBE], 2000).

Accordingly, all teachers can profit from important guideposts for their professional preparation as they face more and more diverse students in their classrooms. In order for both general educators and special educators to accept the standards movement and support special needs students wherever students receive their education, new and developing teachers must understand the knowledge demands of teaching standards and the curriculum. Effective teachers accept or believe in the purposes and the value of having high standards. However, teacher knowledge and ability to integrate high standards into pedagogy is affected by the quality of professional development and the strength of teachers' collaborative efforts to support each other (McLaughlin, 2000).

Unfortunately, even among teachers who survive their early years, many never receive the targeted professional development they need to develop teaching skills that foster high-quality student learning (NASBE, 2000). Thus, in order to strive toward and refine the master teacher process, new teachers benefit from sustained support that takes time and effort, particularly from new teachers and those helping them on the way to becoming master teachers. Activities such as attending professional development events, participating in peer evaluations, and investing considerable time in discussions and observations can make the difference in teachers' attrition (that is, exit from the field) or retention (that is, commitment to remain in the field). These types of activities also contribute to new teachers' job satisfaction in the process of obtaining master teacher status.

Chronic Shortages

At a time when special education teacher preparation programs need to focus on the quality of the professional teaching cohort, it is unfortunate that chronic shortages of well-prepared and qualified special educators loom large (O'Shea, Hammitte, et al., 2000). According to the Office of Special Education Programs (1999), in 1995, more than 28,000 individuals practiced special education without the appropriate credentials, more than 4,000 special education teaching positions were vacant, and there were shortages of qualified teachers to educate exceptional students in urban as well as rural areas. These shortages, continuing into the 21st century, were especially critical in high-poverty areas (O'Shea, Hammitte, et al.). Stemming these chronic shortages, while simultaneously ensuring that teacher education programs prepare the next generation of educators for the responsibilities they will assume, was and will continue to be daunting. Ironically, even in the face of these critical shortages, a focus on quality, rather than any lowering of standards, remains necessary. Quality begins with what teachers can articulate about the job search.

THE JOB SEARCH

Knowing what potential employers seek in job candidates can help to strengthen new teachers' experiences in meeting high professional standards and can increase new teachers' positive prospects for employment. When initiating the job search process, many new teachers will find established local steps. Familiarity with screening procedures, interviewing processes, and faculty selection criteria of school districts will make new teachers' job searches smoother and will aid in their transition to the system. Teachers have an advantage in their job searches when they are familiar with employment procedures.

Equal Opportunity Employment Procedures

Districts nationwide are committed to selecting and employing the most qualified persons for available teaching positions. So that districts do not discriminate on the basis of hiring, promotion, or retention practices, district policies include equal opportunity employment procedures for all candidates. This means that school districts cannot discriminate on the basis of age, cultural or ethnic background, gender, religious orientation, disabling condition, and so forth. Policies for teaching positions must be written in advance of posting teaching opportunities.

Posting Teaching Opportunities

Vacancy or new position notices are based on contract agreements existing in school districts. In the initial screening steps, school district personnel scan applications, review cover letters, and identify key elements in résumés for faculty positions. Many districts have interview teams comprised of school board members, administrators, teachers, and parents. Interview teams most likely are obligated through contractual or union agreements to include the review of substitute lists and appraisal forms prior to selecting interview candidates. This means that, prior to interviewing and/or hiring new district personnel, interview teams will consider first a (1) substitute teacher, (2) permanent substitute teacher, (3) long-term substitute teacher, or (4) half-day teacher.

It is very helpful to get on substitute lists even if no immediate positions are available. Not only does substituting provide the new teacher with experience, but it can

*P*ause and Reflect 11.1

Describe what you believe school district personnel want candidates to do after the personnel office posts available teaching opportunities. List at least three things a new teacher can do to participate in the employee search.

1. _____

_____

_____

_____

2. _____

_____

_____

_____

3. _____

_____

_____

_____

also be the person's means to "get a foot in the door." Importantly, many school district personnel recognize their obligation to screen and employ, as well as to provide a thorough introduction to the school district. Substituting is a fast way to get the initial orientation and name recognition. In this way, new teachers can begin their positions on the best possible grounds. They also have an edge in observing teacher induction criteria for that district.

Employee Searches

School districts nationwide desire to select high-quality professional employees, so they often begin their employee searches by posting available positions in key locations. For example, career counseling centers in colleges or universities receive up-to-date job postings from local, state, and national employment searches. Job postings—vacancy and new position notices—include information on the position(s) available, qualifications, major responsibilities, salary, and application deadlines. Job postings also list the names, addresses, and telephone numbers of contacts.

New teachers wanting a teaching position for the beginning of the school year ideally will initiate job searches in late February to have all necessary data completed. Most positions begin with the start of a new school year; however, some positions are available in January. Teachers having necessary information in district personnel offices by mid-October can be considered for January positions.

When the new teacher locates a desirable teaching position in a geographic area in which he or she would like to work, the next logical step is to write an introduction letter to the district's personnel director. The teacher should identify him- or herself in the introduction letter and express an interest in working for the district. It is a good idea to request more written information on the job listing, including the grade level, subject(s) taught, school name, and geographic region. The introduction letter should also contain a request for the district's professional application form. Teachers should type all introduction letters neatly and then sign and date them. Figure 11.1 illustrates an introduction letter in a simulated "Main Street School District."

Professional Application, Résumé, and Cover Letter

The teacher candidate completes the professional application form by identifying personal information (e.g., name, address, emergency telephone number); professional preparation (e.g., undergraduate institution, degree, graduation date); professional experience (e.g., prior teaching experience, student teaching locations, service length); and references (e.g., people who have supervised the candidate or observed the candidate's teaching experiences).

Further, many personnel directors require documentation in addition to the professional application form. This documentation relates to candidates' background checks and clearances (including fingerprints), FBI clearance for nonresidents, antidrug policy checks, child abuse checks, and communicable disease clearances. The additional data are to eliminate the possibility of hiring people who have criminal backgrounds and/or have been exposed to diseases and illnesses that potentially may be dangerous or life-threatening to others. (Most graduates completing student teaching recently will have fulfilled these background checks prior to their student teaching assignments.) Prospective teachers should type the professional application forms or print them neatly. Figure 11.2 illustrates a professional application form in the Main Street School District.

After the prospective teacher has completed the professional application form, he or she should send the form to the district personnel office. In turn, the personnel office will initiate an individual credentials file for each candidate. (It is wise to make a copy of all information prior to mailing the completed form.) A current résumé and a cover letter should accompany the completed professional application form.

127 Lincoln Drive
Smithtown, Pennsylvania 15249
412-987-6543

February 14, 2002

John Doe, Personnel Director
Main Street School District
One Main Street Drive
Main Street, USA 12345

Dear Mr. Doe,

I am interested in applying for the special education teaching position in Main Street School District that was advertised recently. I will be graduating from Smithtown University in May 2002 and am available to begin teaching in the fall of 2002. Upon completion of my undergraduate studies, I will be certified to teach in special education and elementary education. I am especially interested in consulting with parents and general educators concerning students with mild to moderate disabilities in your school district.

Please send me more information on the posted job position for an elementary-level teacher. I would like more information, including the grade level, subject(s) taught, the school in which the class is located, and its geographic relationship to Main Street River. Also, I am interested in obtaining a copy of your district's professional application form. Please send me all necessary forms I need to complete in order to be considered for an interview.

Thank you for your time and consideration of my request.

Sincerely,

Martha Barton

FIGURE 11.1 An Introduction Letter to Main Street School District

A **résumé** is a one- to two-page written summary supporting the candidate's personal information, professional preparation, and professional experiences. The résumé summarizes (1) the candidate's personal information; (2) references, including the names, addresses, and telephone numbers of contacts; (3) previous employment; (4) teaching certification areas; and (5) career goal expectations. It underscores the teacher's specialized training or experiences.

The **cover letter** briefly highlights pertinent information from the application form and résumé. Often, district personnel offices post more than one position. Therefore, it is helpful to indicate the specific position one is interested in obtaining within the cover letter's initial paragraph. Figure 11.3 illustrates an example of a typed cover letter; Figure 11.4 illustrates an example of a résumé.

An increasing number of districts are accepting candidates' application forms and résumés electronically. With the accesibility of the Internet, e-mail, and Web site tech-

Main Street School District
One Main Street Drive
Main Street, USA 12345

PROFESSIONAL APPLICATION FORM

1. Fill out information as completely as possible. Forward the following application and the materials listed below to **Personnel Office, Main Street School District, One Main Street Drive, Main Street, USA 12345.** Completed applications include: (**A**) cover letter, (**B**) application form, (**C**) three (3) professional reference forms, (**D**) college/university transcripts, (**E**) copy of teaching certificate, (**F**) criminal and child abuse clearances, and (**G**) NTE scores.

2. This application will remain active for a period of 1 year. If you desire to have your application remain active after the termination date, please contact the Personnel Office at the Main Street School District.

3. Appointments for interviews will be arranged by this office for those individuals who meet screening criteria.

PERSONAL INFORMATION

Last Name _____ First Name _____ Middle _____

Business Address _____ Telephone _____

Town _____ Zip Code _____

Home Address _____ Telephone _____

Town _____ Zip Code _____

Number to Call in Case of Emergency _____ Social Security Number _____

Area of Certification _____ Date Issued _____

(Copy of Certificate or Letter of Verification from your college must accompany application.)

Present Position _____ Present Annual Salary _____

Type of Position Desired _____ Date of Availability _____

Salary Expected _____ Total Time Taught _____ Time Taught in State _____

PROFESSIONAL PREPARATION

INSTITUTION & LOCATION	MAJOR/MINOR	DEGREE	GRAD. DATE

High School

Undergraduate

Graduate

Main Street School District Is an Equal Rights and Opportunities Educational Agency

FIGURE 11.2 Professional Application Form

PROFESSIONAL EXPERIENCE

INSTITUTION & LOCATION	POSITION	FROM/TO	YEARS	SIZE/UNIT

OTHER VOCATIONAL OR GENERAL EXPERIENCES THAT YOU BELIEVE ARE PERTINENT

_____

_____

_____

_____

REFERENCES

Please list the names of at least three persons who have supervised your work or teaching and will be providing a completed Main Street School District Reference Form.

Name _____ Position _____

Present Address _____

Town, State, Zip Code _____ Telephone _____

Name _____ Position _____

Present Address _____

Town, State, Zip Code _____ Telephone _____

Name _____ Position _____

Present Address _____

Town, State, Zip Code _____ Telephone _____

SIGNED _____ DATE _____

Main Street School District Is an Equal Rights and Opportunities Educational Agency

127 Lincoln Drive
Smithtown, Pennsylvania 15249
412-987-6543
May 1, 2002

John Doe, Personnel Director
Main Street School District
One Main Street Drive
Main Street, USA 12345

Dear Mr. Doe,

Below is my completed professional application form for the fourth grade, special education consulting position in Main Street School District. Your district personnel office advertised this position and recently sent me the forms to complete. I am very interested in moving to the Main Street area. I include my résumé and a brief summary of my professional endeavors for your perusal.

I completed my student teacher experience at George Roberts Elementary School in April 2002. I worked under the direction of Mr. Tom Mallory. My major instructional responsibilities under Mr. Mallory included planning, implementation, and evaluation of the reading, language arts, mathematics, and science curricula. I worked with third- , fourth- , and fifth-grade students receiving special education services. All of my students had IEPs delivered in the general education setting. My main responsibilities were assessment, programming, and evaluating both learning strategies and positive management practices aimed at assisting the students' success in their general education classes. I received specialized training in computer technology and specially designed instruction while working at George Roberts Elementary. Consequently, I am very familiar with adapting the general education curricula from third to fifth grade, as well as with strategies to adapt and modify computer technology for the curriculum areas. Further, my teaching experiences include work in curriculum-based assessment, portfolio assessments, and classroom management techniques for special education services.

FIGURE 11.3   A Typed Cover Letter to Main Street School District

nologies, many employment searches encourage candidates to post their qualifications electronically. In turn, many job opportunities feature an electronic posting of available positions. This system allows both the candidate and the personnel office to screen potential employee-employer matches more efficiently and effectively. Innovations in electronic applications and résumé inquiry include job banks that are interactive and résumé-friendly, on-line application-interview processes; and local district Web sites that boast available incentives and opportunities.

Professional References

Professional references are important to the job selection process. Most personnel offices will ask the new teacher to name at least three contacts that have supervised the

Finally, while completing my undergraduate degree, I worked nights for the past 3 years at the Smithtown University Student Center. My responsibilities included maintaining product inventories at the University Bookstore.

I am very interested in a third- or fourth-grade teaching position at Main Street School District. My professional contacts who will be able to provide you more information concerning my professional training are the following individuals:

1. Mr. Tom Mallory
Teacher, Elementary Education Department
George Roberts Elementary School
Smithtown, Pennsylvania 15249
412-987-3456

2. Dr. Bob Lennon
Supervisor, Special Education Services
Smithtown School District
Smithtown, Pennsylvania 15249
412-987-1298

3. Dr. Mary Reynolds
Professor, Special Education Department
Smithtown University
Smithtown, Pennsylvania 15249
412-456-7890

Please let me know whether you require any other information from me at this time. Thank you for your time and consideration. I look forward to hearing from you at your earliest convenience.

Sincerely,

Martha Barton

teacher's work or student teaching; thus, the selection of references is vital. (The candidate should not rely on relatives, neighbors, or other individuals unfamiliar with teaching responsibilities or professional job qualifications.) If the candidate is completing the application process prior to graduation, the teacher supervising the candidate during the student teaching or internship assignment is an important reference choice. Further, when the candidate is familiar with a school administrator, such as a program supervisor or principal, the administrator can be another good reference choice. Finally, college or university instructors, supervisors, or professors from whom the candidate took classes can be important contacts.

The contacts most likely will complete a professional reference form, such as illustrated in Figure 11.5. On this form, the individual will rate the candidate in areas such as teacher performance (e.g., knowledge of subject matter, maintenance of classroom

Martha Barton
127 Lincoln Drive
Smithtown, Pennsylvania 15249
412-987-6543
Social Security: 123-45-6789

Educational Background

High School:	**Dates:**
High School Diploma	June 1998
Smithtown High School	
Smithtown, Pennsylvania 15249	
University:	**Dates:**
Bachelor of Science	August 1998–May 2002
College of Education	
Smithtown University	
Smithtown, Pennsylvania 15249	
Professional Certifications:	**Effective Dates:**
Special Education, Instructional I	May 2002
Elementary Education, Instructional I	May 2002
Professional Experience:	**Dates:**
Student Teaching, Grades 3-5	January 2002-April 2002
Special Education Services	
George Roberts Elementary School	
Smithtown, Pennsylvania 15249	
412-987-3456	
Student Teaching, Grades 7-8	August 2001–December 2001
General Education	
Sammel Middle School	
Smithtown, Pennsylvania 15249	
412-987-4000	
Practicum, Ellis Preschool Center	January 2002–April 2002
George Roberts Elementary School	
Smithtown, Pennsylvania 15249	
412-987-1007	
Specialized Training Experience:	**Dates:**
Computer Technology	January–May 2002
Specially Designed Instruction	
Curriculum-Based Assessment	
Portfolio Assessments	
Classroom Management	
(George Roberts Elementary School)	

FIGURE 11.4   Résumé

Professional Organizations:
Association for Retarded Citizens, Member (1998–present)
Council for Exceptional Children, Member (1998–present)
Division on Mental Retardation, Member (1998–present)
Division for Learning Disabilities, Member (1998–present)
Division for Behavioral Disorders, Member (1998–present)

Career Goal Expectations:	**Anticipated Dates:**
Special Education Consulting Teacher	August 2002
Master's Degree, Special Education	May 2007
Previous Employment:	**Dates:**
University Bar and Grill	August 1995–April 2002
Maintenance Supervisor	
Smithtown University Student Center	
Awards/Recognition:	**Dates:**
Dean's List	August 1998–May 2002
College of Education	
Smithtown University	
Smithtown, Pennsylvania 15249	

Professional References:
Mr. Tom Mallory
Elementary Education Department
George Roberts Elementary School
Smithtown, Pennsylvania 15249
412-987-3456

Dr. Bob Lennon
Supervisor of Special Education Services
Smithtown School District
Smithtown, Pennsylvania 15249
412-987-1298

Dr. Mary Reynolds
Professor of Special Education
Smithtown University
Smithtown, Pennsylvania 15249
412-456-7890

control); professionalism (e.g., participation in professional organizations, demonstration of initiative and leadership); and personnel qualities (e.g., display of emotional stability, positive relationships with students, collaboration with administration and staff). Additionally, contacts will rank the candidate, including comparing the new teacher with others in the same position whom the contact has supervised or managed. Finally, most personnel offices ask the contact to provide written comments indicating the candidate's attendance and overall teaching performance. Contacts also provide their name, school address, and telephone number for future reference, if necessary.

College Transcripts, Verification of Previous Employment, and Teaching Credentials

In addition to securing a professional application form, cover letter, résumé, and references, the candidate will often have to provide the school personnel office with copies

Main Street School District
One Main Street Drive
Main Street, USA
12345

Mail to: John Doe, Director of Personnel
Room 1234
Main Street School District
412-123-4567

PROFESSIONAL REFERENCE FORM

Candidate's Name _____ Position Desired _____

Please assist me in my application for a position with Main Street School District by completing the form below and returning it in the enclosed self-addressed envelope. You have my permission to complete this evaluation based on your knowledge of my background.

I further understand that the information provided will be kept confidential by and become the property of Main Street School District.

Applicant's Position _____ Full Time _____ Part Time _____

Exact Dates of Service: From (mo./yr.) _____ Total (mo./yr.) _____

Total Years Served _____

Reason for Leaving Employ/Reemploy? _____

Would You Employ/Reemploy? _____

1. TEACHER PERFORMANCE	Out-standing	Above Average	Average	Unsatisfactory	No Opportunity to Observe
A Has knowledge of subject matter					
B Is consistently thorough in lesson planning; manages learning environment, including student materials, activities, and time					
C Uses a variety of teaching techniques, resources, and materials that relate effectively to the individual needs and maturity of children					
D Exhibits enthusiasm for teaching and has the ability to arouse interest; stimulates intellectual growth					
E Maintains classroom control; is respectful, positive, fair, firm, and consistent with children					

Main Street School District Is an Equal Rights and Opportunities Educational Agency

FIGURE 11.5 Professional Reference Form

2. PROFESSIONALISM	Out-standing	Above Average	Average	Unsatisfactory	No Opportunity to Observe
A Follows ethical and professional practices in ˉworking with others					
B Keeps accurate and up-to-date records (e.g., IEPs, portfolios)					
C Participates in general school activities					
D Participates in a variety of professional organizations					
E Demonstrates loyalty and dependability					
F Shows initiative and leadership skills					
3. PERSONAL QUALITIES					
A Displays emotional stability					
B Has positive relationships with students					
C Collaborates with administration and staff					
D Communicates and works with parents effectively					
E Maintains professional appearance					
F Demonstrates professional oral and written communication skills					
G Responds positively to construc-tive criticism					

4. COMPARATIVE RANKING

How would you rank this person as compared with others in the same position whom you have had under your supervision?

TOP 5%   NEXT 20%   MIDDLE 50%   LOW 25%

Main Street School District Is an Equal Rights and Opportunities Educational Agency

continued

of his or her college or university transcripts (verified on official college or university letterhead). Additionally, the office may request verification of previous employment and a copy of teaching certifications. (Because these are requested by, but not mailed in by the candidate, these additional data can be received in the personnel office at a later date than the application form, cover letter, and résumé.)

Personnel offices will ask candidates to send written documentation of summary grade point averages from college or university course work. In determining which candidates to interview, many personnel directors often assign points on the basis of

5. **PLEASE COMMENT ON THE FOLLOWING:**

    A. OVERALL PERSONALITY AND CHARACTER _____

_____

    B. ATTENDANCE _____

    C. OVERALL PERFORMANCE AS A TEACHER _____

_____

_____

    D. ADDITIONAL COMMENTS _____

_____

_____

EVALUATOR'S NAME (Print/Type) _____

TITLE _____

SCHOOL ADDRESS _____

_____

DAYTIME PHONE NUMBER _____ DATE _____

SIGNATURE _____

Main Street School District Is an Equal Rights and Opportunities Educational Agency

FIGURE 11.5 continued

summary grade point averages. For example, candidates might receive points in the summary grade point averages as follows:

1. *Cumulative College Grade Point Average* (with at least a grade point of 3.0, based on a 4.0 scale, as the cutoff for interviews).

Grade Point Average	Points
4.0-3.6	2
3.59-3.0	1
Below 3.0	No interview

2. *Cumulative Master's Grade Point Average* (if applicable) (with at least a grade point of 3.5, based on a 4.0 scale, as the cutoff for interviews).

Grade Point Average	Points
3.5 or higher	1

3. *Grade Point Average of Certified Area(s)* (with at least a grade point of 3.0, based on a 4.0, scale as the cutoff for interviews).

Grade Point Average	Points
4.0–3.6	3
3.59–3.2	2
3.19–3.0	1
Below 3.0	No interview

P̲ause and Reflect 11.2

How would you rate if the district personnel office were to assign points on the basis of your summary grade point averages? Determine your points and your interview potential on the basis of your grade point average as indicated below. Would you be eligible for an interview?

A. *Cumulative College Grade Point Average* (with at least a grade point of 3.0, based on a 4.0 scale, as the cutoff for interviews).

Grade Point Average	Points
4.0–3.6	2
3.59–3.0	1
Below 3.0	No interview

Your cumulative college grade point average: _____

B. *Cumulative Master's Grade Point Average* (if applicable) (with at least a grade point of 3.5, based on a 4.0 scale, as the cutoff for interviews).

Grade Point Average	Points
3.5 or higher	1

Your cumulative college grade point average: _____

C. *Grade Point Average of Certified Area(s)* (with at least a grade point of 3.0, based on a 4.0 scale, as the cutoff for interviews).

Grade Point Average	Points
4.0–3.6	3
3.59–3.2	2
3.19–3.0	1
Below 3.0	No interview

Your cumulative college grade point average: _____

Are you eligible for an interview on the basis of this rating system? _____

In addition, district personnel offices often request the candidate's score(s) on a national teaching test, such as the National Teachers' Examination. A passing score in core areas, such as in written expression and mathematics, as well as in the candidate's content area specialization (e.g., special education, reading, science) can be determinants in initial candidate screenings.

Completed Credentials Files

Completed credentials files for teaching positions contain many data. Most personnel offices consider a candidate's application to be incomplete until they receive the following in the candidate's credentials file:

- A professional application form
- A cover letter
- The candidate's current résumé
- Recent background checks and clearances
- Letters of recommendation (usually three)

- Official undergraduate and/or graduate transcripts
- Verification of previous employment (if applicable)
- A copy of applicable teaching certification(s).

In some school districts that have insufficient candidates, positions will be readvertised. If the number of candidates is still insufficient, many districts select the highest scoring applicants to interview. Districts hold most candidates' files for only 6 months to a year. Candidates will need to reactivate their files for additional consideration when positions are reposted.

Interview teams often use an "initial screening" form, such as illustrated in Figure 11.6, in choosing the candidates selected for interviews. Interview teams will screen candidates face-to-face during personal interviews and rate candidates' (1) college grades, (2) national teaching scores, (3) professional experience, (4) specialized training or experience, and (5) references. Many interview teams indicate that candidates who have evidence of completing multiple tasks simultaneously (e.g., holding jobs, raising a family, having university or community leadership experiences, in addition to completing college coursework) often receive initial selection for job interviews. Such candidates demonstrate on paper that they have what it takes to be a teacher—a professional required to complete competing, multiple tasks in classroom settings.

Face-to-Face Interviews

The top-rated candidates are chosen for face-to-face interviews by the interview teams. Face-to-face interviews may include the candidate's travel to the district; job fairs that partner local universities, districts, and community resources; or candidate's travel to other states or foreign countries. In preparing for the interview, the candidate's dress choice should be professional (a conservative suit and shoes in neutral colors are the best choices). The procedures involve the new teacher sitting before interview team members, addressing answers to probing questions. Questions either are in a group for-

---

Main Street School District
One Main Street Drive
Main Street, USA
12345

INITIAL SCREENING
Rate based on "0" to "5", 5 being the highest score

Candidate's Name _____   Date _____

Area(s) of Certification:

1. COLLEGE GRADES ASSESSMENT _____
2. NTE SCORE _____
3. PROFESSIONAL EXPERIENCE _____
4. SPECIALIZED TRAINING OR EXPERIENCE _____
5. REFERENCES _____

CANDIDATE QUALIFIES FOR AN INTERVIEW: YES/NO

Main Street School District Is an Equal Rights and Opportunities Educational Agency

FIGURE 11.6 Initial Screening Form

TABLE 11.1 Questions Applicable to the Interview Team and Candidates During Face-to-Face Interviews

Interview Team Questions to Candidates	Candidates' Questions to Interview Teams
What is relevant in your background that qualifies you for this teaching position?	What grade levels does the position entail?
What are some methods that you would use in teaching a reading lesson . . . mathematics lesson . . . science lesson, and so forth?	How many students are in the school? What is the student-teacher ratio?
How do you determine that students have learned what you have taught? What are assessment methods you use?	How many students receive special education services?
What do you do when your students forget homework assignments?	Where do the students receive the special education services?
How would your supervisor determine whether you were well organized in your classroom?	Who attends the IEP meetings with the special education faculty?
What steps would you take if your principal provided constructive criticism on some aspect of your lesson plans?	What peer-mentoring and/or professional development services does the district offer?
How do you promote positive communication with parents?	How often are family members invited to participate in school functions?
What are several ways you use to maintain class-room control?	How are teaching faculty evaluated or observed? What is the process, and who conducts the process?
How would you begin teaching l[subject area] if you were not provided teaching materials?	What are the beginning and ending times for teachers' school attendance?
What are specific consulting strategies you will use with general education teachers if you are to use a learning strategies approach?	How are resources provided for individual students, classes, and teachers?
How will you manage and evaluate your paraprofessionals and classroom volunteers?	What extracurricular duties are expected of teachers?

mat or are provided by individual interview team members. The questions often relate to the candidate's (1) background, (2) instructional techniques, (3) content matter, (4) behavioral support or classroom management, (5) planning ability, and (6) knowledge of teaching.

Importantly, interview teams also look for candidates to demonstrate initiative during face-to-face contacts. To do so, new teachers should be prepared to ask pertinent questions about local practices. The intent of this part of the interview is to allow the interview team to determine a match between the candidate's interests and qualifications and what the district can offer the candidate. By the same token, it gives the candidate an opportunity to decide whether the district is the right employment choice.

Pertinent questions that the new teacher might raise in face-to-face interviews include those related to the district's average class sizes, number of students in the building, number of students receiving special education services, number of students provided special education services through inclusion models in the general education classroom, number of teachers, starting time and ending time for teachers, extracurricular activities, classroom resources, and professional responsibilities. Other pertinent questions relate to specifics of job demands and incentives for employment. Table 11.1 presents questions applicable to the interview team and candidates during face-to-face interviews.

Pause and Reflect 11.3

What pertinent topics might you raise in a face-to-face interview with an interview team? Determine what you would want to ask to help you in deciding whether the position is the right employment choice for you. Write down at least five questions you would want to ask if you were involved in a face-to-face interview.

1. _____

_____

_____

_____

2. _____

_____

_____

_____

3. _____

_____

_____

_____

4. _____

_____

_____

_____

5. _____

_____

_____

_____

Candidate Recommendations

Many districts require top-rated candidates to conduct a classroom demonstration lesson or a computer technology demonstration in front of the interview team and other teachers, administrators, or parents. These requests most likely will take place during a second or third round of face-to-face interviews. Interview teams consider these results prior to recommending the final two or three candidates to the district personnel director. Many district personnel directors will submit top-rated candidate recommendations to the superintendent and board of education. School board members, however, often do the final selection for the faculty position. The board of education approves final faculty selections, with all credentials and processing papers completed in full before final appointment.

PREPARATION OF PROFESSIONAL PORTFOLIOS

Many new teachers will find that it is helpful to include teacher preparation evidence during their job search experiences. A **professional portfolio** is a purposeful collection of pedagogical work that tells the story of the teacher's efforts, progress, or achievements.

Some preparation programs currently use a professional portfolio to document new teachers' accomplishments and how well beginning or developing teachers meet professional standards. Professional portfolios often function as a process to account for assessment decisions, improved teaching, and student performances in teacher preparation. For example, Kenney, Hammitte, Rakestraw, and LeMontagne (2000) coupled their professional portfolios process with the statewide move to teacher preparation coursework delivery. In advocating programmatic changes focused on raising university standards in teacher preparation, these authors detailed how new teachers prepare professional portfolios and receive instructional modeling of effective teaching practices across grade levels, educational settings, and teacher placement in primary through grade 12 classrooms. Kenney et al. also provided data on their college's use of professional portfolios to document performance based assessments, dynamic assessment strategies, programmatic change effectiveness, and special education course work.

Professional Portfolio Purposes

There are reasons for new teachers to prepare professional portfolios. First, a professional portfolio is a means for beginning or developing teachers to specify essential knowledge, skills, and important professional dispositions. Second, professional portfolios can establish usable ways to display teaching progress, efforts, and achievements. Thus, by creating a professional portfolio during preservice experiences, new teachers show evidence that they are ready to assume professional responsibilities. Next, the professional portfolio illustrates to employers the contents, products, and processes new teachers use to solve, create, design, debate, perform, research, collaborate, interact, and explain—all essential behaviors in the master teacher process.

Professional portfolios reveal new teachers' work in situations based on real-world experiences as they explore and learn from active, rather than passive, learning the art and science of teaching. Finally, a reflective professional portfolio allows new teachers to make judgments about their own work as they self-reflect on instructional assessments, management, teaching, and collaborative activities initiated during their teacher preparation experiences.

Portfolio Evidence

Relevant portfolio evidence is similar across teacher preparation programs. For example, evidence (i.e., artifacts) includes academic achievements and tangible rewards, such as accolades earned in college or university programming. Also relevant is community or service recognition that demonstrates teachers' efforts. Actual assessment, instructional, or behavioral materials are valuable products and may include specially designed teaching items, learning strategy materials, curriculum-based assessments, or functional behavioral assessments. Pertinent data also include positive behavioral strategies used during instruction; student work samples; cooperative learning tasks; record-keeping systems used to manage student groups; and Web sites, photographs, video recordings, films, or tape recordings of teacher-student interactions (written parent/guardian permission is necessary for the latter). Finally, written reflections, responses, or notations made during university courses or student teaching seminars and journal entries summarizing professional dispositions, behaviors, or feelings during teaching experiences can be important.

Professional Portfolio Process

Beginning or developing teachers initiating the professional portfolio process begin by collecting artifacts from their initial experiences in university course work, tutoring sessions, field experiences, and/or student teaching opportunities. Artifacts pinpoint multiple examples of the concrete evidence of their growth and development in the content and processes of teaching. Examples of planning or assessments, behavioral support systems or discipline procedures, and collaborative or consultation experiences are many of the items that may be employed in a professional portfolio. Thus, artifacts represent evidence of the new teacher's professional activities with students, families, school-based professionals, and community professionals with whom teachers interact. Artifacts also include examples of the content and processes of teaching that are meaningful to the new teacher's self-esteem as a professional educator.

New teachers begin the professional portfolio process by participating in the teaching-learning process and building reflections. They choose examples of contact with students, parents, and peers that demonstrate that new teachers are acquiring basic pedagogy. That is, the first step is to assemble a collection of artifacts that represents the activities in which new teachers engage during initial teaching experiences. For example, new teachers begin to save and collate examples of their first attempts at writing lesson plans, creating teaching games, or analyzing behavioral charts that they create. Initial examples often are trial-and-error.

As new teachers implement and refine their teaching experiences in classroom settings, a second step is to choose those artifacts that the new teacher deems important to represent him- or herself as a professional. This discrimination step eliminates unnecessary documentation and keys in on meaningful data. Importantly, the teacher must choose to select and highlight collected data that are essential in describing him- or herself as a professional. Through a sorting process—examining and analyzing artifacts—the teacher keeps artifacts that hold self-importance. At the same time, the teacher must be willing to discard certain lesson plans, teaching games, behavioral systems, or other items that hold little or no relevance to the teacher's evolving picture of him- or herself as a professional.

The third step in the process, self-evaluation, is the new teacher's rationalization for artifact inclusion in the professional portfolio. Thus, the new teacher must attest to the inclusion of artifacts presented and refined within the portfolio's parameters. He or she must be willing to evaluate in a written dialogue, synthesizing thoughts on why the included evidence is meaningful and whether/why the included artifacts contribute to the teacher's awareness of individual knowledge, skills, or dispositions in the teaching process. The self-evaluation step includes a dated, individualized self-assessment statement. Insights and mistakes that contributed to professional growth and development are important reflective criteria. New teachers articulate the hows and whys of artifact contribution as they acquire, become fluent in, maintain, refine, and generalize important teaching behaviors.

Many new teachers align their professional portfolio reflections with data from CEC (2000a) and other standards-based teaching references. For example, some personnel preparation programs encourage their teacher candidates to reflect on artifacts aligned with standards setting efforts related to teaching responsibilities (e.g., framework components from Danielson, 1996). Often, with the university's and/or district personnel's attestation to the quality of the professional portfolio artifacts, the artifacts are intended for inclusion in the new teacher's professional credentials.

MOVING FROM STUDENT TEACHER TO MASTER TEACHER: WORKING EFFECTIVELY IN PARTNERSHIPS

Once school districts select personnel for faculty vacancies or new positions, the road for the developing teacher in refining the master teaching process has begun. Cooperative approaches and specific teacher induction efforts structure the master teaching process.

Cooperative Approaches

Cooperative approaches are being used increasingly in U.S. schools. Competence in interaction knowledge, skills, and dispositions often differentiates master teachers from less skilled teachers. Importantly, classrooms are no longer the exclusive domain of teachers. Peer teachers, related services providers, student teachers, paraeducators, instructional assistants, and volunteers are becoming partners in the instructional and management team (Aldinger, Warger, & Eavy, 1991; Dettmer, Dyck, & Thurston, 1996). Many schools now provide core teams to lead and support the entire school community, to model an effective problem-solving approach, and to enhance a child-focused atmosphere. Such schools offer school and community collaboration. All of these instructional arrangements require ongoing cooperation and support.

The 1990s highlighted important changes now being implemented in educational circles during the 21st century. Among factors shaping these changes are elements of partnerships.

- Reports suggesting that cooperative learning experiences to increase teachers' and peers' acceptance of diverse students is a necessary component to effective classroom programming (Slavin, Karweit, & Madden, 1989; U.S. Department of Education [USDE], 1994)
- Awareness that students, especially students with disabilities, demonstrate improved interactions and improved student learning outcomes when community members, school faculty, and staff directly team with, problem-solve together, and support each other and family members (Dettmer et al., 1996; Giangreco, Cloniger, Dennis, & Edelman, 1994)
- Increased recognition that partnerships (e.g., across general education and special education settings) are necessary if learning outcomes for students are to improve (CEC, 2000a; CEC, 2000b).
- Increased recognition that those involved in the education of students with disabilities face major philosophical and logistical changes; as a result of the reauthorized IDEA 97. (Chapter 2 describes IDEA 97 in detail.)

Many individuals contend that school personnel who work together can prevent such issues as school violence and its preceding behaviors by providing a supportive schoolwide climate and responding early to at-risk students' academic and behavioral problems (Dwyer, Osher, & Hoffman, 2000). In fact, schools that are academically responsive and prosocial contribute to prevention. Reflective practices and effective partnerships become part of a school culture whereby new teachers are naturally expected to collaborate with more experienced university and school-based colleagues (Weiss & Weiss,

Pause and Reflect 11.4

What makes your role as a new teacher different from that of teachers working in special education services 20 years ago? Decide at least 10 factors that make teachers' roles in the 21st century different from teachers' roles in the 1980s:

1. _____

2. _____

3. _____

4. _____

5. _____

6. _____

7. _____

8. _____

9. _____

10. _____

Compare and contrast your ideas with those of your peers.

1999). Accordingly, when professionals model partnerships, they provide a supportive schoolwide foundation. Such professionals are more likely to address early students' academic and behavioral problems.

A comprehensive picture of integration trends based on national special education statistics emerged. Sawyer, McLaughlin, & Winglee (1995) found that full-time placement in the general education classroom showed a relatively consistent increase, over time, for most disability categories. Currently, special needs students are served increasingly more often in inclusive services in the general education setting (Hehir, 1999). As discussed in Chapter 2, IDEA mandates that the general education curriculum must be the basis for students' IEPs.

Accordingly, the newly hired teacher will find that many school districts nationwide are changing their special education services to accommodate the needs of diverse students. Many changes in services are controversial. Some proponents report that curriculum changes and emphasis on the general education classroom were long overdue. Such opportunities for integration of students with and without disabilities benefits both groups academically and socially (Kunc, 1992; Snell & Janney, 1994; Stainback & Stainback, 1990; Thousand, Villa, & Nevin, 1994). Other researchers question these changes and the ability of the general education system to meet the many unique learning needs of these students (Baker & Zigmond, 1990; Kauffman & Hallahan, 1995).

Newly hired personnel must become aware of the need for cooperative partnership and a teaming spirit—during school activities, as well as in extracurricular functions.

The close proximity of working together has much influence on what happens to teachers, students, and the classroom environment. New teachers will progress in expanding service delivery roles as they involve themselves in shared decision-making and mentoring experiences. Awareness of a team approach necessitates knowledge of the additional stress and conflicts that partnerships will create.

Team Approach

Even some veteran teachers have had little experience in some of the new service demands (e.g., accommodating or adapting the general education curriculum). In some cases, it may be viewed as an overwhelming or intimidating task—especially so to newly hired personnel. This problem can be overcome by a team of professionals who meet together when needed, to brainstorm and provide suggestions regarding objectives for students and to discuss how the objectives can be fostered in classrooms (Stainback, Stainback, & Stefanich, 1996).

A team is composed of adults and students working together and sharing common activities and experiences. Drury (1986) highlighted attributes of a team as highly involved people who are committed to achieving common objectives, who work well together and enjoy doing so, and who produce high-quality results. Box 11.1 is based on Drury's work of differentiating a team from a collection of individuals.

Box 11.1   **Developing and New Teachers Who Operate as a Team Versus Those Who Operate as a Collection of Individuals**

A Team

Developing teachers who

- listen and try to understand
- share common visions
- share in decision-making by consensus
- use clear communication within and outside the team
- display ability to talk through conflicts and problems in a constructive way
- display openness, honesty, mutual respect, and trust
- focus on the task
- make use of all team resources, including parents and professionals from other disciplines

A Collection of Individuals

Developing teachers who

- fight for their own views without consideration of others
- do not use effective listening skills
- operate on right or wrong premises
- have no clear group vision
- operate on negative assumptions and hidden agendas
- display suspicion, distrust, and competition
- often are sidetracked

Source: Adapted from Drury, S. S. (1986). *Team effectiveness.* Newark: University of Delaware.

Teacher Induction Programs

Teams can help new teachers enormously, especially in teacher induction programs that include mentoring experiences. Mentoring experiences help the new professional by offering support in (1) planning flexible learning objectives, (2) adapting activities to individual students, (3) using multiple adaptations simultaneously to accommodate diverse group needs, and (4) implementing successful curriculum strategies (Stainback et al., 1996).

Teacher induction programs, including opportunities for mentor-protégé partnerships, not only reduce attrition rates among new teachers but also improve teaching capabilities. The availability of formal induction programs and their structure vary among states and local school districts. However, effective programs help new teachers in the hiring and retention processes (Weiss & Weiss, 1999).

Understanding and acting upon the process in mentor-protégé partnerships are germane to effective teacher induction programs. Although there may be some local differences in format and content, the processes involved in hiring and retaining teachers are similar. Most districts follow typical hiring processes and many rely on teacher induction to smooth the transition from preservice to inservice activities. Local school districts' criteria for linking preservice to inservice activities have a research focus. For example, Ralph, Kesten, Lang, and Smith (1998) found that partnerships by those having an interest in the hiring process (e.g., university preparation personnel, public school administrators, and teacher union representatives) contribute jointly to the quality of the preparation, hiring, and induction of new teachers.

Critical faculty shortages in special education underscore renewed attention on the recruitment and retention specifics of qualified educators who will instruct diverse students with special needs. Cooley and Yovanoff (1996) indicated that the national context of shrinking supply and demand for special educators both contributes to and is affected by the high rate of attrition among these professionals. Importantly, new teachers' early job experiences have a huge impact not only on whether teachers remain in teaching for the long term but also on the kinds of teachers they become. Dissatisfying early experiences are relevant to attrition rates among teachers in their first 5 years of experiences—rates that now range from 30% to 50% nationwide (NASBE, 2000). To survive and succeed, all new teachers need exposure to high-quality induction programs that will help them remain committed to their profession.

High-Quality Induction Programs. High-quality induction programs share at least four characteristics: (1) mentoring relationships between new and experienced teachers, such that beginning or developing teachers have a sustained relationship with at least one accomplished, experienced teacher; (2) targeted professional development for participating teachers, so that new teachers have specifically targeted activities based on their needs and concerns as new teachers; (3) a support focus on at least the 1st year of actual teaching experiences; and (4) a system to evaluate the performance of beginning or developing teachers, including remediation and counseling efforts (NASBE, 2000). When preservice and inservice personnel partner to support new teachers' transition, new teachers have increased survival and success rates.

Additionally, school districts have existing team models that may be helpful to the new teacher. For example, many classroom teams that serve students with disabilities rely on partnership models. Such models include collaborative consultation (Idol, 1988), coteaching (Walther-Thomas, 1996), child study/resource teams (Hayek, 1987), and cooperative teaching (Bauwens & Hourcade, 1995). All these models emphasize active participation and stress the importance of trust, mutual respect, and the value of each person's roles and contributions to group effectiveness.

Walther-Thomas (1996) described a popular partnership model that will be helpful to newly hired personnel initiating collaboration attempts. In coteaching, teacher teams provide all students with instruction, discipline, and support. This helps coteachers avoid unintentionally stigmatizing students with identified needs and helps eliminate mental walls that some teachers possess. Coteaching reminds teachers to think about all class members as "our students." It offers new teachers many of the benefits as reported by researchers (e.g., opportunities for teaming, problem solving, joint decision-making, and sharing responsibilities and accountability). It can provide new teachers with assistance in development, delivery, and evaluation of effective instructional programs. It can provide them with many critical data about classroom setting demands, teacher expectations, and current student performance levels. This knowledge enables new teachers to provide more appropriate recommendations regarding the instructional procedures that are most likely to benefit their students with disabilities and many of their students who are low achievers. Coteaching provides professionals with ongoing support, opportunities for problem solving, and professional development—all elements necessary in refining the master teacher process.

Accordingly, teacher preparation programs around the country are recognizing that it is now time to integrate partnershp-building competencies into professional-development and teacher preparation practices. Many of the calls for professional preparation standards reiterate the need for collaboration and team building as essential skills (CEC, 2000a; NASBE, 2000; NBPTS, 1999).

O'Shea, Williams, & Sattler (1999) reported on new teachers' perceptions of collaboration training and the types of collaboration patterns that evolve in university preparation across special education and elementary education course work. They found that most new teachers support collaboration opportunities and welcome activities designed to encourage partnerships across curriculum areas. In their study, O'Shea, Williams, et al. reported that many new teachers indicated that collaboration preparation helped to support their knowledge, skills, and dispositions of inclusion benefits and pitfalls, including the dedication on the part of all educators involved. New teachers offered important insights into why collaboration preparation focusing on curriculum areas can support their readiness for future instructional roles.

Mentoring Activities

Teacher educators are responding to research reports that peer-mentoring opportunities are significant in the preparation and professional growth of teachers (Bauwens & Hourcade, 1995; Billingsley & Cross, 1992; Cooley & Yovanoff, 1996; NASBE, 2000; Weiss & Weiss, 1999). In mentoring activities, new teachers are paired with peers to experience sharing, problem solving, and conflict resolution situations. Many districts offer teacher induction partnerships to support new teachers in addressing these situations. In addition to problem solving with other new teachers, mentorship experiences include opportunities for experienced and inexperienced personnel to work together. Using mentorship opportunities imbues the process with an ethic of caring that teachers, ideally, will translate into their own classrooms. New teachers have opportunities for modeling, observations, dialogue, practice, continuity in caring, teaming, reflection, and confirmation of actions—essential ingredients to the facilitation of cooperation expected in classroom endeavors.

P *ause and Reflect 11.5*

How Do Mentorship Experiences Help You in Your Current Field Placement?

List at least five advantages to you personally of working with other new teachers during your classroom experience. Are there advantages to working with experienced teachers? List at least five advantages to you personally of working with experienced teachers, that are different from the advantages of working with new teachers.

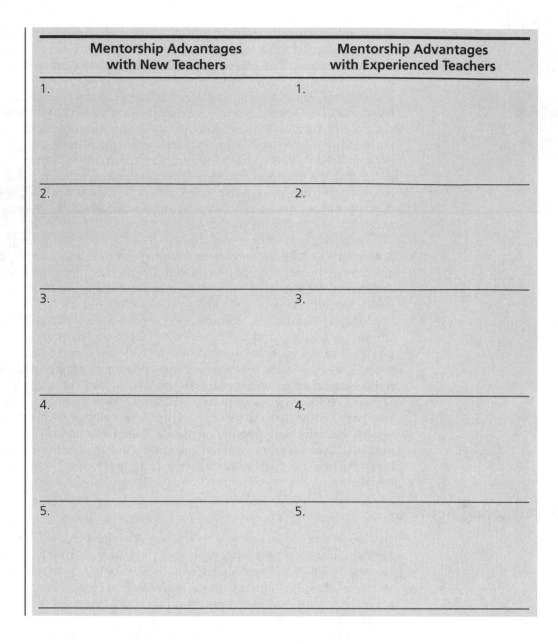

Mentorship Advantages with New Teachers	Mentorship Advantages with Experienced Teachers
1.	1.
2.	2.
3.	3.
4.	4.
5.	5.

Working with Students' Parents or Guardians

Many of the partnership benefits gleaned from teaming, coteaching, or mentorship programs can be used in working collaboratively with students' parents or guardians (Karp, 1993). New teachers can profit from opportunities to practice and model sharing, problem solving, teaming, and reciprocity—while gaining pedagogical knowledge and skills they will need in their work with students' families. (Chapter 9 details family transition approaches.)

Importantly, master teachers recognize variations in beliefs, traditions, and values across cultures and the effect of these relationships among child, family, and schooling. Despite the differences that students bring to school, teachers work actively to support family-friendly schools and to create an environment that encourages family advocacy. Master teachers accept and support the diversity and dynamics of students' families, backgrounds, and communities. In essence, master teachers establish and maintain rapport with students' families while valuing, respecting, and/or accepting others whose backgrounds, cultures, languages, and approaches to child care differ from their own.

When teachers work to support family-friendly interactions between parents of special needs students and the local school system, they are demonstrating master teacher behaviors. They help to ensure that new parents are supported in positive, successful interactions facilitated by their peers and school personnel. Master teachers help parents and guardians new to the system gain knowledge and skills concerning legal rights to family involvement guaranteed by state and federal mandates. Master teachers help family members move in the direction of empowering and supporting, rather than combating or confronting each other. Box 11.2 presents a summary of important strategies that master teachers use with families.

Box 11.2   Important Strategies That Master Teachers Use with Families

1. **Implementing effective communication** (e.g., demonstrating active listening, positive regard, and empathy) **and interaction skills** (e.g., encouraging families to express, share, disagree, problem-solve, form partnerships, decide, and/or reach group goals; considering how individuals share with others)
2. **Overcoming barriers that potentially block effective rapport with students' parents or guardians** (e.g., relying on limited knowledge and skills; ignoring family priorities, values, customs, and traditions)
3. **Providing family members with opportunities for shared planning and decision-making with district officials** (e.g., offering direct support for parents and guardians new to special needs services; setting up opportunities to talk with district officials and teachers about school conferences, grades, consulting reports, IEPs, management strategies, learning supports, adaptations, and modifications)
4. **Creating matched goals and objectives between home and school,** such as family members' desire for school participation (e.g., talking about amount of homework, number of acceptable conferences, resources, persons responsible for task completion, potential outcomes, and individual expectations over the course of the school year; offering choices in meeting times and places conducive to families' involvement)
5. **Encouraging parent or guardian mentoring and leadership opportunities at the local level** (e.g., setting up after-school opportunities for family members to meet with and share information with other families)
6. **Recognizing that families who lack knowledge or are inactive do not necessarily lack interest in their children's education and achievement, but rather need alternatives and choices in school involvement** (e.g., valuing, respecting, and/or accepting others whose training, culture, concepts, skills, and values differ)
7. **Planning and conducting collaborative conferences** (e.g., assisting families in making informed decisions regarding educational opportunities available for their child; helping empower families by sharing, questioning, clarifying, or problem-solving during meetings or activities set up to explain students' learning; clarifying students' work samples and assessment records)
8. **Sharing learning resources for home use when feasible** (e.g., lending media, learning aids, and educational materials appropriate to students' learning skills and abilities; having and sharing reading materials, computer technology, and videos highlighting management and learning strategies; offering a lending library for families' use)
9. **Ensuring that families understand the scope of educational resources available to them and their child** (e.g., when asked, interpreting professional journals and summarizing major findings in language appropriate to parents or guardians; securing local and state resources on programs and services)

10. **Collaborating with general classroom teachers and other school and community personnel** (e.g., when appropriate, integrating students into various learning environments; seeking to improve communications with teachers, administrators, and other school personnel about characteristics and needs of students with diverse needs and strengths)

11. **Being accessible and responsive to family needs; recognizing the strengths and positive attributes of students, families, and other team members**

Acquiring knowledge, skills, and dispositions in working with diversity provides an ideal opportunity for new teachers to imitate concepts and skills that master teachers demonstrate in their partnership with students' families. By observing how effective teachers problem-solve and partnerships toward mutually agreed-on goals with students' families and by imitating experienced peers, new teachers can demonstrate the master teacher process. Working with students' families entails a host of knowledge and skills concerning students' home backgrounds. Table 11.2 lists such knowledge and skills.

Developing teachers who work with students with disabilities will be exposed to family support programs. Effective partnerships require the new teacher to demon-

TABLE 11.2   Examples of Knowledge and Skills that Teachers Require Concerning Students' Home and Community Backgrounds

Knowledge	Skills
• Awareness of the numbers of individuals in the family, sibling makeup, birth order of child with a disability, and type of family structure (e.g., nuclear, single parent, step-family)	Discussing with families expected similarities and differences for the child; including discussions on the impact to siblings, grandparents, neighbors, and so on
• Understanding of the cultural, ethnic, and environmental milieu of the family	Encouraging questions and comments; specifying resources, services, and programs that will help
• Recognition of the effects that problems in ability, behavior, learning, social skills, and so forth may have on one's home life	Contributing and providing personal insights to help facilitate family expectations
• Awareness of the child's self-directness encouraged or expected by parents or guardians	Demonstrating respect for the family's contributions in decisions, and working toward a common goal of successful programming
• Awareness of the family's school and life expectations for their child	Providing information in a variety of forms (e.g., books, materials) to help the child, siblings, and other family members
• Recognition of specific family-school involvement priorities	Using open communication methods often, such as letters home, shared reports, face-to-face contacts, and home visits
• Understanding of unique family differences in coping with the demands and challenges of a child with a disability.	Scheduling time to discuss program issues, student progress, parent options, community input, or other issues
	Modifying IEPs or family programs on the basis of the family's needs for a particular service

strate listening skills and empathy. Communication skills and constructive problem-solving ability are important. Effective interpersonal skills with other professionals are vital, as are the abilities to be task- and resource-oriented. Students with disabilities thrive in respectful and beneficial relationships between families and professionals. Family support involves appropriate management and efforts by all teachers. As in most situations, however, partnership teams are not easy, and conflicts can arise often. Many problems with team approaches will not be observed readily but can be stumbling blocks in new teachers' efforts.

Persistent problems often surface that are related to teachers' lack of planning time, student scheduling, caseload concerns, limited administrative support, and the need for, but often, paucity of staff development opportunities (O'Shea et al., 1999; Walther-Thomas, 1996). Many school districts are electing to serve diverse students in cooperative services. School districts are beginning to address realistic and legitimate concerns of planning, scheduling, and so forth. Nonetheless, master teachers have been able to face these persistent problems, operate in a cooperative mode, and continue to serve their diverse students effectively. New teachers, mindful of both the benefits and pitfalls of teaming, are in good positions. Teachers play many roles with their diverse students, families, and other professionals. However, they need to be cognizant of ways to overcome problems and make teaming work.

Making Teaming Work

The effectiveness and proficiency of teaming is influenced heavily by the teacher's disposition toward having another adult present in the classroom or by working with others on joint projects within the school. For example, in the classroom, students' attention will shift to the other adult to some degree, a factor to which the teacher may react. During schoolwide projects, the teacher may have to share recognition for success, rather than be singled out for individual accomplishment. Special education teachers must work effectively with general education teachers to make IEP's work well for students. At some point, every teacher must cooperate with family members, paraprofessionals, peers, and administrators as they accommodate and/or adapt the general education curricula to individual students' needs. A teacher's disposition and style are important in that they will encourage or sabotage the abilities of other adults to interact effectively with students or to succeed in schoolwide projects. Individual teacher dispositions are especially important to the interplay of individuals and team effectiveness. These skills and abilities are listed in Box 11.3.

Box 11.3   **Important Teacher Attributes Influencing Teaming Effectiveness**

- Skills in organizing and planning for students, adults, and activities
- Leadership ability
- Observational skills
- Ability to communicate needs and wants to all present in the group
- Experience in training, managing, and monitoring students and adults
- Skills in taking and following directions from others
- Educational background and experiences
- Awareness of others' educational background and experiences
- Philosophy of education

Source: Adapted from Lombardo, V. (1980). *Paraprofessionals in special education.* Springfield, IL: Charles C Thomas.

Peer Observations

One way that new teachers can benefit is to interact with more experienced colleagues through peer observations. New teachers observing experienced peers can ask questions to clear up role conflict and ambiguities, can ask for tips on proven practices, and can view how teachers survive in the system and problem-solve. New teachers will sharpen their own personal teaching styles and be able to function more proficiently in teaming models when they observe experienced peers. It is important to keep realistic expectations, initial mistakes are bound to occur until experience accumulates. Many observation benefits will result.

1. Observation of similar activities by peers can confirm in the new teacher's mind the appropriateness of the strategies, materials, procedures, and techniques used in his or her classroom.

2. Observation of experienced peers who model research-based practices will generate new approaches and techniques.

3. Patterns of students' behaviors in various class settings can be recorded and analyzed to compare across settings.

4. Teachers can share observations during team meetings and conferences with families, peers, and supervisors.

5. New teacher's can analyze factors influencing the success of peer teachers' behaviors.

6. Peer teachers can aid in the communication process and corrective feedback. Developing and new teachers can discuss behaviors of concern during peer reviews as a reference for change. Box 11.4 lists classroom observation factors that are important to new teachers' success.

Peer observation can encourage a teacher's professional and skill development. By reviewing with others and sharing information through either formal or informal methods, teachers are implementing a collaborative approach (O'Shea & Hoover, 1986). Teachers can share the benefits of teaching that make the field rewarding and challenging.

Managing Paraprofessionals

In addition to interacting with families and peers, new teachers will use partnership models as resources in their own classes. For example, the vast majority of teachers serving children with problems will have responsibilities supervising paraeducators and/or adult volunteers in the classroom. These individuals are referred to as **paraprofessionals.** Paraprofessionals, or aides, teacher aides, paraeducators, or auxiliaries (used interchangeably here), are all nonprofessionals who relieve teachers of some nonteaching duties, whether they are paid or volunteer their time (Beach, 1973). Often the new teacher is a consultant to the paraprofessionals and must supervise, manage, and evaluate their ability to interact in the classroom. The teacher functions as a leader to paraprofessionals.

The role of paraprofessional is especially important to personnel in new special education roles because students with special needs often require the assistance of more than one adult for a majority of the day. Paraprofessionals make a noticeable, positive impact in school systems if used effectively. Paraprofessionals (1) improve the adult-to-student ratio in the classroom; (2) facilitate the implementation of the curriculum; (3) enable the teacher to develop more effective programs based on the individual or small-group needs of students; (4) make it possible for teachers to use more variety in structured classroom activities; (5) enable the teacher to use more instructional media

---

Box 11.4　　　**Classroom Observation Factors That Are Important to New Teachers' Success**

- Detailed physical description of the classroom, including information on visual, auditory, and/or other environmental factors (e.g., seating arrangements, location of materials, equipment, and other relevant classroom features)
- Descriptions of age levels, cognitive/ability levels, academic grade levels, pertinent behaviors of individual students, learning styles, and other relevant descriptive data
- Behavioral management plan for the entire class, including all classroom rules, strategies for increasing positive student behaviors, and strategies for decreasing negative student behaviors
- Uses of informal assessment and data collection procedures, including teacher-made checklists, rating scales, inventories, and curriculum-based assessment devices
- Uses of formal assessment, including title, publisher, publication date, and brief description of the purpose of the assessment device
- Descriptions of the teaching format used for various subjects (e.g., "used individual instruction for reading skills; used large-group instruction for social skills")
- Descriptions of instructional strategies and teaching methods, including use of learning strategies, peer tutoring, direct instruction, and guided discovery learning
- Uses of volunteers, paraprofessionals, teacher aides, or other adults in the classroom
- Methods of communicating with parents or guardians
- Methods of working cooperatively with other professionals in the school (e.g., administrators, guidance counselors, speech-language pathologist, general education class teachers, other special education teachers)
- Names and locations of relevant personnel (e.g., principal, assistant principal, office secretaries, guidance counselor, special education coordinator, special education teachers, general education teachers, school district superintendent, area superintendent)
- Names and locations of relevant rooms (e.g., teachers' lounge, cafeteria, office, health suite)

---

and materials; (6) provide increased teacher time for evaluating learning situations, using behavioral management techniques, and counseling or guiding students; and (7) relieve teachers of the numerous semi- and nonprofessional tasks that consume a disproportionate amount of the teacher's time and energy.

However, new teachers may be asked to manage a paraprofessional who has been in the class for many years prior to the new teacher's arrival. The new teacher may be assigned to work with an aide who displays an inappropriate disposition or whose personal goals and aspirations conflict with those of the teacher. Without proper management and insight into these sources of difficulty, new teachers may develop a negative working relationship with paraprofessionals, which may affect classroom interactions. Stress and conflict may arise from the difficult situation. Awareness of management techniques to facilitate teaming with paraprofessionals may help the new teacher in encouraging a smooth transition in class supervision and operations.

Strategies Useful With Paraprofessionals

Drury (1986) discussed teaming techniques pertinent to current teachers in their management of teacher aides and volunteers. As a team consultant and leader in the classroom, the new teacher should consider the following:

1. *The team makes major decisions with a team consultant or leader facilitating the decision-making process.* New teachers will consider differences in their roles as group consultees for some teams (e.g., observing peers, consulting with supervisors) or

group consultant-leaders for other teams (e.g., supervising students and paraprofessionals). New teachers must take the lead in determining classroom decisions—no matter how long the aide has been working.

2. *Goal setting and action plans are based on team analyses of problems.* Developing and new teachers must set goals and objectives for classroom activities and follow up with action plans designed to implement team decisions. Problem solving can often be accomplished more quickly when many individuals share strategies. Teacher aides are a good source of information particularly pertaining to their classroom. New teachers can use the suggestions of teacher aides as an additional source of input into goals and objectives. Teachers have the major say, however, in goal setting and action plans.

3. *Team members have input into team decisions.* All members of the educational team can make special contributions to the team. New teachers will benefit from appropriate suggestions of other adults, especially paraprofessionals, who often know students and classrooms well.

4. *Team members need access to all data relevant to decisions.* Sharing information in written form promotes team cohesiveness and effective team functioning. Sharing data with paraprofessionals who are working with particular children will encourage effective communication for all classroom members. (Teachers must remember to safeguard confidentiality of pertinent data.)

5. *Communication is encouraged for all team members.* Being part of a team entails listening to and receiving messages from all other members of the team. By being open with the paraprofessional, the new teacher is encouraging a healthy, working rapport.

Working with Paraprofessionals. Working with paraprofessionals is one area in which the new teacher may be required to lead. The paraprofessional can perform any task that does not require professional training or judgment but may not assume nor be assigned the responsibilities reserved for teachers (Drecktrab, 2000; McKenzie & Houk, 1986). Paraprofessionals may not be given independent responsibility for classroom teaching, management, or organization. A paraprofessional may function in the classroom only if a trained teacher is available for direction and guidance, albeit a new teacher can work within the context of a team model to use teacher paraprofessionals to supplement professional instruction and management. The teacher functions as the team consultant and must facilitate major classroom decision-making. Under the teacher's direction and support, paraprofessionals can assist in classroom management, supplemental teaching, housekeeping chores, and extracurricular activities. If a paraprofessional is to be used to the best advantage, there must be a correspondence between the tasks the teacher expects to have performed and the paraprofessional's ability and opportunities to carry them out. Box 11.5 provides tips to help paraprofessionals get oriented to the special education situation. Orientation in-service conducted by the teacher is a rapport-building technique that new teachers can use to help establish a team model.

O'Shea and Hendrickson (1987) offered these suggestions to classroom teachers to encourage teaming with paraprofessionals. These suggestions are pertinent for today's classroom interactions as well.

1. Treat the paraprofessional with respect in all dealings.

2. From day one, capitalize on the personal strengths of the paraprofessional. Point out these strengths whenever possible in a written fashion and share them with the paraprofessional, administration, and other teachers or paraprofessionals.

3. Give the paraprofessional plenty of compliments on work that is well done.

4. Maintain high performance standards and encourage the paraprofessional to do the same.

| **B**ox 11.5 | **Tips to Orient the Paraprofessional When Working with Special Needs Students** |

Introduce the aide to other adults and the students with whom he or she will be working. The intent is to plan for early interactions with the aide. Help the aide acquire as much information about each student as quickly as possible.

Expose the aide to written guidelines and review these materials (e.g., classroom or board of education policies, teacher's handbook, aide's handbook) with which the aide should become familiar.

Tour the school with the aide if the principal has not already done so. Provide a tour of the classroom and areas where the following necessities are kept: supplies, books, games, charts, desks, curriculum guides, district course of study, picture files, and audiovisual collection.

Have the aide become familiar with the following during his or her first days of work:

- *Personnel names and location within the school:* Principal, assistant principal, dean, other supervisors, psychologist, social worker, speech clinician, therapist, librarian, other ancillary personnel, custodian, nurse, cafeteria director, cooks and lunchroom personnel, teachers, other paraeducators, other aides (e.g., playground, lunch, bus, special education)
- *Location of important school areas:* Special education classrooms, library, supply room, storage areas, workroom, bookstore, cafeteria, auditorium, gymnasium, faculty lounge
- *Location of things within the school:* Audiovisual equipment, storage cabinets, copying machine, art supplies, other machines

Provide the aide with a job description that outlines the functions of the position. Spell out specifically all clerical, housekeeping, technical, and supervised instructional tasks assigned. Also point out tentative activities that might occur irregularly (e.g., field trips, school projects). Help the aide devise his or her own weekly schedule to be filled out each week.

Source: Adapted from O'Shea, D. J., & Hendrickson, J. M. (1987). *Tips for using teacher aides effectively* (Monograph No. 16.). Gainesville: University of Florida Diagnostic and Teaching Clinic.

---

5. Make the communication process as optimal as possible. Be willing to listen and respond with empathy as necessary to the paraprofessional's concerns.

6. Strive for consistency in the working relationship with the paraprofessional. Don't tell the paraprofessional one thing one day and something different the next day.

7. Organize the classroom in a manner that promotes good order and a sense of forward movement. Tell the paraprofessional specifically how the class is to operate. Discuss directly with the paraprofessional what, where, why, when, and how duties are to be done. Demonstrate the correct procedures as well. Elicit feedback and input from the paraprofessional on the success of classroom procedures.

8. Distribute duties in a fair and equitable manner. Get continual feedback from the paraprofessional to assess reasonableness of the type and amount of assigned work. Ask questions and encourage the paraprofessional to do the same.

9. Within a structured conference, explain to the paraprofessional the importance of increasing the quality and quantity of the duties as his or her expertise grows.

10. Help the paraprofessional in observing and following the disciplinary measures used by the teacher; make adjustments only after a conference together.

11. Try to encourage the paraprofessional to handle his or her own disciplinary problems, but if serious problems occur, advice and help from the teacher will be sought.

12. Do not correct the paraprofessional in front of others, especially in front of students. (If you must provide corrective feedback, do it privately at a scheduled conference.)

13. Provide constructive criticism by telling the paraprofessional what can be improved and how it is to be improved. Aim criticism toward the goal of improved performance.

14. Encourage the paraprofessional to keep a sense of humor whenever possible.

Paraprofessionals have lives outside school, and effective teachers get to know and respect the personal side of the people with whom they work so closely. It is important to show interest, when appropriate, in the paraprofessional's personal stories.

Finally, Box 11.6 presents descriptions of tasks that paraprofessionals can do to provide the teacher with more quality time with students. Some of these tasks are supplemental instructional activities; others are housekeeping chores of the classroom. All these tasks can be accomplished by paraprofessionals with direction and guidance from the classroom teacher.

Box 11.6 **Teaming Tasks That Aides Can Do to Assist Special Education Teachers**

- Assist students in academic subject areas in which the teacher believes that tutoring is necessary
- Circulate around the room to check students' progress
- Provide individualized assistance, such as flashcard drill or listening to oral reading
- Prepare charts, graphs, or teaching bulletin boards
- Correct written assignments from the teacher's key or model
- Work with those students who were absent to review or summarize lessons or activities
- Collect assignments from the general classroom teacher for completion in the resource classroom
- Assist students with written compositions, especially with spelling, punctuation, and grammar
- Correct homework and workbooks; note and report weak areas
- Call the class to order
- Collect money for lunch, class pictures, field trips, or special items
- Care for bulletin board appearance and overall appearance of the room
- Help students move from one activity to another
- Assist students in the lavatory
- File correspondence and other reports in students' records
- Keep inventories of classroom stock: equipment, books, and instructional supplies

Source: Adapted from Clough, D. B., & Clough, B. M. (1978). *A handbook of effective techniques for teacher aides.* Springfield, IL: Charles C Thomas.

TEACHER STRESS AND BURNOUT

Whereas some researchers have suggested that teaming will help in reducing teacher stress and burnout, especially through the teacher's involvement in functional and daily decision-making (Dunham, 1983; Fimian & Blanton, 1986; Taylor & Salend, 1983), others have noted the potential ineffectiveness of some teaming models (Gloeckler & Simpson, 1988; Schulz & Turnbull, 1984; Zabel & Zabel, 1980). Stress and burnout are variables that influence the master teaching process whether new teachers perceive conflict from paraprofessionals, from role conflicts and role ambiguities with other professionals, or from ineffectual working conditions and environmental factors.

Ballinger (2000) reported that stress is a significant reason why many teachers leave their jobs for good. Among the factors contributing to teachers' stress are low pay; lack of support; increased problems with student discipline; lack of job knowledge, especially in classroom management; and a top-down management style of administrators. Weiss and Weiss (1999) reported that sometimes 1st-year teachers experience stress because they are frequently left in a "sink or swim" position with little support from colleagues and few opportunities for professional development. Informal, haphazard teacher induction experiences have been associated with high levels of attrition as well as low levels of teacher effectiveness (National Commission on Teaching and America's Future, 1996). As an increasing number of general education teachers continue to instruct students with special needs, stress and burnout are important factors that will influence many teachers' chosen careers.

Stress is part of everyday life and, in manageable doses, can motivate individuals to improve and grow. Too much stress, however, will cause serious repercussions for an otherwise healthy person (Epanchin, 1987). Certain working conditions are very stressful and often lead to burnout and eventual attrition. In other words, teachers often leave their jobs when stress takes over their lives (Billingsley, 1993; Billingsley & Cross, 1992; Brownell & Smith, 1992; Weiss & Weiss, 1999).

Many educators have observed changes over the past few decades that make teaching, especially special education, a stressful profession (Barner, 1982; Billingsley, 1993; Brownell & Smith, 1992; Cooley & Yovanoff, 1996; Crane & Iwanicki, 1986; Dunham, 1983; Frank & McKenzie, 1993; Greer & Greer, 1992; Iwanicki, 1983; Morsink, 1982; Pattavina, 1980). In fact, CEC (2000b) recently identified barriers that obstruct high-quality special education, in which three compelling realities emerged.

1. Many individuals with diverse needs do not receive the quality education they need to reach successful adult outcomes.

2. Many special educators teach under conditions that prevent them from delivering quality instruction.

3. Many special educators are asked to fill roles that are fragmented, ambiguously defined, and obscured by conflicting responsibilities.

Stress is a very real dilemma for educators that cannot be overlooked by new teachers. As reported in Chapter 3, Doyle's (1980) conceptualization of complex organizational pressures portrays the classroom as a public forum requiring frequent and immediate actions by the teacher in the face of almost overwhelming and often unpredictable environmental variables. Developing and new teachers who deal with intense pressures on a daily basis because of the often unpredictable nature of students with special needs and the added responsibilities of working from team models, working with difficult parents, and managing and supervising paraprofessionals will be hit hardest by the pressures of school and classroom stress. Self and others' expectations of what they can accomplish will be problems. Additionally, public demands and increased public expectations reflect the changing roles of educators, making the job of master teacher very difficult.

Stress and Special Educators

Morsink (1982) examined trends in the roles of special educators and reported potential sources of stress to professionals. More recent researchers confirmed stress and resulting burnout in special educators (Ballinger, 2000; Billingsley, 1993; Brownell & Smith, 1992; Cooley & Yovanoff, 1996; Frank & McKenzie, 1993; Greer & Greer, 1992; Weiss & Weiss, 1999). Work-related variables have been found to contribute to burnout issues, including excessive paperwork requirements, student numbers, low salaries, lack of administrative support, collegial isolation, role conflict or ambiguity, student behaviors, and lack of visible student progress (Billingsley, 1993; Brownell & Smith, 1992; Cooley & Yovanoff, 1996; Frank & McKenzie, 1993).

O'Shea, Stoddard, and O'Shea (2000) reported on teachers' stress related to the reauthorized mandates of IDEA 97, that is, stress associated with special education paperwork, functional behavioral assessments, accommodations and adaptations, and overall perceptions of peers to support each other in such areas as procedures, assessment, curriculum, and instruction. The effects of social change on schools and the ways teachers perceive these changes as affecting themselves personally is an impediment to their development as master teachers. Public perceptions and demands on teachers, and the teachers' own self-perceptions of what they believe is expected, are related to the successful completion of their roles.

Increased legal responsibilities of educators are a source of conflict (Barner, 1982; Brownell & Smith, 1992; Cooley & Yovanoff, 1996; O'Shea, Stoddard, et al., 2000). Many teachers consider too much red tape in their jobs as a major source of their discontent. An additional problem pertinent to developing teachers is lack of time-management skills (Algozzine, 1986; Brownell & Smith, 1992). Time-management skills may influence teaming models and opportunities to work with peers, paraprofessionals, families, and students. Pervasive feelings for teachers overwhelmed by changing legal, behavioral, and social responsibilities include the educator's perceived sense of failure and impotence to do a job well; daily confrontation with problems of students, parents, peers, paraprofessionals, and administrators; complex and vast paperwork connected with IEPs; and feelings of loneliness and helplessness, especially in the 1st year of teaching (Fimian & Blanton, 1986; Pattavina, 1980). When added together, all these factors help make teaching, especially teaching special education students, a demanding profession.

Figure 11.7 illustrates potential sources of stress to teachers, factors that new teachers should examine closely. Awareness of stress factors is a first step in lessening the negative effects of stress that will impede a new teacher's desire to remain in the field.

Signs and Signals. Many professionals do not agree on common definitions or strategies for remediation of stress, although most agree on the variable ways that stress and conflict manifest on teachers: loss of productivity, work refusal, physiological disorders that are psychologically based, and loss of quality teachers (burnout—the desire to leave the field because of emotional overload associated with teaching, schools, students, or the entire educational process) (Algozzine, 1986; Bradfield & Fones, 1985; Crane & Iwanicki, 1986; Fimian, 1983; Morsink, 1982; Retish, 1986; Smith & Cline, 1980). Many quality teachers will be lost to the profession because they do not heed warning signals.

Signs and signals of stress are provided in Box 11.7. If a teacher recognizes many of these signs frequently, over time, and to such an intensity that coming to school becomes a daily chore, it is time to reevaluate and redefine personal priorities and coping strategies. Even teachers new to the field will experience some of these after a few weeks in school. It is vital to target strategies to alleviate these sources of conflict as soon as they are recognized.

FIGURE 11.7 Potential Sources of Stress to Special Educators

STRESS FACTORS

Effects of social changes
Increased legal responsibilities
Lack of administrative support
Career stagnation
Lack of training
Teaching competencies
Vast paperwork
Poor salaries/benefits
Public perceptions
Unrealistic expectations
Lack of time-management skills
High teaching loads
Low self-perceptions
Daily confrontations with students
Uncooperative/uninvolved parents
Feelings of loneliness
Feelings of lack of control
Lack of recognition
Little planning time
Lack of input into school policies/procedures

Box 11.7   **Signs and Signals of Stress**

- Avoidance of school through many absences, continual tardiness, or an intense desire to leave the building before the school day is over
- Apathy to students, parents, and teachers
- Lower productivity in teaching, especially in teachers who at one time were highly productive
- Continual negative self-statements concerning teacher effectiveness
- Physical signs, including prolonged headaches, stomach pains, and voice problems
- Real or imagined mental fatigue over time
- Blatant refusal to comply with school policies and rules
- Prolonged crying and depression
- Deep feelings of loss of control over career, personal life, or business matters
- Continual complaints to loved ones

Reducing Stress and Burnout. Cooley and Yovanoff (1996) identified potential interventions at reducing or alleviating burnout and improving retention among special educators. Short-term interventions include individual responses of professionals to the stressors they encounter, the quantity/quality of collegial interactions available to them, and access to appropriate alternatives to administrative support when such support is lacking. There are factors over which teachers themselves have some control or that fall within administrators' purview to address. Other strategies are to equip teachers with coping skills and to reduce collegial isolation that special educators commonly experience. Opportunities for teaming and work-related problem solving are useful. Support and constructive, collaborative dialogue between professional peers can help reduce stress and burnout.

Strategies to reduce stress and burnout are listed in Box 11.8. Some of these strategies are implemented by the external control of others (e.g., administrative support to

---

Box 11.8   **Strategies to Reduce Stress and Burnout**

Externally Controlled Strategies

Administrative support (recognized/supported by administrators)

- Access to counseling
- Reduced class size
- Reduced teacher loads
- Adequate resources/materials
- Adequate paraprofessional and volunteer help
- Tangible incentives for successful teaching
- Increased pay
- Increased job benefits
- Environmental variables (e.g., lighting, acoustics)
- Opportunities for teacher advancement

Administrative interventions (controlled by administrators)

- Increased planning time
- Increased responsibility for job performance
- Teacher's lounge discussion sessions
- Organized personnel social functions
- Functioning feedback mechanisms in school (e.g., school suggestion box)
- Teacher input into curriculum and scheduling
- Increased involvement of teachers in faculty decision-making
- Analysis of school-classroom expectations

Self-Control Strategies

Physical controls

- Relaxation training
- Adequate diet
- Adequate sleep
- Regular exercise
- Self-verbalization of positive dispositions

Interpersonal controls

- Hobbies
- Clubs/organizations
- Family
- Sports/leisure
- Community support systems
- Increased networking
- Increased professional skills and training

---

reduce class size) or by self-control of teachers (e.g., commitment to exercise, adequate sleep). It is important to note that administrators can recognize the need for strategies to help teachers cope better with their jobs, but they do not necessarily have the personal control to change policies (e.g., recognition of the need for increased teacher pay but lack of power to change school financial policies). Administrators also can have a direct influence in their own schools on coping interventions for teachers by enforcing personal policies to lessen teacher stress and burnout (e.g., principals can structure weekly sessions in the faculty lounge so that teachers can discuss concerns or exchange ideas to reduce tensions). Thus, as listed in Box 11.8, external controls can be an administrative support (the administrator recognizes the need for the strategy but will or will not have personal control over the strategy) or an administrative intervention (the administrator has personal control within his or her own school to implement the strategy). Self-control strategies for teachers include physical controls (related to bodily functions) or interpersonal controls (related to commitment of family or community involvement). Self-control strategies can be continually implemented directly by new teachers.

Time-management strategies will also be useful sources of stress reducers to developing teachers (Youngs, 1986). These include the following tips:

1. *Be proactive, not reactive.* Learn to anticipate and plan for stress. By being prepared, new teachers can learn to avoid sources of difficulty.

2. *Plan time.* Try not to be controlled by events and persons around you beyond your own personal limits. Assert yourself so that others do not push you beyond these limits. Communicate to others and yourself what your limits are.

3. *Identify and plan for quality time.* This is a time during the day when you can focus your awareness on a specific task without interruption. Avoid doing more than one thing at a time.

4. *Don't place demands on yourself that you can't meet.* Be honest with yourself and with others. Demanding too much of yourself causes stress and will create failure. Effective teachers will know when to say no as well as yes.

5. *Know where your time goes.* If necessary, make a list of what you did during a day and evaluate whether you spent your time wisely. Developing and new teachers will self-evaluate continually.

6. *Build your strengths and not your weaknesses.* Concentrate on what you can do, rather than on what you cannot do. As with special needs students, new teachers must be kind to themselves.

7. Be aware that, in general, poor time management includes

   a. excess time spent in crisis situations

   b. more time spent on trivia than is necessary

   c. frequent interruptions that destroy planning incentive and momentum

   d. less time spent on high-priority items than low-priority ones

   e. little quality time spent on items requiring creativity and productivity

8. *Set long-term life career goals as well as short-term goals.*

9. *Reward yourself for what you do well.* Put what you don't do well in proper perspective. Time-management strategies can help in reducing stress and can help in facilitating the master teacher process. New teachers can help reduce their feelings of lack of control over their teaching careers and advance within their profession.

Tips For New Teachers' Survival. The issue of new teachers' survival receives attention from policy makers (CEC, 2000a). New teachers are to concentrate on making their foray into the world as a professional special educator by seeking actively to reduce stress. Attending to the following points may help.

1. Get to school early to establish important relationships.

2. Get to know students to become familiar with students' demographics and needs.

3. Organize files to locate previous lesson plans and projects

4. Learn time management, as previously described, including setting priorities.

5. Look professional, including the choice of proper and comfortable attire.

6. Reach out for help, such as locating a mentor.

7. Socialize with peers to initiate collaboration with peer teachers.

8. Sponsor a club or team to know various students and colleagues.

9. Join professional organizations, where questions about concerns or problems can be answered quickly and confidentially.

A TEACHER CAREER CYCLE: FACILITATING THE MASTER TEACHER PROCESS

Continual professional growth and active involvement are components in the master teacher process. By continually upgrading teachers' commitments to the field, individuals in education will be closer to fulfillment as master teachers. Recognition of advancements within teaching, involvement in professional organizations, obtainment of higher degrees, and renewed certifications in areas of specialization all inform, reinforce, and challenge teachers. These steps will help encourage professionalism and continued active involvement through the years (Dudzinski, Roszmann-Millican, & Shank, 2000). As teachers begin to feel confident of their abilities and develop a prolonged commitment to the field, master teachers evolve.

Advancement Within the Field

There are ways other than direct contact with students to effect changes in the field of education and to advance personally within the field. Many teachers change with their jobs and still provide services to their field. Other services that make a noticeable difference include involvement in research, administration, teacher training, service organizations and advocacy groups, curriculum planning and development, parent training, and support services and counseling. Work in each of these areas helps increase benefits to teachers and to all students with special needs, including their parents and peers. Teachers who are committed to these other areas will also become master teachers by making a difference in the field. By expanding services and professional memberships, committed teachers remain in the field but specialize in areas outside direct contact with students.

Involvement in Professional Organizations

Developing and new teachers will be able to maintain knowledge of current strategies and recognized teaching practices through active participation in professional organizations. Many professional organizations provide and promote conferences, workshops, in-services, and continuing education classes. Working actively in local, state, or national professional groups will widen the contacts that teachers have and will aid in professional awareness. By actively participating in professional organizations, new teachers are executing some control over their teaching careers. Increasing professional awareness helps maintain master teachers and invigorate and challenge developing and new teachers.

Involvement in Professional Development Activities

An increasing number of experienced teachers participate in professional development activities that support their continued expertise. Many teachers undergo intense and ongoing professional growth opportunities to keep pace with new, emerging knowledge and skills for teachers' roles. Many districts offer local educational incentives to experienced teachers. For instance, some districts provide tuition toward teachers' recertification or add-on certifications; some offer stipends and books for degree programs related to critical teaching areas, some partner with colleges and universities to offer distance education or on-line course work. Others encourage mid-career change recruitment incentives through fast-track alternative certification programs. Continued professional development activities provide teachers opportunities to collaborate and increase a sense of power to influence major decisions and policies that guide their work. Activities upgrade teachers' skills while fostering collegial support. Teachers can work in both discipline-specific and cross-disciplinary professional communities to exchange and generate new knowledge. When they participate in ongoing professional development, they engage in practice-based inquiry and have opportunities to team with colleagues. They model the reciprocity of roles and collaboration among disciplines that effective special and general educators promote.

Higher Degrees

Many teacher education programs and universities offer courses leading to advanced degrees in education. Often, local school districts provide in-service training modules that can be exchanged for college credit or advanced standing, leading to additional degrees for teachers. Obtaining higher degrees increases teachers' competency levels and mastery of teaching objectives—all relevant to feelings of success and confidence in teaching. When teachers feel successful and confident, teaching abilities increase.

Certifications

Many current general educators and special educators are renewing certifications to teach. With increased numbers of diverse students in general education, more general education and content area teachers are attaining special education certification. Teachers are adding on areas of specialization to broaden their base to instruct and manage students with special needs. Certification provides a mechanism for establishing regulations to carry out the intent of IDEA. It is often the foundation for the establishment of minimum training and experience levels expected of teachers. In a sense, certification provides to teachers and administrators the confidence that certified employees are trained, competent, and able to carry out the responsibilities they have been assigned. Teachers with varied and/or updated certification have obtained more than the minimum necessary to survive in teaching and to maintain their stance as master teachers.

ANALYZING PERSONAL PHILOSOPHIES: WHAT CAN TEACHERS DO TO REMAIN COMMITTED TO THEIR CAREERS?

Teachers with advanced degrees and additional certifications are in an excellent position to effect changes in their individual classrooms and the total school system. Armed with updated information on current research and teaching practices, these teachers help ensure students with disabilities a free and appropriate public education. They remain invigorated and committed over time. Teachers who respect the teaming model and who actively target strategies against stress enhance their own professionalism. As these teachers develop and change in conjunction with the needs of the students they teach, they are on the road to becoming master teachers. These teachers continually observe students and discuss ways of meeting students' needs with their peer teachers. They implement learning strategies and behavioral support strategies consistently.

They work well on team models with parents, professionals, and paraprofessionals. They recognize stress factors and ways of reducing stress when they begin to feel burnout. These teachers are committed to special education success through active professional involvement, additional training and in-services, and continued commitment to specialized areas of expertise. These teachers have made the transition from student teacher to master teacher. They have found that teaching students with diverse needs is rewarding and stays a challenging career over the years.

SUMMARY

The chapter opened with a discussion on professional teaching standards, now common in most education circles. Next, we examined tips on conducting job searches and writing résumés. Typical job interview procedures emphasize skills in oral and written communication to receive a board of education recommendation as a new teacher. We discussed ways and means to create a professional portfolio. Then, we discussed working with families, peer teaming and reviews, and observing fellow educators in other settings. Observation and continual professional discussion lead to positive changes as teachers collaborate and share successful teaching techniques and strategies. Tips on successful teacher induction programs and mentor-protégé relationships received attention.

A portion of the chapter was devoted to strategies for dealing with paraprofessionals. In addition to working with peers, many teachers work in close proximity to other adults, either with paraeducators or volunteers. A team approach was advocated for a successful teacher-paraprofessional relationship.

All teachers must be able to recognize and deal with stress and burnout, factors that impede the master teaching process. We provided a discussion on potential sources, signs and signals of stress and burnout in teachers, and strategies to lessen negative effects that will result when warning signs are not heeded immediately.

We reviewed techniques to facilitate the master teacher process including advancement within the field of special education, involvement in professional organizations, attainment of higher degrees, and renewal of teacher certifications. Master teachers are committed to the field and change in accordance with the needs of their students.

ACTIVITIES TO EXTEND YOUR KNOWLEDGE

1. Choose one local, state, or national professional organization dealing with individuals with disabilities. Write or e-mail for information on how to join, fees, and resource materials available. Analyze (a) your letter sent to the organization; (b) a copy of the information you received; and (c) a one-page summary, written by you, of the organization's purpose and target audience.

2. Compile a list of at least 15 community service agencies (including postal or electronic address, telephone number, contact person, and purpose of the agency) that are available to teachers, students, and/or family members of individuals with disabilities in your area.

3. In a collaboration effort with peers, develop a list of 15 potential educational programming ideas for achieving and maintaining your status as a "master teacher." Include rationales for the ideas based on current reference citations.

4. Participate in an in-class presentation dealing with the prevention and/or amelioration of teacher stress and burnout in modern classroom. Include handouts

and current reference citations for your peers. If you feel comfortable doing so, discuss the possible etiology of a stress and burnout problem as these affect you in your field placement.

5. Explore computer programs and/or library resources to find more information on specific locations in which you can obtain an advanced degree and/or renew your current teacher certification.

6. Discuss with students' families what they believe new professionals can do to demonstrate a commitment to lifelong teaching careers. Compare and contrast your findings with those of your peers.

7. Write down a list of 10 items that you believe personally reflect how you demonstrate positive regard for the culture, religion, gender, and sexuality of students in your field setting. Do not name students, but rather discuss your specific strategies with your peers.

8. Write a paper (without using references) that articulates your personal philosophy of education. Include what you believe your relationship will be with fellow educators, administrators, families, and paraprofessionals. Include important points on how you believe you can personally demonstrate your active involvement with these other individuals. Discuss how you can become and remain a master teacher.

9. Self-reflect on your current knowledge, skills, and dispositions of working with special education students in the general education curricula. Analyze your professional strengths and needs.

POINT AND CLICK

The following Web sites highlight the chapter's theme of new teachers' efforts in participating in and refining the master teacher process. Each of these listings can assist new teachers in their lifelong quest to be a master teacher in their work with diverse students.

National Information Center for Children and Youth with Disabilities (NICHCY)
P.O. Box 1492
Washington, DC 20013-1492
1-800-695-0285 or 202-884-8200 (voice/TTY)
E-mail: nichcy@aed.org
cichy.org/index.html
This Web site provides access to a nationally recognized organization that offers the latest updates on professional efforts to support students with disabilities, their families, and the professionals working with them.

National Association of Developmental Disabilities Councils
1234 Massachusetts Avenue NW, Suite 103
Washington, DC 20005
202-347-1234
E-mail: naddc@igc.apc.org
http//www.igc.apc.orc/NADDC/
New teachers can access this Web site on a national organization that clarifies information from local, state, and national chapters of the Association of Developmental Disabilities Councils.

Center for Effective Collaboration and Practice
American Institutes for Research
1000 Thomas Jefferson St. NW, Suite 400
Washington, DC 20007
1-888-457-1551
http://www.air-.org/ceep/
This Web site provides updated research on collaboration and practices to create school teams both within the school and between the school and community.

American Network of Community Options and Resources (ANCOR)
4200 Evergreen Lane, Suite 315
Annandale, VA 22003
www.ancor.org
This Web site supports teachers' collaboration with community and related service personnel.

Beach Center on Families and Disability
311 Haworth Avenue
University of Kansas
Lawrence, KS 66045
913-864-7600
http://www.lsi.uknas.edu/beach/beachhp.html
This Web site offers collaborative and consulting ideas for working with all members of students' families, including parents or guardians, siblings, extended family members, neighbors, and/or other significant individuals.

REFERENCES

Aldinger, L., Warger, C. L., & Eavy, P. W. (1991). *Strategies for teacher collaboration*. Ann Arbor, MI: Exceptional Innovations.

Algozzine, B. (1986). *Problem behavior management: Educator's resource guide*. Rockville, MD: Aspen.

Baker, J., & Zigmond, N. (1990). Are regular education classes equipped to accommodate students with learning disabilities? *Exceptional Children, 566)*, 515–526.

Ballinger, J. (2000). Programs aim to stop teacher washout. *Journal of Staff Development, 21*, 92, 2833.

Barner, A. (1982). Do teachers like to teach? *Pointer, 27*(1), 5–7.

Bauwens, J., & Hourcade, J. J. (1995). *Cooperative teaching: Rebuilding the schoolhouse for all students*. Austin, TX: PRO-ED.

Beach, R. G. (1973). *Help in the school: Establishment of a paraprofessional program*. Philadelphia: Dorrance.

Billingsley, B. S. (1993). Teacher retention and attrition in special and general education: A critical review of the literature. *Journal of Special Education, 72*(2), 137–174.

Billingsley, B. S., & Cross, L. H. (1992). Predictors of commitment, job satisfaction, and intent to stay in teaching: A comparison of general and special education. *Journal of Special Education, 25*(4), 453–471.

Bradfield, R. H., & Fones, D. M. (1985). Special teacher stress: Its product and prevention. Special report. *Academic Therapy, 21*, 91–94.

Brownell, M. T., & Smith, S. W. (1992). Attrition/retention of special education teachers: Critique of current research and recommendations for retention efforts. *Teacher Education and Special Education, 15*(4), 229–248.

Clough, D. B., & Clough, B. M. (1978). *A handbook of effective techniques for teacher aides*. Springfield, IL: charles C. Thomas.

Cooley, E., & Yovanoff, P. (1996). Supporting professionals-at-risk: Evaluating interventions to reduce burnout and improve retention of special educators. *Exceptional Children, 62*(4), 336–355.

Council for Exceptional Children. (2000a). *What every special educator must know: The standards for the preparation and licensure of special educators.* (4th ed.). Reston, VA: Author.

Council for Exceptional Children (2000b). *Bright futures for exceptional learners: An action plan for quality conditions, teaching, and results for every exceptional learner.* Reston, VA: Author.

Crane, S. J., & Iwanicki, E. F. (1986). Perceived role conflict, role ambiguity, and burnout among special education teachers. *Remedial and Special Education, 7*(2), 24–31.

Danielson, C. (1996). *Enhancing professional practice: A framework for teaching.* Alexandria, VA: Association for Supervision & Curriculum.

Dettmer, P. A., Dyck, N. T., & Thurston, L. P. (1996). *Consultation, collaboration, and teamwork for students with special needs.* Needham Heights, MA: Allyn & Bacon.

Diez, M. (1998). The role of standards and assessment: A dialogue. In M. Dietz (Ed.), *Changing the practice of teacher education: Standards and assessment as a lever for change.* Washington, DC: American Association of Colleges for Teacher Education.

Doyle, W. (1980). *Classroom management.* West Lafayette, IN: Kappa Delta Pi.

Drecktrab, M. E. (2000). Preservice teachers' preparation to work with paraeducators. *Teacher Education and Special Education, 23*(2), 157–164.

Drury, S. S. (1986). *Team effectiveness.* Newark: University of Delaware.

Dudzinski, M., Roszmann-Millican, M., & Shank, K. (2000). Continuing professional development for special educators: Reforms and implications for university programs. *Teacher Education and Special Education, 23*(2), 109–124.

Dunham, J. (1983). Coping with stress in schools. *Special Education: Forward Trends, 10,* 2–6.

Dwyer, K. P., Osher, D., & Hoffman, K. C. (2000). Creating responsive schools: Contextualizing early warning, timely response. *Exceptional Children, 66,*(3), 347–365.

Epanchin, B. C. (1987). Anxiety and stress-related disorders. In B. C. Epanchin & J. L. Paul (Eds.), *Emotional problems of childhood and adolescence: A multidisciplinary perspective.* Upper Saddle River, NJ: Merrill/Prentice Hall.

Fimian, M. J. (1983). A comparison of occupational stress correlates as reported by teachers of mentally retarded and nonmentally retarded handicapped students. *Education and Training of the Mentally Retarded, 18,* 62–68.

Fimian, M. J., & Blanton, L. P. (1986). Variables related to stress and burnout in special education teacher trainees and first-year teachers. *Teacher Education and Special Education, 9,* 9–21.

Frank, A. R., & McKenzie, R. (1993). The development of burnout among special educators. *Teacher Education and Special Education, 16*(2), 161–170.

Giangreco, M. F., Cloniger, C. J., Dennis, R. E., & Edelman, S. W. (1994). Problem-solving methods. In J. S. Thousand, R. Villa, & A. Nevin (Eds.), *Creativity and collaborative learning: A practical guide to empowering students and teachers* (pp. 321–346). Baltimore: Paul H. Brookes.

Gloeckler, T., & Simpson, C. (1988). *Exceptional students in regular classrooms: Challenges, services, and methods.* Mountain View, CA: Mayfield.

Greer, J. G., & Greer, B. B. (1992). Stopping burnout before it starts: Prevention measures at the preservice level. *Teacher Education and Special Education, 15*(3), 168–174.

Hayek, R. A. (1987). The teacher assistance team: A prereferral support system. *Focus on Exceptional Children, 20*(1), 1–7.

Hehir, T. (1999). The changing roles of special education leadership in the next millennium: Thoughts and reflections. *Journal of Special Education Leadership, 12*(1), 3–8.

Idol, L. (1988). A rationale and guidelines for establishing special education consultation programs. *Remedial and Special Education, 9*(6), 48–58.

Interstate New Teacher Assessment and Support Consortium. (1994). *Model standards for beginning teacher licensing and development: A resource for state dialogue.* Washington, DC: Author.

Iwanicki, E. F. (1983). Toward understanding and alleviating teacher burnout. *Theory Into Practice, 22,* 27–32.

Karp, N. (1993). Collaborating with families. In B. Billingsley (Ed.), *Program leadership for serving students with disabilities* (USDOE #H029H10034-93). Richmond: Virginia Department of Education.

Kauf man, J. M., & Hallahan, D. P. (1995). *The illusion of full inclusion: A comprehensive critique of a current special education bandwagon.* Austin, TX: PRO-ED.

Kenney, S. L., Hammitte, D. J., Rakestraw, J., & LeMontagne, M. J. (2000). *Special education and the P-16 Initiative: Addressing CEC standards through portfolio development and assessment. Teacher Education and Special Education, 23*(2), 89–97.

Kunc, N. (1992). The need to belong: Rediscovering Maslow's hierarchy of needs. In R. A. Villa, J. S. Thousand, W. Stainback, & S. Stainback (Eds.), *Restructuring for caring and effective education: An administrative guide to creating heterogeneous schools* (pp. 25–40). Baltimore: Paul H. Brookes.

Lombardo, V. (1980). *Paraprofessionals in special education.* Springfield, IL: charles C. Thomas.

McKenzie, R. G., & Houk, C. S. (1986). Use of paraprofessionals in the resource room. *Exceptional Children, 53*(1), 41–45.

McLaughlin, M. J. (1999). Access to the general education curriculum: Paperwork and procedures for redefining "special education." *Journal of Special Education Leadership, 12*(1), 9–14.

McLaughlin, M. J. (2000). *Reform for every learner: Teachers' views on standards and students with disabilities.* Alexandria, VA: The Center for Policy on the Impact of General and Special Education Reform.

Morsink, C. V. (1982). Changes in the role of special educators: Public perceptions and demands. *Exceptional Education Quarterly (The Special Educator as a Professional Person), 2*(4), 15–25.

National Association of State Boards of Education. (2000, April). *Teacher induction programs.* (Policy Information Clearinghouse). Alexandria, VA: Author.

National Board for Professional Teaching Standards. (1999). *Exceptional needs standards.* Washington, DC: Author.

National Commission on Teaching and America's Future. (1996). *Summary report What matters most: Teaching for America's future.* New York: Author.

Office of Special Education Programs. (1999). *To assure the free appropriate public education of all children with disabilities: Twentieth annual report to Congress on the implementation of the Individuals with Disabilities Education Act.* Washington, DC: Author.

O'Shea, D. J., Hammitte, D. J., Mainzer, R., & Crutchfield, M. (2000). From teacher preparation to continuing professional development. *Teacher Education and Special Education, 23,*(2), 71–77.

O'Shea, D. J., & Hendrickson, J. M. (1987). *Tips for using teacher aides effectively* (Monograph No. 16).

Gainesville: University of Florida Diagnostic and Teaching Clinic.

O'Shea, D. J., Williams, A. L., & Sattler, R. O. (1999, March-April). Collaboration across special education and general education: Preservice level teachers' views. *Journal of Teacher Education, 50*(2), 147–158.

O'Shea, L. J., & Hoover, N. L. (1986). *Conferring with teachers about teacher performance.* Tallahassee: Florida Department of Education.

O'Shea, L. J., Stoddard, K., & O'Shea, D. J. (2000). IDEA '97 and educator standards: Special educators' perceptions of their skills and those of general educators. *Teacher Education and Special Education, 23*(2), 125–141.

Otis-Wilborn, A., & Winn, J. A. (2000). It's the standards and the process. *Teacher Education and Special Education, 23*(2), 78–87.

Pattavina, P. (1980). Bridging the gap between stress and support for public school teachers: A conversation with Dr. William C. Morse about teacher burnout. *Pointer, 24*(2), 88–94.

Ralph, E. G., Kesten, C., Lang, H., & Smith, D. (1998). Hiring new teachers: what do school districts look for? *Journal of Teacher Education, 49*(1), 47–56.

Retish, P. (1986). Burnout and stress among special educators and others. *Journal of Special Education, 10*(3), 267–270.

Sawyer, R. J., McLaughlin, M. J., & Winglee, M. (1995). Is integration of students with disabilities happening? An analysis of national data trends over time. *Remedial and Special Education, 15*(4), 204–215.

Schulz, J. B., & Turnbull, A. P. (1984). *Including handicapped students: A guide for classroom teachers* (2nd ed.). Needham Heights, MA: Allyn & Bacon.

Slavin, R. E., Karweit, N. L., & Madden, N. A. (1989). *Effective programs for students at risk.* Needham Heights, MA: Allyn & Bacon.

Smith, J., & Cline, D. (1980). Quality programs. *Pointer, 24*(2), 80–87.

Snell, M. E., & Janney, R. (1994). Including and supporting students with disabilities within general education. In B. S. Billingsley (Ed.), *Program leadership for serving students with disabilities* (pp. 219–262). Richmond: Virginia Department of Education.

Stainback, W., & Stainback, S. (1990). *Support networks for inclusive schooling: Interdependent integrated education.* Baltimore: Paul H. Brookes.

Stainback, W., Stainback, S., & Stefanich, G. (1996). Learning together in inclusive classrooms. What about the curriculum? *Exceptional Children, 28*(3), 14–19.

Taylor, L., & Salend, S. J. (1983). Reducing stress-related burnout through a network support system. *Pointer, 27*(4), 5–9.

Thousand, J. S., Villa, R., & Nevin, A. (Eds.). (1994). *Creativity and Collaborative learing: A practical guide to empowering students and teachers.* Baltimore: Paul H. Brookes.

Top tips for new teachers. (2000, June/July). *CEC Today, 6*(8), 6–7.

U.S. Department of Education. (1990). *Twelfth annual report to Congress on the implementation of the Individuals with Disabilities Education Act.* Washington, DC: Author.

U.S. Department of Education. (1994). *Sixteenth annual report to Congress on the implementation of the Individuals with Disabilities Education Act.* Washington, DC: Author.

U.S. Department of Education. (1997). *Nineteenth annual report to Congress on the implementation of the Individuals with Disabilities Education Act.* Washington, DC: Author.

Walther-Thomas, C. S. (1996). Inclusion and teaming: Including all students in the mainstream. In T. Dickinson & T. Erb (Eds.), *Teaming in middle schools.* Columbus, OH: National Middle Schools Association.

Weiss, E. M. & Weiss, S. G. (1999, Spring). *New teacher induction.* (ERIC Clearinghouse on Teaching and Teacher Education). Washington, DC: American Association of Colleges for Teacher Education.

Youngs, B. B. (1986). *Stress in children: How to recognize, avoid, and overcome it.* Melbourne, Victoria: Nelson.

Ysseldyke, J., & Olsen, K. (1999). Putting alternate assessments into practice: What to measure and possible sources of data. *Exceptional Children, 65*(2), 175–185.

Zabel, R. H., & Zabel, M. K. (1980). Burnout: A critical issue for educators. *Language Unlimited, 2,* 23–25

Appendix
CEC Code of Ethics and Standards
for Professional Practice
for Special Educators

CEC CODE OF ETHICS FOR EDUCATORS OF PERSONS WITH EXCEPTIONALITIES

We declare the following principles to be the Code of Ethics for educators of persons with exceptionalities. Members of the special education profession are responsible for upholding and advancing these principles. Members of The Council for Exceptional Children agree to judge and be judged by them in accordance with the spirit and provisions of this Code.

Special Education Professionals:

A. Are committed to developing the highest educational and quality of life potential of individuals with exceptionalities.

B. Promote and maintain a high level of competence and integrity in practicing their profession.

C. Engage in professional activities which benefit individuals with exceptionalities, their families, other colleagues, students, or research subjects.

D. Exercise objective professional judgment in the practice of their profession.

E. Strive to advance their knowledge and skills regarding the education of individuals with exceptionalities.

F. Work within the standards and policies of their profession.

G. Seek to uphold and improve where necessary the laws, regulations, and policies governing the delivery of special education and related services and the practice of their profession.

H. Do not condone or participate in unethical or illegal acts, nor violate professional standards adopted by the Delegate Assembly of CEC.

CEC STANDARDS FOR PROFESSIONAL PRACTICE

Professionals in Relation to Persons with Exceptionalities and Their Families

Instructional Responsibilities

Special education personnel are committed to the application of professional expertise to ensure the provision of quality education for all individuals with exceptionalities. Professionals strive to:

(1) Identify and use instructional methods and curricula that are appropriate to their area of professional practice and effective in meeting the individual needs of persons with exceptionalities.

(2) Participate in the selection and use of appropriate instructional materials, equipment, supplies, and other resources needed in the effective practice of their profession.

(3) Create safe and effective learning environments which contribute to fulfillment of needs, stimulation of learning, and self-concept.

(4) Maintain class size and case loads which are conducive to meeting the individual instructional needs of individuals with exceptionalities.

(5) Use assessment instruments and procedures that do not discriminate against persons with exceptionalities on the basis of race, color, creed, sex, national origin, age, political practices, family or social background, sexual orientation, or exceptionality.

(6) Base grading, promotion, graduation, and/or movement out of the program on the individual goals and objectives for individuals with exceptionalities.

(7) Provide accurate program data to administrators, colleagues, and parents, based on efficient and objective record keeping practices, for the purpose of decision making.

(8) Maintain confidentiality of information except when information is released under specific conditions of written consent and statutory confidentiality requirements.

Management of Behavior

Special education professionals participate with other professionals and with parents in an interdisciplinary effort in the management of behavior. Professionals:

(1) Apply only those disciplinary methods and behavioral procedures which they have been instructed to use and which do not undermine the dignity of the individual or the basic human rights of persons with exceptionalities, such as corporal punishment.

(2) Clearly specify the goals and objectives for behavior management practices in the persons' with exceptionalities Individualized Education Program.

(3) Conform to policies, statutes, and rules established by state/provincial and local agencies relating to judicious application of disciplinary methods and behavioral procedures.

(4) Take adequate measures to discourage, prevent, and intervene when a colleague's behavior is perceived as being detrimental to exceptional students.

(5) Refrain from aversive techniques unless repeated trials of other methods have failed and only after consultation with parents and appropriate agency officials.

Support Procedures

(1) Adequate instruction and supervision shall be provided to professionals before they are required to perform support services for which they have not been prepared previously.

(2) Professionals may administer medication, where state/provincial policies do not preclude such action, if qualified to do so or if written instructions are on file which state the purpose of the medication, the conditions under it may be administered, possible side effects, the physicians name and phone number, and the professional liability if a mistake is made. The professional will not be required to administer medication.

(3) Professionals note and report to those concerned whenever changes in behavior occur in conjunction with the administration of medication or at any other time.

Parent Relationships

Professionals seek to develop relationships with parents based on mutual respect for their roles in achieving benefits for the exceptional person. Special education professionals:

(1) Develop effective communication with parents, avoiding technical terminology, using the primary language of the home, and other modes of communication when appropriate.

(2) Seek and use parents' knowledge and expertise in planning, conducting, and evaluating special education and related services for persons with exceptionalities.

(3) Maintain communication between parents and professionals with appropriate respect for privacy and confidentiality.

(4) Extend opportunities for parent education utilizing accurate information and professional methods.

(5) Inform parents of the educational rights of their children and of any proposed or actual practices which violate those rights.

(6) Recognize and respect cultural diversities which exist in some families with persons with exceptionalities.

(7) Recognize that the relationship of home and community environmental conditions affects the behavior and outlook of the exceptional person.

Advocacy

Special education professionals serve as advocates for exceptional students by speaking, writing, and acting in a variety of situations on their behalf. They:

(1) Continually seek to improve government provisions for the education of persons with exceptionalities while ensuring that public statements by professionals as individuals are not construed to represent official policy statements of the agency that employs them.

(2) Work cooperatively with and encourage other professionals to improve the provision of special education and related services to persons with exceptionalities.

(3) Document and objectively report to ones supervisors or administrators inadequacies in resources and promote appropriate corrective action.

(4) Monitor for inappropriate placements in special education and intervene at appropriate levels to correct the condition when such inappropriate placements exist.

(5) Follow local, state/provincial, and federal laws and regulations which mandate a free appropriate public education to exceptional students and the protection of the rights of persons with exceptionalities to equal opportunities in our society.

Professional in Relation to Employment

Certification and Qualification

Professionals ensure that only persons deemed qualified by having met state/provincial minimum standards are employed as teachers, administrators, and related service providers for individuals with exceptionalities.

Employment

(1) Professionals do not discriminate in hiring on the basis of race, color, creed, sex, national origin, age, political practices, family or social background, sexual orientation, or exceptionality.

(2) Professionals represent themselves in an ethical and legal manner in regard to their training and experience when seeking new employment.

(3) Professionals give notice consistent with local education agency policies when intending to leave employment.

(4) Professionals adhere to the conditions of a contract or terms of an appointment in the setting where they practice.

(5) Professionals released from employment are entitled to a written explanation of the reasons for termination and to fair and impartial due process procedures.

(6) Special education professionals share equitably the opportunities and benefits (salary, working conditions, facilities, and other resources) of other professionals in the school system.

(7) Professionals seek assistance, including the services of other professionals, in instances where personal problems threaten to interfere with their job performance.

(8) Professionals respond objectively when requested to evaluate applicants seeking employment.

(9) Professionals have the right and responsibility to resolve professional problems by utilizing established procedures, including grievance procedures, when appropriate.

Assignment and Role

(1) Professionals should receive clear written communication of all duties and responsibilities, including those which are prescribed as conditions of their employment.

(2) Professionals promote educational quality and intra- and interprofessional cooperation through active participation in the planning, policy development, management, and evaluation of the special education program and the education program at large so that programs remain responsive to the changing needs of persons with exceptionalities.

(3) Professionals practice only in areas of exceptionality, at age levels, and in program models for which they are prepared by their training and/or experience.

(4) Adequate supervision of and support for special education professionals is provided by other professionals qualified by their training and experience in the area of concern.

(5) The administration and supervision of special education professionals provides for clear lines of accountability.

(6) The unavailability of substitute teachers or support personnel, including aides, does not result in the denial of special education services to a greater degree than to that of other educational programs.

Professional Development

(1) Special education professionals systematically advance their knowledge and skills in order to maintain a high level of competence and response to the changing needs of persons with exceptionalities by pursuing a program of continuing education including but not limited to participation in such activities as inservice training, professional conferences/workshops, professional meetings, continuing education courses, and the reading of professional literature.

(2) Professionals participate in the objective and systematic evaluation of themselves, colleagues, services, and programs for the purpose of continuous improvement of professional performance.

(3) Professionals in administrative positions support and facilitate professional development.

Professionals in Relation to the Profession and to Other Professionals

The Profession

(1) Special education professionals assume responsibility for participation in professional organizations and adherence to the standards and codes of ethics of those organizations.

(2) Special education professionals have a responsibility to provide varied and exemplary supervised field experiences for persons in undergraduate and graduate preparation programs.

(3) Special education professionals refrain from using professional relationships with students and parents for personal advantage.

(4) Special education professionals take an active position in the regulation of the profession through use of appropriate procedures for bringing about changes.

(5) Special education professionals initiate, support, and/or participate in research related to the education of persons with exceptionalities with the aim of improving the quality of educational services, increasing the accountability of programs, and generally benefiting persons with exceptionalities. They:

- Adopt procedures that protect the rights and welfare of subjects participating in the research.
- Interpret and publish research results with accuracy and a high quality of scholarship.
- Support a cessation of the use of any research procedure which may result in undesirable consequences for the participant.
- Exercise all possible precautions to prevent misapplication or misuse of a research effort, by self or others.

Other Professionals

Special education professionals function as members of interdisciplinary teams, and the reputation of the profession resides with them. They:

(1) Recognize and acknowledge the competencies and expertise of members representing other disciplines as well as those of members in their own disciplines.

(2) Strive to develop positive attitudes among other professionals toward persons with exceptionalities, representing them with an objective regard for their possibilities and their limitations as persons in a democratic society.

(3) Cooperate with other agencies involved in serving persons with exceptionalities through such activities as the planning and coordination of information exchanges, service delivery, evaluation, and training, to avoid duplication or loss in quality of services.

(4) Provide consultation and assistance, where appropriate, to both general and special educators as well as other school personnel serving persons with exceptionalities.

(5) Provide consultation and assistance, where appropriate, to professionals in nonschool settings serving persons with exceptionalities.

(6) Maintain effective interpersonal relations with colleagues and other professionals, helping them to develop and maintain positive and accurate perceptions about the special education profession.

Index